Focus on College Success

D1359350

3rd Edition

Constance Staley

CENGAGE Learning®

Australia • Brazil • Japan • Korea • Mexico • Singapore • Spain • United Kingdom • United States

CENGAGE Learning

Focus on College Success: 3rd Edition

Senior Project Development Manager:
Linda deStefano

Market Development Manager:
Heather Kramer

Senior Production/Manufacturing Manager:
Donna M. Brown

Production Editorial Manager:
Kim Fry

Sr. Rights Acquisition Account Manager:
Todd Osborne

FOCUS on College Success, Third Edition
Constance Staley

For product information and technology assistance, contact us at
Cengage Learning Customer & Sales Support, 1-800-354-9706
For permission to use material from this text or product,
submit all requests online at **cengage.com/permissions**
Further permissions questions can be emailed to
permissionrequest@cengage.com

This book contains select works from existing Cengage Learning resources and was produced by Cengage Learning Custom Solutions for collegiate use. As such, those adopting and/or contributing to this work are responsible for editorial content accuracy, continuity and completeness.

Compilation © 2013 Cengage Learning
ISBN-13: 978-1-285-88610-7

ISBN-10: 1-285-88610-0

Cengage Learning
5191 Natorp Boulevard
Mason, Ohio 45040
USA

Cengage Learning is a leading provider of customized learning solutions with office locations around the globe, including Singapore, the United Kingdom, Australia, Mexico, Brazil, and Japan. Locate your local office at: **international.cengage.com/region.**

Cengage Learning products are represented in Canada by Nelson Education, Ltd.
For your lifelong learning solutions, visit **www.cengage.com/custom.**
Visit our corporate website at **www.cengage.com.**

Printed in the United States of America

Brief Contents

Contents

chapter 5 Developing Information Literacy, Writing, and Speaking Skills 139

chapter 6 Engaging, Listening, and Note-Taking in Class 177

chapter 7 Developing Your Memory 213

chapter 8 Reading and Studying 243

chapter 9 Taking Tests 275

chapter 10 Building Relationships, Valuing Diversity 305

chapter 11 Working Toward Wellness 339

chapter 12 Choosing a College Major and Career 373

Acknowledgments

It's been said that "Achievement is a *we* thing, not a *me* thing, always the product of many heads and hands." There are so many people to thank that this acknowledgements section could be as long as a chapter of *FOCUS*! However, here I'll at least mention those who have contributed the most, including all the students over the last 30-plus years who have taught me more than I've ever taught them.

Family Let me start at the center of my life. My deepest thanks go to Steve, my Sean-Connery-look-alike husband (How do I put up with it?), who almost forgot what I looked like over the last few years. As I *FOCUS*ed away in my attic office day after day and night after night, he brought me too many cups of coffee to count. I cherish his devotion. My daughters Shannon and Stephanie helped bring some much-needed balance to my life, and aside from being the most adorable children on the planet, my grandtwins Aidan and Ailie have been a living learning laboratory for me. As young children mastering one new thing after another, they truly have taught me about of the pure joy of learning. And to my beautiful 80-something Mom, who lovingly alternated between urging me to "slow down and relax" and "hurry up and finish," thanks for all your motherly love.

Reviewers The list of reviewers who have contributed their insights and expertise to *FOCUS on College Success* is long. I'd like to thank the following reviewers, who helped to shape the third edition with their feedback. My heartfelt thanks to all of them: Peg Adams, Northern Kentucky University; Marinda Ashman, Utah Valley University; Doug Gardner, Utah Valley University; Dawn Green, Central Texas College, Killeen; Linda Hensen-Jackson, Arkansas Tech University; Charlene Latimer, Daytona State College; Jen Manson, Lake Sumter Community College; Karen McKinney, Georgia Perimeter College, Clarkston; Deborah Miller, Ohio State University, Newark; Shane Y. Williamson, Lindenwood University.

Thank you also to the students who shared their feedback for this edition: CaSandra Allen; Nicole Bergeron; Courtney Coulter; Spencer Davis; Ashley Fite; Katrina Hanna; Paul Hatfield; Evan Howell; Samuel B. Jones III; Meagan Klomfas; Joe Leslie; Chelsey Lower; Maggie McCormack; Zachery A. McCormick; Tim McCoy; Hillary Presler; Brittany Price; Trashun L. Pringle; Rachel Rhinehart; Kayla Russell; Mai Sawada; Abdool Shakur; Emily Six; Jennifer Skovgaard; Paige Spence; Erin Steinman; Danielle Van Mater; Victoria Williams; Devan Young; Victoria Williams.

I'd also like to thank all the reviewers who helped to shape *FOCUS* in its previous editions: Peg Adams, Northern Kentucky University; Josie Adamo, Buffalo State College; Sandy Aguilar, Florida Community College at Jacksonville-Kent; Barbara Anderson, Midlands Technical College; Jon Aoki, University of Houston-Downtown; Andrew J. Armijo, University of New Mexico; Mercy Azeke, Norfolk State University; Michael Becraft, Austin Peay State University; Lynda Bennett, Blue Mountain Community College; Janet Breaker, Milwaukee Area Technical College; David Borst, Concordia University; Beverly Brucks, Illinois Central College; Toi Buchanan, Fayetteville Technical Community College;

Castell Burton, Valencia Community College; David Campaigne, University of South Florida; Lea Campbell, North Harris Montgomery Community College; Barbara Chavis, Cleveland Community College; Miriam Chiza, North Hennepin Community College; G. Jay Christensen, California State University, Northridge; Regina Vincent Clark, Tennessee State University; Karen Clay, Miami Dade College; Geoff Cohen, University of California, Riverside; Carrie Cokely, Meredith College; Della Colantone, Alderson-Broaddus College; Therese Crary, Highland Community College; Kimberly Cummings, University of Tampa; Allison Cumming-McCann, Springfield College; Janice A. Daly, Florida State University; Vrita H. Delaine, The University of Southern Mississippi; Mark Demark, Alvin Community College; Gigi Derballa, Asheville-Buncombe Technical Community College; Anne Dickens, Lee College; Michael Discello, Pittsburgh Technical Institute; Carmen Etienne, Oakland University; Sally Firmin, Baylor University; Charles Frederick, Indiana University; Becky Garlick, Blinn College; Sharol Gauthier, University of South Carolina Upstate; Jayne Geissler, East Carolina University; Alice Godbey, Daytona State College; Dee Allen Goedeke, High Point University; Laura Goppold, Central Piedmont Community College; Marie Gore, University of Maryland, Baltimore County; Wendy Grace, Holmes Community College; Dawn Green, Central Texas College; Laurie Grimes, Lorain County Community College; Rhonda Hall, West Virginia University; Tuesday Hambrick, North Lake College; Valerie Hewitt, Remington College; Cynthia S. Johnson, Palm Beach Community College; Joseph Jumpeter, Pennsylvania State University, Wilkes-Barre Page Keller, College of Charleston; Amy Koning, Grand Rapids Community College; Lois Lawson-Briddell, Gloucester County College; Kelly Lee, Orange Coast College; Janet Lindner, Midlands Technical College; Brenda Marina, The University of Akron; Marty Marty, Missouri State University; Claudia McDade, Jacksonville State University; Michelle McDaniel, Middle Tennessee State University; Bridgett McGowen, Prairie View A&M University; Aiesha Miller, The University of Akron; Brian Mitchell, Gibbs College of Boston; Karen Mitchell, Northern Essex Community College; Kelly Morales, University of Texas-Pan American; Gail Muse, Holmes Community College; Harriet Napierkowski, University of Colorado; Bonnie Porter Pajka, Luzerne County; Community College; Kate Pandolpho, Ocean County College; Stan Parker, Charleston Southern University; James Penven, Virginia Polytechnic Institute and State University; Karla Pierce, Florida Community College at Jacksonville; Mia Pierre, Valencia Community College; Jeanne Pettit, Northern Kentucky University; Joni Webb Petschauer, Appalachian State University; Amy Poland, Buena Vista University; Margaret Puckett, North Central State College; Terry Rafter-Carles, Valencia Community College; Melanie Rago, Indiana University; Margaret Rapp, Tyler Junior College; Rebecca Reed, Johnson & Wales University; Virginia Reilly, Ocean County College; Saundra Richardson, University of North Carolina at Pembroke; Chuck Rhodes, Sonoma State University; Jennifer Rockwood, The University of Toledo; Lawrence Rodriguez, Palo Alto College; Bea Rogers, Monmouth University; Keri Rogers, Sam Houston State University; Tara Ross, Keiser College; Patty Santoianni, Sinclair Community College; Alan Schlossman, Daytona State College; Cathy Seyler, Palm Beach Community College; Sarah Shutt, J. Sargeant Reynolds Community College; Phebe Simmons, Blinn College; Brenda A. Smith, Norfolk State University; Kim Smokowski, Bergen Community College; Marilyn Starkes, Thomas Nelson

Community College; Angie Walston, Barton College; Janice Waltz, Harrisburg Area Community College; Jodi Webb, Bowling Green State University; Jill Wilks, Southern Utah University; Shane Williamson, Lindenwood University.

The Wadsworth Team No book, of course, gets very far without a publisher, and FOCUS has had the best publishing team imaginable: the dynamic, highly people-skilled Annie Todd, Director of Developmental Studies; the best-in-the-industry, innovative, energetic Shani Fisher, Executive Editor; the meticulous, multi-talented Julia Giannotti, Senior Development Editor; true professionals who combed pages and probably did more than I'll ever know, Jessica Rassile, Content Project Manager; the ultimate on-the-ball Editorial Assistant, Sarah Turner, and Associate Editor, Joanna Hassel, for her work on all the outstanding supplements to *FOCUS*; the obviously talented Art Director, Pam Galbreath; and Ed Dionne, Project Manager at MPS North America. I'd like to especially thank Larry Harwood, the master photographer who took photos of the *FOCUS* cast on the University of Colorado at Colorado Springs campus. And heartfelt thanks to Wadsworth's Annie Mitchell and Sean Wakely, who believed in this project from the very start; Sylvia Shepherd, whose creative vision shaped much of this book, and Lauren Larsen, whose wit and wisdom formed the basis for several of the early chapters.

Other Contributors I'd also particularly like to thank the "*FOCUS* All-Stars," as I call them, my students who modeled for the photo shoots and starred in the "Inside the FOCUS Studio" videos. I'd also like to thank my colleagues at UCCS who have helped me develop many of the ideas in this book, whether they know it or not—all the Freshman Seminar faculty past and present. I also can't go without thanking the many authors who granted me permission to use their work, the career interviewees who shared their expertise and advice in each chapter, and four essential scholars who allowed me to use, apply, and extend their instruments throughout the book: Neil Fleming, Brian French, John Bransford, and John Pelley. And thanks to my expert student research assistants: Phil Wilburn, Sarah Snyder, Jessica Smith, and Lindsey McCormick, my best buddy Liz for all her encouraging words. I'd like to give a special thanks to Aren Moore who worked closely with me to create *FOCUS*Points, the interactive, multimedia PowerPoint designed for *FOCUS*. And finally, I'd like to thank Matt McClain, the comedy writer who brought his innovative humor to the learning process through podcast summaries of the chapters and television scripts for the website TV shows. He took the "big ideas" from *FOCUS* chapters and made them memorable to students by using their own best-loved media.

Above all, *FOCUS* has taught me truly to focus. Writing a book takes the same kind of endurance and determination that it takes to get a college degree. My empathy level for my students has, if anything, increased—and I am thankful for all I've learned while writing. It has been a cathartic experience to see what has filled each computer screen as I've tapped, tapped, tapped away. Ultimately, what I have chosen to put into each chapter has told me a great deal about who I am, what I know (and don't), and what I value. There's no doubt: I am a better teacher for having written this book. May all my readers grow through their *FOCUS* experience, too.

Meet the Cast

© Larry Harwood Photography. Property of Cengage Learning

Chapter 1: Sylvia Sanchez / Alycia

Hometown: I've lived all over Colorado. I consider the whole state to be my home town!

Major: Nursing with a minor in psychology

Lessons Learned: Alycia is still learning lessons about college. She keeps growing and discovering new things about herself and has made life-long friends. She plans to remember college as the best years of her life!

Toughest First-Year Class: Anatomy . . . It was hard to study ALL the time.

Advice to New Students: "Listen to your heart; it will lead you to the right place. Take every opportunity that comes to you because college is about finding out who you are and what you want from life."

© Larry Harwood Photography. Property of Cengage Learning

Chapter 2: Tammy Ko / Jessica

Hometown: Manitou Springs, Colorado

Major: Marketing

Lessons Learned: Juggling a part-time job while in school, Jessica loved living on campus her first term and meeting new people, but she regretted not talking to other students about which professors and courses to take towards her marketing major. In order to succeed, she says, you've "gotta give it all you've got!"

Toughest First-Year Class: Microeconomics because it wasn't like high school courses that just required memorizing a lot of facts.

Advice to New Students: "Talk to other students to learn about the best professors, and make sure you are studying something that you are truly interested in."

© Larry Harwood Photography. Property of Cengage Learning

Chapter 3: Derek Johnson / Derrick

Hometown: Colorado Springs, Colorado

Major: Communications/Recording Arts

Lessons Learned: Even though he's not married and has no children, Derrick and his case study character have much in common—too much to do and too little time! Derrick felt his biggest mistake his first year was not asking enough questions in class. He knows now he should have asked for clarity on content or assignments he didn't understand.

Toughest First-Year Class: English because he and his instructor had differing opinions, but he communicated through the tough spots and earned an "A".

Advice to New Students: "Surround yourself with positive people. As the saying goes, 'you are the company you keep.' I've seen many of my friends drop out because the people they called friends were holding them back from their full potential. Now that I have graduated, I look back at all the people I hold close and know that I wouldn't have made it without them."

Free Time: composing music and producing films

© Larry Harwood Photography. Property of Cengage Learning

Chapter 4: Annie Miller / Meagan

Hometown: Albuquerque, New Mexico

Major: Nursing

Lessons Learned: Meagan admits that her biggest mistake her first term was not asking anyone for help with anything. But she enjoyed moving away from home and being more independent, meeting new people, and having a more laid-back academic schedule than her high school schedule had been.

Toughest First-Year Course: Calculus because she was overconfident and didn't study for exams.

Advice to New Students: "Don't give up! College is amazing! Oh, and don't spend all of your money on food." Restaurant bills and snacks add up!

Free Time: biking, hiking, playing Ultimate Frisbee, and giving campus tours

© Larry Harwood Photography. Property of Cengage Learning

Chapter 5: Dario Jones / Orlando

Hometown: Fountain, Colorado

Major: MA, Communication

Lessons Learned: Start strong, work hard, and finish strong

Toughest First-Year Course: Math 099

Advice to New Students: "Get to know your instructors and fellow classmates. Ask questions in class when you're not sure about something."

Free Time: What free time? To relax, I listen to jazz or classical music, or I'll channel surf until I find something interesting to watch.

© Larry Harwood Photography. Property of Cengage Learning

Chapter 6: Lindsey Collier / Heather

Hometown: Her parents have moved several times while she's been in college—so where is home?

Major: Nursing

Lessons Learned: Heather made the mistake of not making academics her first priority, but she learned from her first-year seminar course that she needed to be willing to sacrifice social time for study time.

Advice to New Students: "College isn't like high school—you do actually have to study three times as much for any course. No matter what course it is, study for it. You'll feel much better about receiving high marks than about partying with friends. And get involved on your campus. It's your home away from home, so why not make the most of it?"

Free Time: College Step and Dance Team

© Larry Harwood Photography. Property of Cengage Learning

Chapter 7: Darnell Williams / Calil

Hometown: Colorado Springs, Colorado

Major: History with a secondary education emphasis

Lessons Learned: Calil noticed many similarities between himself and the FOCUS Challenge Case character he portrayed, besides playing football and watching movies. Calil, too, had problems with the transition from high school to college. He admits he was a student who "coasted" through his senior year of high school, which made his first year of college more difficult. He didn't study as hard as he should have as a first-year student.

Toughest First-Year Class: English, because he wasn't fully aware of the instructor's expectations.

Advice to New Students: "Determination is the key to success. If you are determined, there is nothing in the world that can stop you."

© Larry Harwood Photography. Property of Cengage Learning

Chapter 8: Katie Alexander / Christina

Hometown: Colorado Springs, Colorado. Since she went to college in her hometown, Christina really enjoyed the opportunity college provided to meet new people.

Major: Nursing

Lessons Learned: Spending her free time with her friends watching movies, going bowling or dancing, and just hanging out, Christina found that like her FOCUS Challenge Case character, she, too, would make up excuses to get out of studying and doing her homework. She quickly learned the importance of reading and taking notes. "As weird as it may sound, reading cuts your end study time by more than half. Reading the material ahead of time helps you understand everything so much better."

Advice to New Students: "Stay motivated. College is going to FLY by! If you stay motivated and get good grades, it really will be over before you know it."

© Larry Harwood Photography. Property of Cengage Learning

Chapter 9: Joe Cloud / Alvin

Hometown: Ganado, Arizona (Navajo Nation)

Major: Business

Toughest First-Year Course: Spanish because he came from a place where no other languages are ever spoken.

Lessons Learned: President of the American Indian Science and Engineering Society on campus, Alvin identifies closely with his FOCUS Challenge Case character. He, too, is one of a minority of Native Americans in higher education, so a lot of people in his hometown are carefully watching his academic success. Alvin admits his biggest mistake in his first term was not opening up to people—he came to school for class and left without trying to meet new people. But he learned from his mistakes and eventually came to value meeting all sorts of different people through activities on campus.

Advice to New Students: "Learn from my mistakes: Be open to try new things and get out of your comfort zone. You meet a lot of new people that way and it makes your first year the experience of a lifetime."

© Larry Harwood Photography. Property of Cengage Learning

Chapter 10: Kia Washington / Charmaine

Hometown: Colorado Springs, Colorado

Major: Psychology and Sociology

Toughest First-Year Course: General psychology because there was so much to learn in such a short period of time.

Lessons Learned: In her first-year seminar, Charmaine learned how to manage her time more effectively, as well as how important it is to keep yourself healthy in mind, body, and spirit, something she felt her FOCUS Challenge Case character could have benefited from.

Advice to New Students: "Remember to have fun in everything that you do, both academically and otherwise. Take care of yourself first and don't feel as though you have to do everything all the time; sometimes the best parts of life come during moments of down time. This is where you are able to truly reflect on what it is you're doing and remember why you're doing it in the first place!"

© Larry Harwood Photography. Property of Cengage Learning

Chapter 11: Anthony Lopez / Luis

Hometown: Aguascalientes, Mexico

Major: Spanish with an emphasis in secondary education

Lessons Learned: Luis is extremely involved on campus and within his community—he is President of the Association of Future Teachers, sings with his church choir, plays intramural soccer, and works for the Air Force on weekends—and as a first-year student, in order to cope with stress on a few occasions, he found himself doing the same things his FOCUS case study character did—partying too much. Luis thinks one mistake he made in his first term was that he procrastinated with homework because his new freedom let him think he could have fun first and study later, but he quickly learned he was wrong.

Advice to New Students: "Be smart and get involved, but always do your homework first. If you are involved on campus, you will meet people that will help make your college experience easier and more fun."

© Larry Harwood Photography. Property of Cengage Learning

Chapter 12: Ethan Cole / Josh

Hometown: Fort Morgan, Colorado

Major: Sociology

Lessons Learned: Like his *FOCUS* Challenge Case character, Josh noticed that he, too, didn't always push himself to reach his potential. But he learned through his first-year seminar course that he is responsible for himself and that professors aren't like high school teachers. They will let you fail a class if you don't do what you need to. It's up to you.

Advice to New Students: "Not only did getting involved on campus help me have more fun in school, but it has also helped me academically. It has taught me how to manage my time and has made it so much easier for me to participate with confidence in class. Just make sure you get what you need to do done, and you will enjoy your college experience so much more."

Free Time: "Free time? What's that?! I'm too busy to have free time!" (But he secretly admits he snowboards, plays guitar, draws, and spends time with friends.)

© Larry Harwood Photography. Property of Cengage Learning

MEET THE AUTHOR: Constance Staley

Hometown: Pittsburgh, Pennsylvania (although she never actually lived there. Instead, she lived all over the world and went to ten schools in twelve years.)

Background: Connie has taught at the University of Colorado at Colorado Springs for more than 35 years after getting a bachelor's degree in education, a master's degree in linguistics, and a Ph.D. in communication.

College Memories: Connie remembers loving her public speaking class as a first-year student and having tons of friends, but being extremely homesick for her family.

Advice to New Students: "Earning a college degree is hard work, takes a long time, and requires a substantial investment of your time, energy, and resources. But it's the best investment you can make in your own future—one you'll never regret."

Free Time: Spending time with her husband, her two daughters, and her boy-girl grandtwins; relaxing at her cabin in the mountains; and traveling around the country to speak to other professors who also care about first-year students and their success.

Introduction to Students

Dear Reader,

This book is different. It won't coerce, coddle, caution, or coax you. Instead, it will give you the tools you need to coach yourself. Ultimately, this book is about you, your college career, and your career beyond college. It's about the future you will create for yourself.

FOCUS on College Success stars a cast of twelve of my own students, like a stage play. One student "actor" is featured in each chapter's opening case study. All 12 cast members reappear throughout the book, so that you'll get to know them as you read. I've been teaching for more than 30 years now and worked with thousands of students. Each case study is about a real student (with a fictitious name) that I've worked with or a composite of several students. You may find you have some things in common with them. But whether you do or not, I hope they will make this book come to life for you. You'll also be able to meet these "actors" electronically in videos called, "Inside the FOCUS Studio," on the book's College Success CourseMate.

I love what I do, and I care deeply about students. I hope that comes through to you as a reader. You'll see that I've inserted some of my personality, had a bit of fun at times, and tried to create a new kind of textbook for you. In my view, learning should be engaging, personal, memorable, challenging, and fun.

Most importantly, I know that these next few years hold the key to unlock much of what you want from your life. And from all my years of experience and research, I can tell you straightforwardly that what you read in this book works. It gets results. It can turn you into a better, faster learner. Really? you ask. Really! The only thing you have to do is put all the words in this book into action. That's where the challenge comes in.

Getting a college degree takes time, energy, resources, and focus. At times, it may mean shutting down the six windows you have open on your computer, and directing all your attention to one thing in laser-like fashion. It may mean disciplining yourself to dig in and stick with something until you've nailed it. Can you do it? I'm betting you can, or I wouldn't have written this book. Invest yourself fully in what you read here, and then decide to incorporate it into your life. If there's one secret to college success, that's it.

So, you're off! You're about to begin one of the most fascinating, liberating, challenging, and adventure-filled times of your life. I may not be able to meet each one of you personally, but I can wish you well, wherever you are. I hope this book helps you on your journey.

Constance Staley

READINESS ✓ FOCUS Entrance Interview

Although you may not have experienced life as a new college student for long, we're interested in how you expect to spend your time, what challenges you think you'll face, what strengths you can build on, and your general views of what you think college will be like. Please answer thoughtfully.

INFORMATION ABOUT YOU

Name Jamie Hayward

Student Number ______ Course/Section Criminal Justice

Instructor ______

Gender female Age ______

Your Background

1. **Ethnic Identification (check all that apply):**

✓ American Indian or Alaska Native
___ Native Hawaiian or Other Pacific Islander
___ Asian
___ Hispanic/Latino
✓ Black or African American
___ White
___ Mixed Race (for example, one Caucasian parent and one Asian)
___ Prefer not to answer

2. **Is English your first (native) language?**

✓ yes ___ no

3. **Did your parents graduate from college?**

___ yes, both ___ yes, father only ___ yes, mother only ✓ neither ___ not sure

Your High School Experience

4. **If you are entering college soon after completing high school, on average, how many total hours per week did you spend studying outside of class in high school?**

✓ 0–5 ___ 6–10 ___ 11–15 ___ 16–20 ___ 21–25
___ 26–30 ___ 31–35 ___ 36–40 ___ 40+ ___ I am a returning student and attended high school some time ago.

5. **What was your high school grade point average when you graduated?**

___ A+ ___ A ___ A− ___ B+ ___ B
___ B− ___ C+ ___ C ___ C− ___ D or lower
___ I don't remember. ✓ I earned a GED.

Information About This Semester/Quarter

6. How many credit hours are you taking this term?

____ 6 or fewer   ____ 7–11   ____ 12–14   ____ 15–16   ____ 17 or more

7. Where are you living this term?

____ in campus housing   ____ with my immediate family   ____ with a relative other than my immediate family

____ on my own   ____ other (please explain)

Working While in College

8. In addition to going to college, do you expect to work for pay at a job (or jobs) this term?

____ yes   ____ no

9. If so, how many hours per week do you expect to work?

____ 1–10   ____ 11–20   ____ 21–30   ____ 31–40   ____ 40+

10. If you plan to work for pay, where will you work?

____ on campus   ____ off campus   ____ at more than one job

YOUR COLLEGE EXPECTATIONS

Your Reasons and Predictions

11. Why did you decide to go to college? (Check all that apply.)

____ because I want to build a better life for myself.
____ because I want to build a better life for my family.
____ because I want to be well off financially in the future.
____ because I need a college education to achieve my dreams.
____ because my friends were going to college.
____ because my family encouraged me to go.
____ because it was expected of me.
____ because I was recruited for athletics.
____ because I want to continue learning.
____ because the career I am pursuing requires a degree.
____ because I was unsure of what I might do instead.
____ other (please explain) ________________

12. How do you expect to learn best in college? (Check all that apply.)

____ by looking at charts, maps, graphs
____ by looking at color-coded information
____ by looking at symbols and graphics
____ by listening to instructors' lectures
____ by listening to other students during in-class discussions
____ by talking about course content with friends or roommates
____ by reading books
____ by writing papers
____ by taking notes
____ by going on field trips
____ by engaging in activities
____ by actually doing things

13. The following sets of opposite descriptive phrases are separated by five blank lines. Put an X on the line between the two that best represent your response, like this: For me, high school was easy ____:__X__:____:____:____ hard

I expect my first term of college to:

challenge me academically ____:____:____:____:____ be easy
be very different from high school ____:____:____:____:____ be a lot like high school
be exciting ____:____:____:____:____ be dull
be interesting ____:____:____:____:____ be uninteresting
motivate me to continue ____:____:____:____:____ discourage me
be fun ____:____:____:____:____ be boring
help me feel a part of this campus ____:____:____:____:____ make me feel like an outsider

14. **How many total hours per week do you expect to study outside of class for your college courses?**

___ 0–5 ___ 6–10 ___ 11–15 ___ 16–20 ___ 21–25
___ 26–30 ___ 31–35 ___ 36–40 ___ 40+

15. **What do you expect your grade point average to be at the end of your first term of college?**

___ A+ ___ A ___ A– ___ B+ ___ B
___ B– ___ C+ ___ C ___ C– ___ D or lower

Your Strengths, Personality, and Interests

16. **Please identify your *strengths*—personal characteristics that will contribute to your college success. (Check all that apply.)**

___ a. I am good at building relationships.
___ b. I can usually convince others to follow my plan.
___ c. I like to win.
___ d. I work toward future goals.
___ e. I like to be productive and get things done.
___ f. I have a positive outlook on life.
___ g. I'm usually the person who gets things going.
___ h. I enjoy the challenge of learning new things.
___ i. I am focused.
___ j. I can usually look at a problem and figure out a plan of action.
___ k. I work to keep everyone happy.
___ l. I'm a take-charge kind of person.
___ m. I help other people develop their talents and skills.
___ n. I'm a very responsible person.
___ o. I can analyze a situation and see various ways things might work out.
___ p. I usually give tasks my best effort.

17. **How confident are you in yourself in each of the following areas? (1 = very confident, 5 = not at all confident)**

___ overall academic ability
___ mathematical skills
___ leadership ability
___ reading skills
___ public speaking skills
___ study skills
___ technology skills
___ physical well being
___ writing skills
___ social skills
___ emotional well being
___ teamwork skills

18. **For each of the following pairs of descriptors, which set sounds most like you? (Please choose between the two options on each line and place a checkmark by your choice.)**

___ Extraverted and outgoing or ___ Introverted and quiet
___ Detail-oriented and practical or ___ Big-picture and future-oriented
___ Rational and truthful or ___ People-oriented and tactful
___ Organized and self-disciplined or ___ Spontaneous and flexible

19. ***FOCUS* is about 12 different aspects of college life. Which are you most interested in applying to yourself in your academic work? (Check all that apply.)**

___ Building dreams, setting goals
___ Managing time, energy, and money
___ Developing information literacy, writing, and speaking skills
___ Developing your memory
___ Taking tests
___ Working toward wellness
___ Learning to learn
___ Thinking critically and creatively
___ Engaging, listening, and note-taking in class
___ Reading and studying
___ Building relationships, valuing diversity
___ Choosing a major and career

Your Challenges

20. Of the 12 aspects of college life identified in the previous question, which do you expect to be most challenging to apply to yourself in your academic work? (Check all that apply.)

____ Building dreams, setting goals

____ Managing time, energy, and money

____ Developing information literacy, writing, and speaking skills

____ Developing your memory

____ Taking tests

____ Working toward wellness

____ Learning to learn

____ Thinking critically and creatively

____ Engaging, listening, and note-taking in class

____ Reading and studying

____ Building relationships, valuing diversity

____ Choosing a major and career

21. Which one of your current classes do you expect to find most challenging this term and why?

Which class? (course title *or* department and course number) ____________________

Why? ____

Do you expect to succeed in this course? ____ yes ____ no ____ Perhaps (please explain): ____________________

22. Please mark your *top three areas of concern* relating to your first term of college by placing 1, 2, and 3 next to the items you choose (with 1 representing your top concern).

____ I might not fit in.

____ I might not be academically successful.

____ I'm not sure I can handle the stress.

____ I might overextend myself and try to do too much.

____ I might not reach out for help when I need it.

____ I might not put in enough time to be academically successful.

____ I might be tempted to drop out.

____ I might not be organized enough.

____ I may be distracted by other things, like spending too much time online.

____ Other (please explain) ____________________

____ I might have difficulty making friends.

____ My grades might disappoint my family.

____ I may have financial problems.

____ I might cut class frequently.

____ I tend to procrastinate on assignments.

____ My professors might be hard to communicate with.

____ I might be homesick.

____ I might be bored in my classes.

____ My job(s) outside of school might interfere with my studies.

Your Future

23. How certain are you now of the following (1 = totally sure, 5 = totally unsure)?

____ Finishing your degree

____ Choosing your major

____ Deciding on a career

____ Completing your degree at this school

____ Continuing on to work toward an advanced degree after college

24. What are you most looking forward to in college?

25. Describe the best outcomes you hope for at the end of this first semester/quarter. Do you expect to achieve them? Why or why not?

Artmim/Shutterstock.com

Building Dreams, Setting Goals

CHAPTER 1

© Larry Harwood Photography, Property of Cengage Learning

You're about to discover . . .

- How this book will help you learn
- What motivates you
- What separates performers and learners
- What your core values say about you
- How to develop goals that work

READINESS ✓ What do you KNOW?

Before beginning to read this chapter, take two minutes to answer the following questions on a scale of 1 to 10. Your answers will help you assess how ready you are to focus.

low 1 2 3 4 5 6 7 8 9 10 high

How much do you *already* know?

Based on reading the "You're about to discover . . ." list and skimming this chapter, how much do you think you probably already know about this chapter's subject? 8

See if you can answer these questions about goals and dreams *before* you read.

1. What is the difference between a learner and a performer?
2. What is the difference between intrinsic and extrinsic motivation?
3. Which four factors—all beginning with the letter "C"—are a part of intrinsic motivation—and your college success?

How much do you expect to learn?

In general, how motivated are you to learn more by reading this chapter? ________

How much do you think this information might affect your success overall? ________

How much energy do you plan to put into reading this chapter? ________

If your response isn't as high as you know it could be, explain why. ________

____

____

How ready are you to read *now*?

How ready are you to focus on this chapter? Enter a number for each aspect of your readiness to focus.

Physically ________

Intellectually ________

Emotionally ________

If any of your answers is below a 10, pay attention to whatever is distracting you before you start reading. Then zero in and focus.

How long do you think it will take you to complete this chapter from start to finish?

________ Hour(s) ________ Minutes

Now, as you begin, do you intend to finish reading this chapter?

____ yes ____ no ____ maybe

FOCUS Challenge Case

? challenge

Sylvia Sanchez

College—finally! As Sylvia opened the new package of turquoise sheets for the bed in her dorm room, she felt excited but at the same time, amazingly calm. Sylvia had been counting off the days all summer, and frankly, it felt good to be on her own. No younger brothers and sisters squawking, no parents breathing down her neck, no grandparents expecting regular visits, and no lame boyfriend hanging around all the time. She stopped to check her cell phone—four new texts, probably all from him. And all those pictures of her he had posted on Facebook this morning! She wanted to write back and tell him to get over it, but she thought she'd better wait awhile for that. *Let's just see what college has to offer. That's smarter*, she admitted. Her three suite-mates hadn't arrived yet, so naturally Sylvia claimed the best bedroom. *They'd probably have done the same thing*, she reassured herself. *They should have gotten here earlier.*

Sylvia had always been smart—not brilliant, but smart enough to know how to play the game. She was always rushing around, doing a hundred things at once. Focusing wasn't her strong point, and multitasking didn't always get her the best grades, but truthfully, she'd never even cracked a book during her senior year and still earned all A's and B's, even in AP and IB classes. College, she imagined, would be a slightly harder version of high school. It couldn't be as hard as her parents had warned. She remembered their threats when she brought home a bad grade in high school: *You just wait until you get to college!* How would they know? They'd never even been to college themselves. If all that propaganda from parents and high school teachers were really true, no one would go to college! *How hard can it possibly be?* she asked herself. Her parents were helping with the finances, but they weren't able to afford much. "And we're not paying for anything below a B!" her father had insisted. She just had to keep her grades up enough to hold onto her financial aid, and if she could manage to impress her parents, that wouldn't hurt, either.

Of her four new college courses, Sylvia was least worried about her college success class. *Automatic A*, she predicted. *Everyone knows how to study.*

It's just common sense, she thought to herself. But whether studying enough to "live up to her potential" was on her agenda was another thing. The thought of writing an essay every week for her English Composition class brought on major dread; in fact, she wasn't all that excited about any of her classes. There might be other, more compelling pursuits that took up her time in college, like meeting interesting people and finishing her demo CD.

The one thing Sylvia knew for sure was that she desperately wanted to major in music, and her parents desperately wanted her to major in business. "Who gets a job with a music degree?" they would ask. Her Dad grilled her regularly on the subject. "There are all kinds of possible careers if you earn a business degree, but only one music teacher per school. And when budget cuts come around, it's the arts that always go first. How about if you just pay for a music degree on your own? Your mother and I never had the chance; don't blow this opportunity!" "Yeah, whatever . . ." was her usual retort.

But all Sylvia really wanted in life was to be behind a microphone in front of an audience. And the bigger the audience, the better. Someday—she just knew it—she'd sign a recording contract with a major record label. All her friends told her how good she was. They'd even encouraged her to try out for a TV singing competition. Imagine—fame and fortune. *Sylvia Sanchez, recording artist . . .* even her name had the right ring to it and eventually, everyone would recognize it. They'd download her top hits, and she'd have the clothes, hair, make-up, and money she'd always wanted.

Elif Eren/Shutterstock.com

As she stood at the foot of the bed, admiring her new sheets, Sylvia caught a glimpse of herself in the mirror on the wall. "Looking good!" she whispered. Was she referring to her how her new bedroom was shaping up or how she'd made the right decision on what to wear?

Suddenly, Sylvia heard laughter in the hallway and realized she was just about to meet her new suite-mates. What would they be like? Would she like them? Would they like her? Deep down, Sylvia realized she really did want to be successful in college. She wanted to live her own life and do her own thing. Still, she rationalized, *If this whole college thing doesn't work out, I'll go back home, pick up where I left off, get back my old job at the mall, and wait for the future I* really *want.*

Artmim/Shutterstock.com

© Cengage Learning

AP Photo/PRNewsFoto/Epic Records, Pindyurin Vasily

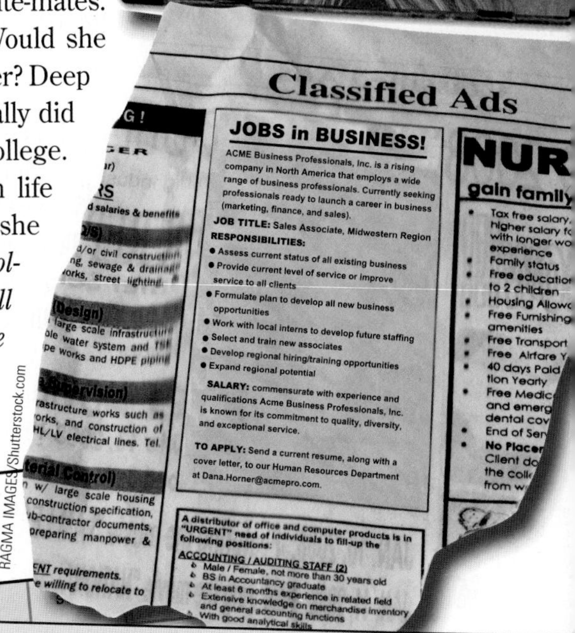

RAGMA IMAGES/Shutterstock.com

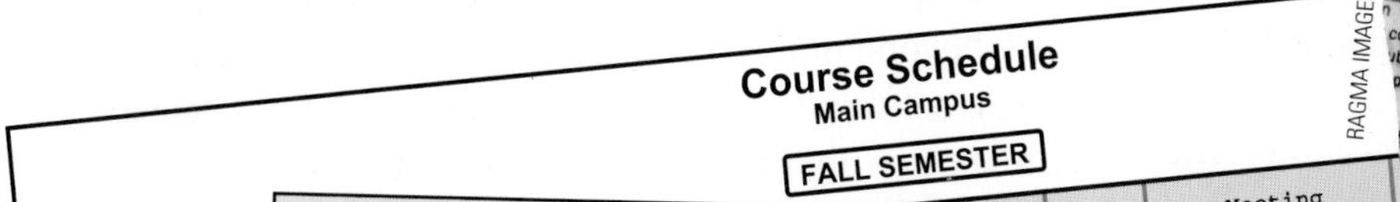

© Cengage Learning

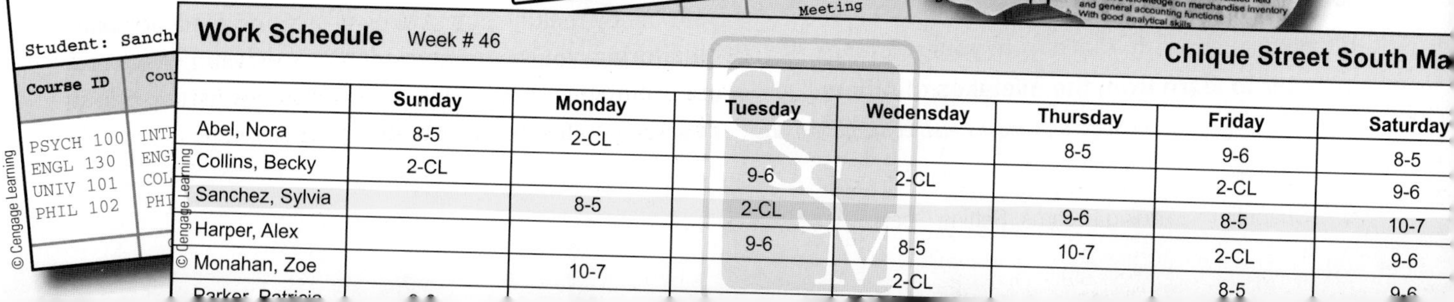

	Sunday	Monday	Tuesday	Wedensday	Thursday	Friday	Saturday
Abel, Nora	8-5	2-CL			8-5	9-6	8-5
Collins, Becky	2-CL		9-6	2-CL		2-CL	9-6
Sanchez, Sylvia		8-5	2-CL		9-6	8-5	10-7
Harper, Alex			9-6	8-5	10-7	2-CL	9-6
Monahan, Zoe		10-7		2-CL		8-5	9-6

© Cengage Learning

What Do You Think?

1. Is Sylvia sufficiently motivated to succeed in college? Why or why not?
2. Describe Sylvia's beliefs about her intelligence. Does she think college is mostly about effort or about ability? Is Sylvia a *learner* or a *performer*?
3. Is Sylvia's vision of becoming a famous singer a goal or a dream? Why?
4. Identify three things that show focus and might help Sylvia make good life management choices.
5. Are any elements of Sylvia's situation similar to your own college experience thus far?

Who Are You? And What Do You Want?

Imagine this voicemail greeting: "Hi. At the tone, please answer two of life's most important questions. Who are you? And what do you want?" Beep. Very clever, don't you think? Can you answer these questions right now? Have you thought much about them? How much do you really know about yourself and what you want from this life of yours?

Don't worry. These aren't trick questions and there are no wrong answers. But there are some answers that are more right for you than others. College is a great time to think about who you are and what you want. In addition to learning about biology or history or business—whatever you choose for a major—college will be a time to learn about yourself: your motivation, values, dreams, and goals. College is a time when you'll make some of the most important choices of your life. Which major will you choose? Which career will you aim for? How many lifelong friends will you make? From this point on, it's up to you. Have you ever heard this phrase with ten two-letter words: "If it is to be, it is up to me"? It's true.

Think about it: a college education is one of the best investments you can make. Once you've earned a college degree, it's yours forever. Someone can steal your car, walk away with your cell phone, or carry off your laptop, but once you've earned a college degree, no one can ever take it from you. Your choice to be a college graduate will pay off in many ways. So even if you aren't sure exactly how you want to spend the rest of your life right now, you can't go wrong by investing in your future.

Yeah, but maybe with some luck I won't need a degree . . .

This book starts with the big picture: your life. It's about managing your life, being fully invested in what you're doing, and using your abilities to their utmost. Notice the phrase "managing your life"—not *controlling* your life. Let's face it: many things in life are beyond our control. We can't control international politics, set tuition rates, or advise characters in our favorite movies about what to do next. But you can manage your life by making smart choices, setting realistic goals, monitoring your time and energy, motivating yourself, and ultimately creating your own future. As the title of this book states boldly, it's about focus.

"It's always smart to learn from your mistakes. It's smarter to learn from the mistakes of others."

Hillel Segal and Jesse Berst, computer experts

> **Furious activity is no substitute for understanding.**
>
> *H. H. Williams, British poet and playwright*

IKO/Shutterstock.com

For many of us, focusing is a challenge. We work too many hours, crowd our lives with obligations, and rush from one thing to the next. We think we're good at multitasking. We can surf the Internet, listen to a new CD, watch a DVD, and read this chapter—all at the same time, right? But think about Gandhi's wise words applied to today's lifestyle: "There is more to life than increasing its speed." The truth is, the more we try to multitask, the more we end up sacrificing the self-discipline required for in-depth study. Recent research indicates that multitasking hurts your brain's ability to learn, and that what you learn while you're distracted by other things is harder to use and recall.[1] In fact, even though technology gives you new access and abilities, according to one study, when you're distracted by e-mail or phone calls, your IQ drops by 10 points.[2] Technology's stimulation gives your brain a squirt of dopamine, which can actually be addictive, and being constantly connected, research shows, can cause brain fatigue.[3] Many experts say that multitasking causes a brownout in your brain; there's just not enough power to go around. Your stress level can skyrocket when you "fragment" your attention in dozens of directions at the same time, and "rebooting" after you've interrupted yourself to bounce out to something else can take from seconds to hours.[4]

Ours is a fast-paced society. We expect results quickly. We've become accustomed to instant gratification, as it's called. We want what we want, and we want it right now! But earning a college degree takes time, commitment, and determination. It won't happen overnight and it won't happen automatically. Unlike almost anything else you can buy, you must invest more than money to become truly educated.

Of course, some people achieve success without a college degree, but by and large, they're the exception. Even Steven Spielberg, self-made billionaire in the film industry and winner of Academy Awards for *Schindler's List* and *Saving Private Ryan,* felt the need to finish the college degree he had started more than thirty years before. "I wanted to accomplish this for many years as a 'thank you' to my parents for giving me the opportunity for an education and a career, and as a personal note for my own family—and young people everywhere—about the importance of achieving their college education goals," he said. "But I hope they get there quicker than I did. Completing the requirements for my degree 33 years after finishing my principal education marks my longest post-production schedule."[5]

If you read this book carefully and follow its advice, it will help you become the best student you can possibly be. It will give you practical tools to help you manage your life. It will take you beyond college into your career. And most of all, it will encourage you to become a true scholar. That is this book's challenge to you as you begin your college career.

EXERCISE 1.1

We'd Like to Get to Know You …

Take a few minutes to finish the following statements. Think about what each sentence says about you. Use your responses to introduce yourself to the class or form pairs, talk over your responses together, and use your partner's answers to introduce him or her to the class.

1. I'm happiest when ______________________.
2. I'm disappointed when ______________________.
3. If I had an extra $100, I'd ______________________.
4. The thing I'm most proud of is ______________________.
5. Once people get to know me, they're probably surprised to find I'm ______________________.
6. My family wants me to ______________________.
7. I'd really like to become ______________________.
8. My friends enjoy me because ______________________.
9. I've been known to consume large quantities of ______________________.
10. I'd rather be ____________ than ____________.
11. When I'm under stress, ______________________.
12. My best quality is ______________________.
13. My worst quality is ______________________.
14. The academic skill I'd most like to develop is ______________________.
15. One thing I'd like to figure out about myself is ______________________.

Spending Time "in the System"

Challenge: How do people learn?

Reaction:

____

____

____

Spending time "in the system"? No, being in college isn't like being in jail—far from it. Many people reflect on their college days as one of the most enjoyable, active, and interesting times of their lives. Get involved on campus, make lifelong friends, and gain as much as you can from your college experience.

"The system" is the approach used in this book to structure productive learning: the Challenge → Reaction → Insight → Action system. It is based on the work of Dr. John Bransford and his colleagues, who together wrote an influential book called *How People Learn*.

Figure 1.1 summarizes how learning requires focus, and focus involves the four steps in this system. Ideally, it would be interesting to hear the conversation going on in your head as you learn—what's called metacognition, or knowing how you come to know something. But because that's impossible, this book asks you to write and discuss things along the way: your reactions, your insights, and the actions you plan to take. You'll come to realize things about yourself.

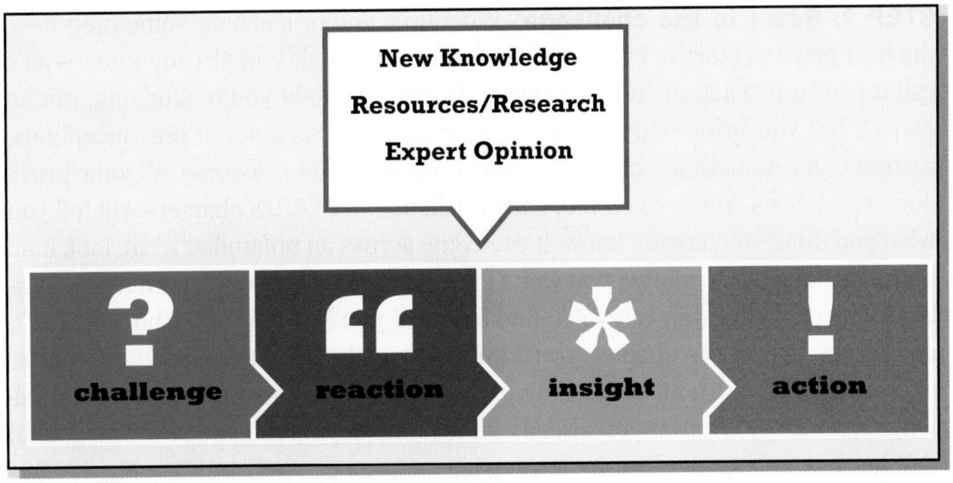

FIGURE 1.1

How People Learn

Source: Based on J. Bransford, et al. (2000). *How People Learn: Brain, Mind, Experience, and School.* Washington, DC: National Academy Press.

This book's goal for you is *transformative learning*: "a process of examining, questioning, validating, and revising [your] perceptions."[6] What you'll learn by reading it has the potential to *transform,* or *change* you, so that you're ready to meet the many challenges that await you in college and in life. Here's a step-by-step explanation of the learning system used in this book.

STEP 1: Accept the *FOCUS* challenge. Every time you study a new subject or take a new course, you are challenged, right? Within each chapter of this book, you'll be presented with challenges, beginning with a case study about a college student—perhaps someone like you or a friend—who is experiencing something new and difficult. Research shows that people can learn more from examples of things going wrong than they can from examples of things going perfectly smoothly. As you continue to read, you'll be presented with additional challenges related to the chapter's content to pique your curiosity, motivate you to keep reading, and start a learning chain reaction. Don't skip over this step; it's an important part of the learning process. Challenge yourself!

I hope things go right for me!

> **Surround yourself with people who take their work seriously, but not themselves, those who work hard and play hard."**
>
> *Colin Powell, former U.S. Secretary of State*

STEP 2: React to the challenge. Whenever you're learning something new, the best place to start is by figuring out what you think you already know—let's call it your gut reaction. You're a novice to any new field you're studying, not an expert, but you bring with you to the learning process a set of preconceptions, assumptions, sometimes biases or misperceptions, and of course, all your previous experiences. Your reaction to each challenge in *FOCUS* chapters will tell you what you think you already know. If you come across an unfamiliar term, look it up in the dictionary. Of course, you won't know everything there is to know in reacting to the challenge yet. But you'll find out what you do know and what you don't, and by the end of the chapter, you'll know more about all the challenges you've encountered throughout your reading. Stop and fill in your reactions to the Challenge questions. What *do* you already know? Check yourself and see. The goal of this book is to help you become a deep learner, as opposed to skimming the surface and simply rushing on to the next assignment and the next course—as many college students do. It will ask you to pause, take stock, focus, and think.

STEP 3: Use new knowledge to gain insights. After your initial reaction, you must pay attention to your inner voice—insights you've gained from new knowledge. An "Insight → Action" activity at the end of every chapter will help you keep track of them. Your instructor may ask you to record your answers online or in a notebook, or you may discuss these questions in class. Let's say, for example, that you read later in this chapter about goal setting. When you first thought about it, the whole idea of setting goals seemed simple, but after reading about it, you decide you really hadn't ever thought about it very deeply and hadn't thought much at all about setting your own goals. The difference between step 2 (whatever reaction you provided to the challenge) and step 3 (the insights you've gained) demonstrates that learning is taking place.

Talk about insight and action—my bathroom scale gave me an insight this morning. I need to lose five pounds, but will I follow through with action? That's another question!

STEP 4: Use your insights to propel you toward action. Insights have no impact unless they become integrated into your life, unless they lead to change. Decide how an insight affects your existing beliefs, how it changes them, and, therefore, what you've learned. Your insights may lead you to change your behavior, develop an informed opinion, or make choices about your education, your job, your family, or your life. The bottom line is: You must use your insights to take action. To become real, new knowledge must lead to personal insights that result in action.

Right! Maybe I'm just recognizing that what I'm reading sounds right. I guess I really didn't know all these things beforehand.

Each step in this four-part system is important. For example, if you skip step 2, *react to the challenge,* by identifying what you *think* you know, you may assume you already know all the new information you're reading or hearing. You may think, "Sure, of course, that makes sense. I already knew that," when you really didn't. Realizing there's a gap between steps 2 and 3—what you thought you knew and the insights you've gained from new knowledge—is important. And actually putting the insights you gain into real, live, honest-to-goodness action is vital.

As you work through this book, the Challenge → Reaction → Insight → Action system will continue cycling back to step 1, presenting you with new challenges. If you follow the system built into this book and integrate it into your other academic pursuits, you can become a lifelong learner. Thinking in terms of the learning cycle will become ingrained. Someone once said that change is accelerating in such mind-boggling ways today that "Learning is what most adults will do for a living in the 21st century." Life management is about knowing how to learn.

How Motivated *Are* You and *How* Are You Motivated?

? challenge
" reaction

Challenge: How intrinsically motivated do you think you are on a scale of 1 to 10 with 10 meaning EXTREMELY ACADEMICALLY MOTIVATED and 1 meaning NOT VERY MOTIVATED AT ALL? Why does this number seem right to you?

Reaction: ____________________

I'd say 5 for me. I just want to get to the fun part—my singing career!

Let's get serious. When it comes to getting a college education, where does motivation come into the picture? In general, motivation is your desire to engage and put forth effort, even when the going gets rough. The word *motivation* comes from Medieval Latin, *motivus,* meaning moving or impelling. What moves you to learn? There are many ways to define motivation, and different people are motivated by different things.

How motivated would you be to learn something difficult, such as a new language, one you'd never studied before? Let's say that you were offered a chance to learn Finnish, a challenging language that is not related to English.

EXERCISE 1.2

Intrinsic Motivation Self-Assessment

Read each of the following statements and circle the number beside each statement that most accurately represents your views about yourself.

	Completely Not True	Somewhat Not True	Neutral	Somewhat True	Completely True
1. I have academic goals.	1	2	3	4	5
2. I am confident I can complete my degree.	1	2	3	4	5
3. I determine my career goals.	1	2	3	4	5
4. I enjoy solving challenging, difficult problems.	1	2	3	4	5
5. I work on an assignment until I understand it.	1	2	3	4	5
6. I am confident I will graduate from college.	1	2	3	4	5
7. I determine the quality of my academic work.	1	2	3	4	5

(continued on next page)

	Completely Not True	Somewhat Not True	Neutral	Somewhat True	Completely True
8. I am pursuing a college degree because I value education.	1	2	3	4	5
9. I feel good knowing that I determine how my academic career develops.	1	2	3	4	5
10. I have high standards for academic work.	1	2	3	4	5
11. Staying in college is my decision.	1	2	3	4	5
12. I study because I like to learn new things.	1	2	3	4	5
13. I enjoy doing outside readings in connection to my future coursework.	1	2	3	4	5
14. I am intrigued by the different topics introduced in my courses.	1	2	3	4	5
15. I study because I am curious.	1	2	3	4	5
16. I look forward to going to class.	1	2	3	4	5
17. I am excited to take more courses within my major.	1	2	3	4	5
18. I enjoy learning more within my field of study.	1	2	3	4	5
19. I like to find answers to questions about material I am learning.	1	2	3	4	5
20. I enjoy studying.	1	2	3	4	5
21. I have pictured myself in a profession after college.	1	2	3	4	5
22. I am excited about the job opportunities I will have when I graduate.	1	2	3	4	5
23. I have pictured myself being successful in my chosen profession.	1	2	3	4	5
24. I believe I will make a substantial contribution to my chosen profession.	1	2	3	4	5
25. I feel good knowing I will be a member of the professional community in my area of study.	1	2	3	4	5
Total each column, then add your scores across.	______ +	______ +	______ +	______ +	______ =

______ OVERALL SCORE

Continue reading to find out what your overall score means.

Source: French, F.B., & Oakes, W. (2003). Measuring academic intrinsic motivation in the first year of college: Reliability and validity evidence for a new instrument. *Journal of the First Year Experience, 15*(1), 83–102.

For example, in Finnish *Kiitoksia oikein paljon* means "thank you very much." Finnish would be a challenge to learn. To determine your level of motivation, it would help to know your attitude toward Finland and Finnish people, whether you needed to learn Finnish for some reason, how you felt about learning it, if you thought you could learn it successfully, if you were reinforced in some way for learning it, and just how stimulating you found the learning process to be.[7] In other words, your motivation level depends on many factors, right?

You'd probably be more motivated to learn Finnish if these sorts of things were part of the picture: (a) you were going to visit relatives in Finland and were excited about it, (b) you'd always excelled at learning foreign languages and you expected to learn this one easily, (c) your boss was planning to transfer you to Helsinki as part of a big promotion, or (d) you enjoyed your Finnish language class, thought the instructor was a gifted teacher, and found the other students to be as motivated as you were. So, whose job is it to motivate you? Your instructor's? Your parents'? This book's? Yours? *Can* anyone else besides you motivate you? This book will ask you: how motivated *are* you to succeed in college? And *how* are you motivated?

To assess your own motivation, it's important to understand the difference between *extrinsic* and *intrinsic* motivation.[8] People who are *extrinsically,* or externally, motivated learn in order to get a grade, earn credits, or complete a requirement, for example. They are motivated by things outside themselves. People who are *intrinsically,* or internally, motivated learn because they're curious, fascinated, challenged, or because they truly want to master a subject. They are motivated from within. Let's be realistic, however. Extrinsic motivation is real and important. You need a particular number of credit hours to graduate. You'd rather get A's than F's. But how intrinsically motivated you are in college will have a great deal to do with just how successful you are. The motivation to become truly educated must come from within you.

Good point. Is it my motivation or my parents'?

Look at Figure 1.2 and circle the three boxes (and only three) that most accurately describe your overall current motivation to attend college. Does your

FIGURE 1.2

Extrinsic versus Intrinsic Motivation

Extrinsic Motivation **Intrinsic Motivation**

Christopher Hall/Shutterstock.com; Yari/Shutterstock.com; Scott Maxwell/LuMaxArt/Shutterstock.com; Andy Dean Photography/Shutterstock.com; Palto/Shutterstock.com; Pling/Shutterstock.com; Yuri Arcurs/Shutterstock.com; Vasilius/Shutterstock.com

motivation vary in the different courses you're taking? When you think about why you're in college, are you generally on the extrinsic side or the intrinsic side—or both? Your instructor may wish to generate a discussion about these questions in class.

You completed the Academic Intrinsic Motivation Scale (AIMS) in the previous exercise, which is designed to measure your intrinsic, or internal, motivation to succeed in college in terms of these four C-Factors. You'll see these C-Factors reappear throughout the book to boost your intrinsic motivation:

CURIOSITY Do you want to learn new things? Are you truly interested in what you're learning? Do you ask questions? Do you allow your curiosity to propel your learning? Many chapters include a short article based on current research, a *New York Times* bestseller, an upcoming trend, or a new way of looking at what's needed to succeed in college. You'll read cutting-edge information that may pique your curiosity and lead you to consider exploring the original source or related material on your own.

CONTROL Do you think the academic investment you make will lead to successful outcomes? Do you believe you can control how successful you'll be? You are encouraged throughout this book to apply what you are reading about to your most challenging class this term and to take charge of your own learning. The challenge in your chosen class may be due to the level, for example—either too high-level because the material is extremely difficult (a killer course) or too low-level (a no-brainer, boring course). This book will help you succeed in your chosen class by prompting you to work with your instructor through an office hours visit or e-mail, for example. Taking charge of your own learning is vital to college success.

I'm goal oriented, but I'm just not sure what it will take . . .

CAREER OUTLOOK Are you goal oriented? Are you future oriented? Can you imagine yourself graduating and getting a job you want? Specific chapters of *FOCUS* include some extremely useful advice about career prospects, perceptions, progress, priorities, or professionalism that will put you ahead of the game by the time you launch your career. (Much of the advice works for your college career, too.) Looking ahead now can do you a world of good later. Employers say that many college graduates are ready in theory, but not in practice. They have the knowledge they've gained while studying for a college degree, but not necessarily the ability to put that knowledge into practice. As Yogi Berra says, "In theory there is no difference between theory and practice. In practice there is." It's time to start practicing for your career now!

CHALLENGE Does your college coursework challenge you appropriately? Too much challenge can cause you to become frustrated and give up. Not enough challenge can cause you to lose interest.[9] In general, if a course is too challenging, you may be tempted to give up. If it's too easy, you may lose interest. Adjusting the level of challenge to one that's right for you is key to keeping yourself motivated to learn, and that's up to you. No one else. Online quizzes for each chapter will challenge you so that you can work at your best. For more practice online, go to www.cengagebrain.com to take the Challenge Yourself online quizzes.

EXERCISE 1.3

The Ideal Student

Create your own personal top-ten list of the characteristics of an ideal student. Bring your completed list to your next class session where everyone can read their lists, and begin to add, delete, merge, and create a master list to which everyone can subscribe. Put your initials next to each of the ten items on the master list that you promise to do throughout the term. Your personal top-ten list, which your instructor may discuss with you individually at a later time, will become your learning contract for the course.

If your overall score on the AIMS in Exercise 1.2 was 100–125, you're intrinsically motivated at a high level. If you scored between 75 and 99, you're intrinsically motivated at a moderate level, but increasing your intrinsic motivation may help you achieve more. If you scored below 75, a lack of intrinsic motivation could interfere with your college success. If you're intrinsically motivated, you'll accept challenges, react to them by identifying what you already know, seek insights from new knowledge, and take action based on what you've learned.

Give Yourself an Attitude Adjustment

There's a difference of opinion on the subject of attitude. Some people say attitude is not all that important. Attitude-schmattitude, they say. Others say that *attitude* is more important than *aptitude*. What do you think?

In research studies conducted by Rick Snyder at the University of Kansas, students who scored high on a measure of hope got higher grades. Snyder explained that students with high hopes set themselves higher goals and know how to work hard to attain them.

Quick quiz. How many times in the past week did you catch yourself saying "Whatever . . . ," rolling your eyes when someone—perhaps a teacher, parent, or friend—offered you feedback or suggestions that you didn't want to hear? Be honest now. Think of all of those moments. Whatever-ness—an attitude of cynicism, apathy, disdain, or impatience—takes a lot less effort than optimism, respect, kindness, or any other positive response. Whether you realize it or not, whatevers chip away at your motivation, and they can contribute to self-sabotaging your opportunities to succeed in life. When it comes to your college education, one good thing you can do for yourself is to purge the word *whatever* from your vocabulary. Your education is much too important for whatevers—and so are you.

Oops! Whatever is one of my favorite words!

Eight Ways to Adjust Your Attitude

The good thing about attitude is that you can change it yourself. In fact, you can give yourself an overall attitude adjustment, which can lead to better control over your learning and deeper investment in your own education.

> **You are never given a wish without the power to make it come true. You may have to work for it, however.**
>
> *Richard Bach, from* Illusions

As you think about benefits of fine-tuning your attitude, keep these eight recommendations in mind:

© Larry Harwood Photography. Property of Cengage Learning

1. **Know that you always have choices.** Regardless of circumstances—your income, your background, or your prior academic record—you always have a choice, even if it's limited to how you choose to perceive your current situation.
2. **Take responsibility for your own outcomes.** Coach Vince Lombardi used to have his players look in a mirror before every game and ask themselves, "Am I looking at the person who is helping me win or the one who is holding me back?" Blaming others simply reduces your own power to work toward constructive responses to challenges.
3. **Convert turning points into learning points.** Instead of beating yourself up when things don't go well, figure out why. See what you can learn from the experience and then move on. As Henry Ford once said, "Failure is the opportunity to begin again, more intelligently."
4. **Choose your words carefully.** "Can't" and "won't" are two of the biggest inhibitors to a healthy attitude. Also pay attention to how you describe things. Is the cup half empty or half full? State things in the positive rather than the negative (for example, "stay healthy" rather than "don't get sick"). Language is a reflection of attitude.

> **"A positive attitude is your most priceless possession, one of your most valuable assets. To a great extent, it determines the overall quality of your life."**
>
> *Keith Harrell, from* Attitude Is Everything

5. **Fill your mind with messages about the attitude you want to have.** The old saying, "garbage in, garbage out," applies to attitudes as well. There are countless books, CDs, and films that offer positive, motivating messages. Paying attention to role models whose traits you admire is also a great way to bolster your outlook.
6. **Remember that negative experiences can be great teachers.** Have you ever watched someone do something so badly that you've said to yourself, "I'm never going to do that! I'm going to do it differently!"? You can also choose to learn from your own mistakes and setbacks. They all offer some sort of lesson—be it greater clarity, personal growth, or a new vision—even if it takes a bit of distance from the event to see what you can learn. It's hard to believe, but Michael Jordan was cut from his high school basketball team. He once observed, "I've failed over and over again in my life. That is why I succeed."

Maybe I do need an attitude adjustment. There are some good points here that I've never thought about . . .

7. **Offer help without expecting something in return.** Give freely of yourself, with no expectations of *quid pro quo*, and life will reward you in unexpected ways—not the least of which is a positive outlook. Offer to help someone study for a test or suggest that a classmate practice a presentation for class in front of you, for example. Engage in random acts of kindness; it'll do amazing things for your attitude.
8. **Acknowledge your blessings.** Taking time at the end of each day to recognize and feel gratitude for the blessings in your life—no matter how large or small—is a great way to amplify a positive attitude.

CAREER OUTLOOK: *KNOW THYSELF*

There is only one success—to be able to spend your life in your own way.

Christopher Morley (1890–1957),
American journalist, novelist, essayist and poet

Expectations. They play a big role in our lives. Your teachers expect you to work up to your full potential. Your grandparents expect you to marry someone who's "good enough" for you. Your parents expect you to give college your best shot. Sometimes it can seem as if you have less input than you should. Although they have your best interests at heart, it is *your* life, after all.

It's true about careers, too. Perhaps your family has talked about it for years: "Our Gabe is going to be a doctor. We've known it since we watched him play with his toy doctor's kit as a little kid." The story has been repeated so many times that it's now turned into a real expectation your family has for you. Or perhaps your parents have decided on a major for you based on economics, despite the fact that you have other interests. "We're not paying tuition for any major that won't lead to a real career with good job prospects. It's just not worth it."

But here's an important question: What do *you* want to do with your life? While your parents will most likely have an important perspective, figuring this out for yourself is one of the most important questions you will begin to answer in college.

Think of it this way: Before you take a road trip, you don't just close your eyes and point to a place on the map, do you? You don't automatically take someone else's recommendation. And you don't just start driving and hope to end up someplace interesting. You take your time and figure things out, realizing that you may end up taking an unexpected detour along the way. That's an important comparison.

Most college students change their majors at least once, and many adults change their careers, too. Our fictitious Gabe above, whose family has decided should be a doctor, may actually become one. But instead, he may eventually decide to head up the hospital as a businessman, rather than practice medicine, or open an emergi-care franchise as an entrepreneur. He may (or may not) choose something related to medicine, but not actually practice it.

Begin your journey with this advice in mind: Don't panic, but do start discovering your own expectations of yourself now. Use college as an opportunity to truly get to know yourself. Pay attention to which disciplines fascinate you as a learner. Make decisions for the right reasons. A career that pays well but holds no real appeal for you may result in major dissatisfaction later on. Project some alternative futures for yourself based on various career possibilities. Imagine yourself wearing different career "hats." As a French Pulitzer-prize winning author once said, "Be faithful to that which exists nowhere but in yourself." And set *your own* course.

Think Ahead: Why are you going to college? Who among your family members or friends has communicated their expectations for your future career? If so, is it a future you really want?

Yikes! This is about me!

CAST ON CAREERS

© Larry Harwood Photography. Property of Cengage Learning

FOCUS: When it comes to careers and majors, what advice do you have for new students?

TAMMY: I'd say, be true to yourself. My parents wanted me to major in accounting because they own a family-run business, but I just didn't have any interest in numbers. And sitting behind a desk all day held no appeal at all. Eventually, I convinced them that it was a better idea to major in business, rather than specialize in accounting. But it took me a semester of mediocre grades to get there.

FOCUS: How can new students be true to themselves when they don't know what they want?

TAMMY: For me, it was important to "go with my gut." I knew myself well enough to know what energized me and which classes I looked forward to, beyond just liking the instructor. I was genuinely interested in the content. Don't worry if you don't have it all figured out right away. Eventually, things will come into FOCUS!

Yes, I totally get this!

Statements That Ought To Be Outlawed in College . . . and Why

Because words reflect attitudes (and help shape them), listen for statements like these escaping from your mouth. They can negatively affect your attitude and therefore your learning:

I can agree with that! But I'm starting to get interested in some of them.

- **"I thought college classes would be more interesting than they are."** Some students, especially those who didn't find high school classes particularly interesting, expect something different in college. *Interesting* is in the mind of the beholder. You may not, but your professors think chemistry, calculus, and psychology are the most interesting things on the planet. It's up to *you* to generate your own enthusiasm for learning, rather than expecting your instructors to do it for you. Not all college classes will be naturally interesting to you, but you'll be much more successful if you decide to learn all you can, regardless of the wow factor.
- **"I didn't learn a thing in that class."** This statement may say more about you than it does about the quality of the instructor, teaching assistant, or course content. Actively search for what you can take away from a class, even if it didn't quite meet your expectations. When you play the blame game, you lose.
- **"The textbook is really dull. Why bother reading it?"** This question is about personal responsibility, too. Hey, it's your college experience. If you choose not to learn because the written material doesn't meet your entertainment criteria, how sad is that?
- **"The professor is soooo-o-o boring."** Again—it's your choice. Life isn't all Comedy Central. In your career, you'll be interacting with many different types of personalities, so it's good to begin now to appreciate that different people communicate differently. Get beneath the surface and you'll be amazed at how much you can learn.
- **"Why do I have to take this required course? What's the point?"** The point is to broaden your horizons, expand your skills as a critical thinker, and become a lifelong scholar. Care enough to give yourself every opportunity to do your best. And, yes, every class, every situation in life, is an opportunity. You're worth it.[10]

Singers don't need to be critical thinkers . . . or do they?

- **I can tell that my instructor doesn't like me.** The instructor may or may not like you (and you may or may not like him or her). That's not really the point. He may be focused on the course content, or she may just be introverted. Even if it were true, you'll still want to give it your best shot.

> **Ability is what you're capable of doing. Motivation determines what you do. Attitude determines how well you do it.**
>
> *Lou Holtz, former college football coach and ESPN sports analyst*

Ability versus Effort: What's More Important?

Successful people have several things in common: they love learning, seek challenges, value effort, and persevere even when things become difficult.[11] They demonstrate both ability and effort. These two things are the basic requirements for success.

EXERCISE 1.4

Your Academic Autobiography

Write a three-page academic autobiography describing your preparation for college. Describe the quality of your primary, middle, and high school learning experiences. Did they prepare you for what you're experiencing now in college? What do you think will be your strengths and weaknesses as a college student? Look back at your academic self throughout your schooling and look ahead to the kind of student you're planning to be in college, then write your academic autobiography. Or as an alternative, create a presentation answering these questions for your classmates.

Many people think ability is more important than effort. Either you have it or you don't. But here's a new way of thinking about the question. Take the notion of genius, for example. Experts used to think that a genius was someone born with extraordinary talent, like Mozart. From an early age, geniuses demonstrate exceptional natural abilities, they thought. But experts have changed their thinking: "What Mozart had, we now believe, was . . . the ability to focus for long periods of time. The key factor separating geniuses from the merely accomplished is not a divine spark. . . . It's deliberate practice. Top performers spend more hours (many more hours) rigorously practicing their craft." A master violinist once said, "I practice the violin eight hours a day for 40 years, and they call me a genius?" Effort counts much more than you might think.[12]

That said, think about some of the possible combinations of ability and effort. If you have high ability and exert great effort, you'll most likely succeed. If you have high ability and exert little effort, and still succeed, you've just proved how smart you must be! But if you have high ability and exert little effort and fail, you can always claim you didn't have the time to invest or you didn't care, right? You can always say that you could have done well if you'd tried harder. Rationalizing can lead to a dangerous strategy, one that's called "self-handicapping."[13] Some college students actually consciously or unconsciously apply this strategy. They exert little effort, perhaps because they have no confidence in themselves or because they fear failure, and then they rationalize when they don't do well.

Denis Scott/CORBIS

Only the curious will learn and only the resolute overcome the obstacles to learning. The quest quotient has always excited me more than the intelligence quotient.

Eugene S. Wilson,

former Dean of Admissions, Amherst College

EXERCISE 1.5

Theories of Intelligence Scale

Using the following scale, indicate the extent to which you agree or disagree with each of the following statements by writing the number that corresponds to your opinion in the space next to each statement. There are no right or wrong answers.

1	2	3	4	5	6
Strongly Agree	Mostly Agree	Agree	Disagree	Mostly Disagree	Strongly Disagree

_____ 1. You have a certain amount of intelligence, and you can't really do much to change it.

_____ 2. You can learn new things, but you can't really change your basic intelligence.

_____ 3. You can always substantially change how intelligent you are.

_____ 4. No matter how much intelligence you have, you can always change it quite a bit.

? challenge

“ reaction

Challenge: What is intelligence? Where does it come from? How do your views of intelligence affect you and your learning?

Reaction:

____

____

____

Research shows that what you *believe* about your own intelligence—your *mindset*—can make a difference in how successful you'll be in college. At first glance this statement seems absurd. What does what you believe about intelligence have to do with how smart you really are?

The scaled questions demonstrate that there are two basic ways to define intelligence. Some of us are *performers*, who agree with statements 1 and 2, while others of us are *learners*, who agree more with statements 3 and 4. *Performers* believe that intelligence is a fixed trait that cannot be changed. From the moment you're born, you have a certain amount of intelligence that's been allotted to you, and that's that. *Learners*, on the other hand, believe you can grow your intelligence if you capitalize on opportunities to learn. Whenever you tackle a tough challenge, you learn from it. The more you learn, the more intelligent you can become. Understanding which view of intelligence you endorse will make a difference in how you approach your college classes, as well as the outcomes—both positive and negative—that you'll achieve.

> **Ho imparato che niente e impossibile, e anche che quasi niente e facile . . . (I've learned that nothing is impossible, and that almost nothing is easy . . .)**
>
> *Articolo 31 (Italian rap group)*

These two contrasting views of intelligence have been revealed through the research of Dr. Carol Dweck of Stanford University, her graduate students, and other social psychologists. Some of their original work began with children, who were first asked to agree or disagree with questions similar to those you just answered to determine which view of intelligence they held. Afterward, they were given eight conceptual problems to solve, problems that were appropriate for their grade level. As they worked on the problems, the researchers asked them to talk aloud about whatever was on their minds, even if it was unrelated to the actual problems. After they had solved the first eight problems successfully, they were given four additional problems that were far too difficult for them to solve. This is where their views about the nature of intelligence made a difference.

As they tried to tackle the problems that were too difficult for them, the *performers* talked about feeling helpless. They became discouraged and anxious, forgot that they had solved the first eight problems successfully, and told themselves they weren't very smart. The *learners,* on the other hand, coached themselves on how to do better, remained optimistic, and actually improved their problem-solving strategies. They wanted to master what they were working on. To *learners,* academic challenges were opportunities for growth; to *performers* academic challenges were threats that might reveal their deficiencies. Performance

I'm not sure I'm really a learner . . .

CONTROL: *YOUR TOUGHEST CLASS*

Think about all the courses you're enrolled in this term. Use the following matrix to analyze your C-Factors for these courses. Describe each course in terms of its *challenge* level, your *curiosity* about the subject, how much *control* you believe you have to succeed, and the way each class impacts your *career outlook.* (Keep in mind that many first-year introductory courses are broad-based. They may seem less directly related to your career than later classes in your major, but it's still important to consider what skills you can gain that will lead to a more successful career.) Once you've determined the levels of challenge, curiosity, control, and career outlook you perceive in your courses, remember that it's your responsibility to adjust them. Instructors can't always meet the differing requirements of each student in a class. But *you* can make your own adjustments to gain as much as possible from each of your courses. Assess your C-Factors in each of your classes, and consider the adjustments you need to make.

Course Title	Challenge	Curiosity	Control	Career Outlook	Adjustments Required
Composition	Very High: never been good at writing	Very Low: had a discouraging teacher in H.S.	Moderate: probably higher than it feels to me	Will need to know how to write in any job	Need to spend more time pre-writing and going to the campus Writing Center for help

Which of the classes you listed will be your most challenging this term? What is the relationship between the four C-Factors and your intrinsic motivation to learn in each one of these courses? What can you do to increase your intrinsic motivation and become more successful?

is about measuring ability, "trying to convince yourself and others that you have a royal flush when you're secretly worried it's a pair of tens."[14] Learning is about investing the effort required to master new things: "Why waste time proving over and over how great you are, when you could be getting better?"[15]

Sometimes students who are highly confident are *performers*. They've always been told they're smart, and they have an image to protect. They become focused on the possibility of failure, which they need to avoid at all costs, instead of developing strategies to help them succeed. If you believe you only have a certain amount of intelligence, whether you realize it or not, your goal in college may be to prove you have enough. When you come to a tough course, you think, "If I have to work hard at this, I must not be very good at it." But if you believe you can develop your intelligence through learning, your goal will be to increase your ability: "If I have to work hard at this, eventually I'll become *very* good at it." Note that the research is not claiming that everyone is equally intelligent. That's not true, but what is true is that for any given individual, intellectual capacity can be increased with effort and guidance. Think of college as your opportunity to do that. According to Dweck, just learning about the importance of mindset can make a difference. Truly mastering something takes more sustained effort; performing can simply be an easy out. Learners are more likely to be intrinsically motivated; performers love the "cheering of the crowd"—external approval. Mindset matters, perhaps more than you've ever even considered.

Like mine?!

Let's admit it: We live in a performance-based society. Getting good grades is what it's all about, we're told. We all want to do well, look good, appear smart, and impress others. Did your previous schooling emphasize the performance mindset? Do you come from a family that overemphasizes grades? Are your parents putting extra pressure on you because they never had the chance to go to college? Are you from an underrepresented population on campus and because of this you feel performance pressure to succeed?[16] That's normal, but your view of intelligence can be changed, and changing it may be your key to academic success. There is evidence that students who are taught the value of a learning mindset over a performance mindset can actually achieve more than students who aren't.[17]

Regardless of what you believe about your precise intelligence level, the fact is this: *intelligence can be cultivated through learning.* And people's theories about their intelligence levels can be shifted.

What Drives You? Values, Dreams, and Goals

? challenge

“ reaction

Challenge: What are your core values? Can you list five?

Reaction:

___

___

___

Before tackling the big questions about what you want to create with your life, it's important to first take a close look in the mirror. Who are you? What makes you tick? What do you value? What are your goals? Where will your dreams take you?

How motivated are you to get there? How will your attitude affect your journey? How much effort versus ability will it take? Everything you're read about so far in this chapter fits into the future you're creating for yourself.

EXERCISE 1.6

Core Values Self-Assessment

Review the following list and check off the items that you value. Don't spend too much time thinking about each one; just go with your initial gut reaction. For each item, ask yourself "Is this something that's important to me?"

For me, it's about fame, success, happiness, creativity, and wealth!

_____ Health	_____ Fame	_____ Financial wealth
_____ Fitness/Physical strength	_____ Independence	_____ Commitment
_____ Loyalty	_____ Honesty	_____ Compassion
_____ Academic achievement	_____ Children	_____ Leisure time
_____ Success	_____ Leadership	_____ Balance
_____ Happiness	_____ Family	_____ Friendship
_____ Social life	_____ Marriage/Partnership	_____ Recognition
_____ Athletics	_____ Spirituality	_____ Status
_____ Creativity	_____ Variety	_____ Wisdom
_____ Meaningful work	_____ Challenge	_____ Time spent alone
_____ Adventure	_____ Personal growth	_____ Other (list here)

Now review all of the items you checked off and circle the five that are most important to you at this point in your life. Then rank them by putting a number next to each of the five circled values with number one as your top priority. Finally, take stock. Is this the person you want to be? Is there anything about your values that you would like to change? If so, why not go ahead and do it?

Values at the Core

One way to gain some insights about who you are is to look at your core values. So what do you value in life? By taking time to examine your personal values, managing your life will become easier and make more sense. Values can be intangible concepts such as love or respect, or tangible things such as family or money, and understanding how they motivate you isn't as simple as it might seem. Values can change as you go through life. For example, if you're single now, you may value the freedom to meet a variety of potential romantic partners. Just get to know people and have fun, that's all. Later, however, you may want a committed relationship because you value companionship and stability more than you used to. For this reason, it's important to reassess your values from time to time and reprioritize them.

Another complicating factor is that values can conflict with one another. Suppose that you value honesty and kindness, and you are at a party and a friend asks you what you think of her new hair color. You honestly think it's hideous, but telling her so would hurt her feelings, thus violating your value of being kind. How do you respond? That would depend on which value

> **It is our choices that show what we truly are far more than our abilities.**
>
> *Albus Dumbledore,* Harry Potter and the Prisoner of Azkaban

Patrik Giardino/Corbis

> **Self-knowledge is far more important than self-confidence.**
>
> *Simon Cowell, long-time* American Idol *judge, from* I Don't Mean to Be Rude, But . . .

is a higher priority for you. You have to make an on-the-spot decision about which value to tap. Once you define your values, however, they can serve as guideposts in helping you make choices every day—everything from the insignificant day-to-day choices to more significant ones such as which major to pursue in college.

In the Challenge → Reaction → Insight → Action system, knowing your values in life is key to understanding your reaction. Once you've defined your values, you can use them in your daily life to guide your actions. For example, if academic achievement is one of your top values, the next time you have the urge to cut class, consider the impact that choice would have on your value system. There is a great inner satisfaction that comes from living a life tied to core values.

Dreams versus Goals

Do you agree or disagree with this statement: "I can be anything I want to be"? If you are like most students, people have probably told you this all your life. Your parents and teachers all want you to have positive self-esteem, and certainly there are many career options available today. But is it true? Can you be *anything* you want to be? What's the difference between a dream and a goal?

As a college student, you may dream of being a famous doctor or a famous athlete or just plain famous. That's the beauty of dreams—you can imagine yourself in any career, any circumstances. When you're dreaming, you don't even have to play by the rules of reality. Dreams are fantasy-based—*you* in a perfect world. But when it's time to come back to reality, you discover that there are, in fact, rules. You may have dreamed of becoming a top-earning NBA player or a top fashion model when you were a child, but you have grown up to be the same height as Uncle Al or Aunt Sue—and that's not tall enough.

Dreams alone are not enough when it comes to "creating the future." As professional life coach Diana Robinson says, "A dream is a goal without legs." And without legs, that goal is going nowhere. Dreaming is the first step to creating the future you want, but making dreams come true requires planning and hard work. Suppose you want to become a fashion designer because you like clothes and people always tell you you look good. As you continue through college, however, you will come to understand the nuts and bolts of the fashion design business. Perhaps you'll learn that famous fashion designer Yves Saint Laurent got his first fashion designer job with Christian Dior after winning an International Wool Secretariat design competition. The fashion industry might be challenging to break into, but that doesn't mean you should abandon your dream. Instead, you must realize that

> **The best way to predict the future is to create it.**
>
> *Peter Drucker, management expert (1909–2005)*

dreams and goals are not the same thing. You must find a reality-based path to help you turn your dreams into goals. Just dreaming isn't enough.

I wonder how I can start doing that . . .

Dreams are exciting; you can let your imagination run wild. Goals are real; you must work out how to actually achieve your dreams. Goal setting is an important part of the life management skills this book will help you develop. Your goals may not seem at all clear to you right now, but the important thing is to learn that there's a right way and a wrong way to go about goal setting. The best way to ensure that the goals you set will serve you well is to make sure you FOCUS. Here's a brief overview of what that means.

F **Fit.** Your goal must fit your values, your character, and who you are as a person. Goals that conflict with any of these things will not only be difficult to accomplish, but they just won't work. If your goal is to become a writer for a travel magazine because you love adventure, but you have a fear of flying, you're in trouble.

O **Ownership.** You must own your goals. In other words, you've got to see it, taste it, want it! It must be your goal, not someone else's goal for you. Ask yourself: Does the thought of achieving this goal get me fired up? Do I genuinely own this goal or do I feel I ought to have this goal because it sounds good or pleases someone else?

C **Concreteness.** For any goal to be effective, it must be real. In other words, you must be able to describe your goal—and it's ultimate outcome—in complete and specific detail, including your deadline for accomplishing it. "To run a mile in less than six minutes by March 4th" is much more concrete than "to eventually run faster." The more concrete, the better.

Maybe I should audition for that new vocal group on campus that I've heard about.

U **Usefulness.** Goals must have utility, or usefulness. They must serve a purpose, and that purpose should be tied to your long-term vision of the person you want to become. For example, if you want to work for an international corporation some day, it would be useful to begin studying a foreign language now.

S **Stretch.** In the business world, people talk about stretch goals. These are goals that require employees to stretch beyond their usual limits to achieve something more challenging. The key to stretching is to find a good balance between being realistic and being challenged. Realistic goals are those whose outcomes are within your control. (Winning the lottery, for example, is beyond your control, and therefore not a very realistic goal.) Goals must be based in reality, but also offer you a chance to grow beyond the person you currently are.

Goals should be set for different time frames in your life to include both short- and long-term goals. Once your long-term goals are set (though they may shift over time as *you* shift over time), you will then want to set some short-term goals, which act as intermediate steps to achieving your long-term goals.

Flying Colours LTD/Getty Images

"What you get by achieving your goals is not as important as what you become by achieving your goals."

Zig Ziglar, Motivational speaker, writer, and trainer

	Long-Term Goals What do I want to accomplish . . .	Short-Term Goals What do I want to accomplish . . .	
Fame!	In my lifetime?	This year?	GPA+++
Grammy award	In the next twenty years?	This month?	Try hard
Platinuum album	In the next ten years?	This week?	Turn everything in
Viral music video	In the next three to five years?	Today?	Go to class!

???

CURIOSITY: *HOW RAPT ARE YOU?*

Stop Tweeting. Close your Facebook. Turn off your smartphone. Crank down the iTunes, and listen up. Attention is a hot new topic that neuroscientists are focusing on.

According to attention expert Winifred Gallagher in her book *Rapt: Attention and the Focused Life*, today we live in a distraction-rich world. Stimulation overload is an ever-present danger, and everybody and everything want your attention. "People don't understand that attention is a finite resource, like money. Do you want to invest your cognitive cash on endless Twittering or Net surfing or couch potatoing? You're constantly making choices, and your choices determine your experience." "Multitasking is a myth. You cannot do two things at once. It's either this or that," Gallagher claims.

Stephen Coburn/Shutterstock.com

You can always tell when people are trying to multitask while you're on the phone with them, for example. Apart from the tapping of keys in the background, there's silence after you ask a question. "Are you still there?" you ask. They're making choices, and at the moment they're choosing something else over talking on the phone with you. According to one expert, most office workers keep eight windows open on their computers at once and skip between them every 20 seconds. Our brains can switch between tasks at astonishing speed, and switching makes us feel efficient. But try this experiment: read this section out loud while you type something else. Just how efficient are you?

Here's a fascinating notion of Gallagher's. If you look back at your life, you'll see that who you are is based largely on what you've chosen to pay attention to. In what ways might that be true for you? If you took countless piano lessons as a kid and spent endless hours practicing the piano, music may matter to you now in ways that other people can't begin to understand. You probably also learned some important lessons about focus. If piano hadn't been your thing, but you'd put the same amount of attention into baseball, you might be a different person with another reality. Your life, Gallagher says, is the sum of what you focus on.

In the "Age of Distraction," is it possible to lead a focused life? Learning how to focus—really focus—like any other skill takes discipline and effort. It takes tremendous brain power to ignore all the "incomings" that hit us every day. We must learn to deliberately create our own "distraction-proof personal pods" to do it. Her recommendation? Spend the first 90 minutes of every day concentrating on your most important task. During that time, don't answer e-mails, don't Google, don't text, don't make phone calls—just focus. Paying attention to how you pay attention leads to a fuller, richer, more successful life.[18]

> We are what we repeatedly do. Excellence, then, is not an act, but a habit.
>
> *Aristotle, Greek philosopher (384–322 B.C.)*

© Larry Harwood Photography. Property of Cengage Learning

College Success: You Make the Call

What does it mean to succeed? Actually, success is difficult to define, and different people define success differently. Right now in college, you may think of success in terms of your future income. But is success simply about material wealth? Is it about fame? Status?

According to motivational author Robert Collier, "Success is the sum of small efforts, repeated day in and day out." Perhaps to you, success is somewhere off in the distant future, and it happens more or less suddenly, like winning the lottery. Actually, success begins right now. You should be the one to define what success will look like in your life, but generally, success is *setting out to do something that's personally meaningful, and then being fully engaged while doing it.* It's that simple. And it applies to your college experience as well. It starts now.

In order to understand your own definition of success in college, first you need to ask yourself why you're here. Why *did* you come—or return—to college, anyway? Do you want to develop into a more interesting, well-rounded, educated human being? Are you working toward a degree that leads to a specific career? Do you have children and want an education in order give them a better life? Did your mom or dad tell you that college wasn't optional?

We will assume that part of your definition of succeeding in college includes *graduating* from college. This book will provide you with an honest look at what that takes, including many opportunities to assess yourself in these areas. It will also offer an array of tools you can use throughout your college career and in your life beyond college.

Graduating from College: What It Takes

Some students think a college degree is a simple financial transaction. Think about this analogy: If you want to buy a gallon of milk, you go to the supermarket, select the kind of milk you want—whole milk, two percent, or nonfat—take it to the cashier, slide your debit card, and the milk is yours. Some students think a college education should work the same way. They think if they select the kind of degree they want—sociology, English, or geography—and pay tuition, the degree is theirs. Not so. There's much more to it than that. A college education requires more than a financial commitment. It requires you to invest your ability, your intellect, your drive, your effort—and yourself.

BOX 1.1 Generation 1: First in the Family?

I'm really glad this was in the first chapter because it's about me, and I hadn't really thought about any of this.

Did both your parents graduate from a four-year college? If not, you are a "first-generation college student." Quite an impressive title, isn't it? Being first at something has some definite pros. You're a trailblazer, a pioneer, someone to be looked up to. "Imagine, our son Dion with a college degree? Isn't that something?" But along with pros come potential challenges. Who will you go to for advice? Will your family understand what it takes? Will they support your efforts? At moments when your confidence is shaken, you may wonder: *can* a first-generation student be successful? The answer? Of course! (Your author is a first-generation college graduate!) In the end, your success is up to you. As you begin your college career, take these suggestions to heart:

1. **Communicate with your family.** Research shows that the *quality* and *quantity* of communication about college that you engage in with your family is key to your success. While they can't empathize because they haven't been there and done that, they can listen and encourage you. Talk to them openly about your college experience.[19]
2. **Keep your stress level in check.** If your family puts extra pressure on you to perform, your stress level may increase dramatically. But stress isn't the best motivator. This is something you want to do, so hone in and hunker down. Pay particular attention to your instructors, keep track of due dates, and focus. All you can do is your best. Think of it this way: you're "demystifying" college. You may just inspire Mom or Dad or your little brother to go to college one day, too.[20]
3. **Get going.** Remember this: when the going gets tough, the tough get going. Sometimes first-generation students are tempted to drop out, scale back (from four classes to three, for example), avoid assessment (thinking, oddly, "If I don't hand my paper in, I can't get a bad grade on it"), or lower their own expectations ("I was hoping for a 4.0 GPA, but maybe a 2.0 will do"). While sometimes these options may be the right ones, sabotaging your own efforts is never a good idea. Keep your eye on the prize—that degree you'll be the first one to earn in your family.[21]
4. **Find a true mentor.** Look for a particular professor or advisor to serve as a mentor—someone you can go to for advice and support. Just knowing that someone cares can be a powerful motivator. Ask this person to help you through rough patches or go to her to get recharged when your "academic batteries" are low.
5. **Get involved.** College may feel like a "foreign" culture to you. You may have conflicting emotions: excitement, confusion, and anxiety. You may not understand what instructors expect, how to fit in, or how to get it all done. But you won't learn these things if you aren't around. If you breeze in for your classes and bolt afterwards, it will be harder to adjust to your new role. Ease into the campus culture and take full advantage of what it means to be in college. Make friends and feel the beat of campus life.[22]

If you follow this advice, you *can* be successful! If you're a first-generation college student, dogear the corner of this page, and refer back to it whenever you need to.

Ryan McVay/Photodisc/Getty Images

Many people falsely assume that the best indicator of whether or not you will graduate from college has to do with the brain matter found between your ears. Wrong! Brains alone—especially brains measured by your high school grade point average or even your SAT or ACT scores—are no guarantee that you'll earn a college degree. What does it take?

> **Though no one can go back and make a brand new start, anyone can start from now and make a brand-new ending.**
>
> *Carl Bard*

EXERCISE 1.7

College Success Factors

Many factors (besides past grades and entrance test scores) impact your success in college. Read down this list and ask yourself how you measure up in each of these areas. Mark an honest response from 1 to 7. If you're just beginning college and you're unsure about how you'll do, use your habits in the past to gauge your responses.

Maybe I should work on my score on this one.

1	2	3	4	5	6	7
NO!	NO	No	Maybe/ Sometimes	Yes	YES	YES!

______ **Ability to adapt.** Are you the type of person who thrives in new environments? Do you enjoy meeting new classmates, new professors, and new counselors? In general, do you like—and do well—with change?

______ **Attitude.** Do you have a positive attitude toward your education? Do you want to be here? Are you motivated to learn and grow? Are you confident that you can do well in school? Are you willing to do the hard work involved in earning a college degree?

______ **Maturity.** Are you emotionally mature? Are you willing to display the level of maturity required to manage your college education over time and earn a degree?

______ **Class attendance.** Do you have a good track record of attending class in the past? Are you willing to commit to attending each of your college classes regularly, regardless of whether or not you actually *feel* like attending on a particular day? Did you know that class attendance is a major predictor of college success?

______ **Study habits.** Do you spend enough time studying? Do you study until you understand the material or do you simply study until you're out of time or need to move on to the next thing? Are you willing to make the necessary commitment to time spent studying even if it takes more time than you're planning on?

______ **Note-taking skills.** Note-taking is not an ability we're born with. It's a skill that must be learned and can be taught to just about anyone. Many of your professors will expect you to learn through lectures. How complete and comprehensive are your notes? Do you work with them after class (color-coding, typing up, and so on)?

______ **Academic support services.** Do you know what resources are available on campus to help you with academic issues? Are you willing to use a tutor or a campus learning center to help with a particular course that overwhelms you?

______ **Personal support system.** How strong is your personal support system? Who cares about your success in college? Do you have parents, siblings, and friends who support you, encourage you, and ask how you're doing?

______ **Faculty connections.** Are you interested in knowing more about your professors, their backgrounds, and their academic interests beyond the particular class you're taking with them? Are you willing to visit your instructors during their office hours if you are having difficulty with a class?

______ **Campus connection.** Do you plan to participate in or attend on-campus events? Sometimes students unknowingly fall prey to the PCP (parking lot, class, parking lot) syndrome. They're only on campus for their classes, and as soon as class is over, they're outta there. Believe it or not, connecting to your campus, other students, and your instructors is critical to your success.

______ **Time management skills.** Are you capable of managing your time effectively so that the important things—not necessarily just the urgent or exciting, fun things—get completed? Do you use a specific system for time management? Are you willing to learn these skills?

(continued on next page)

_____ **Money management skills.** How good are you at managing your money? Some students fall into the trap of using their school loans or grants to pay off credit card debt. Or they work far too many hours, which takes time away from their studies and makes academic success difficult to achieve. While managing your money isn't an academic skill, per se, not knowing how to do it can substantially impact your college career.

Now add up your scores on each item for a final tally. While this list isn't exhaustive, these factors are vital to college success. If your score was 60 or higher, you're in good shape. If not, take a close look at the areas that could affect your college success, read more about them in this book, and develop insights that lead to more effective action.

Did you notice that none of the things listed in Exercise 1.7 is a talent that you're simply born with? That's the good news. All of these factors that support your goal of graduating from college are things you can become better at if you are committed to doing so. And in making commitments to improving these factors *now*, you are making a commitment to graduate from college *later*.

The Bad News: Obstacles along the Way

? challenge
" reaction

Challenge: What are the five most common mistakes new college students make?

Reaction:

____

____

All my friends are going to college, and my parents expect it. But is it what I want? Will I be successful?

Getting accepted to college is a good thing! You should feel proud. But a major national report indicates that "college attendance in the United States has grown so rapidly over the past four decades that now 75 percent of high school graduates get some postsecondary education within two years of receiving their diplomas. Student aspirations are even loftier, with nearly 90 percent saying they hope to attend college. Older adults, too, have recognized the benefits of college study and account for more than one-third of matriculants [new students]. . . . Possession of a college degree today . . . is the passport to most careers, and without it, people can find themselves trapped in unrewarding jobs."[23] While everybody's doing it, or so it seems, not everyone is doing it successfully. Only 28 percent of American adults have college degrees, and nearly one of three Americans in their mid-twenties drops out of college.[24]

Realistically, the distance between getting accepted to college and graduating from college is considerable, and the journey can be both exhilarating and discouraging at times. Of all the college students who began as first-year students in 1992, only two-thirds had graduated eight years later.[25]

> There are a thousand excuses for failure, but never a good reason.
>
> *Mark Twain*

Risk factors include working more than thirty hours per week, going to school part-time, being a single parent or having children at home, and being a first-generation college student.[26] The important thing to keep in mind as you think about risk factors is that they alone cannot determine your ultimate level of success. Don't throw in the towel now if you had a child at age sixteen or are working thirty-five hours per week off campus. These factors are presented merely as information to assist you on your journey. They are simply *predictors*—not *determiners*. Only you can determine your outcomes in life, and that includes college.

It's worth taking a close look at these success inhibitors now, rather than becoming a statistic yourself later. Your effort, attitude,

BOX 1.2 Five Mistakes That Can Cost You Big Time!

Every year, more than 3 million first-year students begin college. Here are the five most common mistakes they make—so you can avoid them.[27]

Mistake 1: Cutting classes. Going to every class session gives you a real advantage; cutting class is a predictor of how well you won't do. If you think about how much each class session has already cost you in tuition, you'll realize that class is an investment you can't afford to blow off. If you're taking an online class, don't put off the work until the end of the semester. Keep up on a regular basis, just as you would by physically going to class.

Mistake 2: Overloading. Some students think it's to their advantage to take as many classes as possible their first semester—even if they're working full or part-time. "Suffering" gives them bragging rights. College isn't something you can just "pile on" to an already very busy life and be successful without putting yourself through some serious stress.

Mistake 3: Overmedia-ing. If you spend hours and hours a day on Facebook, Twitter, and YouTube, obviously, you aren't studying. It may take an hour or more to read a chapter of your textbook, but when you've been jumping between bits and bytes, it may take even longer. Rather than stressing out about how little time you have to study, train yourself to set aside some "media-free" time just for schoolwork, and then reward yourself with the social media fun that's an important part of your life, too.

Mistake 4: Procrastinating. Many students say they can't get serious about their assignments until the adrenaline kicks in at the last minute. What they don't think about is what will happen during a "peak week" when four papers, three presentations, and two exams hit at once. You can do a great deal to pre-manage your own stress level with regular upkeep—like taking care of your car or your relationships. It's your college education, after all, and you're in charge.

Mistake 5: Going it alone. Many students think sending a professor an e-mail or showing up during her office hours is intimidating or an obvious sign of weakness. Professors have office hours because they *want* you to stop in; they don't want to just sit there, waiting for students to show up. Most instructors actually want to get to know you, and they're pleased when you show an interest in their course content. Use *their* office hours to *your* advantage.

Memorize these five mistakes and take them seriously so that you get off to the best start possible!

Source: Jacobs, L.F. and Hyman, J.S., "The 5 Biggest Mistakes College Students Make." *U.S. News and World Report*, September 1, 2010.

BOX 1.3

Campus Resources: HELP Is Not a Four-Letter Word

It's not uncommon for new college students to feel isolated, even at a small school. Everything about your college experience is new, and you're adjusting gradually. As you adjust, remember that everyone needs a little help sometimes. Whatever the problem, your campus has all kinds of resources available for the taking, but you must take them. They won't come to you.

Social Connections

How can I meet other students? Does your campus have a Student or University Center? Take advantage of favorite gathering spots on campus. Not only can you meet people, but you can also scan the bulletin boards for information. If you're finding it hard to meet people, could it be because you're not around? To meet people, it helps to be where they are.

Academic Resources

How can I learn more about how I learn? Check to see if your campus has a Learning Center, an office that helps with learning disabilities, or a place you can go to fill out a learning style instrument. If writing is a struggle, look for your campus's Writing Center. If your calculus class is giving you fits, find the Math Learning Center. Or particular courses may offer what's called Supplemental Instruction, extra help beyond class sessions with basic principles or homework assignments. And get to know your academic advisor as if she or he were your best friend. That person can save you time and money and steer you toward classes in which you're most likely to be successful.

Adjustment

What if I need a counselor? College is a time of accelerated personal development and wonderful discoveries. But it may also be a time when you face challenging issues, such as leaving the comfort zone of your family; breaking up or beginning a new romance; or dealing with feelings of anxiety, isolation, or depression. The Counseling Center on your campus can help you work through a variety of issues. Many students—more than ever, many colleges report—are taking advantage of what Counseling Centers have to offer. And if you find yourself in the middle of a real crisis, call the campus hotline for immediate help.

Finances

Where can I find information about financial aid or get help with money problems? Your campus Financial Aid Office can help with loans, scholarships, and grants to pay for college. If you have a financial emergency—you lost the lease on an apartment, the residence halls are full, and you'll be living out of your car—help is available from the Red Cross or Salvation Army. If it's a matter of just blowing your budget, you can find advice, often free, from consumer credit agencies. Your campus may also offer free workshops on managing your money through a Learning Center or Student Success Center.

Technology

What if I have a technology meltdown? The new version of the old "my dog ate my homework" story relates to numerous variations on a theme: technology crashing. Your campus may not have round-the-clock advice from techies, but the Computer Help Desk can often solve what sounds like a complicated problem with simple advice. Also, use the campus computer labs. You can make good use of short blocks of time—or long ones—between classes. Good point!

Health

Are health services available to students? Many campuses have a Student Health Center where you can find a range of free or inexpensive services—everything from flu shots to strep throat tests to birth control advice if you're sexually active. Join the recreation center, if your campus has one, or an intramural team, coach a children's soccer team, or devote some time to exercise each day to stay healthy.

Majors and Careers

What do I want to be when I grow up? Thinking ahead to a career is sometimes difficult when so much is going on. Sometimes a career is nothing like you imagined—or preparing for one entails much more than you'd predict. Become an intern to try out a career or visit your campus's Career Center. Experts there can give you diagnostic tests to help you discover a major and career for which you are well-suited.

Et cetera

Where can I buy my books? Textbooks are a significant investment these days, and it's important to buy the right editions for your classes. Often you can also rent textbooks or buy e-books instead of print copies. Buying books online may save you money, although you'll have to wait for shipment. The bookstore is a much quicker option, and it's a good idea to find out where it is, no matter where you buy your books. You'll most likely need it for other school supplies.

What if I'm in need of Campus Security? If you feel unsafe walking to your car late at night or you need information about parking permits on campus, check with the Campus Security or Public Safety Office. They're there for your protection.

What's the bottom line? Get to know your campus and its full range of offerings—and take advantage of everything that's in place for your success.

and willingness to get any help you need to succeed are all vital. Henry Ford was right: "Whether you think you can or you can't, you're right."

The Good News: Benefits at the End of the Road

Regardless of how you choose to define success as it pertains to your college experience, it's a fact that there are plenty of benefits to graduating from a college or university. According to a recent study, "The evidence is overwhelming that college is a better investment for most graduates than in the past . . ." even for people in jobs that don't require a degree, like secretaries, plumbers, and cashiers. "And, beyond money, education seems to make people happier and healthier."[28] Here's a quick look at some of them:

1. **Higher earning potential.** On average, college graduates earn twice as much income as their peers with only a high school diploma (see Figure 1.3).[29]
2. **Lower unemployment rates.** College graduates are more employable than their non-degreed peers. This is especially helpful during cyclic downturns in the economy, when many people—even talented and committed employees—find themselves out of work.
3. **Wisdom.** College students have the opportunity to gain understanding about a broad range of topics—politics, sociology, and history, to name a few. A well-educated person knows Sigmund Freud's contribution to psychological theory, Charles Darwin's contribution to evolutionary theory, and Adam Smith's contribution to economic theory. But beyond theories, facts, and dates, a well-educated person knows how to think critically, contribute to society, and manage his or her life.
4. **Insight.** College students have the opportunity to understand themselves better as they participate in the academic, social, and co-curricular opportunities of higher education.

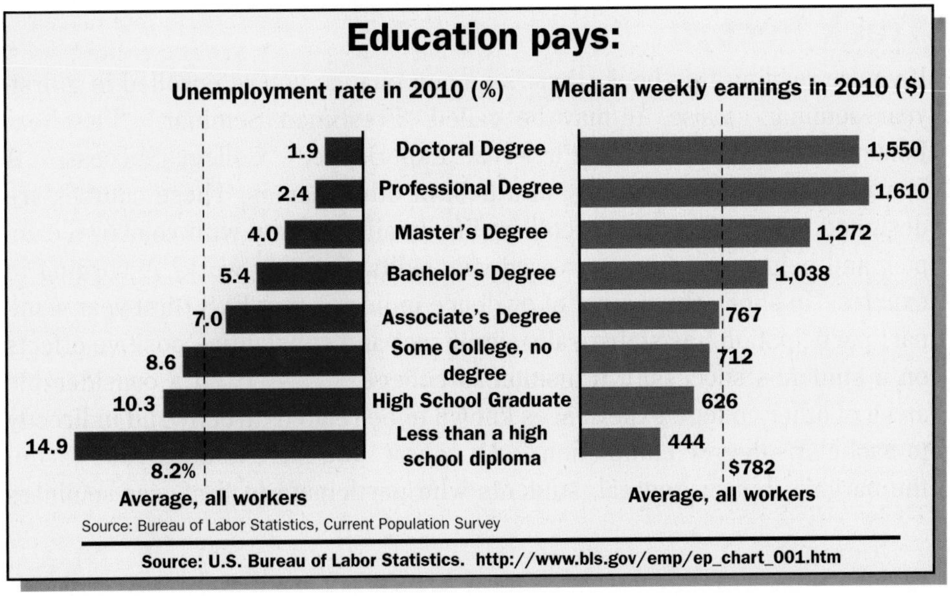

FIGURE 1.3

Education, Earnings, and Employment: The Quantifiable Value of a College Degree

Source: Bureau of Labor Statistics, Current Population Survey. Microsoft® Internet Explorer screenshot reprinted with permission from Microsoft Corporation.

> **Losers make excuses; winners make progress.**
>
> *Brian Tracy*

5. **True scholarship.** College students have the opportunity to become lifelong learners. True scholarship is not about making the grade. It's about becoming the best student-learner you can be—inside or outside of the classroom. The value of this benefit is beyond measure and will serve you throughout your life.

I hope, I hope!

6. **Lifelong friendships.** Many college graduates report that some of their strongest lifelong relationships were formed during their time at college. Choosing to attend college and choosing a specific major puts you in touch with a network of people who share your specific interests.

This Course Has a Proven Track Record

If you're reading this book, there's a good chance you're enrolled in a first-year seminar course. It may be called "Freshman Seminar," "First-Year Forum," "University 101," "First-Year Experience," "College Success," "A Learning Community," or any of a host of other names. These courses are designed to introduce you to college life, familiarize you with your own campus, and help you refine your academic skills. Do they work? According to experts, "In short, the weight of evidence indicates that FYS [first-year seminar] participation has statistically significant and substantial, positive effects on a student's successful transition to college. . . . And on a considerable array of other college experiences known to be related directly and indirectly to bachelor's degree completion."[30] Of course, you have to keep your part of the bargain, but in general, students who participate in first-year seminars

True!

complete more credit hours, adjust to college more quickly, become more involved in campus life, view themselves and their skills more accurately, enjoy and appreciate their college experience, and ultimately, graduate. That's what this course is about. Your instructor and your classmates are rooting for you. Now it's up to you!

How Do I Want to Be Different When I'm Done?

One thing is sure: College will change you. Most every high-intensity experience full of opportunities does. Take advantage, meet new people, and stretch yourself. You may notice that as a result of your college experience, your old relationships may "fit" differently. Your romantic partner may brag about you or secretly envy you. Your family may praise your efforts or hardly notice. But you will. If you finish what you've begun, you will watch yourself become a more sophisticated, more knowledgeable, more confident person. You can't help but be. Ask yourself now, at the beginning of your college experience, just how you'd like to change, and make it happen.

Now What Do You Think?

1. At the beginning of this chapter, Sylvia Sanchez, an ambivalent student, was about to begin her college career. Now after reading this chapter, would you respond differently to any of the questions you answered about the "FOCUS Challenge Case"? Knowing what you know now, how would you advise her? Write a paragraph ending to the story, incorporating your best advice.
2. What do you think about the Challenge → Reaction → Insight → Action system? Does it make sense? Do you understand how it works? Write a few paragraphs describing it in your own words.
3. What types of things fascinate you and fire up your intrinsic motivation? Why are they intrinsic motivators for you?
4. What actions can you take to become more of a *learner* and less of a *performer,* particularly in your most challenging class this term?
5. Think about one of your goals for the future. Run it through a quick check to ensure that it's a FOCUS goal. Circle the appropriate answer:
   - Does this goal fit me? Yes No
   - Do I really want this goal? Do I own it? Yes No
   - Does my goal have concrete details and deadlines? Yes No
   - Is this goal useful to me? Does it serve a purpose? Yes No
   - Does this goal stretch me? Is it challenging, yet achievable? Yes No

   If you answered "no" to any of the previous questions, your goal needs to be more *FOCUS*ed. What must you do to make that happen?
6. Why did you choose to attend college? Be as specific as you can in listing the reason(s). Review your list and put an asterisk next to the most positive, goal-oriented reasons. After reading this chapter, can you identify your greatest challenges and what you'll do to overcome them?

REALITY What did you LEARN?

On a scale of 1 to 10, answer the following questions now that you've completed the chapter.

low 1 2 3 4 5 6 7 8 9 10 high

In hindsight, how much did you already know about this subject before reading the chapter?

Can you answer these questions about goals and dreams more fully now that you've read the chapter?

1. What is the difference between a learner and a performer?
2. What is the difference between intrinsic and extrinsic motivation?
3. Which four factors—all beginning with the letter "C"—are a part of intrinsic motivation—and your college success?

How useful might the information in this chapter be to you?

How much do you think this information might affect your success overall? ________

How much energy did you put into reading this chapter? ________

Did you finish reading this chapter? ________

Did you intend to when you started? ________

If you meant to but didn't, what stopped you? ________

How long did it actually take you to complete (both the reading and writing tasks)?

______ Hour(s) ______ Minutes

Challenge Yourself Online Quiz To find out just how much you've learned, access the College Success CourseMate via www.cengagebrain.com to take the Challenge Yourself Online Quiz.

Take a minute to compare these answers to your answers from the "Readiness Check" at the beginning of this chapter. What gaps exist between the similar questions? How might these gaps between what you thought before starting the chapter and what you now think after completing the chapter affect how you approach the next chapter in this book?

I listened to the mp3 chapter summary and watched the "Inside the FOCUS Studio" TV show at www.cengagebrain.com. Great way to review before taking the online quiz!

CHAPTER 2

Learning about Learning

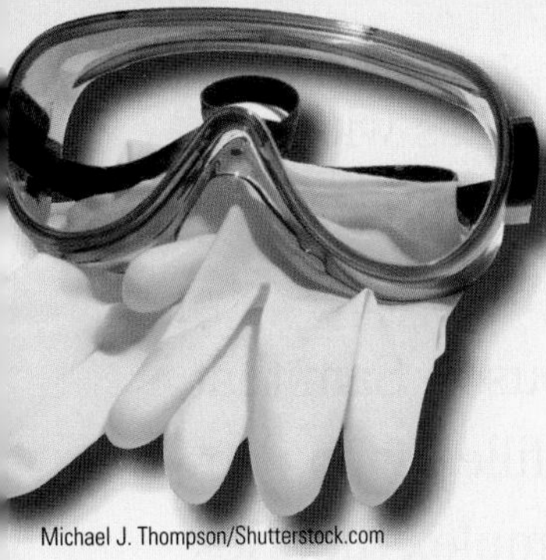

Michael J. Thompson/Shutterstock.com

You're about to discover . . .

- How learning changes your brain
- How people are intelligent in different ways
- How you learn through your senses
- How your personality affects your learning style
- How to become a more efficient and effective learner

© Larry Harwood Photography. Property of Cengage Learning

READINESS What do you KNOW?

Before beginning to read this chapter, take two minutes to answer the following questions on a scale of 1 to 10. Your answers will help you assess how ready you are to focus.

low 1 2 3 4 5 6 7 8 9 10 high

How much do you already know?

Based on reading the "You're about to discover . . ." list and skimming this chapter, how much do you think you probably already know about this chapter's subject? ________

See if you can answer these questions about learning to learn before you read.

1. What does the term "multiple intelligences" mean? Can you name three different types of intelligences?
2. What does VARK stand for? Can you identify the letters as they relate to students' preferences for taking in information?
3. What does your personality have to do with how you learn? Give several examples.

How much do you expect to learn?

In general, how motivated are you to learn more by reading this chapter? ________

How much do you think this information might affect your success overall? ________

How much energy do you plan to put into reading this chapter? ________

How ready are you to read now?

How ready are you to focus on this chapter? Enter a number for each aspect of your readiness to focus.

Physically ________

Intellectually ________

Emotionally ________

If any of your answers is below a 10, pay attention to whatever is distracting you before you start reading. Then zero in and focus.

How long do you think it will take you to complete this chapter from start to finish?

________ Hour(s) ________ Minutes

Now, as you begin, do you intend to finish reading this chapter?

________ yes ________ no ________ maybe

© Larry Harwood Photography. Property of Cengage Learning

FOCUS Challenge Case

? challenge

Tammy Ko

As she walked out of her "Introduction to Criminology" class with her classmate Sam on a dark rainy afternoon, Tammy Ko noticed that her mood was in sync with the weather. "I had no idea what I was getting into," she confessed to Sam. It was obvious to Sam that Tammy and their professor lived in different worlds. Hers was filled with people and excitement. His was filled with dull lecture notes and complex theories in books.

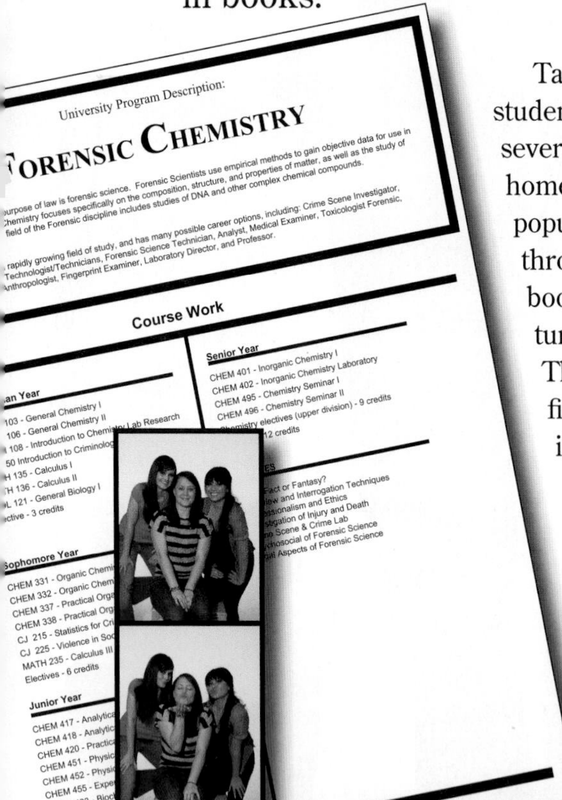

© Cengage Learning

Tammy was a first-semester student at a large state campus several hours from her tiny hometown, where she'd been a popular student. If you leafed through her high school yearbook, you'd see Tammy's picture on nearly every page. There Tammy had been a big fish in a small pond, but now it was the other way around.

Even though she found college life at the large state university overwhelming, Tammy was excited about her major, forensic chemistry. The crime shows on TV were her favorites. She watched them all each week. She rationalized how much time it took by thinking of it as career development. The fun was picturing herself as an investigator solving headline cases: "Man Slain, Found in City Park" or "Modern Day 'Jack the Ripper' Terrorizes Las Vegas." She could envision herself hunched over laboratory equipment, testing intently for fibers or DNA, and actually breaking the case.

When she registered for classes, her academic advisor had told her that taking an "Introduction to Criminology" course from the sociology department would be a good idea. "It'll teach you how to think," he'd said, "and it'll give you the background you need to understand the criminal mind. At the end of this class," he said, "you'll know if you really want to pursue a career in forensics." *Maybe it would teach me how to think,* Tammy thought to herself now that the term was underway, *if only I could understand the professor. Forget understanding the criminal mind—I'd just like a glimpse into his!* Most of the time, Sam agreed with her just to keep the peace although he always aced everything.

© Larry Harwood Photography. Property of Cengage Learning

Loren Rodgers/Shutterstock.com

BorisVian/Shutterstock.com

© Cengage Learning

TheSupe87/Shutterstock.com

Professor Caldwell was quiet and reserved, and he seemed a bit out of touch. He dressed as if he hadn't bought a new piece of clothing in as many years as he'd been at the university. In class, he was very articulate, knowledgeable, and organized with his handouts neatly piled on the desk, and he covered each day's material methodically point by point. Tammy wished he'd leave his notes occasionally to explore fascinating, related tangents. Tammy had always preferred teachers who created exciting things to do in class over teachers who went completely by the book.

Tammy's biggest complaint about Professor Caldwell was that he only talked about *theories* of criminology. When was he ever going to get to the hands-on part of the course? She couldn't help thinking, *When will we stop talking about theories and start working on real cases—like the ones on all those TV shows?*

To make matters worse, learning from lectures was not Tammy's strong suit. She hadn't done well on the first exam because she'd had to resort to memorizing things that didn't make much sense to her, and her D grade showed it. The exam consisted of one question: "Compare and contrast two theories of criminology discussed in class thus far." Tammy hated essay tests. She was at her best on tests with right or wrong answers, like true-false or multiple-choice questions. Making sense out of spoken words that go by very quickly during a lecture and trying to psych out professors' preferred answers on essay tests were challenges to her.

Michael J. Thompson/Shutterstock.com

But her "Introduction to Criminology" class was far from hands-on. In fact, Tammy had noticed that many of her teachers preferred talking about things to doing things. They seemed to take more interest in theories than in the real world. *Too bad, she thought, the real world is where exciting things happen.* Although she hated to admit it, sometimes Tammy couldn't wait for her college career to be over so that she could begin her real career.

A few of Tammy's other friends had taken Professor Caldwell's classes. "Just try and memorize the stuff; that's all you can do," they'd advised her. Regardless of what they happened to be talking about, somehow the conversation always came around to stress, Professor Caldwell, and how impossible it was to learn in his classes.

Kenneth Sponsler/Shutterstock.com

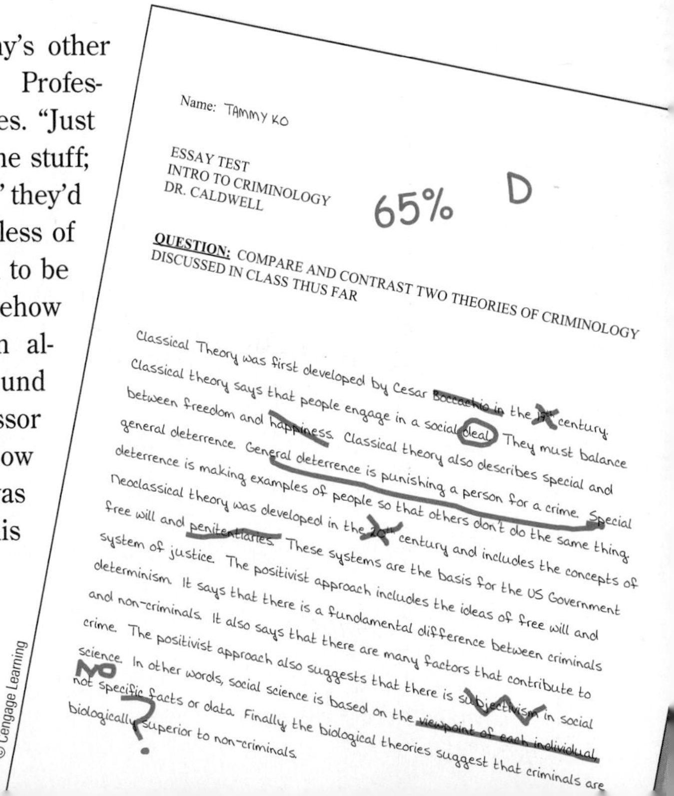

Name: TAMMY KO

ESSAY TEST
INTRO TO CRIMINOLOGY
DR. CALDWELL

65% D

QUESTION: COMPARE AND CONTRAST TWO THEORIES OF CRIMINOLOGY DISCUSSED IN CLASS THUS FAR

Classical Theory was first developed by Cesar Boccachio in the 19th century.
Classical theory says that people engage in a social deal. They must balance
between freedom and happiness. Classical theory also describes special and
general deterrence. General deterrence is punishing a person for a crime. Special
deterrence is making examples of people so that others don't do the same thing.
Neoclassical theory was developed in the 20th century and includes the concepts of
free will and penitentiaries. These systems are the basis for the US Government
system of justice. The positivist approach includes the ideas of free will and
determinism. It says that there is a fundamental difference between criminals
and non-criminals. It also says that there are many factors that contribute to
crime. The positivist approach also suggests that there is subjectivism in social
science. In other words, social science is based on the viewpoint of each individual,
not specific facts or data. Finally the biological theories suggest that criminals are
biologically superior to non-criminals.

NO

?

© Cengage Learning

challenge

reaction

What Do You Think?

1. Why is Tammy having difficulty learning in her "Introduction to Criminology" class?
2. Is Tammy smart? If so, in what ways? What sensory modality does Tammy prefer for taking in information? Does she learn best by watching, listening, reading and writing, or doing?
3. What do you think Tammy's personality type is? How does her personality type relate to her learning style?
4. How would you describe Professor Caldwell's teaching style? His personality type? How does his personality type relate to his teaching style?
5. What should Tammy do to become a better learner in Professor Caldwell's class?

Go to the HEAD of the Class: Learning and the Brain

challenge

reaction

Challenge: What is learning? Can you define the process?

Reaction:

____

____

____

EXERCISE 2.1

Assessing Your Views on Learning

The following statements represent common student views on learning. Think about each statement, and mark it true or false based on your honest opinion.

I'd say number 3 is definitely true—at least for me!

_____ 1. Learning is often hard work and really not all that enjoyable.

_____ 2. Memorization and learning are basically the same thing.

_____ 3. The learning done in school is often gone in a few weeks or months.

_____ 4. In college, most learning takes place in class.

_____ 5. Learning is usually the result of listening to an instructor lecture or reading a textbook.

_____ 6. The best way to learn is by working alone.

_____ 7. Most students know intuitively how they learn best.

_____ 8. Teachers control what students learn.

_____ 9. Learning only deals with subjects taught in school.

_____10. The learning pace is controlled by the slowest learner in the class.

You probably noticed that many of these statements attempt to put learning in a negative light. How many did you mark true? This chapter will help you understand more about learning as a process and about yourself as a learner. As you read, your goal should be to use the insights you gain to become a better learner.

Let's start our exploration of the learning process close to home—in our own heads. What's going on up there, anyway? While your hands are busy manipulating test tubes in chemistry lab, or your eyes are watching your psychology professor's PowerPoint presentation, or your ears are taking in a lecture on American politics, what's your brain up to? The answer? Plenty.

This chapter will help you understand how you learn best. In some ways, learning is learning—everyone learns according to the same general principles. For example, new research shows that in many ways, the old one-two-three method still works best: read, close the book, and write down what you remember. Amazingly, it works like a charm. You just have to discipline yourself to do it, and then go back to the book and continue to fill in the gaps.[1]

In other ways, however, you have your own distinct learning preferences. Perhaps you catch on quickly and prefer that teachers clip right along. Or maybe you like chewing over material at a slower pace, especially if it's complex. Maybe you consider yourself to be a hands-on learner. You learn best when someone gives you some guidance, hands over the controls, and lets you have at it. Many students find it easier to learn by doing things themselves, rather than by watching their instructors do things. Math can be a good example. If that's the case for you, you'll have to create hands-on ways to reinforce your learning either in class or outside of class. This chapter will help you find ways to do that.

This sounds exactly like me!

Use It or Lose It

The human brain consists of a complex web of connections between neurons. This web grows in complexity as it incorporates new knowledge. But if the connections are not reinforced frequently, they degenerate. As you learn new things, you work to hardwire these connections, making them less susceptible to degeneration. When your professors repeat portions of the previous week's lecture or assign follow-up homework to practice material covered in class, they're helping you to form connections between neurons through repeated use—or, in other words, to learn. Repetition is vital to learning. You must use and reuse information in order to hardwire it. Think of it this way: People say that practice makes perfect. But practice also makes learning "permanent, automatic and transferable to new situations."[2]

Giving your brain the exercise it needs—now and in your years after college—will help you form connections between neurons that, if you keep using them, will last a lifetime. From a biological point of view, that's what being a lifelong learner means. New research shows that your brain is "competitively plastic." You get better at what you practice, and you lose what you don't use.[3] The age-old advice "use it or lose it" is true when it comes to learning.

© Larry Harwood Photography. Property of Cengage Learning

"The art and science of asking questions is the source of all knowledge."

Thomas Berger, American novelist

Ask Questions and Hardwire Your Connections

Your professors have been studying their disciplines for years, perhaps decades. They have developed extensive hardwired connections between their brain neurons. They are *experts*. Woodrow

Wilson once said, "I not only use all the brains I have, but all that I can borrow." Think of college as an ideal time to borrow some excellent brains—your professors'!

By contrast, you are a *novice* to whatever discipline you're studying. You've not yet developed the brain circuitry that your professors have developed. This realization points to a potential problem. Sometimes professors are so familiar with what they already know from years of traveling the same neuron paths that what you're learning for the first time seems obvious to them. Without even realizing it, they can expect what is familiar to them to be obvious to you. Sometimes, it isn't obvious at all. One learning expert says this: "The best learners . . . often make the worst teachers. They are, in a very real sense, perceptually challenged. They cannot imagine what it must be like to struggle to learn something that comes so naturally to them."[4] Think of how challenging it is when you try to teach something that you understand thoroughly to another person who doesn't, like teaching someone who has never used a computer before how to upload an assignment.

Definitely Professor Caldwell!

Since you're a novice, you may not understand everything your professors say. Ask questions, check, clarify, probe, and persist until you do understand. Sometimes your confusion is not due to a lack of knowledge, but a lack of the *correct* knowledge. You may be getting interference from misinformation or unproductive habits of thinking and learning that have become hardwired in your brain. For example, you may study for a test by doing only one thing—reading and re-reading the textbook when you actually need to do more than that. It's important to be familiar with an array of study tools and choose the ones that work best for you and the subject matter you're trying to learn.

Think of it this way. Learning often involves "messy journeys back, forth and across" new territory.[5] Some of the neural connections you brought with you to college are positive and useful, and some are counterproductive. When you learn, you not only add new connections, but you rewire some old connections. While you're in college, you're under construction![6]

Take Charge and Create the Best Conditions for Learning

Collin Anderson/Blend Images/CORBIS

Throughout this discussion, we've been talking about internal processes in your brain. *Your* brain, not anyone else's. The bottom line is this: Learning must be *internally initiated*—by you. It can only be *externally encouraged*—by someone else. You're in charge of your own learning. Learning changes your brain.

> **When we come to know something, we have performed an act that is as biological as when we digest something.**
>
> *Henry Plotkin,* Darwin Machines and the Nature of Knowledge *(1994)*

CURIOSITY: *CAN YOU BUILD A BETTER BRAIN?*

Don't look now, but you're a very busy person! If you were watching a movie of your life at this moment, what would the scene look like? A cell phone in your hand, a website open on your computer screen, your iPod plugged in, and this book propped in your lap? So much to do, so little time! All we can hope for is that some scientist somewhere will invent a way to get a bigger, better brain! But let's face it: brain enhancement surgery won't be available any time soon.

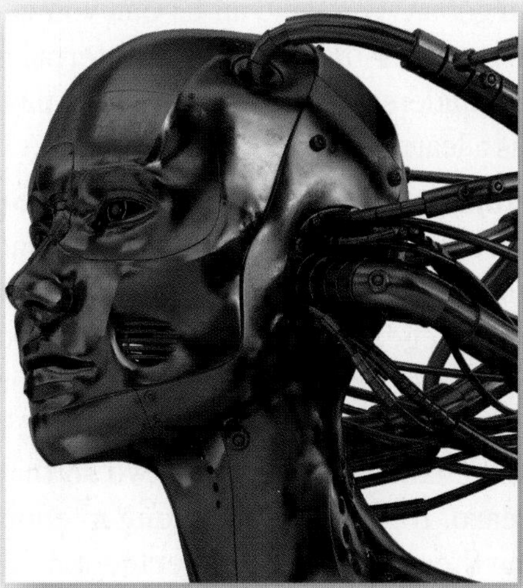
iStockphoto.com/Vladislav Ociacia

Even so, scientists have been busy recently learning more about this heady organ of ours. From birth to adolescence, we lay the brain's basic circuitry. Stimulation is critical. When children grow up in isolated, sterile environments, their brains suffer. But when they grow up in fertile, rich environments, their brains thrive. The more our moms and dads read to us and play learning games with us, the better. Scientists used to think that our basic circuitry is hardwired for life by the time we're adults. But new brain research focuses on *neuroplasticity*. It is possible to build a better brain, especially after traumatic injury, because the brain is more "plastic" than previously thought—not plastic like a Barbie doll, but plastic in that it can "reshape" itself, based on what science has discovered. In a fascinating new book, *The Brain That Changes Itself*, Dr. Norman Doidge recounts miraculous stories of patients whose injured brains have been rewired to work better. If you want some interesting reading, take a look.[7]

What's the secret to a healthy brain? When we think of fitness, most of us think from the neck down—strong abs, bulging pecs, and tight glutes. But brain health tops them all. New evidence shows that physical exercise helps our brains shrug off damage, reinforce old neural networks, forge new ones, and ultimately result in a better brain![8]

Current research focuses on a protein called BDNF (for brain-derived neurotrophic factor). BDNF, sometimes referred to as "Miracle-Gro" for the brain, helps nerve cells in our brains grow and connect, is important for development in the womb, but it's also important in adult brains. Simply put: it helps us learn. According to researchers, rats that eat a high-calorie, fast-food diet and have a couch-potato lifestyle have less BDNF in their brains. Omega-3 fatty acids found in fish normalize BDNF levels and counteract learning disabilities in rats with brain injuries. Scientists are working to see if the same thing may be true for humans.[9]

"Exercise your brain. Nourish it well. And the earlier you start the better," scientists tell us.[10] New research indicates that education is a great way to nourish our brains. People who are less educated have twice the risk of getting Alzheimer's disease in later life, and less educated people who have ho-hum, nonchallenging jobs have three to four times the risk. According to researchers, "College seems to pay off well into retirement."[11] It can help you build a better brain!

Let's look at food as an analogy: If learning is a process that is as biological as digestion, then no one can learn for you, in the same way that no one can eat for you. The food in the refrigerator doesn't do you a bit of good unless you walk over, open the door, remove the object of your desire, and devour it. It's there for the taking, but you must make that happen. To carry the analogy further, you eat on a daily basis, right? "No thanks, I ate last week" is a senseless statement. Learning does for your brain what food does for your body. Nourish yourself!

> Learning is not so much an additive process, with new learning simply piling up on top of existing knowledge, as it is an active, dynamic process in which the connections are constantly changing and the structure reformatted.
>
> *K. Patricia Cross, Professor Emerita of Higher Education, University of California, Berkeley*

Brain researchers tell us the best state for learning has ten conditions. Read each one, along with some suggestions about how to get there.

1. **You're intrinsically motivated (from within yourself) to learn material that is appropriately challenging.**

© Larry Harwood Photography. Property of Cengage Learning

- **Examine where your motivation to learn comes from.** Are you *internally* motivated because you're curious about the subject and want to learn about it or externally motivated to get an A or avoid an F? Can you generate your own internal motivation, rather than relying on external motivators? This book has built-in reminders to boost your intrinsic motivation. Use them to your advantage as a learner.
- **Adjust the level of challenge yourself.** You might think that instructors should be the ones to adjust the level of challenge—to pay attention to what's called "The Goldilocks Principle." But in college, it's your responsibility to get the challenge level "just right" for you.[12] If you're too challenged in a class, you can become anxious. Get extra help if you aren't quite up to the task or bump up the challenge a notch or two so that you're continually motivated to learn. If you're not challenged enough, expect more of yourself. Go further than you're expected to and learn as much as you can or help teach other students who are struggling.

2. **You're appropriately stressed, but generally relaxed.**

- **Assess your stress.** No stress at all is what you'd find in a no-brainer course. Some stress is useful; it helps engage you in learning. How stressed are you—and why—when you get to class? Are you overstressed because you haven't done the reading and hope you won't be called on? Prepare for class so that you're ready to jump in. Or are you understressed because you don't value the course material? Consider how the information can be useful to you—perhaps in ways you've never even thought of.
- **Attend to your overall physical state.** Are you taking care of your physical needs so that you can stay alert, keep up with the lecture, and participate in the discussion?

3. **You enter into a state researchers call "flow" when you're so totally absorbed in what you're doing that you lose track of everything else.[13]**

- **Identify the kinds of learning situations that help you "flow."** Do you get fully engaged by hands-on activities? Do you find that certain courses naturally capture your attention so that you're surprised when it's time for class to end? Understanding your own preferences as a learner is key here.

> **Think about what you can do as a learner to get yourself there.** Not all classes or subjects will naturally induce a flow state in you, so ask yourself what *you* can do to focus on learning and exclude distractions.

"They know enough who know how to learn."

Henry Brooks Adams, American journalist and historian, 1838–1918

4. You're curious about what you're learning, and you look forward to learning it.

> **Get ready to learn by looking back and by looking ahead.** When you're about to cross the street, you must look both ways, right? Keep that image in mind because that's what you should do before each class. What did class consist of last time? Can you predict what it will consist of next time? Considering the big picture can help you fit your learning into a larger whole.

> **Focus on substance, not style.** Despite society's obsession with attractiveness, grooming, and fashion, a student's job is to ask: What can I learn from this person? Passing judgment on physical appearance just encourages you to play the blame game and derails your learning.

Right! But Caldwell needs a major makeover!

5. You're slightly confused, but only for a short time.[14]

> **Use confusion as a motivator.** You may not be getting the lecture's main points because you don't understand new terms used along the way. Look them up early on in the learning process. Ask yourself what background information would help things click—and find out the answers to those questions. As one learning expert explains, "solving problems brings pleasure," which gives you and your brain a sense of satisfaction.[15]

> **Ask questions!** To your professor, questions indicate *interest,* not *idiocy.* Don't be afraid to probe more deeply into the material.

6. You search for personal meaning and patterns.

> **Ask yourself: What's in it for me?** Why is knowing this important? How can I use this information in the future? Instead of dismissing material that appears unrelated to your life, try figuring out how it *could* relate. You may be surprised!

If I do become a CSI, I guess I might have to know some things about the criminal mind.

> **Think about how courses relate to one another.** How does this new knowledge align with other things you're learning in other courses? Does sociology have anything to do with history? Psychology with economics?

William Perugini/Shutterstock.com

"Personal participation is the universal principle of knowing."

Michael Polanyi, Hungarian-British scholar (1891–1976)

7. **Your emotions are involved, not just your mind.**

   - **Evaluate your attitudes and feelings.** Do you like the subject matter? Do you admire the teacher? Remember that high school teacher, the one whose class you just couldn't stand? Not every class will be your favorite. That's natural. But if a class turns you off as a learner, instead of allowing your emotions to take over, ask why and whether your feelings are in your best interest.
   - **Make a deliberate decision to change negative feelings.** Fortunately, feelings can be changed. Hating a course or disliking a professor can only build resentment and threaten your success. It's possible to do a one-eighty and transform your negative emotions into positive energy.

Guess I should …

8. **You realize that as a learner you use what you already know in constructing new knowledge.**[16]

   - **Remember that passive learning is an oxymoron.** When it comes to learning, you are the construction foreman, building on what you already know to construct new knowledge. You're not just memorizing facts someone else wants you to learn. You're a full partner in the learning process!
   - **Remind yourself that constructing knowledge takes work.** No one ever built a house by simply sitting back or just hanging out. In your college courses, you must identify what you already know and blend new knowledge into the framework you've built in your mind. By constructing new knowledge, you are building yourself into a more sophisticated, more polished, and most certainly, a more educated person.

9. **You understand that learning is both conscious and unconscious.**

   - **Watch where your mind goes when it's off duty.** Does learning take place when you're not deliberately trying to learn? Some of what you learn will be immediately obvious to you, and some will dawn on you after class is over. Pay attention to your indirect learning and move it into your line of vision.
   - **Remember that both kinds of learning are important.** Both conscious learning and unconscious learning count. There are no rules about when and where learning can occur.

© Larry Harwood Photography. Property of Cengage Learning

It ain't what you know that gets you into trouble. It's what you know for sure that just ain't so.

Mark Twain

10. You're given a degree of choice in terms of what you learn, how you do it, and feedback on how you're doing.

- **Make the most of the choices you're given.** College isn't a free-for-all in which you can take any classes you like toward earning a degree. However, which electives you choose will be up to you. Or if your instructor allows you to write a paper or shoot a video, choose the option that will be more motivating for you. When you receive an assignment, select a topic that fires you up. It's easier to generate energy to put toward choices you've made yourself.
- **Use feedback to improve, and if feedback is not given, ask for it.** It's possible to get really good at doing something the wrong way. Take a golf swing or a swimming stroke, for example. Without someone intervening to give you feedback, it may be difficult to know how to improve. Your instructors will most likely write comments on your assignments to explain their grades. Assessing your work is their job; it's what they must do to help you improve. Take their suggestions to heart and try them out.

CONTROL: *YOUR TOP-TEN LIST*

Reflect on yourself as a learner in your toughest class this term. How optimal are the conditions for learning? Put a checkmark in the box if any of the following conditions are present. If not, beside each item, write in a suggestion to help create the condition and improve your own learning.

Ten Conditions for Optimal Learning	Course Title:	
1. You're intrinsically motivated to learn material that is appropriately challenging.	☐	
2. You're appropriately stressed, but generally relaxed.	☐	
3. You enter into a state researchers call flow.	☐	
4. You're curious about what you're learning, and you look forward to learning it.	☐	
5. You're slightly confused, but only for a short time.	☐	
6. You search for personal meaning and patterns.	☐	
7. Your emotions are involved, not just your mind.	☐	Hating this class won't help me. I need to adjust my attitude.
8. You realize that as a learner you use what you already know in constructing new knowledge.	☐	
9. You understand that learning is both conscious and unconscious.	☐	
10. You're given a degree of choice in terms of what you learn, how you do it, and feedback on how you're doing.	☐	

Multiple Intelligences: *How* Are You Smart?

? challenge

" reaction

Challenge: Are people smart in different ways? How so?

Reaction:

____

____

____

EXERCISE 2.2

Multiple Intelligences Self-Assessment

On each line, put checkmarks next to all the statements that best describe you.

Linguistic Intelligence: **The capacity to use language to express what's on your mind and understand others ("word smart")**

_____ I'm a good storyteller.

_____ I enjoy word games, puns, and tongue twisters.

_____ I'd rather listen to the radio than watch TV.

_____ I've recently written something I'm proud of.

_____ I can hear words in my head before I say or write them.

_____ When riding in the car, I sometimes pay more attention to words on billboards than I do to the scenery.

_____ In high school, I did better in English, history, or social studies than I did in math and science.

_____ I enjoy reading.

Logical-Mathematical Intelligence: **The capacity to understand cause/effect relationships and to manipulate numbers ("number/reasoning smart")**

_____ I can easily do math in my head.

_____ I enjoy brainteasers or puzzles.

_____ I like it when things can be counted or analyzed.

_____ I can easily find logical flaws in what others do or say.

_____ I think most things have rational explanations.

_____ Math and science were my favorite subjects in high school.

_____ I like to put things into categories.

_____ I'm interested in new scientific advances.

Spatial Intelligence: **The capacity to represent the world visually or graphically ("picture smart")**

_____ I like to take pictures of what I see around me.

_____ I'm sensitive to colors.

_____ My dreams at night are vivid.

_____ I like to doodle or draw.

_____ I'm good at navigating with a map.

_____ I can picture what something will look like before it's finished.

_____ In school, I preferred geometry to algebra.
_____ I often make my point by drawing a picture or diagram.

Bodily-Kinesthetic Intelligence: **The capacity to use your whole body or parts of it to solve a problem, make something, or put on a production ("body smart")**

_____ I regularly engage in sports or physical activities.
_____ I get fidgety when asked to sit for long periods of time.
_____ I get some of my best ideas while I'm engaged in a physical activity.
_____ I need to practice a skill in order to learn it, rather than just reading or watching a video about it.
_____ I enjoy being a daredevil.
_____ I'm a well-coordinated person.
_____ I like to think through things while I'm doing something else like running or walking.
_____ I like to spend my free time outdoors.

Musical Intelligence: **The capacity to think in music, hear patterns and recognize, remember, and perhaps manipulate them ("music smart")**

_____ I can tell when a musical note is flat or sharp.
_____ I play a musical instrument.
_____ I often hear music playing in my head.
_____ I can listen to a piece of music once or twice, and then sing it back accurately.
_____ I often sing or hum while working.
_____ I like music playing while I'm doing things.
_____ I'm good at keeping time to a piece of music.
_____ I consider music an important part of my life.

Interpersonal Intelligence: **The capacity to understand other people ("people smart")**

_____ I prefer group activities to solo activities.
_____ Others think of me as a leader.
_____ I enjoy the challenge of teaching others something I like to do.
_____ I like to get involved in social activities at school, church, or work.
_____ If I have a problem, I'm more likely to get help than tough it out alone.
_____ I feel comfortable in a crowd of people.
_____ I have several close friends.
_____ I'm the sort of person others come to for advice about their problems.

My highest intelligence is in the Interpersonal category. That sounds about right.

Intrapersonal Intelligence: **The capacity to understand yourself, who you are, and what you can do ("self-smart")**

_____ I like to spend time alone thinking about important questions in life.
_____ I have invested time in learning more about myself.
_____ I consider myself to be independent minded.
_____ I keep a journal of my inner thoughts.
_____ I'd rather spend a weekend alone than at a place with a lot of other people around.
_____ I've thought seriously about starting a business of my own.
_____ I'm realistic about my own strengths and weaknesses.
_____ I have goals for my life that I'm working on.

(continued on next page)

Naturalistic Intelligence: **The capacity to discriminate between living things and show sensitivity toward the natural world ("nature smart")**

_____ Environmental problems bother me.
_____ In school, I always enjoyed field trips to places in nature or away from class.
_____ I enjoy studying nature, plants, or animals.
_____ I've always done well on projects involving living systems.
_____ I enjoy pets.
_____ I notice signs of wildlife when I'm on a walk or hike.
_____ I can recognize types of plants, trees, rocks, birds, and so on.
_____ I enjoy learning about environmental issues.

Which intelligences have the most check marks? Write in the three intelligences in which you had the most number of check marks.

_______________ _______________ _______________

Although this is an informal instrument, it can help you think about the concept of multiple intelligences, or MI. How are you smart?

Based on Armstrong, T. (1994). *Multiple Intelligences in the Classroom.* Alexandria, VA: Association for Supervision and Curriculum Development, pp. 18–20.

FIGURE 2.1

Multiple Intelligences

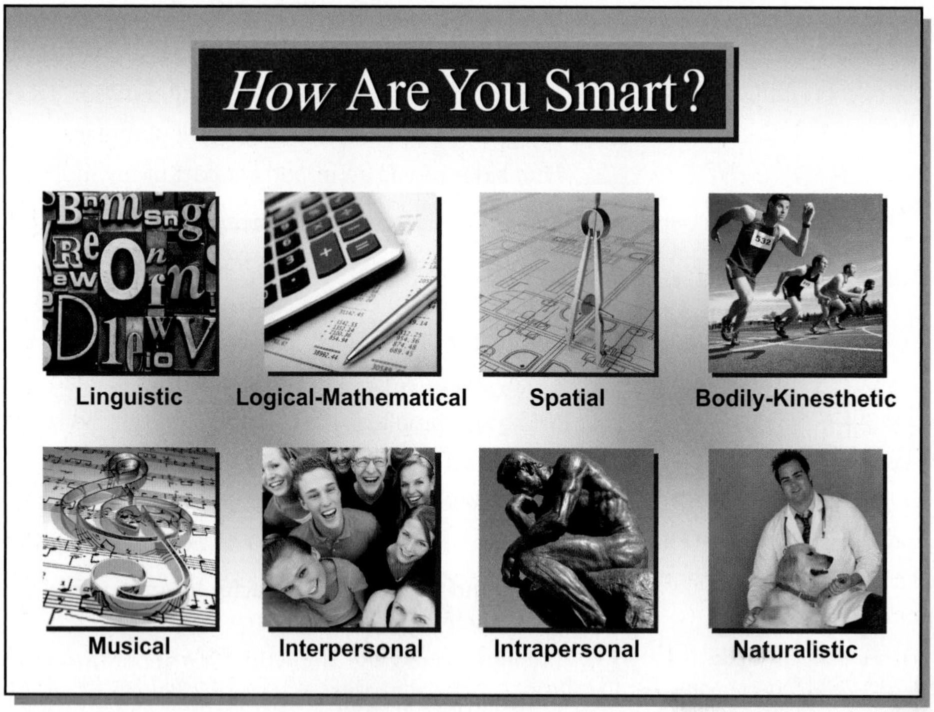

Alan Merrigan/Shutterstock.com; Denisenko/Shutterstock.com; Mopic/Shutterstock.com; Morgan Lane Photography/Shutterstock.com; Yakobchuk Vasyl/Shutterstock.com; Yuri Arcurs/Shutterstock.com; Sean Nel/Shutterstock.com; william casey/Shutterstock.com

Have you ever noticed that people are smart in different ways? Consider the musical genius of Mozart, who published his first piano pieces at the age of five. Olympic Gold Medalist Lindsey Vonn started skiing at when she was two years old. Not many of us are as musically gifted as Mozart or as physically gifted as Lindsey Vonn, but we all have strengths. We're all smart in different ways. You may earn top grades in math, and not-so-top grades in English, and your best friend's grades may be just the opposite.

According to Harvard psychologist Howard Gardner, people can be smart in at least eight different ways. Most schools focus on particular types of intelligence, linguistic and logical-mathematical intelligence, reflecting the three R's: reading, writing, and 'rithmetic. But Gardner claims intelligence is actually multifaceted. It can't be measured by traditional one-dimensional standardized IQ tests and represented by a three-digit number: 100 (average), 130+ (gifted), or 150+ (genius). Gardner defines intelligence as "the ability to find and solve problems and create products of value in one or more cultural setting."[17] Although we all have ability in all eight intelligences, most of us, he claims, are strong in two or three.[18]

So instead of asking the traditional question "How smart are you?" a better question is "How are you smart?" The idea is to find out *how,* and then apply this understanding of yourself to your academic work in order to achieve your best results.

Translate Content into Your Own Intelligences

Do you sometimes wonder why you can't remember things for exams? Some learning experts believe that memory is intelligence-specific. You may have a good memory for people's faces but a bad memory for their names. You may be able to remember the words of a country-western hit but not the dance steps that go with it. The Theory of Multiple Intelligences may explain why.[19]

Examine your own behaviors in class. If your instructors use their linguistic intelligence to teach, as many do, and your intelligences lie elsewhere, can you observe telltale signs of your frustration? Instead of zeroing in on the lecture, do you fidget (bodily-kinesthetic), doodle (spatial), or socialize (interpersonal)? You may need to translate the information into your own personal intelligences, just as you would if your professor speaks French and you speak English. If you're having learning problems in one of your classes, it may be partially due to a case of mismatched intelligences between yours and your instructor's.

Since my highest intelligence is interpersonal, I should probably study for Professor Caldwell's class with someone else. Talking about things would help. Maybe Sam??

Let's say one of your courses this term is "Introduction to Economics," and the current course topic is the Law of Supply and Demand. Basically, "the theory of supply and demand describes how prices vary as a result of a balance between product availability at each price (supply) and the desires of those with purchasing power at each price (demand)."[20] To understand this law, you could read the textbook (linguistic); study mathematical formulas (logical-mathematical); examine charts and graphs (spatial); observe the Law of Supply and Demand in the natural world, through the fluctuating price of gasoline, for example (naturalist); look at the way the Law of Supply and Demand is expressed in your own body, using food as a metaphor (bodily-kinesthetic); reflect on how and when you might be able to afford something you desperately want, like a certain model of car (intrapersonal); or write (or find) a song that helps you understand the law (musical). You needn't try all eight ways, but it's intriguing to speculate about various ways to learn that may work for you, rather than assuming you're doomed because your intelligences don't match your instructor's.

Use Intelligence-Oriented Study Techniques

What if your strongest intelligence is different from the one through which course material is presented? What can you do about it? Take a look at the following techniques for studying using different intelligences. Tweaking the way you study may make a world of difference.

Linguistic --→	1. Rewrite your class notes. 2. Record yourself reading through your class notes and play it as you study. 3. Read the textbook chapter aloud.
Logical Mathematical --→	1. Create hypothetical conceptual problems to solve. 2. Organize chapter or lecture notes into logical flow. 3. Analyze how the textbook chapter is organized and why.
Spatial --→	1. Draw a map that demonstrates your thinking on course material. 2. Illustrate your notes by drawing diagrams and charts. 3. Mark up your textbook to show relationships between concepts.
Bodily–Kinesthetic --→	1. Study course material while engaged in physical activity. 2. Practice skills introduced in class or in the text. 3. Act out a scene based on chapter content.
Musical --→	1. Create musical memory devices by putting words into well-known melodies. 2. Listen to music while you're studying. 3. Sing or hum as you work.
Interpersonal --→	1. Discuss course material with your classmates in class. 2. Organize a study group that meets regularly. 3. Meet a classmate before or after class for coffee and course conversation.
Intrapersonal --→	1. Keep a journal to track your personal reactions to course material. 2. Study alone and engage in internal dialogue about course content. 3. Coach yourself on how to best study for a challenging class.
Naturalistic --→	1. Search for applications of course content in the natural world. 2. Study outside (if weather permits and you can resist distractions). 3. Go to a physical location that exemplifies course material (for example, a park for your geology course).

Choose a Major and Career That Fit Your Intelligences

If linguistic intelligence isn't your most developed type, but spatial intelligence is, architecture would probably be a much better major for you than English. If you've had a job you hated in the past, perhaps the Theory of Multiple

Intelligences can help you understand why. Take a look at Figure 2.2 for ideas about careers that emphasize particular intelligences and famous achievers in each category.

Develop Your Weaker Intelligences

It's important to cultivate your weaker intelligences. Why? Because life isn't geared to one kind of intelligence. It's complex. Even in the particular career fields listed for each intelligence in the preceding chart, more than one intelligence may be required. A photo journalist for *National Geographic*, for

Intelligence Type	Careers in Intelligences	Well-Known Examples
Linguistic	journalist	Diane Sawyer
	teacher	Your instructor
	lawyer	Lin Wood
	talkshow host	Oprah Winfrey
Logical-Mathematical	accountant	Henry W. Bloch (H&R Block)
	engineer	Dean Kamen, inventor
	computer programmer	Bill Gates, entrepreneur
Spatial	architect	Norma Merrick Sklarek, first African American woman architect, designed the Los Angeles International Airport Terminal
	artist	Christo, environmental artist
	artistic director	Grant Major, Academy Award Winner, *Lord of the Rings: The Return of the King*, 2003
Bodily-Kinesthetic	professional athlete	Serena Williams, tennis player
	coach	Mike McCarthy, Green Bay Packers
	actor	Johnny Depp
Musical	musician	Carrie Underwood, country singer
	composer	John Williams, composer/ conductor
Interpersonal	salesperson	Sam Walton, Wal-Mart Founder
	teacher	Your instructor
	counselor	Carl Rogers
Intrapersonal	theorist	Ilya Prigogine, Nobel prize winner, chemistry, 1977
	researcher	John Wheeler, physicist
	philosopher	W. V. Quine, American philosopher
Naturalistic	landscape architect	Frederick Law Olmsted
	anthropologist	Jane Goodall
	botanist	Peter Raven

FIGURE 2.2

Choosing an Intelligence-Based Career

How important will my Interpersonal Intelligence be as a CSI?

> O! this learning, what a thing it is.
>
> *William Shakespeare*

example, might need linguistic intelligence, spatial intelligence, interpersonal intelligence, and naturalist intelligence. Being well-rounded, as the expression goes, is truly a good thing. Artist Pablo Picasso once said, "I am always doing that which I cannot do, in order that I may learn how to do it." Remember that no one is naturally intelligent in all eight areas. Each individual is a unique blend of intelligences, and most people are strong in only two or three.[21] But the Theory of Multiple Intelligences claims that we all have the capacity to develop all of our eight intelligences further. That's good news! Howard Gardner puts it this way: "We can all get better at each of the intelligences, although some people will improve in an intelligence area more readily than others, either because biology gave them a better brain for that intelligence or because their culture gave them a better teacher."[22]

How Do You Perceive and Process Information?

? challenge

" reaction

Challenge: You've lived with yourself for many years now, but how well do you know yourself as a learner?

Reaction: List as many descriptive phrases about your learning preferences as you can. For example, you might write, "I learn best when I listen to an instructor lecture" or "I learn best when I make color-coded binders for each class." Use this activity to discover some specifics about your learning style.

____

____

____

I learn best when I'm actively involved.
I learn best when I work with other people.
I learn best when I can understand the professor!

Style—we all have it, right? What's yours? Baggy jeans and a T-shirt? Sandals, even in the middle of winter? A stocking cap that translates into I-just-rolled-out-of-bed-before-class? When it comes to appearance, you have your own style.

Think about how your mind works. For example, how do you decide what to wear in the morning? Do you turn on the radio or TV for the weather forecast? Jump on the Internet? Stick your head out the front door? Throw on whatever happens to be clean? We all have different styles, don't we?

So what's a learning style? A learning style is defined as your "characteristic and preferred way of gathering, interpreting, organizing, and thinking about information."[23] The way you perceive information and the way you process it—your perceiving/processing preferences—are based in part on your senses. Which sensory modalities do you prefer to use to take in information—your eyes (visual-graphic or visual-words), your ears (aural), or all your senses using your whole body (kinesthetic)? Which type of information sinks in best? Do you prefer teachers who lecture? Teachers who use visuals such as charts, web pages, and diagrams to explain things? Or teachers who plan field trips, use role-plays, and create simulations?

I wish we'd take a field trip to the county jail or a real crime lab as part of class!

To further understand your preferred sensory channel, let's take this example. You decide to buy a new car and you must first answer many questions: What kind of car do you want to buy—an SUV, a sedan, a sports car, a van, or a truck? What are the differences between various makes and models? How do prices, comfort, gas mileage, and safety compare? Who provides the best warranty? Which car do consumers rate highest? How would you go about learning the answers to all these questions?

Which would you be most likely do to?

a) Look up charts that compare different makes and models by cost, gas mileage, buyer satisfaction, and so forth, visually. (V)

b) Ask friends and relatives to tell you how satisfied they are with the last car they bought or listen to various pitches made by salespeople. (A)

c) Buy a copy of Consumer Guide's annual edition on autos or read magazines like *Car and Driver.* (R/W)

d) Go to various showrooms and test drive different makes and models. (K)

iStockphoto.com/Marcela Barsse/MarsBars; Johanna Goodyear/Dreamstime.com; iStockphoto.com/Nadezda Firsova; iStockphoto.com/Pascal Genest

Eventually, as you're deciding which vehicle to buy, you might do all these things, and do them more than once. But learning style theory says we all have preferences in terms of how we perceive and process information.

After reading the car-buying description, you probably have a gut feeling about your own style. However, take a few minutes to answer the questions about yourself in Exercise 2.3—for confirmation or revelation—to verify your hunches or to learn something new about yourself.

You can take the VARK online at http://www.vark-learn.com/english/page.asp?p=questionnaire and your results will be tabulated for you.

Holger Winkler/Corbis

" **Learning how to learn is life's most important skill.** "

Tony Buzan, memory expert

EXERCISE 2.3

VARK Learning Styles Assessment

Choose the answer that best explains your preference and circle the letter. Please select more than one response if a single answer does not match your perception. Leave blank any question that does not apply.

1. You are helping someone who wants to go downtown, find your airport or locate the bus station. You would:
   a) draw or give her a map.
   b) tell her the directions.
   c) write down the directions (without a map).
   d) go with her.

2. You are not sure whether a word should be spelled "dependent" or "dependant." You would:
   a) see the word in your mind and choose by the way different versions look.
   b) think about how each word sounds and choose one.
   c) find it in a dictionary.
   d) write both words on paper and choose one.

3. You are planning a group vacation. You want some feedback from your friends about your plans. You would:
   a) use a map or website to show them the places.
   b) phone, text or e-mail them.
   c) give them a copy of the printed itinerary.
   d) describe some of the highlights.

4. You are going to cook something as a special treat for your family. You would:
   a) look through the cookbook for ideas from the pictures.
   b) ask friends for suggestions.
   c) use a cookbook where you know there is a good recipe.
   d) cook something you know without the need for instructions.

5. A group of tourists wants to learn about the parks or wildlife reserves in your area. You would:
   a) show them Internet pictures, photographs or picture books.
   b) talk about, or arrange a talk for them on parks or wildlife reserves.
   c) give them a book or pamphlets about the parks or wildlife reserves.
   d) take them to a park or wildlife reserve and walk with them.

6. You are about to purchase a digital camera or cell phone. Other than price, what would most influence your decision?
   a) Its attractive design that looks good.
   b) The salesperson telling me about its features.
   c) Reading the details about its features.
   d) Trying or testing it.

7. Remember a time when you learned how to do something new. Try to avoid choosing a physical skill, like riding a bike. You learned best by:
   a) diagrams and charts—visual clues.
   b) listening to somebody explaining it and asking questions.
   c) written instructions—e.g. a manual or textbook.
   d) watching a demonstration.

8. You have a problem with your heart. You would prefer that the doctor:
   a) showed you a diagram of what was wrong.
   b) described what was wrong.
   c) gave you something to read to explain what was wrong.
   d) used a plastic model to show what was wrong.

9. You want to learn a new software program, skill or game on a computer. You would:
   a) follow the diagrams in the book that came with it.
   b) talk with people who know about the program.
   c) read the written instructions that came with the program.
   d) use the controls or keyboard and try things out.

10. I like websites that have:
   a) interesting design and visual features.
   b) audio channels where I can hear music, radio programs or interviews.
   c) interesting written descriptions, lists and explanations.
   d) things I can click on or try out.

11. Other than price, what would most influence your decision to buy a new non-fiction book?
   a) The way it looks is appealing.
   b) A friend talks about it and recommends it.
   c) You'd quickly read parts of it.
   d) It contains real-life stories, experiences and examples.

12. You are using a book, CD or website to learn how to take photos with your new digital camera. You would like to have:
   a) diagrams showing the camera and what each part does.
   b) a chance to ask questions and talk about the camera and its features.
   c) clear written instructions with lists and bullet points about what to do.
   d) many examples of good and poor photos and how to improve them.

13. Do you prefer a teacher or a presenter who uses:
   a) diagrams, charts or graphs?
   b) question and answer, talk, group discussion or guest speakers?
   c) handouts, books or readings?
   d) demonstrations, models, field trips, role plays or practical exercises?

14. You have finished a competition or test and would like some feedback. You would like to have feedback:
   a) using graphs showing what you had achieved.
   b) from somebody who talks it through with you.
   c) in a written format, describing your results.
   d) using examples from what you have done.

15. You are going to choose food at a restaurant or cafe. You would:
   a) look at what others are eating or look at pictures of each dish.
   b) ask the server or friends to recommend choices.
   c) choose from the written descriptions in the menu.
   d) choose something that you have had there before.

16. You have to give an important speech at a conference or special occasion. You would:
   a) make diagrams or create graphs to help explain things.
   b) write a few key words and practice your speech over and over.
   c) write out your speech and learn from reading it over several times.
   d) gather many examples and stories to make the talk real and practical.

Source: N. Fleming. (2001–2010). *VARK, a Guide to Learning Styles*. Version 7.1. Available at http://www.vark-learn.com/english/page.asp?p=questionnaire. Used with permission from Neil Fleming.

(continued on next page)

Scoring the VARK

Let's tabulate your results.

Count your choices in each of the four VARK categories.	(a)	(b)	(c)	(d)
	Visual	Aural	Read/Write	Kinesthetic

My VARK scores are
K = 14, A = 6,
V = 5, R = 4
Since I prefer my chem lab over lecture classes, I'm not surprised that I'm kinesthetic!

Now that you've calculated your scores, do they match your perceptions of yourself as a learner? Could you have predicted them? The VARK's creators believe that *you* are best qualified to verify and interpret your own results.[24]

Using Your VARK Preferences

Knowing your preferences can help you in your academic coursework for reasons like these:

1. You can use your preferences to get the best results.
2. You can pay attention to how you study, not just what you study.
3. You can make conscious choices that positively affect your overall college success.

If your highest score (by 4 or 5 points) is in one of the four VARK modalities, that particular learning modality is your preferred one.[25] If your scores are more or less even between several or all four modalities, these scores mean that you don't have a strong preference for any single modality. It's estimated that 60 percent of the population is multimodal, which gives most of us flexibility in the way we learn.[26] A lower score in a preference simply means that you are more comfortable using other styles. If your VARK results contain a zero in a particular learning modality, you may realize that you do indeed dislike this mode or find it unhelpful. "Why would anyone want to use *that* mode?" you may have asked yourself in the past. It may be helpful to reflect on why you omit this learning modality. To learn more about your results and suggestions for applying them, see Figure 2.3 for your preferred modality.

Your highest score represents your preferred learning style; your lowest score, your least preferred. Most college classes emphasize reading and writing; however, if your lowest score is in the read/write modality, don't assume you're academically doomed. VARK can help you discover alternative, more productive ways to learn the same course material. As Fleming writes, knowing your VARK scores doesn't naturally help you become a better learner any more than jumping on a scale helps you slim down. You must take the next step and do something about it![27]

That's right. I can't change the way Professor Caldwell teaches. I'll guess I'll just have to change the way I study.

Learning style descriptions aren't meant to put you into a cubbyhole or stereotype you. And they certainly aren't meant to give you an excuse when you don't like a particular assignment. You may learn to adapt naturally to a

	Everyday Study Strategies	Exam Preparation Strategies
VISUAL 	• Convert your lecture notes to a visual format. • Study the placement of items, colors, and shapes in your textbook. • Put complex concepts into flowcharts or graphs. • Redraw ideas you create from memory.	• Practice turning your visuals back into words. • Practice writing out exam answers. • Recall the pictures you made of the pages you studied. • Use diagrams to answer exam questions, if your instructor will allow it.
AURAL 	• Read your notes aloud. • Explain your notes to another auditory learner. • Ask others to "hear" you understanding of the material. • Record your notes or listen to your instructors' podcasts. • Realize that your lecture notes may be incomplete. You may have become so involved in listening that you stopped writing. Fill your notes in later by talking with other students or getting material from the textbook.	• Practice by speaking your answers aloud. • Listen to your own voice as you answer questions. • Opt for an oral exam if allowed. • Imagine you are talking with the teacher as you answer questions.
READ/WRITE 	• Write out your lecture notes again and again. • Read your notes (silently) again and again. • Put ideas and principles into different words. • Translate diagrams, graphs, etc., into text. • Rearrange words and "play"with wording. • Turn diagrams and charts into words.	• Write out potential exam answers. • Practice creating and taking exams. • Type out your answers to potential test questions. • Organize your notes into lists or bullets. • Write practice paragraphs, particularly beginnings and endings.
KINESTHETIC 	• Recall experiments, field trips, etc. Remember the real things that happened. • Talk over your notes with another "K" person. • Use photos and pictures that make ideas come to life. • Go back to the lab, your manual, or your notes that include real examples. • Remember that your lecture notes will have gaps if topics weren't concrete or relevant for you. • Use case studies to help you learn abstract principles.	• Role-play the exam situation in your room (or the actual classroom). • Put plenty of examples into your answers. • Write practice answers and sample paragraphs. • Give yourself practice tests.

FIGURE 2.3

Visual, Aural, Read/Write, and Kinesthetic Learning Strategies

particular instructor or discipline's preferences, using a visual modality in your economics class to interpret graphs and a kinesthetic modality in your chemistry lab to conduct experiments.

Of course, you'll be required to use all four modalities in college. You'll have to read your literature assignments and write your English papers, even if read/write isn't your preferred style. Different disciplines require different kinds of information access. As one skeptic of learning styles writes, "At some point, no amount of dancing will help you learn more algebra." Actually, some teachers do use dance to help students learn math, and there are plenty of other kinesthetic techniques that work well, like solving actual problems, rather than simply re-reading a chapter in your math book.[28]

Regardless, you may also find that you need to deliberately and strategically re-route your learning methods in some of your classes, and knowing your VARK

CAREER OUTLOOK: *UNI-TASK INTENTIONALLY*

Our lives have been divided into smaller and smaller increments of focus. We do more things than ever, but we've lost control of our attention.

Tony Schwartz,
The Way We're Working Isn't Working

Multitasking. It's quickly becoming one of the most popular words in the English language. In whatever career you enter, you'll be expected to juggle many things at once. You'll get a phone call while answering one of the two billions e-mails sent daily in the U.S. and at the same time be conducting online research for your boss. Reportedly, the average worker spends 11 minutes at a time on any given project, switching between different aspects of it every three minutes.[29] The odd thing about our so-called ability to multitask is that it makes us feel productive, powerful, and prolific. But not only do interruptions break our focus, they also increase the number of mistakes we make, and often actually *cost*—rather than *save*—us time. This of it this way: would you really want a brain surgeon to stop your operation to check her Facebook wall or answer texts from her kids every so often? Probably not.

To help you get the picture, visualize the prefrontal cortex of your brain as a stage. Instead of allowing any actor on stage who wants some attention, be selective. ("Not now; wait for Act 3, Scene 2!") The stage is only so big; every actor in the play can't fit on it at once.[30] Pulling off an entire production requires maximum effort, and some scenes require an actor doing a monologue, instead of different actors entering "stage left" or "stage right" constantly and chaotically.

To make things even more challenging, we may be tempted to "stray" by our learning style preferences. Someone who prefers an aural modality, for example, may want to discuss everything fully just to hear the sound of his own and others' voices, when a quick "executive decision" would be more appropriate. A reserved, introverted person may prefer e-mail over facing a live human being, even when sensitive issues are at stake. Your learning style preferences could actually jeopardize your ability to focus on one thing when the right decision might be to choose the best modality for that thing, and get it done.

Instead of multi-tasking, try uni-tasking. When a task is both urgent *and* important, put on your blinders. As Jason Fried and David Heinemeier Hansson, the authors of *Rework,* wisely claim, "Interruption is the enemy of productivity. You can't get meaningful things done when you're constantly going start, stop, start, stop. Instead, you should get in the alone zone. Long stretches of alone time are when you're most productive. When you don't have to mind-shift between various tasks, you get a boatload done."[31] So close your office door, zero in, and stick to one thing until you're actually finished—or you've gone as far as you can. Oh, and it works in college, too.

Think Ahead: In whatever career you're thinking of for yourself, what do you expect will be the most challenging, competing tasks? What sorts of things might you be juggling? How well does multitasking work for you now? How well might it work for you then, and what will you do to manage?

I can focus, but only on things I like . . .

CAST ON CAREERS

© Larry Harwood Photography. Property of Cengage Learning

FOCUS: Describe your ability to focus. Are you good at it?

ETHAN: As a brand new student, I was horrible at it. I wanted to jump into everything, and I was so excited by all the new friends I made that I didn't really focus on schoolwork much at all. I'm very extraverted; people matter to me. My residence hall door was always open, and other students came and went at all hours of the day and night. And I'm a kinesthetic learner, so I wanted to "do it all"! Unfortunately, all those things caught up with me and the result was major stress! I'm getting better at it though, and *FOCUS* has helped.

FOCUS: What career plans do you have right now? Is multitasking likely to be an issue?

ETHAN: I have two long-term goals: I'd like to become a teacher, and I'd like to travel internationally. Put those two together, and I can see myself teaching somewhere like New Zealand or Korea after I graduate. If I do that, not only will I have to pay attention to each one of my students, but I'll have to learn a new culture. But I can't wait for those career challenges!

preferences can help you do that. Learning to capitalize on your preferences and translate challenging course material into your preferred modality may serve you well. Remember these suggestions about the VARK, and try them out to see if they improve your academic results.

1. VARK preferences are not necessarily strengths. However VARK is an excellent vehicle to help you reflect on how you prefer to learn and begin to reinforce the productive strategies you're already using or select ones that might work better.
2. If you have a strong preference for a particular modality, practice multiple suggestions listed in Figure 2.3 for that particular modality. Reinforce your learning through redundancy.
3. Remember that an estimated 60 percent of people are multimodal. In a typical classroom of 30 students (based on VARK data):
    - 17 students would be multimodal,
    - 1 student would be visual,
    - 1 student would be aural,
    - 5 students would be read/write,
    - 6 students would be kinesthetic,

    and the teacher would most likely have a strong read/write preference![32]
4. If you are multimodal, as most of us are, it may be necessary to use all your modalities, rather than choosing one, to boost your confidence in your learning. If your VARK preferences are roughly equal for "V" and "K," for example, you may need to create charts (V) and make flash cards (K) in order to feel ready for an exam. Practice the suggestions for all of your preferred modalities.
5. While in an ideal world, it would be good to try to strengthen lesser preferences, you may wish to save that goal for later in life. Fleming's students eventually convinced him that college isn't the place to experiment. Academic results are important, and often scholarships and graduate school acceptance hang in the balance. You, too, may decide it's better to try to strengthen existing preferences now and work on expanding your repertoire later. This book will give you an opportunity to practice your VARK learning preferences—whatever they are—as you read each chapter.

What Role Does Your Personality Play?

? challenge

" reaction

Challenge: How does your personality affect your learning style?

Reaction:

____

____

____

One of the best things about college, no matter which one you've chosen to attend, is meeting so many different kinds of people. At times you may find these differences intriguing. At other times, they may baffle you. Look around and listen to other students, and you'll start to notice. Have you heard students voicing totally opposite opinions about college life by saying things like this?

"There's no way I can study in the dorm. It's way too noisy."	"There's no way I can study in the library. It's way too quiet."
"My roommate is terrific! We're getting along great."	"My roommate is unbearable! I can hardly stand being around him."
"I'm so glad I've already decided on a major. Now I can go full steam ahead."	"I have no idea what to major in. I can think of six different majors I'd like to choose."
"My sociology prof is great. She talks about all kinds of things in class, and her essay tests are actually fun!"	"My sociology prof is so confusing. She talks about so many different things in class. How am I supposed to know what to study for her tests?"[33]

You're likely to run into all kinds of viewpoints and all kinds of people, but as you're bound to discover in college, differences make life much more interesting! Perhaps your friends comment on your personality by saying, "She's really quiet," or "He's the class clown," or "He's incredibly logical," or "She trusts her gut feelings." What you may not know is how big a role your personality traits like these play in how you prefer to learn and your academic success.[34]

The Myers-Briggs Type Indicator® (MBTI) is the most well known personality assessment instrument in the world. Each year, approximately four million people worldwide obtain significant insights about their personalities, their career choices, their interaction with others, and their learning styles by completing it.

This chapter will introduce you to a shorter instrument based on the MBTI, the SuccessTypes Learning Style Type Indicator. Created by Dr. John Pelley at Texas Tech University, this instrument focuses specifically on your personality type and how you prefer to learn. If you are able to complete the full Myers-Briggs Type Indicator in the class for which you're using this textbook, or through your college counseling center

> **This constant, unproductive preoccupation with all the things we have to do is the single largest consumer of time and energy.**
>
> *Kerry Gleeson*

Each person is an exception to the rule.

Carl Jung, Swiss psychiatrist (1875–1961)

or learning center, do so. You'll learn even more about yourself.

Here's an important point: Both the SuccessTypes Learning Style Type Indicator and the Myers-Briggs Type Indicator show you your preferences. These instruments are not about what you *can* do. They're about what you *prefer* to do. That's an important distinction. Here's an illustration. Try writing your name on the line below.

____

Now put the pen in your other hand, and try writing your name again.

____

What was different the second time around? For most people, the second try takes longer, is less legible, probably feels odd, and requires more concentration. But could you do it? Yes. It's just that you prefer doing it the first way. The first way is easier and more natural; the second way makes a simple task seem like hard work! It's possible that you might have to try "writing with your other hand" in college—doing things that don't come naturally. Practice, rehearsal, and focus might be extra important, but you can do it!

Throughout this book, you will find "Your Type Is Showing" features. These articles will summarize MBTI research that investigates the chapter's topic. They are intended to pique your interest and invite you to go beyond what you see in the chapter. Chances are you'll be fascinated by what you can learn about yourself through the MBTI. But in the meantime, let's zero in on how your personality affects your learning style, specifically.

EXERCISE 2.4

The SuccessTypes Learning Style Type Indicator

Each of the following statements represents opposites in your thinking when you are learning. Choose the one that describes the way you really are. It is common to want to choose the one that represents what you want to be or what others think you ought to be. Try to imagine that you are learning for yourself and not for a teacher and that there is no grade involved. For example, you are learning about something that interests you like a new hobby or outside interest. Just choose the description that best fits you, and write the letter associated with that sentence in the box to the left, and you will total them when you are done.

I'd write a lot of S's here. maybe that's because I'm a kinesthetic learner. I like to learn by using my senses (see it, touch it, work with it).

1. ☐ E I study best with other people.
   I I study best by myself.

2. ☐ E When I study with other people, I get the most out of expressing my thoughts.
   I When I study with other people, I get the most out of listening to what others have to say.

3. ☐ E When I study with other people, I get the most out of quick, trial-and-error thinking.
   I When I study with other people, I get the most out of thinking things through before I say them.

4. ☐ E I prefer to start my learning by doing something active and then considering the results later.
   I I prefer to start my learning by considering something thoroughly and then doing something active with it later.

5. ☐ E I need frequent breaks when I study and interruptions don't bother me.
   I I can study for very long stretches and interruptions are *not* welcome.

6. ☐ E I prefer to demonstrate what I know.
   I I prefer to describe what I know.

7. ☐ E I like to know what other people expect of me.
   I I like to set my own standards for my learning.

8. ☐ S I am more patient with routine or details in my study.
   N I am more patient with abstract or complex material.

9. ☐ S I am very uncomfortable with errors of fact.
   N I consider errors of fact to be another useful way to learn.

10. ☐ S I am very uncomfortable when part of my learning is left to my imagination.
    N I am bored when everything I am supposed to learn is presented explicitly.

11. ☐ S I prefer to learn fewer skills and get really good at them.
    N I prefer to keep learning new skills and I'll get good at them when I have to.

12. ☐ S I learn much better in a hands-on situation to see what is.
    N I learn much better when I'm thinking about the possibilities to imagine what might be.

13. ☐ S I prefer to learn things that are useful and based on established principles.
    N I prefer to learn things that are original and stimulate my imagination.

14. ☐ S I always re-examine my answers on test questions just to be sure.
    N I usually trust my first hunches about test questions.

15. ☐ S I emphasize observation over imagination.
N I emphasize imagination over observation.

16. ☐ S I'm more comfortable when the professor sticks closely to the handout.
N I'm likely to get bored if the professor sticks closely to the handout.

17. ☐ T I prefer to have a logical reason for what I learn.
F I prefer to see the human consequences of what I learn.

18. ☐ T I prefer a logically organized teacher to a personable teacher.
F I prefer a personable teacher to a logically organized teacher.

19. ☐ T I prefer group study as a way to give and receive critical analysis.
F I prefer group study to be harmonious.

20. ☐ T I prefer to study first what should be learned first.
F I prefer to study first what appeals to me the most.

21. ☐ T The best way to correct a study partner is to be blunt and direct.
F The best way to correct a study partner is to be tactful and understanding.

22. ☐ J I prefer to study in a steady, orderly fashion.
P I prefer to study in a flexible, even impulsive, way.

23. ☐ J I stay on schedule when I study regardless of how interesting the assignment is.
P I tend to postpone uninteresting or unpleasant assignments.

24. ☐ J I tend to be an overachiever in my learning.
P I tend to be an underachiever in my learning.

25. ☐ J I prefer to structure my study now to avoid emergencies later.
P I prefer to stay flexible in my study and deal with emergencies when they arise.

26. ☐ J I prefer to give answers based on the information I already have.
P I prefer to seek more information before deciding on an answer.

27. ☐ J I prefer to finish one assignment before starting another one.
P I prefer to have several assignments going at once.

28. ☐ J I like well defined learning assignments.
P I like learning from open-ended problem solving.

Let's boil it down to four letters:

E or I ☐ Record the letter which occurred the most for questions 1–7.

S or N ☐ Record the letter which occurred the most for questions 8–16.

OK. Let's see what my answers mean.

T or F ☐ Record the letter which occurred the most for questions 17–21.

J or P ☐ Record the letter which occurred the most for questions 22–28.

Adapted from Table 5.1 in *Success Types for Medical Students*, J. W. Pelley and B. K. Dalley (Texas Tech Univ. Extended Learning, 1997). Used by permission of John W. Pelley.

You can take the SuccessTypes Learning Style Type Indicator online at http://www.ttuhsc.edu/SOM/success/page_LSTI/LSTI.htm.

Interpreting Your SuccessTypes Learning Style Type Profile

Look at your four-letter profile. Are you an ESFP? An ESTP? An INTJ? What do those four letters say about you? There are many sources of information about the sixteen possible combinations of letters, or type, in books and online resources.[35] However, here are some things you need to know about measuring psychological type.

First, most abbreviated type indicators—even this one—are not scientifically reliable. They are designed to illustrate type, not prove it. As the instrument's creator asserts, "Your type is the starting line, not the finish line.... Type is more than the sum of its parts."[36]

Second, the SuccessTypes Learning Style Type Indicator forces you to make a choice between two opposites. That's because, theoretically, you can't simultaneously prefer two opposite things at once. That doesn't mean you'd never under any circumstances choose the other one. It just means that most of the time the one you chose would be your preference.

Third, any Myers-Briggs type instrument answers four questions about you (see Figure 2.4 for further explanations of typical characteristics of the preferences):

1. What energizes you and where do you direct energy? E or I
2. How do you gather information and what kind of information do you trust? S or N
3. How do you make decisions, arrive at conclusions, and make judgments? T or F
4. How do you relate to the outer world? J or P

Using Your SuccessTypes Learning Style Type Profile

What does it all mean? Now that you know some important things about yourself as a learner, there are several other points about learning styles you should know.

First, look at your first and second letters (ES, IS, EN, or IN). Statistically, twice as many instructors as students are Introverted Intuitives (IN). By and large, students are Extraverted Sensors (ES), preferring concrete, practical learning, while instructors often prefer theories and learning for its own sake.[37]

Now look at your second and last letters (SP, SJ, NP, or NJ). Three times as many college students prefer sensing and perceiving (SP) as their professors, who are likely to be intuitive and judging (NJ). Generally, students want a more concrete, flexible approach to learning while instructors like to teach abstract, structured theories.[38]

While simply knowing about these mismatches is good, it's important to go further and act on that knowledge. As a single learner in a larger class, you

Extravert (E)

"How do you recharge your batteries"? Students who prefer extraversion pay attention to people and things around them. That's also where they get their energy. As learners, they:

- Learn best when actively involved
- Like to study with others
- Like backgroud noise while studying
- Don't particularly enjoy writing papers
- Want teachers to encourage discussion in class

Introvert (I)

Students who prefer introversion focus on the world inside their heads. They pay attention to their own thoughts, feelings, and ideas, and draw energy from their inner experience. As learners, they:

- Learn best by pausing to think
- Like to study alone
- Say they aren't good public speakers
- Need to study in quiet
- Want teachers to give clear lectures

Sensing (S)

What kind of information do you rely on? Students who are sensors become aware of things that are real through their senses: sound, touch, taste, feel, and smell. They focus on what is happening in the here and now. As learners, they:

- Look for specific information
- Memorize facts
- Follow instructions
- Like hands-on experiences
- Want teachers to give clear assignments

Intuition (N)

Students who trust their intuition, or sixth sense, look for patterns, possibilities, and the big picture. As learners, they:

- Look for quick insights
- Like theories and abstract thinking
- Read between the lines
- Create their own directions
- Want teachers to encourage independent thinking

Thinking (T)

Students who are thinkers like to make decisions objectively using logic, principles, and analysis. They weigh evidence in a detached manner. As learners, they:

- Use logic to guide their learning
- Like to critique ideas
- Learn through challenge and debate
- Can find flaws in an argument
- Want teachers to present logically

Feeling (F)

Students who are feelers value harmony and focus on what is important to them or to others when they make decisions. As learners, they:

- Want information to apply to them personally
- Like to please their teachers
- Find value or good in things
- Learn when they are supported or appreciated
- Want teachers to establish rapport with students

Judging (J)

Students who are judgers like to make quick decisions, settle things, and structure and organize their worlds. As learners, they:

- Like more formal class structures
- Plan their work in advance
- Work steadily toward their goals
- Like to be in charge
- Want teachers to be organized

Perceiving (P)

Students who are perceivers want to adapt to the world around them. They don't like to close off options; instead they'd rather experience whatever comes up. As learners, they:

- Like infiormal learning situations
- Enjoy spontaneity
- Stay open to new information
- Work in energy bursts
- Want teachers to entertain and inspire

Aha! Here's the biggest problem! I'm an ESFP, and I'll bet Professor Caldwell is an INTJ. We couldn't be more opposite!

FIGURE 2.4

Learning Style Preferences

Source: Based on J. K. DiTiberio & A. L. Hammer. (1993). *Introduction to Type in College.* Palo Alto, CA: Consulting Psychologists Press.

Should I go to him for help in making connections between theories and the real world? Maybe we watch the same TV shows and we can talk about how true to life they are—or aren't.

will need to adjust to the teaching style of your instructor in ways such as the following:

- **Translate for maximum comfort.** The way to maximize your comfort as a learner is to find ways to translate from your instructor's preferences to yours. If you know that you prefer feeling over thinking, and your instructor's style is based on thinking, make the course material come alive by personalizing it. How does the topic relate to you, your lifestyle, your family, and your future choices?
- **Make strategic choices.** While learning preferences can help explain your academic successes, it's also important not to use them to rationalize your nonsuccesses. An introvert could say, "I could have aced that assignment if the professor had let me work on an individual project instead of a group one! I really hate group projects." Become the best learner you can be, regardless. But also realize that you'll need to become more versatile over time. In the workforce, you won't always be able to choose what you do and how you do it. Actively choose your learning strategies, rather than simply hoping for the best. Remember: no one can learn for you, just as no one can eat for you.
- **Take full advantage.** College will present you with an extensive menu of learning opportunities. You will also build on your learning as you move beyond your general, introductory classes into courses in your chosen major—and across and between disciplines. Don't fall victim to the temptation to rationalize and victimize as some students do ("I could have been more successful in college if . . . I hadn't had to work so many hours . . . I hadn't had a family to support . . . my friends had been more studious . . . my roommate had been easier to live with . . . my professors had been more supportive. . . ." If, if, if. College may well be the most concentrated and potentially powerful learning opportunity you'll ever have.

Understanding the central role you play in your own learning may be the single most important thing you take from this chapter. Learning more about learning styles has a valuable byproduct: you pay attention to how you study and why, you know what other options are available, and you motivate yourself to try something different if necessary. Being able to monitor how you learn may be *the* most fundamental of all skills. Learning styles are controversial among researchers who are trying to prove their existence, but they make sense to most students. Most of us can't just read a chapter or hear a lecture and absorb everything. We must go further. The bottom line is that just paying attention to how you learn can help you improve your learning. Being *intentional* about your learning is key.[39]

The three instruments presented in this chapter are separate, free-standing tools. Consider each one to be a window into understanding how you learn best. But it may help you to think about them this way. Everyone has Multiple Intelligences; like most people, you are probably strongest in two or three. Within your multiple intelligences, you have preferences as a visual, aural, read/write, kinesthetic, or multimodal learner. And surrounding those two aspects of your learning is your personality itself. That affects *how* you prefer to learn in many different ways. You know much more about yourself than you did at the beginning of this chapter, or perhaps you've validated what you've suspected all along. Each chapter of this book will remind you of your VARK preferences with special "VARK It!" activities to reinforce your preferred sensory modalities as you read. And you'll have a chance to re-explore your SuccessType Learning Style preferences in short sections called "Your Type Is Showing," in which you'll get a short flash of current research findings on the Myers-Briggs Type Indicator and the chapter's particular focus.

Gaining the insights provided in this chapter and acting on them have the potential to greatly affect your college success. Understand yourself, capitalize on your preferences, build on them, focus, and learn!

VARK It!

Complete the recommended activity for your preferred VARK learning modality. If you are multimodal, select more than one activity. Your instructor may ask you to (a) give an oral report on your results in class, (b) send your results to him or her via e-mail, (c) post them online, or (d) contribute to a class chat.

iStockphoto.com/Marcela Barsse/MarsBars; Johanna Goodyear/Dreamstime.com; iStockphoto.com/Nadezda Firsova, iStockphoto.com/Pascal Genest

Visual: Look back over this chapter to see which photos (and quotes) remind you of yourself and your learning. Mark the photo and write an explanation.

Aural: Discuss your 1) multiple intelligences, 2) VARK preferences, or 3) personality factors that affect learning with your friends or family. Do your results make sense to them? Why or why not?

Read/Write: Choose one major section of this chapter that made an impact on you, and write a paragraph summary about your own learning.

Kinesthetic: Do your own online research to further your understanding of how the three self-assessment tools in this chapter impact you or change the way you think of yourself as a learner.

* insight ! action

Now What Do You Think?

1. At the beginning of this chapter, Tammy Ko, a frustrated and disgruntled student, faced a challenge. Now after reading this chapter, would you respond differently to any of the questions you answered about the "FOCUS Challenge Case"? Knowing what you know now, how would you advise her? Write a paragraph ending to the story, incorporating your best advice.
2. What are your most developed intelligences? Describe a situation in which you excelled as a learner and how the Theory of Multiple Intelligences helps explain your success.
3. What is or are your VARK preferences? Are they what you predicted? How will you capitalize on them to learn at your best?
4. How does your personality affect your learning? Provide an example of how you can make the best use of what you know now about your approach to learning based on your personality type.
5. This chapter asked you to assess your learning in three different ways by thinking about your multiple intelligences, sensory modalities, and personality. We learned from Tammy's notes that she has high Interpersonal Intelligence, is a kinesthetic learner according to the VARK, and that her personality type is ESFP (while Professor Caldwell's is probably INTJ). How do these three assessments fit together for her? How do your three assessments fit together for you? How is the new picture of yourself as a learner similar to or different from what you used to think about yourself? How will it change the way you approach learning in the future?

REALITY What did you LEARN?

On a scale of 1 to 10, answer the following questions now that you've completed the chapter.

low 1 2 3 4 5 6 7 8 9 10 high

In hindsight, how much did you already know about this subject before reading the chapter?

Can you answer these questions about learning more fully now that you've read the chapter?

1. What does the term "multiple intelligences" mean? Can you name three different types of intelligences?
2. What does VARK stand for? Can you identify the letters as they relate to students' preferences for taking in information?
3. What does your personality have to do with how you learn? Give several examples.

How useful might the information in this chapter be to you?

How much do you think this information might affect your success overall? ________

How much energy did you put into reading this chapter? ________

How long did it actually take you to complete this chapter (both the reading and writing tasks)? ________ Hour(s) ________ Minutes

Did you finish reading this chapter? ________

Did you intend to when you started? ________

If you meant to but didn't, what stopped you? ________

Aced the online quiz!

Challenge Yourself Online Quiz To find out just how much you've learned, access the College Success CourseMate via www.cengagebrain.com to take the Challenge Yourself Online Quiz.

Take a minute to compare these answers to your answers from the "Readiness Check" at the beginning of this chapter. What gaps exist between the similar questions? How might these gaps between what you thought before starting the chapter and what you now think after completing the chapter affect how you approach the next chapter in this book?

CHAPTER 3

Managing Your Time, Energy, and Money

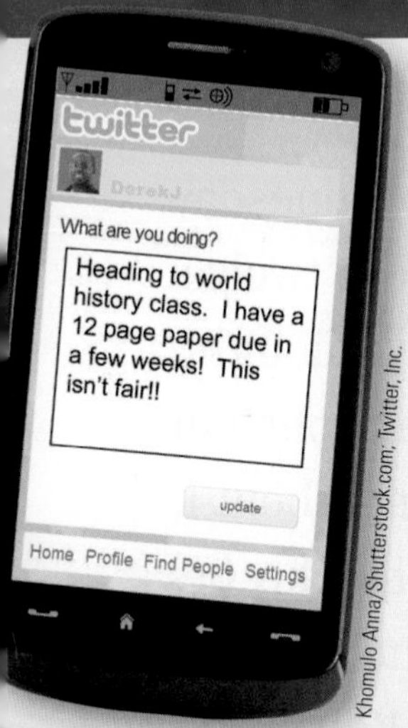

Khomulo Anna/Shutterstock.com; Twitter, Inc.

YOU'RE ABOUT TO DISCOVER...

- WHY TIME MANAGEMENT ALONE DOESN'T WORK
- HOW COMMON TIME-WASTERS CREEP IN, AND HOW TO BUST THEM
- HOW THE P WORD CAN DERAIL YOU
- HOW TO REALISTICALLY BALANCE WORK, SCHOOL, AND PERSONAL LIFE
- HOW TO MANAGE ANOTHER VITAL RESOURCE: YOUR MONEY

© Larry Harwood Photography. Property of Cengage Learning

READINESS ✔ What do you KNOW?

Before beginning to read this chapter, take two minutes to answer the following questions on a scale of 1 to 10. Your answers will help you assess how ready you are to focus.

low 1 2 3 4 5 6 7 8 9 10 high

How much do you *already* know?

Based on reading the "You're about to discover . . ." list and skimming this chapter, how much do you think you probably already know about this chapter's subject? ________

See if you can answer these questions about managing time and energy *before* you read.

1. What's the difference between time management, attention management, and energy management? How are they different, and what do they have in common?
2. What percentage of college students admit to procrastinating on assignments? Why do they procrastinate?
3. What percentage of college students with credit cards have no idea how much interest they pay on their credit card bills?

How much do you expect to learn?

In general, how motivated are you to learn more by reading this chapter? ________

How much do you think this information might affect your success overall? ________

How much energy do you plan to put into reading this chapter? ________

How ready are you to read *now*?

How ready are you to focus on this chapter? Enter a number for each aspect of your readiness to focus.

Physically ________

Intellectually ________

Emotionally ________

If any of your answers is below a 10, pay attention to whatever is distracting you before you start reading. Then zero in and focus.

How long do you think it will take you to complete this chapter from start to finish?

____ Hour(s) ____ Minutes

Now, as you begin, do you intend to finish reading this chapter?

____ yes ____ no ____ maybe

Larry Harwood Photography.
Property of Cengage Learning

FOCUS Challenge Case

? challenge

Derek Johnson

As Derek Johnson walked out of his World History class on Wednesday evening, he felt panicked. The professor had just assigned a twelve-page paper, due one month from today. *How could she?* Derek thought. *Doesn't she realize how busy I am?* The syllabus mentioned a paper, but twelve pages was downright excessive. He sent a tweet complaining about it from his phone on his way to his next class. Twitter was quickly becoming Derek's favorite way to communicate. Writing short tweets was certainly better than dragging something out over 12 pages!

Hintau Aliaksei/Shutterstock.com

Blackpixel/Shutterstock.com

Fotorro/Shutterstock.com

When Derek had decided to go to college after working for a year after high school, he hadn't quite realized what a juggling act it would require. First, there was his family—his Mom and stepdad, his five-year-old sister, Taura, and three other stepbrothers and stepsisters on his Dad's side. Then there was his full-time job, which was really quite demanding for an administrative assistant. He hoped that a degree in business would help him move into the management ranks, where the salaries were higher. No matter what, Derek always ran out of money before the end of the month. Besides his job, there was singing in his church choir, coaching the youth soccer league, competing in cycling races, and working out every morning at the gym. Derek had been a high school athlete, and physical fitness was a priority for him.

His head began to swim as he thought about all his upcoming obligations: his mother's birthday next week, the dog's vet appointment, his stepbrother coming to town for a visit, the mandatory training class for work. Something had to go, but he couldn't think of anything he could sacrifice to make time for a twelve-page paper. Maybe he'd have to break down and buy one of those planners, but weren't most people who use those slightly, well . . . compulsive?

Still, the paper was to count as 25 percent of his final grade in the course. He decided he'd try and think of a topic for the paper on his way home. But then he remembered that his mom had asked him to stop at the store to pick up groceries. Somewhere on aisle 12,

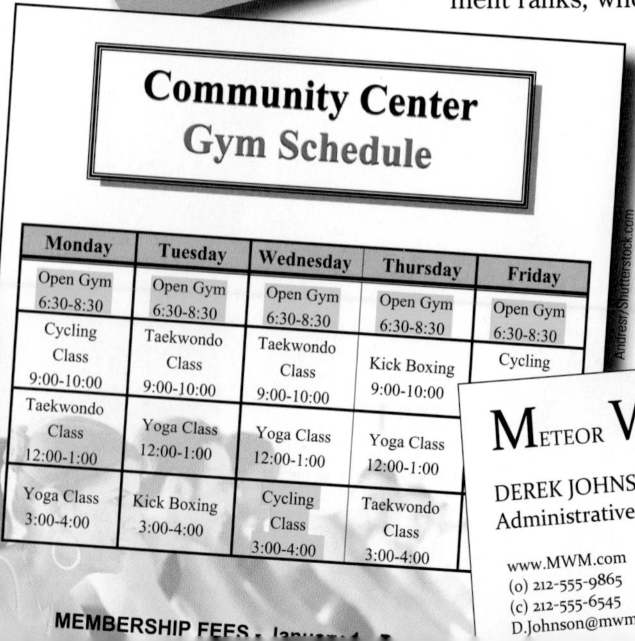

Community Center
Gym Schedule

Monday	Tuesday	Wednesday	Thursday	Friday
Open Gym 6:30-8:30	Open Gym 6:30-8:30	Open Gym 6:30-8:30	Open Gym 6:30-8:30	Open Gym 6:30-8:30
Cycling Class 9:00-10:00	Taekwondo Class 9:00-10:00	Taekwondo Class 9:00-10:00	Kick Boxing 9:00-10:00	Cycling
Taekwondo Class 12:00-1:00	Yoga Class 12:00-1:00	Yoga Class 12:00-1:00	Yoga Class 12:00-1:00	
Yoga Class 3:00-4:00	Kick Boxing 3:00-4:00	Cycling Class 3:00-4:00	Taekwondo Class 3:00-4:00	

MEMBERSHIP FEES -

Andresr/Shutterstock.com

© Cengage Learning

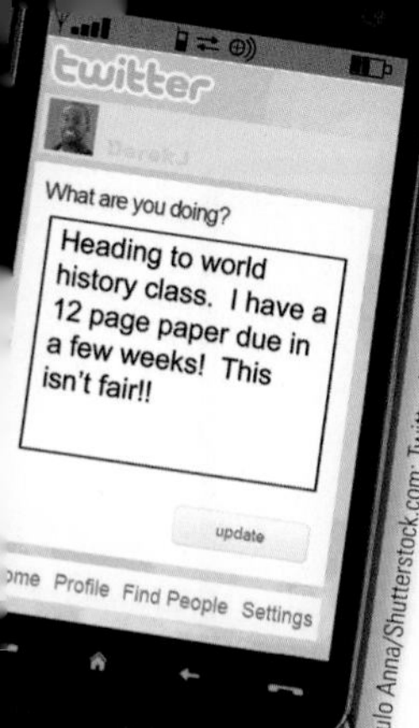

Khomulo Anna/Shutterstock.com; Twitter, Inc.

between the frozen pizza and the frozen yogurt, Derek's thoughts about his research paper vanished.

The following week, the professor asked the students in the class how their papers were coming along. Some students gave long accounts of their research progress, the wealth of sources they'd found, and the detailed outlines they'd put together. Derek didn't raise his hand.

A whole week has gone by, Derek thought on his way back to his car after class. *I have to get going!* Writing had never exactly been Derek's strong suit. Through a great deal of hard work, he had managed to earn a 3.8 GPA in high school—a record he planned to continue. A course in World History—not even in his intended major—was *not* going to ruin things! The week had absolutely flown by, and there were plenty of good reasons why his paper was getting off to such a slow start.

It was true that Derek rarely wasted time, except for occasionally watching his favorite TV shows. But then again, with such a jam-packed schedule, he really felt the need to unwind once in a while. Regardless, he rarely missed his nightly study time from 11:00 p.m. to 1:00 a.m. Those two hours were reserved for homework, no matter what.

At the end of class two weeks later, Derek noticed that several students lined up to show the professor the first drafts of their papers. *That's it!* Derek thought to himself. *The paper is due next Wednesday. I'll spend Monday night, my only free night of the week, in the library. I can get there right after work and stay until 11:00 or so. That'll be five hours of concentrated time. I should be able to write it then.*

Despite his good intentions, Derek didn't arrive at the library until nearly 8:00 p.m., and his work session wasn't all that productive. As he sat at his library computer, he found himself obsessing about things that were bothering him at work. His boss was being difficult, and his team of coworkers argued contantly about their current project. Finally, when he glanced at his watch, he was shocked to see that it was already midnight! The library was closing, and he'd only written three pages. Where had the time gone?

On his way out to the car, his cell phone rang. It was his Mom, wondering if he could watch Taura tomorrow night. She was running a fever. Oh, and his boss had called about an emergency meeting at 7:00 a.m. *If one more thing goes wrong . . . ,* Derek thought to himself. His twelve-page paper was due in two days.

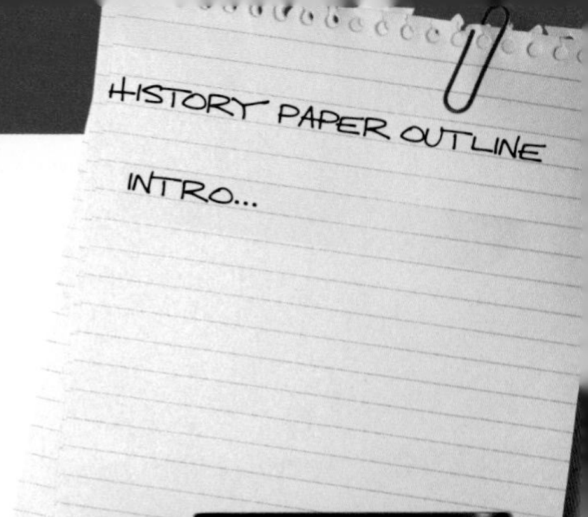

Borodaev/Shutterstock.com

CROM 2009/Shutterstock.com

Studio 10One/Shutterstock.com

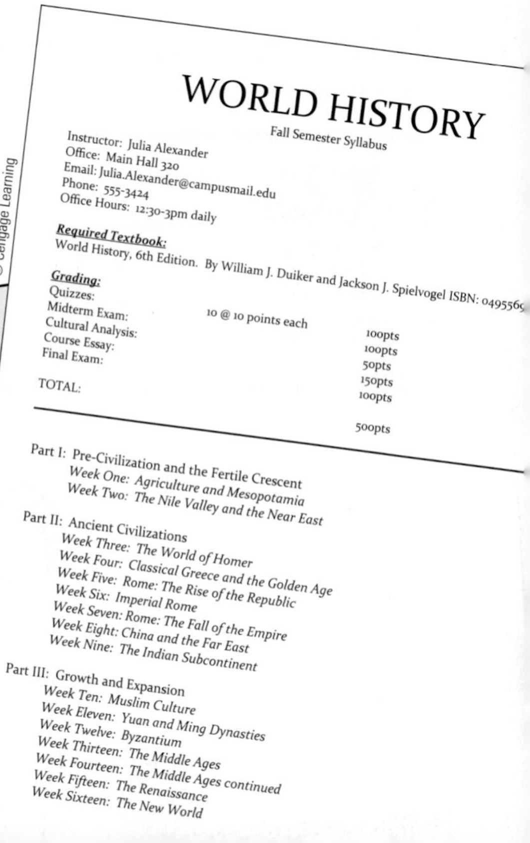

WORLD HISTORY

Fall Semester Syllabus

Instructor: Julia Alexander
Office: Main Hall 320
Email: Julia.Alexander@campusmail.edu
Phone: 555-3424
Office Hours: 12:30-3pm daily

Required Textbook:
World History, 6th Edition. By William J. Duiker and Jackson J. Spielvogel ISBN: 0495569

Grading:

Quizzes:	10 @ 10 points each	100pts
Midterm Exam:		100pts
Cultural Analysis:		50pts
Course Essay:		150pts
Final Exam:		100pts
TOTAL:		500pts

Part I: Pre-Civilization and the Fertile Crescent
Week One: Agriculture and Mesopotamia
Week Two: The Nile Valley and the Near East

Part II: Ancient Civilizations
Week Three: The World of Homer
Week Four: Classical Greece and the Golden Age
Week Five: Rome: The Rise of the Republic
Week Six: Imperial Rome
Week Seven: Rome: The Fall of the Empire
Week Eight: China and the Far East
Week Nine: The Indian Subcontinent

Part III: Growth and Expansion
Week Ten: Muslim Culture
Week Eleven: Yuan and Ming Dynasties
Week Twelve: Byzantium
Week Thirteen: The Middle Ages
Week Fourteen: The Middle Ages continued
Week Fifteen: The Renaissance
Week Sixteen: The New World

© Cengage Learning

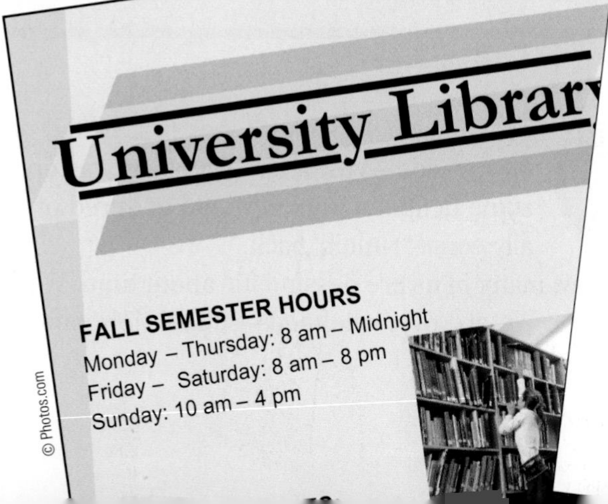

© Photos.com

What Do You Think?

1. Describe Derek's time management strategies. Are they working? Is time management Derek's only problem?
2. Describe the time-wasters that are a part of Derek's schedule. Do you think procrastination is an issue for Derek? What's behind his failure to make progress on his paper?
3. Suggest three realistic ways for Derek to balance work, school, and his personal life.
4. What aspects of Derek's situation can you relate to personally? Besides time management challenges, are you experiencing money management issues as he is in your life right now?

VARK Activity

Complete the recommended activity for your preferred VARK learning modality. If you are multimodal, select more than one activity. Your instructor may ask you to (a) give an oral report on your results in class, (b) send your results to him or her via e-mail, (c) post them online, or (d) contribute to a class chat.

Visual: Buy a set of adhesive colored dots from a local office supply store. As you go through this chapter, put red dots by things you'll try right away, yellow dots by things that sound like a good idea, and green dots by things you're already doing well.

Aural: Listen to the mp3 summary at www.cengagebrain.com for this chapter before you read further. As soon as you've finished, write down three ideas you'll watch for as you read.

Read/Write: Write a case study about yourself and time management, and watch for suggestions that come up that apply to your own issues as you read.

Kinesthetic: Find a YouTube or other online resource on time management that adds to this chapter. Show your YouTube or "compete" with other "K" students to show the best one in class as you begin discussing this chapter.

iStockphoto.com/Marcela Barsse/MarsBars; Joanna Goodyear/Dreamstime.com; iStockphoto.com/Nadezda Firsova; iStockphoto.com/Pascal Genest

Time Management Isn't Enough

Challenge: What is the difference between managing your time and managing your attention?

Reaction:

____

____

____

Years ago, the Rolling Stones first belted out these lyrics: "Time is on my side—yes, it is." The song was optimistic. It predicted that some fictitious woman would get tired of her new love and eventually come "runnin' back."

Today, many of us are pessimistic about time. We feel that time is working against us. We are overwhelmed—school, job, family, friends. The list goes on and on, specific to each of us, but lengthy for all of us. How can we get it all done?

In college and in your career, time management will be one of your greatest challenges. Why? The pace of life is accelerating. Today's world is about high-speed technology, rapid transit, information overload, and a frenetic lifestyle. Leisurely fine dining or family meals around the table have deteriorated into grabbing fast food on the run. Many of us try to cram more into our lives: one more activity, one more experience, one more obligation. As one time management expert notes, "You can be so busy that you don't even take the time to decide what actually does matter most to you, let alone make the time to do it."[1]

> **In truth, people can generally make time for what they choose to do; it is not really the time but the will that is lacking.**
>
> *Sir John Lubbock, British banker, politician, and archaeologist (1834–1913)*

Sometimes we'd like to be able to just hit "insert" on the toolbar, and click on "hours." But when it comes to real-time time management, we're all dealt the same hand. No matter who you are, you have the same 24 precious hours in a day, 168 jam-packed hours in a week as everyone else. We may not be able to change the natural laws of the universe, but we can learn more about making conscious, productive decisions, and—at the same time—finding the key to balance in our lives.

First, let's really understand what we mean by effective time management. It's simply planning, scheduling, and structuring your time to complete tasks you're responsible for efficiently and effectively. Perhaps you're a natural planner. You crave structure and welcome organizing strategies. Or you may be a person who despises the idea of restricting yourself to a schedule. But no matter which of these categories you fall into, you can improve your time management skills.

Before delving into the details of time management skills, however, let's clarify one important point. There's a sense in which the phrase *time management* is misleading. Let's say you decide to spend an hour reading the assigned short story for your literature class. You may sit in the library with your book propped open in front of you from 3:00 to 4:00 o'clock on the dot. But you may not digest a single word you're reading. You may be going through the motions, reading on autopilot. Have you managed your time? Technically, yes. Your planner says, "Library, short story for Lit 101, 3:00–4:00 p.m." But did you get results? The quality of what you do is as or more important than the fact that you did it. Time management expert Jeffrey Mayer asks provactively in the title of his book: *If You Haven't Got the Time to Do It Right, When Will You Find The Time to Do It Over?*. Now that's a good question!

NO KIDDING!

Digital Vision/Getty Images

It's not just about managing your time, it's about managing your attention. Attention management is the ability to focus your attention, not just your time, toward a designated activity so that you produce a desired result. Time management may get you through reading a chapter of your chemistry textbook, but attention management will ensure that you understand what you're reading. It's about *focus*. Without attention management, time management is pointless.

> **Don't confuse activity with accomplishment. 'Time = Success' is a myth.**
>
> *Dr. Constance Staley, University of Colorado, Colorado Springs*

Succeeding in school, at work, and in life is not just about what you do. It's about what gets done. You can argue about the effort you put into an assignment all you want, but it's doubtful your professor will say, "You know what? You're right. You deserve an A just for staying up late last night working on this paper." Activity and accomplishment aren't the same thing. Neither are quantity and quality. Results count. So don't confuse being busy with being successful. Staying busy isn't much of a challenge; being successful is.

Here's a list of preliminary academic time-saving tips. However, remember that these suggestions won't give you a surefire recipe for academic success. To manage your time, you must also manage yourself: your energy, your behavior, your attention, your attitudes, *you*. Once you know how to manage all that, managing your time begins to work. Here are some suggestions worth trying:

- **Have a plan for your study session; include time allotments for each topic or task.** Build predictions of how much time you think each assignment will need into your plan, but make adjustments if you get hung up.
- **Capture killer B's.** You're working on Task A and Task B presents itself—perhaps it's a text or an email, something that seems important at the time. Immediately capture the threatening "Killer B" by writing it in a paper notebook that's always by your side. Why paper? If you use an online journal, you'll be tempted to wander further online. You may end up in Timbuktu.com and make countless stops along the way.[2]
- **Keep track of what derails you.** If you come to understand your patterns, you may be better able to control them: *Oops, there I go again. I'm not going to give in to that temptation!* For example, one new pilot study reports that spending too much time on Facebook highjacks valuable study time and impacts your grades. That makes sense; you only have so much attention to spread around.[3]

TWITTER??

- **Turn off your phone or tell other people you live with that you don't want to be disturbed if a call comes in for you.** Let them know what time they can tell callers to call you back.
- **If you're working on your computer, work offline whenever possible.** If you must be online to check sources frequently, don't give in to the temptation to check your social networking account or e-mail every ten minutes. Even though you may feel you're being highly productive by taking care of all of your online business at once, you'll end up wasting time in the long run.
- **Take two minutes to organize your workspace before beginning.** Having the resources you need at your fingertips makes the session go much more smoothly, and you won't waste time searching for things you need.
- **Learn to say no.** Saying no to someone, especially someone you care about, can feel awkward at first, but people close to you will understand that you can't do everything. Life is about choices, and choosing requires the use of the word no. Practice now: "No, thanks." "Sorry, can't do it this time." See? It's not that hard.

I NEED TO WORK ON THIS!

> Speed is the blessing (and the curse) of the modern age. It is our drug of choice.
>
> *Edward M. Hallowell, M.D., Crazy Busy*

Clayton J. Price/Corbis

- **Slow down.** As they say, "haste makes waste." Working at something a million miles a minute will most likely result in mistakes, superficial thinking, and poor decisions. Ironically, if you rush, you may run out of time and end up settling for less than your best.
- **Actually use a timer.** Forty minutes is thought by some experts to be the optimum amount of time to focus on something before taking a break. It takes 30 minutes to really get in gear, and then you arrive at another 10 minutes of optimal productivity. If you aim for more than that, tedium can set in. And use a real, physical countdown timer. When you hear the "ding," you get a real feeling of accomplishment and a bit of relief from stress. Online timing tools can get buried under layers of other software applications. A real-life timer can force you to face the challenge.[4]

NEVER THOUGHT OF THIS IDEA! CHECK TO SEE IF WE HAVE ONE IN THE KITCHEN.

Energy, Our Most Precious Resource

? challenge / reaction

Challenge: What are ways you can increase your energy throughout the day?

Reaction:

____

____

____

"We live in a digital time. Our rhythms are rushed, rapid-fire and relentless, our days carved up into bits and bytes. . . . We're wired up but we're melting down." So begins a bestselling book, *The Power of Full Engagement: Managing Energy, Not Time, Is the Key to High Performance and Personal Renewal*. The authors, Jim Loehr and Tony Schwartz, have replaced the term *time management* with the term *energy management*. Their shift makes sense. Since most of us are operating in overdrive most of the time, energy is our most precious resource.

Energy management experts say you can't control time—everyone has a fixed amount—but you can manage your energy. And in fact, it's your

> Today is the tomorrow we worried about yesterday.
>
> *Anonymous*

ENERGY GAINS:
- WORKING OUT
- MUSIC
- TAURA!!

responsibility to do so. Once a day is gone, it's gone. But your energy can be renewed. It's not just about managing your time or your attention, it's about having enough energy to do what you need to do.

It's clear that some things are energy *drains*, zapping your drive: bad news, illness, interpersonal conflict, bureaucratic hassles, a heavy meal, rainy days. Likewise, some things are energy *gains*, giving you a surge of fresh vitality: a new job, good friends, music, laughter, fruit, coffee. It's a good idea to recognize your own personal energy drains and gains so that you know how and when to replenish your supply.[5] Energy management experts say it's not just about *spending time*, it's about *expending energy*:

- ***physical*** **energy**
- ***emotional*** **energy**
- ***mental*** **energy**
- ***spiritual*** **energy**

Energy is multi-faceted. Winning a 100-mile cycling competition would leave you physically drained, but mentally sharp and emotionally charged, right?

Of the four dimensions of energy, let's take a closer look at the first two. To do your very best academically, it helps to be *physically* energized and *emotionally* connected. Physical energy is measured in terms of *quantity*. How much energy do you have—a lot or a little? Emotional energy, on the other hand, is measured by *quality*. What kind of energy do you have—positive or negative? If you put them together into a two-dimensional chart with *quantity* as the vertical axis and *quality* as the horizontal axis, you get something like Figure 3.1.

FIGURE 3.1

The Dynamics of Energy[6]

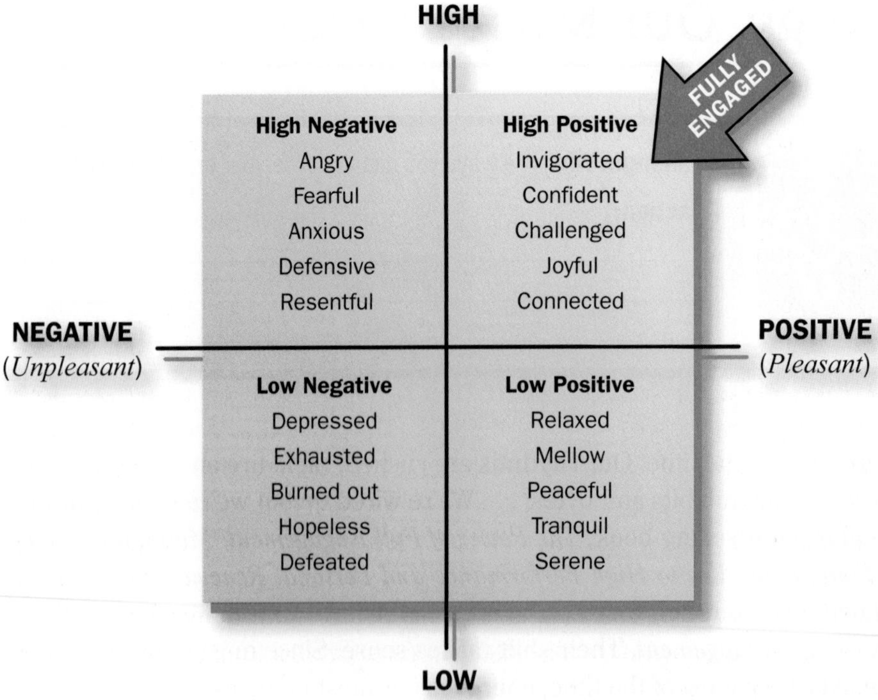

When you're operating in the upper right quadrant with high, positive energy, you're most productive, which makes sense. The question is: How do you get there? How do you make certain you're physically energized and emotionally connected so that you can do your best, academically?

Performance, health and happiness are grounded in the skillful management of energy.

Jim Loehr and Tony Schwartz,
from The Power of Full Engagement

Get Physically Energized

To make sure you're physically energized, try these suggestions.

1. **Go with the flow.** Have you noticed times of the day when it's easier to concentrate than others? Perhaps you regularly crash in the middle of the afternoon, for example. This is partly due to the patterns of electrical impulses in your brain, alpha rhythms that are unique to each individual. In other words, everyone has a biological clock. Paying attention to your body's natural rhythms is important. Plan to do activities that require you to be alert during your natural productivity peaks. That's better than plodding through a tough assignment when the energy just isn't there. Use low energy times to take care of mindless chores that require little to no brainpower.[7]

2. **Up and at 'em.** What about 8:00 a.m. classes? Don't use your body's natural rhythms as an excuse to sleep through class! ("I'm just not a morning person. . . .") If you're truly not a morning person, don't sign up for early morning classes. Some students get into the *social* habit of staying up late into the wee, small hours, and then they just can't get up in the morning. Sleeping through your obligations won't do much for your success—and you'll be playing a continual game of catch-up, which takes even more time.

3. **Sleep at night, study during the day.** Burning the midnight oil and pulling all-nighters aren't the best ideas, either. It only takes one all-nighter to help you realize that a lack of sleep translates into a plunge in performance. Without proper sleep, your ability to understand and remember course material is impaired. Research shows that the average adult requires seven to eight hours of sleep each night. If you can't get that much for whatever reason, take a short afternoon nap. Did you know that the Three Mile Island nuclear meltdown in Pennsylvania in 1979 and the Chernobyl disaster in the Ukraine in 1986 took place at 4 a.m. and 1:23 a.m., respectively? Experts believe it's no coincidence that both these events took place when workers would normally be sleeping.[8]

4. **"Prime the pump."** You've heard it before: Food is the fuel that makes us run. The better the fuel, the smoother we run. It's that simple. A solid diet of carbs—pizza, chips, and cookies—jammed into the fuel tank of your car would certainly gum up the works! When the demands on your energy are high, such as exam week, use premium fuel. If you don't believe it, take a look at how many of your classmates get sick during midterms and finals. Watch what they're eating and note how much sleep they're getting, and you'll get some clues about why they're hacking and coughing their way through exams—or in bed missing them altogether.

Get Emotionally Connected

Physical needs count, to be sure, but emotional connections are part of the picture, too. See if you agree with these suggestions.

1. **Communicate like it matters.** Sometimes we save our best communicating for people we think we have to impress: teachers, bosses, or clients, for example. But what about the people we care about most in our lives? Sometimes these people get the leftovers after all the "important" communicating has been done for the day. Sometimes we're so comfortable with these people that we think we can let it all hang out, even when doing so is *not* a pretty sight. Vow to learn more about communicating at your best in valued personal relationships, and then do it. Communicate as if everything you said would actually come true—"Just drop dead," for instance—and watch the difference! Communicating with people we care about is one of our primary vehicles for personal renewal.

GUESS I COULD CUT BACK.

2. **Choose how you renew.** Finish this analogy: junk food is to physical energy as _____ is to emotional energy. If you answered "TV," you're absolutely right. Most people use television as their primary form of emotional renewal, but, like junk food, it's not that nutritious and it's easy to consume too much. Perhaps for you, it's Facebook or surfing the Internet, rather than TV. Try more engaging activities that affirm you: singing or reading or playing a sport.[9]

3. **Let others renew you.** Remember that people don't just make demands on your time, they can provide emotional renewal. There's pure joy in a child's laugh, a friend's smile, a father's pat on the back. These small pleasures in life are priceless—prize them!

Manage Your Classroom Energy

NEVER THOUGHT ABOUT SCHOOL THIS WAY!

Think of the implications of what you've been reading about—your energy management—on your in-class performance. When your attention meter is on empty and you can't concentrate on your instructor's presentation, energy management could be the problem—and the solution.

It's hard to manage your attention if you bring "High Negative" energy to class. Realistically, how easy is it to learn when you're feeling angry, fearful, anxious, defensive, or resentful? You may be terrified of the upcoming midterm exam or annoyed at the professor who lectures too quickly by simply reading PowerPoint slides as they whiz by. In order to confront your

> Make the most of yourself, for that is all there is of you.
>
> *Ralph Waldo Emerson, American author (1803–1882)*

© Larry Harwood Photography. Property of Cengage Learning

"High Negative" energy and regain control of your attention, you may need to talk with your instructor. Explain how the course is overwhelming you and ask what you can to do ensure success. Make sure you keep up your end of the bargain, though, and do what you can to lower your "High Negative" energy yourself. If your anxiety is stemming from your own lack of preparation, that's an issue you can fix on your own.

It's also hard to manage your attention if you bring "Low Negative" energy to class. Realistically, how easy is it to learn when you're feeling depressed, exhausted, burned out, hopeless, or defeated? In fact, these are times when some students simply don't come to class, period. But that begins a negative chain reaction. Once you get behind on course material, you become more depressed and hopeless about a positive outcome, and so begins a downward spiral. Even "Low Positive" energy can be counterproductive in class. Imagine yourself so relaxed, mellow, peaceful, tranquil, and serene that you zone out and nod off.

Is it possible to have too much "High Positive" energy? What if you're too invigorated, confident, challenged, joyful, and connected? What if you're so thrilled about some exciting news that you can't sit still? As you sit in your seat, some part of your anatomy is continuously moving because of stored-up nervous energy. Things seem to be moving too slowly, and you'd give anything to be able to get up and run around the room. Instead of running around the classroom, run to class or work out beforehand so that you use up some of your spare energy. If you're the kind of person who gets distracted easily, make sure you sit up front. Jump into the discussion by asking questions, and channel your energy into content-related, focused activities. If you find it difficult to manage your attention in a classroom full of friends, meet beforehand for coffee and compare notes on the reading assignment. Do whatever you must to manage your energy productively. It's your responsibility, and it's a vital part of the learning process.

Begin noticing your own energy patterns. Think about the requirements of each day, and the energy that you'll need as you progress from one activity to the next. Working out early in the morning may energize you for the rest of the day. Your most challenging class may temporarily drain you, but after lunch or dinner, you're refreshed and ready to go again.

Finally, although we've focused on physical and emotional energy here, remember that all four dimensions of energy—physical, emotional, mental, and spiritual—are interconnected. If you subtract one from the equation, you'll be firing on less than four cylinders. If you are fully engaged and living life to the fullest, all four dimensions of your energy equation will be in balance. Throughout this book, you'll read about all four dimensions of energy.

▶▶ Your Type Is Showing

What does your psychological type say about your time management preferences? Fill in this quick assessment and find out!

4	3	2	1
Very much like me	Somewhat like me	Not much like me	Not at all like me

1. I am most motivated when I work on active tasks that let me move around or talk to people. (E) _____
2. I avoid tasks that don't fit my own personal value system. (F) _____
3. I don't get around to things I enjoy doing as often as I should. (T) _____
4. I often have to redo work, which takes time, because I've overlooked important details. (N) _____
5. I don't make a schedule; I prefer to be spontaneous. (P) _____
6. I sometimes get locked into a routine, even if it's not particularly productive. (S) _____
7. I have a fairly long attention span and don't mind reading or studying on my own. (I) _____
8. I make schedules and stick to them. (J) _____
9. I work at what's most important first, even if I'd really rather work on something I like. (T) _____
10. I tend to avoid planning and jump right into things even if I make mistakes. (E) _____
11. I like to personalize things I do on my own. (N) _____
12. I prefer e-mail to face-to-face contact when scheduling events with other people. (I) _____
13. I sometimes organize my schedule based on who I'm interacting with. (F) _____
14. I often over-obligate myself with too many commitments. (P) _____
15. I sometimes resist changing my schedule when I should because I already have it so well organized. (J) _____
16. I put-off schoolwork that seems too theoretical. (S) _____
17. I enjoy social connections made in study groups. (E) _____
18. I usually work on the things I like first even if they're not the most urgent. (F) _____
19. I tend to be good at prioritizing and construct schedules that make sense. (T) _____
20. I dislike routines. (N) _____
21. I like to think about things for a while before I get started. (I) _____
22. If I were honest, I'd say I have quite a bit to learn about scheduling and prioritizing. (P) _____
23. I sometimes get bogged down in the details of a project. (S) _____
24. I make schedules and stick to them. (J) _____

Now total your scores for each of the MBTI scales. (There are three items related to each scale.)

Totals: ____ E ____ I ____ S ____ N ____ T ____ F ____ J ____ P ____

High Preference, 12–10 Medium Preference, 9–7 Low Preference, 6 or less

Does your score on this informal time management assessment reflect your SuccessType Learning Style Type Indicator results? All aspects of psychological type can play a role in time management preferences.[10] Take a close look at your scores on the most important scale relating to time management: Judging versus Perceiving. If you scored high on the Judging scale of the MBTI or SuccessTypes Learning Style Indicator, you've probably already bought a planner and have all your upcoming commitments entered—and color-coded, no less.

If you scored high on the Perceiving scale, the words *schedule* and *prioritizing* may not be part of your vocabulary. You just do things when you need to do them, and *most* things get done. The key word in the last sentence is *most.* As you're responsible for more in demanding college classes, what about all the things that will fall into the cracks? That could be a problem, couldn't it?

It's true that some people are natural planners and some aren't. If you're high on the Perceiving scale, you'll have to develop your own coping strategies. Some P's who learn about their preferences make lists for everything. They realize that "Judging" is a requirement for success in most jobs, and they've learned coping mechanisms that serve them well. On the other hand, the spontaneity and curiosity that P's bring to the table can lead to success, too.[11] Take a look at some other possibilities if scheduling doesn't come naturally for you.

1. **Hire a personal assistant.** This advice is mostly facetious, but the principle is a good one. If something isn't a strength of yours, associate yourself with people for whom it is. A friend who can call you and say, "Don't forget that our paper is due Friday" can be a good thing. You don't want to over-rely on people, but perhaps you can learn from them.
2. **Develop a routine that works.** Instead of managing time in increments by scheduling minutes and hours, think in terms of the flow of each day. Perhaps your days go something like this: Exercise → Shower → Class → Lunch → Class → Library → Errands (saved for a low energy time of day) → Dinner → Study. For some people who think in terms of linking events and which order makes the most sense, this approach can work well. There's one caveat—you need to be able to estimate how long each event will take fairly accurately, so that the flow works and you don't run out of time.
3. **Identify one location you can always go to for reminders.** Some people use a well-located whiteboard, notes on the refrigerator, or messages taped to computer screens. Pick one place to go for reminders when you get off track. If you live with other people, you can share this space, and comment on other people's schedules, too.

"I'll Study in My Free Time" . . . and When Is That?

challenge

reaction

Challenge: List all the activities you engage in during an average school day.

Reaction:

____

____

____

Ask ten students when they study, and chances are at least eight will reply, "in my free time." The irony in this statement is that if you actually waited until you had free time to study, you probably never would. Truthfully, some students are amazed at how easily a day can race by without ever thinking about cracking a book. This is why you should actually *schedule* your study time, but to do that, you should first be aware of how you're currently spending those twenty-four hours of each day.

EXERCISE 3.1

Self Assessment—Where Did the Time Go?

Fill in the number of hours you spend doing each of the following, then multiply your answer by the number given (7 or 5 to figure weekly amounts) where appropriate.

Number of hours per day

Sleeping:	____ × 7 = ____
Personal grooming (for example, showering, shaving, putting on makeup):	____ × 7 = ____
Eating (meals and snacks; include preparation or driving time):	____ × 7 = ____
Commuting during the week (to school and work):	____ × 5 = ____
Doing errands and chores:	____ × 7 = ____
Spending time with family (parents, children, or spouse):	____ × 7 = ____
Spending time with boyfriend or girlfriend:	____ × 7 = ____

Number of hours per week

At work:	____
In classes:	____
At regularly scheduled functions (church, clubs, etc.):	____
Socializing, hanging out, watching TV, talking on the phone, etc.:	____

Now add up all the numbers in the far right column and subtract that amount from 168. This is the number of hours you have remaining in your week for that ever-important task of studying.

Is the number you arrived at too low? Are you already below zero? Start over on this chart, and write in studying first (above the first item—sleeping), before anything else. Then make adjustments elsewhere. How many hours per day should you study, based on how many courses you are taking and how challenging they are? Achieving real success in college takes time!

TOTAL = 178
THIS EXERCISE EXPLAINS A LOT! I ENDED UP 10 HOURS IN THE HOLE—WITH NO STUDYING!

Notice that the Exercise you just completed places studying at the bottom of the list, even though it's vital to your success in college. It reflects a common attitude among college students, namely that studying is what takes place after everything else gets done. Where does schoolwork rank on *your* list of priorities?

WORLD HISTORY IS MY HARDEST CLASS. DOES THIS MEAN I SHOULD BE STUDYING HISTORY AT LEAST 12 HOURS PER WEEK? MAN!

If succeeding in college is a top priority for you, then make sure that you're devoting enough time to schoolwork outside the classroom. Most instructors expect you to study two to three hours outside of class for every hour spent in class. If it's a particularly challenging class, you may need even more study time. You can use the following chart to calculate the total number of hours you ought to expect to study—effectively—each week:

Credit hours for less demanding classes:	_____ × 2 hours = _____	hours
Credit hours for typical/average classes:	_____ × 3 hours = _____	hours
Credit hours for more challenging classes:	_____ × 4 hours = _____	hours
	Expected total study time per week = _____	hours

Remember, just putting in the time won't guarantee that you'll truly *understand* what you're studying. You need to ensure that your study time is productive by focusing your attention and strategically selecting study techniques that work best for you. Even though you're a busy person, like everyone else, remember that truly mastering course material takes time.

BOX 3.1 "It's Too Darn Nice Outside" (and Other Lame Excuses for Blowing Off Class)

Do you find yourself skipping class at times in order to do something else: getting an oil change for your car, soaking up the sun's rays, or socializing with some friends you ran into on the way to class? If so, ask yourself this: Would you walk into a gas station, put three $20 bills down on the counter to prepay for a tank of gas, and then put in a dollar's worth and drive off? Absolutely not, you say?

Would you buy a plane ticket for several hundred dollars to see a friend and then just not go because you decided you'd rather do something else instead? No way!

Why, then, would you purchase much more expensive "tickets" to class—the average cost of an hour in class is roughly upwards of $200 per hour—and then toss them in the trash by not attending? Don't you value your money more than that? More importantly, don't you value *yourself* more than that?

The next time you're tempted to opt out of your scheduled classes, ask yourself if you really want to throw away money, in addition to the opportunity. Check your priorities, then put one foot in front of the other and walk into that classroom. In the long run, it's the best investment in your own future.

Schedule Your Way to Success

There is no one right way to schedule your time, but if you experiment with the system presented in this book, you'll be on the right path. Eventually, you can tweak the system to make it uniquely your own. Take an honest assessment of how you currently spend your time and then try following the eight steps to schedule your way into success!

EXERCISE 3.2

Time Monitor

Can you remember how you spent all your time yesterday? Using the following Time Monitor, fill in as much as you can remember about how you spent your time yesterday from 7:00 a.m. to 10:00 p.m. Be as detailed as possible, right down to thirty-minute segments.

7:00	GYM	12:00		5:00	
7:30	GYM	12:30		5:30	
8:00	GYM	1:00		6:00	
8:30	WORK	1:30		6:30	
9:00		2:00		7:00	
9:30		2:30		7:30	
10:00		3:00		8:00	
10:30		3:30		8:30	
11:00		4:00		9:00	
11:30		4:30		9:30	

Now monitor how you use your time today (or tomorrow if you're reading this at night) on the following Time Monitor. Again, be very specific. You will refer back to this exercise later in this chapter.

7:00		12:00		5:00	
7:30		12:30		5:30	
8:00		1:00		6:00	
8:30		1:30		6:30	
9:00		2:00		7:00	
9:30		2:30		7:30	
10:00		3:00		8:00	
10:30		3:30		8:30	
11:00		4:00		9:00	
11:30		4:30		9:30	

STEP 1: Fill out a "Term on a Page" calendar. There's value in having your entire semester or quarter visible on one single page. You can see where things "clump" together around midterms and finals, and when you'll have extra time to work on larger-scale, longer-term projects. Right up front, create a "Term on a Page" calendar that shows the entire school term on one page. (See Exercise 3.3.) You will need to have the syllabus from each of your classes and your school's course schedule to do this step properly. The following items should be transferred onto your "Term on a Page" calendar:

- Holidays when your school is closed
- Exam and quiz dates from your syllabi
- Project or paper deadlines from your syllabi
- Relevant administrative deadlines (*e.g.*, registration for the next term, drop dates)
- Birthdays and anniversaries to remember
- Important out-of-town travel
- Dates that pertain to other family members, such as days that a relative will be visiting—anything that will impact your ability to attend classes or study

CURIOSITY: *CHOOSE TO CHOOSE!*

Have you ever thought about how many dozens, if not hundreds, of choices you make each day? From the second you wake up, you're making decisions, even about the simplest things, like whether to order a cappuccino or a latté; decaf, half-caf, or high-octane; nonfat, two-percent, or the real deal.

Psychologist and professor Barry Schwartz, in his book, *The Paradox of Choice: Why More Is Less*, believes that making nonstop choices can actually cause us to "invest time, energy, and no small amount of self-doubt, and dread." Choosing a new cell phone plan can take some people weeks while they research models of cell phones, minutes available, quotas of text messages, and Internet access, not to mention the fine print. Simply put: Being flooded with choices, while it feels luxurious, can be stressful and even unrewarding. Paralysis, anxiety, and stress rather than happiness, satisfaction, and perfection can be the result of too much "more."

Some of us, Schwartz says, are "maximizers"; we don't rest until we find the best. Others of us are "satisficers"; we're satisfied with what's good enough, based on our most important criteria. Of course, we all do some "maximizing" and some "satisficing," but generally, which are you?

Here are Schwartz's recommendations to lower our stress levels in a society where more can actually give us less, especially in terms of quality of life:

1. **Choose to choose.** Some decisions are worth lengthy deliberation; others aren't. Be conscious of the choices you make and whether they're worth the return on your investment. "Maximize" when it counts and "satisfice" when it doesn't.
2. **Remember that there's always greener grass somewhere.** Someone will always have a better job than you do, a nicer apartment, or a more attractive romantic partner. Regret or envy can eat away at you, and second-guessing can bring unsettling dissatisfaction.
3. **Regret less and appreciate more.** While green grass does abound, so do sandpits and bumpy roads. That's an important realization, too! Value the good things you already have going for you.
4. **Build bridges, not walls.** Think about the ways in which the dozens of choices you've already made as a new college student give you your own unique profile or "choice-print": where you live, which classes you take, clubs you join, campus events you attend, your small circle of friends, and on and on. Remember that, and make conscious choices that will best help you succeed.[12]

© Corbis

STEP 2: Invest in a planner. While it's good to have the big picture, you must also develop an ongoing scheduling system that works for you. Using the "It's all right up here in my head" method is a surefire way to miss an important appointment, fly past the deadline for your term paper without a clue, or lose track of the time you have left to complete multiple projects. Oops!

Although your instructor will typically provide you with a class syllabus that lists test dates and assignment deadlines, trying to juggle multiple syllabi—not to mention your personal and work commitments—is enough to drive you crazy. You need *one* central clearinghouse for all of your important deadlines, appointments, and commitments. This central clearinghouse could be a hard copy planner, a cell phone app an online calendar, a web-based tool you sign up

EXERCISE 3.3

Term on a Page

Take a few minutes right now to create your own Term on a Page using the charts provided.

Term ______ Year ______

Month:	Sunday	Monday	Tuesday	Wednesday	Thursday	Friday	Saturday

MAN, I JUST TRIED THIS, AND I CAN'T BELIEVE IT! THE WEEK OF MIDTERMS IS PACKED WITH MULTIPLE THINGS DUE EVERY SINGLE DAY! GLAD I SAW WHAT THAT'S GOING TO BE LIKE NOW!

Month:	Sunday	Monday	Tuesday	Wednesday	Thursday	Friday	Saturday

Month:	Sunday	Monday	Tuesday	Wednesday	Thursday	Friday	Saturday

Month:	Sunday	Monday	Tuesday	Wednesday	Thursday	Friday	Saturday

Month:	Sunday	Monday	Tuesday	Wednesday	Thursday	Friday	Saturday

© Larry Harwood Photography. Property of Cengage Learning

> **Take care of your minutes, and the hours will take care of themselves.**
>
> *Lord Chesterfield, British statesman and diplomat (1694–1773)*

for, or something else. What's more important than what you choose is whether or not you use it faithfully! And even though it's good to have everything in one central place, redundancy can help, too. If you lose your cell phone, you don't want your entire life to fall apart! Have a scheduling back-up. Many new college students find that an ordinary paper-and-pencil daily calendar from an office supply store works best. Having a full page for each day means you can write your daily to-do list right in your planner (more on to-do lists later), and that can be a huge help.

STEP 3: Transfer important dates. The next step is to transfer important dates for the whole term from your "Term on a Page" overview to the appropriate days in your planner. This may seem repetitious, but there's a method to the madness. While it's important to be able to view all of your due dates together to create a big picture, it's equally important to have these dates recorded in your actual planner because you will use it more regularly—as the final authority on your schedule.

STEP 4: Set intermediate deadlines. After recording the important dates for the entire academic term, look at the individual due dates for major projects or papers that are assigned. Then set intermediate stepping-stone goals that will ultimately help you accomplish your final goals. Working backward from the due date, choose and record deadlines for completing certain chunks of the work. For example, if you have a research paper due, you could set an intermediate deadline for completing all of your initial research or writing a first draft.

STEP 5: Schedule fixed activities for the entire term. Next you'll want to schedule in all fixed activities throughout the entire term: class meeting times and reading assignments, religious services you regularly attend, club meetings, and regular co-curricular activities such as athletics or choir.

CAREER OUTLOOK: *WORK SMARTER, NOT HARDER*

The first hour is the rudder of the day.

????

Henry Ward Beecher, 1813–1887, clergyman, social reformer, abolitionist, and speaker

Imagine yourself off to a great start, impressing everyone, especially your boss, in your long-awaited career after college. But something is gnawing at you. You can't help but notice your stress level inching up. One day, when you power up your office computer, you immediately see 250 new e-mails that weren't there yesterday. A-a-a-a-k!!! When you have multiple projects with deadlines, the bottom line question becomes "Which task do you do first when you're totally overwhelmed?"

Workaholism—that's the answer some people come up with. They come in early, stay late, bring work home, furnish their offices with "sleep-able" sofas, and kill themselves by working around the clock. Our culture seems to admire these "heroes" who try to solve problems by throwing hours at them. But "not only is this workaholism unnecessary, it's stupid. Working more doesn't mean you care more or get more done. It just means you work more."[13]

Instead of working harder, how about working smarter? In the quote above, Beecher's claim is that the first hour sets the course for the day. A rudder is a vertical mechanism at the front of a boat that directs its course. It can either help you get where you need to go or cause you to float aimlessly—or even capsize. If that happens, at the very least, you'll feel frustrated because you don't know how to flip yourself over.

Instead of staying at the office so late that you're doubled over with hunger pangs, try putting a whiteboard on your office wall, and spending the first hour prioritizing your day. Shut the door, turn everything off, and list your goals for the day by creating small boxes to represent your three main projects. Then explore how they can be chunked into smaller subprojects and look for relationships between them and patterns across them. *But then I'll never finish!* you may be thinking to yourself.

A WHITE-BOARD! I'LL TRY IT!

Actually, you'll be able to *save* yourself time and accomplish much more. Your whiteboard will help you prioritize prioritizing (and no, that's not a typo). You're moving the process of priorizing right up to the top of your to-do list.

By prioritizing first, you're guaranteeing that you'll make greater headway than you would otherwise. You're working smarter, not harder. At the end of the day, you can look back at your "wake" in the imaginary river of your work life, satisfied with how far you've come from the shoreline. As Seneca, a wise man who—believe it or not—lived from 4 BC to 65 AD, said "Love of bustle is not industry [hard work]." We get a rush of adrenaline from the hustle-bustle. We wring our hands over the shocking amount of work we have to do. But that's not the same as the true "high" you get from actually *doing* that real, honest-to-goodness hard work. As someone once said, "Efficiency is intelligent laziness." Figure it out *now*. It's all about working smarter and getting things done.[14]

Think Ahead: Why is prioritizing your workload important? What challenges do you see with prioritizing your work? How can you practice prioritizing *now* to develop the skills you'll need in your eventual career?

CAST ON CAREERS

© Larry Harwood Photography. Property of Cengage Learning

FOCUS: How much prioritizing did you do your first semester of college?

KATIE: Oh, that's easy—none. I spent most of my time figuring out excuses for not doing assignments at all. Then I'd panic and do nothing but homework frantically to catch up. But that was an all-or-nothing strategy, alternating between being a slacker and a fanatic, that I wouldn't recommend. It seemed I had no balance whatsoever, and the result was mega stress! But I'm learning how to work smarter by prioritizing. The academic demands are heavy in my major, and you have to come up with a plan to get things done early on.

FOCUS: What are your career plans? Will you benefit from knowing how to prioritize?

KATIE: Absolutely! I'm majoring in nursing. Nurses have to pay attention to many different patients at once. They must also triage, or decide who to treat first; they make life and death decisions on a daily basis. That's just what I'm learning to do with my overwhelming workload. Deciding whether to study chemistry or pharmacology may not be a life and death decision, but it may affect my academic survival! Every day I take stock first thing, and then I feel like I'm making progress and accomplishing real goals as the day goes on.

> **"Hard work is often the easy work you did not do at the proper time."**
>
> *Bernard Meltzer*

THIS IS ONE QUOTE I HAVE TO REMEMBER...

Pando Hall/Getty Images

> **Nothing is so fatiguing as the eternal hanging on of an uncompleted task.**
>
> *William James, American psychologist and philosopher (1842–1910)*

STEP 6: Check for schedule conflicts. Now, take a final look at your planner. Do you notice any major scheduling conflicts, such as a planned trip to your sister's wedding smack dab in the middle of midterm exam week? Look for these conflicts now, when there's plenty of time to adjust your plans and talk with your instructor to see what you can work out.

STEP 7: Schedule unscheduled time. Although scheduling unscheduled time seems like a contradiction of terms, it's important! You do need personal time for eating, sleeping, exercising, and other regular activities that don't have a set time frame, and you need some downtime to reenergize. Besides, despite your planner, life will happen. Several times each week, you can count on something coming up that will offer you a chance (or force you) to revise your schedule. The decision of how high the item ranks on your priority list rests with you, but the point is to leave some wiggle room in your schedule.

STEP 8: Monitor your schedule every day. At this point, you've developed a working time management system. Now it's important to monitor your use of that system on a daily basis. Each morning, take time to preview what your planner has planned for you. Each night, take three minutes to review the day's activities. How well did you stick to your schedule? Did you accomplish the tasks you set out to do? Do you need to revise your schedule for the rest of the week based on something that happened—or didn't happen—today? Don't skip this step. Mentally playing out the day in advance and reviewing afterwards will help you internalize what must be accomplished and help you create a pace for each day. Unless you're willing to take this last step, everything else you do in steps one through seven won't matter!

To Do or Not to Do? There *Is* No Question

Part of your personal time management system should be keeping an ongoing to-do list. While the concept of a to-do list sounds relatively simple, there are a few tricks of the trade.

Important and Urgent: "A" Priorities	Important, but Not Urgent: "B" Priorities
Not Important, but Urgent: "C" Priorities	Not Important and Not Urgent: Scratch these off your list!

FIGURE 3.2

Time Zones

Before the beginning of each school week, brainstorm all the things that you want or need to get done in the upcoming week. Using this random list of to-do items, assign a priority level next to each one. The A-B-C method is simple and easy to use:

A = must get this done; highest priority

B = very important to get done at some point

C = must do it right away, but it's not an extremely high priority

A = 7:30 AM MEETING AT WORK

B = VET APPOINTMENT, COULD DELAY

C = CYCLING RACE DEADLINE

The two factors to consider when assigning a priority level to a to-do item are *importance* and *urgency*, creating four time zones. Use Figure 3.2 as a guide.[15]

After you've assigned a time zone to each item, review your list of A and B priorities and ask yourself:

1. **Do any of the items fit best with a particular day of the week?** For example, donating blood may be a high priority task for you, yet you don't want to do it on a day when you have co-curricular sports planned. That might leave you with two available days in the upcoming week that you can donate blood.
2. **Can any items be grouped together for easier execution?** For example, you may have three errands to run downtown on your to-do list, so grouping them together will save you from making three separate trips.
3. **Do any A and B priorities qualify as floating tasks that can be completed anytime, anywhere?** For example, perhaps you were assigned an extra long reading assignment for one of your classes. It's both important and urgent, an A priority item. Bring your book to read while waiting at the dentist's office for your semi-annual teeth cleaning appointment, a B priority. Planning ahead can really help save time.
4. **Do any priorities need to be shifted?** As the days pass, some of your B priorities will become A priorities due to the urgency factor increasing. Or maybe an A priority will become a C priority because something changed about the task. This is normal.

WHAT CAN I AFFORD TO GIVE UP? MAYBE NOT WORK OUT EVERY DAY?

As for those not-urgent, not-important to-do items, scratch them off the list right now. Life is too short to waste time on unimportant tasks. Give yourself permission to focus on what's important. Since time is a limited resource, one of the best ways to guarantee a successful college experience is to use it wisely. If you don't already use these tools on a regular basis, give them a shot.

EXERCISE 3.4

So Much to Do—So Little Time

Assume this is your to-do list for today (Monday). Assign each item one of the four time zones described earlier: A, B, C (and strike through any items that are not urgent and not important). Finally, renumber the items to indicate which you would do first, which second, and so forth.

Start time: 9:00 a.m., Monday morning, during the second week of the fall term.

1. ______ Return Professor Jordan's call before class tomorrow. He left a message saying he wants to talk to you about some problems with your LIT 101 paper.
2. ______ Pick up your paycheck at McDonald's and get to the bank before it closes at 5:00 p.m. this afternoon.
3. ______ Call the new love interest in your life and ask about going to the party together this weekend before someone else does.
4. ______ Visit the Speech Center to get critiqued on your first speech due Friday. It's closed evenings.
5. ______ Call your favorite aunt. She lives overseas in a time zone seven hours ahead of yours. Today is her fortieth birthday.
6. ______ Stop by the Health Center to take advantage of free meningitis vaccinations today only.
7. ______ Upload the weekend's photos to your Facebook page.
8. ______ Leave a note asking your roommate to please stop leaving messes everywhere. It's really aggravating.
9. ______ Read the two chapters in your History textbook for the in-class quiz on Wednesday.
10. ______ Watch the first episode of the new reality TV show you've been waiting for at 9 p.m. tonight.
11. ______ Write a rough draft of the essay due in your composition class on Thursday.
12. ______ Check with your RA about inviting a high school friend to spend the weekend.
13. ______ Return the three library books that are a week overdue.
14. ______ Call your math Teaching Assistant and leave a message asking for an appointment during her office hours to get help with the homework due on Wednesday. Nearly everyone is confused about the assignment.
15. ______ Go to the campus Athletic Banquet tonight at 6 p.m. to receive your award.

Identify the criteria you used in making your decisions.

How Time Flies!

? challenge

" reaction

Challenge: What are the most common ways you waste time? What can be done about them?

Reaction:

____

____

____

According to efficiency expert Michael Fortino, in a lifetime, the average American will spend:

- Seven years in the bathroom
- Six years eating
- Five years waiting in line
- Three years in meetings
- Two years playing telephone tag
- Eight months opening junk mail
- And six months waiting at red lights[16]

What a waste of time! We can't do much about some of these items, but what *can* we do about other time-wasters? Plan—schedule—organize! Think about the issue of control in time management, and write in examples for the following:

1. Things you think you can't control, and you can't: ______________________
2. Things you think you can't control, but you can: ______________________
3. Things you think you can control, but you can't: ______________________
4. Things you think you can control, but you don't: ______________________
5. Things you think you can control, and you can: ______________________

Perhaps you wrote in something like ***medical emergencies*** for (1). You could have written in ***family or friends barging into your room*** for (2). For (4), maybe you could control your ***addiction to social networking***, but you don't. And for (5), perhaps you wrote in ***your attention***. You're absolutely right. But what about (3)? Did anything fit there? Are there things you think you can control, but you can't? Try and think of something that would fit into (3), and then think of creative ways you really could control this situation if you tried.[17]

A recent ad for a well-known high-tech company asserts, "You can't control your boss, your workload, your weight, your backhand, your weeds, your dog, your life. At least now you can control your cursor."[18] Actually, you can control more than you think you can control—and if not control, at least manage. Your time, attention, and energy are three of these things. Time-wasters lurk in every corner waiting to steal your scheduled time from you. Watch out! Don't let them spend your time *for* you!

> **We cannot waste time. We can only waste ourselves.**
>
> *George Matthew Adams, newspaper columnist (1878–1962)*

The P Word. Read This Section *Now*! . . . or Maybe Tomorrow . . . or the Next Day . . . or . . .

? challenge

reaction

Challenge: What are the most common reasons you procrastinate?

Reaction:

____

____

____

Picture this: You sit down to work on a challenging homework assignment. After a few minutes, you think, *Man, I'm thirsty,* so you get up and get a soda. Then you sit back down to continue your work. A few minutes later, you decide that some chips would go nicely with your soda and off you go again. Again, you sit down to face the task before you, as you concentrate more on eating than on working. Ten minutes go by and a nagging thought starts taking over: *Must do laundry.* Up you go again and throw a load of clothes in the washer. Before long you're wondering where all the time went. Since you only have an hour left before your next class, you think, *Why bother getting started now? Doing this project will take much more time than that, so I'll just start it tomorrow.* Despite good intentions at the beginning of your work session, you've just succeeded in accomplishing zip, nadda, nothing.

GOOD VIDEO ON PROCRASTINATION AT WWW.CENGAGEBRAIN.COM. GLAD TO KNOW I'M NOT THE ONLY ONE WHO PROCRASTINATES, BUT I DO HAVE TO WORK ON IT!

Congratulations! You—like thousands of other college students—have just successfully procrastinated! Researchers define procrastination as "needlessly delaying tasks to the point of experiencing subjective discomfort."[19] And according to researchers, 95 percent of college students admit to procrastinating on their assignments.[20]

You may be in the majority, but alas, in this case, there's no safety in numbers! We're all prone to procrastinate—to put things off until later—from time to time. In fact, in some instances, our society even rewards procrastination: storewide bargains for last-minute holiday shoppers and extended post office hours for income tax slowpokes on April 15, for example. You may think to yourself, if I delay long enough: someone else may do it for me, whatever it was will resolve itself, I can avoid unpleasantness (a difficult encounter with an instructor, for example), or maybe nobody else will do it either, taking some of the heat off.

But academic procrastination is a major threat to your ability to succeed in college. And procrastination in the working world can actually bring your job, and ultimately your career, to a screeching halt. Plenty of people try to rationalize their procrastination by claiming that they work better under pressure. However, the challenge in college is that during some weeks of the term, every single class will have an assignment or test due, all at once, and if you procrastinate, you'll not only generate tremendous anxiety for yourself, but you'll lower your chances of succeeding on any of them.

Before you can control the procrastination monster in your life, it's important to understand *why* you procrastinate. Why is getting started on an assignment difficult until you feel the jaws of a deadline closing down on you?[21] Procrastinators don't tend to be less smart or have a definitive psychological type. They do, however, tend to have lower self-confidence and get lost in their own thoughts.[22] In fact, according to one recent study, procrastination's root cause is a lack of confidence.[23] The reasons for procrastinating vary from person to person, but once you know your own reasons for putting things off, you'll be in a better position to address the problem from its root cause.

The next time you find yourself procrastinating, ask yourself why. Procrastination is self-handicapping: "It's like running a full race with a knapsack full of bricks on your back. When you don't win, you can say it's not that you're not a good runner, it's just that you had this sack of bricks on your back."[24] In addition

EXERCISE 3.5

Who, Me, Procrastinate?

Procrastination is a habit. It may show up as not getting around to doing your homework (if you don't turn it in, you can't get a bad grade on it—which almost guarantees that you'll get a bad grade on it), not vacuuming the carpet because it takes too much energy to lug the machine around, or not getting to work on time because your job is boring. What about you? Think about the following ten situations, and put a check mark next to each one to indicate the degree to which you normally procrastinate:

	Always	*Sometimes*	*Never*
1. Doing homework	____	____	____
2. Writing a paper	____	____	____
3. Studying for tests	____	____	____
4. Reading class material	____	____	____
5. Meeting with your academic advisor	____	____	____
6. Texting/e-mailing a friend	____	____	____
7. Playing a game/hanging out	____	____	____
8. Going to see a movie you've heard about	____	____	____
9. Meeting someone for dinner at a restaurant	____	____	____
10. Watching TV	____	____	____

If you are like many students, you checked "always" or "sometimes" more often for the first five items than you did for the last five items. But procrastination isn't as simple as not procrastinating when you want to do something and procrastinating when you don't. You may actually hate vacuuming but decide to vacuum the entire house so that you don't have to face studying for a test. There are "layers" of procrastination and many reasons why people procrastinate. Which of these apply to you?

____ Avoiding something you see as unpleasant
____ Feeling overwhelmed by all you have to do
____ Being intimidated by the task itself
____ Fearing failure
____ Fearing success
____ Not realizing how important the task is
____ Reacting to your own internal conflict
____ Protecting your self-esteem
____ Waiting for a last-minute adrenaline rush
____ Just plain not wanting to

to understanding why you procrastinate, try these ten procrastination busters to help you kick the habit.

1. **Keep track (of your excuses).** Write them down consistently, and soon you'll be able to recognize them for what they are. Hold yourself accountable. Own your responsibilities—in school and in the rest of your life.
2. **Break down.** No, not psychologically, though sometimes it can feel like you're headed that way. Break your project into its smaller components. A term paper, for example, can be broken down into the following smaller parts: prospectus, thesis, research, outline, small chunks of writing, and bibliography. Completing smaller tasks along the way is much easier than facing a daunting monster of a project.

© Larry Harwood Photography. Property of Cengage Learning

> **Things which matter most should never be at the mercy of things which matter least.**
>
> *Johann Wolfgang von Goethe, German writer and scholar (1749–1832)*

GOOD IDEA FOR MY HISTORY PAPER! →

3. **Trick yourself.** When you feel like procrastinating, pick some aspect of the project that's easy and that you would have to do anyway. If the thought of an entire paper is overwhelming you, for example, work on the bibliography to start. Starting with something—*anything*—will get you into the rhythm of the work.

4. **Resolve issues.** If something's gnawing at you, making it difficult to concentrate, take care of it. Sometimes you must deal with a noisy roommate, your kids vying for your attention, or something equally intrusive. Then get down to work.

5. **Get real.** Set realistic goals for yourself. If you declare that you're going to finish a twelve-page paper in two hours, you're already doomed. Procrastinators are characteristically optimistic. They underestimate how much time something will take. Make it a habit to keep track of how long assignments take you in all your courses so that you can be increasingly realistic over time.

6. **Listen to your self-talk.** Do you say negative things like this to yourself? "I should work on my paper," "I don't want to work on my paper." "I hate having to write this paper," "My instructor is making me do this," "If I just worry about it enough, something will come to me." How much more smoothly would the process go if you said positive things like this? "I will work on my paper" or "I'm choosing to write this paper." As the saying goes, "The difference between 'I can't' and 'I can' is often 'I will.'"[25]

7. **Make a deal with yourself.** Even if it's only spending fifteen minutes on a task that day, do it so that you can see progress.

> **If we did all the things we were capable of doing, we would literally astound ourselves.**
>
> *Thomas Edison, American inventor (1847–1931)*

© Image Source/Corbis

8. **Overcome fear.** Many of the reasons for procrastinating have to do with our personal fears. We may fear not doing something perfectly, or failing completely—or even the responsibility that comes with success to keep succeeding. But as Susan Jeffers, author and lecturer states, "Feel the fear, and do it anyway!"
9. **Get tough.** Sometimes projects simply require discipline. The best way to complete a daunting task is to simply dig in. Become your own taskmaster, crack the proverbial whip, and force yourself to focus on those things that are high priorities, but perhaps not your idea of fun. The thought of diving into that term paper is overwhelming to you, so you're waiting to be inspired. Bah! If you wait for inspiration, you may wait a long time.
10. **Acknowledge accomplishment.** We're not talking major shopping sprees at Neiman Marcus here. We're talking reasonable, meaningful rewards commensurate with the action completed. Go buy yourself a small treat, call your best friend in another state, take a relaxing soak in the bathtub, or do something to celebrate your accomplishments—big and small—along the way. Acknowledgment, from yourself or others, is a great motivator for tackling future projects.

Beyond Juggling: *Realistically* Manage Work, School, and Personal Life

? challenge / reaction

Challenge: How do successful people juggle work, school, and personal life?

Reaction:

____

____

____

Your personal time management needs depend on who you are and how many obligations you have. Today's college students are more diverse than ever. Increasing numbers of college students are also parents, full- or part-time employees, husbands or wives, community volunteers, soccer coaches, or Sunday school teachers. How on earth can you possibly juggle it all?

The answer? You can't. According to work-life balance expert Dawn Carlson, juggling is a knee-jerk coping mechanism—the default setting when time gets tight and it seems that nothing can be put on the back burner. If you, like millions of others, feel overworked, overcommitted, and exhausted at every turn, you may have already learned that you can't juggle your way to a balanced life. It's impossible.[26]

THIS IS HOW I FEEL— LIKE A JUGGLER!

Think about it. A professional juggler—the kind you find at a carnival—focuses every bit of his attention to keep all the balls in the air. The minute he takes his eye off the ball for even a second, down it goes. It's no surprise that you constantly hear people say, "I dropped the ball" with this or that. Not even real jugglers can maintain their trick forever. In fact, a world-record holder in juggling, Anthony Gatto, was only able to keep nine balls in the air (thrown at least twice without dropping) for a whopping 54 seconds.[27] That's it! So why do we even try to juggle our many responsibilities 24/7? Let's face it—it's a losing battle.

Now for the good news. Balance among work, school, and personal life is possible. All of us have three primary areas of our lives that should be in balance, ideally—meaningful work (including school), satisfying relationships, and a healthy lifestyle. In addition to work and relationships, we all need to take care of ourselves. See what you think of these five rebalancing strategies. The idea is you can't have it all, but you can have it better than you do now.

1. **Alternating.** If you use this strategy, your work-life balance comes in separate, concentrated doses. You may throw yourself into your career with abandon, and then cut back or quit work altogether and focus intensely on your family. You may give your job 110 percent during the week, but devote Saturdays to physical fitness or to your family or running all the errands you've saved up during the week. Or you save Tuesdays and Thursdays for homework, and go to classes Mondays, Wednesdays, and Fridays. People who use this strategy alternate between important things, and it works for them. An alternator's motto is "I want to have it all, but just not all at once."
2. **Outsourcing.** An outsourcer's motto might be "I want to have it all, not do it all." This strategy helps you achieve work-life balance by giving someone else some of your responsibilities—usually in your personal life—to free up time for the tasks you care about most. If you have enough money, hire someone to clean the house or mow the lawn. If you don't, trade these jobs among family, friends, or neighbors who band together to help each other. Of course, there are ways this strategy could be misused by college students, like downloading your paper from the Internet with a charge card! Warning: This practice will definitely be hazardous to your academic health! In fact, your college career may be over!

TAKE TAURA WITH ME TO THE GYM? :)

3. **Bundling.** This strategy helps you rebalance your life by killing two birds with one stone. Examine your busy life and look for areas in which you can

> **The trouble with the rat race is that even if you win, you're still a rat.**
>
> *Lily Tomlin, comedian*

© Tetra Images/Tetra Images/Corbis

double dip, such as combining exercising with socializing. If your social life is suffering because of time constraints, take walks with a friend so that you can talk along the way. Do your laundry with your roommate so that you can chat about your classes. A bundler's motto is "I want to get more mileage out of the things I do by combining activities." Bundling is efficient because it allows you to do two things at once.

4. **Techflexing.** Technology allows us to work from almost anywhere, anytime, using technology. If you telecommute from home several days a week for your job, you might get up early, spend some time on e-mail, go out for a run, have breakfast with your family, and then get back on your computer. In the office, you use texting to stay connected to family members or a cell phone to call home while driving to work. Chances are you can telecommute to your campus library and do research online, check in with your professor during online office hours, register for classes online, and pay all your bills online, including tuition. You can use technology, and the flexibility it gives you, to your advantage to merge important aspects of your life. A techflexer's motto is "I want to use technology to accomplish more, not be a slave to it."

5. **Simplifying.** People who use this strategy are ready to cry uncle. They've decided they don't want it all. They've reached a point where they make a permanent commitment to stop the craziness in their lives. The benefit of simplifying is greater freedom from details, stress, and the rat race. But there are trade-offs, of course. They may have to take a significant cut in pay in order to work fewer hours or at a less demanding job. But for them, it's worth it.[28]

These five strategies, used separately or in combination, have helped many people who are dealing with work, school, and family commitments at the same time. They all require certain trade-offs. None of these strategies is a magic solution.

But the alternative to rebalancing is more stress, more physical and emotional exhaustion, more frustration, and much less personal satisfaction. If you focus on rebalancing your life—making conscious choices and course corrections as you go—small changes can have a big impact. Work-life balance isn't an all-or-nothing proposition. It's an ever-changing journey. So take it one step at a time.

Time Is Money!

Challenge: What is your attitude towards money? Think of 3 ways you can get a better handle on your finances.

Reaction:

___

___

___

People say that "time is money." It's true. If you're so efficient with your time that you can call more customers or sell more products, then time does equal money. If your company is the first to introduce a hot new kind of cell phone or a zippy fuel-efficient car, you win. Even if better models come out next year, they may fall flat because people have already invested.

Both time management and money management are key to your college success.

EXERCISE 3.6

How Fiscally Fit Are You?

Before leaving the subjects of time and energy management, let's look at how you manage your money as well. How good are you at managing your finances? Check one of the three boxes for each statement to get a sense of how financially savvy you are.

	Always true of me	Sometimes true of me	Never true of me
1. At any given moment in time, I know the balance of my checking account.			
2. I use my credit card for particular types of purchases only, such as gas or food.			
3. I pay off my bills in full every month.			
4. I know the interest rate on my credit cards.			
5. I resist impulse buying and only spend when I need things.			
6. I have a budget and I follow it.			
7. I put money aside to save each month.			
8. When I get a pay raise, I increase the proportion of money I save.			
9. I keep track of my spending on a daily or weekly basis.			
10. I don't allow myself to get pressured by others into buying things I don't really need.			

Look over your responses. If you have more checks in the "Never true of me" column than you do in either of the two others, you may be able to put the information you're about to read to good use!

> **I'd say it's been my biggest problem all my life . . . it's money. It takes a lot of money to make these dreams come true.**
>
> *Walt Disney, American animator, entrepreneur, and philanthropist (1901–1966)*

Studies show that working too many hours for pay increases your chances of dropping out of college.[29] Many students find themselves working more so that they can spend more, which in turn takes time away from their studies. They may take a semester off from college to make a pile of money and then never come back. While there's evidence that working a moderate amount can help you polish your time and energy management skills, the real secret to financial responsibility in college is to track your habits and gain the knowledge you need to make sound financial decisions.

EXERCISE 3.7

Create a Spending Log

Take a look at this student's spending log, then complete one for yourself. Money has a way of slipping through our fingers. Choose one entire day that is representative of your spending, and use the chart on the next page to keep track of how you spend money. Write down everything from seemingly small, insignificant items to major purchases, and explain why you made that purchase. Your log may look something like this student's:

TIME	ITEM	LOCATION	AMOUNT	REASON
8–9 a.m.	coffee and bagel	convenience store	$3.50	overslept!
9–10 a.m.	computer paper	office supply store	$2.50	English paper due
10–11 a.m.	gas fill-up	gas station	$65.00	running on fumes!
11 a.m.–12 p.m.	burger and fries	fast-food restaurant	$6.00	lunch on the run
12–1 p.m.	toiletries, etc.	drugstore	$18.00	out of stock
1–2 p.m.	bottled water	convenience store	$2.50	forgot to bring
2–3 p.m.	supplies	bookstore	$12.00	forgot to get earlier
3–7 p.m.	WORK			
7–8 p.m.	pizza	pizza place	$12.00	meet friends
8–9 p.m.	week's groceries	grocery store	$61.50	cupboard is bare!
9–10 p.m.	library fines	campus library	$5.00	forgot!
10–11 p.m.	STUDY TIME			
11 p.m.–12 a.m.	weekend movie, online tickets, DVDs, cell phone upgrade	Internet retail websites, phone service	$129.00 $20.00	friend's recommendations, need more minutes

This student has spent $337 today without doing anything special! When you analyze his expenditures, you can find patterns. He seems to (1) forget to plan, so he spends money continuously throughout the day, (2) spend relatively large amounts of money online, (3) be particularly vulnerable late at night, and (4) spend money grabbing food on the run. These are patterns he should be aware of if he wants to control his spending. He could pack food from home to save a significant amount of money, for example. Now create your own chart.

TIME	ITEM	LOCATION	AMOUNT	REASON
8–9 a.m.				
9–10 a.m.				
10–11 a.m.				
11 a.m.–12 p.m.				
12–1 p.m.				
1–2 p.m.				
2–3 p.m.				
3–4 p.m.				
4–5 p.m.				
5–6 p.m.				
6–7 p.m.				
7–8 p.m.				
8–9 p.m.				
9–10 p.m.				
10–11 p.m.				
11 p.m.–12 a.m.				

What patterns do you notice about your spending? What kinds of changes will you try to make to curb any unnecessary spending?

The Perils of Plastic

Credit cards—those attractive, little pieces of plastic that make spending money so convenient and so easy. Why go out of your way and make repeated trips to the ATM to get cash when you can just whip out your credit card instead? Now you can even customize your own with a personal photo of you and your beloved Cocker Spaniel, Rusty, or whatever your heart desires. You can spend, spend, spend until you max out. Many students today find debit cards less tempting because they tap your bank account immediately and help you keep track of your spending. But if you already have a credit card or plan to get one, keep this general advice in mind.

1. **Think about the difference between needs and wants.** You may think you need particular things so that your friends will like you ("Hey, let's stop for a burger"), so that you have a new item (like a new car you can't afford), or so that you look fabulous (like pricey manicures). Here's a rule of thumb: If buying something simply helps you move from acceptable to amazing, it's not an emergency. Do you really need a mocha latté every day? A regular old cup of coffee a day sets you back $500 per year!

2. **Leave home without it.** Don't routinely take your credit card with you. Use cash and save your credit card for true emergencies or essentials, like gas and groceries. Do you really want to risk paying interest on today's ice cream cone years from now?

3. **Don't spend money you don't have.** Only charge what you can pay for each month. Just because your credit card limit is $2,000 doesn't mean you need to spend that much each month. A vacation that costs $1,000 will take 12 years of minimal payments to pay off at an 18 percent interest rate. And that $1,000 trip will eventually cost you $2,115!

4. **Understand how credit works.** It's important to know the basics. In one study, 71 percent of new college students had no idea how much interest they were paying on their credit card bills.[30]

   Here are some terms you need to know:

   - **Credit reports.** Your credit history is based on (1) how many credit cards you owe money on, (2) how much money you owe, and (3) how many late payments you make. Bad grades on your credit report can make your life difficult later.
   - **Fees.** Credit card companies charge you in three ways: (1) annual fees (a fee you must pay every year to use the card); (2) finance charges (a charge for loaning you the money you can't pay back when your bill is due); and (3) late fees (for missing a monthly payment deadline). Think about what's most important to you—no annual fee, frequent flyer miles, lower interest rate—and shop around!
   - **The fine print.** How can you learn more? Read your credit card contract carefully. Credit card companies must give you certain important information, which is often on their website. Go to the Federal Reserve website for vital, bottomline information, and search online to find out more about ways the Credit Card Act of 2009 could affect you.[31]

5. **Track your expenses.** All kinds of tools—technology-based and otherwise—can help you discover where your money actually goes. To control your spending, use a credit card with caution or use a debit card.

6. **If you're already in financial trouble, ask for help.** Talk to an expert who can help you figure out what to do.[32]

BOX 3.2 Top Ten Financial Aid FAQs

Financial aid. Like all good things, you have to know how it works. You can think of financial aid as complicated and time-consuming, or it can be the one thing that keeps you in school. Take a look at these questions students often ask about the mysteries of financial aid. Most students need financial help of some kind to earn a college degree. Here is some information to help you navigate your way financially.[33]

1. **Who qualifies for financial aid?** You may not think you qualify for financial aid, but it's a good idea to apply anyway. You won't know until you try, and some types of aid are based on criteria other than whether or not you actually need the money.
2. **What does FAFSA stand for?** And where do I get a copy? FAFSA stands for Free Application for Federal Student Aid, and you can get a copy from your campus Financial Aid office, a public library, by calling 1-800-4-FED-AID, or by going to www.fafsa.ed.gov and filling out the FAFSA online.
3. **What types of financial aid exist?** You can receive financial aid in the form of scholarships, fellowships, loans, grants, or work-study awards. Generally, scholarships and fellowships are for students with special academic, artistic, or athletic abilities; students with interests in specialized fields; students from particular parts of the country; or students from minority groups. Typically, you don't repay them. Loans and grants come in a variety of forms and from several possible sources, either government or private. Typically, loans must be repaid. In addition, if you qualify for a need-based work-study job on or off campus, you can earn an hourly wage to help pay for school.
4. **When should I apply?** You can apply for financial aid any time after January 1 of the year you intend to go to college (because tax information from the previous year is required), but you must be enrolled to receive funds.
5. **Do I have to reapply every year?** Yes. Your financial situation can change over time. Your brothers or sisters may start college while you're in school, for example, which can change your family's status.
6. **How can I keep my financial aid over my college years?** Assuming your financial situation remains fairly similar from year to year, you must demonstrate that you're making progress toward a degree in terms of credits and a minimum GPA. Remember that if you drop courses, your financial aid may be affected based on whether you're considered to be a full-time or part-time student.
7. **Who's responsible for paying back my loans?** You are. Others can help you, but ultimately the responsibility is yours and yours alone. If your parents forget to make a payment or don't pay a bill on time, you will be held responsible.
8. **If I leave school for a time, do I have to start repaying my loans right away?** Most loans have a grace period of six or nine months before you must begin repayment. You can request an extension if you "stop out," but you must do so before the grace period ends.
9. **If I get an outside scholarship, should I report it to the Financial Aid office on campus?** Yes. They'll adjust your financial aid package accordingly, but those are the rules.
10. **Where can I find out more?** Your best source of information is in the Office of Financial Aid right on your own campus. Or call the Federal Student Aid Information Center at 1–800–433–3243 and ask for a free copy of *The Student Guide: Financial Aid* from the U.S. Department of Education. Financial Aid rules change frequently, so make sure you have the latest information. New rules make financial aid easier to apply for, but also easier to lose if you don't make progress and keep your grades up.[34]

insight ! action

Now What Do You Think?

1. At the beginning of this chapter, Derek Johnson, a frustrated and disgruntled student, faced a challenge. Now after reading this chapter, would you respond differently to any of the questions you answered about the "FOCUS Challenge Case"? Knowing what you know now, how would you advise him? Write a paragraph ending to the story, incorporating your best advice.
2. Do you feel that your energy fluctuates throughout an average day? Describe your biological clock. What actions can you take to regulate your physical and emotional energy for the sake of your own productivity?
3. Here is a list of some of the most common ways students waste time. As you read through the list, check off those that occur in your life most frequently.

   ___ Unscheduled visitors

   ___ Telephone interruptions

   ___ E-mail obsession

   ___ Social networking

   ___ Disorganized workspace/lost items

   ___ Inability to say no

   ___ Lack of focus

   ___ Moving too quickly

   ___ Procrastination

   ___ Poor choices

   ___ Haphazard or, worse yet, a complete lack of scheduling

   ___ Other people's "emergencies"

   If you think time management isn't all that important, but you checked three or more boxes, perhaps the notion of scheduling is sounding more useful. What actions can you take to deal with the issues you marked?
4. If you feel the need to rebalance your life due to the pressures of managing work, school, family, and friends at the same time, take some time to work through the following Rebalancing Plan worksheet.[35]

   Why do I need to rebalance? ______________________________

   What rebalancing strategies will I use? ______________________________

   How will I do it? ______________________________

   How will I let go of ______________ ? ______________________________

   Tasks that I should completely eliminate: ______________________________

   Tasks that I can outsource or give to others: ______________________________

   Expectations of others that affect me: ______________________________

   Time-consuming possessions or relationships that bring little value to me: ______________
5. Describe your "fiscal fitness." Among the following, which issue do you find most challenging: creating and sticking to a budget, spending money on impulse, digging a credit card hole for yourself, or working too much so that you can spend more? What's your best advice to yourself?

Adapted from K. Sandholtz, B. Derr, F. Buckner, D. Carlson (2002). *Beyond Juggling: Rebalancing Your Busy Life.* San Francisco: Berrett-Hoehler Publishing.

REALITY ✓ What did you LEARN

On a scale of 1 to 10, answer the following questions now that you've completed the chapter.

low 1 2 3 4 5 6 7 8 9 10 high

In hindsight, how much did you already know about this subject before reading the chapter?

Can you answer these questions about managing time, energy, and money more fully now that you've read the chapter?

1. What's the difference between time management, attention management, and energy management? How are they different, and what do they have in common?
2. What percentage of college students admit to procrastinating on assignments? Why do they procrastinate?
3. What percentage of college students with credit cards have no idea how much interest they pay on their credit card bills?

How useful might the information in this chapter be to you?

How much do you think this information might affect your success in college? ________

How much energy did you put into reading this chapter? ________

How long did it actually take you to complete this chapter (both the reading and writing tasks)? ________ Hour(s) ________ Minutes

Did you finish reading this chapter? ________

Did you intend to when you started? ________

If you meant to but didn't, what stopped you? ________

Challenge Yourself Online Quiz To find out just how much you've learned, access the College Success CourseMate via www.cengagebrain.com to take the Challenge Yourself Online Quiz.

Take a minute to compare these answers to your answers from the "Readiness Check" at the beginning of this chapter. What gaps exist between the similar questions? How might these gaps between what you thought before starting the chapter and what you now think after completing the chapter affect how you approach the next chapter in this book?

Thinking Critically and Creatively

CHAPTER 4

Joe Gough/Shutterstock.com

You're about to discover . . .

- What critical thinking is
- How to analyze arguments, assess assumptions, and consider claims
- How to avoid mistakes in reasoning
- How you solve problems and make decisions
- How to become a more creative thinker

© Larry Harwood Photography. Property of Cengage Learning

READINESS ✓ What do you KNOW?

Before beginning to read this chapter, take two minutes to answer the following questions on a scale of 1 to 10. Your answers will help you assess how ready you are to focus.

low 1 2 3 4 5 6 7 8 9 10 high

How much do you *already* know?

Based on reading the "You're about to discover . . ." list and skimming this chapter, how much do you think you probably already know about this chapter's subject? ________

See if you can answer these questions about critical and creating thinking *before* you read.

1. What's the difference between thinking and critical thinking?
2. Identify three specific types of faulty reasoning.
3. What's the difference between critical thinking and creative thinking?

How much do you expect to learn?

In general, how motivated are you to learn more by reading this chapter? ________

How much do you think this information might affect your success overall? ________

How much energy do you plan to put into reading this chapter? ________

How ready are you to read *now*?

How ready are you to focus on this chapter?

Enter a number for each aspect of your readiness to focus.

Physically ________

Intellectually ________

Emotionally ________

If any of your answers is below a 10, pay attention to whatever is distracting you before you start reading. Then zero in and focus.

How long do you think it will take you to complete this chapter from start to finish?

______ Hour(s) ______ Minutes

Now, as you begin, do you intend to finish reading this chapter?

______ yes ______ no ______ maybe

© Larry Harwood Photography. Property of Cengage Learning

FOCUS Challenge Case

? challenge

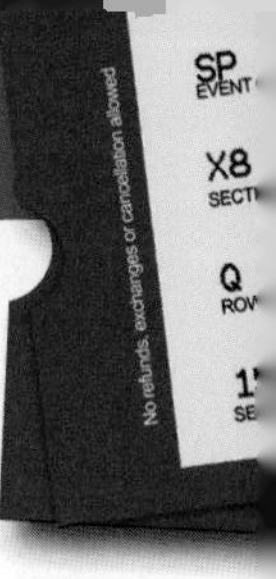

Annie Miller

Growing up in a big city was definitely a good thing. So Annie Miller thought, anyway. Every day that went by, she missed L.A. more and more. She missed the fast pace, the diversity, the lifestyle. Why had she decided to go to such a small college after growing up in such a large city? She knew that it was because she wanted every aspect of her life at college to be different. She wanted to live on a different coast, have new friends, and study something exciting. Her huge high school had been amazing in its own way, but now she wanted a more personal education at a place where everyone knew everyone, like at the small liberal arts college she had chosen on the East Coast. When she finally arrived, eager to begin her new life there, she literally jumped for joy!

Dan Breckwoldt/Shutterstock.com

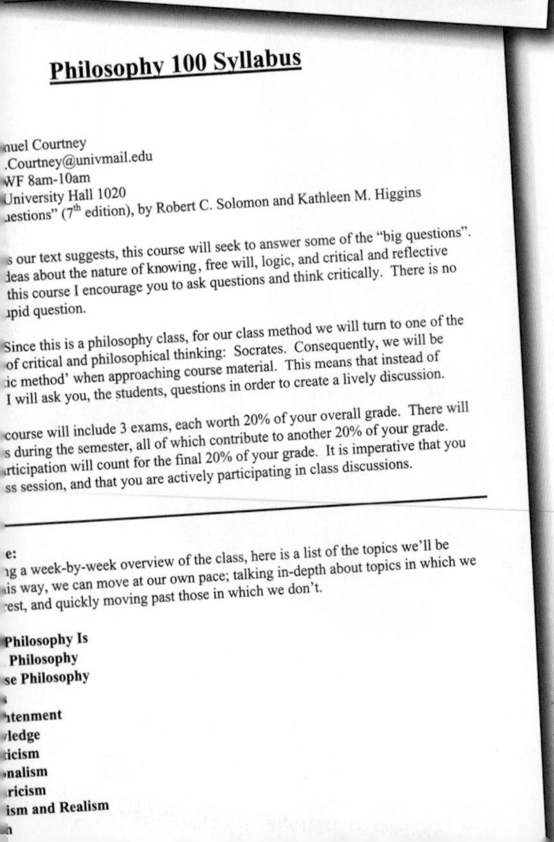

Philosophy 100 Syllabus

nuel Courtney
.Courtney@univmail.edu
WF 8am-10am
University Hall 1020
uestions" (7th edition), by Robert C. Solomon and Kathleen M. Higgins

s our text suggests, this course will seek to answer some of the "big questions". deas about the nature of knowing, free will, logic, and critical and reflective this course I encourage you to ask questions and think critically. There is no upid question.

Since this is a philosophy class, for our class method we will turn to one of the of critical and philosophical thinking: Socrates. Consequently, we will be ic method' when approaching course material. This means that instead of I will ask you, the students, questions in order to create a lively discussion.

course will include 3 exams, each worth 20% of your overall grade. There will s during the semester, all of which contribute to another 20% of your grade. rticipation will count for the final 20% of your grade. It is imperative that you ss session, and that you are actively participating in class discussions.

e:
ng a week-by-week overview of the class, here is a list of the topics we'll be is way, we can move at our own pace; talking in-depth about topics in which we est, and quickly moving past those in which we don't.

Philosophy Is
Philosophy
se Philosophy
s
htenment
ledge
icism
nalism
ricism
ism and Realism
n

© Cengage Learning

Her first semester of classes consisted of a college success course, an English composition class, Introduction to Poetry, and Philosophy 100. She was excited by the idea of learning in small classes with wise and learned professors. But Philosophy 100 had turned out to be a very challenging course. Professor Courtney had announced on the first day of class that he believed in the Socratic method of teaching. He taught by asking questions of students instead of lecturing. "Socrates, perhaps the greatest philosopher of all time," he announced the first day, "is the father of critical thinking. In this class, you'll learn to think critically. *That* is what college is all about."

Professor Courtney began every class session with a hypothetical situation and always randomly chose a student to respond. His opening went something like this:

Assume it's Valentine's Day. A young man makes a trip to the biggest jewelry store in the mall to buy his fiancée a gift. He's saved up for a long time to afford 24 karat gold earrings and he's ready to choose the best money can buy. He finds the perfect pair and hands over his credit card. But when the salesclerk brings the receipt for him to sign, he notices that instead of $300, she has missed a digit, and the receipt reads $30. He now faces a dilemma: Does he

rtusinas/Shutterstock.com

sign and say nothing, or point out the error and pay the full amount? What should he do?

One student responded with, "He should sign his name and then take off quickly. This mistake was the clerk's, not his. If someone catches the mistake later, he can just claim he didn't notice. Maybe no one will ever figure it out, and he'll be $270 richer!" Professor Courtney continued, "On what ethical principle do you base your response?" The student faltered, and the professor moved on to someone else, raising other points that hadn't been considered.

"But what if his fiancée decides to exchange the earrings for another pair? What if the clerk is fired for making a $270 mistake? What if the clerk were your sister or your best friend? What if the hero of a movie did what you're proposing? What if the clerk were you?" he continued. "What would Socrates say about what you should do? According to Socrates, no one errs intentionally. This means that whenever we do something wrong—including something *morally* wrong—it is out of ignorance rather than evil motives. If the young man decides to capitalize on the clerk's error, what are his motives—and are they evil? What would be the *right* thing to do?"

Professor Courtney continued putting students on the spot and raising questions posed by other philosophers they were studying. The questions seemed endless. Annie found herself listening more carefully than in her other classes so that she would be ready to jump in if called upon. And she silently thought through others' answers, too. Even though she had to admit that the learning environment was stimulating, speaking in front of other students made Annie nervous.

"There aren't always right answers," Professor Courtney told them. "What's important is thinking through the problem. The process of learning to think can be more important than the answer itself."

Frankly, that explanation didn't sit well with Annie. *If there aren't right answers, what am I doing in college? Things should be black and white, true or false, right or wrong. I'm paying tuition to hear what the professor thinks, not all the other students in class. He knows the right answers. Why doesn't he just tell us?*

Without fail, Annie always left Professor Courtney's class with a headache from thinking so hard. Her best friend Hannah suggested that she look up his online ratings to find out what other students had said about him. "If his ratings are bad," she said, "just drop the course. At the very least you'll find out if there are secrets to getting an A in his class." But when Annie did that, she found mostly glowing praise: "I thought he was an impossible teacher at the time," wrote one student, "but he really taught me to think. Now I'm grateful!"

Compared to Philosophy 100, all her other classes seemed effortless. She had to admit that she much preferred classes in which she could express herself creatively, like Introduction to Poetry.

Joe Gough/Shutterstock.com

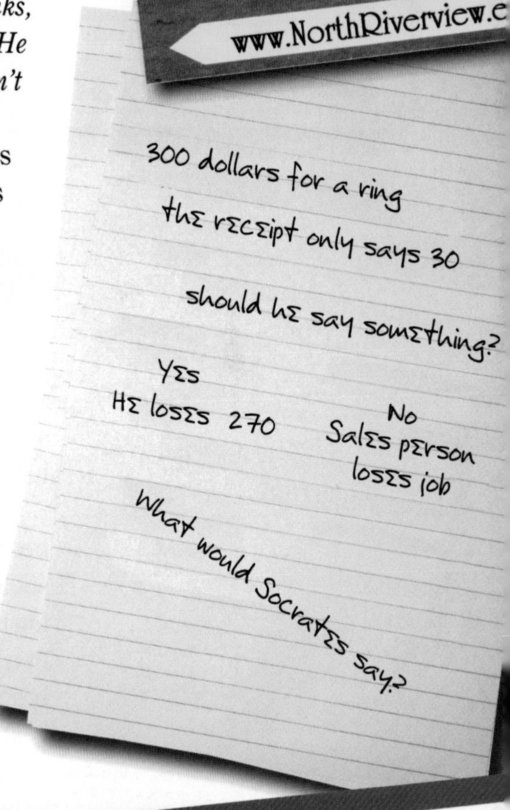

Borodaev/Shutterstock.com

© Ratemyprofessors.com/Used by permission of MTV networks

What Do You Think?

1. Do you agree with Professor Courtney's statement that "there aren't always right answers"? If that's true, why is getting a college education so important?
2. Even though Professor Courtney's teaching methods made her nervous, why did Annie find the learning environment in his class to be stimulating?
3. Annie says she prefers creative thinking to critical thinking. Are they two different things? Why or why not?
4. Identify three things Annie should do to get the most from Professor Courtney's class.

Rethinking Thinking

Challenge: What's the difference between thinking and critical thinking?

Reaction:

Thinking is a natural, ongoing, everyday process we all engage in. In fact, we can't really turn it off, even if we try. We're always on. Some of your college instructors will claim that higher education will teach you to think. But what do they mean? Everyone thinks all the time, right? It happens any time you talk to yourself, doesn't it? However, some experts say school teaches us how to regurgitate, not how to think. Perhaps your instructors are onto something.

In many ways, thinking is like speaking. We all know how to speak; we've been doing it reasonably well since we were toddlers. But if you take a public speaking course, you're bound to be a better speaker by the end of it by knowing more about how to consciously direct your voice, gestures, and delivery. In a similar way, you can become a better thinker by learning how to direct your brain. *Focused thinking*—thinking critically and creatively—is what this chapter is about.

Picture this: You're in the library. It's late, and you're tired. You're supposed to be studying for your political science test, but instead of thinking about foreign policy, your mind begins drifting toward the foreign vacation you took last summer, how tan you were when you returned, how much fun it was to be with your best friends, and where you'd like to visit next.

Would the mental process you're engaging in while sitting in the library be called *thinking*? For our purposes in this chapter, the answer is no. Here thinking is defined as a focused cognitive activity you engage in for a reason. You direct your thoughts toward a particular topic. You're the *active* thinker, not the *passive* daydreamer who is the victim of a wandering mind. Focused thinking is deliberate and intentional, not haphazard or accidental. You choose to do it for a reason.

© Larry Harwood Photography. Property of Cengage Learning

'Knowledge is power.' Rather, knowledge is happiness. To have knowledge, deep broad knowledge, is to know truth from false and lofty things from low.

Helen Keller, American author, activist, and lecturer (1880–1968)

Did you know that developing your critical thinking skills goes hand in hand with developing overall academic abilities as a college student? According to thinking experts like William Perry, who interviewed 400 men in academic difficulty at Harvard roughly fifty years ago, students develop intellectually along a scale. Early on, most students view the world in terms of right or wrong, good or bad, black or white. They see teachers as having the right answers, and students getting the right answers from teachers.

Later they come to understand that knowledge depends on many factors. They no longer wait for the "truth" to be handed down by instructors. Instead, they begin to value their own and others' opinions and perceive multiple points of view as valid. Toward the end of their college careers or in graduate school, students develop their own personal values, recognize that not all views are equal (some are better than others), and learn how to select the best alternative. The point is that your critical thinking skills are developing as you go. Rarely does anyone have already fully developed critical thinking skills as a new college student.[1]

These are subtle patterns. You may not be aware of them. But for now, realize that you may not have mastered critical thinking yet, and that's to be expected. Learning to be a critical thinker is a process each of us undergoes. Ralph Waldo Emerson once said, "Stay at home in your mind. Don't recite other people's opinions. I hate quotations. Tell me what you know." (Ironically, this famous quotation is about how much he hated quotations.) Learn to rely on your own thinking, not other people's.

Focused thinking is like a two-sided coin. Sometimes when you think, you *evaluate* ideas—your own or someone else's. That's *critical* thinking. The word critical comes from the Greek word for *critic (kritikos),* meaning "to question or analyze." The other side of thinking comes when you *produce* ideas. That's what this chapter calls *creative* thinking, and that's something we'll deal with later. When you're thinking critically, you're asking questions, analyzing arguments, assessing assumptions, considering claims, avoiding mistakes in reasoning, problem solving, decision making, and all the while, thinking about your thinking. Which type of thinking is most important, not only to your college success but also to your career success in the future: critical or creative? The answer is both!

© Larry Harwood Photography. Property of Cengage Learning

What we need is not the will to believe, but the will to find out.

Bertrand Russell, British philosopher, logician, and mathematician (1872–1970)

I keep hearing about critical thinking in all my classes, but I have no idea what it is!

What Is Critical Thinking?

Critical thinking is a particular kind of focused thinking. It is purposeful, reasoned, and goal-directed. It's thinking that aims to solve problems, calculate likelihood, weigh evidence, and make decisions.[2] In that sense, movie critics are critical thinkers because they look at a variety of standards (screenplay, acting, production quality, costumes, and so forth) and then decide how a movie measures up. When you're thinking critically, you're not just being critical. You're on the lookout for both faults and strengths. You're looking at how things measure up.[3]

Critical thinkers develop standards they can use to judge advertisements, political speeches, sales pitches, movies—you name it.[4] Critical thinking is not jumping to conclusions; buying arguments lock, stock, and barrel; accepting controversial ideas no matter what; or ignoring the facts.

Unfortunately, some people are noncritical thinkers. They may be biased or closed-minded. Other people are *selective* critical thinkers. When it comes to one particular subject, they shut down their minds. They can't explain their views, they're emotional about them, and they refuse to acknowledge any other position. Why do they believe these things? Only if they understand the *why,* can they explain their views to someone else or defend them under fire. The importance of *why* can't be overstated. Some people, of course, have already thought through their beliefs, and they understand their positions and the reasons for them very well. Arriving at that point is the goal of anyone who wants to become a better critical thinker.

Yeah, I can't believe how superstitious some people are!

In order to develop your critical thinking skills, you must pay attention to the processes and products of your own thoughts. You must become conscious of the way you think and develop a habit of examining the decisions you come to.[5] When your critical thinking skills are well developed, they actually play a role in everything you do. You exist in a state of "critical being."[6]

EXERCISE 4.1

And Just Why Is Critical Thinking Important?

Here is a list of reasons why it's important to improve your critical thinking skills. Beside each entry, mark the degree to which you'd like to concentrate your efforts as a college student, soon ready to enter a new career path. Then read on for more strategies to incorporate critical thinking into your life. On a scale from 1 to 10 with 10 representing the highest degree, would you like to:

1. ______ **Become a more successful college student?** Most college courses require you to think critically (in answering essay questions, for example). In one study of over 1,100 college students, higher scores on critical thinking skills tests correlated highly with better grades.[7] Another study indicates that the more control you believe you have over your academic success, the more likely you are to use your critical thinking skills—and vice versa.[8] There's even evidence that interaction with other students in co-curricular activities can help you develop as a critical thinker.[9] If you participate in a debate, serve as a panelist, organize a campus event, work on a campaign—all experiences outside the classroom—you can sharpen your ability to think critically, too.
2. ______ **Become a better citizen?** Critical thinking is the foundation of a strong democracy. Voters must think critically about candidates' messages and their likelihood of keeping campaign promises. It's easy to talk about balancing the budget, or improving education, but the truth is these highly complex tasks are very challenging to carry out. The American public must sift through information and examine the soundness of politicians' arguments in order to keep our democracy strong.
3. ______ **Become a better employee?** A workforce of critical—and creative—thinkers helps the American economy thrive and individuals become more successful. The U.S. Department of Labor reports that today's jobs require employees who can deal with complexity, learn and perform multiple tasks, analyze and deal with a wide variety of options, identify problems, perceive alternative approaches, and select the best approach.[10] Employers are "practically begging" for employees who can "think, collaborate, communicate, coordinate, and create."[11]
4. ______ **Become a more savvy consumer?** In today's marketplace, everyone wants your dollars. If you acted on every ad you see on the Internet or watch on television, you'd run out of money very quickly. You're told you need whitened teeth, colored hair, softened skin, strong mouthwash, and a host of other things in order to be attractive. Critical thinking will help you evaluate offers, avoid slick come-ons, and buy responsibly.
5. ______ **Build stronger relationships?** Critical thinking helps us understand our own and others' actions and become more responsible communicators. Whether with friends or romantic partners, relationships take work. Sometimes you have to figure out what your partner really means or listen between the lines for important clues. You have to persuade your partner that you're right about something or convince him or her to act on a request. Actually, critical thinking is at the heart of every relationship you care about.
6. ______ **Become a lifelong learner?** Your education doesn't end when you get your diploma. In many ways the real exams begin afterward when you put your classroom learning to the test. And in today's world you must continue to learn as you transition through jobs to give your life more meaning—personally and professionally. You'll need to keep expanding your skills, no matter what your career is. Innovation and change are the watchwords of today's workplace, and continual learning is the only way to survive and thrive.

I put 10's on everything, but I really think 1 and 5 are important.

BOX 4.1 Asking Questions: Inquiring Minds Want to Know

Here's something worth knowing: Good thinkers are good questioners. They're always asking, "who," "what," "why," and "how." "*Who* says so?" "*What* is he trying to convince me of?" "*Why* is he trying to influence me?" "*How* is he trying to do it?" Critical thinkers know how to uncover the truth by asking questions, and they realize that the kind of questions they ask is important. They move beyond the most basic, most obvious questions and stretch their minds to maximize their learning.

The Question Pyramid is an interesting way of looking at focused thinking (see Figure 4.1). As you move up the pyramid, formulating and answering questions become increasingly difficult.

- Level 1 questions are observable, obvious, and one-dimensional. They can be answered with a yes or no answer: "Do philosophers study critical thinking?" Not too challenging.
- Level 2 questions are slightly more challenging. They consist of the standard who and what questions, like, "What is critical thinking?" Level 2 questions are straightforward. They could be answered by memorizing a section of the textbook.
- Level 3 questions require actual critical thinking, "Why is critical thinking studied by philosophers?" You'd need to develop your answer by thinking about possibilities, selecting a response, and backing it up with evidence.
- Level 4 questions require creative thinking, a subject for discussion later in this chapter, "What if no one could think critically? What would societies be like?" "How do you balance critical thinking and creative thinking?" Formulating answers to level 4 questions requires you to think for yourself and come up with your own unique, creative responses.

When you're asking questions instead of answering them, it's easy to get stuck at level 1 or 2, but with effort and a true understanding of how to ask questions, you can challenge yourself to learn more. In fact, most of your college courses will require this of you. So get a head start: After listening to a lecture, create a list of questions to see if you really understand the material. After reading an assigned chapter, create a list of questions to see how much you've digested. Understand the kind of questions you're asking, and move up the pyramid to improve your thinking skills.[12]

FIGURE 4.1

The Question Pyramid

Source: Adapted from Hellyer, R., Robinson, C., & Sherwood, P. (1998). *Study Skills for Learning Power,* p. 18. Houghton Mifflin Company.

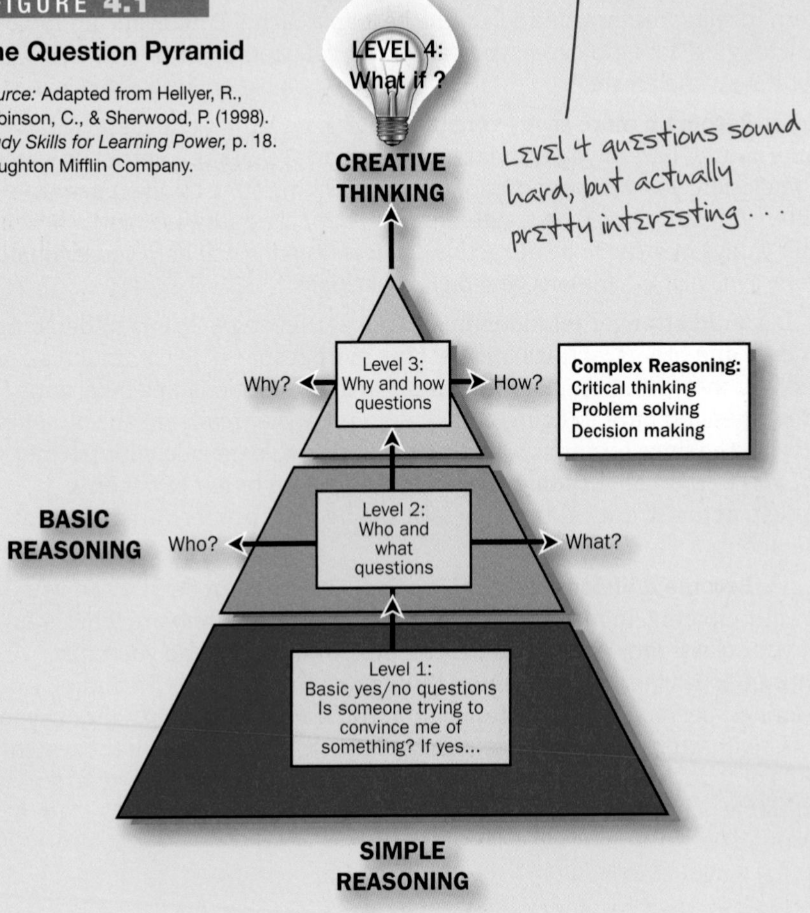

A Four-Part Model of Critical Thinking

Challenge: Reasoning, problem solving, and decision making are all part of critical thinking. How are these three things related?

Reaction:

Like your writing or speaking skills, well-cultivated critical thinking skills can serve as the infrastructure for taking on all of your academic challenges. But let's ask an important question: How do you do it? We'll look at the four primary components of critical thinking, and later in this chapter, we'll use a realistic news story, one that is relevant to many college campuses, to allow you to apply what you've learned and provide a memorable example. Take a look at Figure 4.2 to preview the four-part model of critical thinking.

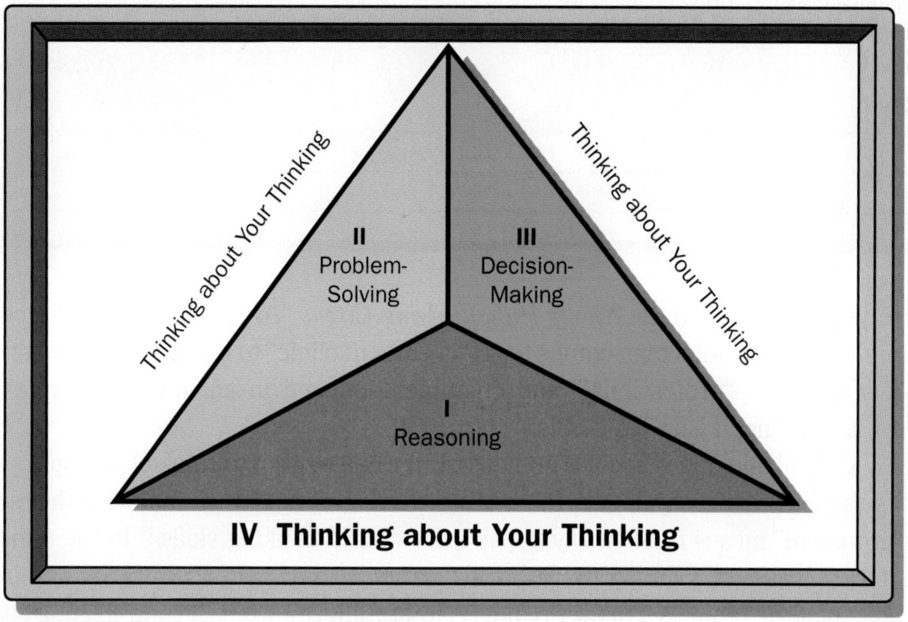

FIGURE 4.2

Critical Thinking Is Focused

Here's a four-part model of critical thinking. Your reasoning skills underlie everything. They are the foundation upon which your problem-solving and decision-making skills rest, and your metacognitive skills, or thinking about your thinking, surround all the focused thinking you do.

I. Reasoning: The Foundation of Critical Thinking

Reasoning, the foundation of critical thinking, is the ability to come to a conclusion based on one or more arguments. A strong argument is convincing because it backs up its claim with evidence. If no one would disagree with what you're saying, it's not an argument. It's self-evident. "Grass is green" is not an argument. But "Cows that are grass-fed make the best meat" (if supporting evidence is provided) is. Do you see the difference? Because reasoning is the foundation for critical thinking, we'll concentrate much of our discussion there.

> **The aim of argument, or of discussion, should not be victory, but progress.**
>
> *Joseph Joubert, French moralist (1754–1824)*

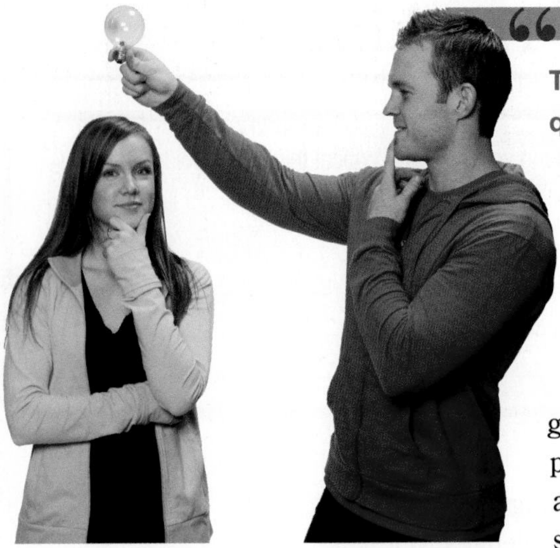

> **The important thing is not to stop questioning.**
>
> *Albert Einstein, theoretical physicist (1879–1955)*

How good are you at creating a sound argument? Let's say that you're trying to convince your roommate to stop inviting people into your room while you're studying for major exams. What evidence would you use to convince her? How good are you at evaluating someone else's argument? For example, you're trying to decide whether an online discount is really a good deal. Would you take the advertiser's word for it or do some research to compare prices on your own? Throughout the rest of this chapter, ask yourself: Are there ways I can improve my reasoning skills?

Analyzing Arguments

? challenge

" reaction

Challenge: What does the term *argument* have to do with critical thinking? Give an example of a "sound" and an "unsound" argument you have heard or read recently.

Reaction:

____

____

____

I love this YouTube vid!

Have you ever seen the *Monty Python Flying Circus* "Argument Clinic Sketch"? In this bizarre skit a man comes to an "argument clinic" to buy an argument. The two arguers—"professional" and customer—engage in an interminably long, "yes, it is" "no, it isn't" squabble.

Critical thinking is about arguments. But when most of us think of an argument, that's the kind of bickering we think of, and having a negative view of what the term "argument" means can actually impair your critical thinking skills.[13] In the middle of the "Argument Clinic" sketch, however, the customer actually makes an important point. He protests that they're not really arguing; they're just contradicting each other. He continues, "An argument is a connected series of statements intended to establish a proposition." That's the kind of argument that's related to critical thinking.

Critical thinking is about an argument that *one* person puts forth. Attorneys—for both the prosecution and defense—put forth their closing arguments at the end of a trial. A politician puts forth an argument about where he stands on the issues. A professor puts forth an argument to persuade her class to learn important content in her discipline.

Arguments are said to be inductive or deductive. *Inductive* arguments go from specific observations to general conclusions. In criminal trials, the prosecution puts together individual pieces of evidence to prove that the defendant is guilty: eyewitnesses put him at the scene, the gun store salesman remembers

> You cannot help but learn more as you take the world into your hands. Take it up reverently, for it is an old piece of clay, with millions of thumbprints on it.
>
> *John Updike, American writer*

Don Hammond/Design Pics/Corbis

selling him a pistol, and his fingerprints are on the weapon. Therefore, the prosecutor argues that the defendant is guilty. Other arguments are said to be *deductive*, meaning they go from broad generalizations to specific conclusions. All serial killers have a particular psychological profile. The defendant has this psychological profile. Therefore the defendant is the killer.

What do arguments do? They try to persuade. Arguments contain clear reasons to believe someone or something. Once you understand what an argument is, you must also understand that arguments can be sound or unsound. If I tell you that two plus two equals four, chances are good that you'll believe me. If, on the other hand, I tell you two plus two equals five, you'll flatly deny it. If I say "Cats have fur." "Dogs have fur." "Therefore dogs are cats," you'll tell me I'm crazy—because it's an unsound argument.

The standard we use to test the soundness of arguments is logic, which is a fairly extensive topic. Let's just say for our purposes here that arguments are sound when the evidence to support them is reasonable, more reasonable than the evidence supporting other opinions. The important point is that a sound argument provides at least one good reason to believe. Let's look at an example:

I don't see why all first-year students have to take Freshman Composition. It's a free country. Students shouldn't have to take courses they don't want to take.

Based on our definition, is this example an argument? Why or why not? Is the statement "It's a free country" relevant? What does living in a free country have to do with the curricula in colleges and universities? Nothing. *Relevancy* is a condition needed for a sound argument.

> Only when we know a little do we know anything; doubt grows with knowledge.
>
> *Johann Wolfgang von Goethe, German writer and scholar (1749–1832)*

Now look at this example:

I don't see why all first-year students have to take Freshman Composition. Many students developed good writing skills in high school, and their Verbal SAT scores are 600 or higher.

Is this second example an argument? Why or why not? The first example doesn't give you a good reason to believe the argument; the second example does. A true argument must contain at least one reason for you to believe it.

Here's another warning. Not everything that sounds like an argument is one. Look at this example:

Everyone taking Calculus 100 failed the test last Friday. I took the test last Friday. Therefore, I will probably get an F in the course.

BOX 4.2 Wanted: Liberal Arts Grads

Congratulations, college grads! Now begins your so-called real life. But here's a bummer: If you took your parents' well-meaning advice and majored in a seemingly useful discipline you really didn't care about, you may have made a mistake. According to research, most parents (75 percent) and college-age kids (85 percent) believe the point of college is to get a practical education to land a good job right out of school. But CEOs in one survey were thinking more about long-term career development; only 37 percent of them said the purpose of a diploma is to acquire work skills. While the parents and kids took a dim view of liberal arts, business leaders called the humanities essential to developing critical-thinking (90 percent) and problem-solving skills (77 percent). Even Steve Jobs, tech guru of Apple fame, believes in the value of a well-rounded education. "... technology alone is not enough—it's technology married with liberal arts, married with the humanities, that yields us the result that makes our heart sing."[15] So while you're in college, it's a good idea to acquire *all* the essential skills you need now for future success![16]

- use a bandwagon appeal ("Everybody's doing it.").
- lie with statistics ("over half" when it's really only 50.5 percent).

On the other hand, we must also keep an open mind and be flexible in our thinking. If you get good evidence to support a view that contradicts yours, be willing to modify your ideas. One way to evaluate the validity of claims is to use the Question Pyramid we discussed earlier. Consider claims by asking these four key questions: "who?" "what?" "why?" and "how?"

Avoiding Faulty Reasoning

? challenge / " reaction

Challenge: List as many reasoning mistakes as you can. Can you provide an example of one or two of them?

Reaction:

____

____

____

> **To treat your facts with imagination is one thing, but to imagine your facts is another.**
>
> *John Burroughs, writer on ecology (1837–1921)*

Although we can certainly improve our critical-thinking skills, it's impossible to be a perfect critical thinker 100 percent of the time. As thinkers, we make mistakes, and sometimes others try to trick us with false arguments. It's important to cultivate both types of critical thinking skills: your *productive* skills, which you use as a speaker and writer, and your *receptive* skills, which you use as a reader and listener. As responsible communicators, we must understand what a sound argument is and know how to construct one ourselves. We must also understand what a defective argument is in order to avoid getting sucked in when we shouldn't.

Here is a top-ten list of logical fallacies, or false logic strategies, we can slip into—or others can use against us—if we're not careful. For each of the ten types, read through the example and then see if you can come up with one of your own.

1. **False cause and effect** (assuming one cause for something when other causes are possible, too)

> **There's a world of difference between truth and facts. Facts can obscure the truth.**
>
> *Maya Angelou, American author and poet (1928–)*

iStockphoto.com/selimaksan

I moved into my new dorm room last month. I've failed every exam I've taken since. Living in the residence hall is blowing my GPA!

2. **Personal attack** (reacting to a challenge by attacking the challenger)

   How could anyone believe our professor's views on ethics? We all know he's a very poor teacher.

3. **Unwarranted assumption** (taking too much for granted without evidence)

   You say universities give women equal opportunities. I say they don't. Reply: It's true. I read it on a website.

4. **Emotional appeal** (appealing to someone's feelings in order to gain acceptance of an argument)

   If you care about the institution that made you what you are today, you'll dig deep into your pockets and send a financial contribution now.

5. **False authority** (attributing your argument to someone else in a supposed position of power to get you off the hook)

   I'd really like to be able to change your grade, but my Department Chair frowns upon that.

6. **Hasty conclusion** (jumping to a conclusion when other conclusions are possible)

   I'm sure my roommate stole my textbook. He's too cheap to buy his own.

7. **Straw man** (attempting to "prove" an argument by overstating, exaggerating, or oversimplifying the arguments of the opposing side)

   We should relax the entrance requirements to help attract more students. Reply: You actually want the quality of students here to take a nose dive? Oh, right, why don't we all just teach high school instead?

8. **Shifting the burden of proof** (shifting the responsibility of proving an assertion to someone else because you have no evidence for what you assert)

   The zero-tolerance policy on alcohol in the residence halls is working. Reply: No, it's not. Reply back: Oh yeah? Prove it.

9. **Oversimplification/overgeneralization** (reducing a complex issue to something very simple or stereotyping)

   College professors have it made. They teach a couple classes a week for a few hours, and then they have free time the rest of the week. That's the kind of job I want!

10. **Either/or thinking** (taking only an extreme position on an issue when other positions are possible)

    Either we ban alcohol on campus or we'll go bankrupt from lawsuits.

VARK It!

Complete the recommended activity for your preferred VARK learning modality. If you are multimodal, select more than one activity. Your instructor may ask you to (a) give an oral report on your results in class, (b) send your results to him or her via e-mail, (c) post them online, or (d) contribute to a class chat.

iStockphoto.com/Marcela Barsse/MarsBars; Joanna Goodyear/Dreamstime.com; iStockphoto.com/ Nadezda Firsova; iStockphoto.com/Pascal Genest

Visual: Create a collage or find an image that represents each letter writer's point of view. Be certain to highlight the faulty reasoning.

Aural: As a group, talk through the case. Focus on questions like these: Does the incident sound realistic? If you ran the university, how would you handle the situation?

Read/Write: Write a press release sent from the university to local media outlets. How would you present this difficult situation to readers in the general public?

Kinesthetic: Assume you are a member of President Bishop's new task force on alcohol policy. Role play members of the task force at their first meeting.

II. Problem Solving: The Basic How-To's

When you have to solve a problem, your critical thinking skills should move front and center. Perhaps you need to find a way to earn more money. You run short each month, and the last few days before payday are nerve-racking. What should you do? Use a gunshot approach and try many different strategies at once or devise a more precise way to get the best results? See if the following steps make sense to you and seem like something you might actually do.

1. DEFINE:
my philosophy class is killing me!

STEP 1: Define the problem. What is the exact nature of the problem you face? You must define the problem if you hope to solve it. For example:

- Is it that you don't monitor your spending and run out of money long before the next paycheck?
- Is it that you've never created a budget and you spend money randomly?

2. BRAINSTORM:
-Drop the class
-Study harder
-Get advice from my advisor
-Form a study group
-Go see Prof Courtney

STEP 2: Brainstorm possible options. List all of the possible solutions you can come up with. For example:

- Eat all your meals in the residence hall instead of hitting the fast-food joints so often.
- Stop ordering in pizza four nights a week when you get the munchies at midnight.
- Ask your parents for more money. They told you to let them know when you need more.
- Look for a job that pays more. Tips at the Pancake House where you work don't really amount to much.
- Capitalize on your particular skills to earn extra money. If you're a whiz at math, you could sign on as a tutor at the Math Learning Center on campus.

3. SET CRITERIA:
a) time
b) effectiveness
c) convenience

STEP 3: Set criteria to evaluate each option. For example:

- *Distance* is important. Your car isn't very reliable, so it would be good to find a job you can walk or ride your bike to.

- *Good pay* is important. In the past, you've always had low-paying jobs. You need whatever solution you arrive at to be worth your while.
- *Time* is important. You're taking a challenging load of classes, and you need to keep up your grades to keep your scholarship.

STEP 4: Evaluate each option you've proposed. For example:

- Eat all your meals in the residence hall. (This is a good idea because you've already paid for those meals, regardless of which solution you choose.)
- Stop ordering in pizza four nights a week. (This is also a good option because impromptu expenses like this can mount exponentially.)
- Ask your parents for more money. (You'd really like to avoid this option. You know they're already making sacrifices to help you through school.)
- Get a job that pays more. (Unfortunately, your campus is half an hour from the center of town where all the posh restaurants are.)
- Capitalize on your particular skills to earn extra money. (Tutors are paid more than minimum wage, and the Math Learning Center is across from your residence hall.)

4. EVALUATE:
-Drop the class (losing my financial aid would be VERY inconvenient!)
-Study harder (I already am!)
-Get advice from my advisor (could take some time to get in to see her)
-Form a study group (when could we all meet?)
-Go see Prof (could work, but he might be hard to talk to)

STEP 5: Choose the best solution. In this case, it looks like the Math Learning Center fits the bill!

5. CHOOSE: Going to see Prof Courtney would be best.

STEP 6: Plan how to achieve the best solution. When you call the Math Learning Center to find out how to apply, you discover that you need a letter of recommendation from a math professor. You e-mail your calculus professor and set up a meeting for later in the week. When the letter is ready, you call the Math Learning Center again to make an appointment to schedule an interview, and so forth.

6. PLAN: E-mail him tonight to make an appointment. Enter the day and time on Google Calendar.

STEP 7: Implement the solution and evaluate the results. A month or two after you take on the tutoring job, you evaluate if this solution is really the best one. You may need to request more hours or different days. Or you may find that this job leads to a better one as a Teaching Assistant for the math department. At any rate, you've used your critical thinking skills to solve a problem, systematically, logically, and effectively. College students who successfully solve everyday problems have higher self-esteem and life satisfaction. As it turns out, improving your problem solving skills has big payoffs! [18]

7. IMPLEMENT: We'll see, but at least I have a plan.

III. Decision Making: What's Your Style?

Arguments lead to decisions, and it's important to make good ones! After you've evaluated the arguments put forth, you must often do something about them. Before you know it, you'll be deciding on a major if you haven't already, a career field, a place to live, a romantic partner—you name it.

When you have an important decision to make, your critical thinking skills should kick into action. The more important the decision, chances are the more thoughtful the process of deciding should be. But people make decisions in their own way. To some extent, decision making is individualistic. Take a

CONTROL: *YOUR TOUGHEST CLASS*

Try out the seven-step problem-solving model for yourself. Think of a problem you're facing right now in your toughest class, and fill in your ideas for steps 1 through 7. Maybe you find the textbook hard to read, or the PowerPoints confusing, or the instructor's accent hard to understand. When you're done, ask yourself whether filling in these steps helped you understand the problem and this problem-solving process better.

STEP 1: Define the problem.

____

STEP 2: Brainstorm possible options.

____

STEP 3: Set criteria to evaluate each option.

____

STEP 4: Evaluate each option you've proposed.

____

STEP 5: Choose the best solution.

____

STEP 6: Plan how to achieve the best solution.

____

STEP 7: Implement the solution and evaluate the results.

____

look at the Decision Style Inventory in Exercise 4.3 to learn more about your decision-making style.

The results of this Decision Style Inventory have been collected from over 2,000 people and provide the basis for the book entitled *Managing with Style* by Alan J. Rowe and Richard O. Mason. After you complete your rankings, total your answers for each letter. Although the Decision Style Inventory is typically used with managers and you may not be one now, it is also a useful way to preview what your style may be when you do have a position of responsibility. The (a) answers represent a *directive* style, the (b) answers represent an *analytical* style, the (c) answers represent a *conceptual* style, and the (d) answers represent a *behavioral* style. What is your decision making style? Which of the four letters (a, b, c, or d) do you have *the most* of?

Interesting! I'd like to know this about myself...

EXERCISE 4.3

Decision Style Inventory

Respond to each of the following twenty statements by marking your response according to the rules that follow. There are no right or wrong answers. Generally, the first impression that comes to mind is the best one to put down. Respond to each statement by assigning an 8 to the answer that is most appropriate (for you), a 4 next to the next most appropriate, then a 2, and finally a 1 for the least appropriate answer. In the following example, an individual prefers blue, brown, gray, and red in that order:

When picking clothes, I prefer Blue 8 Red 1 Brown 4 Gray 2

Each number may only be assigned once for each statement, and each of the four numbers must be used for each statement.

1. In my career, my prime objective will be to:
   - 1 (a) have a position with status.
   - 8 (b) be the best in my field.
   - 4 (c) achieve recognition for my work.
   - 2 (d) feel secure in my job.
2. I enjoy jobs that:
   - 4 (a) are technical and well defined.
   - 1 (b) have considerable variety.
   - 8 (c) allow independent action.
   - 2 (d) involve people.
3. If I were a boss, I'd expect people working for me to be:
   - 8 (a) productive and fast.
   - 1 (b) highly capable.
   - 4 (c) committed and responsive.
   - 2 (d) receptive to suggestions.
4. In my job, I'll look for:
   - 1 (a) practical results.
   - 2 (b) the best solutions.
   - 8 (c) new approaches or ideas.
   - 4 (d) a good working environment.
5. I communicate best with others:
   - 8 (a) on a direct one-to-one basis.
   - 2 (b) in writing.
   - 1 (c) by having a discussion.
   - 4 (d) in a group meeting.
6. As I plan on the job, I'll emphasize:
   - 4 (a) current problems.
   - 1 (b) meeting objectives.
   - 2 (c) future goals.
   - 8 (d) developing the careers of people working for me.
7. When faced with solving a problem, I:
   - 2 (a) rely on proven approaches.
   - 8 (b) apply careful analysis.
   - 4 (c) look for creative approaches.
   - 1 (d) rely on my feelings.
8. When using information, I prefer:
   - 8 (a) specific facts.
   - 4 (b) accurate and complete information.
   - 2 (c) broad coverage of many options.
   - 1 (d) limited information that is easily understood.
9. When I am not sure about what to do, I:
   - 1 (a) rely on my intuition.
   - 8 (b) search for the facts.
   - 4 (c) look for a possible compromise.
   - 2 (d) wait before making a decision.
10. Whenever possible, I avoid:
    - 4 (a) long debates.
    - 8 (b) incomplete work.
    - 1 (c) using numbers or formulas.
    - 2 (d) conflict with others.
11. I am especially good at:
    - 1 (a) remembering dates and facts.
    - 8 (b) solving difficult problems.
    - 4 (c) seeing many possibilities.
    - 2 (d) interacting with others.
12. When time is important, I:
    - 8 (a) decide and act quickly.
    - 4 (b) follow plans and priorities.
    - 1 (c) refuse to be pressured.
    - 2 (d) seek guidance or support.
13. In social settings, I generally:
    - 8 (a) speak with others.
    - 4 (b) think about what is being said.
    - 2 (c) observe what is going on.
    - 1 (d) listen to the conversation.
14. I am good at remembering:
    - 8 (a) people's names.
    - 4 (b) places we met.
    - 1 (c) people's faces.
    - 2 (d) people's personalities.

(continued on next page)

15. The work I do will provide me:
   4 (a) the power to influence others.
   1 (b) challenging assignments.
   8 (c) opportunities to achieve my personal goals.
   2 (d) acceptance by the people I work with.

16. I work well with people who are:
   8 (a) energetic and ambitious.
   4 (b) self-confident.
   1 (c) open-minded.
   2 (d) positive and trusting.

17. When under stress, I:
   2 (a) become anxious.
   8 (b) concentrate on the problem.
   4 (c) become frustrated.
   1 (d) am forgetful.

18. Others consider me:
   1 (a) aggressive.
   2 (b) disciplined.
   4 (c) imaginative.
   8 (d) supportive.

19. My decisions typically are:
   8 (a) realistic and direct.
   1 (b) systematic and abstract.
   2 (c) broad and flexible.
   4 (d) sensitive to the needs of others.

20. I dislike:
   4 (a) losing control.
   8 (b) doing boring work.
   1 (c) following rules.
   2 (d) being rejected.

Totals: (a) 93 + (b) 87 + (c) 66 + (d) 54 = 300

(Note: The sum total for (a) + (b) + (c) + (d) should equal 300.)

Source: Adapted from *Managing with Style: A Guide to Understanding, Assessing, and Improving Decision Making* by A.J. Rowe and R.O. Mason, by permission from Dr. Alan J. Rowe.

Hemera Technologies/Photos.com/Jupiter images

> **Directive (a).** This decision-making style emphasizes the here and now. Directives prefer structure and using practical data to make decisions. They look for speed, efficiency, and results, and focus on short-term fixes. Directive decision makers base their decisions on experience, facts, procedures, and rules, and they have energy and drive to get things done. On the down side, because they work quickly, they are sometimes satisfied with simplistic solutions.

Ian Scott/Shutterstock.com

> **Analytical (b).** This decision-making style emphasizes a logical approach. Analyticals search carefully for the best decision, and they sometimes get hung up with overanalyzing things and take too long to finally make a decision. They are sometimes considered to be impersonal because they may be more interested in the problem than in the people who have it. But they are good at working with data and doing careful analysis.

Hemera Technologies/Jupiter Images

> **Conceptual (c).** This decision-making style emphasizes the big picture. Conceptuals are adaptable, insightful, and flexible, and they look for innovative solutions. They are sometimes too idealistic, but they take risks and are very creative.

my score says behavioral, and it fits.

iofoto/Shutterstock.com

> **Behavioral (d).** This decision-making style emphasizes people. Behaviorals enjoy people and the social aspects of work. They use their feelings to assess situations, communicate well, and are supportive of others. On the other hand, they are sometimes seen as wishy-washy or are criticized because they can't make hard decisions or can't say no.

▶▶ Your TypE Is Showing

Researchers have found a relationship between the Decision Style Inventory and the Myers-Briggs Type Inventory style. Is that true for you? It makes sense that your personality and your decision-making style are related, doesn't it? Locate the two middle letters of your type in Figure 4.3 and see how your type correlates to a decision-making style. This is particularly helpful if you have completed the full MBTI.

Directive decision makers, for example, like well-defined goals, well-developed plans, and detailed calculations. People with those characteristics are typically ST's on the MBTI.

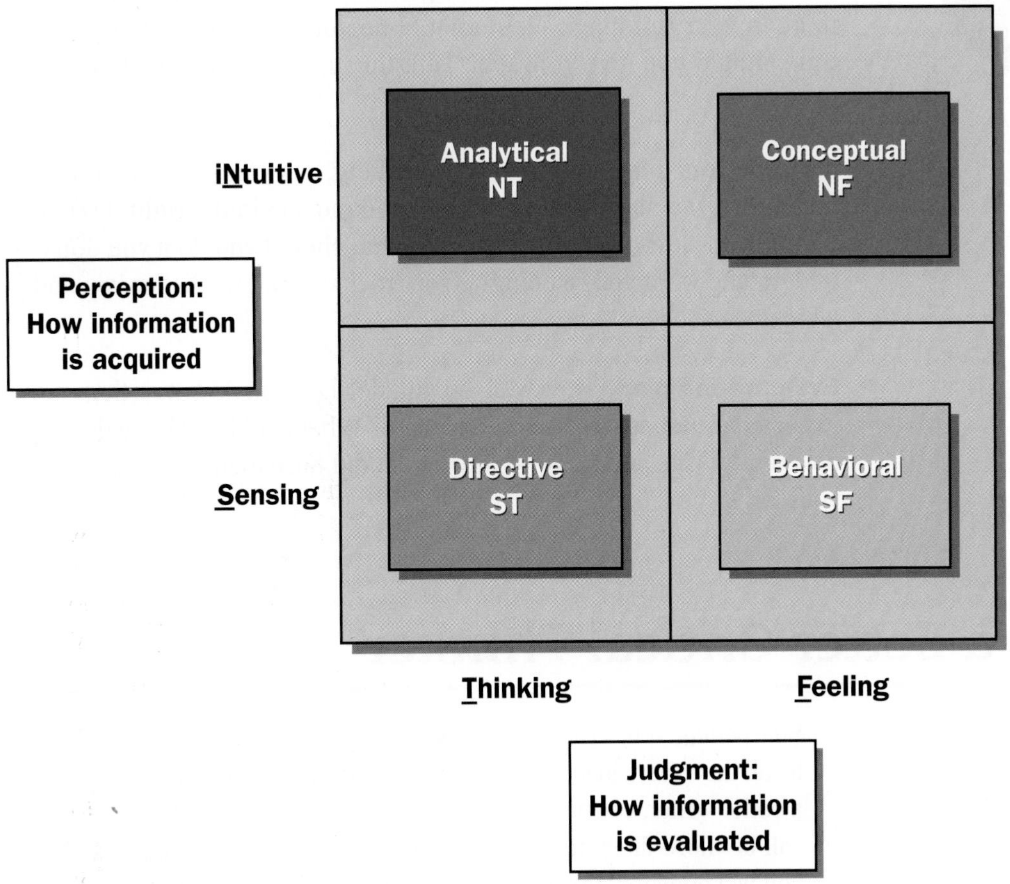

FIGURE 4.3

Relationship between the Decision Style Inventory and the MBTI

Source: From p. 140 of *Managing with Style: A Guide to Understanding, Assessing, and Improving Decision Making* by A.J. Rowe and R.O. Mason. © 1987 by Jossey-Bass. Reprinted by permission from Dr. Alan J. Rowe.

IV. Thinking about Your Thinking

One of the most important aspects of critical thinking is that it evaluates itself. As you're solving problems, for example, you're thinking about how you're thinking. You're assessing your progress as you go, analyzing the strengths and weaknesses in your thinking, and perhaps even coming up with better ways to do it. We call that metacognition, and that's one reason this book contains "Insight → Action" exercises—to give you opportunities to think about how you're thinking and make note of those thoughts. Whenever you're faced with learning something new, metacognition involves three elements. Ultimately, these elements should become the foundation of all your learning experiences so that you improve your metacognitive skills as you go.

© Larry Harwood Photography. Property of Cengage Learning

> **Education is nothing more, nor less, than learning to think!**
>
> *Peter Facione, professor, administrator, author, consultant, and critical thinking expert*

- **Develop a plan of action.** Ask yourself what you already know that can help you learn something new. What direction do you want to go in your thinking? What should be your first task? How much time should you give yourself? Talk through your plan with someone else.

- **Monitor your plan.** While you're working, ask yourself how you're doing. Are you staying on track? Are you moving in the right direction? Should you slow down or speed up? What should you do if you don't understand what you're doing? Keep track of what works for you and what doesn't.

- **Evaluate the plan.** How well did you do? Did you do better than expected or not as well as you expected? What could you have done differently? Can you apply what you just did here to future tasks? Give yourself some feedback.[19]

Becoming a Better Critical Thinker

Akom Production Company/Starstock/Photoshot

Sharpening your critical thinking skills is vital because these skills underlie all the others in your academic repertoire. If you think well, you will be a better writer, a better presenter, a better listener, and a better reader. You will be more likely to engage more fully in your academic tasks because you will question, probe, analyze, and monitor yourself as you learn. Here are some suggestions for improving your skills. As you read them, think about how they pertain to you.

1. **Admit when you don't know.** If you don't know enough to think critically about something, admit it, and then find out more. With the volume of information available in today's world, we can't possibly know everything about anything. But the good news is that information is readily available. All you need to do is read, listen, point, and click to be well informed on many issues.

> **And how is education supposed to make me feel smarter?**
>
> *Homer Simpson, television cartoon character,* The Simpsons

CAREER OUTLOOK: *EXAMINE YOUR THINKING*

Optimism is the faith that leads to achievement. Nothing can be done without hope and confidence.

Helen Keller (1880–1968), American author and educator

Consider a job that you've held in the past. If someone asked you to come up with five adjectives that describe the most memorable boss you've ever had, what words would come to you? Words like *encouraging, smart, visionary, responsive*, or *supportive*—or words like *hasty, unfair, mean, hypocritical*, or *irrational*? What do all the words you think of have in common? Were they mainly *positive* or *negative*?

When asked this question, most people go in one direction: either entirely positive or negative. No one ever says, "What I really love about my boss is his critical nature. He doesn't miss a single mistake I make." Or "My boss has a temper you wouldn't believe. When she nails you on something, you know exactly where you stand."[20] It's natural to lean one way or the other. Critical thinking skills are a useful tool in the workplace. They can help you adjust your thinking appropriately and keep you from getting locked into particular patterns, especially negative ones.

Unfortunately, sometimes negativity is effortless to generate. Imagine a scenario like this. You're desperately looking for a part-time job and meet someone at a party who could be an important resource for you. He says, "E-mail me your résumé, and I'll take a look and get back to you tomorrow." So, you rush home, send off your résumé, and check your e-mail a hundred times the next day, expecting a response. Then you check your e-mail periodically the following day and the day after that. Finally, you give up in disgust, assuming your contact just had a big ego. A month later, while checking your spam folder, you find his message, sent shortly after you met. "I hope this reaches you," the e-mail says. "My e-mail crashed, and I had to set up a new account. Here's my new e-mail address." Like many of us, you assumed the worst and created a derogatory story which you chose to believe. That's normal, too, but the negativity you've generated wasn't necessarily in your best interest: "We can't change the facts, but we do have a choice about what to make of them."[21] Too much pessimism can hurt us: our immune systems degenerate, our relationships dissolve, and our careers get derailed.

In the workplace, the most desirable kind of thinking is "realistic optimism." It's not blind faith or false hope; it's looking for the best in things and then working to make them happen. It's accepting what's going on around you, but at the same time admitting what needs to be changed. It's about resilience, "getting back on the horse," and trotting on. It's a productive pattern of thinking.[22]

Remember that term!!

If "realistic optimism" sounds like an oxymoron to you, have faith! Remember the words of the environmentalist and founder of Patagonia, the well-known outdoor gear company: "There's no difference between a pessimist who says, 'Oh, it's hopeless, so don't bother doing anything,' and an optimist who says, 'Don't bother doing anything, it's going to turn out fine anyway.' Either way, nothing happens." It's your thinking and your career, and you're in the driver's seat. You want to do things, go places, and make things happen. That's what it's all about.

Think Ahead: You're in the process of preparing for your future; examine your thinking *now*. Are you a "glass half full" person or a "glass half empty person?" Reflect on some of your patterns of thinking and how they could affect your about-to-be career.

CAST ON CAREERS

© Larry Harwood Photography. Property of Cengage Learning

FOCUS: As a brand new student, were you optimistic or pessimistic?

DARIO: I'd say I was optimistic—maybe overly optimistic. For example, I never asked questions in class. I just assumed I'd find the answer in the textbook later. But "later" never quite arrived because I'd forget about it. Then when I was preparing for an exam, I'd check my notes from class and find gaps in what I had written down. I just always assumed I'd do fine and everything would be manageable. For the most part, that was true, eventually. But sometimes I wish I had been a little more realistic as a first-year student and saved myself some major stress!

FOCUS: What are your career plans? How will your thinking patterns play a role?

DARIO: I've decided to be a Student Affairs Professional, like a Director of Residence Life or Campus Activities. I loved college so much that I want it to continue! How I think about students, how I deal with student issues, how I can help them mature, have a good time, and do well academically by being more realistic than I was—all those things will be important!

2. **Realize you have buttons that can be pushed.** We all have issues we're emotional about. That's normal. It's natural to feel strongly about some things, but it's also important to understand the reasons why so that you can explain your views to someone else. And of course, realize that you're not the only one with buttons. Your teacher, roommate, significant other, boss, everyone else has them, too.

3. **Learn more about the opposition.** Many times, it's more comfortable to avoid what we don't agree with and selectively validate what we already believe. But part of being a well-educated person means learning about the history, backgrounds, values, and techniques of people you disagree with so that you can anticipate and deal with their arguments more effectively.

I watched the video on critical thinking at www.cengagebrain.com. Really helped me get it!

4. **Trust and verify.** During the cold war, President Ronald Reagan liked to quote an old Russian saying to his Soviet counterpart, Mikhail Gorbachev: "Doveryay, no proveryay," or "Trust, but verify." Being a good critical thinker means achieving a balance between blind faith and healthy skepticism.

5. **Remember that critical thinking is the cornerstone of all academic achievement.** There's nothing more important than learning to think critically. In college and in life, the skills discussed in this chapter will make you a better college student, a better citizen, a better employee, a savvier consumer, a better relational partner, and a better lifelong learner.

CURIOSITY: *ARE YOU TALENTED?*

Who me? Creative? Talented? Gifted? Nah! Some people say: "I'm not creative. I have no talent. I'm just an ordinary guy." Other people settle for good instead of reaching for great: "I'm pretty good. I'm good enough. I have enough to get by." What does it take to be come a truly great thinker, a great creator, a great athlete, a great musician, a great anything?

According to Daniel Coyle, best-selling author of the acclaimed book, *The Talent Code*, talent is something you grow into, not something you're born with. Coyle traveled the world to visit "talent hotbeds," little places that produce great talent: a tennis camp in Russia, a music academy in upstate New York, and an inner city school in California, for example. As he examined these origins of greatness, he discovered that talent is grown by a combination of three principles:

© Photos.com

Deep Practice: Deep practice isn't just practicing regularly or even practicing a great deal, it's practicing a certain way: very slowly and deliberately. That's how your brain gains mastery. At a music academy Coyle visited, young cellists are told that if anyone walking by can recognize the song they're practicing, they're playing too fast. Deep practice is also based on stops and starts, on mistakes, on analyzing what went wrong, and trying over and over again until you can do it perfectly. The trick, Coyle says, is to reach just beyond your grasp.

Ignition: Any kind of practice, let alone deep practice, would be torture unless you really cared. Something or somebody must light a spark in you and ignite the fire that fuels your learning. You must be motivated from within to be great. Only then, with this burst of magnetic attraction to a skill, are you willing to work toward greatness.

Master Coaching: To become truly great, it takes an older, wiser, and more experienced teacher, someone who can show you things you don't see in yourself and help you reach your potential. Olympic athletes need coaches, just as great minds need teachers. To become truly excellent, someone must show you precisely how.

So the next time someone asks you if you're creative, talented, or gifted, you may want to explore what it would take before immediately answering. Talent, according to Daniel Coyle, is something that can be grown depending on how much you want it and hard you're willing to work to get it.

Unleash Your Creativity!

Whether you're eighteen or eighty-one, it's safe to say that your life has been changed by an unending stream of new inventions. Which of the following have come into existence during your lifetime? iPods? GPS systems in cars? The Xbox? DVDs? Microwavable mac and cheese? IMAX movies? Side-impact air bags? Singer Bob Dylan crooned memorable words in 1964: "The times, they are a-changin'." He was right then, and it's still true now. According to creativity expert and best-selling author Daniel Pink, the past was built by logical, left-brained people. But the future belongs to right-brained "artists, inventors, designers, storytellers, caregivers, consolers, big picture thinkers." A "seismic shift" is underway, he tells us, and what we will need most in the future is creativity.[23]

Creativity affects us all. It's true that some of these items haven't made a big impact. But other inventions affect you every single day. In his bestselling book, *The Rise of the Creative Class*, Richard Florida discusses the accelerating role of creativity in our lives today: "We live in a time of great promise. We have evolved economic and social systems that tap human creativity and make use of it as never before. This in turn creates an unparalleled opportunity to raise our living standards, build a more humane and sustainable economy, and make our lives more complete."[24]

> **I can't understand why people are frightened by new ideas. I'm frightened by the old ones.**
>
> *John Cage, American composer (1912–1992)*

Florida notes that in 1900, less than 10 percent of American workers were doing creative work. Farms and factories were most people's work sites. Eighty years later, the figure had only risen to 20 percent. But today, a full third of our working population engages in employment that gets their creative juices flowing, whether they're artists, designers, writers, analysts, musicians, or entrepreneurs. The creative sector of our economy accounts for nearly half of all wage and salary income—$1.7 trillion per year. Today's "no collar" workplace is fueled by creativity. And Florida says, we've barely scratched the surface. Human creativity is virtually limitless.[25]

Diversity in our surroundings is one thing that increases the potential for creativity. Creativity comes in all sizes, ethnicities, preferences, and genders. If you're around other open-minded, flexible, tolerant, forward-looking, innovative people, you're more likely to live up to your own creative potential. And in case you're wondering, you don't have to be an artist to be creative. Creativity simply means finding new and better ways to do things. In many ways, it's a choice you make; you *decide* to be creative.[26]

What does all this have to do with you as an entering college student? Florida says that the rise of the creative sector has also changed the way people work and their expectations. No longer are many Americans' aspirations to make a million dollars and buy the house of their dreams. It's about having enough money to be comfortable while doing enjoyable, interesting, and creative work. The best people in any field aren't motivated solely by money. They are motivated by passion for what they do. Can it be true? Are our values changing?

College is a time to sort through your values and determine what you really want from this life of yours. It's about finding out who you are, what you want, why you want it, and how you can get it. Unleash your creativity now and begin building the future you'd like to live. Remember the warning of thinking expert

I just don't know if I see myself as creative . . .

Edward de Bono, "If you take no part in the design of your future, it will be designed for you by others."

Creativity: "Thinking Outside the . . . Book"

? challenge

" reaction

Challenge: What's the difference between *critical* thinking and *creative* thinking?

Reaction:

____

____

____

Do you believe this statement? *Everyone has creative potential.*[27] It's true. Most of us deny it, however. "Me, creative? Nah!" We're often unaware of the untapped ability we have to think creatively. Try this experiment. Look at the following list of words, and divide the list into two (and only two) different categories, using any criteria you devise. Take a few moments and see what you come up with.

dog, salad, book, grasshopper, kettle, paper, garbage, candle

Whenever this experiment is tried, people always come up with very creative categories. They may divide the words into things that you buy at a store (dog, salad, kettle, paper, candle), things that move on their own (dog, grasshopper), things that have a distinct smell (dog, candle, garbage), words that have two consonants, and so forth. People never say it can't be done; they always *invent* categories. Interesting, isn't it? Our minds are hungry for the stimulation of a creative challenge.

Some people might assert that what the experiment demonstrates is intelligence, not creativity. People with average or above average IQs can come up with distinctive categories easily. Smart people, they'd say, are good at tasks like this, and people who come up with the best ideas must be geniuses.

The fact is that intelligence has more to do with coming up with the right answer, and creative thinking has more to do with coming up with many right answers. Often we get so focused on the *right* answer that we rush to find it instead of exploring all the possibilities. Creative thinking is thinking outside the box, or in terms of getting an education, perhaps we should call it thinking outside the book. Going beyond the obvious and exploring possibilities are important parts of becoming an

© Larry Harwood Photography. Property of Cengage Learning

A mind that is stretched to a new idea never returns to its original dimensions.

Oliver Wendell Holmes, American poet (1809–1894)

educated person. Employers report that many college graduates today have specific skills, but that what they rarely see "is the ability to use the right-hand side of the brain—creativity, working in a team."[28] Here's one way to explain it. You see, there's a difference between thinking *reproductively* and thinking *productively. Reproductive* thinking asks: "What have I learned or experienced in the past that will help me solve this problem?" But when you're thinking *productively*, you generate as many approaches as possible.

> **If you have an apple and I have an apple and we exchange these apples, then you and I will still each have one apple. But if you have an idea and I have an idea and we exchange these ideas, then each of us will have two ideas.**
>
> *George Bernard Shaw, Irish literary critic, playwright, and essayist, 1925 Nobel Prize for Literature (1856–1950)*

In Figure 4.1 we looked at the Question Pyramid. Creative thinking is at the top of the pyramid. It goes beyond critical thinking, is predictive, and multidimensional. It asks "What if . . .?" questions. Here are some interesting ones: "What if everyone was allowed to tell one lie per day?" "What if no one could perceive colors?" "What if universities didn't exist?" "If you looked up a word like *squallizmotex* in the dictionary, what might it mean?"[29]

Exercise 4.4

Creative Potential Profile

All of us have the potential to think creatively, but interestingly, we do so in different ways. Complete the Creative Potential Profile to explore your creative thinking potential by marking your responses on these twenty-five items. Place a 1 next to the item MOST like you, a 2 for the item MODERATELY like you, a 3 for the item that's a LITTLE like you, and a 4 for the item that's LEAST like you. Don't use a number more than once for an item, and use all four numbers each time.

1. I often wonder how to
   ____ (a) introduce change.
   ____ (b) discover new solutions.
   ____ (c) make ideas exciting.
   ____ (d) work best with people.

2. My strength is being
   ____ (a) decisive.
   ____ (b) thorough.
   ____ (c) imaginative.
   ____ (d) understanding.

3. Successful people are
   ____ (a) ambitious.
   ____ (b) disciplined.
   ____ (c) willing to take risks.
   ____ (d) self-confident.

4. I get my best results by
   ____ (a) focusing on current problems.
   ____ (b) applying careful analysis.
   ____ (c) trying new approaches.
   ____ (d) gaining the support of others.

5. I see the future as
   ____ (a) unknown.
   ____ (c) a challenge.
   ____ (b) providing many opportunities.
   ____ (d) facilitating change.

6. I appreciate teachers who
   ____ (a) explain ideas clearly.
   ____ (b) make learning interesting.
   ____ (c) recognize original ideas.
   ____ (d) involve others in learning.

7. People see me as
   ____ (a) energetic.
   ____ (b) persistent.
   ____ (c) a perfectionist.
   ____ (d) committed.

8. People who make things happen
   ____ (a) are highly motivated.
   ____ (b) enjoy experimenting.
   ____ (c) have the courage of their convictions.
   ____ (d) challenge the status quo.

(continued on next page)

9. Discoveries depend on
    ____ (a) being committed.
    ____ (b) being curious.
    ____ (c) being open-minded.
    ____ (d) having a broad perspective.

10. A good writer
    ____ (a) is convincing.
    ____ (b) presents new ideas.
    ____ (c) provides a unique perspective.
    ____ (d) has a compelling vision.

11. Breakthrough thinking
    ____ (a) makes progress possible.
    ____ (b) helps to solve difficult problems.
    ____ (c) explores new frontiers.
    ____ (d) encourages teamwork.

12. I dislike
    ____ (a) losing control.
    ____ (b) doing boring work.
    ____ (c) following rules.
    ____ (d) being rejected.

13. I communicate best by being
    ____ (a) direct.
    ____ (b) informative.
    ____ (c) interesting.
    ____ (d) open.

14. I am committed to
    ____ (a) achieving results.
    ____ (b) being the best at what I do.
    ____ (c) exploring new ideas.
    ____ (d) contributing to society.

15. Creative organizations
    ____ (a) look for good answers.
    ____ (b) encourage experimentation.
    ____ (c) allow freedom of expression.
    ____ (d) support new ideas.

16. Achieving results depends on being
    ____ (a) responsive.
    ____ (b) systematic.
    ____ (c) original.
    ____ (d) cooperative.

17. I prefer situations where I
    ____ (a) am in charge.
    ____ (b) have challenging assignments.
    ____ (c) can use my own ideas.
    ____ (d) can introduce change.

18. Change depends on
    ____ (a) gaining support.
    ____ (b) exploring options.
    ____ (c) independent thinking.
    ____ (d) inspiring others.

19. My goal is to
    ____ (a) accomplish my objectives.
    ____ (b) discover new approaches.
    ____ (c) have my ideas recognized.
    ____ (d) achieve progress.

20. Leaders
    ____ (a) assume responsibility.
    ____ (b) deal with complexity.
    ____ (c) visualize opportunities.
    ____ (d) empower others.

21. Ethical behavior
    ____ (a) is expected.
    ____ (b) requires honesty.
    ____ (c) emphasizes integrity.
    ____ (d) enhances society.

22. The arts
    ____ (a) help to improve designs.
    ____ (b) contribute new perspectives.
    ____ (c) broaden education.
    ____ (d) enrich people's lives.

23. Creative thinkers
    ____ (a) accomplish important goals.
    ____ (b) make significant discoveries.
    ____ (c) have leaps of imagination.
    ____ (d) turn their dreams into reality.

24. Breaking with tradition
    ____ (a) is seldom desirable.
    ____ (b) needs to be done carefully.
    ____ (b) provides new opportunities.
    ____ (d) helps to accomplish goals.

25. When under pressure, I
    ____ (a) trust my instincts.
    ____ (b) rely on known approaches.
    ____ (c) carefully explore my options.
    ____ (d) avoid conflict.

Totals: (a) ____ (b) ____ (c) ____ (d) ____

Source: Adapted from *Creative Intelligence: Discovering the Innovative Potential in Ourselves and Others* by A. J. Rowe. © 2004 by Pearson Education, Inc., by permission from Dr. Alan J. Rowe.

According to creativity expert Alan Rowe, also an author of the Decision Style Inventory in Exercise 4.3, our creative intelligence demonstrates itself in four major styles. Look at your totals and see if the description for your lowest score (meaning your most preferred category) makes sense to you. Each of us has aspects of all four styles, but your raw scores may also tell you something about your creative potential. Which of the four letters (a, b, c, or d) do you have *the lowest number* in? That category best describes you.

PhotoObjects.Net/ Jupiter Images

- **Intuitive (a).** This creative style is best described as *resourceful.* If you are an Intuitive, you achieve goals, use common sense, and work to solve problems. You focus on results and rely on past experience to guide your actions. Managers, actors, and politicians are commonly Intuitives.

PhotoObjects.Net/ Jupiter Images

- **Innovative (b).** This creative style is best described as *curious.* Innovatives concentrate on problem solving, are systematic, and rely on data. They use original approaches, are willing to experiment, and focus on systematic inquiry. Scientists, engineers, and inventors typically demonstrate the Innovative creative style.

PhotosToGo.com

- **Imaginative (c).** This creative style is best described as *insightful.* Imaginatives are willing to take risks, have leaps of imagination, and are independent thinkers. They are able to visualize opportunities, are artistic, enjoy writing, and think outside the box. Artists, musicians, writers, and charismatic leaders are often Imaginatives.

This is so ME!

PhotosToGo.com

- **Inspirational (d).** This creative style is best described as *visionary.* Inspirationals respond to societal needs, willingly give of themselves, and have the courage of their convictions. They focus on social change and the giving of themselves toward achieving it. They are often educators, motivational leaders, and writers.[30]

According to the Creative Potential Profile, which is your predominant style? Do your results seem accurate for you? Think about how you can make the best use of your natural style. How will your creativity affect the major or career you choose? Most people have more than one creative style. Remember that motivation, not general intelligence, is the key to creativity. You must be willing to tap your creative potential and challenge yourself to show it.[31]

Ten Ways to Become a More Creative Thinker

Becoming a more creative thinker may mean you need to accept your creativity and cultivate it. Consider these suggestions on how to think more creatively.

1. **Find new eyes.** Find a new perspective on old issues. Here's an interesting example. Years ago, a group of Japanese schoolchildren devised a new way to solve conflicts and build empathy for others' positions, called the Pillow Method. Figure 4.4 is an adaptation of it, based on the fact that a pillow has four sides and a middle, just like most problems.

1. I'm a student paying tuition for PHIL 100.
2. Professor Courtney is an expert in philosophy.
3. 1 and 2 are true.
4. 1 and 2 are false. Just because I pay doesn't mean I can buy knowledge. Being an expert doesn't always make the professor a great teacher.

mu = It really doesn't matter. He's here to teach, and I'm here to learn.

FIGURE 4.4

The Pillow Method

Position 1—I'm right and you're wrong.
Position 2—You're right and I'm wrong.
Position 3—We're both right.
Position 4—We're both wrong.

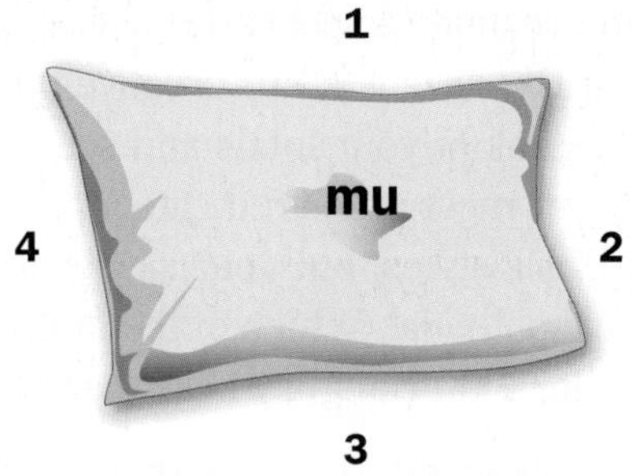

The middle or *mu* is the Zen expression for "it doesn't really matter." There is truth in all four positions. Try it: take a conflict you're having difficulty with at the moment, and write down all four sides and a middle.[32]

2. **Accept your creativity.** Many mindsets block creative thinking: "It can't be done!" "I'm just not the creative type." "I might look stupid!" Many people don't see themselves as creative. This perception can become a major stumbling block. If creativity isn't part of your self-image, you may need to revamp your image. Everyone has creative potential. You may just have to learn how to tap into yours.

3. **Make your thoughts visible.** For many of us, things become clear when we can see them, either in our mind's eye or displayed for us. Even Einstein, a scientist and mathematician, had a very visual mind. Sometimes if we write something down or sketch something out, we generate a new approach without really trying.

4. **Generate lots of ideas.** Thomas Edison held 1,093 patents, until recently, still the record. He gave himself idea quotients. The rule he set for himself was that he had to come up with a major invention every six months and a minor invention every ten days. Bach wrote a cantata every week, even if he was ill. According to two-time Nobel Prize winner Linus Pauling, "The best way to get a good idea is to get lots of ideas."

5. **Don't overcomplexify.** In hindsight, many of the most ingenious discoveries are embarrassingly simple. Biologist Thomas Huxley said, after reading Darwin's explanation of evolution: "How extremely stupid not to have thought of that!" It's common to bemoan our problems and allow anxiety to make them worse. But sometimes the most simple solution is the best one.[33]

6. **Capitalize on your mistakes.** Remember that Thomas Edison tried anything he could think of for a filament for the incandescent lamp, including a whisker from his best friend's beard. All in all, he tried about 1,800 things before finding the right one. Afterwards he said, "I've gained a lot of knowledge—I now know a thousand things that won't work."[34]

7. **Let it flow.** Mihaly Csikszentmihalyi, the author of *Flow: The Psychology of Optimal Experience* and many other books on creativity, discovered something interesting. For his doctoral thesis, he studied artists by taking pictures of them painting every three minutes. He was struck by how engaged

> **A hunch is creativity trying to tell you something.**
>
> *Frank Capra, Italian American film director (1897–1991)*

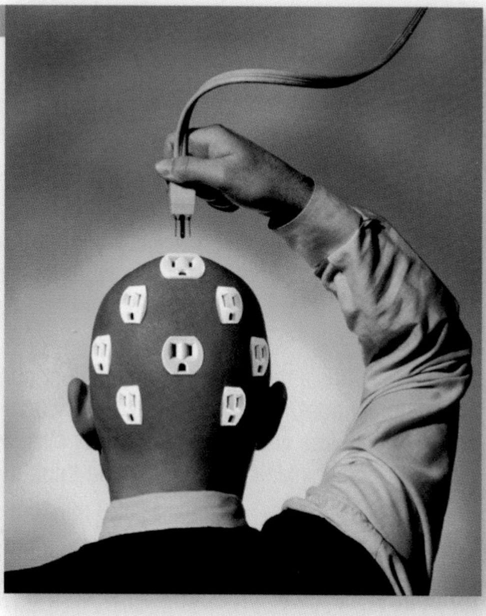

William Whitehurst/Corbis

they were in their work, so engaged that they seemed to forget everything around them. He began studying other "experts": rock climbers, chess players, dancers, musicians, surgeons. Regardless of the activity, these people forgot the time, themselves, and their problems. What did the activities have in common? Clear, high goals and immediate feedback. Athletes call it being in the zone. Csikszentmihalyi's suggestions for achieving flow are these: Pick an enjoyable activity that is at or slightly above your ability level, screen out distractions, focus all your senses and emotions, and look for regular feedback on how you're doing.[35]

8. **Bounce ideas off others.** One good way to become more creative is to use your family or friends as sounding boards. Sometimes just verbalizing something helps you understand more about it. Each person who provides a critique will give you a new perspective, possibly worth considering.
9. **Stop searching for the "right" answer.** This advice doesn't pertain to your upcoming math exam. But it does to apply to situations in which there are many ways to solve a problem. There may be more than one acceptable solution. Fear of mistakes can be debilitating.
10. **Detach your self-concept.** For most of us, creativity is often linked to self-concept. An idea is your brainchild, and you want it to win approval. You've invested part of yourself in giving birth to it. But there's nothing like self-imposed judgment to shut down your creative juices. Your idea may not succeed on its own, but it may feed into someone else's idea and improve it. Or an idea you have about this problem may inform the next problem that challenges you. In the end, in addition to finding a workable solution, what's important is engaging in the creative process with others.

These are all great ideas!

> **Every day is an opportunity to be creative—the canvas is your mind, the brushes and colours are your thoughts and feelings, the panorama is your story, the complete picture is a work of art called, 'my life.' Be careful what you put on the canvas of your mind today—it matters.**
>
> *—Innerspace*

insight / *action*

Now What Do You Think?

1. At the beginning of this chapter, Annie Miller, a frustrated student, faced a challenge. Now after reading this chapter, would you respond differently to any of the questions you answered about the "FOCUS Challenge Case"? Knowing what you know now, how would you advise her? Write a paragraph ending to the story, incorporating your best advice.
2. Identify a time, subject, or event in which you used your critical thinking skills for your own benefit. Perhaps you investigated the salary range for a new job or read blogs on a particular subject to gain new perspectives. Explain what you did, how you went about it, and why. What did you learn about yourself?
3. Provide real examples of critical thinking from any of your current classes. Are you being asked on exams to compare and contrast? To sort through evidence and make decisions? In class discussions are you encouraged to disagree with your instructor or classmates for the sake of a healthy, vigorous debate? How do you handle these situations? Do you think they help you learn? If so, how?
4. Do you see yourself as a creative person? Instead of thinking about whether you're creative or not, ask yourself this question, "*How* am I creative?" Describe the ways.
5. Think of a problem you're facing right now. Use the Pillow Method described in Figure 4.4 to analyze the problem. Why could this approach be helpful?

REALITY ✓ What did you LEARN?

On a scale of 1 to 10, answer the following questions now that you've completed the chapter.

low 1 2 3 4 5 6 7 8 9 10 high

In hindsight, how much did you already know about this subject before reading the chapter?

Can you answer these questions about critical and creative thinking more fully now that you've read the chapter?

1. What's the difference between thinking and critical thinking?
2. Identify three specific types of faulty reasoning.
3. What's the difference between critical thinking and creative thinking?

How useful might the information in this chapter be to you?

How much do you think this information might affect your success in college? ______

How much energy did you put into reading this chapter? ______

How long did it actually take you to complete this chapter (both the reading and writing tasks)? ______ Hour(s) ______ Minutes

Did you finish reading this chapter? ______

Did you intend to when you started? ______

If you meant to but didn't, what stopped you? ______

Challenge Yourself Online Quiz To find out just how much you've learned, access the College Success CourseMate via www.cengagebrain.com to take the Challenge Yourself Online Quiz.

Take a minute to compare these answers to your answers from the "Readiness Check" at the beginning of this chapter. What gaps exist between the similar questions? How might these gaps between what you thought before starting the chapter and what you now think after completing the chapter affect how you approach the next chapter in this book?

Developing Information Literacy, Writing, and Speaking Skills

CHAPTER 5

YOU'RE ABOUT TO DISCOVER...

- HOW TECHNOLOGY IMPACTS OUR LIVES
- HOW E-LEARNING (ONLINE) IS DIFFERENT FROM C-LEARNING (CLASSROOM)
- HOW TO CULTIVATE YOUR RESEARCH AND INFORMATION LITERACY SKILLS
- HOW TO BEST PRESENT RESEARCH THROUGH WRITING AND SPEAKING
- WHAT PLAGIARISM IS AND HOW TO AVOID IT

READINESS ✓ What do you KNOW?

Before beginning to read this chapter, take two minutes to answer the following questions on a scale of 1 to 10. Your answers will help you assess how ready you are to focus.

low 1 2 3 4 5 6 7 8 9 10 high

How much do you *already* know?

Based on reading the "You're about to discover . . ." list and skimming this chapter, how much do you think you probably already know about this chapter's subject? ________

See if you can answer these questions about information literacy, writing, and speaking skills *before* you read.

1. How would you define research? What steps are involved?
2. What is information literacy?
3. Identify the three stages involved in the writing process.

How much do you expect to learn?

In general, how motivated are you to learn more by reading this chapter? ________

How much do you think this information might affect your success overall? ________

How much energy do you plan to put into reading this chapter? ________

How ready are you to read *now*?

How ready are you to focus on this chapter?

Physically ________

Intellectually ________

Emotionally ________

Enter a number for each aspect of your readiness to focus. ________

If any of your answers is below a 10, pay attention to whatever is distracting you before you start reading. Then zero in and focus.

How long do you think it will take you to complete this chapter from start to finish?

________ Hour(s) ________ Minutes

Now, as you begin, do you intend to finish reading this chapter?

________ yes ________ no ________ maybe

© Larry Harwood Photography. Property of Cengage Learning

FOCUS Challenge Case

CLM/Shutterstock.com

Dario Jones

Ever since grade school, Dario Jones had been called a geek. It was a label he hated, but, honestly, most people probably thought of him that way. As a kid, Dario lived for computer games. He played them nearly every waking hour. In the morning, he'd shower in record time, throw on whatever clean clothes he could find, and use any spare minutes for computer games. When he got home, he'd log right back on again. His Dad tried threatening him: "You'll lose your eyesight and flunk out of school."

Once he faked a sore throat and played World of Warcraft at home for a week, while his parents were at work. As he got older, his Dad warned: "You'll never get a date." But Dario wasn't worried. Second Life relationships were enough. Real-life relationships were too much trouble. His cyber life was much more exciting than his real life. Dario spent more time—even sacrificing precious hours of sleep—surfing the Internet, envisioning how he could improve websites, and grooming his Facebook page than he spent talking to any living being. So Dario graduated from a technical high school and got a job immediately as a tech support specialist. "No degree required," the ad had said.

Cengage Learning

But a few months down the road the obvious truth dawned on him. Why was he wasting his time in a dead-end job? The world of computer glitches didn't really interest him. The world of web design did. But somehow after high school, he hadn't thought about it much and went to work for the first company that offered him a job.

Eventually, Dario made a decision. He needed to change his life. He drove to the college campus across town and parked in the parking lot. He sat in his car for a while, and then bit the bullet, walked through the door, and talked with someone. As it

Copyright © Mike Margol / Photo Edit

Luciana Bueno/Shutterstock.com

turned out, that was the last official day to enroll for the semester. So with the help of a friendly advisor, who took him to the Financial Aid office and helped him fill out the application, Dario was in college. He'd have to increase his hours at work to afford tuition, but he thought it would be worth it.

But Dario quickly discovered that *talking* on the phone with customers about computers and *studying* computers were two very different things. Right off the bat, he discovered that Introduction to Computer Science required a research paper with an accompanying oral presentation, which, he had to admit, freaked him out. The assigned topic was Globalization and Internet Commerce. Even though he had always considered himself to be a technology expert, frankly, he didn't know where to start. *Step one*, Dario thought to himself, *is to Google*. He always Googled everything: the directions to a new Mexican restaurant—his favorite food—or some little-known fact that he wondered about, like how many Chihuahuas were sold in the United States last year. (He had just bought one.) But when he Googled "Internet Commerce," he got 22 million hits. *Better regroup*, he advised himself.

But how? Should he go to the library on campus, or try to do his research online in the comfort of his own apartment? Physically going to the library seemed unnecessary when so much information was available online. Then he had a flash of inspiration: Wikipedia. He found a page on "Electronic Commerce." At least that was a start—that is, until he looked at his instructor's handout on the assignment. Students were discouraged from using Wikipedia as a primary research source. The handout said "Information literacy is required." He got another idea: He'd close Wikipedia and go back to Googling. This time he'd try "Electronic Commerce." *Ah, only 7 million hits this time*. He was on a roll. He plugged in "E-Commerce," "E-Business," and "Globalization." He tried "Global Issues," but before he knew it, he found himself knee-deep in articles about global warming. He was so far afield now that he couldn't find his way back to his topic. Should he shut everything down and start over or just give up?

Dario's paper was due the following day. At the last minute, he panicked. He found a few useful things online, and in the interest of time, he cut and pasted from the Internet until he'd filled ten pages. At least he had something to turn in. He wondered if this was the way to do research and whether he'd broken any rules. *Well, at least there will always be computer glitches*, he thought pessimistically. But to be honest, a career solving other people's technical problems wasn't at all what he wanted to do with his life.

Yuri Samsonov/Shutterstock.com

John Coudriet/Shutterstock.com

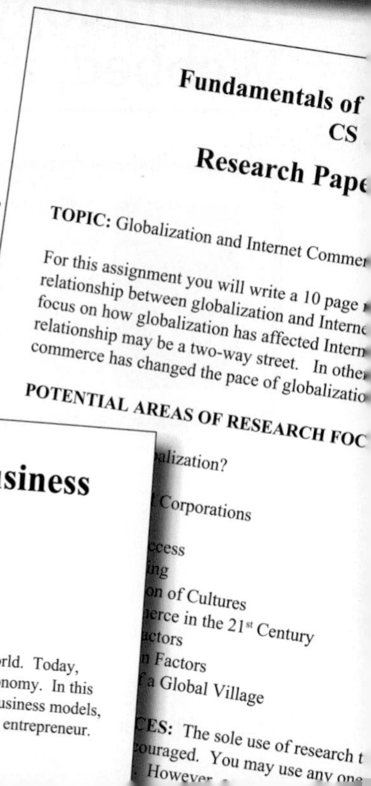

© Cengage Learning

© Cengage Learning

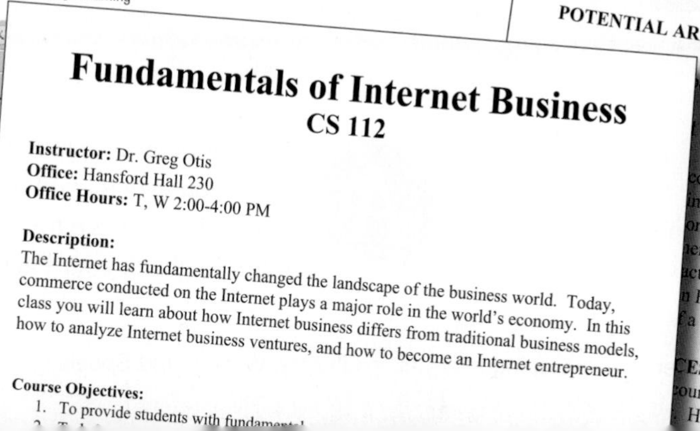

What Do You Think?

1. The instructor's assignment required "information literacy." What is information literacy? Dario is tech-savvy, but does he have the right skills? Why or why not?
2. What mistakes does Dario make in researching his paper?
3. Did Dario plagiarize his paper—or did he simply find the sources he needed and use them? Give the reasons behind your answer.
4. Dario is not only having trouble researching his paper, but he's also worried about his upcoming presentation. What can be done to overcome speaking anxiety?

VARK It!

Complete the recommended activity for your preferred VARK learning modality. If you are multimodal, select more than one activity. Your instructor may ask you to (a) give an oral report on your results in class, (b) send your results to him or her via e-mail, (c) post them online, or (d) contribute to a class chat.

Visual: As you read, highlight things you'll do for a current paper or speech you're working on right now. If you don't have a current speaking or writing assignment, propose one you'd expect in a course you might take next term, and do the same.

Aural: At some point while you're reading this chapter, interview a reference librarian on campus to get his or her take on the most common mistakes first-year students make while conducting research. See if your librarian's items match those listed by the reference librarian cited in this chapter.

Read/Write: As you read, watch for an information-rich paragraph that you relate to in this chapter, and practice closing your book and paraphrasing the paragraph in your own words. Paraphrasing is an important skill to cultivate as you learn to do academic research.

Kinesthetic: Before you read further, find a "Ted Talk" (at www.ted.com) that fascinates you by clicking on the subject of technology on the ted.com website. Email the link to your instructor or show it in class with permission. In your view, how effective is the video presentation, based on the speaking guidelines presented in this chapter?

iStockphoto.com/Marcela Barsse/MarsBars; Joanna Goodyear/Dreamstime.com; iStockphoto.com/Nadezda Firsova; iStockphoto.com/Pascal Genest

Technology Skills: Wireless, Windowed, Webbed, and Wikied

Challenge: In what ways does technology improve our lives, and in what ways does it complicate it? See if you can identify three of each.

Reaction:

____

____

Ah, technology . . . Does it make our lives simpler or more complicated? Have you ever stayed up until the wee, small hours playing an online game? Do you live to text? Do you run, not walk, to any nearby computer to check your Facebook account? Or, on the other hand, do you ever get annoyed because your cell phone is going off continuously—sometimes at the most inopportune moments, like when you can't get to it?

Many of us have a love-hate relationship with technology: We love the convenience but hate the dependence. But in college, information literacy and technology skills will be other keys to your academic success. You'll need to know things like how to use Microsoft Word with agility to produce a polished essay, how to design an information-rich and visually compelling PowerPoint presentation, and how to use one or more of the many course management systems available like Blackboard. You don't have to be a technology guru, but you will need to call upon your technology skills to conduct research for your college classes. Many college students are tech savvy, but their skills are more about entertainment than education. In fact, a recent study suggests that many students actually overestimate their technology skills when it comes to using software that is often related to class assignments.[1]

HMM . . . ARE MINE???

Use Technology to Your Academic Advantage

? challenge

Challenge: How will technology help you in your college coursework? List three ways that you've already experienced or expect to experience.

" reaction

Reaction: ______________________________

____

When you first arrive on campus or even before, you'll see evidence of technology everywhere. Your school may send out regular updates about campus events on Twitter. You may be asked to respond to an on-screen quiz in class by using your cell phone. You'll get an e-mail account and be sent official college documents, like your tuition bill and weather alerts. You will take entire courses or parts of courses online so that you can learn on your own time at your own pace. Many of your instructors will use course management systems, streaming video, and websites in the classroom to increase your learning. Soon, experts say, you will be able to access your course materials via your mobile device from anywhere, direct your computer's operations using hand gestures, and read books *with* other people as a social activity.[2] In fact, these trends are already emerging, and undoubtedly technology will become an even more highly integrated part of learning in the future.

What academic benefits does technology provide?[3] Let's look at some examples of the advantages technology will offer you in college. Technology will help you:

- **Manage your courses.** Many of your college classes will be conducted partially or wholly online, using technology shells, like Blackboard, eCollege, Moodle, Desire2Learn, or eCompanion. Course management systems help you easily track your grades, access syllabi, and upload assignments, for example, all from one place. About two-thirds of college students use them in their classes.[4]

WEB 2.0 IS MY LIFE!

- **Interact with course content, classmates, and your instructor.** You may have heard the term "Web 2.0." It's not a new version of the Internet. It refers to creative uses of it, like Facebook, Wikis, and blogs, where instead of just reading passively, users help create the content. For example, your instructor may post a question or comment and ask you to post your responses online and to respond to those of your classmates. Everyone can get to know you by your online personality, and some students say they become better writers by reading other students' responses to their blogs (Web logs). You may watch a YouTube clip in class, insert one into a presentation you create as a class assignment, or post one yourself related to your life as a student. Or you may be asked to contribute to a Wiki, today's online, editable encyclopedia. Anyone can add information or change content (currently there are more than 17 million articles in more than two hundred and seventy languages on the most extensive of these sites[5]). In addition to these Web 2.0 possibilities, you will undoubtedly use e-mail, Facebook your classmates, and listen to podcasts, if your professor posts an audio version of her lecture. Typically, aural learners enjoy podcasts and kinesthetic learners enjoy the interactivity of Web 2.0.
- **Complete assignments.** Your college classes will ask you to use at least three types of software in your academic work:
  - Microsoft Word allows you to type, edit, alphabetize, index, footnote, and do many other things to prepare papers for your classes.
  - Microsoft PowerPoint, used as an electronic visual aid for oral presentations, allows you to create an on-screen guide for your listeners (and you, if you glance periodically and subtly for clues).
  - Microsoft Excel spreadsheets are good for tabulating, record keeping, and organizing.

  The industry standard for these applications is generally the Microsoft products listed here, although other possibilities exist. If you need help learning any of these applications, your campus techies, instructors, or online tutorials (which can easily be found by Googling) can help. If you're a techie yourself, you can venture into other software applications like Flash, Camtasia, iMovie, or Adobe Acrobat to make your academic work look even more professional.
- **Increase your learning.** You may also find yourself using textbook websites, like the one you're using for *FOCUS on College Success.* Often these websites are tied closely to they textbook you're using in class, and they contain information and activities to enrich your learning experience, like videos, quizzes, and iAudio chapter summaries. Use these resources to help you master course material.

One final point: while our focus here has been on using technology to your academic *advantage*, it can also put you at a *disadvantage*, if you let it. If you bring your laptop to class to take notes, but actually spend your time surfing online instead, you'll miss out on what's going on. If you don't finish your assignments because Facebook takes up all your free time, your grades will show it. A word to the wise: Excess technology or "misplaced" technology can lead to academic self-sabotage.

EXERCISE 5.1

How Tech Savvy Are You?

Many college students spend hours on the Internet downloading their favorite tunes and uploading their favorite photos. They think they know technology. But do they? Here's an important question: What kinds of computer skills will help you excel in college and what kind of skills are employers looking for? Look at the lists below. Which of the following tasks can you perform *right now* (without clicking on "help" or Googling)? These software applications are considered to be the "industry standard" used in most organizations.

	Basic	Moderate	Advanced
MS Word	____ open a document ____ bold text ____ cut and paste ____ undo and redo ____ change the page orientation	____ count words ____ highlight text ____ insert page numbers ____ justify a paragraph ____ add bullets	____ alphabetize lists ____ create footnotes ____ use Autocorrect ____ record/run macros ____ merge documents
MS PowerPoint	____ create slides ____ delete slides ____ insert images ____ choose a design template ____ add new slides	____ animate slides ____ change background colors ____ add transitions between slides ____ create and run a slide show ____ print slides, handouts, and outlines	____ merge slides from another slideshow ____ insert hyperlinks ____ edit hyperlinks ____ change animation timing ____ change animation order
MS Excel	____ create spreadsheets ____ move data around ____ make calculations ____ create a chart ____ copy/merge cells	____ use the SUM function to create formulas ____ use the fill handle to copy a cell ____ use a VBA macro ____ freeze panes ____ format cells, rows, and columns	____ create formulas using the IF function ____ use absolute references ____ use Excel as a database ____ use VLOOKUP ____ use PivotTables

In one recent study, college students overestimated their software skill levels, particularly on Word and Excel. Although they perceived their skills as average or high, when tested, their performance didn't measure up. Computer literacy is a critical job requirement. If you're surprised by how few checkmarks you were able to make above, now is the right time to gear up! Take an online tutorial, sign up for a workshop on campus, or enroll in a computer literacy class. Not only will you be able to apply your skills to all your classes, but you'll be ramping up for the job waiting for you in the world of work.[6]

I THOUGHT I'D HAVE MORE CHECKMARKS ON THIS.
I'M GOING TO ACTUALLY TRY DOING SOME OF THESE.

The Internet: The Good, the Bad, and the Ugly

The Good

For many of us, the Internet is how we get our news, our research, our entertainment, and our communication. When it comes to all the potential benefits of the Internet, think about advantages like these:

- **Currency.** While some of the information posted on the Internet is outdated, much of it is up-to-the-minute. Reports, articles, and studies that might take months to publish in books or articles are available on the Web as soon as they're written. The Internet keeps us current.

HADN'T THOUGHT ABOUT THESE SPECIFIC FEATURES.

- **Availability.** The Internet never sleeps. If you can't sleep at 2:00 a.m., the Internet can keep you company. Unlike your real instructor who teaches other classes besides yours and attends marathon meetings, Professor Google is always in. For the most part, you can check your e-mail or log onto the Internet from anywhere, any time.
- **Scope.** You can find out virtually anything you want to know on the Internet from the recipe for the world's best chocolate chip cookie to medical advice on everything from **A**thlete's Foot to **Z**its. (Of course, real human beings are usually a better option for serious questions.)
- **Interactivity.** Unlike other media, the Internet lets you talk back—instantly and constantly. You can add to your Facebook page daily or edit a Wikipedia entry whenever you like.
- **Affordability.** As of March 2011, there were 2,095,006,005 online Internet users worldwide; 245 million Americans are online today.[7] For most, when it comes to the Internet, the price is right. After you buy a computer, and pay a monthly access fee, you get a great deal for your money.

The Bad

Too much of a good thing can be bad. When anything becomes that central to our lives, it carries risks like the following:

- **Inaccuracy.** Often we take information presented to us at face value, without questioning it. But on many Internet sites, the responsibility for checking the accuracy of the information presented there is yours. Bob's Statistics Home Page and the U.S. Census Bureau's website are not equally valid. Not everything published online is true or right.
- **Laziness.** It's easy to allow the convenience of the Internet to make us lazy. Why go through the hassle of cooking dinner when you can just stop for a burger on the way home? The same thing applies to the Internet. Why bother doing hours of library research on the topic for your paper when others have already been there, done that, and published it on the Internet? And today's global online "paper mills" make it easy to plug in your credit card number and buy your paper online, perhaps one even authored by someone on the other side of the globe![8] For one thing, if you don't give the rightful author credit, that's plagiarism, which can give you a zero on an assignment, or even cause you to fail a course. But another thing worth considering is that the *how* of learning is as important as the *what*. If all you ever did was cut, paste, and download, you wouldn't learn how to do research yourself. You may never have to give your boss a five-page paper on the poetry of Wordsworth—but you may need to write a five-page report on your customers' buying trends over the last six months. No one's researched that particular topic before. Your job *now* is to develop your skills so that you can do it *then*.

Teo Lannie/Getty Images

"**For a list of all the ways technology has failed to improve the quality of life, please press three.**"

Alice Kahn, technology author

BOX 5.1 Netiquette: Online Manners Matter

Professionalism is important in college, and it doesn't just apply to how you act in class, like getting there on time or turning in your assignments when they're due. Online communication like e-mail has netiquette (or network etiquette) rules like these:

1. **Don't send a message you don't want to risk being forwarded to someone else.** Once you send a message, you can't take it back, and it may reappear in a very awkward place!
2. **Don't hit the "send" key until you've given yourself time to cool off, if you're upset.** You may want to edit what you've written into a more humane, more polite version of the same message.
3. **Don't forward chain e-mails.** At the very least, they're a nuisance, and sometimes, they're illegal.
4. **Don't do business over your school e-mail account.** Sending all 500 new students in your residence hall an invitation to your family's restaurant grand opening is off-limits. Besides, sending messages to lots of people at once is called "spam," and doing so might even cause your school's e-mail server to crash.
5. **Don't spread hoaxes about viruses or false threats.** You can get into big trouble for that.
6. **Don't type in all CAPS.** That's called SHOUTING, and it makes you look angry.
7. **Don't be too casual.** Use good grammar and correct spelling. Your instructors consider e-mails to be academic writing, and they'll expect professionalism from you.
8. **Don't forget important details.** Include everything the reader needs to know. For example, if you're writing to an instructor, give your full name and the name of the course you're writing about. Professors teach more than one class and have many students. And remember to use your "official" school e-mail address, rather than your personal one. (Or set up your personal account to forward all your school e-mail automatically.) Your instructor and institution will most likely use your school e-mail account to communicate "officially" with you. With so many types of different e-mail systems out there (gmail, hotmail, yahoo, etc.), that's the best option.
9. **Don't hit the "Reply to All" key, when you mean to hit the "Reply" key.** Many e-mail message writers have been horrified upon learning that hundreds or thousands of people have read something personal or cranky that was meant for just one reader.
10. **Don't forget to fill in the subject line.** That gives readers a chance to preview your message and decide how soon they need to get to it.

- **Overdependence.** A related problem with anything that's easy and convenient is that we can start depending on it too much. National studies report that many of us lack basic knowledge. We can't name the Chief Justices of the Supreme Court or the President of Pakistan. Are we so dependent on the Internet that we're relying on it for information we should learn or know?[9] Using the Internet as your sole source of information can lure you into surface, rather than deep learning. When information is reduced to screen shots, soundbites, and video clips, it's easy to become an information "nibbler," someone who takes nothing but quick "bytes." Many questions don't have quick answers, and many problems don't have simple solutions.[10]

The Ugly

The Internet can be used in foul ways. Spam, viruses, spyware, and phishing cost American consumers billions of dollars in damage, affecting 40 percent of U.S. households.[11] The global personal publishing trend has had unintended, sometimes negative, consequences as well. "If you have ever written a blog entry, posted a comment or reply on a website, uploaded a video to YouTube, posted a picture to Facebook, or uploaded an audio podcast to a website, you've

EXERCISE 5.2

How *Not* to Win Friends and Influence People Online

All five of these e-mail messages from students violate the rules of netiquette. See if you can identify the rule number from Box 5.1 that's been violated in each case.

UGH—MY EMAILS ARE JUST LIKE HERS!

From Matt Rule: ____

Professor X,

I just looked at the online syllabus for Academic Success 101. Why didn't you tell us that our first paper is due on Monday? I will be very busy moving into a new apartment this weekend. Writing an essay for your class is the last thing I want to have to think about.

From Tiffany Rule: ____

Prof X,

i didn't know u were makin us write a paper over the weekend. i won't be able to do it. i hop you don't mind.

From Xavier Rule: ____

PROFESSOR X,

I CAN'T GET MY PAPER DONE BY MONDAY. LET ME KNOW WHAT I SHOULD DO.

From hotchick13@email.com Rule: ____

Prof X

I don't know where to start on the paper you assigned. Can you send me some advice?

From Dameon Rule: ____

Hey, Section 3

Can you believe our instructor? She assigns a big writing assignment after only one day of class! Who in their right mind would be remotely interested in sitting in their crummy little room writing a bunch of meaningless junk, when we haven't even learned anything yet? What kind of teacher are we stuck with here? Somebody out there respond to me, OK? I'm totally hacked off!

As a class, discuss your responses and see if you all agree on which rules were broken in the five examples provided.

participated in personal publishing."[12] Are you making good decisions or potentially harmful ones? Think about these potential dangers:

Social Networking Take a look at one student's social networking page in Figure 5.1 and see if you can guess where things are headed. Like the hypothetical Victoria Tymmyns (or her online name, VicTym) featured there, some students publish inappropriate, confidential, and potentially dangerous information on their Facebook pages. Victoria has posted her address, phone numbers, and moment-by-moment location. Look at the final entries on her page to find out what potential threat she may be facing. Aside from the risk of serious harm, other types of "danger" can result from bad judgment, too. What some students post just for fun on a social networking site can later cost them a job opportunity. If your webpage has provocative photos of you or descriptions of rowdy weekend activities that you wouldn't want your grandmother to see, remove them! (Employers regularly check these sources for insider information on applicants.) "Living out loud," as social networking is sometimes called, requires constant vigilance so that the details of your life aren't on display. Some recent research indicates that younger users

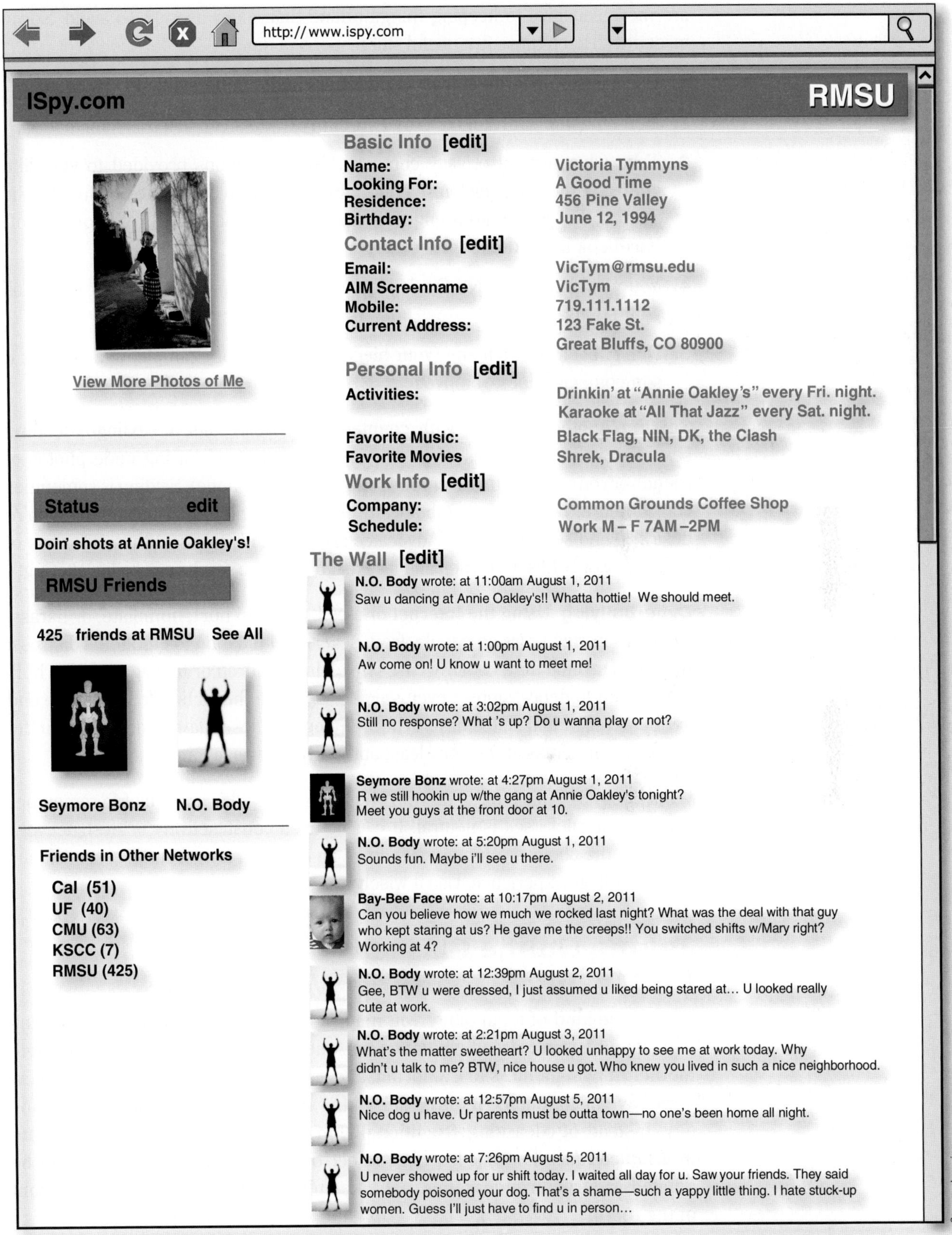

WHOA! MAYBE I SHOULDN'T POST WHAT I'M DOING ALL THE TIME.

FIGURE 5.1

Fictional Ispy.com page

Companion, M. (2006). Victoria Tymmyns Ispy.com. Used with permission.

are more sensitive to keeping things offline than older users.[13] To avoid "social insecurity," keep these five useful suggestions in mind:

1. Use a password with at least eight letters and numbers, like FO34$&CuS.
2. Don't include your full birth date. Identity thieves can use this information.
3. Take advantage of privacy controls. Use the options provided to you, like choosing the "Friends Only" option. Be sure not to check the box for "Public Search Results." Search engines can find your Facebook profile on and off Facebook if you do.
4. You wouldn't put a "No One's Home" sign on your door, so don't post it as your status.
5. Don't post a child's name (your niece or nephew, for example) in a caption. If someone else does, remove it.[14]

Sexting Another example with counterproductive results is sexting—sending sexually explicit messages or posting nude photos (and having nude photos of friends or romantic partners on your computer or cell phone). Sexting is sometimes considered to be a status symbol—an "electronic hickey" that means that you're desirable and sexually active. Advocates argue that it's safe sex: there's no risk of pregnancy or S.T.I's. But when and if sexts go viral, the results can be life-altering![15]

Cyberbullying Using the Internet or a cell phone to hurt, humiliate, or harass, can leave lasting scars on people, from severe intimidation to emotional distress. In some extreme, newsworthy cases involving children or teenagers, cyberbullying has led to depression or even suicide. If you're the victim, tell someone and get help. Individual states have cyberbullying policies or laws, and these hurtful behaviors are crass at the very least and perhaps even against the law.[16]

What does all of this have to do with you? Everything! It's important to remember that the Internet itself is neutral. It can be used constructively or destructively, based on the choices you make. It can be an exciting, invigorating, essential part of your college experience. Use it wisely!

Taking Online Classes: Strategies for Making E-Learning Work for You

Here's one kind of technology you may well run into during your time in college, if you haven't already. What do an American soldier in Germany, a single mother of twin toddlers in California, and a student with cerebral palsy in New York have in common? All three are taking the same online course in psychology. Instead of c-learning (traditionally, in the classroom), they're engaging in *distance education* or e-learning (electronically, online). E-learning can be defined as structured learning that takes place without a teacher at the front of the room.

Many of your college courses are hybrids or blended courses with an online component *and* a classroom component. But chances are you'll be engaged in distance learning in a totally online environment for at least one of your college classes. Distance education is gaining momentum fast and the demand for these courses hasn't peaked yet.[17] "Distance education is

THIS COULD TOTALLY BE ME!

CURIOSITY: *ARE YOU CAUGHT IN THE NET?*

It's noon. You decide to check your online life while you chow down a giant burrito. Five new requests from potential Facebook friends. *Who are these people?* you wonder. After a bit of browsing, you decide to update your photo albums by uploading several shots from your weekend adventures. Then you notice an amazing item on eBay that you've been looking for, and a bidding war is underway. You decide to join in, and you cast the winning bid. *Man, how am I going to pay for that?* you wonder. The clock ticks away. You order a new pair of shoes from your favorite website, and then check your watch. It's already 4:30. Four and a half hours have just gone by, and your chem class has already started!

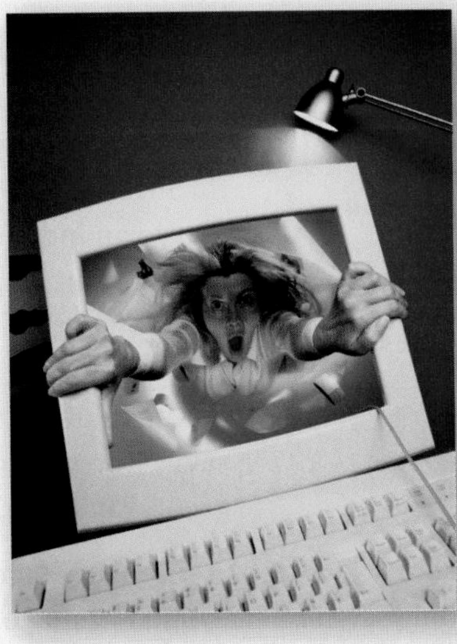

James Cotier/Getty Images

Does this scenario sound uncomfortably familiar? A few minutes start a chain reaction that stretches out for several hours. You hate to admit it, but you're caught in the Net, spending so much time on the Internet that you're neglecting other areas of your life. Just why is the Internet so addicting? Is it the novelty of things like Facebook or eBay? Is it because it allows us to do so much without moving from one spot? Is it because our real lives seem less interesting than the online potential? One addict confessed, "Sometimes I'll sign-off Facebook and just stare at the login screen like a cocaine addict looking at the edge of his coffee table, thinking to myself, 'Well, I've really got nothing better to do right now,' and then I sign right back on. That's when you know you're really addicted."[18]

Are *you* addicted? Ask yourself these questions: Do you obsess about your online life and get nervous if you haven't checked your e-mail or Facebook account for a while? Do you spend more time with your online friends than your real friends? Do you interrupt yourself constantly to check your e-mail or update your online profile while doing Internet research for your class projects? If the answers to the questions in this paragraph are yes, are *you* ready to consider that you may be overly dependent on the Internet?[19]

Don't get caught in the Net. Think about the impact it could have on your college success. Try these suggestions:

1. **Monitor your time online.** Estimate right now how much time you spend online per week. Then actually time yourself. Is your estimate accurate? Or are you way off base? Give yourself a hard-and-fast time limit, and stick to it. Being online tends to distort time. You may think you've only been on for an hour, when three hours have actually gone by. Set an old-fashioned timer, and when it goes off, get up and do something else.
2. **Separate work and play online.** It's easy to find yourself on a fun-seeking detour when you're supposed to be working on a research paper. When work and play are combined, it's easy to lose track of what's what. You end up wasting time because it feels as if you're doing something productive when you really aren't. Facebook, for example, can be a big temptation. Although it's not a clear case of cause and effect, a pilot study found that students who spend more time on Facebook spend less time studying and earn lower grades. However, 79 percent of these same students didn't believe that Facebook impacted their studies.[20]
3. **Take a tech vacation.** Without getting freaked out, think about this option: Turn off your computer, cell phone, or other mobile device for a day, and then extend the time to a week or more. Use a computer lab on campus to do your assignments, rather than tempting yourself to spend hours online at home. Train yourself to withdraw, little by little. Being tied to a electronic device can easily overtake your life. Why disengage from face to face communication to interface with the cyberworld when real-life friends or family members are sitting right beside you or across the table?[21]
4. **Get a life.** Take up yoga, chess, or swimming. Make some new friends, start a relationship, or join a club on campus. Your real life might actually become more interesting.
5. **Talk to people who care about you—a family member or a counselor on campus.** Recognizing the problem and admitting it are the first steps. Being one-sided isn't healthy. There are experts and support groups available to help you deal with your problem and make your real life more fulfilling.[22]

Digital Vision/Jupiter Images

> Any occurrence requiring undivided attention will be accompanied by a compelling distraction.
>
> *Robert Bloch, American fiction writer, (1917–1994)*

becoming a staple of college life."[23] Institutions offer online courses, not only because their convenience makes them popular with some students, but because they save on resources, like classroom space. Your instructors and advisors can help you determine if e-learning is right for you. But keep in mind that some first-year students procrastinate their way through online courses—to their own detriment. If you're an independent, self-motivated learner, online courses can be great, because *you* are in control. On the flip side, however, you have to motivate yourself to actually take control of your own learning. But if you value the control factors below and are tech-savvy (or willing to learn), online classes can be a great way to go.[24] Consider these **benefits**:

- **You control when you learn.** Instead of that dreaded 8:00 a.m. class—the only section that's open when you register—you can schedule your e-learning when it's convenient for you. If you want to do your coursework at midnight in your pajamas, who's to know?
- **You control how you learn.** If you are an introvert, e-learning may work well for you. You can work thoughtfully online and take all the time you need to reflect. If you are an extravert, however, you may become frustrated by the lack of warm bodies around. Jumping into threaded discussions and chatting online may satisfy some of those needs. If you're a kinesthetic learner, the keyboard action may suit you well. You can do whatever you need to do to accommodate your own learning style.
- **You control how fast you learn.** Students learn at different rates. With e-learning, you don't have to feel you're slowing down the class if you continue a line of questioning or worry about getting left in the dust if everyone else is way ahead of you.

E-learning can be a very effective way to learn, but it does require some adjustment. In fact, some research suggests that online learners, particularly those who aren't self-motivated, are more likely to give up and drop out of a course than classroom learners are.[25] Here are some **strategies** to help you make the best of your e-learning opportunities:

CAN'T THESE APPLY TO MY REGULAR COURSES, TOO? THEY SOUND LIKE GOOD IDEAS . . .

1. **Stay motivated and organized.** Instead of listening to your professor lecture at the front of the room, you will have to get information yourself by downloading files or listening to pre-recorded lectures. Just because you're learning

online and you like technology doesn't mean it's easier. Online courses can be highly challenging and actually require more work than face-to-face classes. They often require frequent upkeep. Rather than appearing one, two, or three times a week in a classroom, you may have to post a discussion response every day or every other day online. Over the course of the term, you may spend the same amount of time concentrating on the subject matter, but your time may be chunked differently. Online courses require discipline and focus; you must be intrinsically motivated.[26] Some students find that setting a regular, specific time to do online work is the best route to success.

2. **Communicate your needs to your professor.** Your professor won't be able to see your "huh?" looks when you don't understand something. Take direct action by e-mailing her, for example.
3. **Stay in touch with other students in the course.** Use e-mail to communicate with your cyber classmates to build an online learning community. They may be able to clarify an assignment or coach you through a tough spot.
4. **Keep your antivirus program up to date.** When you upload assignment files, you run the risk of infecting your professor's computer with whatever viruses your computer may have. Make sure your antivirus software is up to date!

I NEED TO DO THIS ASAP!

5. **Create a productive learning environment.** Since you'll most likely do your online coursework at home or in your residence hall room, make sure that environment is right for learning. If your computer is next to the TV, it may take superhuman self-control to stay focused on your online course. Do your work in a computer lab, or if you have a laptop, find a spot that's calm, well lit, and quiet.
6. **Use each login session as an opportunity to review.** Begin each online session by reviewing what you did or how much progress you made last time. Physically logging on can become a signal to take stock before moving forward with new course material.
7. **Call on your time management skills.** If your e-course is self-paced, you'll need to plan ahead, schedule due dates, and discipline yourself to make continual progress. If you're sharing a computer with other family members, create a master schedule. Remember that you may need to be online at particular times to engage in class chats or discussions.[27]
8. **Have a tech back-up plan.** If your Internet provider has a technical problem, that doesn't have to translate into an academic disaster for you. Make sure you have a backup solution—using a campus computer lab or a friend's computer, for example. And if you run into a real snag, don't be afraid to ask for help. Tech support experts on campus can save you hours of frustration, sometimes with a simple solution. Take advantage!

Research Skills and Your College Success

Many of your class assignments in college will require you to conduct research by using technology or by spending time in the real library on campus. Why? Aren't you in college to learn from your instructors? Why do they ask *you* to do research on your own?

There are unanswered questions all around us in everyday life. Some questions are simple; others are complex. How much time will it take to get across town to a doctor's appointment during rush hour? What can you expect college tuition to cost by the time your kids are old enough to go? What are the chances that someone you know who has cancer will survive for five years? Research isn't necessarily a mysterious thing that scientists in white coats do in laboratories. Research is simply finding answers to questions, either real questions you encounter every day or questions that are assigned to you in your classes. Doing research on your own can be a powerful way to learn, sometimes even more so than hearing answers from someone else, even if those people are your instructors. While going off to a research expedition in the actual, physical library on campus may sound like frustrating busywork, the skills you stand to gain are well worth the effort. And knowing how to do research online in today's world of Internet-based resources is vital!

Conducting research teaches you some important things about how to formulate a question and then find answers. And it's not just finding answers so that you can scratch a particular assignment off your to-do list. It's about learning an important process. When you get into the world of work, your instructors won't be there to supply answers, so knowing how to figure things out on your own will be key to your success. So, exactly what is college-level research?

NEVER THOUGHT ABOUT THIS . . .

What Research Is *Not*	What Research Is
Research isn't just going on a "search and employ" mission. It's not just seeing what all you can find and then using it to get an assignment out of the way.	**Research starts with a question.** If an assignment is broad, you must come up with a specific question to research yourself. More about that later.
Research isn't just moving things from Point A (the library) to Point B (your paper).	**Research is a process with a plan.** A plan is something many students lack. They jump in without a question—or a plan.
Research isn't random rummaging through real or virtual files to find out something.	**Research is goal-oriented.** You've formulated a question, developed a plan, and now you begin to find answers by using both online sources and ones that sit on your library's shelves.
Research isn't doing a quick Internet search. The cutting and pasting some students do to fill a paper's page requirements is actually plagiarism!	**Research often involves breaking a big question into several smaller ones.**[28]

Navigating the Library

Being "exiled" to the library to do research for a paper may seem like torture that can ruin a perfectly good weekend. But if you look at things differently, it can be a mind-expanding trip into places unknown. Beyond navigating the web to find research for your assignments, it's important to learn your way around the actual, physical space of the library on your campus. The library has many useful resources, including real, very knowledgeable librarians who are there to help you.

I SHOULD GET TO KNOW A LIBRARIAN ON CAMPUS SO I CAN GET HELP WITH MY PAPER!

Let's say, for example, that you are assigned a research paper for your English Composition class. The field is wide open; you may select any topic you wish. How should you proceed? Here are some of the resources your library offers and how you should use them when you're assigned a research project like this one:

- **Card catalog.** Explore your library's online catalog that lists all of the books available to you. Go to your college's website, and from there, you can find your way to your college library's home page. Click on the library's catalog button. You'll come up with a list of books. Let's say the first one has a call number of HF5415.1265W43, based on the Library of Congress classification system, which most college libraries use. (Some libraries, like your community's public library, may use the Dewey Decimal system. One advantage of the Library of Congress system is

BOX 5.2 The Top Five Research Mistakes First-Year Students Make: Advice from a Reference Librarian

Are you guilty of any of these common mistakes first-year students make?

1. **Selecting a topic that is too broad.** Students often start out with a very general topic, and sometimes have a hard time narrowing the focus. Trying to write a paper on "fossil fuels" sets you up for an impossible task. Entire books have been written on that subject. But if you begin to zero in on "the advantages (or disadvantages) of offshore drilling," you're going in the right direction. Figuring out which words to use in the search process can be tricky, too. If you're writing about sustainability, and you enter "green," you'll get everything from "lime, mint, olive, and avocado" (meaning shades of green, not foods) to "Kermit, the frog." Brainstorming different search words and noting the usable results is half the battle.
2. **Taking short cuts.** Major search engines are a great place to start, but don't stop there. Just using Google or Foxfire is the equivalent of academic "wimping out," like just grabbing something quick from a vending machine when there's so much more nutritious and satisfying food out there. Libraries purchase many different electronic databases that have a wealth of information: articles, books, and book chapters, for example. Learn how to use these specialized library databases and really mine them for information. Finding useful information takes time and patience!
3. **Devoting too little time.** Students frequently underestimate how long the research process will take. There are multiple steps required to doing thorough research. It's not a last-minute process, and procrastination isn't the answer. Even if you write like a pro, you can't complete a research paper in an hour or two. Just getting in materials you've ordered from another library can take several weeks.
4. **Not evaluating sources.** Many students don't look closely enough at the sources they find, and then they end up making poor choices or using the first items that come up in search results. Instead, as you scan your results, look for hints about authenticity and accuracy. Compare your findings with other authoritative sites. Note the domain extension (like .gov, for example). One hit may lead you to another, which leads you to yet another. Evaluate your search results and be selective about what you use. Not all sources are created equal; make sure your sources are credible ones that support your argument.
5. **Copying and pasting.** Students sometimes use someone else's work without correct and thorough documentation of the source, especially when time is running out. You can end up plagiarizing unintentionally just because you don't understand how to cite your sources. Or you may intentionally cut and paste to save yourself time and effort. But either way, you're putting your academic success at high risk.

The biggest mistake students make is not asking the reference librarian for help at the beginning of the research process! That's why librarians are there—to provide guidance and help with all of the above. Continue reading this chapter for more strategies on making the most of your research time.[29]

Marvy!/Corbis

> Finis origine pendet (The end depends on the beginning.)
>
> *Manlius, first century Roman poet*

2. **Who is my audience, and what do I want them to know or do?** You write differently for different audiences—for your composition class or for the school newspaper, for example. If you're writing for the school newspaper, you may aim for catchy phrasing, short sentences, and an intriguing title. Once you know who you're writing to or for, then you can ask: What do I want them to know? Am I trying to inform, persuade, or entertain them? You'll use your research differently, depending on your specific purpose.
3. **Have I done enough research?** If you've followed the guidelines provided so far in this chapter about research, it's now time to ask: Do I have enough support for my thesis? Have I gathered sufficient statistics, expert testimony, and examples to persuade my reader?
4. **Can I compose a strong thesis statement?** Your paper's thesis statement should be the specific argument you're making, summarized into one sentence, ideally. For example, for the scenario we've been using, your thesis may be something like: "In today's world, social media marketing works better than conventional methods for three reasons: visibility, speed, and cost." Formulating a strong thesis is half the battle.
5. **Set in-between target dates for the three stages of writing, even if your instructor doesn't.** Some instructors will ask to see your work at each stage of the writing project. If you try to print your paper at 9:50 a.m. for your 10 a.m. class, you can count on something going wrong, like your printer cartridge shriveling up or your hard drive plummeting to an untimely death. To beat the odds, schedule in-between deadlines for yourself for prewriting, writing, and rewriting to keep the project moving along.

Writing

Have you ever experienced writer's block, or nowadays, the "tyranny of the blank screen"? You sit down to write and suddenly go blank? Whatever you call it, you'll be relieved to know there are ways around it.

Some professional writers resort to strange, almost ritualistic strategies to get themselves going. Victor Hugo supposedly wrote in his study at the same time every day—naked! His valet was ordered to lock away all Hugo's clothes until he had finished each day's writing.[40] Apparently, the method worked—witness *Les Misérables.* But this technique may not be well received by your roommate or your family. Just write freely about whatever comes into your head, whether it's on target or not. But, how do you start? Take a look at these techniques for starting the writing process.

1. **Begin by writing what's on your mind.**

   I'm having trouble starting this paper because there's so much to talk about in terms of social media and marketing. All businesses want to grow, but there are different ways to do it. Why not just go with tried true marketing methods like making cold calls, sending flyers through bulk mail, or creating radio and TV ads? Today, thanks to social media, there are better ways. When visibility, speed, and cost are factors—and they usually are—you need to update your marketing strategies.

   Now stop and look at what you've written. Based on your "stream of consciousness," you now have the beginnings of a paper. You can talk about how new social media marketing techniques can work better for the three reasons you've identified, and you're on your way.

2. **Begin with the words, "The purpose of this paper is. . . ."** and finish the sentence. You may be surprised by what comes out of your fingertips.

3. **Work with a tutor in your campus Writing Center.** Sometimes talking through the assignment with someone else can help, particularly if that person is a writing expert. Or talk it through with your roommate or a family member.

4. **Change the audience.** If it helps, assume you're writing your paper to someone who sharply disagrees with you or to a middle school student who just asked you a question. Sometimes thinking about your audience—instead of the topic in the abstract—helps you zero in on the writing task.

5. **Play a role.** Imagine yourself as a nationally-known tech guru or a network newscaster deciding what to include on the evening news. Separate yourself from the task, and see it from another perspective.

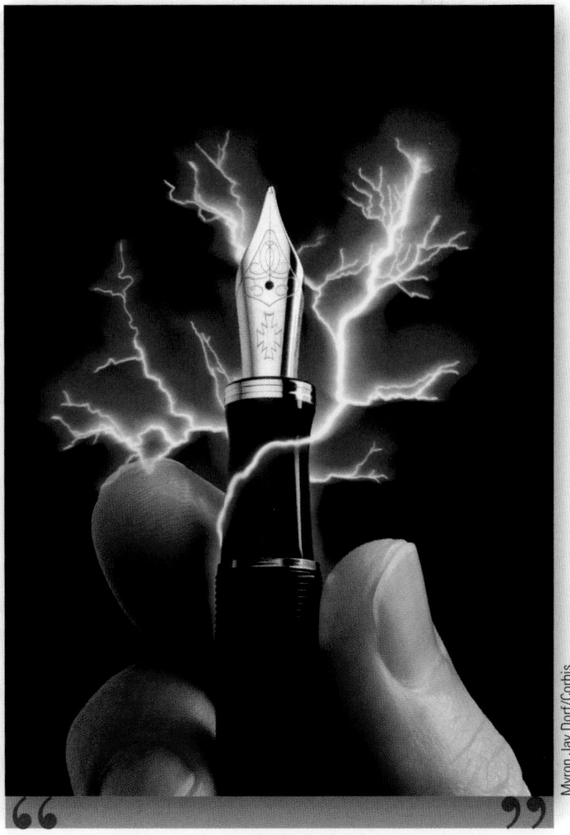

Myron Jay Dorf/Corbis

"I must write it all out, at any cost. Writing is thinking. It is more than living, for it is being conscious of living."

Anne Morrow Lindbergh, American writer and aviation pioneer (1906–2001)

Rewriting

Rewriting is often called "revision," and that's a powerful term. It means not merely changing, but literally re-seeing, re-en*vision*ing your work. Sometimes students think they're revising when they're actually just editing: tinkering with words and phrases, checking spelling, changing punctuation. But the word revision actually means more than that. It means making major organizational overhauls, if necessary. According to many writing experts, that's what you must be willing to do. You're on a search and destroy mission, if that's what it takes.[41] Try these suggestions for rewriting to see if they work for you:

1. **Leave it alone.** To help you see your paper as others will see it, set it aside for a while. If you can wait an hour,

EXERCISE 5.4

What's in an "A"?

Take a look at this first-year student's essay and offer the writer advice.

Assignment: Describe a problem you have faced as a first-year student and identify a possible solution.

> Last summer, I worked for a bank in my hometown to earn money for college. I was told to show up for the interview at 8:30 a.m. I usually don't get up that early, so on Thursday night, I set my alarm clock, my cell phone alarm, and my clock radio to make sure I didn't miss it. Afterward, I thought that I had really hit it off with the interviewer. When I first got the job on a Friday, I was thrilled. Imagine me working for a bank! I thought that sounded like a prestigious job. When I told my Dad about getting the job, he said that he thought banks really shouldn't hire young people because they don't know the value of money. I decided he was probably kidding around.
>
> But after my first week at Citizen's National Bank, I found myself bored stiff. Counting bills and tallying numbers really aren't that interesting. I did meet this girl named Nicole, and she was kind of cool, but everyone else at the bank was a little standoffish, including my supervisor, Ned. I didn't want to have a strained relationship with my supervisor, so I was friendly with him and serious about getting my work done. But by the following Wednesday, I was ready to quit. I heard about an opening at the coffee shop close to my house that included free food. So that's where I ended up. The moral of this story is to only take a job if you are really interested in the work. And I've definitely decided not to major in accounting.

What's the main problem with this essay? The writer has written about a problem she faced as a first-year student. The essay contains no grammatical errors. But is it likely to earn an "A"? Actually, the assignment calls for a problem-solution organizational pattern. Instead, it follows a chronological pattern (and then this happened, and then this . . .). What is the writer's thesis statement? Is it the next-to-the last sentence? *Only take a job if you are really interested in the work.* Instead of telling a story from start to finish, how would the essay change if the writer had asked a question like this: What mistakes do students make when looking for a job to help them pay for college? Then the writer could have organized the essay around the thesis statement (only take a job if you are really interested in the work) and found evidence, including her own experience, to back up the claim. Meeting the specific requirements of an assignment is the first step in earning a good grade.

Yes, many of us will be able to figure out what these sentences mean, though perhaps we'll need to check the dictionary. Sometimes beginning college students decide they must write to *impress* rather than to *express*. They assume instructors like this kind of convoluted writing. They think it sounds more academic. Instructors see through that guise. Mean what you say, and say what you mean.

2. **Be Complete.** Ask yourself what your reader needs to know. Sometimes we're so close to what we're writing that we leave out important information, or we fail to provide the background the reader needs to get our meaning. Put yourself in your reader's shoes.

3. **Be Correct.** If your writing is littered with grammatical, spelling, and punctuation errors, readers may generalize that you also don't know what you're writing about either. If grammar, punctuation, and usage aren't your strong points, ask someone you know who's a crackerjack writer to look over your first draft.

7 "C's"—INTERESTING WAY OF REMEMBERING HOW TO WRITE WELL!

4. **Be Concise.** In the past, you may have used tricks like enlarging the font or increasing the margins to fill an assigned number of pages. But college students sometimes face the opposite problem: they find that writing less

“ ”

Don't agonize. Organize.

Florynce Kennedy, American lawyer and African American activist

Hans Neleman/Corbis

is more challenging than writing more. Think of this formula: A given idea expressed in many words has relatively little impact. But that same idea expressed in few well-chosen and well-combined words can be penetrating. You could say:

> *"Whether or not a penny, or any amount of money, is earned or saved, it has the same or at least a similar value, fiscally speaking, in the long run."*

Compare that weak, wordy blather with this concise expression of Ben Franklin's:

> *"A penny saved is a penny earned."*

5. **Be Compelling.** Your writing should be interesting, active, and vivid, so that people want to read what you have to say. Compare these two headlines. Which article would you want to read?

   - *Protests against tuition increases have been led by student government.*
   - *SGA leaders urge campus-wide protests over tuition hikes.*

   The sentences create different images, don't they? The first sentence makes the situation sound like something that happens every day. The second sentence uses the active voice *(leaders urge campus-wide protests)* instead of the passive voice *(protests have been led),* and the second sentence uses a more descriptive verb *(urge* versus *lead)* and noun *(hikes* versus *increases).* Of course, you can go too far *(SGA leaders spearhead crushing student fury over radical tuition upsurge).* But this principle is a good one to remember.

6. **Be Courteous.** Courtesy is important in any kind of writing. E-mail is often one place where people are discourteous to one another in writing—perhaps because distance gives them courage or they're out of sorts. Having a meltdown on paper or your computer screen is rarely the right choice.

7. **Be Convincing.** You'll be a more successful writer if you support your views with solid evidence and credible testimonials. Give specific examples to illustrate your point—anecdotes, testimonials from experts, experiences, analogies, facts, statistics—and your writing will be more credible.

“ ”

I am returning this otherwise good typing paper to you because someone has printed gibberish all over it and put your name at the top.

English Professor, Ohio University

Keep these seven C's in mind. The secret to learning to think in college is to become a better writer. And as you're learning critical thinking skills, you'll also become a more clear, complete, correct, concise, compelling, courteous, and convincing writer.

BOX 5.3 Ten Ways to Oust Speaking Anxiety

High anxiety. It's the bane of many a speaker. Although doing your best on a writing assignment can certainly generate stress, giving a presentation is an even more personal, more immediate representation of you and your work. There you are, up front, doing your thing. If you can harness your anxiety and actually look forward to opportunities to speak, you'll build more confidence and get better at doing it. See if you think the items on this checklist of fear-suppressing suggestions might work for you.

1. **Ready, set, go.** Being unprepared will cause your anxiety to skyrocket, and winging it won't help your presentation fly! The best antidote to anxiety is to prepare, prepare, prepare!
2. **Dress for success.** Confidence in your physical appearance can increase your confidence overall. Looking good isn't everything, but it helps.
3. **Ease the tension with humor.** Humor can ease tensions, both for your audience and for you. Say something funny that occurs to you at the moment, rather than repeating a joke you read on the Internet.
4. **Don't be a mannequin.** Move around. Use gestures. Look at your audience. Talk as if you were conversing with each individual in the room alone. Be real, be yourself, and you'll feel more confident. Let your personality shine through.
5. **Practice in your presentation room.** Doing so can help put you at ease during your actual speech.
6. **Find some guinea pigs.** When you practice your presentation, do it in front of a live audience to prepare yourself for natural distractions, like people coughing or sneezing. Practice in front of your roommate or your family. Research indicates your grade is likely to go up.[45]
7. **Channel your energy.** Harness your fear, and turn it into positive energy that increases your dynamism.
8. **Visualize success.** When you see yourself giving your presentation in your mind's eye, visualize success, not failure.
9. **Remember that mistakes are made to be corrected.** If disaster strikes, remember that how you handle it is what's important. Perhaps you fear making a "tip of the slung." Don't worry; instead, make the most of a few moments of lightheartedness!
10. **If you can't shake it, fake it.** If your nerves get the better of you, fake it. Pretend you're confident. You assume the role, and before you know it, your confidence begins to rise.

In a Manner of Speaking . . .

Instead of using your research for a paper, your assignment may ask you to use it for a presentation. Your public speaking skills will be on the line. You may be thinking something like this: *I'm not going to be a public speaker. I'm going to be a surgeon. I'll spend all my time hunched over an unconscious person lying on an operating table. All I'll need to know how to do is hold a scalpel with a steady hand.* But is that really true? What about the communicating you'll need to do with totally conscious hospital administrators, other physicians, and patients before and after surgery?

Most people think of public speaking as an episode, a one-time event. You stand up to give a speech, and when you're finished, you sit down. But actually, there's a sense in which all the speaking we do is public. By contrast, what would *private* speaking be? Thinking? On the job, you'll communicate with others every day. Unless you join a profession that requires you to take a vow of silence, you'll be speaking publicly all the time!

Craft a Winning Presentation: The Seven P's

? challenge

" reaction

Challenge: Without looking further in this section, can you identify seven useful key points, all beginning with P, that relate to presentations? When preparing a presentation, it's important to think about 1) purpose, etc.

Reaction:

1. ______________________

2. ______________________

3. ______________________

4. ______________________

5. ______________________

6. ______________________

7. ______________________

When you prepare for a presentation in one of your classes, what is your primary goal? To impress your instructor? To amaze your classmates? To get your presentation over with?

Many of the suggestions about using your research in this chapter apply to both writing and speaking. As both a writer and a speaker, you should be clear, complete, correct, concise, compelling, courteous, and convincing. You should choose an organizational pattern and use it to help your audience understand what you're saying. (Unlike reading a written paper, they only have one chance to hear your words go by.) You must have a strong thesis in a speech, just as you must in a paper. But let's examine some other advice that relates primarily to speaking. Use these suggestions to create winning presentations that set you apart in all your courses.[46]

1. **Purpose.** What is the purpose of your presentation? Often the purpose is given to you directly by your instructor: Prepare a five-minute speech *to inform*. . . . But other assignments will allow you to select your own purpose: "The Trials and Tribulations of a Commuting Student" (to inform), "Sustainability in an Age of Materialism" (to persuade), "Five Sure-Fire Ways to Flunk Out of College . . . Not!" (to entertain), "How Being President of the Student Body Can Change Your Life" (to inspire). Knowing exactly what you're trying to accomplish helps!

2. **People.** Who will be your listeners? Generally, you'll be speaking to an audience of students in your classes, right? But what are their specific characteristics as they relate to your purpose? For example, if you're addressing parents and friends at commencement, you might create a different speech than the one you'd present to your co-members of a student club on campus.

3. **Place.** Where will you deliver your presentation? The location of your presentation may affect its tone and style. A presentation you might give to a group of tourists at a national park would allow for informality, and your visual aid would be the scenery around you. But if you gave the same presentation as a geography major to high school seniors, you'd be

> **The trouble with talking too fast is you may say something you haven't thought of yet.**
>
> *Ann Landers, syndicated advice columnist (1918–2002)*

NOW THE 7 "P's" OF PRESENTATIONS—I LIKE IT!

more formal and scholarly, using a PowerPoint presentation or maps in the classroom.

PREPARATION WILL HELP LOWER MY ANXIETY!

4. **Preparation.** How should you prepare your speech? Developing the content of a speech is often similar to writing a paper. You'll need to develop a thesis statement and find support for each point by researching examples, statistics, and expert testimonies. Depending on the assignment, you might write out your speech or create a set of PowerPoint slides with talking points. Then, after you know what you're going to say, you'll need to write an attention-grabbing introduction and a memorable conclusion.

5. **Planning.** What planning should you do? For example, are visual aids available, or do you need to bring your own? Is there a plug in the room, if you need one? Should you bring a backup of your presentation on a flash drive? Should you test the LCD projector to make any necessary adjustments? Many a speaker has been unnerved at the last minute by some overlooked detail.

I'M AN INTROVERT. THIS MIGHT BE A CHALLENGE!

6. **Personality.** How can you connect with the audience? How can you demonstrate your competence, charisma, and character to your listeners? Eye contact is important. Look at each person individually, if possible. Inspire trust by telling a story or relating your topic to some aspect of your own experience. Rather than playing a role, act natural and be yourself.

GOOD ADVICE. THAT'S WHAT I HAD PLANNED TO DO . . .

7. **Performance.** This last P relates to delivering your presentation. Rehearsal is important (although too much rehearsal can make your presentation sound singsongy and memorized). Beware of bringing a full written draft to the podium. If you do, you may be tempted to read it, which is the last thing you want to do. Aim for a dynamic delivery, both verbally and nonverbally, that helps keep your listeners listening.

One final thing: After you've finished a major research project that leads to a paper or presentation, you're not finished. It's time to sit back and think about what you've accomplished. Are you pleased with your work? What have you learned? What will you do differently next time? If you do this every time you finish a research project, you'll build your skills over time and take them with you to your other college classes, graduate school, or the world of work.

EXERCISE 5.5

Technology Project: Group Ad

I HOPE WE'RE GIVEN THIS ASSIGNMENT!

Working with two or three classmates and using PowerPoint, Flash, or iMovie, create a television ad (as professional-looking as possible) for the course for which you're using this book. Use text, images, and music. The advertisement shouldn't be long—two or three minutes, or the length of the song you use—but it should describe what the course is about and why other students should take it. Be as creative as you like! Play your ad for the class.

CAREER OUTLOOK: *"WRITE" YOUR REPUTATION*

"Writing is making a comeback all over our society. Look at how much people e-mail and text-message now rather than talk on the phone. Look at how much communication happens via instant messaging and blogging. Writing is today's currency for good ideas."
Jason Fried and **David Heinemeier Hansson**, *Rework*, 2010, p. 222.

Wow! THIS IS TRUE!

You've just graduated from college and landed a great job. All that hard work paid off. But now what? How will people in—for example—a large company begin to form an impression of you? The simple answer is that they will *listen* to you—in meetings, during presentations, and while hanging around the proverbial water cooler. But how else will they judge you and your work? One way you may not have thought about yet provides great opportunity, but also significant risk. It can do you in quickly. At times it's ever so subtle; at other times it's totally in your face.

Imagine this example. Your new boss asks, "Can you get an email out about that new policy?" As the eager company newbie, you reply, "Sure." You quickly compose an email message to send out to everyone in the organization: **The new company policy will go into effect soon.** *Short and sweet,* you think and hit the "send" key. But immediately, you get back a barrage of emails from other employees, "What company policy?" "There's a new company policy?" "What new shenanigans is the corporate office up to now?" The request from your boss sounded simple enough. But in your short, sweet message, you've just communicated something relatively meaningless: some new policy from somewhere is about to start sometime. Will your new colleagues assume you're uninformed, unthinking, or unconscious? Think about how composing that one message could start to shape your company reputation right out of the gate.

Instead, you could have sent out an email message like this: **The new software system to report travel expenditures, which has been mandated by the corporate office in response to violations of company travel policy, will go into effect on November 1, 2012, upon the recommendation of the general manager's task force appointed to examine ways to streamline operations and cut company waste.** This message certainly isn't guilty of leaving out all the good stuff like the first one. In fact, you've overloaded your sentence with "TMI"—so much extraneous verbiage that most people will have to read it twice, if they read it at all. Your colleagues may assume you're as boring and stuffy as your message. Even people who haven't met you yet are forming an impression of you through your writing. Are you getting the idea? Pressure? Yes. Overstatement? No. Your writing broadcasts all kinds of information about you.[47]

To make sure that people form the right impression of you, your writing must be clear, powerful, and bold. And actually, if you put some thought into it, the texting and tweeting you do now can help you develop the clear and concise business writing skills you'll need later.[48] (Our second bolded example above wouldn't fly as a tweet, would it? Too many characters.) Writing short, eye-catching, lively messages that people actually *will* read speaks volumes about your potential on the job. If you rock, make sure your writing rocks, too. That kind of writing tells people how effective you will be and "writes" your reputation for ongoing career success.

I ROCK— THAT'S FOR SURE! :)

Think Ahead: Look back at the last three texts or tweets you composed. Are they clear, powerful, and bold? Since you're not actually around when the message is read, does the way you communicated reflect the person that you are? What are you saying about *yourself* behind the actual words? Think of an example of a message you sent recently and how you could have communicated a more positive message about yourself.

CAST ON CAREERS

© Larry Harwood Photography. Property of Cengage Learning

FOCUS: Do you think writing skills are really all that important after you graduate from college?

DARNELL: To be honest, writing isn't my forté. In fact, making myself write research papers and journals as a first-year student was sheer torture. I'm what you'd call a casual person. I'd rather just talk things over. But that's not the way it works. However, as difficult as writing is for me, I do know it's important. It's not just teachers telling you that to get you to write. Everyone I know who has a career as a professional tells me that, too.

FOCUS: What are your career plans?

DARNELL: I'm planning to be a high school history teacher. History is a fascinating collection of stories, and I want to share my passion for them with my students. I plan to ask them to write the same kinds of research papers and journals that I was asked to write in school so that they develop these skills *before* they get to college. I also plan to text and tweet them, and as a teacher, I want to use that kind of writing as potential examples of how to write concise messages with impact.

CONTROL: *YOUR TOUGHEST CLASS*

Identify your most challenging assignment this term, one that will require you to use your research and information literacy skills. What is the specific assignment? For example, it could be "write a five-page paper in which you take a position on a controversial theme relating to our course topic." On a scale of 1 to 10 (with 10 being extremely difficult), how challenging do you expect this assignment to be? What would make it easier? Describe your research assignment here.

Now take a look at the website to the right and answer the following questions (without Googling):

iStockphoto.com/Antonio Nunes

1. Does this website appear to be authentic? Why or why not?
2. Would this service be useful to a student like you with a challenging research assignment?
3. In your opinion, is this website acceptable for college students to use? Why or why not?
4. Are there differences between the three available options and their degree of acceptability?
5. What's the difference between using these professional services and using the professional services of a campus reference librarian?
6. Do you know students who use "professional" research services? What are their views on the acceptability of these services?
7. If you were a college instructor, what would you tell your students about these services?

After you answer these questions on your own, your instructor may wish to generate a discussion among all the members of your class.

BOX 5.4 PowerPoint or PowerPointless? Five Ways to Make Your Presentations Stand Out

Instead of (or in addition to) writing a research paper, your instructor may require you to present your findings in an oral presentation using PowerPoint. While PowerPoint has the potential to be a powerful visual aid, it can also be PowerPointless if some simple rules are ignored. Keep these five suggestions in mind to turn presentations you create for class assignments into powerful ones:

1. **DO use your whole brain.** When it comes to designing PowerPoint presentations, the challenge is to combine useful information with attractive

design. Think of it as using both sides of your brain—your logical left hemisphere and your creative right hemisphere. For example, if you're giving a presentation on teaching young children, you might want to use a font that looks like this (children's writing) on your title slide. (Just make sure it's legible from a distance. A good rule of thumb is to use 24-point font size or larger and keep your fonts simple unless you have a particular reason to change them.) You also might want to include a high-quality graphic like this one here.

ardni/Shutterstock.com

2. **DO use color to your advantage.** Choose an attractive color scheme and stick to it. That doesn't mean that every background on every slide must be the same. In fact, if you do that, your listeners may die of boredom. But if your title slide is blue, orange, and white, then use one, two, or all three of these colors in some hue or shade on every slide. Some speakers create PowerPoint presentations that seem fragmented and messy because the individual slides aren't connected visually.
3. **DON'T crowd your slides with text.** Your listeners won't pay attention to you if they're spending all of their time reading. Be kind, and spare them the trouble by limiting the text on your slides. Some of the most deadly PowerPoint presentations are those in which the speaker turns around, faces the screen, and flies through slide after slide. The only way your listeners can live through that is if oxygen masks drop from the overhead compartments!
4. **DON'T let your slides steal the show.** Always remember that YOU are the speaker. Your slides shouldn't be so fascinating that your audience ignores you. Gunshots and screaming sirens shouldn't be used as sound effects unless, of course, you're speaking on gun control or ambulance response times. Any special effects should be used sparingly to make a point, rather than to shock your listeners.
5. **DO include a bibliography slide, both for words and images.** Some students assume that plagiarism only pertains to writing papers. Not so! Always give credit where credit is due. List your references, either on individual slides (if you use a direct quote, cite it) or on one slide at the end.

GREAT INFO! I JUST FOUND OUT ABOUT PREZI.COM, AND THAT'S A GREAT PRESENTATION TOOL, TOO!

Downloading Your Workload: The Easy Way Out?

? challenge / reaction

Challenge: In your opinion, is the following passage plagiarized? Compare these two examples:

Original passage: The emotional importance of a spoken message is conveyed by its semantic content ("what" is said) and by the affective prosody used by the speaker ("how" it is said). The listener has to pay attention to both types of information in order to comprehend the emotional message as a whole.

Source: Vingerhoets, G., Berckmoes, C., & Stroobant, N. (2003). Cerebral hemodynamics during discrimination of prosodic and semantic emotion in speech studied by transcranial doppler ultrasonography. *Neuropsychology*, 17(*1*), 93–99.

Student paper: The emotional importance of a spoken message is transmitted by its meaning ("what" is said) and by the emotional overtones used by the speaker ("how" it is said). The listener has to pay attention to both types of content in order to understand the emotional message as a whole.

Reaction: Has this student committed plagiarism? Why or why not?

One of the trickiest aspects of writing papers for your college courses can be expressed in these three words: *What is plagiarism?* First, you should understand the difference between *intentional* and *unintentional* plagiarism. Intentional plagiarism is deliberately downloading a paper from an online source or cutting and pasting text from a website or book, for example. However, you run the risk of committing unintentional plagiarism if you don't understand what plagiarism is or you forget which book you used so you don't cite the words you've borrowed from someone else. Technology today makes plagiarism all too convenient and easy, but by the same token, finding plagiarism in students' papers has become easy for instructors, too.[49] The bottom line? Follow the guidelines you get from your instructors, or ask your instructor questions if you're not sure. Both intentional and unintentional plagiarism can hurt you academically. These FAQs will help.

Q1: If I just list all the sources I used in writing a paper in the bibliography, won't that cover everything? List all your sources in the bibliography at the end of your paper, but also mention that they are other's ideas as you present them. Generally, it's a good idea to cite the original author soon after you present that idea in your paper or speech. In a research paper, it's also useful to name the author(s) ("According to Staley, college success skills are critical in the first year of college.") Each discipline uses a particular format to cite references. These are called *style sheets,* such as

> **The first principle is that you must not fool yourself, but you are the easiest person to fool.**
>
> *Richard P. Feynman (1918–1988), Nobel Prize Winner, Physics, 1965*

- *MLA* (Modern Language Association) is often used in the humanities (English, art, and philosophy, for example).
- *APA* (American Psychological Association) is often used in the social sciences (psychology, communication, and sociology).
- *Chicago Manual of Style* is used in history.

Check with your instructor if you're not certain which one to use, and Google these terms to find the specifics of formatting.

Q2: Must I cite all my sources if I just put ideas into my own words? Yes, you must cite all your sources, even though you may think that your paper looks cluttered. In academic writing, you must cite all the information you use, whether you paraphrase it, quote it, or summarize it. Some students are even taught bad habits in high school, for example, "It's not plagiarism if you change every fifth word," so they write papers with a thesaurus close by. Unfortunately, that's not the way it works. Try reading what you'd like to paraphrase, and then cover the text with your hand and write what you remember. In this case, you'd still need to cite the reference, but because you're paraphrasing, you wouldn't use quotation marks.

Q3: But I didn't know anything at all about this subject before I started this assignment. Does that mean I should cite everything? Some ideas are common knowledge that need not be cited. For example, it's a well-known fact that the Civil War lasted from 1861 to 1865. If you cited this piece of common knowledge, who would you cite? Generally, however, your motto should be, "Better safe than sorry." As a rule, you must cite quotations, paraphrases, or summaries. If you use the exact words of someone else, put quotation marks around them, or if they're longer than four lines, indent them in a block. (And generally, only use long quotes if something has been said in a remarkable way.) Also cite specific facts you're using as support and distinctive ideas belonging to others, even if you don't agree with them.

Q4: I've been doing a lot of reading for this paper. Now I'm not really sure which ideas came from others and which are my own. How do I avoid plagiarism? The best solution here is to take careful notes as you do your research and document where you found each piece of information. Avoid cutting and pasting text. That practice can backfire later when you can't remember what you've extracted and what represents your own thoughts and wording. And remember this: Plagiarism applies to speaking as well as writing!

Now look back at your answer to the Challenge → Reaction at the beginning of this section and see if you would change anything.

> **Borrowed thoughts, like borrowed money, only show the poverty of the borrower.**
>
> *Lady Marguerite Blessington, English socialite and writer (1789–1849)*

insight **action**

Now What Do You Think?

1. At the beginning of this chapter, Dario Jones, a confused college student, faced a challenge. Now after reading this chapter, would you respond differently to any of the questions you answered about the "FOCUS Challenge Case"? Knowing what you know now, how would you advise him? Write a paragraph ending to the story, incorporating your best advice.
2. Which of the Five Steps to Information Literacy is the most difficult for you? Which ones do you resist and which ones to you delve into with eagerness? Explain why.
3. Which of the three stages of the writing process is most challenging for you? Explain why. Are you eager to get going, so you skip prewriting? Do you have trouble getting your thoughts on paper as you write? Is time management an issue for you, so that there's no time left for rewriting?
4. Of the seven P's, which will you most need to work on? Do you tend to give one factor less attention than you should? List three specific ways that you can improve your speaking skills in college.
5. List three specific actions you will take to avoid plagiarism at all costs. For example, you may decide to begin taking notes on index cards and list a reference at the top of every card when you do research.

REALITY ✓ What did you LEARN?

On a scale of 1 to 10, answer the following questions now that you've completed the chapter.

low 1 2 3 4 5 6 7 8 9 10 high

In hindsight, how much did you already know about this subject before reading the chapter?

Can you answer these questions about information literacy, writing, and speaking skills more fully now that you've read the chapter? ________

1. How would you define research? What steps are involved?
2. What is information literacy?
3. Identify the three stages involved in the writing process.

How useful might the information in this chapter be to you?

How much do you think this information might affect your success in college?________

How much energy did you put into reading this chapter? ________

How long did it actually take you to complete this chapter (both the reading and writing tasks)? ________ Hour(s) ________ Minutes

Did you finish reading this chapter? ________

Did you intend to when you started? ________

If you meant to but didn't, what stopped you? ________

Challenge Yourself Online Quiz To find out just how much you've learned, access the College Success CourseMate via www.cengagebrain.com to take the Challenge Yourself Online Quiz.

Take a minute to compare these answers to your answers from the "Readiness Check" at the beginning of this chapter. What gaps exist between the similar questions? How might these gaps between what you thought before starting the chapter and what you now think after completing the chapter affect how you approach the next chapter in this book?

Engaging, Listening, and Note-Taking in Class

CHAPTER 6

You're about to discover . . .

- How to get engaged in class
- How to listen with focus
- How to vary your listening styles according to lecture styles
- How to take good notes
- How to use your notes to achieve the best results

© Larry Harwood Photography, Property of Cengage Learning; cynoclub/Shutterstock.com

READINESS What do you KNOW?

Before beginning to read this chapter, take two minutes to answer the following questions on a scale of 1 to 10. Your answers will help you assess how ready you are to focus.

low 1 2 3 4 5 6 7 8 9 10 high

How much do you *already* know?

Based on reading the "You're about to discover . . ." list and skimming this chapter, how much do you think you probably already know about this chapter's subject? ________

See if you can answer these questions about engaging, listening, and note-taking in class *before* you read.

1. What does in mean to sit in the "T zone" in class and why is it important?
2. This chapter discusses "hard" and "soft" listening skills. What's the difference between the two and which one is the right one to use in class?
3. Identify three possible formats for taking notes in class.

How much do you expect to learn?

In general, how motivated are you to learn more by reading this chapter? ________

How much do you think this information might affect your success overall? ________

How much energy do you plan to put into reading this chapter? ________

How ready are you to read *now*?

How ready are you to focus on this chapter? Enter a number for each aspect of your readiness to focus.

Physically ________

Intellectually ________

Emotionally ________

If any of your answers is below a 10, pay attention to whatever is distracting you before you start reading. Then zero in and focus.

How long do you think it will take you to complete this chapter from start to finish?

_____ Hour(s) _____ Minutes

Now, as you begin, do you intend to finish reading this chapter?

____ yes ____ no ____ maybe

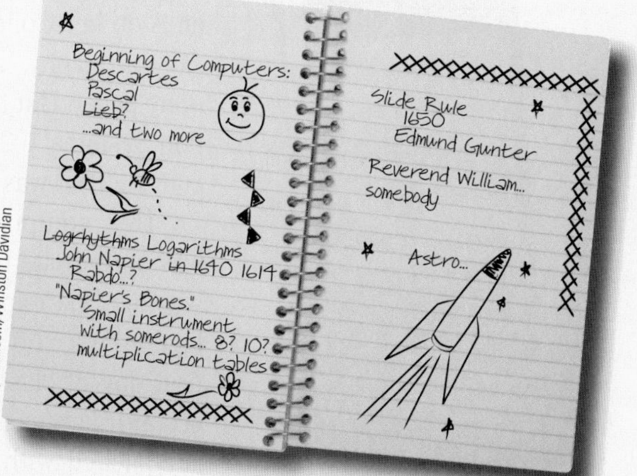

iStockphoto.com/Winston Davidian

© Larry Harwood Photography. Property of Cengage Learning

FOCUS
Challenge Case

? challenge

Lindsey Collier

Felixco/Shutterstock.com

It was Lindsey Collier's first trip home since classes started. Thanksgiving! In addition to the family's traditional feast, she was eager to see her six-year-old sister, her brother who was a sophomore in high school, and her parents. After she left home, she began to appreciate her family more than ever. What great people they are, she kept thinking. Still, she wondered: Will they be glad to see me? Will I fit back into the family? Will Mom have converted my bedroom into a guest room? Will Dad still want to watch our favorite TV shows together? A million questions were running through her mind. Even though they talked on the phone and sent e-mails and text messages nearly every day, actually seeing her family for the first time in three months was going to seem strange. And she hadn't even seen Honey and Nougat yet, the two brand new labrador retriever puppies, except in pictures on her cell phone! How much fun would they be?

Johan Swanepoel/Shutterstock.com

Johan Swanepoel/Shutterstock.com

Johan Swanepoel/Shutterstock.com

Sergey Peterman/Shutterstock.com; Johan Swanepoel/Shutterstock.com

She knew one thing for sure: Her parents would ask questions about how her classes were going. *Pretty well*, she thought. She'd gotten a B on her English paper, a B on her first math exam, an A on her College Success "Academic Autobiography," and an A– on her philosophy paper. But then there was Information Systems 102, her computer literacy course. That was a different story.

Her computer literacy instructor was a graduate teaching assistant. This was his first experience teaching a college course, he had announced on the first day of class, and English was his second language. His lectures were jam-packed with information that went right over Lindsey's head. Take last Wednesday's lecture, for example:

> The real beginning of modern computers goes back to the seventeenth century and intellectual giants such as Descartes, Pascal, Leibnitz, and Napier. In mathematics, particularly, tremendous progress was made in revolutionizing how people saw the world, and their calculations became so laborious that they needed a more sophisticated computing machine.
>
> The development of logarithms by the Scottish mathematician John Napier in 1614 stimulated the invention of the various devices that substituted the addition of logarithms for multiplication. Napier published his great work of logarithms in the book called Rabdologia. This was a remarkable

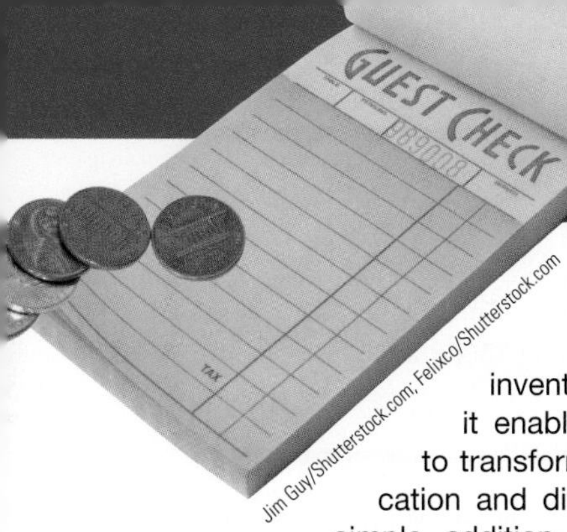

Jim Guy/Shutterstock.com; Felixco/Shutterstock.com

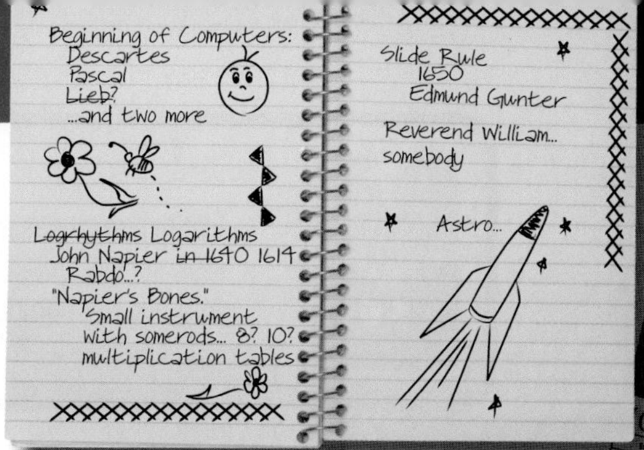

iStockphoto.com/Winston Davidian

Juriah Mosin/Shutterstock.com

invention since it enabled people to transform multiplication and division into simple addition and subtraction. His logarithm tables soon came into widespread use. Napier is often remembered more by another invention of his, nicknamed "Napier's Bones." This was a small instrument constructed of 10 rods, on which were engraved the multiplication tables. They are referred to as bones because the first set was made from ivory and resembled a set of bones. This simple device enabled people to carry out multiplication quickly if one of the numbers was only one digit (i.e., 6 × 6,742).[1]

Robert Davies/Shutterstock.com

Lindsey tried to pay attention to his words and copy down the writing scribbled all over the board, but no matter how hard she tried, her mind seemed to drift to the new guy she'd just met. Frankly, she just wasn't interested in all this stuff. Information seemed to fly out of her instructor's mouth at mach speed, and she used his accent as an excuse. Taking notes that quickly was just plain impossible. She tried giving him quizzical looks to communicate "Slow down, please," but he probably couldn't see her face in the back row.

Because nothing the professor said caught her interest, she knew that asking questions in class would only prove that she wasn't paying attention. Trying to read and take notes from the textbook chapters *before* class took more discipline than she could muster. Once she even tried bringing her laptop to class to take notes, but she couldn't type fast enough, and none of it made much sense. So she drifted to her Facebook page and passed the time in class that way, even though she knew that wasn't a good idea.

Lindsey had thought about trying to stop in during the instructor's office hours some morning, but she worked off-campus as a breakfast server at a local restaurant. She could try making an appointment with him, she thought, but was he really willing to meet with every single student who had a scheduling conflict? *That's why he has office hours*, she told herself. And after all, he was working hard at the same time to earn an advanced degree himself. Besides, did she really want to discuss how poorly she was doing? It was too late in the term to drop the class, and she needed the credits for financial aid. Still, she had to figure something out or computer literacy was going to blow her GPA and her parents' impression that she was doing great in college.

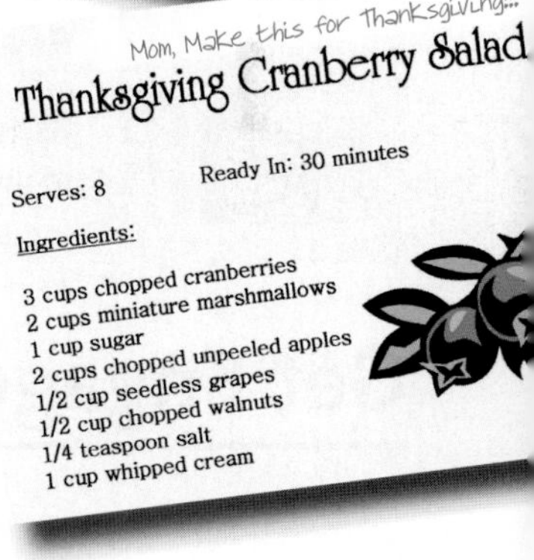

Cengage Learning

Courtesy of Facebook; © Larry Harwood Photography. Property of Cengage Learning

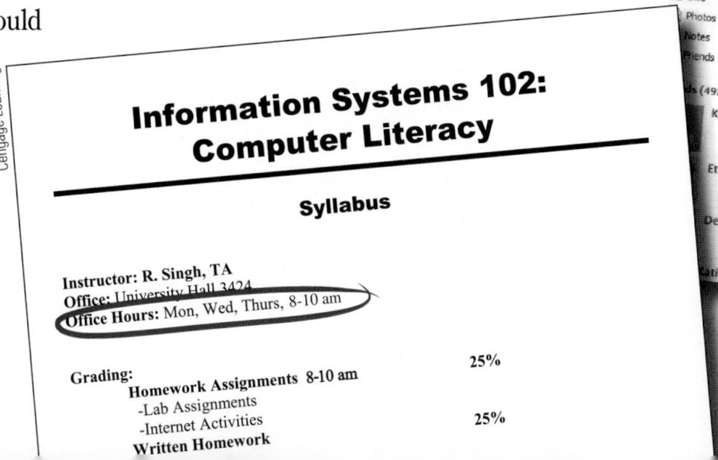
Information Systems 102: Computer Literacy

Syllabus

Instructor: R. Singh, TA
Office: University Hall 3424
Office Hours: Mon, Wed, Thurs, 8-10 am

Grading:
Homework Assignments 8-10 am 25%
-Lab Assignments
-Internet Activities 25%
Written Homework

Cengage Learning

What Do You Think?

1. List five mistakes Lindsey is making.
2. Now list five things that Lindsey should do immediately to improve her computer literacy classroom experience.

VARK It!

Complete the recommended activity for your preferred VARK learning modality. If you are multimodal, select more than one activity. Your instructor may ask you to (a) give an oral report on your results in class, (b) send your results to him or her via e-mail, (c) post them online, or (d) contribute to a class chat.

iStockphoto.com/Marcela Barsse/MarsBars; Joanna Goodyear/Dreamstime.com; iStockphoto.com/Nadezda Firsova; iStockphoto.com/Pascal Genest

Visual: Color-code the notes you take as you read this chapter to mark important themes (blue highlighter for main points, yellow highlighter for examples, etc.).

Aural: As you read this chapter, read the most important sections (that apply to you) aloud, as if you were a TV anchorperson with breaking news. ("This just in . . .")

Read/Write: As you read this chapter, outline it using the major headings as your guide.

Kinesthetic: As you read, decide which of the highlighted quotes in this chapter is most motivating to you. To keep reminding yourself, make a poster of it to tape on the wall by your personal computer.

Get Engaged in Class

Challenge: What is *engagement*? Exactly what does it take to become engaged in class?

Reaction:

___

___

___

No, this chapter isn't about buying a ring and getting down on one knee. It's about your willingness to focus, listen, discuss, ask questions, take notes, and generally dive into your classes. It's about being a full participant in what you're learning, not just a spectator sitting on the sidelines. It's about not just memorizing information for exams and then forgetting it. You see, the secret to college success hinges on this one word: *engagement*.

Think about this analogy. How did you learn to swim? Did you read books about swimming? Did you Google the word and check out all the hits? Did you get advice from your friends about swimming? Did you sit on the edge of the pool and watch other people swim? No, you probably jumped in and got wet, right? The same thing is true with your college classes. The more willing you are to jump in and get wet, the more engaged you'll be in the learning process. It's your education, after all, so take the plunge!

Getting the most out of class means reading, listening, asking questions, participating, and taking good notes. Perhaps you think you've already learned all of these skills, but the truth is they are so important to your college success that it's worth the effort to find out for sure.

> **What actually correlates with success are not grades, but 'engagement'—genuine involvement in courses and campus activities. Engagement leads to 'deep learning,' or learning for understanding. That's very different from just memorizing stuff for an exam, then forgetting it.**
>
> *John Merrow, reporter,* USA Today

Dare to Prepare

If you want to get a head start on developing good academic habits in class, then start before you get there. Preparation separates students into two categories: those who excel at learning and those who don't. Although not all students see the value of preparation, do more than your classmates do—dare to prepare! Follow these suggestions and you'll find that it's easier to get engaged in class because you're ready.

1. **Look ahead.** By checking your course syllabus before class, you'll be prepared for the upcoming topic. You'll also avoid the "oops" factor of sitting down, looking around, and noticing that everyone else knows something you don't about what's supposed to happen today.

2. **Do the assigned reading.** If you have a reading assignment due for class, do it, and take notes as you read. Write in the margins of your textbook or on sticky notes. Question what you're reading and enter into a mental dialogue with the author. Having some background on the topic will do you a world of good in class. You will be able to listen more actively and participate more intelligently during any discussion: *Yes, I remember the chapter covering that topic*, you'll think when the instructor begins talking about something you recognize. Instead of hearing it for the first time, you'll *reinforce* what you've already read. According to one study, as few as one-third of your classmates will have done the assigned reading prior to class. That factoid isn't a reason to excuse yourself from reading; instead it gives you insider information on how *you* can shine in class by comparison.[2]

Read chapter 6 for IS 102 tonight!!!!

3. **Show up physically.** Not only is attending class important for your overall understanding of the material, but it may move your grade up a few notches. Even if attendance isn't required by your instructor, require it of yourself. Research says that missing classes is definitely related to your academic performance.[3] And once you give yourself permission to skip one single, solitary class, it becomes easier to do it the next time, and the time after that, and so on. Studies indicate that on any given day, approximately one-third of your classmates will miss class, that most students think that several absences during a term is "the standard," and that among students who miss class often, only one-quarter do the reading to catch up.[4] Exercise good judgment, even if your classmates don't!

4. **Show up mentally.** Showing up means more than just occupying a seat in the classroom. It means assessing what you bring to the class as a learner on any particular day. Just as each chapter of this book asks you to do a "Readiness Check" before you begin reading, it's a good idea to do a mental "Readiness Check" when you arrive in class. Are you *physically, intellectually,*

I've cut IS 102 three times already!!! Ugh!

> Every person in this life has something to teach me—and as soon as I accept that, I open myself to truly listening.
>
> *John Lahr, drama critic*

No more Facebook in class either!

I'll sit in the "T zone" next class and see if it helps.

and *emotionally* ready to give it your best shot? If not, what can you do to rally for the cause?

5. **Choose your seat strategically.** Imagine paying $150 for a concert ticket, just like everyone else, and then electing to sit in the nosebleed section as high up and far away from the action as you could get. Sitting in the back means you're more likely to let your mind wander and less likely to hear clearly. Sitting in the front means you'll keep yourself accountable by being in full view of the instructor and the rest of the class. Studies show that there is a definite connection between students' academic performance and their seat location. What's the best spot for great concentration? Front and center, literally—the "T zone"! In one study, students who sat at the back of a large auditorium were six times more likely to fail the course, even though the instructor had assigned seats randomly![5] Not only will sitting in the T zone keep you alert throughout the class, but instructors tend to have higher opinions of the students who sit there.
6. **Bring your tools.** Bring a writing utensil and notebook with you to every class. Your instructor may also ask you to bring your textbook, calculator, a blue book for an exam, or other necessary items. If so, do it. Question: how seriously would you take a carpenter who showed up to work without a hammer, nails, and screwdriver? Get the point?
7. **Don't sit by your best friend.** Resist the temptation to sit next to your best buddy in order to catch up on all the latest campus news during class. Of course, it's important to have friends, but class is hardly the best time to devote yourself to helping your friendship blossom. You're there for a reason; now capitalize on it!
8. **Posture counts!** Your parents may have told you more than once as a kid: "Sit up straight!" Sitting up straight in class will help you develop a healthy

Not my issue. I'm good here.

mind. It's hard to focus when you're slouched into a position that screams, "I could really use a power nap about now!" When your body says, "I'm ready to learn," your mind follows suit.

9. **Maintain your health.** Being sick can wreak havoc on your ability to concentrate, listen well, and participate. Take the preventative approach by getting enough sleep, eating well, and exercising. Remember, *energy management* is key to your ability to focus. Depleted energy can lead to serious *dis*engagement.

10. **Focus.** After sitting down in class each day, take a moment to clear your head of all daydreams, to-do's, and worries. Take a deep breath and remind yourself of the opportunity to learn that lies ahead. Promise yourself you'll get the most from this class. Think of yourself as a reporter at a press conference, listening intently because you'll be writing a story about what's going on. You *will* be writing a "story"—often in response to an essay question on an exam!

© Larry Harwood Photography. Property of Cengage Learning

Follow the Rules of Engagement

Just as is the case with most places you can think of, college classrooms have rules about how to behave. You don't find people yelling in church or staring at other people in elevators or telling jokes at funerals. There are rules about how to behave in a variety of contexts, and college classrooms are no exception. Here are a few rules of engagement that you should know about up front:

"**Politeness is the art of choosing among one's real thoughts.**"

Adlai Stevenson II, U.S. Presidential candidate (1900–1965)

1. **Be aware that gab is not a gift.** In class, talking while others are speaking is inappropriate. And it's certainly not a gift—especially to your instructor. In fact, side conversations while your professor is lecturing or your classmates are contributing to the discussion is downright rude. If you're seated next to a gabber, don't get sucked in. Use body language to communicate that you're there to learn, not to gab. If that's not enough to set the gabber straight, politely say something like, "I really need to pay attention right now. Let's talk more later, okay?" Don't let other students cheat you out of learning.

2. **Control your hunger pangs.** If your class meets through a meal hour, get in the habit of eating before or after class. Crunching and munching in the classroom may get in the way of others' learning, not to mention the distraction caused by enticing smells. Instructors differ on their preferences here. It's a good idea to find out what your instructors' preferences are, and then abide by them.

3. **Turn off your cell phone, please!** There's a reason why people are asked to turn off their cell phones before concerts, athletic events, or movies. Imagine being in a jam-packed theater trying to follow the film's

plot with cell phones going off every few seconds. You've paid good money to see a film. The same thing goes for your college classes. In one study, a "planted" ringing cell phone caused students to score 25 percent worse on a course quiz, even though the information had just been presented by the instructor before the distraction and was projected up front on a screen during the 30 second ringing.[6] As a general rule, your instructor's presentation deserves the same focus you'd give a feature film, so turn your cell phone off and put it away. (We can hear it when it's set on vibrate, too.) And texting in class shows everyone where your mind *really* is. The bottom line is that you're in school to learn, so give class your undivided attention.

4. **Better late than never?** Not to some instructors. Students arriving late and leaving early are annoying, not only to your instructor, but to your classmates. To them, it looks like you don't value the other students or the class content. How would you like dinner guests to arrive an hour late, after you'd slaved over a hot stove all day? Your instructors have prepared for class, and they feel the same way. Build in time to find a parking place, hike to the building where class is held, or stop for a coffee. Do everything you can to avoid coming late and leaving early. And don't schedule a lube job for your car during class or volunteer to watch your aunt's kids. Many things in your life are important—it's true—but while you're in school, coming to class and doing your coursework should be at the top of your list. Preserve class time as a priority.

5. **Actively choose to engage, not disengage.** Engagement isn't something that just happens to you while you're not looking. You're sitting there, minding your own business, and zap—you suddenly realize that you've become engaged in learning. It's a choice you make, and sometimes it's a difficult choice because the material isn't naturally appealing to you, or the course is a required one you didn't choose, or you're just plain out of sorts. Choose to engage, anyway. Instead of actively choosing to *dis*engage in class by sleeping through lectures, surfing the Internet, or texting friends, choose to engage by leaning forward, processing information, finding your own ways to connect to the material, and formulating questions to ask. Technology offers a particularly strong temptation to disengage. Taking notes on a laptop may work well for some kinds of subject matter, but it may also take away from what handwriting allows you to do: process information more slowly and thoroughly. And upright laptop screens block your view, making eye contact between your instructor and you difficult to maintain. Even though about two-thirds of college classrooms are now wireless, some instructors are banning laptops in large lecture classes or exerting control over what can be accessed, so that students aren't tempted to surf and check messages continuously during class. According to one study conducted in the business world, employees addicted to e-mail and text messages showed the equivalent of a ten-point drop in IQ—another piece of evidence that multitasking costs![7]

If you're investing in a college education, then play by the rules of engagement. They're in place for your benefit.

Listening with Focus

Challenge: What is *focused listening*? How can you achieve it?

Reaction:

___

___

___

Listening with focus is more than just physically hearing words as they stream by. It's actually a complicated process that's hard work.

"Easy Listening" Is for Elevators— Focused Listening Is for Classrooms

Stores, restaurants, and elevators are known for their programmed, background easy listening music. Chances are you hardly notice it's there. Listening in class, however, requires actual skill, and you'll be doing a great deal of it as a college student. Experts estimate that the average student spends 80 percent of class time listening to lectures.[8]

Many of us naively believe that listening is easy to do. If you happen to be around when there's something to listen to, you can't help but listen. Not so! Did you know that when you're listening at your best, your respiration rate, heartbeat, and body temperature all increase? Just as with aerobic exercise, your body works harder when you're engaging in focused listening. When all is said and done, listening is really about energy management. You can't listen well when your energy is zapped, when you've pulled the mother of all all-nighters, or when your stomach is growling with a vengeance. Focused listening means that you've cleared the deck for class, and you're focusing on engagement.

I did not know that!

Here are some techniques for improving your listening skills in the classroom. Read through the list, then go back and check off the ones you're willing to try harder to do in class this week. It's not always easy to be a good listener, but the investment you make in improving your listening skills will pay off in countless ways.

- ☐ **Calm yourself.** Take a few deep breaths with your eyes closed to help you put all those nagging distractions on the back burner during class time.
- ☐ **Be open.** As you listen in class, you may wonder how you'll ever use this information in your career. But keep an open mind and view your class as yet another opportunity to strengthen your intellect and learn something new. Wisdom comes from a broad understanding of many things, rather than from a consistently limited focus on practical information.

✓ Like IS 102!!

© Lucidio Studio Inc./Corbis

Listening looks easy, but it's not simple. Every head is a world.

Cuban proverb

- ☐ **Don't make snap judgments.** Remember, you don't have to like your instructor's wardrobe to respect his knowledge. Focus on the content he's offering you. You may not even agree with what he's saying, but he may be leading up to a point you can't predict and turn the argument around. Don't jump to conclusions about content or style.
- ☐ **Assume responsibility.** Speak up! Ask questions! Even if you have a professor with an accent who's difficult to understand, an instructor who talks too fast (or too slow), or a professor who seems not to notice that students are in the room, the burden of clarification rests with you. You will interact with people with all sorts of accents, voices, and speech patterns throughout your life. It's up to you to improve the situation.
- ☐ **Watch for gestures and speech patterns that communicate "Here comes something important!"** Some typical examples include raising an index finger, turning to face the class, leaning forward from behind the podium, walking up the aisle, or using specific facial expressions or gestures. Listen, too, for changes in the rate, volume, or tone of speech, longer than usual pauses, or repeated information.
- ☐ **Appreciate your instructor's prep time.** For every hour of lecture time, your teacher has worked for hours to prepare. Although she may make it look easy, her lecture has involved researching, organizing, creating a PowerPoint presentation, overheads, or a podcast, and preparing notes and handouts.
- ☐ **Trick yourself into focused listening.** Some students are very good actors. They know how to look like they're listening. In class, they sit down, get out their notebooks, find a pen, assume a listening posture, and then mentally go somewhere else. While these students aren't fooling themselves, it *is* possible to trick yourself into focused listening. You may find many of your classes to be naturally fascinating learning experiences. But for others, you will need to be convinced. Even if you don't find Intro to Whatever to be the most engaging subject in the world, you may find yourself intrigued by your instructor. Most people are interested in other people. What makes him tick? Why was she drawn to this field? If you find it hard to get interested in the material, trick yourself by paying attention to the person delivering the message. While tricking yourself isn't always a good idea, it can work if you know what you're doing and why.

I wonder what does make my instructor tick?!

Listening Is More Than Hearing

Perhaps you've never thought about it, but, actually, listening and hearing aren't the same thing. Hearing—the physiological part—is only the first stage of a four-stage process. Listening is a much more complex process—especially *focused listening*, or listening at your best. The four stages of focused listening are as follows and are shown in Figure 6.1:

1. **Sensing:** receiving the sounds through your auditory system. As you sit in class, sound waves enter your ears and register in your brain.

2. **Interpreting:** understanding the message. Sounds themselves don't mean anything until you assign meaning to them. Instead of just random noise, the instructor's message must mean something to you.

Not sure I ever get to stage 2 in IS 102!

3. **Evaluating:** weighing evidence. You decide if something is true or important by sorting fact from opinion. Both interpretation and evaluation in class may involve asking questions to clarify things.

4. **Responding:** providing feedback or taking action. You respond by participating in the discussion, asking significant questions, and taking down clear, meaningful notes to study later.[9]

BOX 6.1 Listening Tips If English Is Your Second Language

It's normal to feel overwhelmed in the classroom as a new student, but especially if your first language isn't English. The academic environment in higher education can be stressful and competitive. It's even more stressful if you're also dealing with a new and different culture. You will need to give yourself time to adapt to all of these changes. In the meantime, here are some suggestions for improving your ability to listen well in class:

- Talk to your instructor before the course begins. Let her know that English is not your native language, but that you're very interested in learning. Ask for any suggestions on how you can increase your chances of success in the class. Your instructor will most likely be willing to provide you with extra help, knowing you're willing to do your part to overcome the language barrier.
- Try to get the main points of your professor's lecture. You don't have to understand every word.
- Write down words to look up in the dictionary later. Keep a running list and check them all after class. Missing out on one important term can hurt your chances of understanding something else down the line.
- Don't be afraid to ask questions. If you're too uncomfortable to ask during class, make use of your professor's office hours or e-mail address to get your questions answered. Also, teaching assistants and peer tutors may be available to help you.
- Use all support materials available for the class. Find out if your instructor posts his notes on the course website or if they are available as handouts. Some professors offer guided notes or skeleton outlines for students to fill in throughout the lecture. Some large lectures are videotaped for viewing by students at a later time. Make full use of podcasts of lectures, if they're available, so that you can listen more than once to portions you found confusing in class. Use any tools available to help reinforce lecture content.
- Team up with a classmate whose native language is English. Clarify your notes and fill in gaps.
- Form a study group with other classmates. Meet on a regular basis so that you can help one another. Remember: just because your native language isn't English doesn't mean you don't have something to offer the other members of your study group.
- Be patient. It will take some time to adjust to the accents of your various instructors. After a few weeks of class, you'll find it easier to understand what is being said.
- Practice your English comprehension by listening to talk radio or watching television or movies. You'll hear a variety of regional accents, for example, and broaden your understanding of American culture.
- Take an "English as a Second Language" course if you think it would help. It's important to keep up with the academic demands of college, and further development of your English skills may improve your comprehension and boost your confidence.
- If you continue to feel overwhelmed and unable to cope after several weeks in school, find out if your campus has an International Students Office, and enlist support from people who are trained to help.[10]

Different Strokes for Different Folks: Note-Taking by the System and Subject

? challenge

" reaction

Challenge: Does taking notes help students learn? Why or why not?

Reaction:

____

____

____

This chapter has been leading up to something. Yes, getting engaged and listening in class are essential. But you must have a way to take what's transpired in class with you when you leave. That's where your note-taking skills come in. It's true that you must be a good listener to take good notes, but being a good listener alone doesn't automatically make you a good note-taker. Taking notes in class is actually a very complicated process; there's much more to it than jotting down a grocery list so you won't forget something. After listening carefully, (without taking notes) during Exercise 6.1, how many main points did you remember well enough to write down? How many details? How much more of that lecture would you remember later if you had taken notes? Note-taking is a crucial and complex skill, and doing well on tests isn't based on luck. It's based on combining preparation and opportunity, in other words, knowing how to take useful notes in class that work for you.

Actually, one reason that note-taking is so important in the learning process is that it uses all four VARK categories: *visual* (you see your professor and the screen, if overheads or PowerPoint slides are being used), *aural* (you listen to the lecture), *read/write* (you write what you see and hear so that you can read it later to review), and *kinesthetic* (the physical act of writing opens up a pathway to the brain). As it turns out your transcription fluency—how quickly you can write clear, complete notes to review later—is a critical skill.[20]

Marc Romanelli/Getty Images

According to one study, 99 percent of college students take notes during lectures, and 94 percent of students believe that note-taking is important.[21] These are good signs, but are these students taking notes correctly, as a result of focused listening? If 99 percent of college students are taking notes, why isn't nearly everyone getting straight A's? Here are some reasons:

- Students typically only record less than 40 percent of the lecture's main content ideas in their notes.[22]
- Only 47 percent of students actually review their notes later to see what they've written.

> **Luck is what happens when preparation meets opportunity.**
>
> *Darrell Royal, football coach*

- Only 29 percent edit their notes later by adding, deleting, or reorganizing material.
- A full 12 percent do nothing other than recopy them verbatim.
- Some students never do anything with their notes once they leave class![23]
- In a recent study, students taking notes on laptops ended up with 5 percent lower GPAs than their counterparts using the old-fashioned paper-and-pencil method. Why? Perhaps these results were due to techies' inability to stay focused on task, or the interference of the clicking sounds, or because the physical act of typing is quicker, giving note-takers less time to process information.[24]

Oops! Better try harder to stay focused.

Does note-taking make a difference? Absolutely. During lectures, it serves two fundamental purposes: it helps you understand what you're learning at the time and it helps you preserve information to study later. In other words, both the *process* of note-taking (as you record information) and the *product* (your notes themselves) are important to learning. There is strong evidence that taking notes during a lecture leads to higher achievement than not taking notes, and working with your notes later increases your chances for academic achievement even more. The more notes you take (up to a point—it's possible to get too bogged down in trying to capture every detail), the higher still are your chances of succeeding, and vice versa. Studies show that if you take notes, you have a 50 percent chance of recalling that information at test time versus a 15 percent chance of remembering the same information if you didn't take notes.[25]

But when it comes to note-taking, "different strokes for different folks" is literally true. Many different note-taking systems can work, and different systems work best for different learning styles. Find a system that works well for you. Try taking notes on a stack of index cards in front of you. You can sort them and use them as flashcards later, for example. If your mind works in an orderly fashion, work from an outline—or try one of the four major methods presented in this chapter. Increasingly, professors are providing online lecture notes, miniatures of PowerPoint lecture slides, lecture outlines as handouts, audio support, or some other form of note-taking assistance. There's no doubt these tools may help, but the most helpful learning aids are those you create yourself.

Whichever strategy you choose to use, an important question to ask is: What constitutes *good* notes? The answer is: Writing down an *accurate, complete, organized* account of what you hear in class (or read in your textbook, which is discussed elsewhere in this book). The last thing you want is a "What in the world did I mean by this?" reaction later. How will you know if your notes are good? Show them to your instructor and get input, or assess your strategy after you see your results on the first exam. Your note-taking skills should steadily improve as you evolve as a student.[26]

So what are the various note-taking methods? What are the steps involved in using each one? Knowing your options, developing your skills, and learning flexibility as a note-taker are keys to your success.

Outlining

Outlining is probably the oldest, and perhaps the most trusted form of taking notes. The problem, of course, is that not all instructors speak from an outline. But if yours does, listen for key points, like the five traits, and list examples beneath each one, like in Figure 6.2:

FIGURE 6.2

Outlining

Psych 100: Week 9

I. Five Factor Trait Theory: 5 traits common to all people
  A. Extraversion: related to where energy is directed
    1. Outward directed
      a. talkative
      b. social
      c. like to be with others
    2. Inward directed
      a. quiet
      b. reserved
      c. comfortable on their own
  B. Neuroticism: degree of emotional stability/instability
    1. High neuroticism
      a. temperamental
      b. worrisome
      c. pessimistic
    2. Low neuroticism
      a. even-tempered
      b. calm
  C. Openness: degree to which individuals thoughtfully consider new ideas

At the end of the lecture, include a summary of your notes. Summarizing is an excellent way to make sure you've understood the gist of all the information you've written down in Figure 6.3.

FIGURE 6.3

Summarizing

Summary:
The most widely accepted trait theory in psychology is the five factor theory, which consists of scaled (high to low) traits common to all people: Extraversion, Neuroticism, Openness, Agreeableness, and Conscientiousness.

Of course, if your instructor's lecture is less organized, you can elect to use an informal variation of outlining, like listing bullets, and perhaps even color-coding them and drawing a picture so they're easier to remember, as shown in Figure 6.4.

FIGURE 6.4

Informal Outlining (with Bullets)

Psych 100: Week 9

✓ **Extraversion:** Where is your energy directed?

✓ **Neuroticism:** How stable are you?

✓ **Openness:** Can you think through (accept) new ideas?

✓ **Agreeableness:** Do you get along with others?

✓ **Conscientiousness:** Do you pay attention to others and tasks/details?

Remember the acronym **OCEAN.**

The Cornell System

The Cornell system of note-taking, devised by educator Walter Pauk, suggests this. On each page of your notebook, draw a line from top to bottom about one and a half inches from the left edge of your paper. (Some notebook paper already has a red line there.) Take notes on the right side of the line. Your notes should include main ideas, examples, short phrases, and definitions, for example—almost like an outline.

Leave the left side blank to fill in later with key words or questions you'd like answered, as shown in Figure 6.5. After class as you review your notes, put your hand or a sheet of paper over the right side and use the words or questions you've written on the left side as prompts to see if you can remember what's on the right side.[27] By doing this to recall the lecture, you can get a good idea of how much of the information you've really understood.

FIGURE 6.5

Five Factor Trait Theory: Cornell System Example

	KEY WORDS and QUESTIONS	SHORT PHRASES, EXAMPLES, DEFINITIONS
	Five Factor Trait Theory	– most commonly accepted trait theory.
	Original source:	– Paul Costa and Robert McCrae
	What year was their work published? Check!	– 1992?
	Five Factors	A. Extraversion: related to where energy is directed
		1. Outward directed
		a. talkative
		b. social
		c. Like to be with others
		2. Inward directed
		a. quiet
		b. reserved
		c. comfortable on their own
		B. Neuroticism: degree of emotional stability/instability
		1. High neuroticism
		a. temperamental
		b. worrisome
		c. pessimistic
		2. Low neuroticism
		a. even-tempered
		b. calm
		C. Openness: willingness to consider and accept new ideas

Mind Maps

An alternative to the Cornell system, or a way to expand on it, is to create mind maps. Mind maps use both sides of your brain: the logical, orderly left side and the visual, creative right side. What they're particularly good for is showing the relationship between ideas. Mind maps are also generally a good note-taking method for visual learners, and even the physical act of drawing

Notes, College Algebra 100, Friday, Oct. 5

Determine which of the x values are solutions to the equation

$$x^4 + x^3 - 5x^2 + x - 6 = 0$$

a) $x = -3$, b) $x = -2$, c) $x = 1$, d) $x = 2$

STEPS TO SOLUTION	CALCULATIONS	RESULTS
1) Try answer a Substitute -3 into the equation for x and see if the equation is satisfied.	$(-3)^4 + (-3)^3 - 5(-3)^2 + (-3) - 6 \overset{?}{=} 0$ $81 \quad -27 \quad -45 \quad -3 \; -6 = 0$ $0 = 0$	YES since both sides are 0.
2) Try answer b Substitute -2 into the equation for x and see if the equation is satisfied.	$(-2)^4 + (-2)^3 - 5(-2)^2 + (-2) - 6 \overset{?}{=} 0$ $16 \quad -8 \quad -20 \quad -2 \; -6 = 0$ $-20 \neq 0$	NO since the two sides are unequal.
3) Try answer c Substitute 1 into the equation for x and see if the equation is satisfied.	$(1)^4 + (1)^3 - 5(1)^2 + 1 - 6 \overset{?}{=} 0$ $1 \quad +1 \quad -5 \quad +1 - 6 = 0$ $-8 \neq 0$	NO since the two sides are unequal.
4) Try answer d Substitute 2 into the equation for x and see if the equation is satisfied.	$(2)^4 + (2)^3 - 5(2)^2 + 2 - 6 \overset{?}{=} 0$ $16 \quad +8 \quad -20 \quad +2 \; -6 = 0$ $0 = 0$	YES since both sides are 0.

FIGURE 6.10

Math Note-Taking Example

From http://www.math.armstrong.edu/MathTutorial/exerciseSoln/LinearEqSoln/LinearEq1Soln/13LinearEq1.html

EXERCISE 6.4

"Focused" Multitasking

One reason it's hard to focus in class is because of distractions. You may be tempted to check your Facebook account or text someone about something that pops into your mind. Being pulled in different directions at once is what happens when you multitask. It breaks your concentration and disrupts your learning. Try this experiment instead. Let's call it "Focused Multitasking," meaning that all your attention is directed at one thing. Before you listen to an in-class lecture, divide into groups with each group trying out a different note-taking strategy presented in this chapter. For example, Group 1 members should use outlines. Group 2 should use the Cornell System, Group 3 should create mind maps, etc. Then begin the lecture. The lecture could be your instructor lecturing about this chapter of FOCUS. Or it could be something different, like listening to an NPR podcast that the instructor or the whole class chooses. You are intentionally using all of your VARK preferences at once to focus on a single topic. After the lecture, take a quiz provided by your instructor and see which note-taking group's method earns the highest score!

helps you make those same connections in your brain. Successful note-taking does mean "different strokes for different folks"—and different subjects. Be sure to make the right choices about which note-taking system makes the most sense for the course material being presented.

Using Lecture Notes

Taking good notes is only part of the equation. To get the most value from your notes, you must actually *use* them. As soon as possible after class, take a few minutes to review your notes. If you find sections that are unclear, take time to fill in the gaps while things are still fresh in your mind. One professor found that students who filled in any missing points right after class were able to increase the amount of lecture points they recorded by as much as 50 percent. And students who worked with another student to reconstruct the lecture immediately after class were able to increase their number of noted lecture points even more![32]

I never thought to look at my notes right after class, but that makes sense—when everything is still fresh in my mind...

This part of the note-taking process is often overlooked, yet it is one of the most helpful steps for learning and recall. If you don't review your notes within twenty-four hours, there's good evidence that you'll end up re*learning* rather than re*viewing*. Reviewing helps you go beyond just writing to actually making sure you understand what you wrote. These three techniques help you get the best use of your notes: manipulating, paraphrasing, and summarizing.

- **Manipulating** involves working with your notes by typing them out later, for example. Some research indicates that it's not writing down information that's most important. Manipulating information is what counts. Work with your notes. Fill in charts, draw diagrams, create a matrix, underline, highlight, organize. Cut a copy of the professor's lecture notes up into paragraphs, mix them up, and then put the lecture back together. Copy your notes onto flash cards. Manipulating information helps develop your reasoning skills, reduces your stress level, and can produce a more complete set of notes to study later.[33] And one other point worth noting: Research indicates that graphically organized notes may help you learn better than notes that are in a traditional linear form.[34]
- **Paraphrasing** is a process of putting your notes into your own words. Recopy your notes or your professor's prepared lecture notes, translating them into words you understand and examples that are meaningful to you. Paraphrasing is also a good way to self-test or to study with a classmate. If you can't find words of your own, perhaps you don't really understand the original notes. Sometimes students think they understand course material until the test proves otherwise, and then it's too late! Advance practice testing helps. Practice paraphrasing key concepts with a friend to see how well you both understand the material. Or ask yourself, if I had to explain this to someone who missed class, what words would I use?
- **Summarizing** is a process of writing a brief overview of all of your notes from one lecture. Imagine

> **I make progress by having people around me who are smarter than I am and listening to them. And I assume that everyone is smarter about something than I am.**
>
> *Henry J. Kaiser, American industrialist (1882–1967)*

CAREER OUTLOOK: *INCREASE YOUR SPQ*

When all is said and done, a lot more is said than done.
Lou Holtz

Do you know people like this? When you start a story, they one-up you: "Oh, you think *that's* something? You should hear what *I* did. . . ." They spend their time (and yours) bragging about what they've done and how good they are at things. They "dot" every sentence with an "I." Let's face it: They're just plain annoying. *Everything* is about them.

Other people are humble. When it comes up in conversation that they won a full scholarship to your school, and you say, "Wow! That's incredible!" they say, "Oh, it was just good luck." When they get the top grade on the economics test that everyone else failed, they say, "I don't know. I just remembered stuff and wrote it down." You stand amazed.

But once you're settled into that new job after college, you have to show your stuff. No one will know exactly what you're capable of, nor can they read your mind (or your growing résumé) on a day-to-day basis. Regardless, you will be evaluated formally by your boss at least annually and informally by your colleagues daily. In order for your career to survive—and to thrive—you need high SPQ. In *FOCUS,* you're reading about IQ, EQ, and CQ, but what is SPQ? It's a fairly new fun, pop concept: Self-Promotion Intelligence (Quotient). It's vital to your career, and getting good at it can be a challenge.[35]

Peggy Klaus, Fortune 500 consultant and author of *Brag: The Art of Tooting Your Own Horn Without Blowing It* says "Today, bragging is a necessity, not a choice. Staying quiet about your achievements only leads to being underappreciated and overlooked. . . . You don't have to be an over-the-top cheerleader. Just realize how much you have to offer" and let others know through true-life, engaging stories you pull from your "brag bag." No hype; "Just the facts, ma'am."

Here are some other ideas: Note what makes you unique, and be prepared to talk about it, as if you were creating your own personal "brand." If you have a particular area of expertise, become known as the go-to person for it. Like an athlete, "play back" incidents in your head and remember what you did well (or not). Don't be afraid to speak up, even if you're an introvert (although self-promotion is generally better received if you answer questions about your accomplishments, rather than always bring them up yourself.[36] Conversely, ask questions of others and listen carefully to what they have to say about themselves.). Volunteer for visibility by offering to write, speak, or run a meeting. Connect other people so that you become known as a networker. Use the pronoun "we" more than you use its complement, "I." (Rarely is anything accomplished by a single individual in isolation.) And finally, be generous in your praise of others; it *will* come back to you.[37]

Think Ahead: What particular strengths will you bring to the organization you join? How can you let others know about them? As you consider your SPQ and how important it is to your future career, think about it from your current vantage point. Which suggestions above do you follow now? Which ones will you try to incorporate into your repertoire of career skills?

SPQ–a very interesting idea I've never even thought about...

CAST ON CAREERS

© Larry Harwood Photography. Property of Cengage Learning

FOCUS: Have you ever thought about SPQ? In your opinion, is it important in a career?

SYLVIA: I've never really thought about it before, but it makes perfect sense to me. I have friends now who accomplish great things, but I only find out about it through a mutual friend or read about it on someone else's Facebook page. One friend of mine was invited to join the freshman national honor society because she had a 3.9 her first semester. I didn't even know about this invitation until much later, but I would have enjoyed going to the induction ceremony with her to celebrate. She was always taught that bragging was "wrong," so she kept it to herself. Really, it depends on how you do it. It's possible to talk about your accomplishments and have other people listen without sounding egotistical.

FOCUS: What are your career plans?

SYLVIA: I'm planning to be a nurse. My grandmother was a nurse, and my mother is a nurse. It's not just a tradition in my family; it's genuine interest in helping others. Nursing is a competitive field right now, and in order to get the job I want, I'll have to be able to talk about my college achievements during interviews. I've worked hard and been very active on campus. I'll need some good examples to share with interviewers. I plan to start paying more attention to my SPQ now so that I can do that!

trying to take all your lecture notes from one class session and putting them on an index card. If you can do that, you've just written a summary. Why is it so important to rewrite your notes in this extremely condensed version? Research shows that students who use the summarizing technique have far greater recall of the material than those who don't. In one study, students were given a multiple-choice quiz immediately following a lecture. One group in the study had written summaries; the other had not. There was no noticeable difference in the students' performance immediately following the lecture; however, when the same quiz was given twelve days later, the students who had used the summarizing technique did much better on the quiz than those who had not.[38]

Some students think that simply going over their notes is the best way to practice. Research shows that simply reading over your notes is a weak form of practice that does not transfer information into long-term memory.[39] You must actually *work with* the material, rearrange or reword it, or condense it to get the most academic bang for your buck. Active strategies always work better than more passive ones.

Manipulating, paraphrasing, and summarizing are more effective learning techniques. Even if your instructor provides you with verbatim notes online or hands you hard copies of her PowerPoint slides, you will still need to work with the information in order to learn it. Think of it this way. If you came to class with a friend you'd "hired" to take notes for you, who do you think would do better on the exam—him or you? Even if someone else hands you a set of notes, the truth is your ability to focus, listen, discuss, ask questions, take notes yourself, and get engaged in class are the things that help you learn best.

* insight ! action

Now What Do You Think?

1. At the beginning of this chapter, Lindsey Collier, a frustrated college student, faced a challenge. Now after reading this chapter, would you respond differently to any of the questions you answered about the "FOCUS Challenge Case"? Knowing what you know now, how would you advise her? Write a paragraph ending to the story, incorporating your best advice.
2. Look over the ten "Dare to Prepare" suggestions at the beginning of this chapter.
   - Look ahead.
   - Do the assigned reading.
   - Show up physically.
   - Show up mentally.
   - Choose your seat strategically.
   - Bring your tools.
   - Don't sit by your best friend.
   - Posture counts!
   - Maintain your health.
   - Focus.

   Which of the suggestions do you find most difficult to do? For which of your classes? What can you do to help you prepare better for these classes?

(continued on next page)

3. How well do you take notes? Which behaviors will you target in order to become a better note-taker? Select three of the items in Exercise 6.3 to focus on. Start with any item that you marked as "Never True of Me" and practice doing that behavior in class for several days. Then practice with an additional behavior from that column, and so on. Put the insights you've gained about yourself from reading about note-taking into action in class and describe your results.
4. Do you understand Bloom's Taxonomy? Can you provide examples of questions for each level you'd ask that relate to the information in this chapter?
   - Remembering ____________
   - Understanding ____________
   - Applying ____________
   - Analyzing ____________
   - Evaluating ____________
   - Creating ____________
5. What are your strengths and weaknesses as a note-taker? Are you a good listener? Can you write quickly and legibly? Do you ask questions easily? Use this opportunity to critique yourself and identify some areas for improvement.

REALITY ✓ What did you LEARN?

On a scale of 1 to 10, answer the following questions now that you've completed the chapter.

low 1 2 3 4 5 6 7 8 9 10 high

In hindsight, how much did you already know about this subject before reading the chapter?

Can you answer these questions about engaging, listening, and note-taking in class more fully now that you've read the chapter?

1. What does in mean to sit in the "T zone" in class and why is it important?
2. This chapter discusses "hard" and "soft" listening skills. What's the difference between the two and which one is the right one to use in class?
3. Identify three possible formats for taking notes in class.

How useful might the information in this chapter be to you? How much do you think this information might affect your success in college?

How much energy did you put into reading this chapter?

How long did it actually take you to complete this chapter (both the reading and writing tasks)? _____ Hour(s) _____ Minutes

Did you finish reading this chapter? _____

Did you intend to when you started?_____

If you meant to but didn't, what stopped you?_______

Aced it!

Challenge Yourself Online Quiz To find out just how much you've learned, access the College Success CourseMate via www.cengagebrain.com to take the Challenge Yourself Online Quiz.

Take a minute to compare these answers to your answers from the "Readiness Check" at the beginning of this chapter. What gaps exist between the similar questions? How might these gaps between what you thought before starting the chapter and what you now think after completing the chapter affect how you approach the next chapter in this book?

CHAPTER 7

Developing Your Memory

© Larry Harwood Photography. Property of Cengage Learning

You're about to discover . . .

- *Why memory is a process, not a thing*
- *How your memory works like a digital camera*
- *How to improve your memory using twenty different techniques*
- *How your memory can fail you*
- *How drugs affect your memory*

READINESS ✓ What do you KNOW?

Before beginning to read this chapter, take two minutes to answer the following questions on a scale of 1 to 10. Your answers will help you assess how ready you are to focus.

low 1 2 3 4 5 6 7 8 9 10 high

How much do you *already* know?

Based on reading the "You're about to discover..." list and skimming this chapter, how much do you think you probably already know about this chapter's subject? ________

See if you can answer these questions about developing your memory *before* you read.

1. What are the three "R's" of remembering?
2. This chapter discusses twenty ways to master your memory. Can you identify five?
3. What is the role of health and wellness in how well your memory works?

How much do you expect to learn?

In general, how motivated are you to learn more by reading this chapter? ________

How much do you think this information might affect your success overall? ________

How much energy do you plan to put into reading this chapter? ________

How ready are you to read *now*?

How ready are you to focus on this chapter? Enter a number for each aspect of your readiness to focus.

Physically ________
Intellectually ________
Emotionally ________

If any of your answers is below a 10, pay attention to whatever is distracting you before you start reading. Then zero in and focus.

How long do you think it will take you to complete this chapter from start to finish?

________ Hour(s) ________ Minutes

Now, as you begin, do you intend to finish reading this chapter?

________ yes ________ no ________ maybe

Darko Kovacevic/Shutterstock.com

© Larry Harwood Photography. Property of Cengage Learning

FOCUS Challenge Case

? challenge

Darnell Williams

Quite honestly, Darnell Williams hadn't found high school all that challenging. Playing football his last two years had made it bearable. But at his school, if you showed up and had a pulse, you could count on passing your courses. There wasn't anything in particular he really wanted to do after high school, but he'd decided to go to the college in his hometown anyway. Maybe something there would appeal to him. So he increased his hours at the chain store where he worked to 40 hours per week and enrolled as a full-time student.

Laurin Rinder/Shutterstock.com

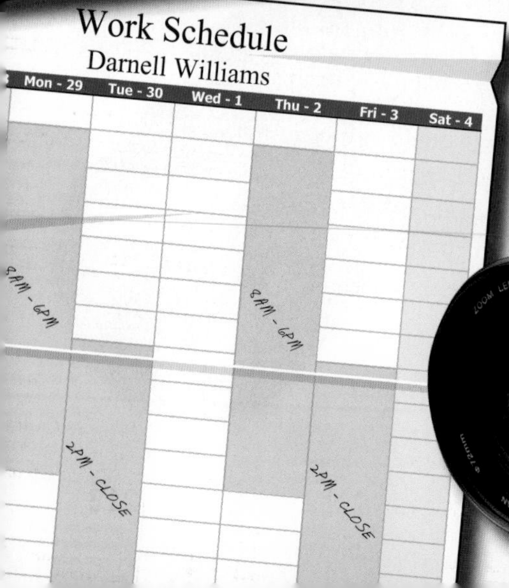

Cengage Learning

But after two weeks, Darnell admitted that he didn't find his classes all that engaging. Although he was strong physically from working out for football, he knew he was out of shape academically. In high school, he never cracked a book or did any homework, but just how well would that work here? Now he wished he'd buckled down more in high school instead of blowing it off.

What Darnell really liked to do could be summarized in three words: sports, movies, and photography. Armed with a couple of burgers, fries, and a shake, he spent most weekends watching movies half the night; cheering on his favorite football teams; or uploading his artsy shots to Flickr. He was a pretty good photographer, if he did say so, and increasingly, most of his friends were other online amateur photographers.

Since Darnell had no idea which college classes to take, he figured he'd just get some basic requirements out of the way during his first term: Introduction to Physics, Introduction to Psychology, Public Speaking, and English Composition. *Might as well start at square one*, he thought. But after his first few classes, Darnell had already decided that college might not be for him. His writing instructor assigned weekly papers, and his public speaking instructor required outlines for every speech.

By mid-semester, Darnell was really starting to get stressed out, especially about his two hardest classes. His psychology professor blasted through

Darko Kovacevic/Shutterstock.com

several chapters of the textbook every week, and his physics professor acted as if the entire class was made up of budding scientists. *Not quite*, Darnell privately objected. He had no idea college consisted of such challenging coursework, and he had no idea how to memorize all the information he needed to know for midterms. The psychology exam would cover the first twelve chapters of the book, and he knew his entire final grade in that class would be based on a midterm exam and a final exam, each worth 50 percent. Twelve chapters—at once? His Introduction to Psychology textbook had a twenty-five-page glossary at the end of the book. Twenty-five pages of new terms to memorize! Impossible!

The physics midterm would require him to have memorized all kinds of mathematical formulas. The syllabus said: "The laws of nature can often be stated in words or written as a mathematical formula. In this course, you will learn to use mathematics and the rules of algebra to make predictions.... Students sometimes try to memorize the formula as just symbols and don't understand the meaning of the symbols."[1] *No kidding*, Darnell thought, cynically. He saw the words and symbols on the page of his physics book, but what did they mean?

$$X = \tfrac{1}{2}at^2 + vt + x$$

X = distance traveled,
a = acceleration,
t = time,
v = starting velocity,
x = starting position
If X is what?

When it came time to study for his two midterm exams, Darnell stared at his open textbook for a while, trying to memorize complicated formulas or psych terms that made no sense to him. He'd think he had a handle on a term, and then the next thing he knew, it had flown out of his head. *How does __anyone__ memorize all this stuff?* Darnell wondered. *Nobody takes a class to learn how to memorize even though that's what college is all about.* The only solution Darnell could think of was pulling a couple of all-nighters, which he did regularly when he got on a movie marathon jag, anyway. But he noticed that watching a movie when you're tired and studying physics when you're tired are two different things, so he just gave up and finished up the night on Flickr. Besides, posting his photos online was much more fun.

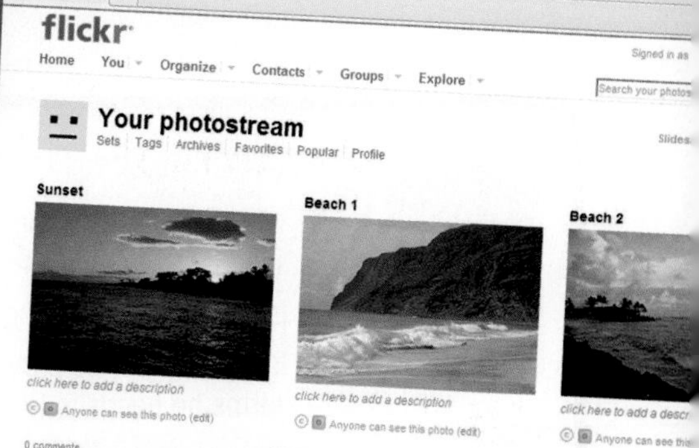

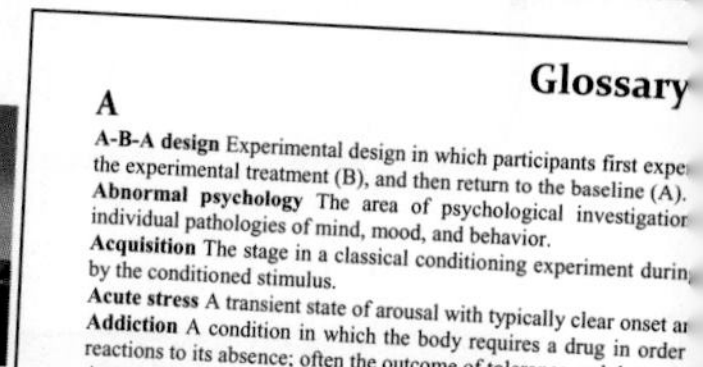

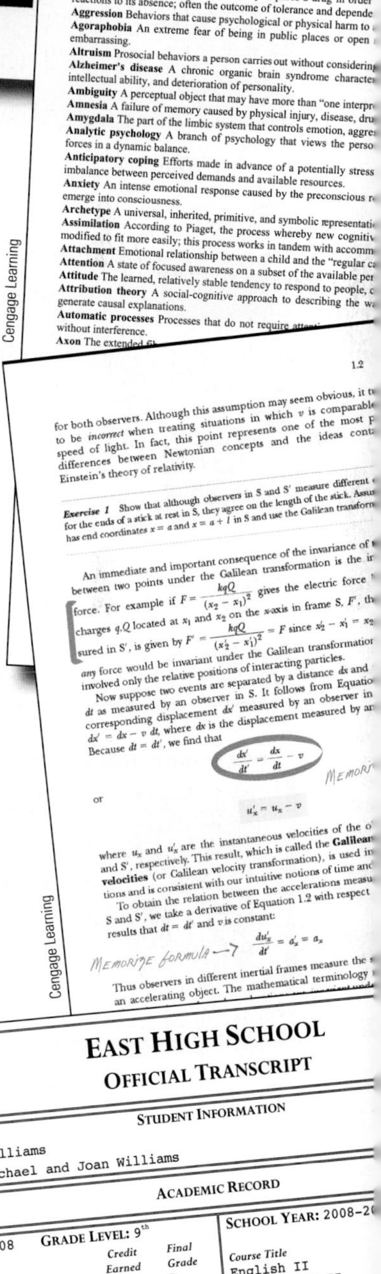

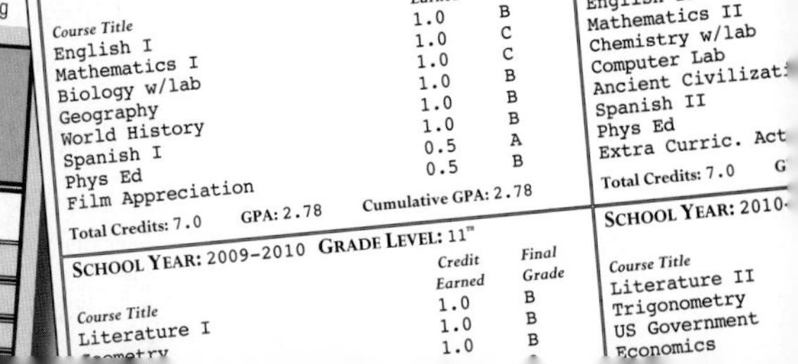

EAST HIGH SCHOOL
OFFICIAL TRANSCRIPT
STUDENT INFORMATION
FULL NAME: Darnell Williams
PARENTS/GUARDIAN: Michael and Joan Williams
ACADEMIC RECORD

SCHOOL YEAR: 2007–2008 GRADE LEVEL: 9th

Course Title	Credit Earned	Final Grade
English I	1.0	B
Mathematics I	1.0	C
Biology w/lab	1.0	C
Geography	1.0	B
World History	1.0	B
Spanish I	1.0	B
Phys Ed	0.5	A
Film Appreciation	0.5	B

Total Credits: 7.0 GPA: 2.78 Cumulative GPA: 2.78

SCHOOL YEAR: 2008–2…

Course Title: English II, Mathematics II, Chemistry w/lab, Computer Lab, Ancient Civilizat…, Spanish II, Phys Ed, Extra Curric. Act…

Total Credits: 7.0

SCHOOL YEAR: 2009–2010 GRADE LEVEL: 11th

Course Title	Credit Earned	Final Grade
Literature I	1.0	B
…ometry	1.0	B
	1.0	B

SCHOOL YEAR: 2010–…

Course Title: Literature II, Trigonometry, US Government, Economics

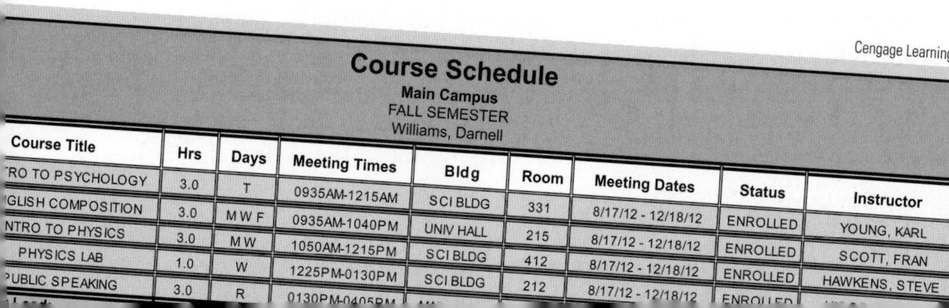

Course Schedule
Main Campus
FALL SEMESTER
Williams, Darnell

Course Title	Hrs	Days	Meeting Times	Bldg	Room	Meeting Dates	Status	Instructor
…RO TO PSYCHOLOGY	3.0	T	0935AM-1215AM	SCI BLDG	331	8/17/12 - 12/18/12	ENROLLED	YOUNG, KARL
…GLISH COMPOSITION	3.0	M W F	0935AM-1040PM	UNIV HALL	215	8/17/12 - 12/18/12	ENROLLED	SCOTT, FRAN
…NTRO TO PHYSICS	3.0	M W	1050AM-1215PM	SCI BLDG	412	8/17/12 - 12/18/12	ENROLLED	HAWKENS, STEVE
PHYSICS LAB	1.0	W	1225PM-0130PM	SCI BLDG	212	8/17/12 - 12/18/12	ENROLLED	
…UBLIC SPEAKING	3.0	R	0130PM-0405PM	…		8/17/12 - 12/18/12	ENROLLED	

What Do You Think?

1. Why is Darnell having problems remembering course content in his classes? List five reasons you identify from the case study.
2. Is Darnell overreacting? Is his situation common to first-year students? To you? Why or why not?
3. Identify three memory techniques that Darnell should use to help him memorize all the formulas and terms he needs to know.
4. If you were asked to explain how the memory process works and the scientific explanation behind his problems, what would you say?

VARK It!

Complete the recommended activity for your preferred VARK learning modality. If you are multimodal, select more than one activity. Your instructor may ask you to (a) give an oral report on your results in class, (b) send your results to him or her via e-mail, (c) post them online, or (d) contribute to a class chat.

Visual: As you read, create a mind map of the twenty ways to master your memory presented in this chapter.

Aural: As you read, create an auditory mnemonic device to help you remember the five major ways to master your memory. Announce it during an in-class discussion. (It may help other people!)

Read/Write: Do whatever you need to do to memorize one paragraph from this chapter. Look for the paragraph as you read. Close the book and write it down. Then check to see how close you were.

Kinesthetic: As you read, think of real examples of times when your memory failed you or times when you've been surprised at how well you remembered something. Bring these examples up in class discussion.

iStockphoto.com/Marcela Barsse/MarsBars; Joanna Goodyear/Dreamstime.com; iStockphoto.com/Nadezda Firsova; iStockphoto.com/Pascal Genest

Memory: The *Long* and *Short* of It

Challenge: List something you memorized as a child: perhaps a poem, a song, or lines from a school play. Why do you remember this passage verbatim after all these years?

Reaction:

____

____

____

Your grandparents used to dance to a popular song called "Memories Are Made of This." Of what, exactly? What are your earliest memories and how old were you? Most of us have "childhood amnesia," as Sigmund Freud called it, until we're three and a half or so. You may remember playing in the sand on the beach during a family vacation, dressing up to attend your cousin's wedding, or riding on an airplane for the first time. Before that age, you may not remember things because you weren't paying attention, because you didn't have the language skills to encode the memories, or because you hadn't yet formed the web of interconnections in your brain that you have now.[2]

Whenever it was that those first memories became available to you, and no matter what they are, think about how chock full your memory is now with both significant and seemingly insignificant memories, going all the way back to that poem your teacher asked you to memorize in fourth grade, the one you still remember ten or more years later, oddly enough. Through the years, your memories will continue to accumulate, and interestingly, you'll never run out of room! It's a good thing, too. Imagine what life without memory would be like. We'd have the same conversations with the same people over and over again, and we'd need to relearn how to drive each time we got behind the wheel of a car. Fortunately, our memories do an amazing job of streamlining life for us. But how much do we really understand about how our memories work—and why they sometimes don't?

EXERCISE 7.1

Subjective Memory Test

How good is your memory? Fill out Parts A and B to begin applying the information in this chapter to your own memory.

	Excellent			Good			Poor
How would you rate your memory overall?	1	2	3	4	5	6	7

A. How often do the following general memory tasks present a problem for you?

	Excellent			Good			Poor
1. Names	1	2	3	4	5	6	7
2. Where I've put things	1	2	3	4	5	6	7
3. Phone numbers I've just checked	1	2	3	4	5	6	7
4. Words	1	2	3	4	5	6	7
5. Knowing if I've already told someone something	1	2	3	4	5	6	7
6. Forgetting things people tell me	1	2	3	4	5	6	7
7. Faces	1	2	3	4	5	6	7
8. Directions	1	2	3	4	5	6	7
9. Forgetting what I started to do	1	2	3	4	5	6	7
10. Forgetting what I was saying	1	2	3	4	5	6	7
11. Remembering what I've done (lock the door, etc.)	1	2	3	4	5	6	7

B. How often do the following academic memory tasks present a problem for you?

	Excellent			Good			Poor
12. What I've just been reading	1	2	3	4	5	6	7
13. What I read an hour ago	1	2	3	4	5	6	7
14. What I read last week	1	2	3	4	5	6	7
15. Assignment/Exam due dates	1	2	3	4	5	6	7
16. Appointments with instructors	1	2	3	4	5	6	7
17. Assignment details	1	2	3	4	5	6	7
18. Factual information for exams	1	2	3	4	5	6	7
19. Theoretical information for exams	1	2	3	4	5	6	7
20. Information from readings for exams	1	2	3	4	5	6	7
21. Information from in-class lectures for exams	1	2	3	4	5	6	7
22. Including everything I should study for exams	1	2	3	4	5	6	7

My score's definitely worse in Part B—I'm a kinesthetic learner.

Part A #2 is a problem for me tho.

Informal assessments, like this one, may help you understand your own perceptions of how well your memory works. The lower your score on each portion, the better you perceive your memory to be. Do your scores for Part A and Part B differ? The general tasks in Part A are presented in the order of concern reported by older adults cited in one study (with the top items perceived as most problematic).[3] Did you find items toward the top of each list to be more problematic for you, too?

In one recent study in which college students were asked which aspects of memory they most wanted to improve among general and academic tasks, the top three items were improving schoolwork or study skills, remembering what was read, and remembering specific facts and details.[4] Understandably, the academic aspects of memory were those most personally valued. Is that true for you, too? Are the items in Part B generally higher priorities for you now as a college student?

> **Memory is the mother of all wisdom.**
>
> *Aeschylus, ancient Greek dramatist and playwright, known as the founder of Greek tragedy (525–456 B.C.)*

Most of us may not even realize just how important memory is. We talk about our memories as if they were something we own. We say we have good memories or bad memories, just like we have a crooked smile or nice one. But no one would ever say, "Hey, that's one nice-looking memory you've got there!" in the same way they'd say, "Wow, you have a really nice smile!" No brain surgeon could open up your head and evaluate your memory. Memory isn't a thing; it's a process. You can't see it or touch it or hold it. Even one specific memory has many different features: You can remember something by what you saw, smelled, heard, or felt. And even within one of these categories, individuals may differ in what they recall. You may be able to rehear lines from the script as if they were being spoken, but your friend may remember specific details about the cinematography, like the angle of particular shots and close-ups of the main actors.

Don't believe it when someone claims to have a one-size-fits-all, magic formula to help you unlock the secrets of your memory. It isn't that easy. Still, there are techniques which, when applied to the way you read your assignments or study for exams, can help you do your best, academically. We can only begin to grasp the rich complexities of memory by understanding it as a process. This chapter will examine how your memory works and suggest how you can best use it as a learning tool. However, it's important to recognize first that mastering memory depends on the answers to several questions like these:[5]

1. **Who is learning?** A calculus professor and a beginning calculus student would approach memorizing the main points of an article on math differently.
2. **What needs to be learned?** How you learn your lines for a play would differ from how you learn the Dutch masters' paintings for your art appreciation test.

> **The existence of forgetting has never been proved: We only know that some things don't come to mind when we want them.**
>
> *Friedrich Nietzsche, German philosopher (1844–1900)*

3. **How will learning be tested?** Learning information to *recall* uses different memory techniques than learning information to *recognize*. Recognition requires that you select from several alternatives; recall requires that you come up with memorized information on your own.

4. **How long must the information be remembered?** Learning your multiplication tables as a child is something that must remain with you throughout your life. You use them on a daily basis to do routine things like figure how much it will cost you to fill up your gas tank. On the other hand, learning the date of the Battle of Hastings isn't quite as crucial to remember for the long haul.

EXERCISE 7.2

Test Your Memory

For a more objective assessment of your memory, try this test. Study the following list of words for up to one minute. Then cover them with your hand and see how many you can remember and list them in the right-hand column.

theory ____________
rehearsal ____________
student ____________
bone ____________
frostbite ____________
camera ____________
rose ____________
calculus ____________
lecture ____________

Man! I only got 5 the first time!

How many words were you able to remember? Which words did you forget? Unfamiliar words? Words that had no relevance to your life? What memory techniques did you use to help you remember?

The Three R's of Remembering: Record, Retain, Retrieve

? challenge

" reaction

Challenge: Think of three ways in which using your memory is like taking pictures with a digital camera.

Reaction:

____

____

____

Improving your memory is easier if you understand how it works. Memory consists of three parts: your *sensory memory,* your *working memory* (called short-term memory by some psychologists), and your *long-term memory.* These three parts of the memorization process are connected to these three memory tasks: *recording, retaining,* and *retrieving* memories—the "Three R's of Remembering."[6]

Let's take a closer look at how all these things figure into your success in college. To do so, we'll compare the three R's of remembering to the process involved when taking pictures with a digital camera: record, retain, retrieve.

Your Sensory Memory: Focus

Consolidating memories in your brain is similar to taking pictures with a digital camera. Before we discuss the first R of remembering—namely, *Record*—we have to talk first about focus. Before you even push the button to snap a picture, you have to focus on your subject. Most digital cameras today focus on things automatically, and unlike older cameras, you don't have to turn the focus knob until the image is clear. But you do need to decide what to focus *on*. What do you want to take a picture of? Where will you point the camera? When it comes to your college classes and the role your memory plays in your success, remember that focus doesn't come automatically. It requires consciously deciding where to direct your attention.

I totally get this! What a cool comparison!

Imagine this: You're on your way to class. You walk through a student demonstration and get brushed by members of the crowd. Then you cross a busy intersection a little too slowly and get honked at by a speeding car. Finally, you see a billboard you've never noticed before: "I love you, Whitney. Will you marry me? Carl." *How romantic,* you think to yourself.

You're engulfed in stimuli as you walk, but three major sensations just passed through your *sensory memory* in a few seconds, in this case, your *haptic* memory (touch, the crowd), your *echoic* memory (sounds, the car horn), and your *iconic* memory (sight, the billboard), all parts of your sensory memory. You have a different channel for each of these three senses. Most experts believe that your sensory memory retains an exact copy of what you've seen or heard—pure and unanalyzed—for less than a second.[7] Some of these images, or icons, will be transferred to your working memory, which we'll discuss next. This transfer depends on attention and focus.

To help you with attention management, consider the following suggestions:

1. **Slow down; you move too fast.** Imagine trying to take a photo of something on the way to class if you were running. Everything would be a blur; trying to take a picture would be futile. The busyness of everyday life is sometimes overwhelming. It's no wonder with so much going on—school, family, friends, romantic partners, work—that your attention gets splintered in many different directions. Focus requires your full attention aimed at one thing at a time. Turn down the music, turn off the television, shut down the six windows open on your browser, and focus. That's a challenge.
2. **Deal with it.** If something is driving you to distraction, maybe you need to take care of it first so that you *can* focus. Getting stuck won't help, but sometimes dealing with an urgent priority is an important first step toward managing your attention.

© chris brignell/Alamy

> **I have a photographic memory but once in a while I forget to take off the lens cap.**
>
> *Milton Berle, comedian (1908–2002)*

> **The true art of memory is the art of attention.**
>
> *Samuel Johnson, British poet, essayist, and biographer (1709–1784)*

© Larry Harwood Photography. Property of Cengage Learning

3. **Notice where you go.** Wandering thoughts are normal. In one study, college students were asked to identify what they were thinking about eight random times each day for one week. On average, they weren't thinking about what they were doing 30 percent of the time. Some students were "elsewhere" 80 to 90 percent of the time.[8] When *your* attention wanders off, where does it go? Is it often the same place? Knowing your mental tendencies is part of understanding what makes you tick. Then you can recognize the pattern when you notice it and work on changing it.

4. **Watch for signals.** As a college student, you'll probably take at least forty different courses from all sectors of your college and be exposed to literally thousands of facts. Not even a memory expert could master them all at once. You must be selective about focus. Interestingly, journalist David Shenk wrote in his book *Data Smog,* "Education is actually the limiting of information."[9] In a funny way, that's true, isn't it? Of all the things you could learn about a subject, you're most likely to learn the material presented by your instructor and through your course readings. Your textbooks will guide you as you read by using bold fonts, different colors, charts, tables, and headings. Think of them as animated .jpegs on the page, calling out, "Hey, look at me!" Then zoom in on those things. In class, watch the instructor's body language; listen to her inflection; notice what gets written on the board or which PowerPoint slides stay on the screen longer than others. Keep those handouts handy. Plenty of subtle signals exist, but you have to pay attention to them.

5. **Get help if you need to.** If you have been diagnosed with ADHD, your brain is wired somewhat differently, affecting your memory and your ability to concentrate.[10] If you've not been diagnosed with a learning disability, but your attention appears to be extremely challenging to harness and you're not sure why, seek help from a counselor or learning specialist on campus. Challenges to your memory can be addressed by learning particular strategies.

Record: Your Short-Term Memory

After you've focused your camera on your subject, you're ready to take a picture, right? But with a digital camera, you don't just click and walk away. You actually click and then review the picture on the small viewing screen to decide whether you want to save it or delete it.

Similarly, *recording* sensory impressions involves an evaluation process that takes place in your short-term or *working memory.* Your working memory is like a review screen, where you review recently acquired sensory impressions, enhancing them with related information that you retrieve from your long-term memory. In fact, your working memory is often involved in the focus process. You give selected, focused attention to some of what you see and hear because it has personal meaning for you or relates to something in your past experience. In our example of you

CAREER OUTLOOK: *FAIL FORWARD*

If you don't make mistakes, you're not working on hard enough problems. And that's a big mistake.

Frank Wilczek, 1951–,
Winner Nobel Prize, Physics, 2004

There's no doubt about it: Failure isn't fun. But have you ever read the professional backgrounds of highly successful people? Believe it or not, most of them didn't skyrocket to the top. If you graphed their careers, you'd see just as many lows as highs. Their histories are littered with failures.

Take Scott Adams, the creator of the Dilbert cartoons, who says "If you're taking risks, and you probably should, you can find yourself failing 90% of the time. The trick is to get paid while you're doing the failing and to use the experience to gain skills that will be useful later. I failed at my first career in banking. I failed at my second career with the phone company. But you'd be surprised at how many of the skills I learned in those careers can be applied to almost any field, including cartooning . . . failure is a process, not an obstacle."[11]

Although it's a radical departure from what most people think—that to fail is to "crash and burn"—try thinking of failure as *forward motion*. You're moving along toward a goal when you suddenly trip and fall forward. The act of falling isn't fun, but at least you end up further along than you were beforehand.

Instead of "*falling* forward," try to wrap your brain around the concept of "*failing* forward." What would that one attitude tweak do for you? It might change everything.

For example, one thing it might do is help you be more realistic about yourself. Nobody is exceptional at everything. But most of us are pretty good at multiple things. For example, maybe you're good at remembering key dates for your history class but not so great at remembering equations for your calculus class. And even though one comes more easily than the other, you still wouldn't consider yourself to be a history genius. You're moderately good at it.

The question is: how can you creatively combine the things you're moderately good at into one package? The Dilbert creator continues, "I succeeded as a cartoonist with negligible art talent, some basic writing skills, an ordinary sense of humor and a bit of experience in the business world. The 'Dilbert' comic is a combination of all four skills. The world has plenty of better artists, smarter writers, funnier humorists and more experienced business people. The rare part is that each of those modest skills is collected in one person." Creating your value by creatively piecing together your unique talents is the secret. Acting on that one realization can propel you and your career forward.

I love Dilbert!

Perhaps you've heard the old quotation, "Good things come to those who wait." In today's competitive career world, that's hardly the case. The action won't move toward you, and luck won't come knocking at your door. You have to move to where the action is to *attract* luck. You will fail at some things; there's no doubt about that. But when you do fail, look around to see where you've landed. Are you ahead of where you were? Take note, collect yourself, get out the superglue, and piece together your own success. Over time, failing forward can not only provide the best lessons, but it can advance your career in ways you can't possibly anticipate now.

Words of wisdom here...

Think Ahead: Think about a college class in which you've not succeeded or not done as well as you hoped you would. What lessons did you learn? As you look ahead to your eventual career, can these lessons apply in the world of working professionals, too? If so, how?

I've never thought about failure this way...

CAST ON CAREERS

© Larry Harwood Photography. Property of Cengage Learning

FOCUS: What mistakes did you make your first semester of college?

JOE: I came to college from out of state, and at first I found it hard to fit in. I spent as little time as possible on campus, and I really didn't want to make connections. Actually, I isolated myself. I tend to be very reserved anyway, and I didn't want to take any unnecessary risks. Eventually, I discovered new things about myself and went on to achieve several leadership positions on campus. As I reached out to other students, I found myself doing better in my classes, too. Now, in many ways, I'm a different person!

FOCUS: What are your career plans?

JOE: Women's and ethnic studies is my major and creative writing is my minor. My long-term goal is to go to law school and specialize in indigenous law—the relationship between Native Americans and their government, or more broadly, the rights of indigenous peoples across the world.

walking to class, which of these three specific sensations you just experienced are you likely to remember: the crowd, the car, or the billboard? To stay true to the analogy, which one would you take a picture of? It depends, right? You may remember the billboard because you plan to show it to someone else later, or the demonstration because you disagree with its cause, or the car horn because it scared you.

The problem with working memory is that the length of time it can hold information is limited. You probably don't remember what you ate for dinner last Monday, do you? You'd have to reconstruct the memory based on other clues. Where was I? What was I doing? Who was I with?

The other problem with working memory is that it has limited capacity. It fills up quickly and then dumps what it doesn't need. If that weren't the case, our working memories would be cluttered with a chaotic array of useless information. Picture someone in the act of juggling with a number of balls in the air at once. Working memory helps us process the world as we encounter it, and it guides our actions, second by second. It's what you're using when you speak or listen (imagine if you forgot the beginning of a sentence by the time you got to the end), work math problems in your head, do a puzzle, follow directions, and read a book, for example.[12] If you look up a number in the campus directory, you can usually remember it long enough to walk over to the phone, right? A few minutes after you've dialed, however, the number is gone. Current estimates are that you can keep something in working memory for one to two minutes, giving your brain a chance to do a quick review, selecting what to save and what to delete.[13] Just how much information can your working memory hold? Look at these letters in the first example, and then close your eyes and try to repeat them back in order.

I don't remember phone numbers at all anymore thanks to cell phones.

SAJANISMOELIHHEGNR

Can't do it? This task is virtually impossible because the string contains eighteen letters. Researchers believe that working memory can recall only seven pieces of information, plus or minus two.[14] (There's a reason why telephone numbers are prechunked for us.) Chunking these eighteen letters into five units helps considerably. Now look at the letters again in this second example and try to recall all eighteen.

SAJA NISM OELI HHEG NR

If we rearrange the letters into recognizable units as in the third example, it becomes even easier, right?

AN IS MAJOR ENGLISH HE

And if the words are rearranged to make perfect sense as in example four, the task becomes simple.

HE IS AN ENGLISH MAJOR

The principle of chunking is also used to move information from your working memory to your long-term memory bank, and it's used in memorization techniques that we will describe later in this chapter.

Retain and Retrieve: Your Long-Term Memory

Let's go back to our camera analogy. Once your camera's memory card gets full, you probably transfer the photos to your computer, or you print them out, put them in photo albums or picture frames, or upload them to Flickr. However,

Monkey Business Images/Shutterstock.com

> **How we remember, what we remember, and why we remember form the most personal map of our individuality.**
>
> *Christina Baldwin, author (1946–)*

think of how terrible it would be to lose your room key and get a case of *frostbite* from spending the night in your car in the parking lot. Now without looking back, try it and see if it works for you. Of course, the optimal way the Loci system works is if the locations are familiar to *you*. Its main benefits are that it uses cues, incorporates associations, and orders information into a sequence, all of which aid in memory transfer and storage.[30] Joshua Foer, ordinary person turned 2006 U.S. Memory champion, puts it this way in his book, *Moonwalking with Einstein: The Art and Science of Remembering Everything,* "The idea is to create a space in the mind's eye, a place that you know well and can easily visualize and then populate that imagined place with images representing whatever you want to remember."[31]

11. **Link or narrate.** Instead of a Loci system, you can create a linking mnemonic to help you memorize a list. To do this, you must connect item A to item B, item B to item C, and so forth. Consider again the list of words you were challenged to remember and write down: theory, rehearsal, student, bone, frostbite, camera, rose, calculus, and lecture. Your visual links might go like this: (1) (theory + rehearsal) You imagine a *theoretician* at a *rehearsal* dinner. (2) (rehearsal + student) The rehearsal dinner is attended by student friends of the bride and groom. (3) (student + bone) One student is in a leg cast because of a broken bone, and so forth.

    Another way to use this method is to create a story that links each cue: A geeky theoretician went to a rehearsal dinner, where he sat next to a student from one of his classes who had a broken leg (bone). The student injured his leg in a hiking accident in which he suffered a fall and got frostbite from exposure, and so forth. Each item is linked to the item before, except for the first one. You must find a cue to remember it independently to get the chain started.

12. **Peg.** The Peg system can be traced back to the mid-1600s, and it was extended to its modern method of using rhyming syllables by England's John Sambrook in 1879.[32] Remember the old nursery rhyme, "One, two, buckle my shoe"? The Peg system uses these rhyming pairs:

one—bun	six—sticks
two—shoe	seven—heaven
three—tree	eight—gate
four—door	nine—wine
five—hive	ten—hen

To use the Peg system, create *specific* images for yourself: a big, fat hamburger *bun*, a stiletto-heeled *shoe*, a weeping willow *tree*, and so forth, and hang the items you're trying to memorize on these mental "pegs" in order. To continue with our example, you'd picture a *theoretical* treatise stuffed between the hamburger *bun*, an image of a teenage girl's *rehearsal* of how to walk in her first pair of stiletto high-heeled *shoes*, a *student* sprawled out studying under a weeping willow *tree,* and so forth. Other types of Peg systems have been devised, but the rhyming system is the most common. But does it work with information other than lists, you might wonder? Try it for yourself to find out.

Manipulate It

Although some of us tend to favor other modalities than kinesthetic learning, all of us can benefit from memory techniques with a kinesthetic basis. Actively doing something with information is a better way to commit it to memory than remaining passively disengaged. If you had three hours to study a textbook chapter that takes one hour to read, what should you do: read the chapter three times, or work with the material after reading it once? The second option is generally more effective. So what kinds of things should you *do*?

13. **Mark it up.** Be an active reader; interact with the text. People who are used to reading complex material—your instructors, for example—read slowly, chew on each word, and make copious notes in the margins, arguing, questioning, summarizing, or explaining. Take notes as you read, "talk" with the author, and write out your reactions. Highlighting can be somewhat helpful, but it's often not enough. Every time you reach for your highlighter, ask yourself why you want to highlight that passage. Why is it important? To commit information to memory, you must go beyond simply coloring.[33]

14. **Mark it down.** If you want to give yourself a break, don't bother committing something unimportant to memory. Just write it down. (Of course, you still have to remember where you put that piece of paper.) Writing something

down is an obvious memory alternative; save your memory for more important tasks. If it's something you do want to remember, however, the physical act of writing itself can help. Unless the exam is open-book, however, actually bringing your notes with you at exam time could be hazardous to your academic health!

I'm a kinesthetic learner—maybe I could cut up my notes and put the pieces back together like a puzzle . . .

15. **Organize.** Arrange and rearrange the material you're trying to memorize. Outline it—putting concepts into hierarchical order can help you figure out important relationships. If you're trying to learn the responsibilities of the various branches of the government for your political science class, actually drawing a kind of written organizational chart is likely to help your essay answer flow better.

16. **Picture.** Drawings and mind maps can also be effective memory tools, particularly for visual learners. Think of drawing pictures to help you remember ridiculous visualizations or word associations. If you're trying to remember bones for your anatomy and physiology class, try Farsighted *Fibula*, Tempting *Tibia*, Party Girl *Patella*, Feathered *Femur*, and Pretty *Pelvis*. Any time you can engage in what's called dual coding, using more than one channel—verbal and visual—you'll likely reinforce what you're trying to memorize.[34]

17. **Act.** If you've always had a hankering to be a star on *Grey's Anatomy* or some other drama, consider putting motions to your memorizing. Act it out. If you're trying to memorize a famous speech like Martin Luther King, Jr.'s "I Have a Dream," deliver it in front of a mirror. Write a short script and ask your roommate to play opposite you, if it helps you remember who said what to whom for an exam in history, or obviously, theater.

18. **Produce.** There's good evidence that putting things in your own words is highly beneficial to remembering.[35] Redeliver the professor's lecture. Can you explain the concepts he explained, or do you stop after a few minutes and puzzle? Producing information requires you to dig deeper into your memory and reconstruct information, a process that engages you more actively and benefits you and your memory beyond simple recognition tasks. One of the very best ways to produce is to teach something to someone else. To do that successfully, you have to know it yourself, inside and out. Teaching adds another layer of responsibility for knowing something, yours *and* someone else's.

19. **Test.** Rather than assuming you remember something, test yourself. Create a multiple-choice, matching, or true-and-false test. Doing so requires you to ask: amidst this sea of information, what's important? Better yet, create essay questions that require you to organize and write what you know about a subject. Swap tests with a study mate, or create flashcards so that you can quiz yourself. Research shows that tests are "powerful memory enhancers." The simple act of taking a test helps you recall information, even if what you studied isn't on the test![36]

Make It Funny

Humor is an excellent memory-enhancing tool. Think about how easy it is to remember the plots of comedies you've seen at the movies or on television. For example, you may be able to remember conversations between *Friends* or *The Simpsons* cast members in shows you've watched once or twice, almost verbatim, just because they tickled your funny bone.

I never thought about it, but it's true! I have a ton of lines memorized from my favorite funny movies!

20. Mock it. Experts on learning and the brain believe that the optimal condition for learning is *relaxed alertness*. Sounds like an oxymoron, doesn't it? How can you be relaxed and alert at the same time? Actually, it is possible when the challenge is high, but the threat is low.[37] What better way to create those conditions than through humor? And what better way to engage your memory than to be a stand-up (or sit-down) comic?

Think back to some of the funniest scenes you've ever seen from *Saturday Night Live* or *Monty Python's Flying Circus*. They're probably still vivid in your memory. Have you ever seen *Monty Python's* "Hell's Grannies" skit: a gang made up of the Monty Python men, dressed up as little old ladies, cigarettes hanging out of their mouths, beating up passers-by with their purses, and tearing through the streets on souped-up motorcycles? Even if you haven't, you can picture it. One way to generate humor is to put incongruous things together in a new context. Images like these are memorable, and you should ask yourself how you could apply your own humor to the material you're attempting to trigger your memory to learn. If you're having trouble separating Socrates and Plato, draw a picture of a crate full of socks next to Socrates' name and a can of PlayDoh® next to Plato's.

> **Whenever I think of the past, it brings back so many memories.**
>
> *Stephen Wright, comedian (1955–)*

Create a David Letterman–like top-ten list of the reasons why Shakespeare's ten tragedies are tragic. Or rewrite a play—put Shakespeare's *Romeo and Juliet* into contemporary slang so that you can remember what "O Romeo, Romeo! Wherefore art thou Romeo?" really means. (Hint: it's not about his location.)[38] "Hey, Romeo. Why you gotta be a Montague, man?" Or if you can never remember which character is from the Montague family and which is a Capulet, write a silly limerick to help you remember:

There once was a girl named Cap

Who fell for a guy and was hap

But her family and his

Wouldn't stand for the biz

So they both ended up playing taps.

Set it to music. Be imaginative. We tend to remember what's bizarre, funny, or even obscene![39]

CONTROL: *YOUR TOUGHEST CLASS*

Think about your most challenging class this semester. What kind of information in this class is difficult for you to commit to memory: complex readings, formulas, lecture material? Answer the following questions to help you realize the role sharpening your memory can play in your success.

- So far in this class, have you been engaging in **maintenance rehearsal** (keeping information in your short-term memory) or **elaborate rehearsal** (transferring information to your long-term memory)?

  ____

- How can you better study for quizzes or exams in this class using memory strategies? Provide examples for each of the five principles discussed in this chapter:

  Make the material stick. ______________________________

  Make it meaningful. ______________________________

  Make use of mnemonic devices. ______________________________

  Manipulate the material to help learn it. ______________________________

  Make it funny. ______________________________

- How successful have your memory strategies been? What will you do differently now?

  ____

  ____

Send your instructor in this class an e-mail, if appropriate, indicating your efforts and detailing your progress.

LET'S SEE . . . Which of THESE should I TRY for PHYSICS?

How Our Memories (uh...hmmm...) Fail Us

Imagine this: You meet someone at a school reception who says, "Hey, I know you! Remember? We met a year ago—it was September—at that fraternity party, and we even went out a few times. I've never forgotten you." You rack your brain. This person doesn't even look familiar. You wonder, *Am I being confused with someone else? Am I crazy? I have no recollection at all!* Later, you comb through your calendar to reconstruct that month. You weren't even attending your current school then. It couldn't have been you.

Digital cameras can malfunction, files we've saved can become corrupted, and sometimes our memories fail us, too. We forget things or alter them in our thinking. Think of how many times you have had to e-mail someone for a password because you've forgotten your original one. Think about the details of a past experience that would probably look a bit different now in instant replay mode. While our memories are one of the most complex tools we have, they're not perfect, and those imperfections fascinate scientists. In one famous experiment, researchers asked sixty-seven men in their late forties questions about their lives as high school freshmen—the same questions the researchers had asked them as actual students thirty-four years earlier. Interestingly, their memories of things were often a far cry from what they had indicated to be true so long ago.[40]

There are certainly things you can do to boost your memory. For example, sleep strengthens your memories and protects them. Exercise at any age, but particularly as we get older, helps improve our memories. Even diet plays a role: eating a healthy balance of protein and carbohydrates, for example, strengthens cognition and memory. If you're running on no sleep, eating junk food like there's no tomorrow, and there's an impression in your couch from where you sit, your memory may be at risk![41]

Nevertheless, our memories do malfunction on occasion. Here are seven ways our memories fail us from *The Seven Sins of Memory: How the Mind Forgets and Remembers.* See how many cause you to nod your head in recognition.

1. **Fading.** Memories are transient; they fade over time. You probably remember what you wore yesterday, but how about on October 5 a year ago? As time goes by, memories generally weaken.

I could SWEAR this section is about me!

2. **Absentmindedness.** Sometimes there's a disconnect between your focus and your memory. You were doing several things at one time—talking to the girl next to you after class and checking your cell phone while stuffing your backpack—and now you have no idea what you did with your history textbook. It's not that the information is lost over time; it probably never registered in the first place because your attention was elsewhere. The famous musician Yo-Yo Ma once absentmindedly left his 2.5 million dollar cello in the trunk of a taxi. Fortunately, it was recovered by the police right away.
3. **Blocking.** It's right on the tip of your tongue, but you just can't quite retrieve it. You can see the face, but you can't conjure up the name. But later that day, without even trying, suddenly it comes to you. Psychologists call it TOT, the Tip of the Tongue phenomenon. You feel as if you're about to sneeze, but can't, and the word—whatever it is—just won't come to you.
4. **Misattribution.** You say to your friend, "Hey, that was an interesting story you told me about the new girl in our composition class." "What story?" your friend replies. Someone told you something, but you're wrong about who it was. Or you read a passage in one book, but think you've read it in another. Or you've dreamed about something for so long that the fantasy actually becomes real in your mind. Your memory deceives you by mistaking one source for another or tricks you by inventing a memory where none actually exists.
5. **Suggestibility.** Sometimes you retain bits of information that you think are memories, but they really aren't. Here's an example: perhaps your mother has told you the cute anecdote about yourself as a two-year-old toddler so many times that you can now envision it, and you think you remember it. You were actually too young to remember anything, but the event has become real at someone else's suggestion.
6. **Bias.** Sometimes we knowingly, or more often unknowingly, rewrite history. We insist on some detail that, if we had the ability to go back in time to verify it, is actually wrong. But we remember it differently—and we're so sure! Perhaps someone has caught you in a trap in one of those instances by finding a piece of real evidence, and you've had to back down and admit that your memory is off a bit.
7. **Persistence.** Another way that memory plagues us is by nagging. You'd really like to forget something, but you just can't. You wake up in a cold sweat at 3 a.m., remembering the embarrassing thing you did at work or said in class. You'd like to be able to push the memory away, but it won't budge.

On today's college campuses, there's another kind of peddling going on. Someone may offer to sell, swap, or give you a substance that promises great results, socially or academically. These aren't the kind of chemicals for which you need eye goggles and rubber gloves, but they are hazardous to you and your memory, and you need to know the risks.

Let's start with the most common drug of all, alcohol, one of the most powerful amnesic agents available. With even one or two drinks, alcohol can disrupt your ability to move information from short-term to long-term memory, and as the amount of alcohol increases, so does your memory impairment. High doses of alcohol can seriously affect your ability to learn something new and even lead to blackouts, such that you can't remember anything that happened while you were under the influence.[48] And research shows that binge drinking causes physiological changes to your brain that affect working memory.[49] In one study, subjects' memories were even impaired when they *thought* they were drinking alcohol and weren't. Participants were asked to drink tonic water, but half were told they were drinking vodka and tonic, before participating in an eyewitness memory experiment. Subjects who believed they had drunk alcohol were more swayed by misleading information afterward, and although they were wrong about the accuracy of their views, interestingly, they were even more confident that they were right than the group of students who didn't think they'd drunk alcohol! The results suggest that even *thinking* you're under the influence can influence your memory![50]

Wow! I had no idea.

Ecstasy, a popular club and party drug, is another chemical that's hazardous to your memory. According to the National Institute on Drug Abuse (NIDA), people who regularly use MDMA (3,4-methylenedioxymethamphetamine) are subjecting themselves to possible brain damage. In a brain imaging study using positron emission tomography (PET) scans, the brain images of regular users of ecstasy showed damage of serotonin nerve endings. Ecstasy users performed worse than control groups on tests measuring attention, memory, and learning, and the heavier the drug use, the more adverse the effects on memory.[51] One study that surveyed "X" users in Europe, the United States, and Australia, found that regular users were 23 percent more likely to report memory problems than nonusers.[52]

That's not all the sobering news. Besides alcohol and drugs, other substances you put in your mouth can affect your memory, too. All those double cheeseburgers and orders of fries wreak havoc on more than your waistline. Extensive studies with mice "provide direct evidence that fast food diets, particularly a diet high in saturated fats, can have an adverse effect on learning and memory."[53]

Deepen Your Memory

The point of this chapter is this: In a classic study conducted in the mid-1970s, two Swedish scholars decided to find out the difference between effective and ineffective learners. They gave students this task: read an essay, summarize it, and solve a problem. Then they interviewed the students to find out how they had approached the task.

Nathan B Dappen/Shutterstock.com

Elisei Shafer/Shutterstock.com

FIGURE 7.5

Memory Processing

I'll remember this image—skipping a stone across the water is much different than deep sea diving!

The interviews revealed two types of learners illustrated in Figure 7.5. One group of students said things like, "I just tried to remember as much as I could" or "I just memorized what I read." Other students said, "I tried to look for the main idea" or "I looked for the point of the article." The professors who conducted the study then characterized the difference between *surface-level processing*, looking at words and numbers alone, and *deep-level processing*, searching for underlying meaning.[54] To become a truly focused learner, you must process information as you go. Dig deep!

* insight

! action

Now What Do You Think?

1. At the beginning of this chapter, Darnell Williams, a discouraged college student, faced a challenge. Now after reading this chapter, would you respond differently to any of the questions you answered about the "FOCUS Challenge Case"? Knowing what you know now, how would you advise him? Write a paragraph ending to the story, incorporating your best advice.
2. Of the list of twenty ways to master your memory, which are your "regulars"? How well do they work for you, generally?
3. Which techniques have you never tried? Why not?
4. Choose a specific technique for an upcoming exam, do it with gusto, and note your results afterward. Make a list of techniques that would work well for you, considering your psychological type and VARK preferences.

REALITY ✓ What did you LEARN?

On a scale of 1 to 10, answer the following questions now that you've completed this chapter.

low 1 2 3 4 5 6 7 8 9 10 high

In hindsight, how much did you already know about this subject before reading the chapter? ______

Can you answer these questions about developing your memory more fully now that you've read the chapter?

1. What are the three "R's" of remembering?
2. This chapter discusses twenty ways to master your memory. Can you identify five?
3. What is the role of health and wellness in how well your memory works?

How useful might the information in this chapter be to you? How much do you think this information might affect your success overall? ______

How much energy did you put into reading this chapter? ______

How long did it actually take you to complete this chapter (both the reading and writing tasks)? ______ Hour(s) ______ Minutes

Did you finish reading this chapter? ______

Did you intend to when you started? ______

If you meant to but didn't, what stopped you? ______

Challenge Yourself Online Quiz To find out just how much you've learned, access the College Success CourseMate via www.cengagebrain.com to take the Challenge Yourself Online Quiz.

Take a minute to compare these answers to your answers from the "Readiness Check" at the beginning of this chapter. What gaps exist between the similar questions? How might these gaps between what you thought before starting the chapter and what you now think after completing the chapter affect how you approach the next chapter in this book?

CHAPTER 8

Reading and Studying

You're About to Discover . . .

- Why reading is important
- How to engage in focused reading
- What metacognition is and how it can help you
- How to become an intentional learner
- How to integrate your learning

© Larry Harwood Photography. Property of Cengage Learning

READINESS ✓ What do you KNOW?

Before beginning to read this chapter, take two minutes to answer the following questions on a scale of 1 to 10. Your answers will help you assess how ready you are to focus.

low 1 2 3 4 5 6 7 8 9 10 high

How much do you *already* know?

Based on reading the "You're about to discover . . ." list and skimming this chapter, how much do you think you probably already know about this chapter's subject? ________

See if you can answer these questions about reading and studying *before* you read.

1. How many words per minute does the average college student read?
2. What does SQ6R stand for?
3. What's the definition of the word "metacognition"?

How much do you expect to learn?

In general, how motivated are you to learn more by reading this chapter? ________

How much do you think this information might affect your success overall? ________

How much energy do you plan to put into reading this chapter? ________

How ready are you to read *now*?

How ready are you to focus on this chapter? Enter a number for each aspect of your readiness to focus.

Physically ________

Intellectually ________

Emotionally ________

If any of your answers is below a 10, pay attention to whatever is distracting you before you start reading. Then zero in and focus.

How long do you think it will take you to complete this chapter from start to finish?

________ Hour(s) ________ Minutes

Now, as you begin, do you intend to finish reading this chapter?

________ yes ________ no ________ maybe

Chas/Shutterstock.com

© Larry Harwood Photography. Property of Cengage Learning

FOCUS Challenge Case

? challenge

Katie Alexander

College would be a lot more fun if it weren't for the stress that all the reading and studying caused. That was Katie Alexander's take on things. She wasn't much of a reader; she much preferred playing softball or volleyball with her friends to sitting in one spot with a book propped open in front of her. Reading for fun wasn't something she'd ever even consider doing—at least not reading books. To Katie, reading 75 text messages a day was necessary; reading books was boring. *Anyway, why read the book when you can just watch the movie?* she always asked. Katie was an energetic, active, outgoing person, and "doing" and "socializing" were her things. Reading and studying definitely weren't.

MalibuBooks/Shutterstock.com

The stress began before school even started when Katie Facebooked her future roommate. Amanda was her name, and she was from the Midwest, too. But here was the challenge. As active and physically fit as Katie was, she was shocked to find out that Amanda was handicapped. She'd been in a wheelchair since an automobile accident in third grade. *Can I handle that?* Katie wondered. *She seems nice, but how can I possibly take care of someone else? I can hardly take care of myself!* But as they communicated on Facebook over the summer, they became great friends before school ever started. And as things turned out, Amanda was the one who took care of Katie, not the other way around. When it came to academics, Amanda wanted to become Katie's personal trainer!

For Katie, reading and studying were hard work. She was smart enough to make it in college—she was sure of that—and she was motivated, especially with Amanda as a roommate. But reading was a labor-intensive activity that tried her patience, and after she'd read something, she was hard-pressed to summarize what it had been about. Before she knew it, she was off in some other world, thinking

Photos.com

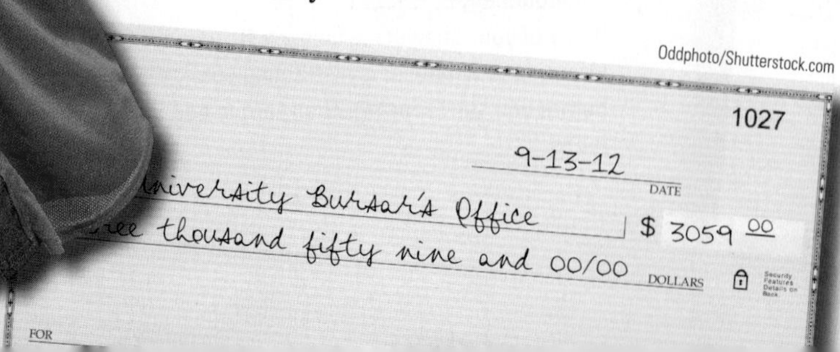

Oddphoto/Shutterstock.com

Johanna Goodyear/Shutterstock.com

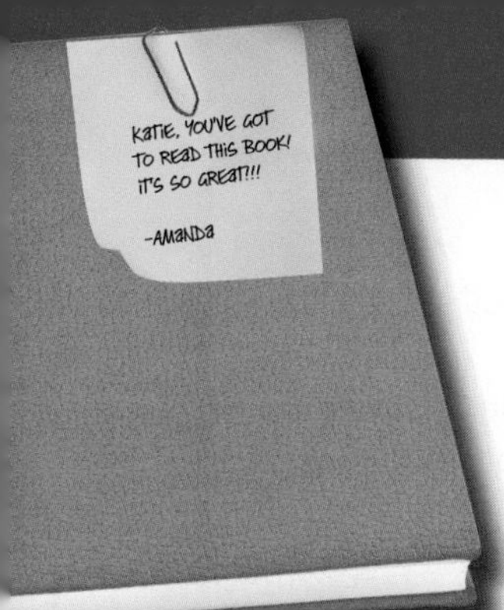

ristoph Weihs/Shutterstock.com; rTwister/Shutterstock.com

Chas/Shutterstock.com

about her friends, or her schedule at work, or everything else she had to do, which resulted in more stress.

Amanda, on the other hand, was an English major who loved to read. In fact, that's all she ever seemed to do. Her other best friend, Brittney, however, had a different strategy. "There's so much required reading in all my classes that I don't even know where to start," Brittney admitted, "so I just don't do it. I go to class, listen to the lectures, and write down what the instructor has said on the essay tests. Learn to play the game'!"

delihayat/Shutterstock.com

But Brittney's strategy definitely wasn't going to work for Katie in Professor Harris-Black's Introduction to Ethnic Studies class. She'd assigned a shocking number of articles to read. The professor didn't even go over the readings in class, and her lectures didn't even relate to the reading. Whenever she sat down to read an assignment, Katie found what to her were unfamiliar words and unnatural phrasing. The professor had suggested that students read with a dictionary at their sides, but who'd ever want to keep stopping to look up words? You'd never finish!

With a midterm exam coming up in her Ethnic Studies class next week, Katie's stress level was starting to skyrocket. She'd only read one of the nine articles assigned. In fact, she hadn't made it through the first article when she got discouraged and gave up. She knew the midterm essay test would be challenging. Winging it wouldn't work, and choosing to "watch the movie" instead of reading the book wasn't an option. Exactly what did Ethnic Studies have to do with anything, she puzzled, and why had her advisor suggested the course in the first place?

The night before the test, Katie decided to get serious. Amanda was already asleep, so she sat down at her desk, armed with her yellow highlighter. As she began reading, however, she realized she didn't know exactly what to highlight since she didn't really understand what she was reading. Looking back at the page she had just finished, she saw that she had basically highlighted everything. Exasperated, Katie told herself that she couldn't go to bed until she'd finished reading everything, no matter when that was. She started with the second article, since she'd read the first one, and by morning, she'd be as ready as possible. Anyway, it wasn't up to her—it was up to Professor Harris-Black; she was the one making up the test.

Getting an A on her Introduction to Ethnic Studies midterm exam was probably out of the question since Katie really didn't know the first thing about how to study. But if she could just manage to pass, Katie knew she would have to settle for that. On the other hand, she secretly hoped that maybe she'd just luck out.

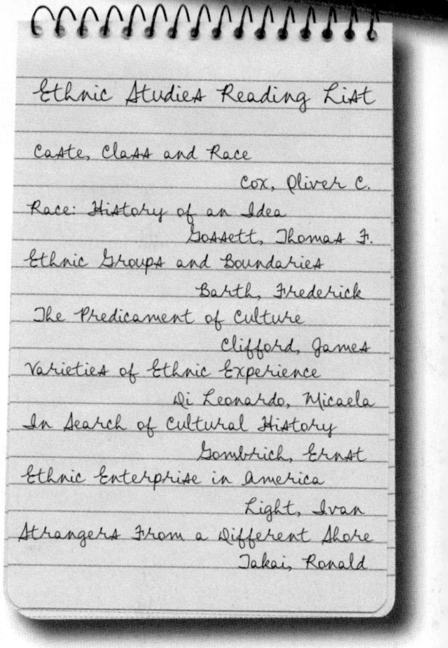

Lars Lindblad/Shutterstock.com

© Cengage Learning

Cross Cultural Dialogue:

A Participant Observer Study by an American Teacher in Ch

Aaron Mohr

The recent growth of international connectivity has increased the possibility for international communication and education. International students now have the opportunity to study in the United States, and Americans have a variety of options for study abroad. Additionally, the need for American educators overseas has increased. Often, American teachers are given incentives to teach classes internationally. While the internationalization of education is certainly beneficial, how do American teachers overcome intercultural differences?

Many researchers have examined willingness to communicate (WTC) in regard to culture (Roach & Olaniran, 2001; Lin & Rancer, 2003). These studies have found that some cultures are less prone to communicate openly, while other cultures display a strong preference for open communication. Other studies have looked at how intercultural interaction can affect WTC, and how interaction between cultures with varying levels of WTC is affected.

This study will look at willingness to communicate among Chinese students. Specifically, the WTC of Chinese students will be examined in an intercultural environment. The research will investigate how these students interact with American teachers in China and native Chinese teachers. This study will take a qualitative approach to determine the WTC of Chinese students interacting with an American teacher over time. The study will also address the WTC of the students in their interactions with their native Chinese teachers.

Literature Review

Many studies in recent years have looked at the willingness to communicate of international students and teachers. One such study investigated how international teaching assistants in the U.S. communicate (Roach & Olaniran, 2001). The study showed that international students willing to come to the U.S. are generally willing to communicate in intercultural settings. Another study looked at the willingness to communicate of Japanese students learning English (Yashima, Zenuk-Nishide & Shimizu, 2004). Other studies have sho differences in WTC can be p that are normally considered would argue that the culture U.S. are fairly similar, beca English-speaking western-s Hackman and Barthel-Hac otherwise. In the study, th that the level of WTC am students was much highe Zealand (Hackman and B

Similarly, this st to communicate among on possible changes in t over time during instru Additionally, the study differences in students instructors versus nati difference that makes age of the students b looking at WTC use study, on the other (ages 11-14); a diff variation. RQ1: I the willingness to change after four RQ2: How will t Chinese students Chinese instruct

This quantitati and how the w students chan American tea with native C determine if changes bas will be coll American case of thi and Ame a researc

Adisa/Shutterstock.com

What Do You Think?

1. How would you characterize Katie as a student? Identify five specific problems described in this case study that could interfere with her college success.
2. Katie is probably an intelligent student, but she has decided that she dislikes reading and studying, so she avoids it. How important will these two skills be as she continues to pursue a college degree? Is she likely to succeed her second time around?
3. Is Katie like students you know? If so, in what ways, specifically?
4. Identify three specific things Katie should do to get her college career on track.

VARK It!

Complete the recommended activity for your preferred VARK learning modality. If you are multimodal, select more than one activity. Your instructor may ask you to (a) give an oral report on your results in class, (b) send your results to him or her via e-mail, (c) post them online, or (d) contribute to a class chat.

Visual: As you begin reading this chapter, start constructing a chart or graph comparing how much time you spend on three things this week: talking on your cell phone, using social media and studying. Which activity has the longest line?

Aural: Choose a classmate as a discussion partner for this chapter. IM, text, or talk through main points and how they relate to both of you as you read. (These are all aural strategies, according to VARK.)

Read/Write: Start reading this chapter with a stack of blank index cards next to you. On each card, write a word you couldn't define in this chapter. When you're done reading, look them up in the dictionary and write out the definitions. Then compare your stack with the ones of other classmates.

Kinesthetic: Watch the Focus TV episode for this chapter at www.cengagebrain.com and answer the questions that go along with it. See if doing that beforehand helps you understand what you're reading.

iStockphoto.com/Marcela Barsse/MarsBars; Joanna Goodyear/Dreamstime.com; iStockphoto.com/Nadezda Firsova; iStockphoto.com/Pascal Genest

Who Needs to Read?

What's so important about reading? Teachers seem to think it's important, and parents consider it to be an admirable pastime, but times have changed, haven't they? Now you can just skim predigested information on websites, get a summary of the day's news from television, and watch movies for entertainment. Who needs to read? Look around the next time you're in a doctor or dentist's waiting room. You'll see some people staring at the TV screen mounted on the wall and others plugged into iPods. A few may be skimming through magazines, but does anyone ever pick up a book to actually read it cover to cover anymore? Does it matter?

The answer, according to many experts, is a resounding yes, it does![1] Reading helped create civilization as we know it and taught us particular ways of thinking. "We are losing a sort of psychic habit, a logic, a sense of complexity, an ability to spot contradictions and even falsity," says Neil Postman, author of

Amusing Ourselves to Death.[2] Eventually, he predicts, our culture will see the effects. What kinds of changes might experts like Postman predict?

- **Reading skills will deteriorate.** One fairly predictable result of doing anything less is that eventually you may not do it as well. Practice keeps your skills sharp. Even an Olympic athlete who doesn't stick with training gets rusty after a while. According to the National Survey of Adult Literacy, "The average American college graduate's literacy in English [has] declined significantly. . . . In 1992, 40 percent of the nation's college graduates scored at the proficient level . . . on the 2003 test, only 31 percent of the graduates demonstrated those high-level skills." Why? "Literacy of college graduates had dropped because a rising number of young Americans in recent years had spent their free time watching television and surfing the Internet."[3]

  Wow! I did not know this!

  As students read less, their reading skills deteriorate and they don't enjoy doing it. Conversely, the better you get at reading, the more you may enjoy it. Falling down every ten minutes the first time you get on skis isn't all that much fun, but once you can zip down the mountain like a pro, you begin to appreciate the sport.

- **Reading will become less popular.** Some might say that reading was much more essential to previous generations because they didn't have all the choices we have today.[4] Words like *lazy* and *bookworm* were used to describe Abraham Lincoln as a child because reading was all he ever wanted to do. Today, you'd be unlikely to hear those two particular insults combined. A hundred years ago, books took us places we could not easily go otherwise. Now there are much easier ways of getting there. Thomas Jefferson once told John Adams, "I cannot live without books." Evidently, today many people can.[5] According to experts, when we do read in today's fast-paced world, we often do so while doing something else—quickly and with less focus.

  Perhaps reading isn't your favorite pastime. You may feel about reading like many people do about eating cauliflower. You know it's good for you, but you'd prefer to avoid it. However, this chapter wouldn't be worth its weight in trees if it didn't try to convince you otherwise. One aspect of reading some people particularly dislike is that reading is not a social or physical activity. You can read with someone else in the room, of course, or talk about what you read afterward with friends, but basically, reading is something you do alone. It's a solitary activity that involves you, words on a page, an invisible author, and your brain. You need to do it with a

  cauliflower—yuck! That's right!

Copyright © Tom McCarthy / Photo Edit

> **You don't have to burn books to destroy a culture. Just get people to stop reading them.**
>
> *Ray Bradbury, science fiction writer, (1920–)*

minimum of physical movement. Reading while playing a game of volleyball would be tough to pull off.

If you enjoy reading, congratulations! When you settle in with an exciting novel, you can travel to the far corners of the Earth, turn back the clock to previous centuries, or fast-forward to a future that extends beyond your lifetime. You can inject yourself into the story and be someone else for a while. Novelist Scott Corbett once said: "I often feel sorry for people who don't read good books; they are missing a chance to lead an extra life."

EXERCISE 8.1

What Is Your Reading Rate?

Before continuing, you'll need a stopwatch or a watch with a second hand. Keep track of how long it takes you to read the following article about "a good life." The object of the exercise isn't to race through; it's to read at your normal speed. After you read the article, you'll be asked to record your reading time and answer some questions to check your comprehension.

Six Ingredients of a Good Life by Tony Swartz

From author's blog, December 7, 2010. (http://blogs.hrb.org/schwartz/2010/12/six-ingredients-of-a-good-life.html). Reprinted with permission from Harvard Business Publishing.

Tony Swartz is a best-selling author, speaker, performance expert, and CEO of "The Energy Project," a company that helps people and organizations perform better and more sustainably.

I ended my most recent post with this line:

"The true measure of greatness is our capacity to navigate between our opposites with agility and grace—to accept ourselves exactly as we are, but never to stop trying to get better."

Over the past week, I've thought about this more deeply. What's dawned on me is just how much a good life requires embracing paradox.

Constantly seek to learn and grow, but accept yourself exactly as you are. Learning and growing require a willingness to look honestly and unsparingly at our shortcomings. Start with your own greatest strength. When you overuse it, it's almost surely a window into your own greatest weakness.

In my case, the strength is drive and passion. Overused, it turns into aggressiveness. Some months ago, I had an encounter with a client in which I felt treated unfairly and dishonestly. I reacted with righteousness, and it probably cost us the client.

There wasn't much value in beating myself up about what happened, or in holding on to a sense of outrage. The client acted badly, but more important, so did I. By accepting responsibility, but also forgiving myself—recognizing that overreaching is an undeniable part of me, but not all of me—I had an opportunity to grow and learn.

Just last week, I was in a meeting with another client, and I felt the urge to press my case just a little harder. Instead, I consciously chose to step back and let the outcome take care of itself. Sure enough, it did. By being aware of my inclination to overuse a strength—by recognizing my own vulnerability—I was able to make a different choice.

Add Value to Others and Take Care of Yourself

Gratifying our most immediate needs and desires provides bursts of pleasure, but they're usually short-lived. We derive the most enduring sense of meaning and satisfaction in our lives when we serve something larger than ourselves. Giving to others generates an extraordinary source of energy.

When we worked with cardiac intensive care nurses at the Cleveland Clinic, for example, we were consistently amazed by their commitment. These nurses spent 12 to 14 continuous hours at their patients' bedsides, often without time to eat, sit down or even go to the bathroom.

Even so, nearly all of them found their work on behalf of critically ill patients deeply satisfying. The problem was that, over time, the jobs became overwhelming.

Encouraged by the hospital, the nurses put the needs of their patients before their own, and believed it was selfish to do otherwise. Many nurses suffered from a phenomenon known as compassion fatigue. Turnover was high.

Consistently sacrificing yourself to serve others is ultimately no better than focusing solely on yourself at the expense of others.

Selfishness is about making your own gratification paramount. Self-care is about making sure you're addressing your own most basic needs, so you're freed and fueled to also add value to others.

Focus Intensely and Renew Regularly

We live in a world in which we're forever juggling demands, but rarely focusing on any one thing for long.

Absorbed attention—the capacity to delay other gratifications to focus on one thing at a time—is the *sine qua non* of achieving and sustaining excellence at anything.

Unlike machines, however, human beings aren't meant to operate at the highest intensity for very long. Instead, we're designed to pulse between spending and renewing energy approximately every 90 minutes.

It's not the hours you work that determine the value you generate, but rather the energy you bring to whatever hours you work. The more skillfully you renew, the more energy you'll have.

I wrote *The Way We're Working Isn't Working* in three uninterrupted 90 minute "sprints" every morning—each one followed by a relatively short period of real renewal, ranging from deep breathing, to eating something, to taking a run. It was a time for both restoration and reflection. I finished the book in half the number of hours than I had any previous book, when I worked ten to 12 hour days.

The world's best performers—musicians, chess players, athletes—typically practice the same way: for no longer than 4½ hours a day. They also sleep more than the rest of us, and take more naps.

These great performers figured out that when they push for too long, their attention wanders, their energy flags, and their work suffers. But because they're so focused when they are working, they get more done, in less time.

Choose a set of the paired opposites above. What could you do to better right the balance between them in your own life? ____________________

Now let's see how you did.

Reading Speed: Stop! Look at your watch. Mark down how long it took you to read the article: _____ Minutes _____ Seconds. If you read this article in four to six minutes, your reading rate is average for a college student. (Note: Article contains 776 words. College students read 200–300 words per minute, on average.) If you read faster or slower than that, what does that mean? If it took longer than four minutes, but you answer the three questions in the "Reading Comprehension" that follows correctly, reading slowly may not be as much of a problem for you as you may think it is. Right about now, however, you may be thinking, *Hey, I don't have time to spare! I'm juggling several different courses, a job, family responsibilities—a dozen things.* That's the point! Read with focus so that you can record, retain, and retrieve information. If you don't understand what you read, it's difficult, if not impossible, to learn it. Reading without comprehension is just going through the motions.

Yikes! Took me 6 min. 30 sec. I'm slower than average :(

Reading Comprehension: Answer the following questions without going back and rereading the article.

1. What was this article's main point? ____________________
2. How did the author write his book, *The Way We're Working Isn't Working?* ____________________
3. Why do the world's best performers limit how long they practice every day to four ½ hours? ____________________

Now go back and check the accuracy of your answers. Are you "reading right"?

- **Academic skills will be affected.** Whether or not you enjoy reading, it will be one of the primary skills you need to cultivate in college. According to one study, 85 percent of the learning you'll do in college requires careful reading.[6] First-year students often need to read and comprehend 150–200 pages per week in order to complete their academic assignments.[7]

  What's more, reading skills go hand in hand with writing skills, which makes them even more important. The better you get at reading, the more you raise your probability of academic success. Believe it or not, some students choose to skip the reading. But this is a dangerous, self-sabotaging strategy. Many of your classes will require intensive reading of complex material, including primary sources by original authors and scholarly research. Sometimes reading in college is just plain difficult. It takes focus, even if you do find the material to be highly engaging and truly fascinating! However, if you complete reading assignments, and your classmates don't, think about how much ahead of the nonreaders *you* will be! Now is the time to begin enhancing these skills. But how do you become a better reader?

Read Right!

? challenge

" reaction

Challenge: Are there right ways to read? What have you learned about reading in college thus far? Provide as many suggestions about reading right as you can.

Reaction:

____

____

What do we know about reading? How *should* you tackle your many reading assignments in college? Consider these twelve essential points:[8]

1. **Understand what being a good reader is all about.** Reading isn't a race. Remember the old children's story about the tortoise and the hare? The turtle actually won the race because he plodded along, slowly and steadily, while the rabbit zipped all over the place and lost focus. The moral of that story applies to reading, too. Reading is a process; understanding is the goal. The point isn't simply to make it through the reading assignment by turning pages every few minutes so that you can finish the chapter in a certain amount of time. When your instructors read difficult material, which they do regularly in their profession, they don't rush. They chew on the tough parts, reread sections, and make notes to themselves in the margins. Reading requires you to back up occasionally, just like when you back up a DVD to catch something you missed: "What did he say to her? I didn't get that." Students sometimes mistakenly think that good readers are speed-readers.[9] But reading actually has two components: speed

and comprehension. Often, comprehension is sacrificed when speed is increased because most speed-readers actually just skim. Yes, you can improve your reading speed with focused effort, but more importantly, you can improve your comprehension skills by managing your attention. Science fiction writer Isaac Asimov once wrote, "I am not a speed reader. I am a speed understander."

2. **Take stock of your own reading challenges.** Which of the following are reading issues for you? Put a checkmark next to any that apply to you.[10]

___ boredom	___ vision	___ speed	___ comprehension	___ time
___ amount	___ interest	___ motivation	___ surroundings	___ fear
___ fluency	___ fatigue	___ level	___ retention	___ laziness

✓ boredom
✓ amount
✓ interest
✓ speed
✓ motivation

Many people find reading challenging. You may have worked with an impatient teacher as a youngster, or you may have been taught using a method that didn't work well for you—factors that still cause you problems today. Reading involves visually recognizing symbols, transferring those visual cues to your brain, translating them into meaningful signals—recording, retaining and retrieving information (here's where your memory kicks in)—and finally using these meanings to think, write, or speak. Reading challenges can be caused by *physical factors* (your vision, for example) and *psychological factors* (your attitude). If you want to become a better reader in the future, it's a good idea to assess honestly what's most challenging about the process for you right now.[11]

Huh...this is news to me—why didn't anyone teach me this??

3. **Adjust your reading style.** Reading requires versatility. Contrast these two situations: reading the menu on the wall at your local fast-food joint and poring over the menu at a fancy, high-end restaurant. You'd just scan the fast-food menu in a few seconds, wouldn't you? You wouldn't read word by word and ask: "Is the beef in that burger from grass-fed cattle?" "What, exactly, is in the 'special sauce'?" If you did, the exasperated attendant would probably blurt out, "Look, are you going to order something or not?" That kind of situation requires quick skimming. But you'd take some time to study the menu at a pricy restaurant you might go to with friends and family to celebrate your college graduation. It's an entirely different situation, and the information is more complicated. And if it's a fancy French restaurant, you might even need to ask the definitions of some terms like *canard* (duck) or *cassoulet* (a rich,

Andersen Ross/Brand X Pictures/Jupiter Images

> **Outside of a dog, a book is man's best friend. Inside of a dog, it's too dark to read.**
>
> *Groucho Marx, American comedian, actor, and singer (1890–1977)*

> **It matters, if individuals are to retain any capacity to form their own judgments and opinions, that they continue to read for themselves.**
>
> *Harold Bloom, literary critic (1930–)*

hearty stew). That kind of situation requires slow, considered study, word by word. You're going to pay for what you choose, and you want the best results on your investment. That's true about college, too. You're investing in your college degree, so reading right is important!

You don't read a textbook or a novel in the same way you skip around when you read a magazine, only choosing articles that interest you: "How to Totally Redecorate Your Apartment on Fifty Bucks" or "Does Your Love Life Have a Pulse?" Books require starting at the beginning and reading straight through. The plot of most novels would be very different if readers just picked certain sections to read! You'll face an enormous amount of reading in your combined college classes. The question is, what's fast food (to carry through with the analogy) and what's fine dining? According to research on reading, good readers know the difference and adjust their reading styles.[12]

It's important to devote more time to reading and studying than you think you'll actually need. If you don't understand difficult material, go back and reread it, instead of assuming it will be explained by your instructor in class. Keep a dictionary at your side, and check unusual new terms. You'll be able to digest what you're reading much better.

4. **Converse with the author.** In every book you read, the author is trying to convince you of something. Take this book, for example. We have been engaged in a conversation all the way through. What do you know about me? What am I trying to persuade you to think about or do? Even though I'm not right in front of you in person on every page, you are forming impressions of me as you read, and I'm either convincing you to try the suggestions in this book or I'm not. As you read any book, argue with the author ("That's not how I see it!"), question her ("What makes you say that?"), agree with her ("Yes, right on!"), relate something she said earlier to something she's saying now ("But what about ...?"). Instead of just coloring with your yellow highlighter, scribble comments in the margins, or keep a running commentary in a notebook. Make small ticks in the margins to mark words you'll look up in your dictionary at a good breaking point. Reading is an active process, not a passive one in which the words just float by you. In fact, mark up this page right now! How do you decide what's really important? One thing you can do is ask your instructor in this course to show you his or her mark-ups in this book, and see if the two of you agree on what's important.

OK, author, you're persuading me!

EXERCISE 8.2

A Press Conference with the Author

If you could interview the author of this text, what would you ask her? What would you like to know about her? What would you argue with her about? Play devil's advocate and come up with a list of challenging questions and the responses you think she'd provide. Then role-play this activity with one student playing the role of the author in a press conference on television and the rest of the class playing reporters from major newspapers and magazines of their choosing or as assigned by your instructor.

This poem is hard for me and English is my first language!

CURIOSITY: *READING WHEN ENGLISH IS YOUR SECOND LANGUAGE*

Hints on Pronunciation for Foreigners

I take it you already know
Of laugh and bough and cough and dough?
Others may stumble but not you,
On hiccough, thorough, laugh and through.
Well done! And now you wish, perhaps,
To learn of less familiar traps?

Beware of heard, a dreadful word
That looks like beard and sounds like bird,
And dead: It's said like bed, not bead—
For goodness' sake don't call it "deed"!
Watch out for meat and great and threat
(They rhyme with suite and straight and debt.)

A moth is not a moth in mother
Nor both in bother, broth in brother
And here is not a match for there
Nor dear and fear for bear and pear,
And then there's dose and rose and lose—
Just look them up—and goose and choose,
And cork and work and card and ward,
And font and front and word and sword,

And do and go and thwart and cart—
Come, come, I've hardly made a start!
A dreadful language? Man alive.
I'd mastered it when I was five.

—T.S.W. (only initials of writer known) or possibly written by George Bernard Shaw

Go ahead. Try reading the preceding poem aloud. Even if English is your first language, you probably had to pause and think about how to say a word occasionally. Most anyone would. English isn't exactly the easiest language in the world to learn, non-native English speakers say. It's filled with perplexing irregularities. Think about the raw courage it would take to pursue a college degree by reading and writing in a language other than your native tongue. If English is your first language, could *you* do it in German or Arabic or Hindi? That being acknowledged, what strategies can ESL (English as a Second Language) students use to help with challenging reading assignments?

1. Remember that spoken English differs from the written English you'll find in textbooks and academic articles. In casual conversation, you'll hear, "And she's . . . like, 'wow!' and I'm . . . like, 'really?'" If you read that in a book, you'd have no idea what the speakers were communicating about. But if you're standing next to the conversationalists in the hallway, you have a chance of figuring it out. Learning to speak informally in conversation is very different from learning to read scholarly discourse. When you read, there's no body language to rely on or real-live author around to whom you can address questions. Address these questions to your instructor or study-group mates instead.
2. Ask your English-speaking friends and instructors to coach you. For example, ESL speakers sometimes struggle with the hundreds of idioms found in English. Idioms are groups of words with a particular, nonliteral meaning. For example, "I have a frog in my throat" means your voice is hoarse, not that you literally have swallowed a green amphibian. Idioms must be learned as a set of words in order to communicate their intended meaning. If you change one word ("I have a *toad* in my throat"), the idiom doesn't work. Considering how many idioms English has and how freely English speakers use them without consciously thinking about it, non-native speakers may find learning them all to be a challenge. You'll more likely hear idioms spoken, rather than read them; however, you may come across them frequently in fiction or poetry assigned in a literature class. If you're an international student, ask about unique phrases that don't make sense to you.
3. Use the Internet or an online course to improve your language skills. According to one study, international students in an online course made significant gains in their language skills, compared with a control group of students who sat through the same course in a classroom. Online courses provide good exposure and practice in your reading and writing skills via e-mail, web searching, threaded discussions, and online postings.[13]
4. Try explaining what you're reading to someone else. Talking something through while you're reading, especially with a native English speaker, can help you clarify meanings on the spot—and may help the other student achieve better comprehension, too.
5. Mark up the textbook so that you can pursue difficult passages in greater detail later. Insert question marks in the margin. Read with your English–native tongue dictionary in front of you. If you get completely stuck, find another book that may explain the concepts differently.

5. **Dissect the text.** Whether you did it virtually online or physically in a real lab, cutting up those little critters in your biology class helped you figure out what was what. The ability to dissect text is important in reading. As you read and make notes in the margins, write what and why statements. Try it: beside each paragraph on this page, write a one-sentence summary statement: a *what* statement. Put the author's words into your own words. Then write another sentence that focuses on *why* the paragraph is included. Does it contain *evidence* to make a point? Is it an *example* of something? If you can tackle this recommendation, you'll do wonders for yourself when exam time rolls around. Think of an essay question on a test that asks, "Discuss three reasons why it's important to read right." You'd remember the why statements you've written in the margins of this section, and be ready with your answer!

EXERCISE 8.3

Marginal Notes

Go back through the section of this chapter on reading that you just completed. If you used a highlighter, make notes to yourself in the margins (or on another sheet of paper) about *why* you underlined a word, phrase, or section. Why did you consider that part to be important? Knowing the answers to these questions is more important than the act of "coloring."[14]

6. **Make detailed notes.** Knowing how to use a highlighter while you read is most students' idea of good study skills. Highlighting skills are important, but there's more to it. Choose headings, phrases, and individual words that relate to main points, rather than just highlighting everything that could possibly be important. But even if you highlight selectively, you'll be much more likely to actually master a challenging reading assignment if you keep a notebook beside you and take full-blown notes as you read. Go back and forth, detailing main points and supporting evidence, so that you have a set of notes using the Cornell note-taking system, for example, by the time you've finished reading. If you're reading onscreen, open a new document and annotate there. The physical act of writing or typing can consolidate what you're reading and act as a form of rehearsal that helps you remember it later.

7. **Put things into context.** Reading requires a certain level of what's called cultural literacy, core knowledge that puts things into context and gives them meaning. Authors assume their readers have a common background. They refer to other books or current events, or historical milestones, and unless you know what they're referring to, what you're reading may not make sense to you. An example you might be familiar with is how the television show *Seinfeld* made real words that everyone now knows and uses out of fake ones: *yada yada yada*, for example. Those words are now part of our cultural literacy that have meaning for you and everyone you know, probably, but may not for people from another culture. They know the literacy of their own culture instead.

   Imagine the "Far Side" cartoon in which a caveman and cavewoman (Mom and Dad) are reviewing the report card that Junior (who is slouched

> **Perhaps the most valuable result of all education is the ability to make yourself do the thing you have to do, when it ought to be done, whether you like it or not.**
>
> *Thomas Henry Huxley, British biologist (1825–1895)*

in the foreground) brought home to the cave. Dad says, "Oh look...this get better. 'F' in history! You even flunk something not happen yet." Getting the joke requires an amazing amount of cultural literacy:

- That American Moms and Dads typically review report cards with their children.
- That report cards are important to American parents.
- That students worry when their grades are poor.
- That cavemen and women spoke a rudimentary form of human language.
- That history is a subject taught in school.
- That history is a cumulative record of events over time.

These examples of cultural literacy are fairly easy to figure out, but what about this less familiar historical reference? You might think, for example, that Walt Whitman's 1888 poem "O Captain! My Captain!" is something a sailor wrote when his skipper died. Instead, it's a poem about Abraham Lincoln, who was assassinated as the Civil War drew to an end.

O captain! my captain! our fearful trip is done;
The ship has weathered every rack, the prize we sought is won;
The port is near, the bells I hear, the people all exulting,
While follow eyes the steady keel, the vessel grim and daring.

But O heart! heart! heart!
O the bleeding drops of red!
Where on the deck my captain lies,
Fallen cold and dead.

I had to learn this in school! It never made sense until now!

Lincoln was the captain, the ship was the United States, the storm was the Civil War, and the prize was keeping the union together, surviving the war, and abolishing slavery. At the time, the poem held a highly prominent place in American cultural literacy. Whitman said he was asked to recite it so often that he was almost sorry he had ever written it.[15] Today, far fewer people in our culture know this once familiar reference. Did you? If you come across it in a book now, you are culturally literate and understand the reference. You're an insider, which is an important aspect of reading. Keep your eyes and ears open, read and listen, or buy a cultural literacy dictionary so that, as a reader, you're "in the know."[16]

8. **Read to learn with the SQ6R method.** Much of the reading you'll do in college includes complicated sentences that are difficult to navigate. When you try reading complex passages aloud, you may stumble because you don't immediately recognize how the words are linked into phrases. But practicing reading aloud is one way you can become more familiar with difficult language. Many instructors teach their first-year students a common approach to reading and studying called SQ3R:

Survey—Skim to get the lay of the land quickly.

Question—Ask yourself what, why, and how questions. What is this article or chapter about? Why is it included? How might I use this information?

"slows down forgetting." Your brain is continually seeking stimulation, and when you change something, your brain "reboots," relearns some of what you've forgotten since you last studied the material, and kick in harder. New research is proving that some of the old standard advice about study habits (always study in the same room) isn't accurate![33]

7. **Review, review, review!** Review your course material often enough that you can retain and retrieve information at the level expected by your instructor. If you have to start fresh each time you come to class, trying to work from your memory of what was discussed during the last class, you'll always feel behind. To be even more focused, some students review *lecture* course material right after class (to help you remember it) and *discussion* course material right before class (so that you can participate in the discussion).

Good reason to talk to that cute guy in class!

8. **Find a study buddy.** Find a classmate who also values studying, and commit to keeping one another focused during study sessions. Create quizzes and hypothetical test questions for each another, and use your study partner to keep you on track.

9. **Don't be an ostrich!** Some students fall prey to "the Ostrich Syndrome." If reading or homework assignments seem too hard or feel like busywork, they just don't do them. Instead, they bury their heads in the sand and pretend like nothing's at stake. Somehow they may even think that they can't get a bad grade if they don't turn in an assignment for the instructor to grade. It goes without saying (but here it is anyway) that "ostriching" is the opposite of making an intentional study plan, and the results are disastrous. Estimate how long an assignment will take and follow through. Honest-to-goodness realism and continuous upkeep in your courses work wonders.

10. **Vary your study techniques by course content.** Studying productively is more than just learning a few general rules that apply to any type of subject matter. You need to zoom in on whatever subject or discipline it is that you're studying. Look over the pages of your textbook. Does the material synch with your learning style? Is it text-heavy (read/write)? Do graphs or charts explain the text and seem important? Are color-coding or bulleting used to call your attention to particular items (visual)? If the material isn't presented as you'd prefer, what can you do to "translate"? For example, if you're a kinesthetic learner, can you make flash cards? Can you create and complete practice tests? If you learn by listening, can you read the material aloud (aural)? And finally, what kind of exam (multiple-choice, essay, problem sets, etc.) does the material lend itself to? What are you likely to need to know and what will you be asked to do on an exam? When you study math, it's important to do more than read. Working problem sets helps you actually develop the skills you need. When you study history, you study differently. You might draw a timeline of the events leading up to World War I, for example.[34]

JUNIORS BILDARCHIV

"An ostrich with its head in the sand is just as blind to opportunity as to disaster."

Anonymous

EXERCISE 8.5

"Disciplined" Studying

Assume you are taking two classes this term: calculus and music. For the two textbook pages here, describe how you would go about studying the material, based on what the content in these two subjects requires. Among other things, which particular VARK learning style preferences should be used: V, A, R, and/or K? Fill in specifics about how you would study each subject's textbook page. After you're done, compare notes with your classmates.

2 **Chapter P** Preparation for Calculus

P.1 Graphs and Models

- **Sketch the graph of an equation.**
- **Find the intercepts of a graph.**
- **Test a graph for symmetry with respect to an axis and the origin.**
- **Find the points of intersection of two graphs.**
- **Interpret mathematical models for real-life data.**

iStockphoto.com/Georgios Kollidas

RENÉ DESCARTES (1596–1650)

Descartes made many contributions to philosophy, science, and mathematics. The idea of representing points in the plane by pairs of real numbers and representing curves in the plane by equations was described by Descartes in his book *La Géométrie*, published in 1637.

The Graph of an Equation

In 1637 the French mathematician René Descartes revolutionized the study of mathematics by joining its two major fields—algebra and geometry. With Descartes's coordinate plane, geometric concepts could be formulated analytically and algebraic concepts could be viewed graphically. The power of this approach was such that within a century of its introduction, much of calculus had been developed.

The same approach can be followed in your study of calculus. That is, by viewing calculus from multiple perspectives—*graphically*, *analytically*, and *numerically*—you will increase your understanding of core concepts.

Consider the equation $3x + y = 7$. The point $(2, 1)$ is a **solution point** of the equation because the equation is satisfied (is true) when 2 is substituted for x and 1 is substituted for y. This equation has many other solutions, such as $(1, 4)$ and $(0, 7)$. To find other solutions systematically, solve the original equation for y.

$y = 7 - 3x$ Analytic approach

Then construct a **table of values** by substituting several values of x.

x	0	1	2	3	4
y	7	4	1	-2	-5

Numerical approach

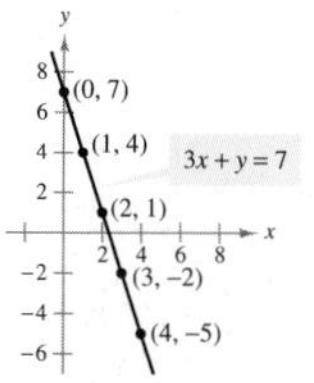

Graphical approach: $3x + y = 7$
Figure P.1

From the table, you can see that $(0, 7)$, $(1, 4)$, $(2, 1)$, $(3, -2)$, and $(4, -5)$ are solutions of the original equation $3x + y = 7$. Like many equations, this equation has an infinite number of solutions. The set of all solution points is the **graph** of the equation, as shown in Figure P.1.

NOTE Even though we refer to the sketch shown in Figure P.1 as the graph of $3x + y = 7$, it really represents only a *portion* of the graph. The entire graph would extend beyond the page. ■

In this course, you will study many sketching techniques. The simplest is point plotting—that is, you plot points until the basic shape of the graph seems apparent.

EXAMPLE 1 Sketching a Graph by Point Plotting

Sketch the graph of $y = x^2 - 2$.

Solution First construct a table of values. Then plot the points shown in the table.

x	-2	-1	0	1	2	3
y	2	-1	-2	-1	2	7

Finally, connect the points with a *smooth curve*, as shown in Figure P.2. This graph is a **parabola**. It is one of the conics you will study in Chapter 10. ■

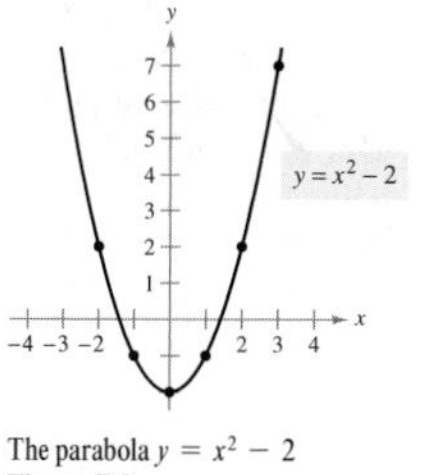

The parabola $y = x^2 - 2$
Figure P.2

How would you study this?

____

____

(continued)

Measures

As you performed the different meters, you may have lost your place momentarily. Even if you didn't, you can see that it would be difficult to play a long piece of music without losing one's place. For this reason, music is divided into **measures** with vertical lines called **bar lines**.

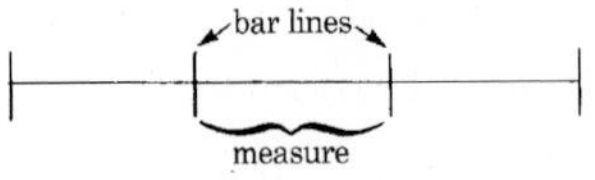

A bar line occurs immediately before an accented pulse. Thus, duple meter has two pulses per measure, triple meter has three pulses per measure, and quadruple meter has four pulses per measure. The following example shows the common meters again, this time with bar lines included. Notice how much easier it is to read and perform the meter when it is written this way.

duple meter 

triple meter 

quadruple meter 

Double bar lines have a special meaning: Their two most common uses are to signal the beginning of a new section in a large work and to mark the end of a work. Put double bar lines at the end of any exercises or pieces you write.

MUSIC IN *Action*

Hearing Pulse and Meter

As members of the class listen, clap a steady pulse without any noticeable accents. Slowly change the pulse to duple, triple, or quadruple meter. You may want to have a contest to see how quickly members of the class can detect the shift to a measured pulse.

Note Values

Learning to read music involves mastering two different musical subsystems: pitch notation and rhythmic notation. Pitch is indicated by the placement of a note on a five-line staff (the higher the note on the staff, the higher the pitch). You will learn about that later in this chapter. Rhythm, on the other hand, is written with

How would you study this?

____

____

Finally, what have you learned about studying and about yourself as a learner by completing this exercise?

11. **Study earlier, rather than later.** Whenever possible, study during the daytime rather than waiting until evening. Research shows that each hour used for study during the day is equal to one and a half hours at night. Another major study showed that students who study between 6:00 P.M. and midnight are twice as likely to earn A's as students who put off their studying until after midnight.[35]

12. **Create artificial deadlines for yourself.** Even though your professors will have set deadlines for various assignments, create your own deadlines that come before the ones they set. This will allow for any unforeseen emergencies, as well as give you time to give your assignment one last review before turning it in. "The dog ate my homework" story is so overused that it's become a cliche, and it's well known that exam times bring great danger to students' relatives, especially fictitious ones! Remember that Murphy's Law is alive and well: "Whatever can go wrong will." Printer cartridges always run dry midway through printing your paper, and hard disks invariably crash while you're typing the last entry in your bibliography. Finish early, and you'll save yourself some trauma.

13. **Treat school as a job.** If you consider the amount of study time you need to budget for each hour of class time, and you're taking 12–15 credits, then essentially you're working a 36–45 hour/week job on campus. Arrive at "work" early and get your tasks done during "business hours" so you have more leisure time in the evenings.

14. **Show up.** Once you've decided to sit down to read or study, really commit yourself to showing up—being present emotionally and intellectually, not just physically. It's easy to look like you're "there" when you're really off somewhere in your head. If you're committed to getting a college education,

BOX 8.1 Can You Read the Future?

Imagine you're a college student ten years from now. Will all the reading and studying you're doing now be different then? Although no one has a crystal ball, experts are already busy describing your successors: "Generation C" which stands for connected, communicating, content-centric, computerized, community-oriented, and always clicking. In many ways, they'll be like you, only more so. Here's what the prognosticators are saying about students, reading, and studying.[36]

Since everyone will be connected virtually all the time, reading will become a more *social* activity. Readers will be able to see additional "layers" of information: comments written by others (alongside what they're reading), the results of debates and polls on whatever they're reading about, extra facts that verify the reliability of the sources, ongoing discussions in the popular media from various perspectives, and others' recommended booklists. They'll be able to touch the screen to drag a book recommendation to a contact's profile or even contribute themselves by performing certain on-screen actions, unlocking secret chapters, and adding their own content.[37]

In the future, college students' lives will be organized around PDDs (primary digital devices) that will keep them connected at home, in transit, and at school. They'll be able to read textbooks, attend lectures, do research, take exams, pay bills, shop online, watch videos, listen to music, and communicate with friends instantly, 24/7, from one portable device. Much of this you do now, but when it comes to academic success, FOCUSING will be just as important, if not more.

FIGURE 8.2

The Relationship Between Challenge and Skill

Source: Hallowell, E. M. (2011). *Shine.* Boston, Harvard Business Review Press, p. 57.

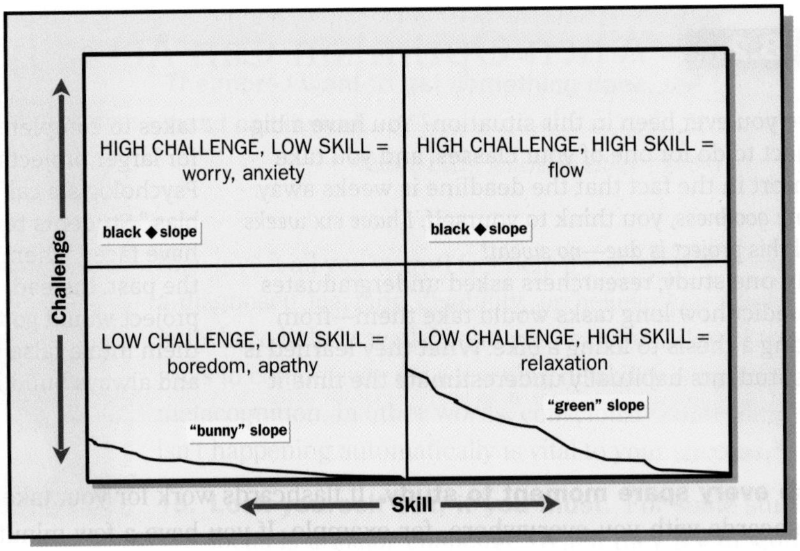

because the academic challenges you're facing demand much more. Look at Figure 8.2, which explores the relationship between *challenge* and *skill.* Think of it this way: if you put a novice skier at the top of a "black diamond" expert slope, she may be frozen with fear. But if you put an Olympic Gold Medal skier there, she'll fly down the mountain and have great fun doing it. She'll probably find a gentle slope with the label "green" to be relaxing; she'll just cruise along taking in the scenery. And most anyone—novice or expert skier—will find the "bunny slope" for kiddies to be boring. Now look at the chart again, and modify the examples—from skiing skills to academic skills. Where do you fit? Is your anxiety level high because your academic skill level isn't up to the challenge? It's time to fully develop your study skills by following the advice in this chapter. Polished skills will help you meet greater challenges, gain more knowledge, and "flow" through your college experience.

Integrated Learning: Learning Is Greater Than the Sum of Its Parts

? challenge

" reaction

Challenge: What is *integrated* learning? Can you define the term or predict what it means?

Reaction:

____

____

____

Integrated learning involves forming connections. It's easy to develop target fixation and think, "I'll put my psychology book away and study math now." In your mind, math and psychology are unrelated. They're requirements that help you check off squares toward getting your college degree.

Although that's true—they *are* separate classes—they're interrelated in daily life. Most of the important problems you will face in your life won't have simple solutions. You won't be able to check off a square and be done with them. Turning to page 225 in your psychology book probably won't give you the answer in a flash. Even if a problem you face on the job requires a mathematical solution, you'll still need to integrate some psychology in order to convince your boss that your answer is right! Problems are multilayered and unscripted; they require you to come at them from different directions. Instead of just knowing X amount of math and Y amount of psychology, it's integrated learning that counts ultimately—the ability to make connections between classes and disciplines, between something you learned earlier and something you're trying to learn now, and between the classroom and your other experiences on campus, in the community, or on the job.[42] As you work to become a truly educated person, you begin to realize that knowledge intersects and overlaps. You may experience integrated learning as "aha moments":

> **What do you consider to be the end purpose of education? Is it not to bring about an integrated individual?**
>
> *Krishnamurti, Indian speaker and educator (1895–1986)*

- **Between disciplines** "My psychology professor was talking about this kind of math learning disability, just yesterday in class."
- **Over time** "This point in my psychology textbook relates to what I studied in my history course last term."
- **Between contexts** "My service learning project teaching fourth-graders is helping me understand what I'm learning in my psychology class."

That's precisely what you'll be doing in your career—applying what you're learning in class! The time to start watching for connections is now at the beginning of your college career, and you can help make them happen. Here are some ways to begin.

1. **Take interdisciplinary courses.** Some classes are all about connections between disciplines. See if your college has a department of "Integrated Studies" or offers classes that bring two or more disciplines together.
2. **Find connections yourself.** Many of your instructors will make connections for you. Your poetry instructor, for example, may also discuss how the poet was affected by the art, literature, music, and philosophy of the day. But if those connections aren't made for you by your instructors, search for them yourself.
3. **Look for links between classes.** Your instructors don't know what other classes you're taking, but you do. Find areas of overlap between them. Most courses are "separated" by discipline, but there's no reason you can't connect them in your head. Your college experience may seem fragmented to you, but work to develop what playwrights call the "through line," the central idea of the play from start to finish. When it comes to getting a college education, keep the concept of a through line in your head. If you approach learning with a high level of self-awareness, you can bridge the breadth of your courses and deepen your learning.

This semester I'm taking Ethnic Studies, algebra, English Composition, and biology. What do all those things have in common???

4. **Join a learning community.** On many campuses, first-year students have an opportunity to be a part of a community of learners who take a particular set of classes—English, psychology, and physics, for example—together. When you do this, it's easy to talk with your classmates about overlap between the courses.

5. **Examine a single skill across multiple courses.** Take your writing skills, for example: How does your writing compare in your composition class, your political science class, and your sociology class? Think outside the box of the "serial" classes you're taking, one after the other, and look at what you're doing in several at the same time.

6. **Connect contexts.** One of the main points of getting an education is being able to apply it. Connect what you're learning in the academic curriculum with your co-curricular experience. ("If I apply what I'm learning in my anatomy course, maybe I can improve my performance on the track team.") Connect what you're learning in class to what you do on the job. ("We just learned about the primacy-recency effect in my psychology class, and the chef asked us to push the specials tonight. That means I should welcome guests by first going over the list of specials, then let them talk for a while and bring their drinks, and then mention the specials again before I take their orders.")

7. **Build a learning portfolio.** While some institutions require their students to create a learning portfolio, electronically or on paper, it's a great idea to do it on your own. A learning portfolio is a file (online or hard copy) in which you reflect on your work, measure your progress, provide evidence of what you've accomplished, and assess what you're learning *across* your courses. In many professions—art and architecture, for example—professionals build a portfolio to show their work to galleries or builders. A learning portfolio uses the same principles. In creating your own learning portfolio, you'll need to decide what to include and why, and in the process of building a portfolio you'll make some important discoveries about yourself as a learner. Think about all the knowledge, skills, sensitivities, and values a graduate should be able to demonstrate. Here's a sample list:

Effective communication	Diversity
Information literacy	Ethics
Critical and creative thinking	An appreciation for the arts
Quantitative reasoning	Breadth of knowledge
Collaboration skills and teamwork	Depth of knowledge

A learning portfolio provides evidence of the quality of your work. Select assignments to include that represent your strengths. Include papers from your classes, reflective essays, multimedia projects, an *academic* résumé that lists your courses and what you've learned from them, and a *co-curricular* résumé that lists all the activities and positions of leadership you've held in campus organizations. By the time you graduate, your learning portfolio will be an integrated summary of your entire college experience that you might even show to a potential employer or a graduate school interviewer.

Why is integrated learning so important? Making connections is the route to memory power and to learning itself. You learn best when you relate what you're learning to what you already know, to your life, and to the world around you. In other words, connections count.

The more we learn about the world, the more we realize it is an increasingly complex place. According to one scientist who studies air pollution, "What happens in Beijing will affect Boston, what happens in Boston will affect Paris, et cetera . . . this connectivity of the planet will come back at us time and time again."[43] Connectivity affects us all in ways we don't even realize. Becoming an integrated learner will help you build the skills you need to navigate the world in your chosen career and throughout your life.[44] If you can begin to think about integrated learning now, as a first-year student, imagine how much further ahead of your classmates you'll be by the time you graduate.

> ***Non scholae sed vitae discrimus.*** **(We do not learn for school, but for life.)**
>
> *Lucius Annaeus Seneca, Roman philosopher and statesman (4 B.C.–A.D. 65)*

In your career, you'll need to be able to solve complex problems that require you to integrate your learning. Knowing isolated facts won't be enough. You will need to pull together what you've learned in many different courses to come up with a solution. The time to become an intentional, integrated learner is now!

I think I'm an ESFJ. After reading this, I see that I need to make a study plan!

▶▶ Your TypE Is Showing

What does your psychological type have to do with your reading and studying skills? What would you predict? See if these descriptions apply to you.

Type, Reading, and Studying

Extravert (E)

Extraverts sometimes have difficulty concentrating on reading assignments for long periods of time. Reading aloud may help them to stay focused and benefit comprehension, too.

Introvert (I)

Introverts find it easier to concentrate for longer periods, but they sometimes wander off in their thoughts, either related to what they're reading or into something else entirely in a daydream.

Sensing (S)

As children, sensors sometimes find learning to read more challenging than intuitive children do. Sensors may learn to "break the code" of written language with the help of a teacher using experienced-based reading or phonics instruction.

Intuition (N)

Intuitives find it easier to understand and manipulate symbols, generally. However, they sometimes fall into the trap of neglecting the facts of a text and focusing more on the larger concepts or big picture.

Thinking (T)

Generally, thinkers are more tolerant of "dry" reading assignments than feelers are. They often focus more on the information content than they do on tone or style. They also tend to be more critical readers.

Feeling (F)

Feelers care about the tone and style of what they read, and they may choose to read something simply because they enjoy those qualities in an author. They also tend to be more eager about reading materials that have personal meaning for them.

Judging (J)

Judgers reach conclusions about what they're reading more quickly; however, they may rush to judgment on something they're reading, and then find when they reread it, that they've drawn the wrong conclusions.

Perceiving (P)

Perceivers sometimes enjoy reading because it helps them explore things they don't know much about. They tend to read more slowly or become so bogged down in their reading that they take too long to get to the related assignment.

When it comes to studying, the Sensing-iNtuition and Judging-Perceiving scales relate most to college success. For sensors studying means learning facts. That's something they're good at. But instructors often want to know more than that on exams: How do the facts connect? What do they mean? What's the bottom line? Intuitives, on the other hand, want to know what things mean right away. Where is this leading? What's the main point here? While the big picture is important, details count, too. Judgers like to study with a plan. As soon as they receive an assignment, they often organize the steps involved and sketch out a timeline so that they feel they're making continual progress. Perceivers may prefer to look at all the angles first, and sometimes they spend so much time doing so that they are forced to make a snap decision at the last minute on exactly how to proceed.[45]

Do any of these descriptions fit you? What do they tell you about how to read and study to *your* best advantage?

I should remember that: "Never regard study as a duty..."

Albert Einstein said this: "Never regard study as a duty, but as the enviable opportunity to learn to know the liberating influence of beauty in the realm of the spirit for your own personal joy and to the profit of the community to which your later work belongs." Reading and studying are what college is all about. Take his advice: consider the opportunities before you to become an expert thinker, an integrative and intentional learner, and a contributor to the community and world in which you live.

insight **action**

Now What Do You Think?

1. At the beginning of this chapter, Katie Alexander, a frustrated and disgruntled college student, faced a challenge. Now after reading this chapter, would you respond differently to any of the questions you answered about the "FOCUS Challenge Case"? Knowing what you know now, how would you advise her? Write a paragraph ending to the story, incorporating your best advice.
2. How would you characterize your reading skills, based on all your years of schooling and feedback you have received from teachers? Are you an above average, average, or below average reader? Why?
3. Considering how important reading will be to your college success, what can you do to improve? For example, would it be worthwhile to try reading for pleasure to see if you can become better at it? Can you set a timer to give yourself reading goals, or create practice quizzes to assess your comprehension?
4. Choose two classes you're taking this semester. How are they connected? What overlap do you note in the content of both courses?
5. If you began building a learning portfolio this term, what would you include and why?

REALITY ✓ What did you LEARN?

On a scale of 1 to 10, answer the following questions now that you've completed the chapter.

low 1 2 3 4 5 6 7 8 9 10 high

In hindsight, how much did you already know about this subject before reading the chapter? ______

Can you answer these questions about reading and studying more fully now that you've read the chapter?

1. How many words per minute does the average college student read?
2. What does SQ6R stand for?
3. What's the definition of the word "metacognition"?

How useful might the information in this chapter be to you? How much do you think this information might affect your success overall? ______

How much energy did you put into reading this chapter? ______

How long did it actually take you to complete this chapter (both the reading and writing tasks)? ______ Hour(s) ______ Minutes

Did you finish reading this chapter? ______

Did you intend to when you started? ______

If you meant to but didn't, what stopped you? ______

Challenge Yourself Online Quiz To find out just how much you've learned, access the College Success CourseMate via www.cengagebrain.com to take the Challenge Yourself Online Quiz.

Take a minute to compare these answers to your answers from the "Readiness Check" at the beginning of this chapter. What gaps exist between the similar questions? How might these gaps between what you thought before starting the chapter and what you now think after completing the chapter affect how you approach the next chapter in this book?

CHAPTER 9

Taking Tests

You're about to discover…

- Why you should change your thinking about tests
- What to do before, during, and after a test
- What test anxiety is and what to do about it
- How to take different kinds of tests differently
- How cheating can hurt your chances for success

© Larry Harwood Photography. Property of Cengage Learning

READINESS ✔ What do you KNOW?

Before beginning to read this chapter, take two minutes to answer the following questions on a scale of 1 to 10. Your answers will help you assess how ready you are to focus.

low 1 2 3 4 5 6 7 8 9 10 high

How much do you *already* know?

Based on reading the "You're about to discover . . ." list and skimming this chapter, how much do you think you probably already know about this chapter's subject? ________

See if you can answer these questions about taking tests *before* you read.

1. What are the four components of test anxiety?
2. Identify three hints for managing your time during tests.
3. Why are subjective (essay) tests often perceived to be more challenging than objective (true-false, multiple-choice) tests?

How much do you expect to learn?

In general, how motivated are you to learn more by reading this chapter? ________

How much do you think this information might affect your success overall? ________

How much energy do you plan to put into reading this chapter? ________

How ready are you to read *now*?

How ready are you to focus on this chapter? Enter a number for each aspect of your readiness to focus.

Physically ________

Intellectually ________

Emotionally ________

If any of your answers is below a 10, pay attention to whatever is distracting you before you start reading. Then zero in and focus.

Finally, how long do you think it will take you to complete this chapter from start to finish?

________ Hour(s) ________ Minutes

Now, as you begin, do you intend to finish reading this chapter?

________ yes ________ no ________ maybe

© Larry Harwood Photography. Property of Cengage Learning

FOCUS Challenge Case

? challenge

Joe Cloud

"Joe College," that's me, Joe Cloud kept thinking to himself. His long-awaited opportunity to leave his small rural community on the reservation had finally arrived. He was at college in the big city, where life was vastly different. He would be different, too, he had convinced himself—somehow more outgoing, more athletic, more popular, more successful—more of everything.

Sergey Skleznev/Shutterstock.com

Kavram/Shutterstock.com

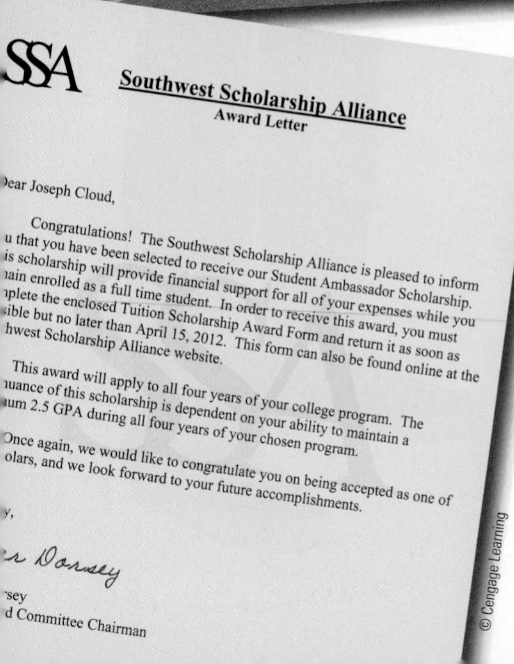

SSA **Southwest Scholarship Alliance**

Award Letter

)ear Joseph Cloud,

Congratulations! The Southwest Scholarship Alliance is pleased to inform u that you have been selected to receive our Student Ambassador Scholarship. is scholarship will provide financial support for all of your expenses while you nain enrolled as a full time student. In order to receive this award, you must nplete the enclosed Tuition Scholarship Award Form and return it as soon as sible but no later than April 15, 2012. This form can also be found online at the hwest Scholarship Alliance website.

This award will apply to all four years of your college program. The uance of this scholarship is dependent on your ability to maintain a um 2.5 GPA during all four years of your chosen program.

Once again, we would like to congratulate you on being accepted as one of olars, and we look forward to your future accomplishments.

y,

r Dorsey

sey

d Committee Chairman

© Cengage Learning

Growing up in his town of 1,000, he had been the science fair king, the after-school grocery store shelf stocker, and the smartest guy in his high school of thirty-five. He was leaving a trail of victories behind him, and everyone in town appeared to have a stake in his future success in college. As the end of the summer approached, whenever people saw him in the grocery store, they'd yell out, "Hey, Joe, when are you leaving for college?"

Much to his parents' delight, Joe had even won a scholarship that would pay for all of his expenses. The condition was that he would be successful, graduate, and return to the reservation to give back to the community in some capacity.

As midterms approached, Joe figured things were going well, except for his killer calculus course. There were 350 students in the lecture course, and Professor Buchanan was very businesslike and aloof. Joe was building up a great deal of anxiety over the course. Never before had he failed at anything, and if he didn't keep his grades up, he'd lose his scholarship.

The first week had been a review of what he had learned in his high school calculus class. But things became more challenging quickly. The pace quickened to the point that Joe found himself frantically trying to keep up. Math had never been his best subject.

However, as the midterm exam approached, Joe began experiencing a funny sensation when he entered class each week. As he approached the door, his breathing became shallow and rapid, his heart was pounding, and he felt lightheaded when he sat in his seat. He finally had to get up and leave before passing out. Unfortunately, it was exam review day, too.

That evening at dinner, he talked over his experience with his friend, Chris. "I've been telling you to eat breakfast!" Chris said. "You have to start rolling out of bed earlier, man!" But deep within himself, Joe knew his problem was more

Sean MacD/Shutterstock.com

GraÃ§a Victoria/Shutterstock.com

than just skipping breakfast.

Although he hated to admit it, calculus had become so distasteful that Joe hadn't cracked the textbook since the day he had to get up and leave. He knew cramming was a bad idea, but he also knew that he had given himself no choice. The night before the midterm, Joe started his studying by spending an hour looking up websites on how to cram for tests on the Internet; lots of coffee was the common theme. As the clock ticked into the wee hours of the morning, he was making trips to the coffee machine every forty-five minutes. He figured he had to pull an all-nighter if he wanted to pass at all. Dr. Buchanan had said the test would consist of calculus problems with the answers in multiple-choice format, so Joe got out his highlighter and started reading the textbook chapters.

The morning of the exam, Joe woke up suddenly and when he glanced at his alarm clock, he saw that he had overslept. The exam would start across campus in fifteen minutes. His palms were sweaty, and his heart was racing again. He leaped out of bed, threw on some clothes, and ran out the door. When he got to class, he noticed that he'd forgotten his watch and his book bag with his calculator in it. As he sat down in a random empty seat, a student next to him leaned over and whispered, "I am totally freaked out about this test, aren't you?" That didn't help.

Joe finally worked up the nerve to look at the first question and realized he couldn't answer it. Frantically, he paged through the rest of the exam. It all looked unfamiliar. He was so tired that he was having trouble focusing. His seat gave him a perfect view of another student's answer sheet one row down and over. He struggled with the temptation. It was the longest fifty minutes of his life, and when Dr. Buchanan called "time," Joe put down his pencil and slumped back into his chair.

The next week when the exams were handed back, Joe expected the worst—and he got it. What he stared at was the worst grade he'd ever gotten on any test in his entire life. Disgusted, he threw his exam in the trash can at the front of the lecture hall on his way out. *Why is there so much emphasis on exams in college, anyway? I'll never have to take a test again when I get out of here,* he muttered to himself. He was only halfway through his first term, and his scholarship was already on the line.

objectsforall/Shutterstock.com

© Cengage Learning

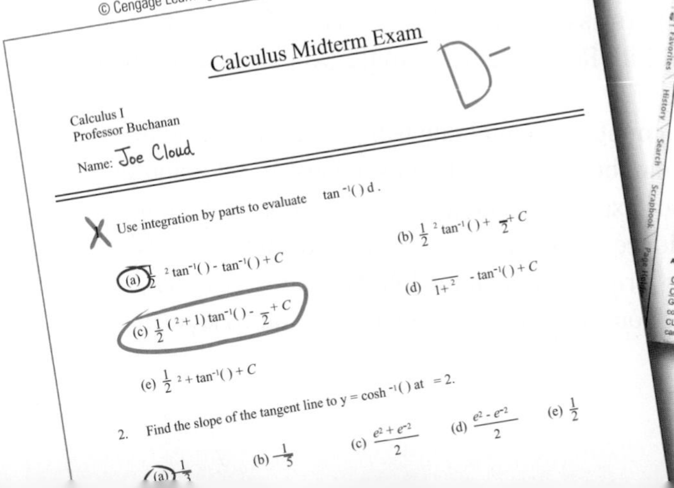

wikihow.com

What Do You Think?

1. What should Joe have done differently *before, during,* and *after* the exam?
2. Does Joe have test anxiety? Why or why not?
3. What's the *right* way to study for a multiple-choice exam in a calculus course?
4. Does cramming work? Why or why not?
5. What do you think about Joe's temptation to cheat to save his scholarship? Why should or shouldn't he do it?

VARK It!

Complete the recommended activity for your preferred VARK learning modality. If you are multimodal, select more than one activity. Your instructor may ask you to (a) give an oral report on your results in class, (b) send your results to him or her via e-mail, (c) post them online, or (d) contribute to a class chat.

Visual: As you read, make a flow chart to show how you will proceed *before, during*, and *after* the next test in one of your more challenging classes. Personalize the chart to show exactly what you will actually do.

Aural: Talk to yourself as you read about how to study for an upcoming exam that will challenge your test-taking knowledge and skills. Ask yourself questions that you predict will appear on the exam and answer them aloud.

Read/Write: As you read key points that pertain to you, write a press release describing your ideal performance on an upcoming exam. For example, "Midwestern first-year student aces exam by trying new study techniques" and then describe the new techniques used.

Kinesthetic: Before you begin reading, construct a challenging practice test for an upcoming actual exam. When you finish the chapter, actually take the practice test and time yourself while taking it (to simulate the stress you'll face during the real exam).

iStockphoto.com/Marcela Barsse/MarsBars; Joanna Goodyear/Dreamstime.com; iStockphoto.com/Nadezda Firsova; iStockphoto.com/Pascal Genest

Testing 1, 2, 3 ... *Show* What You *Know*

Let's face it, life would be very different without grades in college, or time clocks on the job, or performance reviews throughout your career, wouldn't it? You wouldn't have to show up at work if you didn't feel like it, and you'd get a paycheck anyway. You wouldn't have to do a good job because no one would care. And you wouldn't have to write papers, or give presentations, or take tests in college. Not only would you benefit by having more free time, but your instructors wouldn't have to forge their way through stacks of papers assigning grades, either. What a wonderful world that would be—or would it? Realistically, it would probably bring total chaos.

Life's not like that. Results count. Accountability is the bottom line. Achievement is taken seriously. You may be thinking, "I'll never have to take another test once I get out of here," but exams are actually realistic representations of life's requirements. The experience of taking a test is similar to running a critical meeting or giving a high-stakes presentation on the job. You'll need to walk into the room, ready to show what you know, and answer unanticipated questions.

The anxiety you feel before taking a test isn't much different from the anxiety you might feel in stressful situations in your career. Exams ask you to demonstrate your knowledge on the spot at a particular juncture in your learning. They help you compare your progress to that of other students and to your professor's set of expectations about what all students should know.[1] On the job, every day will be a test of your skills and abilities, and you'll get your "grade" when your supervisor gives you an accounting of your performance over the last six months or year. Tests are inevitable; so rather than bemoan them, perhaps we should change the way we think about them.

I watched the Focus TV episode on testing at www.cengagebrain.com, and it says this!

The first step of test-taking, of course, is to make sure you're prepared. All of the information in this chapter is worthless if you haven't gone to class or read the textbook or taken good notes during lectures. Miracles, by their very definition, are in very short supply. Nothing can substitute for being conscientious about your work. Think about preparing for an exam as you would for an athletic event. Imagine running the 26 mile, 385 yard Boston Marathon, billed as "the world's oldest and most prestigious road racing event." You'd have to work for months to develop the stamina you would need to finish successfully. You wouldn't want to just show up for kicks and wing it. If you did, at the very least, you'd probably pull a muscle. At the very worst, they'd carry you away on a stretcher.

The same principle holds true for exams in college. In order to have the stamina required and avoid the "injury" of not doing well, tests require this same kind of step-by-step, long-term preparation. Tests in your courses will usually ask you to do one or more of the following:

- *Remember* or *recognize* specific facts
- *Compare, contrast, synthesize,* or *interpret* information
- *Apply* theories and principles to recognizable or new problems
- *Predict* the outcomes to a set of variables
- *Evaluate* the usefulness of ideas, theories, or methods for a particular situation

Look at all those italicized verbs, and you begin to see the span of what will be required of you in all your courses.

Think about taking tests as a three-stage project with a beginning, middle, and end. What do you do *before* the test to get ready? What do you do *during* the test to do your best? What do you do *after* the test to ensure a productive learning experience you can use for future exams? Taking a test can actually be a learning experience, and you can improve your performance incrementally as you learn to master the principles you'll read in this chapter.

© Larry Harwood Photography, Property of Cengage Learning

"Today the greatest single source of wealth is between your ears."

Brian Tracy, leadership and business speaker

Before the Test: Calm Your Nerves by Preparing Carefully

?
challenge

"
reaction

Challenge: List your five best specific ideas about how to prepare for tests. What works for you? Assume you are giving advice to a brand new student.

Reaction:

1. ____
2. ____
3. ____
4. ____
5. ____

As you read the upcoming sections about *before, during,* and *after* a test, evaluate how many of these suggestions apply to you. Put a plus sign (+) in front of each item you already do regularly and a (✔) in front of items you could start doing more regularly to improve your test-taking skills.

1. ________ **Begin preparing for an exam on the first day of class.** Nothing can replace consistent, regular study before and after each class. If you work along the way, then when it comes time for the exam, you won't need to panic and begin sudden heroic efforts. Keep up with the reading, even if there are things you'd rather be doing. Learning experts talk about the differences between *spaced* and *mass* learning. Spaced learning takes place over time; mass learning takes place all at once. For example, if you took piano lessons as a child, your teacher probably had you learn parts of a piece of music a few bars at a time until you learned the whole song. Imagine sitting at the piano as a six-year-old and trying to learn all of "Für Elise" in one sitting. While mass learning may work for some simple tasks, spaced learning is said to enhance retention by as much as 40 percent.[2]

2. ________ **Identify the days and times of all your exams for the whole term in your planner, cell phone, online calendar, or PDA.** At the beginning of the term, write in the days and times of all the exams in all your courses—even finals, which will seem very far off. You'll thank yourself many times over for completing this essential task.

3. ________ **Find out exactly what the test will cover.** There's nothing more terrifying than having a classmate next to you say something like this before the exam begins, "I can't believe this test covers the entire first six chapters," when you thought it only covered the first four chapters. Clarify whether handouts will be included, previous quiz questions—anything you're not sure of. Phone, text, or e-mail several other students, or better yet, ask your instructor questions like these: How long will the test be? What material will it cover? Which topics are most important? It's also a good idea to ask about criteria that will be used in grading. Do punctuation and grammar count? Will there be an in-class review? All these questions are usually fair game.

> If you would hit the mark, you must aim a little above it.
>
> *Henry Wadsworth Longfellow, American poet (1807–1882)*

Comstock/Jupiter Images

4. ______ **Understand that specific types of preparation are required for specific types of tests.** Objective and subjective tests should be approached differently, as described in later sections of this chapter. Online tests require that you know the answers to important questions up front. For example, will the test time out? Must you complete the exam once you start, or can you save your answers and come back to finish later? Should you compose essay answers elsewhere and paste them into the online exam so that you don't lose all your work in the case of a technology hiccup? Is the campus wireless system reliable enough for completing tests online?

5. ______ **Make a study schedule.** How many days are left to study? What will you accomplish each day? Don't decide you'll use whatever time is left over to study for your test. Usually there isn't any time left over. Time has a way of filling up all by itself. Remember—don't let what is "urgent" crowd out what is important.

6. ______ **Begin serious reviewing several days before the test.** The best strategy is "tending" the class material, just as you take care of other things you care about on an ongoing basis, like your car or your dog. After each lecture, work with your notes, revising, organizing, or summarizing them. Then several days before the exam, step up your effort. Divide up the work by days or study blocks. Begin consolidating your lecture notes and reading notes. Make flashcards, outlines, charts, summaries, tables, diagrams, practice quizzes that are often available on your textbook websites, whatever works for your learning style and fits the material.

7. ______ **Maximize your memory.** Research indicates that elaborate rehearsal is more effective than shallow rehearsal and specific techniques help transfer information from short-term to long-term memory. Remember to "Make It Stick" (rehearse, overlearn, space it out, separate it, and mind the middle), "Make It Meaningful" (feel, connect, and personalize), "Make It Mnemonic" (spell, locate, link or narrate, and peg), "Manipulate It" (mark it up, mark it down, organize, picture, act, produce, and test), and "Make It Funny" (mock it).

8. ______ **Get everything ready the night before.** To calm your nerves, lay out your clothes the night before the exam and pack your book bag with things you'll need: several pencils, erasers, scrap paper, your calculator, and a watch that works. Remove as much hassle as you can from test day.

I sure blew this one!

9. ______ **Manage your energy so that you're ready to focus and work quickly.** You've heard it before, but if you're exhausted or feverish, you're not as likely to "show what you know" as you will if you're healthy and rested. Exams tend to take their toll, energy-wise, so have reserves built up to sustain you. And don't resort to artificial stimulants, like drinking excessive

amounts of coffee to stay awake. "All-nighters" are a college ritual. They may make you feel heroic, and people sometimes brag about having suffered through them, but they catch up with you, and they're a bad habit to get into. According to one expert, "for every hour of sleep we lose, we drop one IQ point."[3] A series of all-nighters during midterms or final exams can seriously impair your intellectual performance.

I think I do this a lot.

10. ________ **Don't give in to a nonproductive, negative attitude.** Emotions are contagious. Stay away from other students who are freaked out or pessimistic about the exam. Think—and feel—for yourself. Make sure your self-coaching is productive ("I've studied this section for an hour; if it's on the exam, I'll nail it."), rather than punishing ("I'm so stupid. Why didn't I keep up with the reading?").

11. ________ **Study with other students.** Have you ever heard this quotation before: "To teach is to learn twice" (Joubert, French moralist, 1754–1824)? It's true. When you teach something to someone else, you must first learn it thoroughly yourself. Why not study with other students? You can take turns teaching one another, comparing class notes, and making practice exams for each other. Don't wait to be invited; take responsibility and start a study group yourself. And if you're concerned that a study group of several students may degenerate into a social club, study with just one other person—find a study partner and commit to doing the work.

12. ________ **Remind yourself of your long-term goals.** Why are you going to college? All this sweat and toil is worth something or you wouldn't be doing it. Keep your sights on the finish line! Enjoy the feeling of accomplishing something now that contributes to your goal-oriented success later. Ask people who finish the Boston Marathon how they feel. The answers you'll get won't focus exclusively on the ordeal; they will celebrate the accomplishment—guaranteed!

13. ________ **Arrive at the classroom early, but not too early.** Get there early enough to get a seat where the lighting is good and you won't be distracted by other students, but don't arrive so early that you build up excessive anxiety during a long wait.

14. ________ **Don't pop pills to stay awake.** You may know students who use Ritalin, Adderall, Vicodin, and OxyContin as study aids. This is a bad idea. When these drugs are used for the wrong reasons, they can help you stay awake for hours and enter a dreamy state. The potential side effects include insomnia, nausea or vomiting, dizziness, palpitations, headaches, tremors and muscle twitching, even seizures. With such horrible potential health risks staring you in the face, not to mention possible legal sanctions if you obtain these drugs without a prescription, why not make things simple? Just study.[4]

Wakako Tsuchida wins the 2011 Boston Marathon Woman's Wheelchair Division

CJ GUNTHER/EPA /Landov

15. ________ **Don't let open-book or take-home tests lull you into a false sense of security.** What could be easier than an open-book test? What could be better than taking a test in the comfort of your own home? Actually, these two types

of tests require substantial preparation. Time is the issue here. If you're unfamiliar with the material, flipping through pages of notes or skipping around in the textbook won't help. Create a reference guide for yourself so that you can find various topics in your notes or textbook and use your time efficiently.

16. ________ **Don't mess with success.** If you're doing well and earning the grades you deserve, don't discard what is working for you. Honestly assess the efficiency and effectiveness of your current practices, and then decide what ideas from this chapter you should add to your test-taking preparation repertoire.

BOX 9.1 Test Tips from A+ Students

- "I rewrite my notes immediately after each class, which helps me retain information. I schedule my classes at least an hour apart so I can do this."
- "When I rewrite my notes, I put them in test format. This helps enormously during the review process."
- "I find that flashcards are a great way to learn math formulas, definitions, or important concepts. For a foreign language class, I put the word on one side of the index card, and I draw a picture of the object on the other."
- "I go through the exam quickly and assign each question a level of difficulty: 1, 2, or 3, with 3 being the hardest. Then I answer all the 1's first and the 2's second. I know the 3's will take me some extra time."
- "I make flow charts to help me learn processes and relationships. As I create charts and tables, I 'play with' the information by labeling columns and rows, and that's how I learn it."
- "I rewrite my notes several times, and each time I do, I condense them into smaller and smaller amounts of information. Working with the same material over and over helps me learn."
- "I divide up the amount of material I have to study by the number of days before the test. That way I know exactly what I need to master each day."
- "If I have three tests scheduled for the same day, I study in three hour blocks and alternate among the three subjects. That keeps things interesting and energizes me."
- "In my experience, most of what is on tests comes from lectures. I think this is because teachers are most familiar with their own views."
- "In my experience, most of what is on tests comes from the textbook. I think this is because it saves teachers time to use the questions in the instructor's manual, rather than making them up from scratch."
- "I reread all my notes an hour before the test so that everything is fresh in my mind. I make sure I clear my schedule so that's possible."
- "When I finish studying for the night, I reward myself with a treat and then turn in."
- "I bring a candy bar to the exam. When I start feeling tired and my mind begins to wander, I refresh myself with a sugar high."
- "I always wear my 'lucky shirt' on exam day. It's worked for me so far!"[5]

These are great ideas, but I think I have test anxiety—I feel like I need some professional help ...

Cramming: Does "All or Nothing" Really Work?

? challenge

reaction

Challenge: Why is cramming for tests a bad idea? List as many reasons as you can.

Reaction: ____

____

____

Imagine yourself as the actor in the following scenarios. Compare these situations to cramming for tests.

- You don't eat for a week, and then at one sitting, you gorge for several hours on everything you can stuff into your mouth. Does that sound appealing to you? Probably not. It wouldn't work well either, would it? You can only hold so much.
- You haven't called your significant other since last year. Suddenly you appear at her door with candy, flowers, concert tickets, and dinner reservations at the most exclusive restaurant in town. You can't understand why she isn't happier to see you.
- You don't feed your dog for several months. When you finally bring him a plate loaded with ten T-bone steaks to make up for your neglect, you notice he's up and died on you. Oops!

Of course, these tongue-in-cheek, all-or-nothing situations are ridiculous, aren't they? How could anyone ever neglect such basic necessities of life? There's an important point to be made here. Many things in life require continuous tending: pets and people, for example. If you ignore them for a time, catching up is next to impossible. Your college courses should be added to the list.

▶▶ Your TypE Is Showing

How would you answer the following yes or no questions about your test-taking strategies as they may relate to your type?

1. I usually end up changing answers to some questions on exams, and usually lose points in the process. ________ yes
2. Essay questions are much harder for me than true-false or multiple-choice questions. ________ sometimes
3. If I had a choice, I'd take an exam in a room all by myself so that I could really concentrate. ________ yes
4. I prefer open-ended questions that allow me to include everything I know. ________ no
5. Organizing my response to an essay question is difficult for me. I prefer to just start writing and see where the answer goes. ________ not really
6. I sometimes read more into a question than is really there. ________ no
7. I usually end up making careless mistakes on exams. ________ yes
8. I feel most comfortable answering questions that have a specific, concrete clue about the answer. ________ yes
9. I take my time on tests, reading and rereading questions. ________ sometimes
10. I understand my strengths and weaknesses as a test-taker, and I'm consciously working to improve. ________ maybe I will now

Does personality type impact test-taking strategies? If so, how? You'd probably assume that an *introvert* would say yes to item 3, or that a *perceiver* would agree with item 4. Look at your responses and see how they relate to what you know about your type. According to one study, *judgers* are less likely than *perceivers* to change answers, and *introverts* who change their answers—as opposed to *extraverts*—are more likely to gain, rather than lose, points by doing so.[6]

Actually, the MBTI scale that shows the biggest differences on test-taking is the Sensing-iNuition scale. *Sensors* are less likely than *iNtuitives* to trust their hunches when answering text questions. They may read a question over and over, searching for some kind of concrete clue, so much so that they read into the question. They may miss the big picture, answer theoretical questions based on their own practical experience, and lose points by changing answers. People who are *iNtuitives* tend to jump to conclusions when they read test questions. They may fill in a missing word with their mind's eye, or make an inference upon which they base another inference until they are far afield from the answer the question is seeking.[7]

Do these research results apply to you? I'm an ISTJ

Believe it or not, some students give themselves permission to follow this all-or-nothing principle in their academic work. They sail along without investing much time or energy in their studies, and then they try to make up for lost time right before an exam by cramming. The word *cram* provokes a distinct visual image, and rightly so. Picture yourself packing for spring break in a warm, sunny place and hardly being able to close your suitcase because it's crammed full. You can't decide what to bring so you bring everything you can think of.

The same holds for cramming for a test. You try to stuff your brain full of information, including things you won't need. Since you haven't taken the time to integrate the information and gather it into related chunks, you end up with random bits of unconnected data. Cramming is an attempt to overload information into your unreliable working memory. It's only available for a very short time. However, there are other reasons why cramming is a bad idea:

- Your anxiety level will surge.
- Your sleep will suffer.
- Your immune system may go haywire.
- You may oversleep and miss the exam altogether. ← almost did that one!

Despite the warnings here, most students cram at some time or other during their college careers, and doing so may even give them a temporary high and make them feel like they're suffering for a cause.[8] But generally, slow and steady wins the race.[9]

Test-Taking: High Anxiety?

EXERCISE 9.1

Do You Suffer from Test Anxiety?

What is test anxiety? What are the symptoms? Do you have it? Fill out the following informal survey to determine whether or not you may have test anxiety. For each of the twelve statements, rate your degree of agreement or disagreement.

1	2	3	4	5
Disagree Completely	Disagree Somewhat	Unsure	Agree Somewhat	Agree Completely

1. I cringe when I suddenly realize on the day of an exam that a test is coming up. 4
2. I obsess about the possibility of failing an upcoming exam. 2
3. I often experience disappointment, anger, embarrassment, or some other emotional reaction during an exam. 4
4. I think that instructors secretly get enjoyment from watching students squirm over exams. 1
5. I experience physical symptoms such as an upset stomach, faintness, hyperventilation, or nausea before an exam. 3
6. I tend to zone out during exams; my mind goes blank. 4
7. I feel extreme pressure to please others by doing well on exams. 2
8. If I'm honest, I'd have to admit that I really don't know how to study for tests. 2
9. I'd much rather write a paper or give a presentation than take an exam. 3
10. I usually fear that my exam grade will be lower than that of other students. 4

(continued on next page)

51—see, I thought I had test anxiety!

11. After taking an exam, I obsess on my performance, going over and over questions that I think I may have missed. 3
12. I convince myself that I'm not good at taking exams even though I often do fairly well on them. 2

If your score equals 49–60, you are a likely candidate for test anxiety. For suggestions on how to manage your anxiety, read on.

If you scored between 37 and 48, you have some signs of anxiety and may need help in managing your stress level.

If you scored 36 or below, you most likely experience a normal amount of anxiety and have already developed coping skills to help you.

Professor Marlin's (tongue-in-cheek) Rule: If you have an open-book test, you will forget your book. If you have a take-home test, you will forget where you live.

Anonymous

Test anxiety—what is it? And, more importantly, does it affect you? While most people think of text anxiety as a negative, the truth is, it's natural to be anxious before, during, and even after an exam. Most everyone is. In fact, some anxiety is useful. The adrenaline rush that accompanies anxiety can keep you alert and focused.

But for some students test anxiety takes over and sabotages their efforts. They may say, "I knew it all before the test, but when I saw the questions, everything I knew vanished before my very eyes." These students experience fainting spells or even gastric distress that requires them to leave the testing room periodically. Some of them may be reacting to prior bad experiences with exams. Others may put intense pressure on themselves because they're perfectionists. Clearly, there's evidence from medical science that too much anxiety can work against you. Corticosterone, a hormone released during times of extreme stress, can actually impair your ability to retrieve information from long-term memory.[10] Regardless of the reason, the first part of the solution is understanding exactly what test anxiety is. It has four different, but related, components:[11]

If I flunk, I'll lose my scholarship!

These all sound like me!

- **cognitive aspects**—nonproductive thoughts that run through your head before, during, and after an exam ("I have to get an A on this test. If I don't, I'll flunk out of school.")
- **emotional aspects**—negative feelings you experience related to the exam (disappointment, frustration, sadness, and so on)
- **behavioral aspects**—observable indications of stress (fidgeting, drumming your fingers on the desk, walking quickly, and so on)
- **physiological aspects**—counterproductive physiological reactions (dry mouth, butterflies in your stomach, palpitations, a tension headache, lightheadedness, and so on)

Since you can't expect the tests you take in college to change for your sake—to alleviate your anxiety—the possibility for change must come from within *you*. Consider these suggestions as they relate to the four indicators of test anxiety.

Cognitive

- **Understand your testing strengths and challenges, based on your learning style.** Although research indicates that most students prefer multiple-choice tests over essay tests, you have your own strengths and preferences.[12] Your psychological type may provide insights into some of these.

> **Positive thinking will let you do everything better than negative thinking will.**
>
> *Zig Ziglar, motivational speaker and author*

Chase Jarvis/Getty Images

catastrophize—good word!

- **Don't catastrophize!** Stop yourself from engaging in negative, unproductive self-talk. It's easy to imagine worst-case scenarios: "If I fail this exam, I'll lose my scholarship, and if I lose my scholarship, I won't be able to afford to go to college, and if I don't go to college, I'll probably end up as a homeless person, begging for change on the street." Negative thinking can easily spiral downward, and before you know it, you're thinking about major life catastrophes and the end of the world. Although some exams do have important outcomes, it's important to put things in perspective. Twenty years from now, who will know if you earned an 85 or an 88 on your philosophy test this week? Although this argument can be taken too far (so that you convince yourself that nothing matters much), if your test anxiety stems from perfectionism, this is an important point to remember.

Emotional

- **Monitor your moods.** Your emotions fluctuate based on many factors; they vary by type, intensity, and timing.[13] If you eat well and get enough sleep before an exam, your moods are more likely to be even-keeled than if you skip meals, ride the carbohydrate roller coaster, and pull all-nighters. An eight-hour sleep debt will cause your mood to take a nosedive.[14]
- **"Park" your problems if you can.** When you go into a store, you leave your car outside in the parking lot and come back to it when you're finished shopping. Think about how that analogy relates to taking a test. Everyone has problems. If we didn't we wouldn't be human. But obsessing on them during a test is counterproductive to say the least. Park them for a while. Focus on your work, and challenge yourself to do your best. Your worries won't go away, unfortunately; they'll be around after you're done, when you're better able to take steps to deal with them.

Behavioral

- **Relieve some stress with physical activity.** Expend some of that extra, pent-up energy before the exam. Sprint to class or take a walk to clear your head in the hour before the test begins.
- **"Step out of your life" by spending time outdoors.** Being in the outdoors is liberating. There's a big world out there; it's easy to forget that when you're spending large amounts of time in classrooms or at work.

Physiological

- **Teach yourself how to relax.** Relaxation training can be used to overcome test anxiety. As simple as it sounds, that may involve learning how to breathe. Watch a new baby sleep, and you'll see instinctive, deep, even breathing in which only the baby's stomach moves up and down. As adults, when we're anxious, we breathe rapidly and shallowly, which

CURIOSITY: *REDUCE MATH ANXIETY AND INCREASE YOUR TEST SCORES*

Honestly, most people feel some twinge of anxiety about working a complex set of math problems on an exam. But if your level of anxiety interferes with your test success, you may suffer from math anxiety. One expert estimates that roughly 20 to 25 percent of college students are in that category.[15] Some estimates are that as many as 85 percent of college students in introductory math classes experience some degree of math anxiety.[16]

If you're one of them, admitting the problem is the first step. Next, it's important to understand how math anxiety can work against you during exams so that you can do something about it. The most effective strategies to cope are direct and uncomplicated.[17]

Think back; perhaps you can pinpoint where your fears began. It may have been a teacher or a class or a particular test. Experts believe math anxiety is learned, and that it's up to you to "unlearn" it.

James Noble/CORBIS

Why and how does math anxiety affect people? Try this experiment: multiply 86 × 7. To arrive at the answer, you must first multiply 6 × 7, make note of the 2, and carry the 4. Then you must multiply 7 × 8 and add the 4 to arrive at 602. Notice the steps involved in this simple math problem. You have to keep certain numbers in your head while you continue to work through it, which is often the case with math. Your working memory allows you to pull it off.

Working memory is your short-term, temporary-storage, limited-space memory. It's the memory you use to hold certain pieces of information—your brain's scratchpad— keeping them available for you to work with and update.[18] A task like multiplying 639 × 924 would be too much for most people's working memories, but some people have more capacity than others. Here's the kicker: Math anxiety actually eats up your working memory.

Why? Managing anxiety takes up working memory space that could be used to solve math problems. When you reduce your anxiety, you have more room to use your working memory productively. Math anxiety also causes people to take longer to do math and to make more mistakes.[19]

It's not the case that you use up your working memory because you think and think and think about how to work the problem and get the right answer. Instead, your working memory is hijacked by negative thoughts, causing you to choke.[20]

The solution? Practice for stressful exams under pressure. Set a timer, and tell yourself you must finish before it goes off. Make a game of it: for every question you miss on a practice exam, you must put a quarter in the kitty and pay off your friend, significant other, or mom. In other words, practicing in an equally stressful environment (or nearly so) can help during the actual test.[21] Since math anxiety is a learned fear, it can be unlearned.

doesn't sufficiently oxygenate our brains. Conversely, when we learn to breathe with our diaphragms by drawing in air through our nostrils, filling our entire lungs (not just the upper third), and exhaling completely and smoothly, as if trying to blow out a candle a foot in front of you, we begin the process of learning to relax.[22] Meditation, massage, and biofeedback can work, too.

- **Seek help from a professional.** An expert who works with anxiety-ridden college students can diagnose your problem and help you through it. While helping you learn to relax, a counselor or learning expert on or off campus may help you engage in "guided visualization." Guided visualization asks you to visualize yourself doing the things you need to do, leading up to your goal—in this case succeeding on your test. At each step

Ah-ha! I thought so—I'll look up the campus number tonight.

of the way, you envision success, and then continue to rehearse those images in your mind.[23] Or a counselor might help you engage in "systematic desensitization," a technique in which you work to overcome your anxiety incrementally in very small steps.[24]

During the Test: Focus and Work Hard

? challenge

" reaction

Challenge: List five ways to focus and work hard during an exam. Choose methods that work well for you. List one other technique you've never tried that you suspect would help you.

Reaction:

1. ____________________
2. ____________________
3. ____________________
4. ____________________
5. ____________________

____

During an exam, the heat is on! Do you use these strategies? If not, which ones can you incorporate to improve your performance? Put a plus sign (+) in front of each item you already do regularly and a (✔) in front of items you could start doing more regularly to improve your test-taking skills.

1. ________ **Jot down what you don't want to forget right away.** When you first receive your exam, turn it over and jot down everything you want to make sure you remember—mnemonic devices, charts you've created, acronyms—assuming, of course, that writing on the test is allowed. Some students treat the exam itself as if it were a sacred document, but marking up your exam is usually allowed. Circle key words and strike through answers you eliminate.

2. ________ **Preview the exam.** Just going through all the questions may help you review terms you know. And you'll notice which questions are easier and which are harder right away. It's also likely that reading sample questions will trigger your memory and help you come up with information you need. After the first few minutes, you may relax a bit, and answers will come to you more easily.

3. ________ **Start with what you know.** Make sure you get credit for answers you know; don't waste time early on struggling with the more difficult questions. This strategy will also boost your confidence and help you relax. Studies show that running up against extremely difficult test questions at the beginning of a test can actually negatively impact accuracy on simpler questions later on.[25]

Just like my test! I always feel like this!

4. ________ **Manage your time.** Allocate your time based on the relative weight of the questions. Don't wrestle with one question for ten minutes when it's only worth one point. Go on to a more heavily weighted one.

William Whitehurst/CORBIS

> Ability will never catch up with the demand for it.
>
> *Malcolm S. Forbes, U.S. art collector, author, and publisher (1919–1990)*

5. _______ **Read directions thoroughly.** Misreading or skipping the directions altogether can be a lethal mistake. Remember that your instructor can't read your mind. ("But that's not what I meant!") Slow down and make sure you understand what you're being asked to do.

6. _______ **Read questions carefully.** Sometimes skipping over a word in the sentence (or filling one in where none exists) will cause you to jump to a false conclusion. Don't let your eyes (or your brain) play tricks on you!

7. _______ **If the test has a mixed format, complete the multiple-choice questions first.** Often instructors create exams using both *objective* (multiple-choice, true-false) questions and *subjective* questions (fill in the blank, essay). Generally, objective questions ask you to *recognize* answers from several alternatives, and subjective questions ask you to *recall* answers from memory. A multiple-choice question may remind you of something you want to include in an essay. Keep a pad of paper nearby during the exam. Jot down ideas as you answer multiple-choice questions. You'll feel more confident and do a better job if you keep a running list of ideas that occur to you as you go.

8. _______ **Explain your answer to an ambiguous question in the margin of your test.** You may point out a problem your instructor wasn't aware of or get partial credit.

9. _______ **Change your answers if you're convinced you're wrong.** Despite advice you've probably always received from teachers and classmates alike, changing answers when you're sure you've made a mistake is usually a good idea, not a bad one. In one study, less than 10 percent of students made changes that decreased their scores, while 74 percent made changes that increased their scores.[26]

Whoa!

10. _______ **Ask your instructor for clarification.** If the exam appears to have a typo or something seems wrong, ask your instructor or proctor to clarify for you. Of course, if you ask for the definition of a word that is a clue, you probably won't get an answer, but if you have a technical question or a question about the test-taking process, don't be afraid to ask.

11. _______ **Pay attention to "aha" moments.** Don't let your "aha" moments turn into "oh, no" moments. If you remember something you couldn't think of earlier, go back to that question and finish it right away.

BOX 9.2 Chew Your Way to an A, by Gum!

If you're an average American, you're chewing your life away—300 sticks of gum per year! Children in the United States spend about half a billion dollars on bubble gum every year.[27] For sure, Americans are loyal to their favorite pastime, chewing away the hours. But here's a provocative question out of the blue: Can chewing gum during an exam help you academically?

According to some researchers, chewing gum can actually improve your brain power.[28] In a study conducted by British scientists, people who chewed gum scored 24 to 36 percent higher on memory tests than those who didn't. Dr. Andrew Scholey, a researcher in human cognitive neuroscience at the University of Northumbria in Northern England, conducted an experiment in which three groups of 25 subjects took part. The first group chewed gum throughout, the second group had no gum, and the third group pretended to chew gum by making chewing motions.

Dr. Scholey speculates that the improved memory of gum-chewers may be due to the fact that chewing gum increases the heart rate, which then supplies more oxygen to the brain. Or the effect may have to do with the fact that chewing stimulates insulin production, which affects the part of the brain involved in memory.[29] Researchers say chewing gum doesn't improve your concentration, but it may improve your recall. Of course, some scientists are skeptical of Dr. Scholey's research. But chew it over yourself!

12. _______ **Don't give in to peer pressure.** If, while you're working away, you look around and see that many students are leaving because they're already finished, don't panic. Take as much of the allotted time as you need. Everyone works at a different rate.

13. _______ **Save time for review.** When you're finished, go back over all your answers. Make sure you've circled the right letter or filled in the correct bubble. Be certain you've made all the points you intended to make in your essay. Look at your work critically, as if you were the instructor. Careless errors can be costly!

14. _______ **Be strategic about taking online tests.** Often tests posted online are timed. If you're taking a distance education course or a classroom course with an online test component, watch for e-mail announcements that tests have been posted, and note particular instructions. When will the test expire and disappear? Can you reenter the test site and redo answers before you hit the submit button? Can you take tests collaboratively with other students? With online tests, of course, the other recommendations in this chapter for true-false or multiple-choice tests apply as well.

© Larry Harwood Photography. Property of Cengage Learning

"We all have ability. The difference is how we use it."

Stevie Wonder, singer and composer, (1950–)

Taking Objective Tests

Challenge: Are there specific strategies you should use to take objective tests? Identify five suggestions that apply to true-false and multiple-choice tests.

Reaction:

1. ____________________
2. ____________________
3. ____________________
4. ____________________
5. ____________________

Many of the exams you'll take in college will be objective, rather than subjective, tests. Let's examine the best strategies for taking objective tests.

True-False: Truly a 50–50 Chance of Getting It Right?

True?

Exam questions that test your recall are always more challenging than questions that test your recognition skills. T or F?

True-false tests may seem straightforward, but they can be tricky. You assume you have a 50–50 chance of answering correctly. But don't forget, you also have a 50–50 chance of answering incorrectly. Sometimes the wording of the statements makes the *process* of taking true-false tests more challenging than their *content*. Consider these helpful guidelines:

- **Watch for parts of statements that make the entire statement false.** The statement must be all true to be "true," and a few words may make an otherwise true statement "false." Here's an example:

Got me on this one!

Derek Bok, who was president of Harvard University for thirty years, once said, "If you think education is expensive, try ignorance." T or F

The main part of the statement is true; the quotation does belong to Derek Bok. Actually, however, Bok was president of Harvard from 1971 to 1991 (and returned to serve on an interim basis in 2006–2007), making the detail about him, buried in the middle of the sentence, false. The entire statement, then, must be marked "false."

- **Assume statements are true until you can prove them false.** Statistically, exams usually contain more true answers than false ones.

You have a better than 50 percent chance of being right if you guess "true." But teachers vary; yours may not follow the norm.

- **Watch for *absolutes*; they often make a statement false.** Words like always, never, and entirely often make otherwise true statements become false. "You can always get an A on an exam if you study for it." Unfortunately, no.
- **Look for *qualifiers*; they often make a statement true.** On the other hand, words like sometimes, often, and ordinarily often make statements true. "You can sometimes get an A on an exam if you study for it." Fortunately, yes.
- **Remember that negatives can be confusing.** Is this statement true or false? "Students who don't lack motivation are likely to excel." "Don't lack" really means "have," right?

Multiple *Choice* or Multiple *Guess*? Taking the Guess Work Out

Which of the following statements is (are) true?

a. Richard Greener, who became Harvard's first African American graduate in 1870, later became a lawyer, educator, and distinguished U.S. consul and diplomat.
b. Elizabeth Blackwell, who graduated from Geneva Medical College in New York, was the first woman in the United States to earn a medical degree.
c. Oberlin College was the first U.S. college to admit women and the last to admit African-American students on an equal footing with Caucasians.
d. a and b
e. a, b, and c

e? Nope

Are multiple-choice tests difficult for you? Often what's difficult about multiple-choice tests has more to do with the structure of the test than the content. Studying for these tests requires a particular approach, and if you master the approach, you'll find taking multiple-choice tests to be much easier. You can actually think of them as variants of true-false tests. [The correct answer to the question, by the way, is (d).]

- **Think of answers on your own before reading your choices.** You may get hung up on the wording of an answer. Answer it on your own so that you can recognize it, no matter how it's worded. You may want to do this by covering up the alternatives initially, and then proceeding after you know what you're looking for. Sometimes the alternatives will differ by only one or two words. It's easy to become confused.
- **Line up your test and answer sheet.** This sounds like a simple suggestion, but getting off a line can be very disruptive when you have to erase like crazy and start over!

This is a good strategy, if I can overcome my anxiety!

- **Determine the TPI (time per item).** Divide the number of questions by the allotted time. If there are seventy-five questions to answer in an hour, you know that you'll need to work faster than one question per minute. Remember to save some time for review and revision at the end.
- **Don't decide answers based on the law of averages.** If you flip a coin three times, and it comes up "heads," most of us assume it's probably time for "tails" to come up next. Likewise, on exams, if you've answered (d) for three questions in a row, you may think it's time for an (a), (b), or (c). It may not be.
- **Using a process of elimination, guess if there's no penalty.** Some instructors subtract points for wrong answers, but if you do guess, guess wisely. And don't skip questions. Always mark something unless you're penalized for doing so. Take a look at this example:

> Before you write an answer on an essay test, you should do all but the following:
> a. Read all the questions.
> b. Begin with the hardest question.
> c. Look at what the questions are asking you to do, specifically.
> d. Underline key words in the question.

You know that you should do (a). Reading all the questions before you start is a must. You know that option (d) makes sense, and so does (c). But you're not quite sure about option (b). You can eliminate (a), (c), and (d), so (b) must be the right answer based on a process of elimination. As you work, eliminate answers that you know are incorrect by marking through them like this.

- **Look for highly similar pairs.** Sometimes two options will differ by a single word or the order of words. Often one of these is the right choice.
- **Look for contradictory answers.** If two statements are complete opposites, one of them is often the right choice.
- **Watch out for tricks intended to separate the prepared from the unprepared!** For example, avoid answers that are true in and of themselves, but not true when attached to the sentence stem or question being asked. For example, imagine this question option on a multiple-choice exam:

Sounds right . . .

> Global warming is considered to be a serious issue among some scientists because:
> a. Former President Bill Clinton describes global warming as a greater threat to the world than terrorism.

Image Source/Corbis

"**I am easily satisfied with the very best.**"

Winston Churchill, Prime Minister of England (1874–1965)

While Clinton did espouse this view in a 2006 speech, it is not the reason for scientists' concern, so (a) isn't the correct answer.[30] Two other tips: generally, when numbers are in each alternative, choose numbers in the middle range. Choosing answers that are longer and more descriptive usually pays off, too.

- **Consider each answer as an individual true-false question.** Examine each option carefully, as if you had to decide if it were true or false, and use that analysis to make a decision about which option is correct.
- **Be wary of "all of the above" or "none of the above" options.** While instructors sometimes make these options the correct ones, it's also possible they resort to these options because making up enough plausible answers is challenging.
- **Watch for terminology that has been emphasized.** Look for key terms that appeared in your lecture notes and in chapters of the text. These words may provide links to the correct answer. Remember when taking multiple-choice tests that you are looking for the *best* answer, not simply the *right* one.[31]

EXERCISE 9.2

Multiple Choice Test

Answer the following multiple-choice questions. Beneath each question, identify which of the principles of test-taking from this chapter you are using to identify the correct answer.

1. "I know of no more encouraging fact than the unquestionable ability of man to elevate his life by conscious endeavor." These words were said by:
   a. Bill Clinton
   b. Abraham Maslow
   c. Ronald Reagan
   d. Henry David Thoreau

2. Which of the following statements about the ACT test is not true?
   a. The ACT includes 215 questions.
   b. ACT results are accepted by virtually all U.S. colleges and universities.
   c. Students may take the ACT test as many times as they like.
   d. None of the above.

a, d, e?
Got two out of three right!

3. Which of the following suggestions about preparing for college is (are) true?
   a. Get involved in co-curricular activities in high school.
   b. Always take challenging courses that show your effort and ability.
   c. Involve your family in your decisions and preparation for college.
   d. Find a mentor, a teacher, or counselor who can give you good advice.
   e. All of the above.

[Answer key: (d), (c), (e)]

CAREER OUTLOOK: *COMMAND CRUCIAL CONVERSATIONS*

The way we communicate with others and with ourselves ultimately determines the quality of our lives.

Anthony Robbins,
American author and success coach

Imagine this: You're appealing to your professor to change an exam grade: *"Why did you give me a D? Now I'm going to lose my scholarship."* "Open mouth, insert foot." Often during challenging conversations, you know intuitively that your communication choices are crucial. You also know intuitively (by that sinking feeling in the pit of your stomach) when you've said the wrong thing. Unfortunately, by implying that your poor grade is your professor's fault, you've probably "failed the test." You're unlikely to get the results you were seeking. There are ways in which crucial conversations are tests of our communication skills, and it's clear that most of us don't always know how to get the "grade" we want.

In this example, like many others in your life—with teachers, friends, family, bosses, colleagues, romantic partners, you name it—you're smack dab in the middle of a *crucial conversation*. When is a conversation crucial instead of just plain important? Crucial conversations are said to be those with results that could potentially change the quality of your life. It may be true that whether or not you get your grade changed actually *will* affect your scholarship and impact your ability to stay in school. According to experts, crucial conversations have three components: high stakes, strong emotions, and differing opinions—a potentially toxic triangle. Not to add pressure to the discussion, but it's safe to say that they're the most important conversations of our lives.[32]

At times like these, results are on the line, and sometimes our communication skills don't rise to the occasion. We underreact with silence, overreact with a meltdown, or choose a safe, but inappropriate medium (like sending a text message that says, "The wedding is off," for example). Other times, we somehow get it right. The question is: How do we develop the communication skills we need for these inevitable crucial conversations? When we're at our best, we demonstrate a willingness to speak up when we disagree, deal with issues head-on rather than resorting to the "silent treatment," and dive into dreaded conversations with bravery and resolve, rather than fear. Underneath it all is this advice—"engage brain before opening mouth." Intentionality and planning make a crucial conversation work.[33]

On down the road, "Could the ability to master crucial conversations help your career? Absolutely. Twenty-five years of research with twenty thousand people and hundreds of organizations has taught us that individuals who are the most influential—who can get things done, and at the same time build on relationships—are those who master their crucial conversations.... As it turns out, you don't have to choose between being honest and being effective. You don't have to choose between candor and your career. People who routinely hold crucial conversations and hold them well are able to express controversial and even risky opinions in a way that gets heard."[34]

In your coming career, crucial conversations will be nothing short of crucial. When you're seeking an opportunity, responding to criticism, giving your boss feedback, asking a difficult teammate to cooperate, or requesting help, your career may be on the line. How well you communicate will make all the difference.

I need to improve my communication skills.

Think Ahead: Think about a recent crucial conversation you've had. If you could hit the "redo" button, what would you do or say differently? Can the lesson you just identified be applied to your future career in the workplace? If so, how?

CAST OF CAREERS

© Larry Harwood Photography. Property of Cengage Learning

FOCUS: Looking back, what crucial conversations did you have as a first-year student?

KIA: I had some awkward conversations with my roommate, friends, and boyfriends, like most college students. But the ones I remember most are the crucial conversations I had with my advisor. Sometimes I wanted to take a course she didn't recommend, sign up for more hours that I should, or change my major yet another time. She helped me work my way through these issues, and looking back, if I'd had my way, the results wouldn't have worked in my favor. I had to learn to listen, not only to her, but to myself. The stakes were high (how long it would take me to graduate), my emotions were strong (just let me do what I want to do!), and the two of us had differing opinions. She taught me a lot about how to communicate more effectively.

FOCUS: What are your career plans?

KIA: I love college so much that I want it to continue! I'm majoring in psychology, but I'm planning to continue on and get a master's in student affairs to become an academic advisor or campus life specialist. Working with students is something I know I'll enjoy!

Short-Answer, Fill in the Blank, and Matching Tests

Short-answer tests are like essay tests, which we'll discuss shortly, in many ways. You're required to come up with an organized, well-thought-through answer on your own. But instead of a long essay, you only need to write a paragraph or two. Is that easier? It may be, but sometimes it's just as hard or harder to condense what you have to say about difficult concepts into fewer words. Generally, however, the suggestions for essay tests hold.

For fill in the blank tests, first think the statement through. What does it mean? Try inserting different words. Which one sounds best? Which one was used during lectures or appeared in the textbook? If one word looks awkward, try another one. Although it's not a completely reliable hint, look at the number of words, placement of spaces, and length of the space. If you don't know the exact terminology the question is looking for, insert descriptive words of your own. You may earn partial credit.

Matching tests require particular strategies, too. First of all, you must determine whether items should be used only once or if they can be reused. If it's not clear from the test directions, ask for clarification. Match the items you're certain about first and cross them out if once only is the rule. If you mismatch an item early on, the rest of your choices will be wrong, too.

Taking Subjective Essay Tests

Essay Question: Please discuss the value of brain research in relation to our current knowledge of how learning takes place.

Essay questions are difficult for some students because details are required. Rather than being able to *recognize* the correct answer, you must be able to *recall* it totally from your own memory. Here are some recommendations you should consider:

- **Save enough time for essays.** If the test has a mixed format, it's important to save enough time to write well-thought-through essays. Often objective questions such as multiple choice or true-false only count a point or two, whereas essay questions often count into the double digits.
- **Read all the questions before you start.** To sharpen your focus and avoid overlap, give yourself an overview of all the questions before you start writing.
- **Make brief notes.** Somewhere on the exam or on scratch paper, write a brief plan for your responses to essay questions. A few minutes of planning may be time well spent. As you plan your answer, keep basic questions in mind—*who, what, when, where*, and *why*—as an organizing framework.

- **State your thesis up front.** How will you handle this question? What's your plan of attack? Your first paragraph should include your basic argument in a thesis statement.
- **Provide support for your thesis.** Writing an answer to an essay question requires you to make assertions. However, it's not enough that you assert things; you must try to prove that they are true. If your thesis asserts that college students cheat more today than they did when your parents went to college, you must present evidence—statistics, examples, or expert testimony—to demonstrate that what you're asserting is true.
- **Zero in on the verb.** The heart of an essay question is its verb. Take a look at this list and think about how each verb dictates what is required:

  Analyze—break into separate parts and examine or discuss each part

  This is something I've never even thought about. It's like a hint about how to respond to the question!

  Compare—examine two or more things, find the similarities and differences (usually you emphasize the similarities)

  Contrast—find the differences between two or more things

  Critique, criticize, or evaluate—make a judgment, describe the worth of something

  Define—provide the meaning (usually requires a short answer)

  Describe—give a detailed account, list characteristics or qualities

  Discuss—describe a cause/effect relationship, the significance of something, the pros and cons, or the role played by someone or something

  Enumerate—list qualities, characteristics, events, and so on

  Explain—similar to discuss

  Illustrate—give concrete examples

  Interpret—comment on, give examples, provide an explanation for, discuss

  Outline—describe the plot, main ideas, or organization of something

  Prove—support an argument with evidence from the text or class notes

  Relate—show the relationship or connection between two things

  State—explain in precise terms

  Summarize—give a condensed account of key points, reduce to the essential components

  Trace—describe a process or the development of something
- **Use terminology from the course.** Perhaps more than any other type of exam, an essay test allows you room to truly display your knowledge. Use the opportunity! Reflect new terms you have learned, and tie your answer directly to course content.
- **Rifle your answer, don't shotgun.** Here's an analogy: A shotgun fires many small metal pellets. A rifle fires a single bullet. When writing an essay answer, some students write down everything they know, hoping

Good analogy!

that something will be correct. You may actually lose points by doing this. It's better to target your answer and be precise.

- **Generalize if you're unsure of small, exact details.** You can't quite remember, was it 1884 or 1894? The best idea is to write, "Toward the end of the nineteenth century" instead of choosing one of the two and being wrong.
- **Follow all the rules.** When answering an essay question, it's important to be as concise yet thorough as possible. Enumerate your ideas ("There are three major ..."). Avoid slang ("Wordsworth elaborated ..." not "Wordsworth jazzed up the poem."). Refer to researchers or authors or noteworthy people by their last names ("Jung wrote ..." not "Dr. Carl Jung wrote ...").
- **Watch your grammar.** The reason why its important, to do this, is because many student's dont and there answers are marked wrong. They wish they would of done better afterwards. You get the point.
- **Write an answer that corresponds to how much the question is worth.** It's important to be concise, but generally, if one essay answer is worth 10 points and another is worth 25 points, your instructor will expect you to write more for the question that's worth more. A more detailed, thorough response is what is called for.
- **Put down what you do know.** If you see a question you didn't predict, don't panic. If you've studied, you know something that might help give you partial credit even if you don't know the answer in full.

CONTROL: *YOUR TOUGHEST CLASS*

Think about your most challenging class this term. Identify one key challenge you face in this class that relates to test-taking. For example, one key challenge might be that the exams in your toughest class only include essay questions, which you find more difficult that multiple-choice type exams. Now develop a step-by-step action plan to deal with this one challenge. For example, your action plan might look like this:

1. Reread the sections of the chapter on preparing for tests and test anxiety.
2. Meet with my professor to discuss my problems in her class.
3. Show her this action plan, and ask for her suggestions.
4. Keep a journal of my progress to note improvement and meet with her four more times this term.

This is what my list should be, I think.

Now do the same for your most challenging class.

What is your key challenge? ______________________

1. ______________________

____

2. ______________________

____

3. ______________________

____

4. ______________________

____

> Knowing is not enough; we must apply. Willing is not enough; we must do.
>
> *Johann Wolfgang von Goethe, German writer and scholar (1749–1832)*

- **Proofread and make sure your handwriting is legible.** While most instructors will count the number of points you covered and use specific standards, grading essays is a slightly subjective process. That means instructors must use their own judgment. A good essay answer is taken less seriously if it's littered with mistakes or a real mess to read. This is the real world; neatness counts. Anything you can do to create a positive impression may work in your favor.
- **If you run out of time, jot down any remaining points in the time that's left.** You may not get full credit, but partial credit is better than none.
- **Include a summary statement at the end.** Your essay answer should read like a real essay with an introduction, a body, and a conclusion. Don't just stop mid-sentence without wrapping things up.[35]

Don't Cheat Yourself!

What if you were in one of these situations? How would you respond?

- You must get a good score on your anatomy and physiology test so that you don't lose your scholarship. You and your classmates all share homework answers on Facebook. The professor is known for using the same tests over and over again. He doesn't invest time in updating his exams, and students know it. If he doesn't care, why should you?
- Your parents are paying out-of-state tuition, and you can't afford to fail the midterm exam in your killer physics course. Your best friend teaches you how to make a fake ingredients list (with your physics formulas) and paste them on the inside label of your water bottle to bring in to the exam. Very clever!
- Many students in your communication major get through difficult exams by sharing answers via their cell phones. It's easy to dial your phone using one hand under the desk and text message answers to each other. "Hey, what did you put down for 2, 8, and 15?" "b, d, and c," your friend replies in an instant. The professors never notice, and the courses aren't all that interesting anyway.
- A friend of yours sends herself an e-mail of all the names and dates she'll need to know for her history exams. With just one click on her smartphone she can call up whatever

Vera Berger/Corbis

> For nothing can seem foul to those that win.
>
> *William Shakespeare, British poet and playwright (1564–1616)*

information she needs. "Try it," she says. "Everyone else does it, and you'll feel cheated if you don't cheat. If you don't do what other students do, you'll graduate with mediocre grades, and you'll never be able to compete for the jobs you've always wanted. Besides getting away with it here just helps prepare you for the business world where things are *really* cutthroat!"

- You hear about an online paper mill that will write your paper for you. For a set per-page price, they will even "doctor" each sentence so that the source can't be found on the Internet. You have four papers, a presentation, and an exam all due the same week, and one or two ghostwritten papers may cost you, but what choice do you have? That's not all that much considering the tips you make as a server. Hmm. . . .

I've heard of people doing this kind of stuff for some of my classes.

How did you respond to these five scenarios? Are you aware of cheating schemes on your own campus? Could students you know be the ones in these situations? Notice that most of these students have practical-sounding reasons for what they are doing. If you want to cheat, it's not hard (in fact, technology makes it easy), and you can always blame someone else like your teachers or parents. What's the harm?[36] You get better grades, your parents are pleased, your teachers feel gratified, your school brags about the fine academic record of its students, and you pat yourself on your back for skillfully managing a very busy, demanding life. Everyone wins, right? Wrong.

According to some studies, fifty years ago, one in five college students admitted to cheating. Today's figures range from 75 to 98 percent. Here's some straight talk about cheating:[37]

1. **Remember that cheating snowballs.** What started as secretly pocketing some kid's CD or glancing at your neighbor's reading test in grade school turns into writing a math formula between your fingers or hiding the names of the constellations under your shirt cuff in middle school. Then these juvenile violations turn into full-fledged, sophisticated infractions as students "download their workload" in high school and knowingly violate their school's Academic Integrity Policy in college. Where does it stop? With corporate scandal and newspaper headlines?
2. **Instead of saving time, cheating can take time.** Everyone is busy. Many students are working at jobs for pay in addition to taking classes. How can anyone get everything done that needs to get done? But instead of devising elaborate cheating schemes, which take time, why not just use that time to study?
3. **If you cheat now, you'll pay later.** Sooner or later, cheating will catch up with you. You may get past your history professor or your calculus instructor this time, and you may even get good grades on others' work you turn in as your own. But someday your boss will ask you to write something, or do some research, or use a skill a student is expected to have mastered in college, and you won't know where to start.
4. **If you do get caught, cheating may do you in.** Some students cheat because they know other students have gotten away with it. Cheating for them is a thrill, and not getting caught is like beating the system. Roll the dice and see what happens, they say. But you should know that professors are in the know these days. Academic hallways are abuzz with faculty talk about cheating. If you do get caught, your academic career may come to an abrupt halt.

5. **Cheating is just plain wrong.** You may or may not agree with this point, but it deserves some serious consideration. How would you like to be cheated out of money that's owed you or days off that are due you? The Golden Rule may sound old-fashioned, but the fact that it's been around for a long time with roots in a wide range of world cultures tells you something. "Intellectual Property" and "Academic Integrity" may not be as tangible as money you deserve or eight hours of free time, but they are increasingly protected by every college and university.

What are your personal ethical standards? Are you willing to cut corners? Would you cheat to achieve top grades in college? What kind of "devil's bargain" would you be willing to strike?

If you're tempted, remember this. Sooner or later, cheating costs you—big time! Don't cheat yourself out of learning what you need to learn in college. Learning is not all about *product*—the exams, papers, grades, and diplomas themselves—it's about *process,* too. The process involves gaining skills that will prepare you for life after college. That's a goal worth working toward.

cheating is too easy— I'm a better pesron than that ... and I have a lot of people looking up to me.

You can't go through life devising elaborate schemes, or hiring someone else to do your work for you, or rationalizing about finding a way to beat the system because you're too busy to do your own work. Cheating in your college classes now just makes it that much easier to risk cheating your employer—and yourself—later on the job. Look through newspapers or watch the evening news to see who's been caught lately. It's a competitive world out there, but more and more companies find that having a good reputation, which comes from valuing integrity, is good business. The bottom line is "Employees don't follow leaders they don't trust. Employers don't hire people or promote employees they don't trust. Clients don't buy from suppliers they don't trust."[38] Integrity starts now: *earn what you learn.*[39]

After the Test: Continue to Learn

? challenge

" reaction

Challenge: What suggestions can you come up with for things to do after an exam—to help you remember the information, perhaps for a later exam or for another course, or do better next time?

Reaction: ______________________________

____

____

discouraged! But I think I CAN DO THIS now.

After you finish an exam and get your results, you may be soaring or discouraged. Regardless, exams can be excellent learning experiences if you take these steps. Put a plus sign (+) in front of each item you already do regularly and a (✔) in front of items you could start doing more regularly to improve your test-taking skills.

1. ________ **Analyze your results.** Conduct a thorough analysis of your test results. For example, an analysis like this one might tell you what kinds of questions are most problematic for you.

Type of Question	Points Earned/Right	Points Deducted/Wrong	Total
Multiple Choice	32	3	35
Fill in the Blank	15	2	17
True-False	20	8	28
Essay	10	10	20
Total	77	23	100

Or analyze your results by examining lecture questions versus textbook questions to find out where to concentrate your efforts on future tests. Or do an analysis by chapter content to tell you where to focus your time when studying for the final exam.

2. _______ **Read your instructor's comments and take them to heart.** Some students throw their exams away immediately. Instead, they should use them to ask: What was the instructor looking for? Was my writing ability critiqued? Does the test make more sense now than it did while I was taking it? Are there instructor's comments written on the test that I can learn from? What do the results of this exam teach me about preparing differently, perhaps, for the next test?

Oops! I threw my test away immediately.

3. _______ **Explain your grade to yourself.** Where did you go wrong? Did you misread questions? Run out of time? Organize essay answers poorly? Does the grade reflect your effort? If not, why not? Did test anxiety get the better of you? On the other hand, if you studied hard and your grade reflects it, that's an explanation, too!

4. _______ **Be honest.** It's easy to get caught up in the blame game: "I would have gotten a better grade if the exam had been fairer, if the test had been shorter, if the material hadn't been so difficult, if I'd had more time to study. . . ." Your instructors have heard every excuse in the book: "my dog ate my notes," "a relative died," "a family emergency made it impossible to study," "my hard drive crashed," "my roommate was sick"—you name it. Of course, sometimes crises do overtake events. But rather than pointing fingers elsewhere if you're disappointed with your results, be objective and look at what *you* can do differently next time.

5. _______ **Make a specific plan for the next test.** Most courses contain more than one exam. You'll probably have an opportunity to apply what you've learned and do better next time.

6. _______ **Approach your instructor politely if you believe your exam has been mismarked.** Sometimes teachers make mistakes. Sometimes they're interrupted while grading and forget to finish

© Larry Harwood Photography. Property of Cengage Learning

"A man's errors are his portals of discovery."

James Joyce, Irish novelist (1882–1941)

reading an essay answer, or the answer key is wrong, or they miscalculate. Even if the scoring is correct, it may be a good idea to approach your instructor for help about how to improve your next test score.

7. _______ **Reward yourself for good (study) behavior.** After you've worked hard to prepare and the exam is over, reward yourself—take in a movie, go out with friends, do something to celebrate your hard work.[40]

*
insight
!
action

Now What Do You Think?

1. At the beginning of this chapter, Joe Cloud, a frustrated and disgruntled college student, faced a challenge. Now after reading this chapter, would you respond differently to any of the questions you answered about the "FOCUS Challenge Case"? Knowing what you know now, how would you advise him? Write a paragraph ending to the story, incorporating your best advice.
2. Is test anxiety a problem for you? What are your reactions to taking tests in each of the four areas of test anxiety (Cognitive, Behavioral, Emotional, Physiological)?
3. Reflect on your own situation and answer the following questions. As you assessed your own test-taking strategies earlier in this chapter, how many checkmarks did you make for the suggestions on *before*, *during*, and *after* tests, indicating potential areas for improvement? Which of the suggestions from all three sections will you try to focus on in the future? What test-taking problems have you had in the past, and how will this information help you?

REALITY ✓ What did you LEARN

On a scale of 1 to 10, answer the following questions now that you've completed the chapter.

low 1 2 3 4 5 6 7 8 9 10 high

In hindsight, how much did you already know about this subject before reading the chapter? _______

Can you answer these questions about taking tests more fully now that you've read the chapter?

1. What are the four components of test anxiety?
2. Identify three hints to managing your time during tests.
3. Why are subjective (essay) tests often perceived to be more challenging than objective (true-false, multiple-choice) tests?

How useful might the information in this chapter be to you? How much do you think this information might affect your success overall? _______

How much energy did you put into reading this chapter? _______

How long did it actually take you to complete this chapter (both the reading and writing tasks)? _______ Hour(s) _______ Minutes

Did you finish reading this chapter? _______

Did you intend to when you started? _______

If you meant to but didn't, what stopped you? _______

Challenge Yourself Online Quiz To find out just how much you've learned, access the College Success CourseMate via www.cengagebrain.com to take the Challenge Yourself Online Quiz.

Take a minute to compare these answers to your answers from the "Readiness Check" at the beginning of this chapter. What gaps exist between the similar questions? How might these gaps between what you thought before starting the chapter and what you now think after completing the chapter affect how you approach the next chapter in this book?

CHAPTER 10

Building Relationships, Valuing Diversity

© Cengage Learning

You're about to discover...

- What emotional intelligence is and how it relates to college success
- How to improve communication with people you care about
- Why diversity makes a difference
- Why service-learning is valuable
- Why global learning is important

© Larry Harwood Photography. Property of Cengage Learning

READINESS ✔ What do you KNOW?

Before beginning to read this chapter, take two minutes to answer the following questions on a scale of 1 to 10. Your answers will help you assess how ready you are to focus.

low 1 2 3 4 5 6 7 8 9 10 high

How much do you *already* know?

Based on reading the "You're about to discover . . ." list and skimming this chapter, how much do you think you probably already know about this chapter's subject? ________

See if you can answer these questions about building relationships and valuing diversity *before* you read.

1. What is emotional intelligence and how does it relate to college success?
2. Identify one of five basic conflict styles.
3. Describe three benefits of valuing diversity.

How much do you expect to learn?

In general, how motivated are you to learn more by reading this chapter? ________

How much do you think this information might affect your success overall? ________

How much energy do you plan to put into reading this chapter? ________

How ready are you to read *now*?

How ready are you to focus on this chapter? Enter a number for each aspect of your readiness to focus.

Physically ________
Intellectually ________
Emotionally ________

If any of your answers is below a 10, pay attention to whatever is distracting you before you start reading. Then zero in and focus.

How long do you think it will take you to complete this chapter from start to finish?

________ Hour(s) ________ Minutes

Now, as you begin, do you intend to finish reading this chapter?

______ yes ______ no ______ maybe

FOCUS Challenge Case

© Larry Harwood Photography. Property of Cengage Learning

? challenge

Kia Washington

An emotional wreck. That's what Kia Washington was. Since she first arrived on campus, it seemed that everything had gone wrong. Her best friend, Alicia, had decided to go to a different school at the last minute, she was closed out of what probably would have been her favorite class—Introduction to Literature—and she hadn't been able to get into campus housing because of a computer mix-up. If she lived off campus now, the Housing Office told her, they'd guarantee her a room next term. To top it off, she was questioning her choice of classes and wondering why she couldn't decide on a major that would lead to a good job.

© Cengage Learning; Lori Howard/Shutterstock.com

The apartment she'd managed to find close to campus on Craigslist was run down and barely affordable. She bought an inexpensive microwave, a mattress, and some towels, but she really didn't have the money to fix it up. Feeling completely alone and isolated, she found herself in tears more than once those first few weeks. Home, for all its faults, was looking better than it had when she lived there.

© Larry Harwood Photography, Property of Cengage Learning

For most of her teenage years, Kia had lived with her Mom, who worked two jobs to support her and her brother, William. Although they got along well, her Mom was always too tired to do anything, it seemed, so they rarely spent much time together. And she never saw her father anymore. He'd remarried after the divorce and moved to another state. All through school, her family life had been rocky. Kia's parents, who probably cared for each other deep down, just couldn't get along. As a child, Kia sometimes retreated to her bedroom to wait out the arguments. Their decision to divorce five years ago had actually come as a relief.

Despite trouble at home, Kia had been a very good student in high school. Perhaps because home was a difficult place, she threw herself into her studies. She liked to read anything she could get her hands on, and doing homework had been a good escape. In fact, Kia kept to herself a good deal of the time. Meeting new people was one aspect of college she'd never really looked forward to. She preferred to just do her own thing, like listen to music by herself with her earplugs in between classes. Visiting

© M4OS Photos/Alamy

© Cengage Learning

the University Center to meet people and get connected wasn't something that interested her at all. Honestly, Kia felt completely isolated on campus, even though there were students everywhere.

There really was only one other person that Kia cared about—Quentin. Throughout all of her high school years, Kia and Quentin had been inseparable. He was older than she was, and that was definitely part of the appeal. Quentin also happened to be smart, and he was the funniest person Kia knew. They spent most evenings on their cell phones, sometimes into the early morning hours. No wonder every member of the female species was after him or so it seemed to Kia. Luckily, he always told her that he wasn't in the market. But now that she'd gone off to college, she worried that it would become harder to keep him. Holding onto Quentin was her most important goal right now.

Tiplyashin Anatoly/Shutterstock.com

Most of the time, they got along really well, and fights were over quickly. Whenever a conflict came up, Kia exploded and Quentin just took it. He was the proverbial nice guy and she was—as her mother put it—moody. She often felt as if she was on an emotional roller coaster, and her temper got the best of her. Trying to communicate her way through a disagreement never seemed worth it to Kia. She'd spit out a few rude comments and then walk away or hang up. Fortunately, Quentin never seemed to hold a grudge.

But last Thursday, they'd had the worst fight ever on the phone over something silly; she couldn't even remember what. Suddenly she heard herself yelling into the phone, saying things she knew she'd regret. Quentin managed to get the words "control freak" out, and then this time *he* hung up. She hadn't heard from him since. He didn't return voicemails or e-mails, and his text messages abruptly stopped. She found herself obsessing about him, not able to sleep well or eat much over the weekend, and she couldn't face going to her classes on Monday or Tuesday. By Wednesday, she was so sick with worry that she couldn't drag herself out of bed.

Why does this have to be so hard? Kia kept asking herself. She'd decided to go to college to make a better *future* for herself. But right now the most important thing she had to do was get through the *present. My life is a soap opera,* she thought. And to anyone watching right now, she was right.

Courtesy of Apple

© ICP/Alamy

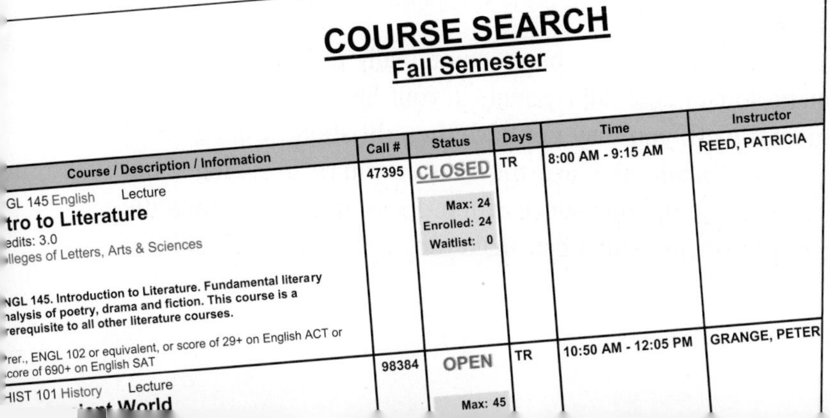

COURSE SEARCH
Fall Semester

Course / Description / Information	Call #	Status	Days	Time	Instructor
GL 145 English Lecture **tro to Literature** edits: 3.0 lleges of Letters, Arts & Sciences **NGL 145. Introduction to Literature. Fundamental literary nalysis of poetry, drama and fiction. This course is a rerequisite to all other literature courses.** rer., ENGL 102 or equivalent, or score of 29+ on English ACT or core of 690+ on English SAT	47395	CLOSED Max: 24 Enrolled: 24 Waitlist: 0	TR	8:00 AM - 9:15 AM	REED, PATRICIA
HIST 101 History Lecture ... World	98384	OPEN Max: 45	TR	10:50 AM - 12:05 PM	GRANGE, PETER

© Cengage Learning

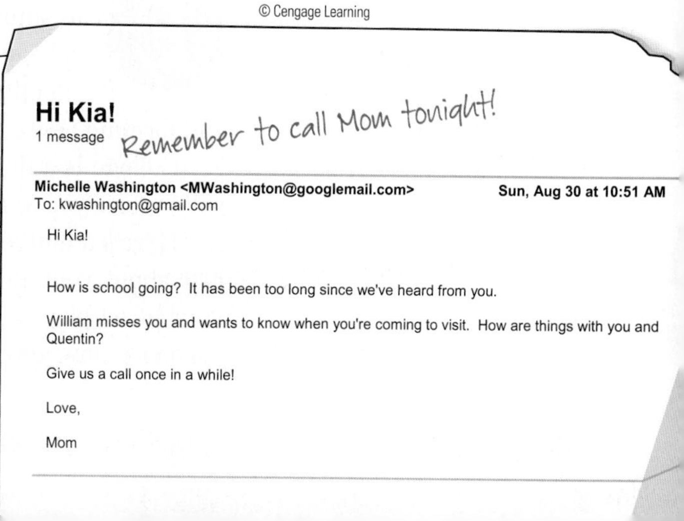

Hi Kia!
1 message

Remember to call Mom tonight!

Michelle Washington <MWashington@googlemail.com> **Sun, Aug 30 at 10:51 AM**
To: kwashington@gmail.com

Hi Kia!

How is school going? It has been too long since we've heard from you.

William misses you and wants to know when you're coming to visit. How are things with you and Quentin?

Give us a call once in a while!

Love,

Mom

© Cengage Learning

What Do You Think?

1. How would you characterize Kia's adjustment to college? Identify five specific problems described in this case study that could interfere with her college success.
2. To have done so well in school, Kia must be an intelligent person. But is her emotional quotient (EQ) different from her intelligence quotient (IQ)? Why or why not?
3. Kia's relationship with Quentin is the most important one in her life. What is she doing to contribute to the problems in the relationship? Will the relationship survive? If so, what would it take?
4. Describe Kia's conflict management style compared to Quentin's. What clues does the case study provide you?
5. Identify three things Kia should do to get her college success and her life on track.

VARK It!

Complete the recommended activity for your preferred VARK learning modality. If you are multimodal, select more than one activity. Your instructor may ask you to (a) give an oral report on your results in class, (b) send your results to him or her via e-mail, (c) post them online, or (d) contribute to a class chat.

Visual: As you read about emotional intelligence in this chapter, think about your own strenths. Make a chart of the five scales of emotional intelligence and select representative artwork or graphics for each scale to help you remember its meaning and importance.

Aural: As you start this chapter, write an email to an "email partner" in class about a past relationship—good or bad—and what you think made it that way. (Your instructor may assign "email partners" or let you choose your own.) While you read the chapter, find things that relate to your partner's story.

Read/Write: Before you start reading this chapter, write a case study about a real relationship using fictitious names. After you finish the chapter, look back at your case study to see how information from the chapter could have helped to improve the relationship. Maybe I'll write about myself . . .

Kinesthetic: Before you start reading this chapter, interview an international student on your campus about how college life differs between what he or she experiences on your campus and what would be different at colleges in his or her home country. When you get to class, relate what you found out to your classmates.

iStockphoto.com/Marcela Barsse/MarsBars; Joanna Goodyear/Dreamstime.com; iStockphoto.com/Nadezda Firsova; iStockphoto.com/Pascal Genest

The Heart of College Success

Every day, in many ways, you make choices about how you react to situations and other people. College is no exception. As a new college student, you're on your own, continually adapting to new situations, adjusting your past relationships with friends and family, and forming new ones rapidly.[1]

College is a time of transition; it can be an emotionally turbulent time that will require you to make some major adjustments in your life.

Here's a fundamental truth you may not have thought about: College isn't just about your head. Yes, academics are the reason you're in college, but your heart plays a critical role in your success, too. From friends to romantic partners, how you handle relationships can make or break you academically.

Could this refer to me??→

Emotional reactions to troubling circumstances have the raw potential to stop you dead in your tracks. Some students, for example, have the *academic* skills required for success, but *nonacademic* issues can interfere. There's no doubt about it: How you manage your emotions and respond to stressful situations will impact your college success.

In college and in life, your EQ (emotional quotient), or *emotional intelligence,* can be just as important as your IQ (intelligence quotient). Studies show that first-year students often feel overwhelmed, lonely, homesick, or friendsick. Friendsickness can interfere with your adjustment to college.[2] In one study, freshmen who felt the loneliest and most socially isolated had weaker immune systems than their counterparts who didn't report these feelings.[3] According to a former university administrator at a large, prestigious school, "More students leave college because of disillusionment, discouragement, or reduced motivation than because of lack of ability."[4] *That's* how important emotional intelligence is to college success! According to emotional intelligence expert, Daniel Goleman, "Even the most academically brilliant among us are vulnerable to being undone by unruly emotions."[5]

EXERCISE 10.1

How Would You Respond?

Read these five scenarios and identify your most likely reactions.[6]

Hmm, let me try this...

1. You peer over a classmate's shoulder and notice she has copied your online response from a class chat and submitted it as her paper in the course, hoping the professor won't notice. What do you do?
   a. Tell the student off to set the record straight, right then and there.
   b. Tell the professor that someone has cheated.
   c. Ask the student where the research for the paper came from.
   d. Forget it. It's not worth the trouble. Cheaters lose in the end.

1. a

2. You're riding on a plane that hits a patch of extreme turbulence. What do you do?
   a. Grab hold of the person in the next seat and hold on for dear life.
   b. Close your eyes and wait it out.
   c. Read something or watch the movie to calm yourself until things improve.
   d. Panic and lose your composure.

2. b

3. You receive a paper back in your toughest course and decide that your grade is unacceptable. What do you do?
   a. Challenge the professor immediately after class to argue for a better grade.
   b. Question whether or not you're really college material.
   c. Reread the paper to honestly assess its quality and make a plan for improvement.
   d. Deemphasize this course and focus on others in which you are more successful.

3. d

4. While kidding around with your friends, you hear one of them tell an offensive, blatantly racial joke. What do you do?
   a. Decide to ignore the problem and thereby avoid being perceived as overly touchy.
   b. Report the behavior to your residence hall advisor or an instructor.

(continued on next page)

c. Stop the group's conversation. Make the point that racial jokes can hurt and that it's important to be sensitive to others' reactions.

4. d

d. Tell your joke-telling friend later that racial jokes offend you.

5. You and your romantic partner are in the middle of a heated argument, and tempers are flaring. What do you do?

5. b

a. Stop, think about what you're trying to communicate, and say it as clearly and neutrally as possible.

b. Keep at it because if the issue generated that much emotion, it must be important to get to the bottom of it.

c. Take a twenty-minute time out and then continue your discussion.

d. Suggest that both of you apologize immediately and move on.

Perhaps you've found yourself in settings such as those described in Exercise 10.1. You might need more actual details to make the best choice in these five scenarios, but according to some experts, choice (c) is the most emotionally intelligent one in each case. Do you agree? How do *you* make decisions such as these? What constitutes an emotionally intelligent response?

What Is Emotional Intelligence?

? challenge

" reaction

Challenge: Have you ever heard the term emotional intelligence? How would you define it?

Reaction:

____

____

____

Many experts believe that intelligence is multifaceted. Rather than a narrow definition of intelligence, they believe in Multiple Intelligences: Linguistic, Logical-Mathematical, Spatial, Kinesthetic, Musical, Interpersonal, Intrapersonal, and Naturalistic.[7] Emotional intelligence may well be a combination, at least in part, of *intrapersonal* and *interpersonal* intelligences.

Emotional intelligence is a set of skills that determines how well you cope with the demands and pressures you face every day. How well do you understand yourself, empathize with others, draw on your inner resources, and encourage the same qualities in people you care about? Emotional intelligence involves having people skills, a positive outlook, and the capacity to adapt to change. Lack of emotional intelligence has the potential to derail you.

Emotional intelligence can propel you through difficult situations. Take the case of the window washer during the September 11, 2001, World Trade Center terrorist attack. Six men—five of whom were executives—were trapped in an elevator after the first tower was hit. The sixth man, Jan Demezur, was a window washer who showed the others that the end of his squeegee could be used to pry open the elevator door. When the group finally forced the door open only to find the number 50 painted on the wall of the elevator shaft, they realized that their express elevator didn't stop at floor 50. There was no way out. Demezur began using the sharp edge of his squeegee to poke a hole in the wall. The six men took turns, scratching through three layers of drywall to safety. Under extreme pressure and the threat of imminent death, the window washer demonstrated ingenuity, confidence, optimism, teamwork, leadership, and emotional intelligence.[8]

In that elevator, the most effective individual wasn't the one who earned the most money, dressed the best, or had the highest status. It was the person who could rally others to extraordinary effort—the person who could connect with other people.

© Larry Harwood Photography. Property of Cengage Learning

Research describes the powerful effects of emotional intelligence. For example, in a forty-year study of 450 boys who grew up in Somerville, Massachusetts, two-thirds came from poor families and one-third had below average IQs. Later in life, however, intelligence as traditionally defined had little to do with their success. What was more important was how well they handled frustration, controlled their emotions, and got along with others.[9] In another study looking back over the careers of scientists now in their seventies, social and emotional abilities were four times as important as IQ in determining professional success.[10] Of course, there's no doubt that IQ is important. You must be smart to become a scientist, or any type of professional, for that matter. But assuming you're qualified and prepared, how your career unfolds and how successful you actually are may have more to do with your EQ than it does your IQ.[11]

Research demonstrates that your emotions and your thought processes are closely connected.[12] There's also evidence that being in a happy mood can help you generate more creative solutions to problems.[13] The bottom line? New research links emotional intelligence to college success, and learning about the impact of EI in the first year of college helps students stay in school.[14]

> **Our emotions are the driving powers of our lives.**
>
> *Earl Riney, American clergyman (1885–1955)*

As you read about the five scales of emotional intelligence, begin assessing your own competence in these areas. We'll discuss how to gain a better understanding of your actual capabilities later in this chapter. As each scale is introduced, ask yourself whether you agree or disagree with the sample statement presented as it pertains to you.[15]

Hemera Technologies/Jupiter Images

Intrapersonal Skills (Self-Awareness)

"It's hard for me to understand the way I feel." Agree or disagree?

To what extent are you in tune with your emotions? Do you fully realize when you're anxious, depressed, or elated? Or do you just generally feel up or down? Are you aware of layers of emotions? Sometimes we show *anger*, for instance, when what we really feel is *fear.* (For example, you might scream at your brother in anger when you're actually

> **Managing your emotions is an inside job.**
>
> *Doc Childre and Howard Martin, performance experts*

really afraid he'll embarrass you in front of your friends.) Are you emotionally self-reliant, rather than emotionally dependent on others? Do you realize that no one else can truly make you happy, that you are responsible for creating your own emotional states? Do you set goals that relate to things *you* value and work toward achieving them? How well do you understand yourself and what makes you tick?

Hemera Technologies/Jupiter Images

Interpersonal Skills (Relating to Others)

"I'm sensitive to the feelings of others." Agree or disagree?

Are you aware of others' emotions and needs? Do you communicate with sensitivity and work to build positive relationships? Are you a good listener? Are you comfortable with others, and do you have confidence in your relationships with them?

I'm sensitive to the feelings of others sometimes, but I'm not always sensitive enough to Quentin ...

Hemera Technologies/Jupiter Images

Stress Management Skills

"I feel that it's hard for me to control my anxiety." Agree or disagree?

Can you productively manage your emotions so that they work *for* you and not *against* you? Can you control destructive emotions? Can you work well under pressure? Are you in control, even when things get tense and difficult?

Hemera Technologies/Jupiter Images

Adaptability Skills

"When trying to solve a problem, I look at each possibility and then decide on the best way." Agree or disagree?

Are you flexible? Do you cope well when things *don't* go according to plan? Can you switch to a new plan when you need to? Do you manage change effectively? Can you anticipate problems and solve them as they come up? Do you rely on yourself and adapt well?

Photos.com

General Mood

"I generally expect things will turn out all right, despite setbacks from time to time." Agree or disagree?

Are you optimistic and positive most of the time? Do you feel happy and content with yourself, others, and your life in general? Are you energetic and self-motivated? Do people tell you you're pleasant to be around?

From EQ-i: HEd version. Reprinted by permission.

Emotional intelligence and its effects reverberate throughout our lives. For example, researchers study related concepts: "hardiness," "resilience," and "learned optimism."[16] Some people are more resistant to stress and illness. Hardy, resilient, optimistic people are confident, committed to what they're doing, feel

Look up these words!

greater control over their lives, and see hurdles as challenges. Emotional intelligence is part of the reason why.

Emotional intelligence and its five scales are important in all aspects of life, including your future career.[17] When *Harvard Business Review* first published an article on the topic in 1998, it attracted more readers than any article in the journal's previous forty years. When the CEO of Johnson & Johnson read it, he ordered copies for the company's 400 top executives worldwide.[18]

Why? Emotional intelligence is a characteristic of true leaders. Immediately after the first shock of the September 11, 2001, tragedy, the world tuned in to a press conference with New York's Mayor Rudy Giuliani. He was asked to estimate the number of people who had lost their lives in the World Trade Center collapse that day, and his reply was this: "We don't know the exact number yet, but whatever the number, it will be more than we can bear." In that one sentence, Giuliani demonstrated one of the most important principles of true leadership. Leaders inspire by touching the feelings of others.[19]

Can Emotional Intelligence Be Improved?

Everyone wants well-developed emotional intelligence, but how do you get it? Can EI be learned? While researchers admit that genes definitely play a role, most experts believe that emotional intelligence can be increased. One of the most convincing pieces of evidence is from a study that followed a cohort of students over seven years. Students assessed their emotional intelligence, selected particular competencies to strengthen, and then each created an individual plan to develop them. Seven years later, their competencies remained high.[20]

Recent physiological research, indicating that the human brain's hippocampus is more "plastic" than originally thought, also endorses the notion that EI can be improved. New "mindfulness" training to help people regulate their own emotions actually alters parts of the brain. A group of scientists who received mindfulness training an hour a week for eight weeks had measurable changes in their brains and reported more positive emotions than their non-trained counterparts at the end of the eight weeks, and again four months later.[21] Researchers continue to study emotional intelligence to fully grasp its implications in many different areas of life, but its central role in college success is increasingly understood. So what can you do to improve your EI skills?[22]

Seek honest input from others. It's hard to be objective about yourself. But it is possible to tap some of that necessary objectivity from those who interact with you regularly. How do they see you? Use other people as coaches to help you see which aspects of your emotional intelligence need strengthening.

Robert Recker/Corbis

"What's going on in the inside shows on the outside."

Earl Nightingale, success consultant

Find an EI mentor. A mentor on the job is someone who's older and more experienced than you are and can help you navigate your way through tough problems and manage your career. Mentors help, and an EI mentor—someone with finely honed EI skills you admire—can provide you with invaluable advice about handling challenging emotional situations.

CURIOSITY: *BUILD RELATIONSHIPS, ONE DROP AT A TIME*

After the Korean War, the U.S. Army's chief psychiatrist studied the psychological warfare used against 1,000 American prisoners of war who had been kept at a North Korean camp. He made a startling discovery: negativity kills.[23]

The prisoners had not been treated cruelly. They were given food, water, and shelter. They hadn't been tortured, yet many American soldiers died in the camp. They weren't surrounded by barbed wire and armed guards, yet no one ever tried to escape. Instead, many of them turned against each other, formed relationships with their North Korean guards, and when they were finally freed, many didn't even bother to call home when given the opportunity to let their loved ones know they were alive.

Many of these men died of extreme hopelessness caused by a total removal of emotional support. Soldiers were rewarded for informing on one another and required to stand up in groups of their peers and tell all the bad things they had ever done, as well as the good things they should have done. All positive letters from home were withheld, but negative ones telling of relatives passing away or wives divorcing their husbands were delivered right away. Even notices of overdue bills from collection agencies were passed along. Eventually, many of these American prisoners simply gave up. They died of "give up-itis," as they called it, raising the overall death rate in the camp to 38 percent—the highest American POW death rate in U.S. history.

The record of what happened raised this fundamental question, described in the *New York Times* and *Wall Street Journal* bestseller *How Full Is Your Bucket*? If negativity can have such a devastating impact, what can positivity do? That's where the analogy of buckets and dippers begins. Most of us will never endure the kind of psychological warfare these soldiers did, but all of us can examine the negativity we inflict on others, and by contrast, the positivity we can bring to others' lives.

How Full Is Your Bucket? by Tom Rath and Donald Clifton claims that each of us has an invisible bucket; we function at our best when our buckets are full. We each also have an invisible dipper. In every interaction, we use our dipper to fill others' buckets or to dip from them. The principle of the book is simple; following its advice, however, is challenging. *How Full Is Your Bucket?* makes these five recommendations:

1. **Dip less.** Get in the habit of listening to yourself. Are your words cynical, insensitive, or critical? If so, push the pause button and rephrase what you're trying to communicate. Keep track by scoring your interactions as positive or negative, and set a goal of five positive exchanges for every negative one.
2. **Bring out the best.** By filling others' buckets, we set off a chain reaction that comes back to us. Imagine a scenario in which something really annoys you about your romantic partner, and you find yourself being critical much more often than you should be. If you make a conscious decision to focus instead on all the good things instead of the one bad thing, you'll have a positive impact on the relationship, and your partner will begin responding more positively to you. Watch and see!
3. **Make more than one best friend.** Who ever said people are only allowed one best friend? High-quality relationships improve the quality of your life. Bucket filling from the start is the way to begin a new best friendship, and regular bucket filling is how to keep it.
4. **Fill a drop at a time.** Giving a small unexpected gift is a great way to fill someone else's bucket. It needn't be much: a token, a trinket, a compliment, or a thank you. Put your positive comments in an e-mail or a note to make them last. Make a habit of giving "drops."
5. **Apply the Golden Rule backwards.** Rather than "Do unto others as you would have them do unto you," try this: "Do unto others as *they would have you do unto them.*"

How full is your bucket? In your interactions, are you filling or dipping? Building a relationship is a process that occurs one drop at a time.

This section makes me realize how much I've been dipping lately...

Complete an assessment tool. Other than just feeling generally up or down, is there a way to know more about your own level of emotional intelligence? The oldest and most widely used instrument to measure emotional intelligence is the Emotional Quotient Inventory, the EQ-i, from which the sample statements for the five scales we have been discussing come. It was the first instrument of its kind to be published and the first to be validated by psychologists in the well-respected *Mental Measurement Yearbook* (1999).[24] The results provide you with a self-assessment of your emotional intelligence on each of the five major scales and further subscales.

As a part of the course for which you're using this textbook, you may have an opportunity to complete the EQ-i or an equivalent instrument. (But be careful of fully trusting the results of online "pop" instruments.)

Work with a counselor to learn more. Some areas of emotional intelligence may be too challenging to develop on your own. You may need some in-depth, one-on-one counseling to work on areas that need enrichment. Recognize that doing so isn't a stigma. Instead, you are taking advantage of the resources available on your campus and maximizing the potential for growth that can come during your college years.

Call next week???

Be patient with yourself. Learning to become more empathetic or more attuned to a friend or romantic partner's emotions in a close relationship aren't skills you can enhance overnight using cookbook techniques. Building emotional skills is a gradual process that involves awakening insights, acting on them, and noting the results over time.

This is making me think . . .

Keep at it: It's safe to say that EI is something all of us can strengthen, if we're willing to work at it. Relationships that are important to us require the best of our emotional intelligence skills. In fact, studies show that the way in which we provide emotional support is strongly related to relationship satisfaction.[25]

EXERCISE 10.2

How Do You Relate?

Are you are involved in an intimate relationship right now? If so, which of these ten statements describe it? Put a checkmark in the "yes" or "no" column for each one.

	Yes	No
1. My partner is a very good listener.	____	____
2. My partner does not understand how I feel.	____	____
3. We have a good balance of leisure time spent together and separately.	____	____
4. We find it easy to think of things to do together.	____	____
5. I am very satisfied with how we talk to each other.	____	____
6. We are creative in how we handle our differences.	____	____
7. Making financial decisions is not difficult.	____	____
8. Our sexual relationship is satisfying and fulfilling.	____	____
9. We are both equally willing to make adjustments in the relationship.	____	____
10. I can share feelings and ideas with my partner during disagreements.	____	____

Now continue reading to find out how other couples responded in a national study.

BOX 10.1 What Is This Thing Called Love?

Ah, romance.... Relationships—they're what make the world go 'round. Although 80 percent isn't a hard and fast number, Brian Tracy has a point in his quote below. Relationships count, and for many of us, romantic ones count as much or more than others.

Most of us have strong ideas about what we want in someone else: good looks, intelligence, or honesty, for example. But if your parents, a friend, or a previous partner were to put your profile on a matchmaking website, what would they say about you? What qualities do you bring to a relationship—loyalty, humor, caring?

Anthropologist Helen Fisher defines love in ways you may not have thought about before: the psychological and physiological characteristics of love. Fisher asked her 437 American subjects to agree or disagree with statements about their romantic partners such as "My heart races when I hear ______'s voice" and "When I'm in class/at work my mind wanders to ______." Interestingly, Fisher found that neither age, gender, sexual orientation, religion, nor ethnic group made a difference. Love is love, she found. Participants in the study shared characteristics such as these five.[26]

1. *Extreme energy*. When you're in love, your heart pounds, you are breathless, you feel as if you could "leap over tall buildings with a single bound." Your brain is "hopped up" on chemicals, and you have energy to spare.
2. *Imagined betterment*. Although most people in love can easily point out faults in their romantic partners, they tend to persuade themselves that these characteristics are unimportant, or even charming.
3. *Interfering thoughts*. People in love spend huge amounts of time thinking about their partners. No matter how hard they try to think about other things, their thoughts return to him or her. In some studies, participants report that they spend more than 85 percent of their waking hours thinking about their romantic partners.[27]
4. *Mood swings*. Lovers soar with ecstasy and sink to the depths of despair, based on their romantic partners' responses. "She loves me; she loves me not" is a realistic obsession.
5. *Hypersensitivity*. People in love continuously watch and wait for clues about how their romantic partners feel about them. They hover by the phone or computer, and search endlessly for a meaningful sign, reinterpret a facial expression, or translate a word or phrase into relational terms.

When you're newly infatuated with someone, your brain has elevated levels of dopamine and norepinephrine, chemicals that result in the characteristics just explained. Scientists also believe that lovers have lower levels of serotonin in their brains. These three chemicals appear to be the physiological basis for passionate, exhilarating, romantic love. However, later in life, after years of marriage, perhaps, these chemicals are overtaken by others. None of us could tolerate a continuous rush of stimulating chemicals and their intense effects forever! Unbridled passion and wild ecstasy are replaced by feelings of contentment and security. However, many couples remain "in love" for twenty, thirty, fifty, or more years. They may even describe themselves as more in love than when they first met. In one remarkable study, couples married more than twenty years rated themselves higher on romantic love than couples married only five years. Researchers noted that some long-term couples' results looked like those of high school seniors![28]

The chemistry of love points to a truth worth noting: Love is not just an emotion. Chemicals wax and wane; emotions come and go. Commitment goes beyond attraction, beyond emotion. It's a *decision* to invest—and continually *reinvest*—in a relationship. As Fisher writes, "Don't assume the relationship will last forever; build it one day at a time. And never give up."

© Larry Harwood Photography. Property of Cengage Learning

Eighty percent of life's satisfaction comes from meaningful relationships.

Brian Tracy, personal and career success author

Communicating in Important Relationships

Think of all the kinds of communicating you do—and with whom. For example, you have friends you care about. You may think the primary thing friends help you do is fill up your spare time. But new research shows that friends can actually help you fight illness and depression, boost your cognitive functioning, and even prolong your life. In one study, student participants were taken to the bottom of a steep hill while wearing a heavy backpack. They were asked to estimate the steepness of the hill. Participants standing next to friends, rather than by themselves, thought the hill looked much less steep, and friends who had know each other longer gave increasingly less steep estimates. Researchers summarized that "People with stronger friendship networks feel like there is someone they can turn to. Friendship is an undervalued resource. The consistent message of these studies is that friends make your life better." If that's true, then how you communicate with them is more important than you may even realize.[29]

Or consider family members. These people make up the core of who you really are. Your kid brother may drive you crazy at times, and a parent may seem to smother you, but generally, these people care about you most. Often we "let it all hang out" with family members, perhaps because we know they'll overlook our flaws. When we're tired or stressed, this is often where we "veg" or vent. But because of the central, enduring role they play in our lives, they deserve more quality communication than we sometimes give them.

Classmates and instructors, too, deserve your best communication, even when you disagree with the perspective they're voicing in class. You may see your instructors as intimidating or helpful, but you'll need to make the first move to get to know them, rather than the other way around. Take the initiative to meet them during their office hours and bring up points from class that you'd like to know more about. It's unlikely a professor will single you out ("John, you looked puzzled when I got to the part of the chapter on pages 160–170. Did you understand what I was talking about?"). You have many classmates, and your instructor may not be able to pay attention to each individual student. It'll be your job to go to your professor to get the clarification you need. You'll want to get to know your classmates, too, to make your classes more engaging. You're likely to work with them on class projects. Do some of your best communicating here. Chances are your group-mates—and the group's grade—will depend on it. Participate, do your part, and keep your word. No one will appreciate it if you promise to come to every planning meeting outside of class and turn out to be a no-show every week. And if you volunteer to do the group's PowerPoint and then don't come through in the end, you'll get a reputation that may follow

© Larry Harwood Photography. Property of Cengage Learning

At the extreme, we are so enmeshed in our connections that we neglect each other.

Sherry Turkle, Alone Together: Why We Expect More from Technology and Less from Each Other

Walt Disney/courtesy Everett Collection

> **Piglet sidled up to Pooh from behind. "Pooh!" he whispered." "Yes, Piglet?" "Nothing," said Piglet, taking Pooh's paw. "I just wanted to be sure of you.**
>
> *A. A. Milne, British author (1882–1956)*

you to other courses. Group work in your college classes is a great place to practice the exact skills that will be required of you in the workplace. Whatever the type of important relationship—friends, family, classmates, or instructors—how you communicate is vital. Some would go so far as to make this broad generalization: the quality of your communication directly affects the quality of your life.

Beyond friends, family, classmates, and instructors, think about how very important communication is in romantic relationships. If you're in a romantic relationship right now, you may have wondered from time to time if it's truly a good one. In one study, 94 percent of college students reported having been in love, and over one-third reported three or more past love relationships.[30] Perhaps it was love at first sight, and you immediately announced to your friends or family that this was the one for you. Instead, perhaps right now you're with someone you've never really gotten to know very well; you're going through the motions. The relationship is convenient, fun for the time being, but emotional intimacy isn't at the heart of it. If you're not in a romantic relationship at all right now, perhaps you're on the lookout for someone with potential. It's not easy to know exactly what characterizes a healthy relationship. If you look around at others' relationships, you only see what those two people choose to display. What does it take? A study of 21,501 couples across the country compared the answers of the happiest couples to those of the unhappiest.[31] The areas of maximum difference between the two groups were found on responses like the following.

	Happy Couples	Unhappy Couples
1. My partner is a very good listener.	83%	18%
2. My partner does not understand how I feel.	13%	79%
3. We have a good balance of leisure time spent together and separately.	71%	17%
4. We find it easy to think of things to do together.	86%	28%
5. I am very satisfied with how we talk to each other.	90%	15%
6. We are creative in how we handle our differences.	78%	15%
7. Making financial decisions is not difficult.	80%	32%
8. Our sexual relationship is satisfying and fulfilling.	85%	29%
9. We are both equally willing to make adjustments in the relationship.	87%	46%
10. I can share feelings and ideas with my partner during disagreements.	85%	22%

[Note: numbers do not total 100 percent because of the study's design.]

Look at the highest percentages in the "Happy Couples" column. These results point to an all-important truth: Communication is at the heart of every quality relationship.

In relationships we sometimes communicate in ways that aren't productive. The work of communication specialist Deborah Tannen focuses on miscommunication between men and women. Remember the *Seinfeld* episode in which George's date asks him if he'd like to come up to her apartment for coffee when he takes her home? George completely misses the point and replies that he never drinks coffee late at night. She meant, "Would you like to continue our date?" but he took the question at face value. Later he kicked himself for being so slow-witted. Trying to "listen between the lines" in romantic relationships is a challenge. We say one thing and mean another, or we hope a partner can read our minds and then resent it when they do.

The classic work of psychiatrist Dr. George Bach and others can help relational partners communicate more openly and honestly and meet conflict head on. He described types of "crazymaking" that cause communication breakdowns and, at their worst, relationship failures. See if you recognize people you know—romantic partners or even friends—in these six types of crazymakers.[32]

- The TRAPPER: *Trappers* play an especially dirty trick by requesting a desired behavior from the other person and then attacking when the request is met.
- The BLAMER: *Blamers* are more interested in whose fault the problem is than they are in solving it.
- The MINDREADER: *Mindreaders* try to solve the problem by telling their partners what they're really thinking.
- The GUNNYSACKER: *Gunnysackers* save grudges. They fill up proverbial gunnysacks, and then dump all the contents on their partners at some "opportune" moment.
- The HIT AND RUN FIGHTER: *Hit and run fighters* attack and then leave the scene quickly without giving their partners a chance to explain or defend themselves.
- The "BENEDICT ARNOLD": *Benedict Arnolds* like to stir up trouble behind the scenes by playing "let's you and someone else fight."

I've definitely been all these things with Quentin ...

If you think you're a victim of crazymaking communication, what should you do about it? Try these five suggestions:

1. **Step back and try to figure out the situation.** Is the crazymaker making a request of you (to be more open, reliable, or responsible, for example)? If so, is the request reasonable, and are you willing?
2. **Become aware of the feelings behind the crazymaking.** Is your partner feeling powerless or vulnerable, for example?
3. **Try not to respond with anger, even though it's difficult.** Piling more wood on the fire certainly won't help to put it out.
4. **Check out your assumptions with the other person.** Ask, "Are you feeling frustrated? Is that what this is about? What would you like me to do?"
5. **Try and reach a mutually agreeable solution by changing communication patterns that aren't productive.**

Once you've identified any unproductive communication habits, you can work on improving your skills as well as your relationships. The following five suggestions are a place to start. These recommendations work for any type of close relationship—friends or romantic partners.

Choose wisely. When it comes to selecting someone you may want to build a future with, as a friend or romantic partner, don't settle. Seek someone who shares your values, whose background is compatible, but who is different enough to make life interesting. Choose someone who values productive communication as much as you do.

Let go of unrealistic expectations. Remember that although people live happily ever after in movies, in truth, all relationships have ups and downs. We're human; we make mistakes as communicators. Metaphorically speaking, one blip on the screen doesn't necessarily indicate that the whole program should be scrapped. Conversely, working on problems together strengthens your relationship.

Engage in preventative maintenance. You take your car in for a checkup every so many thousand miles to prevent major breakdowns; it's a good idea to do the same with relationships you care about. Keep the channels of communication open, and talk about small issues before they escalate into colossal ones. Make deposits into a positive "memory bank." Experts say that doing interesting new things together—going on a vacation, for example—can trigger renewed romantic love.[33] In the same way, going through an intense experience with a friend may strengthen your relationship.

I wish I'd known more about this sooner . . .

Monitor your own communication. You can't change someone else, but you can change your own communication: "Although it takes two to have a relationship; it takes only one to change its quality."[34] Eliminate an annoying behavior or modify your conflict style. Be more tolerant of someone else's communication faults, too. Communicate your needs; relationships aren't guessing games. Check, don't assume. Remember that listening is one of the highest compliments you can pay someone. (You're important to me!) Instead of attacking, own your emotions by using the X-Y-Z formula: When you do X in situation Y, I feel Z. ("When you tease me [X] in front of other people [Y], I feel embarrassed and never know how to react [Z]" as opposed to "You always embarrass me! Stop it, will you?")[35] Working to increase your emotional intelligence doesn't mean denying all negative feelings; that would mean cutting off part of your psyche! How you choose to communicate those negative feelings is where the monitoring comes in.

Take the high road. Don't give in to momentary temptations that may lead to regret and possibly the end of a relationship with great potential. Without trust as the bedrock of your communication, little else matters. If your friend is truly your friend, don't join in when someone else is badmouthing her. If you've promised yourself to someone, keep your promise.[36]

Managing Conflict: Life Is Not a Sitcom

Research documents the far-reaching effects of bad relationships. They can hurt your job performance, your finances, your physical and mental health—even your life span.[37] Conflict with romantic partners, or with anyone you're in close proximity to—roommates, for example—can bring on major stress that affects your academic performance, not to mention your overall happiness.[38]

▶▶ Your Type Is Showing

Which of the four type scales is best represented in each of the following sample dialogues between sets of romantic partners? Extravert or Introvert (E vs. I)? Sensing or iNtuition (S vs. N)? Thinking or Feeling (T vs. F)? Judging or Perceiving (J vs. P)? Conflict can emerge between partners when they differ on a scale or when they both display the same preference. For each scene, identify the psychological type you believe is being demonstrated by the two players and a rationale for the choice you've identified. Your instructor may ask for volunteers to play these roles in class, so that you can discuss them. Also, try reversing the roles, and see if the perceptions are different based on male-female stereotypes that exist in our society.

SCENE 1

She: Hey, I've been wondering about something.

He: Yes, what's that?

She: How come you don't like to go to parties with me?

He: What do you mean?

She: I mean, you always want to stay home and watch a movie or do something alone—just the two of us.

He: I hate parties; you know that. I'd rather just be with you. Why would I want to spend an evening with a bunch of people I don't even know?

She: Because it's fun! I love being around people!

He: Well, I don't. It's a drag. Besides all you do at parties is flirt with other men, and frankly I don't like that. If you like parties so much, maybe you'd better find yourself a new boyfriend who likes them, too!

She ______ vs. He ______ Rationale: ________________

SCENE 2

He: Hey, I have a great plan for Saturday.

She: Yes, what's that?

He: We'll sleep in until 9, and then drive to the city to that new mall. Later we can have dinner at that restaurant I told you about, and get back home around 10 or so.

She: Why don't we just wait until Saturday and see what we feel like doing?

He: Because we have to plan ahead. I know you. You'll just sleep in until noon, and the day will already be half gone.

She: I don't like schedules; you know that. Why are you always trying to force me into following a "plan"?

He: Because somebody has to be in charge. And if it's not going to be you, it's going to have to be me!

She ______ vs. He ______ Rationale: ________________

SCENE 3

She: We need to talk.

He: Why?

She: Because we need to reconnect. We've both been so busy. I feel like we need some time together this weekend.

He: Of course, we've been busy. I'm taking six courses, and they've increased my hours at work. You know I need the money for school.

She: I know all that, but I don't want all these other things to get in the way of "us."

He: What do you mean "get in the way of us"? We're still together, aren't we?

She: Yes, we're still together, but I want us to be really happy.

He: What do you mean "really happy"? I thought we were really happy. Don't we go out every weekend? Don't we eat dinner together every night? Don't we text message each other all day long?

She: Yes, we do, but I keep wondering how close we really are.

He: Oh, brother. You're not making any sense at all.

She ______ vs. He ______ Rationale: ________________

Researchers who study relationships and psychological type have found the following:

- Between the two adages "birds of a feather flock together" and "opposites attract," when asked to identify the type of an ideal mate, most of us opt for similarity, particularly on the Sensing versus iNtuition scale.
- As a culture, we find extraversion more attractive than introversion.
- People have mixed feelings about Thinking versus Feeling, based on their own type, cultural stereotypes for men and women, and a natural preference for the feeling mode in a romantic partner.
- The highest potential for conflict is generated between an introverted man and an extraverted woman. Extraversion in women can be misinterpreted as flirting, which may generate jealousy in a partner.[39]

Unfortunately, movies and television often communicate—subtly or not so subtly—that conflict can be resolved by the end of the show. Just lighten up or settle down and you can resolve almost any problem. And if you can't, just swallow, take a deep breath, and move on. But life isn't like that, nor should it be. Managing the conflict in your life takes time, energy, and persistence. It requires understanding your natural tendencies, considering why you communicate as you do, and making productive choices as a communicator.

If you've ever monitored yourself during a particularly heated conflict, you may remember doing something like this: yelling in anger at someone at the top of your lungs, being interrupted by a phone call and suddenly communicating calmly and quietly to the caller, and then returning to the original shouting match after you hang up.

Interesting . . . I usually only think about it in terms of who wins and who loses.

Why? We make *choices* as communicators. Sometimes our choices are productive ones, and sometimes they aren't. And that goes for electronic communication, too. You can pump yourself full of e-courage and send a text or email you'd never actually say to someone face-to-face--and regret it later! As a child, you may have heard the phrase: "Sticks and stones can break my bones, but words will never hurt me!" Actually, words *can* be used as weapons, and lethal ones at that! It's important to remember that we *do* choose what we say and how we behave. Our choices affect both the *process*—how things go during the conflict—and the *product*—how it turns out in the end. Negative choices produce destructive conflict that includes personal attacks, name calling, an unwillingness to listen, or the crazymaking strategies described earlier in this chapter. Positive choices are much more likely to bring

EXERCISE 10.3

What's Your Conflict Style?

For each of the following statements, please rate your response on a scale of 1 to 5, with 1 representing "strongly agree" and 5 representing "strongly disagree."

1. __1__ I usually end up compromising in conflict situations. (CO)
2. __2__ Someone always loses in a conflict. (CP)
3. __3__ I usually let other people "win" in conflicts because I often feel less strongly about the outcome than they do. (AC)
4. __1__ When I really care about a relationship, I devote unusual amounts of time and energy into coming up with creative solutions so that each of us can get what we want. (CL)
5. __2__ "Don't rock the boat" is a good philosophy. (AV)
6. __4__ "Winning" in conflict situations gives me a real "high." (CP)
7. __1__ Sacrificing what I want so that someone else can achieve a goal is often worth it. (AC)
8. __1__ It's possible for both parties to "win" in conflict situations. (CL)
9. __2__ Sometimes you have to settle for "part of the pie." (CO)
10. __1__ I try to avoid conflict at all costs. It's not worth it. (AV)

Now find a partner in class and compare your responses. Circle the items on which the two of you differed most, for example, where one of you marked a "1" and the other a "5." See if you can explain your own choice and also come to understand your partner's thinking. On how many items did you differ? If the answer is "several" or "many," you might experience substantial conflict as roommates or romantic partners.

FIGURE 10.1

Conflict Management Styles

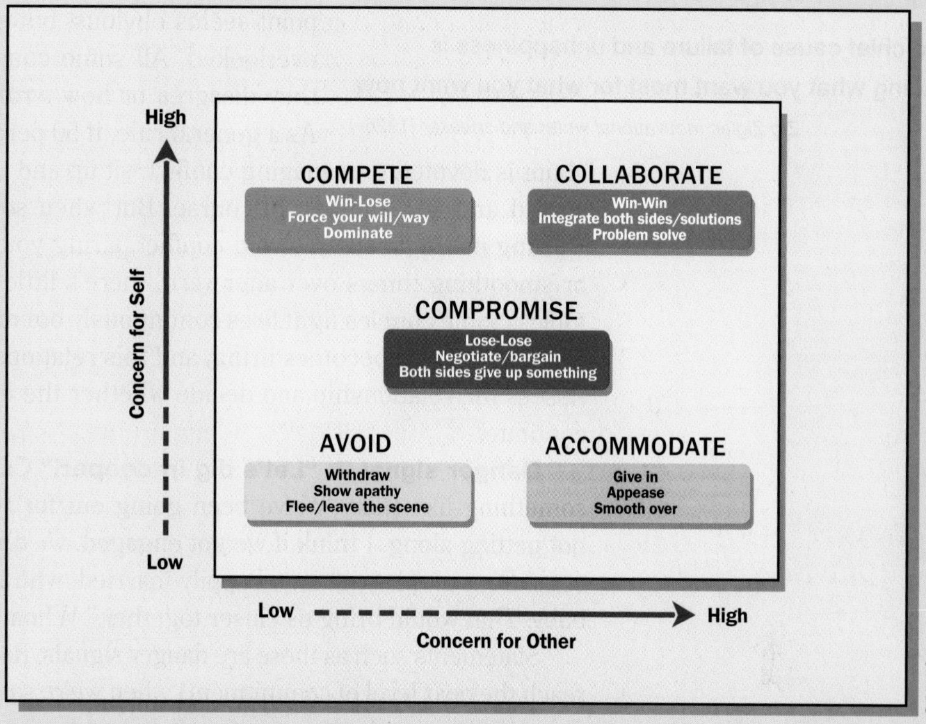

I compete. Quentin usually accommodates... or avoids.

People often come at conflicts using differing styles. Not only do you disagree on the topic at hand—whatever it is—but you approach conflict itself differently. This quick quiz is based on a well-known, five-part model of conflict styles (see Figure 10.1). In our version of the model, the horizontal axis is labeled "Concern for Other" (or cooperativeness) and the vertical axis is labeled "Concern for Self" (or assertiveness).[40]

Where are your highest scores? Notice the letters at the end of the ten statements.

If you like to win and care most about your own goals, you *compete* (CP).

If you care more about the other person's goals, and give in or sacrifice your own, you *accommodate* (AC).

If you don't care about your goals or your partner's, you *avoid* (AV).

If you care somewhat about both and are willing to settle for "part of the pie," you *compromise* (CO). Strictly speaking, when you compromise, neither of you gets exactly what you want.

If you care about your own goals and your partner's, and you're willing to devote the time and energy required to reach a win-win solution, you *collaborate* (CL).

What's your style? Do you have a conflict style you're most comfortable with? Do you fall into the habit of using one style, even if it's not productive in particular situations? Flexibility is the key to managing conflicts productively, and if the relationship really counts, collaboration is the ideal.

productive conflict that helps us learn more about ourselves, our partners, and our relationships.

Just like healthy relationships, unhealthy ones have identifying characteristics, too. They may be unfulfilling, nonsupportive, or even abusive, for example. While every relationship can teach us something important about future ones, some red flags are worth our attention. Here are three to think about.[41] If you see these danger signals, it may be time to end the relationship, or if you and your partner both agree, to devote more time and energy toward improving it.

> The chief cause of failure and unhappiness is trading what you want most for what you want now.
>
> *Zig Ziglar, motivational writer and speaker (1926–)*

Danger signal 1: "All we ever do is fight!" This point seems obvious, but sometimes it's so obvious it's overlooked. All some couples talk about is how much they disagree or how wrong things are between them. As a general rule, if 50 percent or more of what you talk about is devoted to managing conflict, sit up and take notice. Fifty percent isn't a hard and fast number, of course. But when so much of your time is spent walking on eggshells to avoid conflict, airing your differences during conflict, or smoothing things over afterward, there's little time or energy left for other topics. Some couples fight fires continuously but never put them out. Eventually, running in place becomes tiring, and this relationship may have run its course. Assess the relationship and decide whether the investment is one you want to continue.

Danger signal 2: "Let's dig in deeper!" Can you imagine anyone saying something like this: "We've been going out for two years now, but we're just not getting along. I think if we got engaged, we'd both be more committed." Or consider a couple who is unhappily married, who say, "Maybe we should have a baby. That would bring us closer together." Whoa!

Statements such as these are danger signals. Relationships should escalate (or reach the next level of commitment) when we're satisfied with them, when we find them fulfilling, and when we are ready to take the next step together. Trying to force intimacy doesn't work. While this point makes sense intuitively, it's surprising how many couples fall into this trap. Sometimes it's one partner who becomes insecure and forces the issue. Forced escalation may even provide some short-term CPR; something new and interesting is happening. But if the effort isn't mutual and genuine, the brief revitalization won't last. People escalate relationships when they're happy with them, when they're afraid of losing them, or when they don't know what else to do. Only the first one of these reasons really works.

FIGURE 10.2

Moving to the Next Stage

I've never thought about this—very cool way to think about relationships.

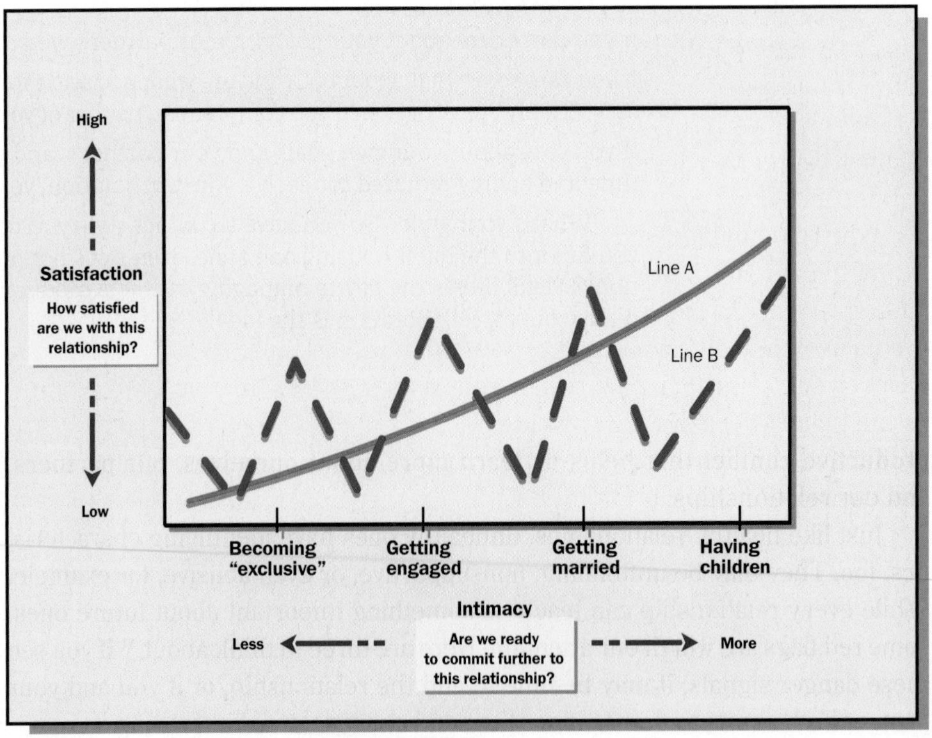

Figure 10.2 provides a visual example of a traditional pattern of relationship stages in our society. (Of course, the steps don't always occur in this order, nor are they even these particular steps.) At each step, the couple is making a decision about staying together. Ideally, relationships should escalate naturally along Line A; however, sometimes participants mistakenly force them to escalate unnaturally along Line B.

> **I'm very loyal in relationships. Even when I go out with my mom I don't look at other moms.**
>
> *Garry Shandling, comedian*

Danger signal 3: "This relationship just isn't worth it!" From two unique individuals, a third entity—a unique relationship—is born. The relationship you create with one person is unlike the one you'll create with anyone else. In a sense, you're a different person with Jack than you are with John or Mary. Not only are *you* different in many ways, but *your relationship* with each of these individuals is unique, too. Relationships, like individuals, have their own attitudes, values, and sensitivities. They can be liberating or smothering. That's why people talk about "taking part in" relationships, almost as if the relationship was separate from or beyond the two people themselves. Interestingly, relationships have a way of taking on a life of their own.

Being in a relationship comes with certain *costs* (giving up free time, not dating other people) and *rewards* (status, security, caring). Generally, people choose to stay in relationships they find rewarding, and they leave relationships they find too costly. But that's not always true; not all costs (or rewards) are equal. For the time being, you may decide that *security* (having *someone*) is a reward that outweighs the cost of putting up with the minor annoyances (costs) that come with a particular person, for example.

At some point, you may decide that a relationship just isn't worth it anymore. The costs outweigh the rewards. The relationship is suffocating or lifeless, and you find yourself thinking about having a relationship with someone else, or you're actually on the lookout for a new one. You may decide that greater rewards exist in a different relationship with someone else (even though that may be a false assumption). While subtle, a pervasive, persistent feeling that a relationship is no longer worth it, despite your best efforts, is worth your attention. It may be best to face this realization squarely and end the dissatisfying relationship honestly, rather than allowing another one to develop in secret.

Was Quentin thinking this??

When relationships end, the quality and quantity of communication between the two participants change. You may talk less frequently or less productively. It may happen over time as you drift apart or suddenly over a particular conflict. But as the golden oldie goes, "Breaking Up Is Hard to Do," and applying all the emotional intelligence you can muster will help you through it.

© Ron Nickel/Design Pics/Corbis

> **The difference between friendship and love is how much you can hurt each other.**
>
> *Ashleigh Brilliant, author and cartoonist*

CAREER OUTLOOK: *MAKE IT PERSONAL*

When something is missing in your life, it usually turns out to be someone.

Robert Brault

Have you ever been accused of taking things personally? Your Mom looks askance at your new, multi-tone hair color or your ever-so-stylish "runway" outfit, or your roommate makes an ambiguous, offhanded comment about something that's dear to your heart. *How dare she?* you think to yourself! When you relay the story to your best friend, she provides a reality check, "Oh, lighten up. You don't have to take it personally."

People count. We care about what they think of us. But what about the often overlooked reverse point of view? They care, too. People prop us up, validate us (or not), and meet our personal needs—and we do the same for them. Even though we know it, we don't always show it. It explains why some very intelligent, highly capable people fail and why misunderstandings are common. It's not so much that people always take things personally; it's that they sometimes forget to *make* things personal.

Take a look at these post-college examples: imagine that your co-worker is just about out the door to pick up a sub for lunch, and you yell out, "Hey, can you get me a six-inch combo with a diet drink?" He looks miffed. *What's the big deal?*, you wonder. ***It's just a sandwich; he's always so cranky!*** But maybe your regular, last-minute orders are starting to get to him and he resents serving as your "errand boy." Maybe he was hoping you'd stop what you're doing and come along for once, but you're so into your work that the thought never occurs to you. Maybe he's dealing with big challenges outside the office. "Maybe you need to cut him some slack. Give him the benefit of the doubt. 'Be kind,' a common saying goes, 'for everyone you meet is fighting a hard battle.'"[42]

Or consider this scenario: You're on a team with a colleague who's a bear to work with. She may be the hardest worker in the company, have the best ideas, and sport a sales record that no one can touch. But ultimately she fails miserably in your organization and moves to another one … again. She moves from job to job, and she just can't figure out why she's not seen as successful. But to her, the job is all about the work. The people she works with are invisible to her. She doesn't realize that the people are *how* the work gets done. According to one career expert, "There's a simple reason for it: we rarely take the time to pause, breathe, and think about what's working and what's not. There's just too much to do and no time to reflect." Making things personal is about listening carefully to the layers of communication and remembering that people count. Actually, it's less about time and more about mindset. Appreciate your differences, explore your commonalities, and above all, remember that work, like the rest of life, is about building productive relationships.[43]

Here's a recommendation: At the end of every workday, take five minutes to reflect, not only about the work, but also about your *co-workers*. Ask yourself these three questions:

1. What went well today and what didn't?
2. What lessons from today will help me do a better job tomorrow?
3. Who contributed to my success? Is there someone I should update or thank? If so, do it.[44]

Doing so will not only help you do your best, but it will do the same for others. Remembering to "make it personal" will affect your career more positively than you can possibly imagine now.

This is advice I should remember . . .

Think Ahead: Think about a time that you were involved in a college project (a group presentation, for example) when things either did or didn't work well. Which principles you've just read about were (or would have been) important?

CAST OF CAREERS

© Larry Harwood Photography. Property of Cengage Learning

FOCUS: How important are people to you—and how do you show it?

ANNIE: I'm one of those people who collects friends—and not just Facebook ones! I genuinely like people. Everyone tells me that I'm a good friend, and that's part of it. I'm very close to my family, too, and we're in constant communication. It's not uncommon for me to get emails, calls, and texts from various family members all day long.

FOCUS: What are your career plans?

ANNIE: I'm majoring in nursing, so people will be my job! My goal is to be competent and caring. Often in medicine, kindness can boost a patient's spirits even more than medicine could. That's why I'm drawn to the field.

Diversity Makes a Difference

EXERCISE 10.4

What Are Your Views on Diversity?

Look at the following ten statements and indicate the extent to which you agree or disagree.

Strongly Agree	Agree	Not sure	Disagree	Strongly Disagree
1	2	3	4	5

1. Race is still a factor in hiring decisions today.
2. Multiculturalism implies that all cultures have equally valid viewpoints.
3. Workforce diversity improves the quality of work.
4. The number of male versus female corporate CEOs is nearing the halfway mark in the United States.
5. In some situations, sexual orientation is a justifiable basis for discrimination.
6. All cultures tend to see the rest of the world through their own cultural lens.
7. Feminism is a set of beliefs held by females.
8. A global perspective ensures objectivity.
9. Religious persecution is a thing of the past.
10. There is less racism in the United States today than there was ten years ago.

As you continue reading this section of the chapter, search for points relating to these topics. Also, your instructor may wish to use these ten items to begin a discussion in class.

These ten statements are intentionally provocative to stimulate your thinking. They relate to diversity: the differences between human beings based on gender, race, ethnicity, age, culture, physical features and abilities, mental capability, socioeconomic status, religion, politics, sexuality, gender identity, and points of view. Diversity is a fact of life.

You may be American, male, White, 21, heterosexual, tall, athletic, smart, good-looking, and from a well-to-do family—and inadvertently, without ever realizing it, think anyone who isn't like you is somehow "less" than you are. It's not that you intend to look down on others. In fact, some of these traits identified above aren't chosen ones; they're qualities a person is born with or grew up with. But others unlike you may see you very differently. You see yourself as "fortunate"; they may see you as "privileged." Perceptions are important in discussions about diversity. They influence our interactions with others, and sometimes perceptions can lead to bias. Let's take a closer look:

Type of Diversity	Possible Perceptions	Things to Consider
Age Diversity	"Those youngsters with all the tattoos and piercings! What do they know?"	Trends change, and outward expressions vary from one generation to the next.
	"Older drivers! They're so slow!"	Reaction times slow down, and vision can worsen.
Gender Diversity	"I'm all for women's rights, but a female President? I'm not sure we're ready for that!"	Actually, in the last Presidential race several women rose to prominent roles at the top of their parties.
	"Why would a guy want to be a nurse? That's a woman's job."	Nursing is a top career field for men or women, now and in the future.
Geographic Diversity	"The South is so backwards."	Southerners are proud of their traditions.
	"Northerners are such snobs."	Regional accents can carry particular stereotypes.
Physical Diversity	"Boy, if I only had a handicapped sticker, I could park anywhere on campus."	Physical challenges warrant access capability.
	"That professional signer in class is really distracting!"	In-class signers help deaf students follow lectures and discussions—like a language translator.
Sexual Orientation Diversity	"Call me homophobic, but all my friends are straight."	Homophobia can be a highly negative hidden bias.
	"Bisexual? How can somebody be attracted to both sexes? That's just not normal!"	College will be a time to become aware of differences, including things you may never have been exposed to.
Religious Diversity	"Religious people are unthinking."	Religious beliefs are highly personal, and spirituality in some form can bring balance and meaning.
	"I'm glad I was raised believing in the right religion."	While it can be natural to see your family traditions as "right," realize that others may feel equally strong about theirs.

> **You must look into people, as well as at them.**
>
> *Lord Chesterfield, British statesman (1694–1773)*

Each of us is a unique human being. Some of us are taller, some are shorter, some are older, some are younger. Some aspects of our uniqueness are visible. It's not hard to tell the difference between someone who's five feet tall and someone who's seven feet tall or someone who's 20 versus someone who's 80. But other aspects of our uniqueness aren't as obvious. Would people necessarily know your religion, your sexual orientation, or even your race, just by looking at you? If you had a stack of photos—a headshot of every student who attends your school—could you sort them by race into the same stacks they'd sort themselves into? Anyone can tell an Asian-American from an African-American, just by looking. Or so they may think.

Race is often the first thing people think of when they hear the word diversity. But some experts say race is a relatively modern idea. Centuries ago people tended to classify other people by status, religion, or language, for example, not by race. Actually, diversity is about much more than physical appearance. It's becoming more and more impossible to draw clear lines between what separates us physically. Keanu Reeves is Hawaiian, Chinese, and Caucasian; Mariah Carey is Black, Venezuelan, and Caucasian; and Johnny Depp is Cherokee and

EXERCISE 10.5

Facing the Race Issue

Take a look at the faces below. Can you categorize them into common racial types: White, Black, Hispanic/Latino, Native American, or Asian? After you've identified each one, check the answers below. How accurate were you? Does this activity confirm the point above that although race is used as a common identifier, it isn't an easy or accurate way to classify people?[45]

Answers: (top row): B, H, NA, A, H and (bottom row): B, H, H, W, W.

From top lieft: iStockphoto.com/Andresr; iStockphoto.com/Bill Noll; iStockphoto.com/Thomas Gordon; iStockphoto.com/Goldmund Lukic; iStockphoto.com/Jacom Stephens; iStockphoto.com/Lisa Marzano; iStockphoto.com/Jason Lugo; iStockphoto.com/Roberto A Sanchez; iStockphoto.com/TriggerPhoto; iStockphoto.com/erel photography

Caucasian.[46] Most of us are a blend of ethnicities, and how we perceive ourselves may be different from the way others see us. People may assume that a Pacific Islander with light brown skin, dark hair, and dark eyes, for example, is Hispanic. And a classmate you may assume is White may think of himself as Black. Or consider this: If you have a Chinese mother and a White father, you may not know which "race box" to check on standard forms. Should you choose Mom or Dad?[47] Biologists tell us that there's more variation within a race than there is between races. Race isn't biological, they say, but *racism* is real.[48]

And Exactly Why Should Diversity Be Valued?

? challenge

" reaction

Challenge: Identify three advantages diversity brings to any society.

Reaction:

___

___

___

Although some of you may have grown up in a fairly homogeneous community with less racial, ethnic, or cultural diversity than others, no doubt you have experienced the multicultural nature of our society in many different ways, even in terms of food, music, and clothing, for example. The media have introduced you to aspects of diversity vicariously, and perhaps you've even traveled to other parts of the United States or the world yourself.

But here's the challenge: Have your experiences with diversity and your learning about it in school truly made a difference in the way you think and act? Do you choose to diversify your awareness, your relationships, and yourself as a person? Do you think that the fact that we live in a multicultural society in which we've all been taught to respect and appreciate diversity means that discrimination no longer exists?

> **I take as my guide the hope of a saint: In crucial things, unity; in important things, diversity; in all things, generosity.**
>
> *George H. W. Bush, forty-first president of the United States*

Many college students today do believe that racial discrimination is no longer a problem. Been there; done that, they've concluded. According to a recent survey, "helping to promote racial understanding" was considered "essential" or "very important" by only slightly more than one-third of incoming first-year students.[49] In another study, students were asked to identify the five most critical and two least critical outcomes of a college education from a list of sixteen possibilities. Tolerance and respect for people of other races, ethnicities, and lifestyles were identified as among the least important goals for college learning.[50] Why do you think they responded that way? Do they think they've already achieved these goals, or do they devalue them for other reasons?

If you conducted a survey on your campus to find out if discrimination exists, you might be surprised at the results. Research continues to show that minority students experience discrimination at higher rates than majority students. Many of us downplay the prejudice all human beings harbor to one extent or another. Our brains are "programmed" to group like entities and standardize our views about these groups, resulting in stereotypes. We feel safe around others like us and fear those unlike us.

Refraining from stereotyping groups of people and appreciating individuals for what they are could drastically alter the way we think and act. Perhaps you've always assumed that all nerds are A, all athletes are B, and all sorority women are C. What if you switched the labels around? Are the results ludicrous? When labels come to us easily, they are probably negative, and it's likely they apply to groups *other than* the ones *we* belong to. However, when you liberate yourself to think differently, you're not bogged down by tired, old labels. If you open up your thinking to new possibilities, all kinds of new options present themselves. Imagine a band made up of only trombones, a meal with nothing but potatoes, a song played on one note, or a world where everyone looks exactly like you. Diversity enriches our lives.

A University of Michigan study demonstrated that students who had more positive interactions with diverse peers, and in particular took a college course on diversity, were more likely to have more academic self-confidence, be more personally proactive, and be more disposed to developing better critical thinking skills.[51] Research also shows that having a roommate of a different race can not only reduce prejudice but it can also diversify your friendships. Although it can be a challenge to communicate through your differences, having a roommate of a different race can also teach you what it's like to be someone other than yourself.[52] Learning to deal effectively with diversity can actually change you as a college student!

> **We have become not a melting pot, but a beautiful mosaic. Different people, different beliefs, different yearnings, different hopes, different dreams.**
>
> *Jimmy Carter, thirty-ninth president of the United States*

Actually, college is a perfect time to immerse yourself in diversity—in the classroom and beyond it. Classrooms are becoming more diversely populated; it's true. By the standard definition, only 27 percent of today's college students are "traditional" (meaning a high school graduate who immediately goes on to college, depends on parents fully for financial support, and doesn't work or works only part-time). Most traditional students today don't fit the traditional definition of "traditional."[53] Adult nontraditional learners have varied backgrounds, interests, and approaches to getting an education. Often they try to work their way through systems that are designed around the needs of younger students.[54] Today, twice as many minority students are enrolled in college than were enrolled twenty years ago, and the number of Hispanic college students has tripled since 1980.[55] According to a recent report issued by the National Center for Education Statistics, "Between 1984 and 2004, minority undergraduate enrollment increased from 1.9 million to 4.7 million, or 146 percent."[56] Diversity in higher education gives you an opportunity to expand your world view and develop empathy for others who have vastly different experiences.

Aside from meeting students of other races and ethnicities in college, taking advantage of diversity can help you become a more sophisticated thinker, one who can see problems from multiple perspectives, and a better-prepared employee, ready to hit the ground running in today's highly diverse workplace. Appreciating diversity also helps us become better citizens. Diversity is what our society is based on. In a democratic society such as ours, citizens must be able to recognize and endorse creative solutions to complex problems. A former Chief Justice of the U.S. Supreme Court, Charles Evans Hughes, once said, "When we lose the right to be different, we lose the privilege to be free."

One mistake many college students make is not taking advantage of what diversity offers them. Because like attracts like, they join groups of people just like themselves based on religion, sexual orientation, or majors, for example. You can choose to belong to the Young Republicans; the Gay, Lesbian, Bisexual, Transgender (GLBT) student group; or the Chemistry Honor Society. Joining a group of like students assures you a place where people accept you for who you are and you feel comfortable. Think about the groups you belong to and what they say about you.

Of course, being comfortable and feeling accepted are important. But instead, imagine choosing to join groups composed of very different types of people. Consider what philosopher and educator John Dewey once said, "Conflict . . . shocks us out of sheep-like passivity," or political philosopher Edmund Burke's words, "Our antagonist is our helper. He that wrestles with us strengthens our nerves, and sharpens our skill." A famous American lawyer, Louis Nizer, once put it like this: "Where there is no difference, there is only indifference." Valuing

EXERCISE 10.6

What's the Difference?

Find a partner to work with on this exercise. Individually, list all the various ways in which you differ: age, height, gender, eye color, hometown, and so on. When your instructor calls "time," read your lists aloud. The point of the exercise is to begin a discussion on the meaning of diversity, to explore its many different facets—beyond just external appearance—and to appreciate the fact that each individual is unique.[57]

EXERCISE 10.7

25 Things We Have in Common

Conflict is based on differences. Two people each want different things—or two people want the same thing, but only one can have it. But when you think about it, we have many things in common as human beings. Try this experiment: work with three classmates (in a group of four), and when your instructor announces "go," begin listing things that all four of you have in common. The first group to reach 25 items wins! After the exercise, discuss the kinds of things you listed and how easy or hard it was to create a list of 25 different items.[58]

diversity relates directly to your empathy skills and your emotional intelligence. What about stretching ourselves to learn fully what diversity has the potential to teach us?[59]

Imagine you were engaged in a service-learning project for a class, working in your local soup kitchen. It's easy to look at a homeless person with a critical eye and think, "Why doesn't he just get a job?" But when you actually sit down and share a bowl of soup across the table, you might see things differently. You might hear stories of personal illness, family tragedy, unbelievable trauma—a string of coinciding misfortunes, the likes of which you've never contemplated. Rather than assigning all homeless people to a group with a negative label, learn more about the individuals that make up that group. You might change your views.

One professor says this: "I tell my students to keep in mind that everything they see is a snapshot. That guy drinking from a bottle in a paper bag, he's a photograph. How did he get to where he is? From there, we can share some of the rage at the inherent injustice that awaits so many of our poor children as they grow up. As we examine people, the snapshots become a motion picture that links the past, present, and future—what was, what is, what can be."[60]

Choose a stereotype you recognize, one you suspect you subscribe to if you're honest, and decide what you can do to test it. Ask yourself whether it affects your thinking and actions. For example, are you aware of these facts attesting to the persistence of stereotypes in our culture?

> **If you help others, you will be helped, perhaps tomorrow, perhaps in one hundred years, but you will be helped. Nature must pay off the debt. . . . It is a mathematical law and all life is mathematics.**
>
> *G. I. Gurdjieff, philosopher (1872?–1949)*

- **Sexism is still an issue in corporate America.** In 2008, 12 of America's top 500 companies were run by a woman, up from 1 out of 40 in 1995. Then, only one of those companies had a female CEO; by 2003, seven did. Experts predict that by 2020, it could be 1 in 5; however, the numbers remain grossly lopsided.[61]

BOX 10.2 Service-Learning: Learning by Serving

One of the best ways to learn about diversity in college is by serving others. Instead of spending all your time in a classroom, imagine a class on aging in which you team up with an elder in your community and work together on a term project. You might help a senior write her memoirs, for example, or help an elderly man create a family tree for the next generation. You might be wondering, *How would that work? What could we possibly have in common—an 18-year-old teamed up with an 88-year-old?* You might be surprised.

What might you learn in a college reading course in which you tutor first graders at an inner-city elementary school, or a college success course in which you teach middle school students how to apply what you're learning right now about academic achievement? Centuries ago, a French philosopher wrote, "To teach is to learn twice." You need to know your stuff in order to teach it to someone else effectively, and you learn twice as much if you serve others who differ from you in important ways.

Campus Compact, a national organization with 950 member colleges, estimates that college student volunteering was worth $7 billion to the communities they served in 2006–2007. They report that nearly one-third of students in member colleges regularly do community service for approximately five hours per week.[62]

Beyond the dollars calculated, college students' community service provides invaluable support. Literally thousands of college students volunteered to help with Hurricane Katrina and Rita relief efforts in 2005, for example, to help displaced victims of one of the country's worst natural disasters ever.

However, here's an important point: *community service* and *service-learning* aren't quite the same thing.[63] Service-learning is specifically about the learning. It's a learning experience in which you connect what you're learning for credit in the classroom with what you're learning in the community. You're applying what you're learning, which in turn solidifies—and modifies—your perspective. "Service, combined with learning, adds value to each and transforms both."[64] While you're engaged in a service-learning experience, you'll also be engaged in critical reflection. Critical reflection is like critical thinking, recalling or looking back at the service experience and writing about what you're learning in a continuous, connected, challenging, and contextualized way.[65] That's not the same thing as donating your time for a good cause, as important as that is, in terms of you and your own personal development and the lives of the people you help.

Years ago, learning expert John Dewey wrote that the best learning experiences:

- Generate interest
- Are intrinsically worthwhile
- Present problems that evoke new curiosity and require new information
- Cover a considerable time span so that your learning evolves as you go.[66]

Think about it: Might a service-learning project like helping an 88-year-old person, someone who's lived through nearly a century of triumphs and tragedies, record her life's story meet these four requirements?

The average number of college professors who include service-learning in their courses nearly tripled between 2000 and 2005. Search out these opportunities to enhance your own learning and your appreciation for diversity by serving other people.[67]

Sounds interesting—maybe I'll look for a service learning course for next semester . . .

> **We make a living by what we get, but we make a life by what we give.**
>
> *Winston Churchill, Prime Minister of England (1874–1965)*

Great quote!

EXERCISE 10.8

Circles of Awareness

Write your name in the center of the drawing, then label each of the surrounding circles with a word that represents a group with whom you identify. You may use categories such as age, gender, ethnicity, social, political, and so forth. After your drawing is labeled, your instructor will ask you to circulate around the room and find three classmates who have listed at least three of the same subgroups. Following that, you will be asked to find three students who listed at least three categories that you did not. In the second group you formed, based on differences, use the activity to discuss diversity, differences between individuals and groups, and how awareness can change behavior. Look over everyone's list, and to diversify your thinking, select one group on someone else's list, but not on yours. Find out more about that group, or decide to attend a group meeting to raise your awareness of differences between yourself and the group or between your preconceptions of what the group would be like, and what it's actually like.[68]

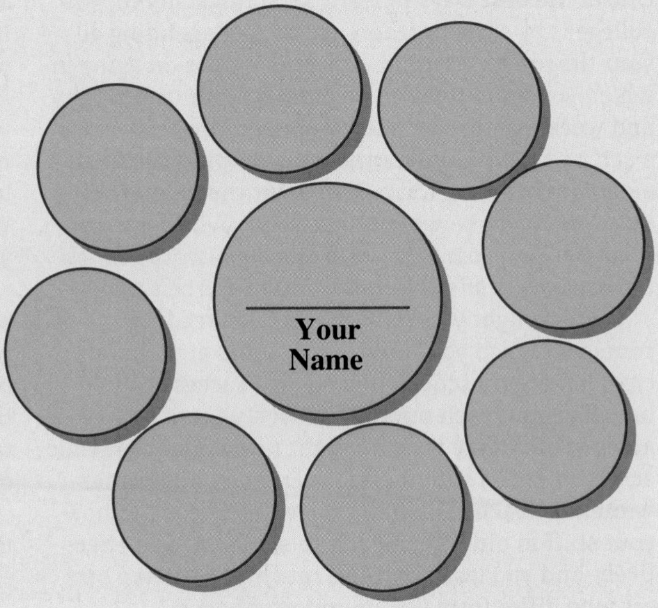

- **Racism is still an issue in hiring decisions.** A recent Gallup poll asked: "Do you feel that racial minorities in this country have job opportunities equal to whites, or not?" Among Caucasians, the answer was 55 percent yes and 43 percent no. (The rest were undecided.) Among African Americans, the answer was 17 percent yes and 81 percent no. You might also be shocked to read about an experiment conducted by University of Chicago and MIT economists in which fabricated applicants of one race were 50 percent more likely to be called for interviews than applicants of another race, based solely on racially based fictitious names! As one *Wall Street Journal* reporter noted, "Someday Americans will be able to speak of racial discrimination in hiring in the past tense. Not yet."[69]

- **Discrimination and stereotypes persist.** Students with disabilities report a "chilly classroom climate" for students with disabilities in higher education.[70] According to one college president, "With all [the change in racial demographics], diversity has become the largest issue behind unrest on campus, accounting for 39 percent of student protests."[71] A recent study of closeted and out gay and lesbian college students reported that these students perceived unfair treatment and a need to hide their identity from most other students. Both groups reported experiencing a similar amount of antigay attacks.[72] In 2009, 7,621 hate crime incidents were reported in the U.S., according to the United States Department of Justice. Racially motivated crimes accounted for approximately 51 percent, religious bias accounted for 18 percent, bias against sexual orientation for 17 percent, bias against disabilities for 1 percent, and bias against ethnicity or national origin accounted for 13 percent.[73] People still harm one another out of hatred for differences they may not understand.

Diversity makes a difference, and as educator Adela A. Allen once wrote, "We should acknowledge differences, we should greet differences, until difference makes no difference anymore." What can we do about it? Some campuses have launched programs in Sustained Dialogue, used in the past to deal with international tensions. This structured approach brings together students with different backgrounds for a year of deep conversation in small groups. Other colleges have developed similar programs to allow students to dialogue about deeply rooted prejudices—sometimes buried to an extent that they are not even realized—to discuss commonalities, and to recognize the potential for conflict—and change.[74] Raising awareness is a first step on the road to recognizing the reality and the richness of diversity.

What's Your CQ?

EXERCISE 10.9

Diagnosing Your Cultural Intelligence[75]

These statements reflect different aspects of cultural intelligence. For each set, add up your scores and divide by four to arrive at an average. As you answer, think about your answers in each category as they compare to the other two categories.

Rate how much you agree with each statement, using this scale:
1 = strongly disagree 2 = disagree 3 = neutral 4 = agree 5 = strongly agree

____ Before I interact with people from a new culture, I think about what I'm going to communicate.
____ If I come up against something unexpected in a new culture, I use the experience to think about how I should respond in other cultures in the future.
____ I plan how I'm going to relate to people from a different culture before I even meet them.
____ When I'm communicating in a new culture, I have a clear sense of whether things are going well or not.
____ **Total divided by 4 = ____ COGNITIVE CQ**

____ It's easy for me to change my body language (eye contact or posture, for example) to match that used by people from a different culture.
____ I can change my expression when I need to interact with people from another culture.
____ I can modify my speech (for example, accent or tone) when interacting with people from another culture.
____ I can easily change the way I act when a cross-cultural situation seems to require it.
____ **Total divided by 4 = ____ PHYSICAL CQ**

____ I have confidence that I can deal well with people from another culture.
____ I am certain that I can make friends with people from a culture that's different from mine.
____ I can adapt to the lifestyle of another culture when I need to fairly easily.
____ I am confident that I can deal with a cultural situation, even if it's unfamiliar.
____ **Total divided by 4 = ____ EMOTIONAL/MOTIVATIONAL CQ**

Generally, an average lower than three identifies an opportunity for improvement, and an average greater than 4.5 identifies a true CQ strength.

An advertisement for an international bank gets the point across well. It shows a picture of a grasshopper. Below the grasshopper are these three sentences that describe three different cultural views of grasshoppers: USA—Pest, China—Pet, Northern Thailand—Appetizer.[76] One insect, three cultural

The education you get now must prepare you to solve the problems of the future. It will require you to look beyond the walls of your classrooms, refine your critical and creative thinking skills, and expand your worldview. The course for which you're using this textbook is a good place to start.

insight / action

Now What Do You Think?

1. At the beginning of this chapter, Kia Washington faced a series of challenges as a new college student. Now after reading this chapter, would you respond differently to any of the questions you answered about the "FOCUS Challenge Case"? Knowing what you know now, how would you advise her? Write a paragraph ending to the story, incorporating your best advice.
2. Of the five EI scales, which do you experience as most challenging? Why? What can you do to improve your emotional intelligence in this area?
3. Do you agree with the suggestions for effective communication in this chapter? Which one do you think is most important? Why? Give an example of its importance from your own experience.
4. Do you think most college students value diversity? Why or why not?
5. Are there particular groups on campus you'd like to learn more about to develop and diversify your awareness? What might you learn by doing so?
6. Have you traveled outside the United States? If so, have those experiences broadened your worldview? How? If not, how might you do so even without the opportunity to travel and see differences firsthand?

REALITY What did you LEARN?

On a scale of 1 to 10, answer the following questions now that you've completed the chapter.

low 1 2 3 4 5 6 7 8 9 10 high

In hindsight, how much did you already know about this subject before reading the chapter?

Can you answer these questions about building relationships and valuing diversity more fully now that you've read the chapter?

1. What is emotional intelligence and how does it relate to college success?
2. Identify one of five basic conflict styles.
3. Describe three benefits of valuing diversity.

How useful might the information in this chapter be to you? How much do you think this information might affect your success overall?

How much energy did you put into reading this chapter?

How long did it actually take you to complete this chapter (both the reading and writing tasks)? ________ Hour(s) ________ Minutes

Did you finish reading this chapter? ________

Did you intend to when you started? ________

If you meant to but didn't, what stopped you? ________

Challenge Yourself Online Quiz To find out just how much you've learned, access the College Success CourseMate via www.cengagebrain.com to take the Challenge Yourself Online Quiz.

Take a minute to compare these answers to your answers from the "Readiness Check" at the beginning of this chapter. What gaps exist between the similar questions? How might these gaps between what you thought before starting the chapter and what you now think after completing the chapter affect how you approach the next chapter in this book?

CHAPTER 11

Working Toward Wellness

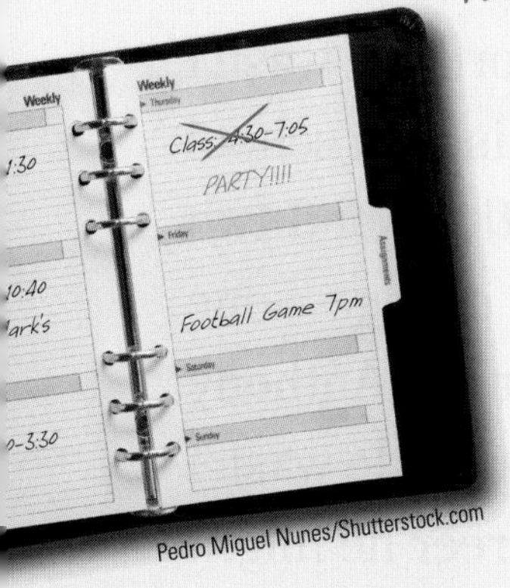

Pedro Miguel Nunes/Shutterstock.com

You're about to discover...

- *How wellness is defined*
- *The importance of physical, mental, and spiritual health*
- *How to assess your own wellness choices by creating a Wellness Wheel*
- *How to deal with six aspects of wellness that affect first-year students: stress, nutrition, exercise, sleep, alcohol and drugs, and sex*
- *How to create a wellness plan for yourself that will impact your college success*

© Larry Harwood Photography. Property of Cengage Learning

READINESS ✓ What do you KNOW?

Before beginning to read this chapter, take two minutes to answer the following questions on a scale of 1 to 10. Your answers will help you assess how ready you are to focus.

low 1 2 3 4 5 6 7 8 9 10 high

How much do you *already* know?

Based on reading the "You're about to discover. . ." list and skimming this chapter, how much do you think you probably already know about this chapter's subject? ______

See if you can answer these questions about working toward wellness *before* you read.

1. Identify three of the fifteen specific symptoms that should signal you to seek medical attention right away.
2. How would you define wellness? Is it more than just not being sick?
3. What's the formal definition of binge drinking?

How much do you expect to learn?

In general, how motivated are you to learn more by reading this chapter? ______

How much do you think this information might affect your success overall? ______

How much energy do you plan to put into reading this chapter? ______

How ready are you to read *now*?

How ready are you to focus on this chapter? Enter a number for each aspect of your readiness to focus.

Physically ______
Intellectually ______
Emotionally? ______

If any of your answers is below a 10, pay attention to whatever is distracting you before you start reading. Then zero in and focus.

How long do you think it will take you to complete this chapter from start to finish?

______ Hour(s) ______ Minutes

Now, as you begin, do you intend to finish reading this chapter?

______ yes ______ no ______ maybe

© Larry Harwood Photography. Property of Cengage Learning

FOCUS Challenge Case

? challenge

Anthony Lopez

Somos/Veer/Getty Images

Anthony Lopez was average in nearly every sense of the word. He wasn't a record-breaking athlete, nor was he the top student in his high school class. He was even sandwiched between two older brothers and two younger sisters. His brothers had excelled in college—one was an attorney and the other a computer engineer. Anthony knew that measuring up would be difficult for him. He wasn't exactly sure why he was in college or what career he might aim for, but he knew his parents expected him to be successful. They never had the opportunity to go to college, so they wanted to make sure their children did.

© Cengage Learning; ifong/Shutterstock.com

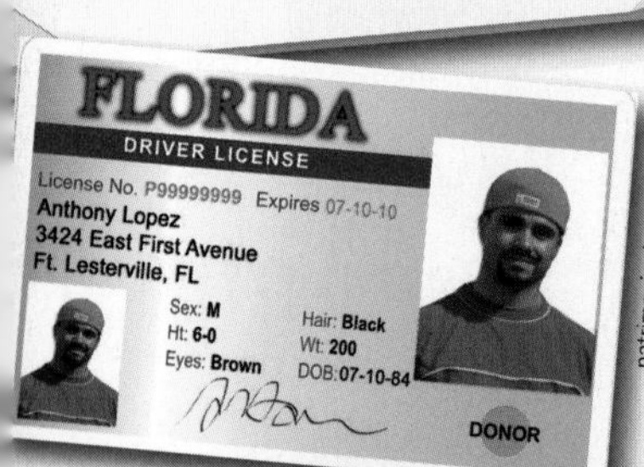

patrimonio designs limited/Shutterstock.com

© Cengage Learning

Now that he was here at the university, Anthony was going to make his mark. He was away from home for the first time ever, and he was having the time of his life! He'd already made loads of friends, and even the ladies, who regularly snubbed him in high school, thought he was worth getting to know here.

In the first weeks of school, Anthony did his part to help Huntington Hall live up to its reputation. Partying was especially heavy on Tuesday ("Booze-day") and Thursday ("Thirstday"), not to mention the weekends. Besides, drinking helped him forget his academic worries, which were beginning to mount, and bolstered his confidence with the opposite sex.

Weekends were supercharged with partying before and after football games and hitting all the bars within walking distance. Fake IDs weren't hard to get, and no one ever questioned him anyway. Most students got a buzz on before even leaving Huntington for a night of drinking so that they could keep their bar tabs down. The freedom he had in college was overwhelming. No one seemed to care if he cut class, turned in his assignments, or drank too much.

After he didn't call home for a week and ignored several texts, Anthony's Mom called him as he walked from his history class back to Huntington Hall for one of the regular Thursday night gatherings—this time in his room. He'd already decided to skip math because it was a huge lecture course, and he figured he was invisible among so many students anyway.

"Anthony, what's going on?" his Mom asked. "We haven't heard from you!" Suddenly Anthony realized she was right. "I've been really busy," he replied.

© Photos.com

Pedro Miguel Nunes/Shutterstock.com

"You know, college is hard work, Mom." He tried to sound convincing. "I'm sure you're working hard, Anthony, but I want to know about you. How are *you* doing?"

Then she started in with the usual list of parental questions: "Are you eating well?" "Sure, Mom," was his answer, although he knew his diet had changed radically since he left home—and not for the better. He hadn't gotten up in time for breakfast once, and his fast-food cravings were particularly hard to ignore. He'd been on the track team in high school, but even running had fallen by the wayside. "Are you getting enough rest?" "Yeah, Mom," he replied, although he and his buddies regularly played Texas Hold 'Em online late into the night. "Are you feeling okay? You sound like you have a cold." "It's nothing, Mom," he said, although his throat was awfully sore. "Are you making some friends?" "Am I ever!" he answered a little too enthusiastically. "How about girls? Have you met anyone worth mentioning?" "I'm a popular guy in college, Mom. You'd be surprised! I'm making my mark!" At the moment, he was juggling three different relationships, and although it was his least favorite of the three, one had recently become intimate, and without much warning, too. That reminded him: he really should go on one of those medical websites to get some information about a couple of new symptoms that were starting to worry him. Why hadn't anyone told him that college could be so stressful?

When the questions came around to academics, Anthony's answers weren't so well rehearsed. "Have you had any exams in your math course yet? How did you do?" Anthony faltered, "Not too well, but I'll bring my grade up next time." Anthony didn't like the way the conversation was going. "Let me call you back later, Mom," he interrupted. Academics were down on his list of priorities, and his Mom's barrage of questions was making him very uncomfortable. What *was* foremost on his mind was the huge off-campus party coming up on Friday night.

However, Friday night was when Anthony's social life came to a screeching halt. The party was so big and noisy that neighbors called the campus police. Anthony and a few other students were issued an MIP, "Minor in Possession" ticket, a class C felony that came with a $500 fine and twelve hours of community service. According to state law, Anthony would lose his driver's license and insurance for thirty days, too. He'd had far too much to drink that night, and it showed.

Now what? An MIP was something that would definitely require a phone call home, and he'd have to face the consequences. He knew how disappointed his parents and older brothers would be. *I'm making my mark all right,* he thought to himself, *but this wasn't exactly what I had in mind.*

hfng/Shutterstock.com

Galina Barskaya/Shutterstock.com

Galina Barskaya/Shutterstock.com

Andresr/Shutterstock.com

Copyright Rodale Inc. 2008. All rights reserved; Konrad Bak/Shutterstock.com

? challenge

reaction

What Do You Think?

1. Is Anthony representative of students on your campus? In your opinion, why do these types of wellness problems arise among college students?
2. Do you predict that Anthony will be successful in college? Why or why not?
3. What would be required to reverse Anthony's rocky start to college?

VARK It!

Complete the recommended activity for your preferred VARK learning modality. If you are multimodal, select more than one activity. Your instructor may ask you to (a) give an oral report on your results in class, (b) send your results to him or her via e-mail, (c) post them online, or (d) contribute to a class chat.

Visual: Start this chapter by drawing a circle to represent a Wellness Wheel. As you read each section, redraw the Wellness Wheel in pie chart fashion by giving each of the six sectors different sized slices, based on how important they are to you and your personal college success.

Aural: Before you start reading this chapter, write an email to a friend who has wellness issues (he or she isn't getting enough sleep, doesn't exercise, is totally stressed out, etc.). As you read, add specifics to your email.

Read/Write: As you read, compile a list of issues about your own personal wellness issues. What do you need to work on? Bring a list to class (if you're willing to discuss it) or submit it to your instructor via email, if asked.

Kinesthetic: Find a YouTube with some good ideas about working toward wellness to share with the class. Email the link to your instructor.

iStockphoto.com/Marcela Barsse/MarsBars; Joanna Goodyear/Dreamstime.com; iStockphoto.com/Nadezda Firsova; iStockphoto.com/Pascal Genest

EXERCISE 11.1

Wellness Survey

This chapter will focus on the relationship between wellness and college success. Six specific aspects of wellness are impacted by regular choices you make. Before you begin reading the chapter, complete this wellness survey. For each statement, rate yourself on a scale of 5 to 1.

Yes!	Yes	Not Sure	No	No!
5	4	3	2	1

1. STRESS

_____ 1. I control my stress level.
_____ 2. I find ways to relax and let off steam that are healthy and productive.
_____ 3. I'm aware of my limits and don't take on too much.
_____ 4. I make time for social activities that are reenergizing.
_____ 5. I learn from poor wellness choices I make and change my behavior.
_____ 6. I don't pattern my own wellness choices on those of my friends, particularly if they may cause problems for me.
_____ 7. I think before I act when it comes to choosing wellness.
_____ 8. I plan ahead to achieve a healthy lifestyle.
_____ 9. I understand the relationship between wellness and academic success and act accordingly.
_____ 10. I know that working toward wellness is key to the future I want for myself.
_____ **TOTAL SCORE for STRESS**

2. NUTRITION

_____ 1. I am knowledgeable about what constitutes a well-balanced, nutritious diet.

_____ 2. I eat frequently throughout the day to keep up my energy, as opposed to overeating at mealtimes.

_____ 3. I eat at least five servings of fruits and vegetables per day.

_____ 4. I eat breakfast most or all mornings.

_____ 5. I use food for nourishment, rather than to comfort myself or relieve boredom.

_____ 6. I eat when I'm experiencing stomach hunger, rather than simply mouth hunger.

_____ 7. I avoid skipping meals to lose weight.

_____ 8. I avoid unhealthy foods, such as fast food or foods high in sugar, fat, or sodium.

_____ 9. I read food labels to learn the nutritional value of foods.

_____ 10. I pay attention to my body's signals about which foods make me feel fit and healthy.

_____ **TOTAL SCORE for NUTRITION**

3. EXERCISE

_____ 1. I recognize when I need to get some exercise.

_____ 2. I take advantage of natural opportunities to exercise, like climbing stairs instead of using elevators.

_____ 3. I am satisfied with the amount of exercise I get.

_____ 4. I enjoy exercising.

_____ 5. I try to get some exercise, even if in small amounts, every day.

_____ 6. I exercise moderately without overdoing it, which can be unhealthy.

_____ 7. I walk or ride my bike instead of driving whenever I can.

_____ 8. I have a regular exercise routine that I follow.

_____ 9. I exercise to help elevate my mood when I feel anxious or depressed.

_____ 10. I use physical exercise to relieve stress.

_____ **TOTAL SCORE for EXERCISE**

4. SLEEP

_____ 1. I go to bed when I'm tired.

_____ 2. If I nap during the day, I make sure it's a short one in the early afternoon.

_____ 3. I get seven or more hours of sleep per night.

_____ 4. I don't vary the times I go to sleep and wake up by more than two hours during the week.

_____ 5. I don't study or read assignments in bed.

_____ 6. I am able to fall asleep on my own without resorting to pills.

_____ 7. I don't use alcohol to help me fall asleep.

_____ 8. I exercise regularly to help my sleeping habits.

_____ 9. I avoid caffeine late in the day.

_____ 10. I understand the importance of sleep to my academic success.

_____ **TOTAL SCORE for SLEEP**

(continued on next page)

5. ALCOHOL and DRUGS

_____ 1. I drink responsibly or not at all.
_____ 2. I don't need alcohol or drugs to have fun.
_____ 3. I don't drink with the intention of getting drunk.
_____ 4. I intervene when my friends are intoxicated or high and help them.
_____ 5. I limit my drinking episodes per week.
_____ 6. I associate with others who drink responsibly or not at all.
_____ 7. I think while I'm drinking and don't lose my good judgment.
_____ 8. I plan ahead when I'm out with friends and choose a designated driver beforehand.
_____ 9. I don't use alcohol or drugs to escape from my problems.
_____ 10. I don't let alcohol and parties affect my academic performance.
_____ **TOTAL SCORE for ALCOHOL**

6. SEX

_____ 1. I am sexually responsible and practice safe sex or abstain from sex.
_____ 2. I am considerate and appropriate in the ways I talk about sex.
_____ 3. I explore my own sexuality in ways that are both positive and pleasurable.
_____ 4. I feel good about my body.
_____ 5. I am comfortable with my sexual orientation.
_____ 6. I understand birth control options and exercise them, if appropriate.
_____ 7. I communicate clearly what I want or don't want from a partner, if appropriate.
_____ 8. I avoid unplanned sex.
_____ 9. I am content with the amount of sexual activity I engage in.
_____ 10. I allow others to express their sexual orientation, even if it is different from mine.
_____ **TOTAL SCORE for SEX**

I hope we don't have to discuss this in class! Some of my scores don't look so good!

You will use your scores on this survey later in the chapter to better understand yourself and your wellness choices and how they may be affecting you.

Health, Education, and Welfare

From 1953 to 1979, the United States government had a Department of Health, Education, and Welfare, and the secretary of HEW was a member of the president's cabinet. The history isn't important here, but the point that those three things—health, education, and welfare—are connected is. Although you may not have thought much about it, your health and well-being significantly impact your college success.

Without good health, education is at risk. Your physical, mental, and spiritual health affect your ability to learn. In a letter to John Garland Jefferson in 1790, Thomas Jefferson encouraged his studious young cousin to remember that "Exercise and recreation … are as necessary as reading. I will rather say more necessary because health is worth more than learning." What did Jefferson mean? Is his advice centuries ago still pertinent today?

Think about this: College is about learning and understanding, cultivating the "life of the mind," as it's sometimes called. However, the life of the mind is

> **When health is absent, wisdom cannot reveal itself; Art cannot become manifest; Strength cannot be exerted; Wealth is useless; and Reason is powerless.**
>
> *Herophilus, Greek physician, called the father of scientific anatomy*

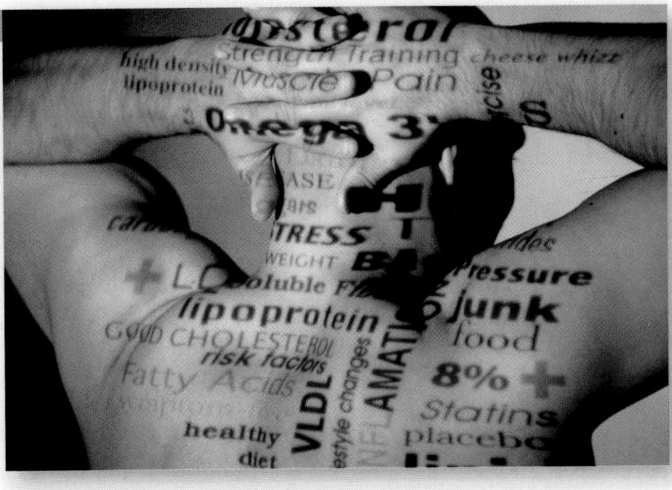

Strauss/Curtis

related to the state of the body. Your brain is obviously connected to the rest of you. Wellness—or a lack of it—can get in the way of an otherwise productive academic career. Wellness isn't merely the absence of illness. It's a process that moves you toward optimal health, based on smart choices. This chapter is about six specific areas of wellness that you can influence to improve your college success.

Physical health is only part of the picture. Mental health issues—depression or anxiety, for example—can also affect your efforts. Spiritual health that comes through searching and self-understanding provide the motivation to make the right wellness choices in the first place.

Here's a sobering wake-up call about wellness and first-year college students. First-year students represent 40 percent of undergraduate deaths from natural causes; 40 percent of all undergraduate suicides; 50 percent of all undergraduate deaths from falls from windows, balconies, and rooftops; and 47 percent of the undergraduates who die on campus.[1] Unfortunately, some first-year students seek thrills, ignore danger, or seriously overextend themselves and become one of these statistics. One reason is because the brains of young college students are still developing the circuitry that acts as an "early warning system" in the brains of older adults.[2]

Whoa! Those are scary numbers.

These statistics are alarming, to be sure, but at the same time, knowing the risks and making wise choices can keep you safe. This chapter's intention isn't to alarm you, however; it's to equip you with the information you need to be at your best physically, psychologically, and academically. Unwise decisions may make adjusting to college more difficult than it needs to be; wise ones bolster your academic efforts. As one headline puts it boldly, "Grades in College Directly Linked to Health-related Behaviors."[3]

Wellness is about making *informed* choices: knowing the range of choices you have, understanding why making productive choices is important, and then doing it. Wellness requires you to slow down, think, listen to your inner voice or your gut, and plan ahead.

It's easy to observe other people and pinpoint all the wellness mistakes they're making. As you watch them, you may think, *That's not a good idea!* or *You're going to regret doing that*! It's not so easy, however, to be objective about your own wellness choices. What's easy is going with the flow and zipping right along without stopping to think. That's where this chapter comes in. Its goal is to change some *counterproductive* choices you may be making—and to validate *productive* ones. As you read, you will explore your physical, mental, and spiritual health; and you'll learn more about where to go if you need help. Later, you'll use the wellness survey you filled out in Exercise 11.1 to create your own Wellness Wheel to identify areas for improvement.

I think this chapter is going to make me uncomfortable . . . :(

> To keep the body in good health is a duty … otherwise we shall not be able to keep our mind strong and clear.
>
> *Buddha (c. 563–483 B.C.)*

Did my mom write this???

Thomas Jefferson said that health is worth more than learning. Fortunately, you don't have to choose between the two in college. You can achieve both. But you do have to make choices—positive, productive ones—in order to achieve wellness. Much of the responsibility for a healthy lifestyle rests squarely on your own shoulders, and if tough problems do surface, getting the help you need is vital. Find out the kinds of wellness resources available on your campus, where they're located, how to contact them, and what kind of help you can expect if you go.

In many ways, your degree of wellness is up to you. After all, who decides when you'll tuck yourself in at night, go back for seconds or thirds, or skip meals so that your jeans fit better? Who monitors your visits to the doctor, your stress levels, and your alcohol consumption? Who requires you to take the necessary precautions for safe sex or suggests you exercise to stay fit? Who does all these things? None other than you! Responsibility for wellness is the place to start this discussion. If you don't agree with this principle, you'll be in denial throughout much of the rest of the chapter.

Physical Health: In Sickness and in Health

? challenge
“ reaction

Challenge: Fill in the blanks for the following statement.

Reaction: I would seek the help of a physician if I had:

1. a fever above ________ degrees.
2. a headache accompanied by ________.
3. a mole that ________.
4. digestive problems that included alternating ________ and ________.
5. a persistent symptom of ________ that won't go away.

Of course, everyone loses at "germ warfare" from time to time. A virus may assault you, seemingly out of nowhere, or an infection may attack when you least expect it. What kinds of physical health problems do college students generally face?[4]

Acute Medical Problems. (Urgent—and important.) You need help fast! Appendicitis or toxic shock syndrome, for example, require immediate, life-or-death medical attention. Unfortunately, sometimes serious health problems occur among college students because they delay treatment by waiting for a convenient time between assignment due dates. Acute complications can set in.

Chronic Medical Problems. (Somewhat less urgent, but very important.) Approximately one-third of asthma sufferers and one-fourth of diabetics are diagnosed by the time they're in their thirties. While most college students are a relatively healthy group, cancer is the fifth leading cause of death among people between the ages of fifteen and twenty-four, following AIDS, accidents, homicide, and suicide.

Infectious Diseases. (An ounce of prevention ...) In many developing countries, infectious diseases such as mononucleosis (known to many as the kissing disease) occur in early childhood when they can be fought off fairly easily. In the United States, however, these infections are often contracted later, during your college years. Complications can sometimes occur, and illnesses in this category can be major reasons for medical withdrawals from college. Life-threatening infectious diseases, such as meningitis, have the capability to spread rapidly on a college campus where students are in close proximity. Or take another kind of infectious disease: sexually transmitted infections. Two-thirds of STIs occur in people under age twenty-five, and many of these diseases can have long-term consequences such as infertility or even cancer. Contagious illnesses are hard to avoid when you're surrounded by classmates or roommates who have them, so anything in this category is worth paying attention to.

You're likely to have your share of aches and pains, colds, and flu symptoms during your first year of college, but you should seek medical attention if you have any of these symptoms:

- Fever of 102.5 degrees or higher
- Headache accompanied by a stiff neck
- Unexplained, significant weight loss
- A mole that bleeds, itches, or changes shape, color, or size
- Sudden vomiting
- Difficulty swallowing
- Blood that is vomited or coughed up
- Alternating diarrhea and constipation
- Pain or blood with urination
- A lump or thickening in the breast
- Unusual discharge from your genitals
- Change in your menstrual cycle
- Pain in your abdomen that won't go away
- Persistent cough, chest pain, or trouble breathing
- *Any* symptom that doesn't seem to go away and worries you

Hmmm ... I do worry about a couple of these ...

Take care of your body. It's the only place you have to live.

Jim Rohn, business philosopher and author

Mental Health: Up or Down

? challenge / **" reaction**

Challenge: Fill in the blanks for the following statement.

Reaction: I would seek the help of a counselor if I:

1. had negative feelings such as __________, __________, or __________.
2. experienced changes in habits such as __________.
3. had trouble doing academic tasks requiring __________.
4. lost interest in __________.
5. experienced troublesome symptoms of depression for longer than __________.

go with you. Medication and counseling can help.[16] For example, drugs such as Zoloft, Paxil, or Lexapro help many people who suffer from depression, and lithium carbonate helps sufferers of bipolar disorder. Left untreated, depression can push people to the edge.

According to recent data, every year about 1,300 college students commit suicide and another 31,469 attempt to.[17] Always take suicidal thoughts, impulses, or attempts—your own or someone else's—seriously and get help right away. Tell your residence hall advisor, a teacher, a coach, a staff member—someone you know and trust—that you need professional help immediately. If you suspect a friend is contemplating hurting herself, ask her. Show your concern and persuade her to get help, rather than risking her decision to become a statistic. Call 911 or a suicide hotline. Experts say that talking about suicide to someone who is considering it doesn't push him over the edge. The most important factor is getting help, and you may play a role in saving his life.

The long list of public figures—historical and contemporary—who have suffered from depression might surprise you.[18] Abraham Lincoln (1809–1865), now considered one of the greatest American presidents, suffered from "melancholy" much of his life, and after he broke off his engagement to Mary Todd in 1841, his friends feared he would commit suicide and watched him around the clock. Eventually, he harnessed his depression by pouring all his energies into his political career. Sigmund Freud (1856–1939), the revolutionary psychoanalyst, was also a patient. He was fixated on his sex life and wrote 900 love letters to the woman he loved. He suffered from depression and despair and was, in fact, susceptible to many of the same problems he diagnosed in his patients. Marilyn Monroe (1926–1962), actress and "silver screen siren," couldn't beat depression and overdosed, it's believed, on barbiturates. She was under the constant care of a psychiatrist, even during the height of her career. Greg Louganis (b. 1960), winner of five Olympic medals and perhaps the best diver in history, had attempted suicide three times by the time he was eighteen. Louganis experienced severe inner turmoil about being gay, and he learned in 1987 that he was HIV-positive. He now speaks across the country about his life experiences as a role model for young people.

I had no idea about these famous people!

Today many modern-day celebrities are open about their battles with depression—Tipper Gore, Carrie Fisher, and Drew Barrymore, for example.[19] Historically, effective medications weren't available, and often people chose to suffer in silence. Today depression has come out of the closet. Public awareness is the goal, and getting help is the path to wellness.

Anxiety

For some students, anxiety skyrockets out of control, and some develop full-fledged anxiety disorders. Anxiety disorders are real, common, often linked to depression, and treatable. They include:

- *Generalized Anxiety Disorder (GAD):* six months or more of extreme worry about things that aren't true immediate concerns, like health, loved ones, money, or jobs—or a generalized anxiety about everything
- *Obsessive-Compulsive Disorder (OCD):* uncontrollable urges to perform repeated actions (like hand washing); making yourself follow specific, unrealistic rules (like forcing yourself to always do X before you do Y and Z)

and becoming upset when you can't; and checking and rechecking something over and over even though you've already made sure

- *Panic Disorder:* an attack in which your heart pounds, your chest hurts, you tremble, sweat, feel out of breath, and are overcome by dread; the attacks occur out of the blue, repeatedly, and without a recognizable physical cause
- *Phobias:* deep fears that are irrational yet guide your behavior. Everyone has certain fears, but phobias are extreme. Some people have phobias related to heights (acrophobia) or confined spaces (claustrophobia), for example, and these fears are debilitating.

Help is available on your campus at the Counseling Center or Student Health Center. Check these online sources for further information, too:[20]

Mental Health America: www.nmha.org

Anxiety Disorders Association of America: www.adaa.org

Anxiety/Panic Attack Resource Site: www.anxietypanic.com

National Anxiety Foundation: http://lexington-on-line.com/naf.html

National Institute of Mental Health: www.nimh.nih.gov

Check these out next time I'm online...

According to a recent study, nearly one-third of students have had counseling at some point in the past.[21] And experts say about 10 percent of the student body on most campuses visits the campus counseling center each year, and many more could be helped by doing so.[22] The percentage of students seeking counseling increases from freshman to senior year.[23] But why wait? If you think you could be helped, take action now!

Spiritual Health: Department of the Interior

? challenge

" reaction

Challenge: How can college help you examine your values, find direction, and ponder the meaning of life?

Reaction:

____

____

____

Who are you? What do you want? For most students, college is a time of personal exploration and growth.[24] Many students are searching for meaning in their lives. For some, it can be a time of struggle as they try to envision what appears to be a distant future. "What am I going to do with my life?" is a pervasive question. Nearly three-quarters of college freshmen report having discussions about the meaning and purpose of life with friends.[25]

According to a national study of 112,232 college students, four out of five first-year students are interested in spirituality, and nearly three-fourths report feeling a sense of connection with a higher power. Eighty-one percent say they attend religious services occasionally or frequently. Most college freshmen

Religion is part of my background, but I'm really not sure how spiritual I am...

CAREER OUTLOOK: *KEEP YOUR BALANCE*

The reinvention of daily life means marching off the edge of our maps.

Bob Black

You're a winner. You're working hard as a highly motivated, ultra competent employee. Your boss is impressed—so much so that you get promoted. Your new position requires you to work harder, and before you know it, you're promoted again. This cycle keeps repeating itself, and over time, you have success written all over you. You're well on your way to mapping out a great future.

There's an underlying question worth exploring, however. Why are you working so hard? Is it because you're passionate about your work? Perhaps it fuels you, gives you purpose, direction, and fulfillment. You love it.

But what if your success isn't about fulfillment at all? What if it's about moving up, making more money, reveling in the prestige? What if you actually dislike your work? You're tethered to your computer, your weekends have disappeared, your weeknights are filled with "homework," and your family has forgotten your name. It can happen gradually, sometimes so gradually that you hardly notice that someone is cranking up the heat. Suddenly, it hits you like a ton of bricks: you've become a classic "workaholic." The company owns you, and you've lost your balance. One work-life balance expert asks, why do people "work long hard hours doing things they hate to enable them to buy things they don't need to impress people they don't like"?[26] Good question. The why of success is fundamentally important.

If you ever lose your professional balance, "march off the edge of your map," and take charge of your own future. Your company is unlikely to say, "You know what? You've been working far too hard. You need to chill for a few weeks." Corporations won't fix things *for* you. They'll usually use as much of you as you let them. You have to do it yourself. You must take control and assume responsibility for living the type of life you want to live. For example, make a rule for yourself that evenings are for family or your romantic partner, and stick to it. Or make a pact that you'll only check your email once a day on weekends so that you can let your mind "idle" for a while. "If you don't design your life, someone else will design it for you. And you may just not like their idea of balance."[27]

A recent study asked dying people to identify their biggest regrets. "Their most common regret? 'I wish I'd had the courage to live a life true to myself, not the life others expected of me.' Their second most common regret? 'I wish I didn't work so hard.' There are two ways to address these regrets. One, work less hard and spend your time living a life true to yourself, whatever that means. Or two, work just as hard—harder even—on things you consider to be important and meaningful. If you put those two regrets together, you realize that what people really regret isn't simply working so hard, it's working so hard on things that don't matter to them. If our work matters to us, if it represents *a life true to us* . . . . then we will have lived more fully."[28]

What does a balanced life look like? It's a life that *you* create, based on who you are and what you want. It's about making your career work for you, not the other way around.

Think Ahead: Think about the idea of balance. What does it mean to you as a college student? What will it mean in your anticipated profession?

CAST ON CAREERS

© Larry Harwood Photography. Property of Cengage Learning

FOCUS: Is finding balance important to college students?

LINDSEY: Absolutely! And it's one of the things that was very hard for me. I wanted to do it all: dance team, campus involvement, a high GPA. But in the end, I had to make choices. I learned the hard way that I had to prioritize and find the right balance for me.

FOCUS: What are your career plans?

LINDSEY: I'm majoring in nursing. I will have to find balance between helping people and practicing medicine. I think I can do it, but finding balance will always be a challenge. Not letting the bureaucracy of a hospital and the potential burnout of the job get in the way of the human element will be important. My goal will be to always remember that!

> It is not what we get but who we become, what we contribute...that gives meaning to our lives.
>
> *Anthony Robbins, motivational speaker and author*

Eric Robert/CORBIS SYGMA

consider it "essential" or "very important" that college help increase their self-understanding (69 percent), help prepare them to be responsible citizens (67 percent), develop their personal values (67 percent), and assist in their emotional development (63 percent). Nearly half believe that college should help encourage their expression of spirituality.

Many college students are on a spiritual quest. Over half of first-year students report questioning their religious beliefs (57 percent) and nearly as many (52 percent) disagree with their families on religious matters. They also report a high level of religious tolerance and concern for others who are in difficulty.[29] Eighty-two percent report doing volunteer work while in high school. However, by the end of the first year of college, students report spending less time volunteering their time or attending religious services.[30]

Can college help you examine your values, find inner direction, and ponder the meaning of life? Think about the courses you're taking this term. Are questions that relate to spiritual health explored, directly or indirectly? A course in philosophy might be a natural place to begin thinking about them, or a course in psychology, or many others, actually. How about the course for which you're using this textbook? Are you being asked to explore your values and your aspirations? In the end, where any course takes you is determined partly by you, and many issues related to spirituality can be examined on your own while you're in college, not necessarily during any particular class. There are also many ways to work on "your interior," such as yoga, meditation, prayer, or exercise. The point is to free up your mind and slow down long enough to search on your own. According to one recent study, college students who integrate spiritual components that help them make choices and assess risks into their lives report better health.[31]

If these values are important to you, make a conscious decision to pursue your personal search for meaning and purpose, despite the many conflicting demands of college life. Your college experience is as much about these vital questions as it is about preparing for a particular career.

You Take the Wheel!

We've already established that some aspects of wellness, like genetic predispositions, are outside your control. But other aspects are mostly or entirely up to you. The remainder of this chapter examines six areas of wellness that impact your college success. The bottom line? Your decisions in these six areas will greatly affect how quickly and how well you adjust to college.

FIGURE 11.1

The Wellness Wheel

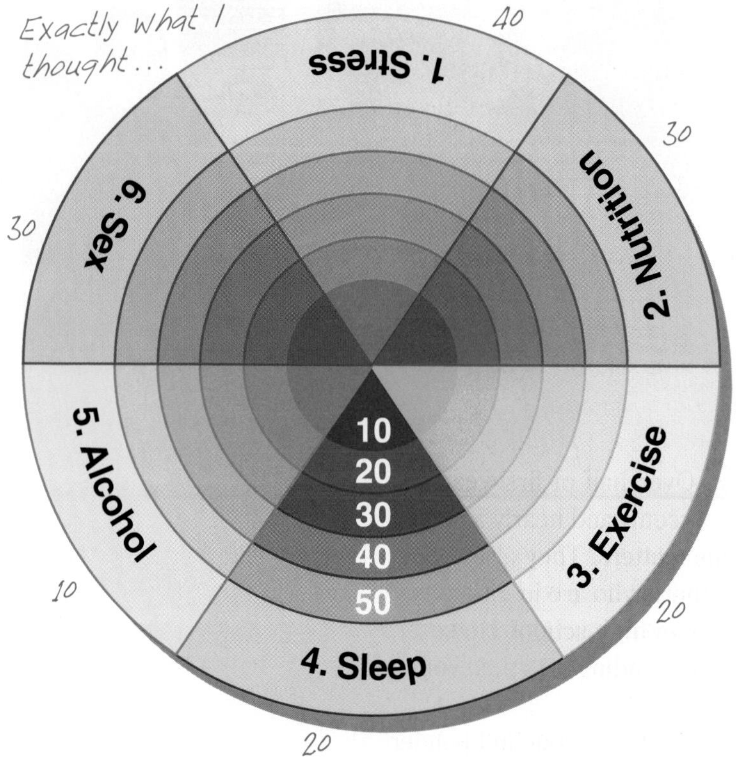

Now return to your completed wellness survey at the beginning of this chapter, and enter your scores for each of the six sectors on the Wellness Wheel in Figure 11.1 by placing a dot on or near the appropriate concentric circle (10, 20, 30, 40, or 50). Then connect the dots. While the survey isn't truly scientific, you will get a clear visual sense of where you are now and where to concentrate your future wellness efforts. For which of the six sectors did you score the lowest total? Were you surprised by your scores, or could you have predicted them?

How is your wheel shaped? Is it dented? Does the figure you get when you connect the dots fill up most of the wheel (representing healthy decisions), or is it smaller, closer to the hub (representing less healthy decisions)? Dots closer to the center represent areas for improvement. Visualize how well your wheel will "roll" in its current shape (and how well *you* will function), and then decide what to do about it. Where do *you* need to focus?

Stress: Fast and Furious

? challenge
" reaction

Challenge: Identify five sources of stress for first-year college students.

Reaction:

1. ______
2. ______
3. ______
4. ______
5. ______

Stress—isn't some stress good for you? Don't Olympic athletes, who train for years and perform on the world's stage, subject themselves to unbelievable stress, and isn't that stress part of what helps them achieve excellence? It's true that stress can produce results. Short-term stress—giving a speech or doing a tough math problem in your head—can actually bring out the best in you. However, long-term stress such as living through a natural disaster or caring for a disabled relative can take its toll. Stress can also come from distant trauma, such as child abuse in your past that continues to haunt you. Short-term stress "revs up" your immune system and protects you, but long-term or chronic stress tears it down, making you more vulnerable to illness.[32]

In some ways, stress is in the eye of the beholder. What's stressful to you may not be stressful to your best friend. There's a difference between stressors (the actual events or circumstances) and *perceived* stressors (how you react to them). Some experts say stress results from being both anxious and fatigued. Anxiety spikes your energy level, but if you're in a state of exhaustion at the same time, your body interprets the cross signals as stress.[33]

Ahhh, I see—when I make bad choices, my stress goes up. I get it—makes sense.

How do you know when you're reacting adversely to stress? Pay attention if you are depressed, irritable, anxious, fearful, lethargic, if you can't sleep (or sleep too much and still feel tired), wake up frequently, experience stomachaches, headaches, shakiness, excessive sweating, heartburn, nausea, rapid and shallow breathing, or frequent colds. Not coping well with stress can show up in your health, your relationships, your job, and your academic work.

So what's so stressful about college? Aside from the adjustment factor, basically, everything! Try these common factors on for size, and see if they produce stress in you, perhaps even in just reading about them.[34]

Goodbyes. For many students, homesickness and friendsickness generate stress. Perhaps you left an ill family member behind or a favorite pet that rarely left your side.

Hellos. Meeting so many new people, while exciting, can feel like pressure. Will you make friends quickly and easily? Will you be accepted for who you are? Nevertheless, forging connections helps provide you with the support system you need in a new situation.

Grades. Perhaps you're attending college on a scholarship, and keeping your grades up is a top priority for you, or test anxiety gets the better of you. If you're a perfectionist, you may put unrealistic expectations on yourself, too, and that can seriously up your stress.

Oh yeah!

Peaks and valleys. Terms in college—quarters or semesters—have a rhythm to them. Your energy requirements are continuous, but they spike for midterm and final exams. Peak times can bring stress that affects your immune system. Just listen to the hacking and coughing during exams; it's a fairly common soundtrack.

Academic load. College brings a relentless lineup of assignments. As soon as you turn in one assignment, another one is waiting right behind it. Each class by itself would require a substantial investment of time, let alone the entire lot.

Academic challenge. At the beginning of the term you may be reviewing material from high school in some of your courses, and your confidence may climb. You may even become overconfident. But soon your instructor will be moving into uncharted territory, and the learning curve will take off, perhaps bringing your stress level right along with it.

Finances. Are you working more hours than you should? Everyone has legitimate bills, but are lifestyle choices adding to your financial burden? If you can afford luxuries like tanning sessions or a gas-guzzling truck, that's one thing. But if you can't and they compound your stress, that's another.

Eating and sleeping habits. Now that you're in college, you may be running from one thing to the next, grabbing the wrong food (or no food at all), and not getting the sleep you need in order to cope. Stress begets stress, you could say, and the results can be unhealthy.

What can you do about stress that seems to be spiraling out of control in your life? Here are five suggestions that may help.

For fast-acting relief, try slowing down.

Lily Tomlin, Comedian

1. **Change the situation.** If you're living with an impossible roommate who stays up all night making a racket while you're trying to get some decent shut-eye, consider moving. Do what you can to take control of the situation that's generating the stress.
2. **Change your reaction.** If you can't change the situation, try to change the way you react to it. Rather than letting the anxiety continue to build up, bunk with a friend and get the sleep you need until the situation is resolved.
3. **Keep up.** Keep up with your academic work in all your classes. Letting assignments slip in even one class is a guaranteed stress inducer.
4. **Improve your problem-solving skills.** If you can figure out what to do about what's stressing you, and you have confidence in your problem-solving skills, you'll be better off.[35] Take a class in problem solving or read up on increasing your skills on your own.
5. **Work with an expert.** If none of these techniques helps, you may benefit from working with a physician or a counselor on campus. Stress has the potential to adversely affect your college experience. Research shows a relationship between stress, low self-esteem, poor health habits, and reduced perceptions of health status.[36] You needn't continue to struggle with unmanageable stress when help is readily available close by. Take action to change things.

EXERCISE 11.2

Workplace Stress Survey

If you work for pay in addition to going to school, describe the organization for which you work. How many employees work there? What kind of work does the organization do? Describe your job. How long have you worked for this organization? What is your role?

Check the items that you consider to be workplace stressors in your current position. Each item includes several examples for clarification.

_____ 1. Economic uncertainty: the possibility of layoffs, mergers, acquisitions, closings

_____ 2. Superiors: a boss or bosses who are difficult to work for or who micromanage

_____ 3. Coworkers: peers who don't pull their share, take credit for your work, or engage in destructive behavior

_____ 4. Subordinates: people you manage who are unmotivated or challenging to lead

_____ 5. Workload: too much work, too little work, not enough variety in the work

_____ 6. Pace: constant pressure, unrealistic deadlines

_____ 7. Communication: being kept in the dark about decisions, an overactive grapevine, gossiping about other employees

_____ 8. Role: unclear expectations, conflicting job demands

_____ 9. Physical environment: noise, air quality, working conditions

_____ 10. Safety: threats, fears, harassment

Elaborate on your stress management techniques for one of the items you checked.

Nutrition: Feast or Famine

Challenge: What do you think the heading of this section refers to, specifically? Can you identify the two ends of the nutrition continuum as they refer to college students?

Reaction:

Many first-year students change their eating habits in college; specifically, they eat too much or too little. Some students pack on double-digit pounds, resulting in what is commonly known as the "freshman 15." If you're paying for a meal plan that includes all you can eat, you may unknowingly (or knowingly) max out your diet and your time to socialize with friends while you eat. College students are at particular risk of packing on the pounds and keeping them into adulthood.[37] Current estimates by the American College Heath Association are that 3 of every 10 college students are overweight or obese.[38] Or perhaps you dislike the food at your school, or are trying to save money by eating tons of Ramen Noodles on your own. Did you know that Ramen Noodles are high in carbohydrates, low in vitamins and minerals, and high in sodium and fat (see Figure 11.2)?

Nutrition Facts

Serving size 1 container, individual (64.0 g)

Amount Per Serving	
Calories 296	Calories from Fat 127
	% Daily Value*
Total Fat 14.1g	22 %
Saturated Fat 6.3g	31%
Cholesterol 0mg	0%
Sodium 1434mg	60%
Total Carbohydrates 36.8g	12%
Protein 5.6g	
Vitamin A 8% •	Vitamin C 0%
Calcium 0% •	Iron 12%

*Based on a 2000 calorie diet

http://www.calorie-count.com/calories/item/6582.html

FIGURE 11.2

Nutritional Label for Ramen Noodles

In fact, many college favorites are loaded with calories. If you chow down on a cheeseburger and fries for lunch (600 + 600 = 1,200 calories) and four pieces of pizza with "the works" (2,400 calories), a side of garlic bread (400 calories), and a large soda (300 calories) for dinner, you've just weighed in with a grand total of 4,300 calories for the day, not including breakfast. (By the way, skipping breakfast in order to sleep in or cut down on calories is one of the biggest mistakes you can make. Breakfast *breaks* your overnight *fast,* replenishes the glucose in your body, and keeps your metabolism going all day.) To burn up 4,300 calories, you'd need to walk briskly for nearly six hours! Think of it this way, "If you eat 100 more food calories a day than you burn, you'll gain about one pound in a month. That's about 10 pounds in a year. The bottom line is that to lose weight, it's important to reduce calories and increase activity."[39]

In one study, 764 college students (53 percent women, 47 percent men) had their height and weight measured and completed questionnaires about their exercise and dietary patterns. At the beginning of their first year, 29 percent reported that they didn't exercise, 70 percent didn't eat the recommended five servings of fruits and vegetables per day, and over 50 percent reported eating high-fat fast food at least three times during the previous week. Two hundred and ninety students were reassessed at the end of their second year, and 70 percent had gained weight.[40] Although researchers didn't find major changes in

I have no clue what my weight is—I'm sure I've put on weight with Huntington Hall's all-you-can-eat food plan.

students' behaviors over that time, their incoming unhealthy behaviors may have caught up with them.

Does that mean you should totally avoid foods you love? In our culture, food is a social activity. We don't eat to live, some would say; we live to eat. However, if you begin to notice that your jeans are shrinking, and you just can't understand why, you may find the answer on the end of your fork! The United States has the highest obesity rate of any developed country, and obesity in America has become a leading national health concern with 66.3 percent of adults either overweight or obese today.[41] Grocery store shelves are stocked with a huge selection of tempting treats and prepackaged foods, and fast foods are readily available. Portion sizes have increased over time, too, and a less active lifestyle is part of the problem. Choosing taste and convenience over good nutrition has become far too common.

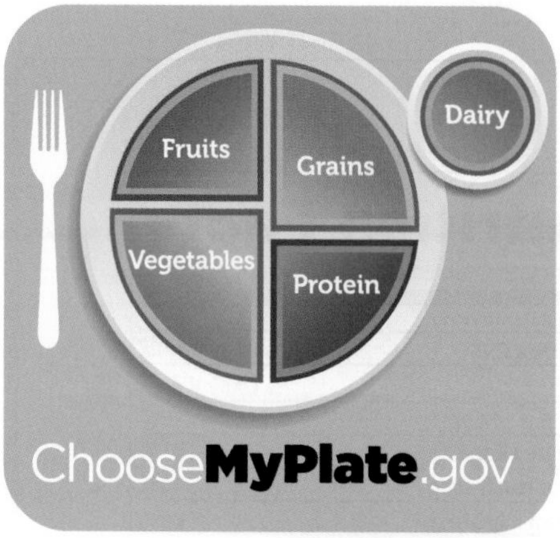

USDA

Think of yourself as an athlete in training. Eat sensibly—and pay attention to nutrition. Here are some key recommendations from the U.S. Department of Agriculture:[42]

1. Take a look at what your dinner plate looks like and then compare it with the image on the left. Overall, aim for fewer calories and make half your plate fruits and vegetables, and make at least half your grains whole grains.[43]
2. Limit less healthy foods. Saturated and trans fats, cholesterol, added sugars, and salt make food taste good, but they don't do your health any favors.
3. Balance the calories you take in with the energy you expend. If you're physically active, you need more fuel for your body. If you're not, eat moderately. Spending three hours on your Facebook page, for example, may do wonders for your social life, but it doesn't require much physical exertion.
4. Replace solid fats with oils when you can. The average American diet is fat-rich, but be aware! Many fat-free or low-fat food items contain more calories than their fat-laden counterparts. Become a faithful label reader, and pay particular attention to ingredients if you have food allergies.[44]
5. Choose fruits and vegetables, and vary your selections. Grab an apple instead of a bag of chips.
6. Consume fat-free or low-fat milk or milk products (like cheese or yogurt).
7. Choose lean meats or poultry—bake, broil, or grill it, and vary your selections with fish, beans, nuts, seeds, and peas.
8. Consume less than one teaspoon of salt (or sodium) per day.
9. Choose foods that are rich in calcium, vitamin D, dietary fiber, and potassium. The average American doesn't get enough of these important nutrients.
10. When in doubt, toss it out! Many foods spoil within two hours or less.[45]

Stephen Welstead/Corbis

"

Fear less, hope more, eat less, chew more, whine less, breathe more, talk less, say more, love more, and all good things will be yours.

"

Swedish proverb

EXERCISE 11.3

"How Do I Love Thee? Let Me Count the Ways"

What are your favorite foods? Are you a chocoholic? Do you crave salty snacks with a vengeance? Do you scarf down pizza like there's no tomorrow? Do you have any idea how many calories you devote to your food passions in one sitting? Next time you indulge, take note. Measure the volume of food (six slices of pizza, half a bag of chocolate kisses), and then tabulate the results via an online calorie calculator or by reading the label and doing the math. Fill in the number of calories here: ________. Are you surprised by the grand total? If the average adult needs roughly 2,000 calories per day, how much of your daily intake did you just consume? Remember, there's no need to abstain; just refrain from eating too much of your "love object" at one sitting.

While general guidelines are good, in the daily rush of campus life, it's even better to have a more specific plan for managing your weight. Many Body Mass Index (BMI) calculators are available online, which is a good place to start as you "weigh" these issues. Online BMI calculators give you an immediate assessment of whether you're underweight, normal, overweight, or obese by simply entering your height and weight.

I'm a Reese's Pieces junkie, but I had no idea how many calories are in a bag!

For some students, college isn't one long feast, it's the origin of famine. The most common age for the onset of an eating disorder is eighteen, and a majority of American college women exhibit at least a few symptoms. In fact, over 90 percent of the 5 million Americans with eating disorders are female. One percent of adolescent girls develop anorexia and 2 to 3 percent develop bulimia.[46]

Anorexics see themselves as fat or flabby, even when others don't. They may literally starve themselves, induce vomiting, or exercise obsessively. Bulimics

EXERCISE 11.4

Which Dinner Would You Order?

Consider these three dining options and decide which one would be the healthiest choice. Think in terms of fats, calories, and the various nutritional recommendations made in this chapter. Assume that you had cereal and a banana for breakfast and a slice of cheese pizza and a soda for lunch.

1. Vegetable Lasagna
   Caesar Salad
   Wheat roll with Butter
   Neapolitan Ice Cream
2. Roast Pork with Gravy
   Garlic Mashed Potatoes
   Corn on the Cob with Butter
   Chocolate Cake
3. Taco Salad
   Apple Pie a la Mode

I'd guess number 1. Vegetables are healthy.

Once you've made your choice, go to an online calorie and nutrient calculator to see how your selection measured up. Were you on target or surprised by the nutritional analysis you found online? The answers are upside down at the bottom of this page.

(Answers to Exercise 11.4: Meal 1: 1,059 cal, 67 g fat, 1,400 mg sodium; Meal 2: 770 cal, 29 g fat, 1,111 mg sodium; Meal 3: 1,993 cal, 95 g fat, 2,786 mg sodium. Note: Calorie count varies by portion size, preparation method, and restaurant/brand. Nutritional information sources: http://www.calorie-count.com/; http://www.benjerry.com/.)

CURIOSITY: *A SUSTAINABLE LIFESTYLE? "IT ISN'T EASY BEING GREEN."*

What does staying healthy mean to you? Eating more vegetables, walking instead of taking the bus, or getting at least 7 hours of sleep a night? For Colin Beavan, a New York City journalist searching for a new writing project, health meant not only taking care of himself, but taking care of the earth.

Colin "grew up all long hair to my shoulders, designer labels are silly… short on cash, save the whales, and we don't want to be rich anyway because we hate materialism" kind of guy. He happened to marry his philosophical opposite, another journalist Michelle Conlin, who "grew up all Daddy's gold Amex and taxi company charge account and huge boats and three country clubs." When his book idea about an eco "life experiment" was accepted by a publishing company, he knew it would not only impact his life, but the lives of Michelle and their young daughter, Isabella. The life experiment was that he and his family would try to live with no impact on the environment for one year, and that he would write a book about their experience.[47]

Convincing Michelle to go along with the project was the first challenge. Actually living green in the middle of Manhattan with its 22.2 million people and boundless opportunities for consumerism was the real one. The average American creates 1600 pounds of trash a year. His goal was to create none. So Colin and Michelle swore off toxins and plastic; ate vegetarian; bought only local, seasonal, fresh foods; and turned off the refrigerator. They took stairs instead of elevators, used no electricity, played games and talked instead of watching television, gave up toilet paper (yes, that's right), and walked or biked everywhere.

A writer in *The New Yorker* labeled Colin's project an "eco-stunt." Critics fixated on what the toilet paper alternative could possibly have been. But at the end of the year-long experiment, what began as a book project became a new lifestyle. Both Colin and Michelle agreed that, despite the hardships, it was mostly worth it—and not just because of the financial payoff. (Colin's popular book, *No Impact Man*, led to an award-winning documentary film.)[48]

What were the lessons of Colin's grand experiment? Did he continue making sacrifices to "save the planet"? Yes and no. Colin lost twenty pounds without trying, and Michelle, a high-fructose junkie who lamented not being able to "eat anything that tastes good," reversed her pre-diabetic condition by eating healthier food. They kept the new habits that were most practical and useful, but not everything. Most of all, they learned about eliminating the meaningless waste in their lives, becoming masters of their own destiny, and reconnecting with each other.

You may think that Colin Beaven took drastic steps to prove a point—or that his year-long experiment was supremely admirable. Regardless, the question worth asking is: what can *I* do? Even if it's just pledging to recycle *all* of the time, rather than hit or miss, or turn out the lights *every* time you leave a room, small actions—collectively—can have a big impact. And while you're going green for the sake of the planet, remember to go green for yourself, too. Make a trip to your local farmers' market, and replace the curly fries with a red leaf lettuce and arugula salad. Going "green" on your plate can do wonders for your wellness.

Courtesy of Oscilloscope Pictures

This movie rocked, even though I'm not sure I could do it!

You have to give Colin Beavan credit; the man put his money where his mouth is.

The Boston Globe

What might seem inconvenient to the point of absurdity instead teaches lessons that all of us need to learn. One person can make a difference.

Marion Nestle, author of What to Eat

From their first baby steps (no takeout) to their giant leap (no toilet paper), the Beavans' experiment in ecological responsibility was a daunting escapade in going green.

Booklist

binge on food until they can't eat any more or are interrupted, and then induce vomiting or take large doses of laxatives and diuretics. Both anorexia and bulimia can have serious medical consequences.

In one study of college women attending a large pubic university, 17 percent of the 578 respondents were found to be struggling with a probable eating disorder. They indicated they would prefer to be helped by a friend.[49] "Friends don't let friends drive drunk" can be extended to many areas of wellness. Medication and therapy can be essential, too. Research indicates that body image and self-esteem are related, particularly for women.[50]

Exercise: Don't Be a Couch Potato!

Research shows that just twenty minutes of exercise can help to calm you for as long as twenty-four hours. Vigorous exercise helps you get rid of excess adrenaline and pumps in endorphins that block pain and anxiety.[51] Research also shows that people who get regular exercise fall asleep more quickly and report fewer sleep difficulties. Pilots, who have bizarre sleep schedules due to long transoceanic flights, follow this advice. Morning walks are a good way to expose yourself to daylight and to get your exercise early in the day. In one study of college freshmen, students who increased their exercise during the first several months of school reported feeling more vigorous, less tired, and less stressed than those who exercised less than they had previously.[52] On the other hand, another study comparing the exercise patterns of college students from Costa Rica, India, South Korea, and the U.S. found that American students watched more television and videos than students from the other three cultures, resulting in less exercise.[53]

Not only does exercise help you burn off cheeseburgers, recent brain-imaging and neurochemical studies indicate that "sweating makes you smart." Physical exercise helps reinforce existing connections between neurons and forge new ones via a protein called BDNF (brain-derived neurotrophic factor). A dense neural network helps you process and store

Herbert Kratky/Shutterstock.com

> **Lack of activity destroys the good condition of every human being, while movement and methodical physical exercise save it and preserve it.**
>
> *Plato (c. 428–348 B.C.)*

▶▶ Your Type Is Showing

Have you ever started a new exercise plan and then up and quit on yourself? If so, have you ever wondered why? Maybe you made a New Year's resolution to slim down or you decided to get buff to try out for the team. Over time you lost interest, however, and your new exercise plan died a slow death. One possible explanation might have been that the type of exercise you chose didn't fit your psychological type. Now there's a thought!

It makes sense that introverts would prefer activities they can pursue alone or with one close friend, like jogging or cycling. Extraverts might go for team sports or coordinated exercise, like volleyball or rowing. Sensors may like practical, results-oriented activities, like lifting weights, whereas iNtuitives may like creative activities such as aerobics set to music. Thinkers may prefer physical activities that require reasoning and logic, like timing your laps across the pool and figuring out ways to beat your own record. Feelers may prefer activities in which others can be part of an interconnected group effort, like team relay races. Judgers may prefer structured exercise routines, like yoga or aerobics. Perceivers, on the other hand, may enjoy spontaneity while they work out, like dancing or exploring new hiking paths, for example.

According to Canadian researcher Dr. James Gavin of Concordia University in Quebec, exercise regimens should "fit" people's personalities. Today, only one out of five North American adults participates in some type of regular exercise. But Dr. Gavin asks, "Does it fit with who the person is? Will it challenge long-standing habits? You might think of it this way: people have personalities . . . and so do sports and fitness activities. People generally feel better when they do activities within their comfort zones, i.e., that match their styles."[54]

Of course, when it comes to exercise, body type, strength, and endurance count; but think, too, about your exercise preferences and your psychological type. Does your new fitness program fit you? If so, it may be much more likely to become part of your lifestyle.

information: "Learning is taking signals that come in from your senses and embedding them into brain anatomy," according to Dr. Vassilis Koliatsos, a psychiatrist at Johns Hopkins University. BDNF affects memory and mood; it literally helps rewire your brain.[55]

Sleep: Are You a Night Owl?

Yes!

Does this describe you? You're running on no sleep . . . no sleep! You have bags under your eyes. You're dizzy, moody, irritable, anxious, or depressed. You can't keep your eyes from closing while reading your assignments, and you have to prop your head up to stay awake in class. You could be starring in a movie called *Sleepless in School.*

Unfortunately, this description fits thousands of first-year college students. When you're running on no sleep, being at your academic best is next to impossible. In fact, you can't really be at your best at anything. Sleep affects your academic performance and—believe it or not—may even adversely affect your decision to stay in college and succeed![56]

Many college students don't get enough sleep and don't get the right kind of sleep. Researchers believe the average college student needs eight to

image100 (RF)/Jupiter Images

Oh sleep! It is a gentle thing, Beloved from pole to pole.

Samuel Taylor Coleridge, English critic and poet (1772–1834)

nine hours of sleep per night; some experts say as much as ten hours! But the actual number of hours college students are sleeping has been decreasing steadily for years.[57] And the results of going without enough sleep are cumulative. The negative impact on your ability to think and learn gets worse as time goes by.[58] Today, many college students average six hours or less per night, or go to bed at 4 a.m. and sleep until noon, upsetting the natural rhythm of their bodies based on nature's cycle of daylight and darkness. A once-in-a-while upset in your equilibrium isn't the end of the world, but if not getting enough sleep is your normal practice, you're building up sleep debt. Think of sleep debt as a buildup of the cumulative amount of sleep you owe yourself to be at your best. If sleep debt were tracked like credit card debt, just how high would your bill be?

Sleep restores us physically and emotionally. It recharges our batteries. College students who don't get enough sleep—particularly REM (rapid eye movement) sleep that takes place most during the last few hours while dreaming occurs—may be hurting their chances at college success. Sleep deprivation causes problems like these:[59]

1. Learning. During REM sleep, your brain creates sleep spindles: one- to two-second bursts of brainwaves that help transfer information to long-term memory. Sleeping less than six hours may block the production of sleep spindles and result in less learning.[60] In tests comparing sleep-deprived students' learning with students who get eight hours of sleep, nonsleepers were less able to learn new information. Interestingly, many students rated their cognitive abilities as higher when they were sleep deprived, but all the evidence indicated the reverse was true.[61]

2. Grade Point Average. In one study that compared college students who were short sleepers (six hours or less), average sleepers (seven to eight hours), and long sleepers (nine or more hours), average GPAs reported for the three groups were 2.74, 3.01, and 3.24, respectively.[62]

3. Relationship Strain. Who wants to interact with a cranky, sleep-deprived person? Sleep deprivation may put your relationships at risk because of increased irritability and decreased interpersonal sensitivity. What's more, getting less sleep may start a chain reaction. In one study of college students' sleep troubles, worrying about relationships was the most often cited reason for not getting enough sleep.[63]

4. Anxiety, Depression, and Illness. Sleep deprivation triggers all sorts of emotional, psychological, and physical risks. Students who report getting less sleep appear to be less psychologically healthy and more prone to catching every bug that comes along.[64] Research indicates that sleep deprivation definitely puts a dent in your emotional intelligence and your ability to think constructively.[65]

5. Car Accidents. According to the National Highway Traffic Safety Administration, fatigue accounts for approximately 1,550 deaths, 71,000 injuries, and more than 100,000 police-reported automobile crashes on our highways each year. Young drivers (ages 16–29) are particularly at risk.[66]

I certainly didn't know all these statistics!

6. Lowered Life Satisfaction. In the grand scheme of things, getting less sleep seems to throw off everything. One study, for example, examined students' reported average length of sleep and their scores on a well-known life satisfaction scale. Getting less sleep was significantly related to being less satisfied with life in general.[67]

© Larry Harwood Photography. Property of Cengage Learning

FOCUS Challenge Case

? challenge

Ethan Cole

Stockbyte/Jupiter Images

One thing was certain: Ethan Cole was unsure. Unsure of his abilities, unsure of which major to choose, unsure of what he wanted to do with his life, unsure of himself. Unsure of almost everything.

Ethan came from a good family, and his parents were actually his best friends. They had been very successful, and they wanted to share the wealth—literally—with their three children. They supported Ethan, no matter what. When he ended up in the principal's office time after time in grade school, they defended him. When he totaled his car in high school, they bought him another one. When he wanted to take a term off to travel and "find himself," they said yes without raising one, single eyebrow. And now that he was thinking of dropping out of college, they said he could move back home, so long as he agreed to a few ground rules and promised to take back his old chores, like mowing the yard. That seemed only fair to him.

The only thing Ethan was sure of was that skateboarding was his life right now. It's all he wanted to do and all he ever thought about. He'd look at a curve on a window frame or an arc in a picture and imagine what skating on it would feel like. All his friends were skateboarders, too, and he read skateboarder magazines and dreamed of the day he might even go pro. He realized not many people make a living at it, but a few really talented athletes did, and maybe—just maybe—he'd be one of them. Recently, he'd found out about the largest concrete skatepark on the globe, Black Pearl in the Grand Cayman Islands—62,000 square feet! He'd made a promise to himself to skate there someday. *Life couldn't get much better than that*, he thought.

But school . . . that was a different story. Schoolwork had never captured his attention. In primary school, his physician had diagnosed Attention Deficit Disorder (ADD), and in middle school, a learning

Lisa F. Young/Shutterstock.com

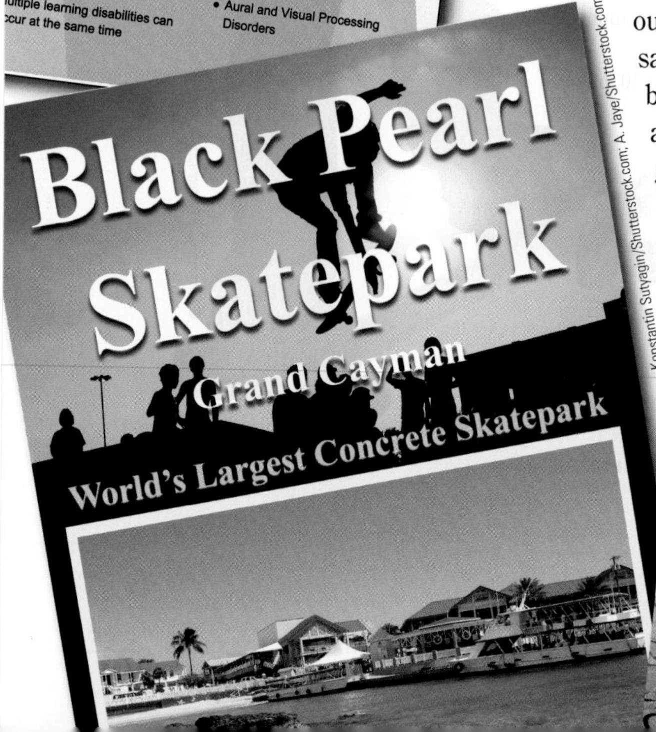

Konstantin Sutyagin/Shutterstock.com; A. Jaye/Shutterstock.com

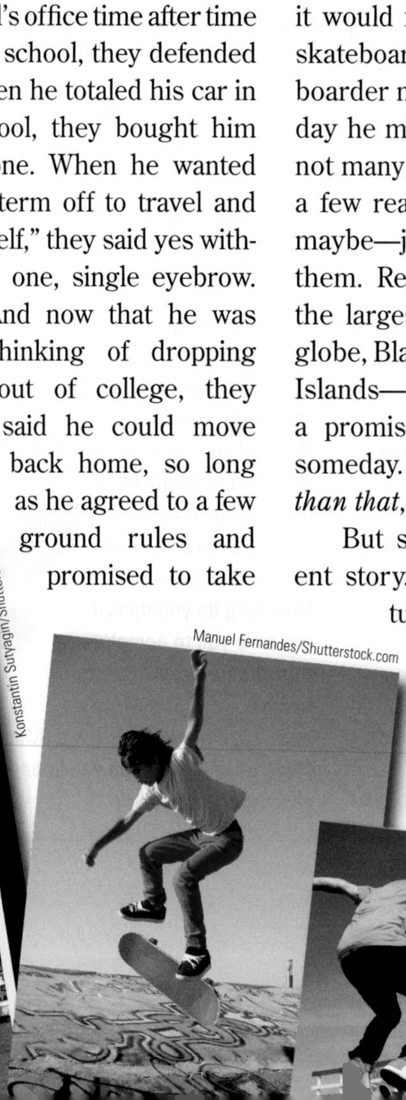

Manuel Fernandes/Shutterstock.com

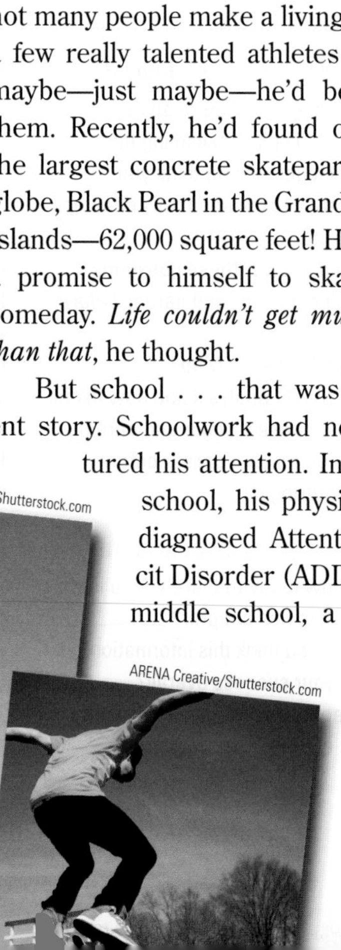

ARENA Creative/Shutterstock.com

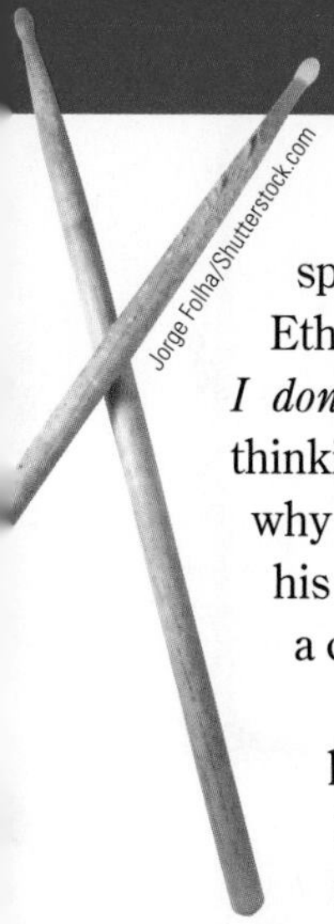
Jorge Folha/Shutterstock.com

specialist had discovered that Ethan was dyslexic. *No wonder I don't like school*, he remembered thinking then. But finally knowing why he couldn't focus didn't change his attitude. He still hated sitting in a classroom.

Despite these challenges, his parents had always told him he was smart. "You can do anything you want to do," they'd said. "Look at you: you're a good-looking kid with plenty of talents. The world is your oyster!" *What a funny phrase*, he'd always thought when they said that. By the time he finally learned what it meant, he totally believed it. His life would become whatever he chose to make of it.

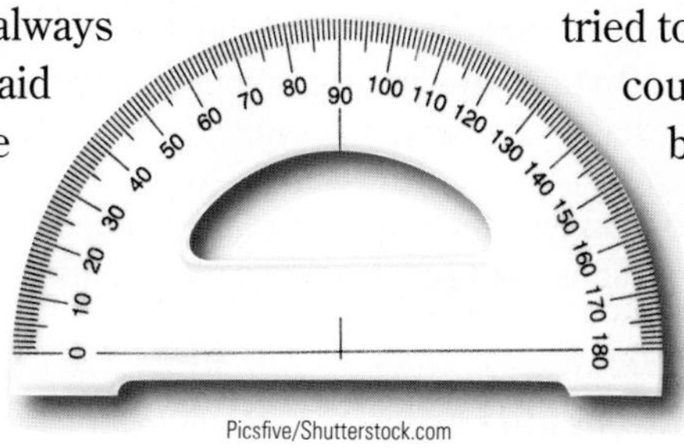

Picsfive/Shutterstock.com

The problem was there were too many choices. How could anyone decide what he wanted to be when he was only nineteen? Ethan remembered liking geometry, he was good at creative writing, he played the drums like a real jazz musician, and he was an incredible artist. *But what do you do with that combination of skills*? he'd asked himself more than once. What possible college major and career would really fit him? He'd spent plenty of time on career websites to try and figure it out.

He'd managed to pull decent grades his first term—a B average—at the arts college close to home. He'd taken Freshman Composition, Introduction to Communication, Drawing 101, and Study Skills, and while he'd done well, none of the course material really sparked a genuine interest. His professors didn't take much of an interest in him, either. His Study Skills instructor was friendly and tried to interest him in the course, but Ethan had been hearing that information repeated in school for years now. He claimed he already had all those skills; he just wasn't motivated to apply them. Instead, he skateboarded every minute he could.

The more he thought about it, the more he thought it was a good idea to take a year off from college. He could get a job delivering pizzas, think about his life, and try to figure it all out. He'd have nobody to tell him what to do, nobody to hold him accountable, nobody to pressure him to study, nobody to force him into making decisions—and plenty of free time to skateboard.

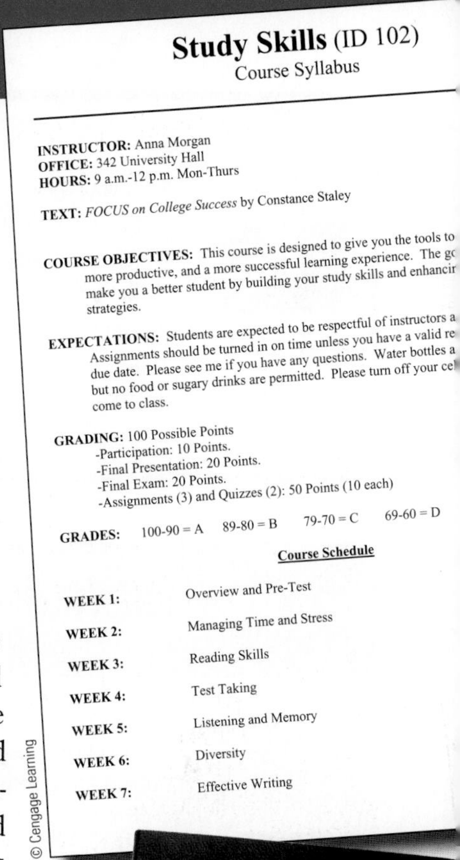
Study Skills (ID 102)
Course Syllabus

INSTRUCTOR: Anna Morgan
OFFICE: 342 University Hall
HOURS: 9 a.m.-12 p.m. Mon-Thurs

TEXT: *FOCUS on College Success* by Constance Staley

COURSE OBJECTIVES: This course is designed to give you the tools to more productive, and a more successful learning experience. The g make you a better student by building your study skills and enhancin strategies.

EXPECTATIONS: Students are expected to be respectful of instructors a Assignments should be turned in on time unless you have a valid re due date. Please see me if you have any questions. Water bottles a but no food or sugary drinks are permitted. Please turn off your ce come to class.

GRADING: 100 Possible Points
-Participation: 10 Points.
-Final Presentation: 20 Points.
-Final Exam: 20 Points.
-Assignments (3) and Quizzes (2): 50 Points (10 each)

GRADES: 100-90 = A 89-80 = B 79-70 = C 69-60 = D

Course Schedule

WEEK 1:	Overview and Pre-Test
WEEK 2:	Managing Time and Stress
WEEK 3:	Reading Skills
WEEK 4:	Test Taking
WEEK 5:	Listening and Memory
WEEK 6:	Diversity
WEEK 7:	Effective Writing

© Cengage Learning

Bryce Newll/Shutterstock.com

Sir Edward Burne-Jones/The Bridgeman Art library/Getty Images

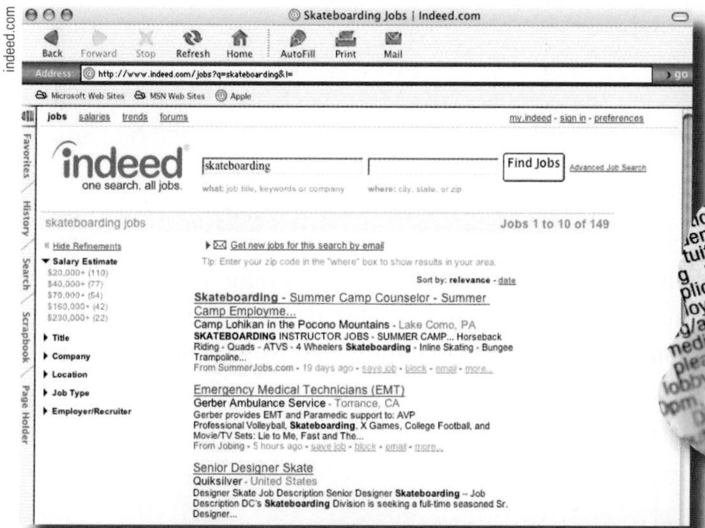

indeed.com

VanHorn/Shutterstock.com

What Do You Think?

1. In your view, what will become of Ethan? What are his prospects for the future? Do you think he'll decide on a major and finish college? Why or why not?
2. Why is Ethan experiencing problems? Are these problems serious? Should they hold him back? List all the problems you can identify.
3. Which majors and careers might Ethan be well suited for? If you were an academic advisor, what advice would you give him?
4. Who would you send Ethan to on your campus for help? What are his options? What do you think he should do at this point?

VARK It!

Complete the recommended activity for your preferred VARK learning modality. If you are multimodal, select more than one activity. Your instructor may ask you to (a) give an oral report on your results in class, (b) send your results to him or her via e-mail, (c) post them online, or (d) contribute to a class chat.

Visual: As you scan this chapter, before you actually start reading, find a quotation that fits you. When you finish reading, use glogster.com to create a poster about yourself and your career planning, using the quote as a theme.

Aural: When you get to the section of this chapter about the "Circle of Learning," talk it through aloud to help you remember the connections between academic disciplines. It's a brand new way of thinking about things.

Read/Write: When you get to the halfway point in this chapter, stop. Find a Harvard Business Review blog that extends what you're reading in FOCUS. Share the gist of the article in class.

Kinesthetic: Before you start reading this chapter, go on a "field trip" to the Career Center on your campus. Collect resources you find there and see if they reinforce what you're reading about here. If you find a new idea in your local Career Center, share it in class.

iStockphoto.com/Marcela Barsse/MarsBars; Joanna Goodyear/ Dreamstime.com; iStockphoto.com/Nadezda Firsova; iStockphoto.com/Pascal Genest

What's the Connection?

Challenge: Is there a connection between what you study in art, psychology, engineering, and chemistry? If so, how would you try to explain the relationships?

Reaction:

As a student, it's natural to try to be as efficient as possible. You're busy taking classes, working at a job, dealing with family issues, participating in co-curricular activities, developing relationships, and on and on. It's easy to get overwhelmed, and a common reaction we humans have to complexity is to try to simplify. So some students simplify by only studying what's on the test. Nothing more.

> **It takes courage to grow up and become who you really are.**
>
> *e. e. cummings, American poet (1894–1962)*

Brand X Pictures/Jupiter Images

But college is not just a collection of random courses—a smattering of this and a smattering of that. And when you finally check off enough boxes, you get a degree in whatever you have the most credits in. That's not the way it's supposed to work.

College is about becoming an educated person, learning how to think, solving problems, and making decisions. College is much more than the "sum of its tests." It's about developing yourself as a person and becoming well-educated. What does it mean to be well-educated? Simply put: Being well-educated is about the pursuit of human excellence.[1]

Why do societies have colleges and universities? Why have they been around so long? Ancient Greece had Plato's Academy and Aristotle's Lyceum. The Sorbonne flourished in France in the Middle Ages. England's Cambridge and Oxford are two of the oldest English-language universities in the world. And Harvard, founded in 1636, was one of the first American institutions of higher education.

Colleges and universities help societies *preserve the past* and *create the future.* Studying the history of the U.S. Constitution in a political science course (past) as opposed to studying potential cures for cancer in a cell biology course (future) are concrete examples. Colleges and universities help us look back (preserve the past) and look ahead (create the future).

College in a Box?

Have you ever thought about the fact that college courses appear to exist in discrete "boxes"? Schools tend to place courses in academic departments, and your class schedule reflects these divisions. For example, your schedule this term might look something like the one in Figure 12.1.

	M	T	W	Th	F
9–10	ENG			SOC	
10–11		PHY			
11–12			PSCI		PSCI

FIGURE 12.1

Most Schools Compartmentalize Learning

huh . . . never thought of it like that!

This organizing system helps you keep things straight in your head, and it also helps your school organize a complex institution. The English department's budget is separate from the physics department's budget. Professors normally work in one department or another. And classes are categorized into particular academic disciplines.

That's the bottom line. But something first-year students often wonder about is how to connect the dots. What's the big picture? Knowledge isn't quite as neat as departments and boxes; it's messy. It overlaps and converges. Despite the convenient institutional compartmentalization of knowledge on a college campus, you might be able to take a somewhat similar course in visual art from the art department, the computer science department, or the communication department. You've probably noticed that you sometimes hear something discussed in one of your classes that's also being discussed in another one. Knowledge is interconnected. College in a Box isn't an accurate way of looking at things.

Even though each discipline has its own history and identity and way of asking questions and finding answers, the disciplines aren't as distinct as your class schedule might lead you to believe. Let's explore how academic disciplines interrelate.

How Do the Disciplines Connect?

The Circle of Learning (see Figure 12.2) illustrates the interconnectedness of knowledge. Although this circle could be drawn in many different ways, using many different traditional academic disciplines, here is an example to get you thinking.[2]

It works like this. Let's start at the top of the circle with *math,* which is a basic "language" with rules and conventions, just like spoken language. You

FIGURE 12.2

The Circle of Learning

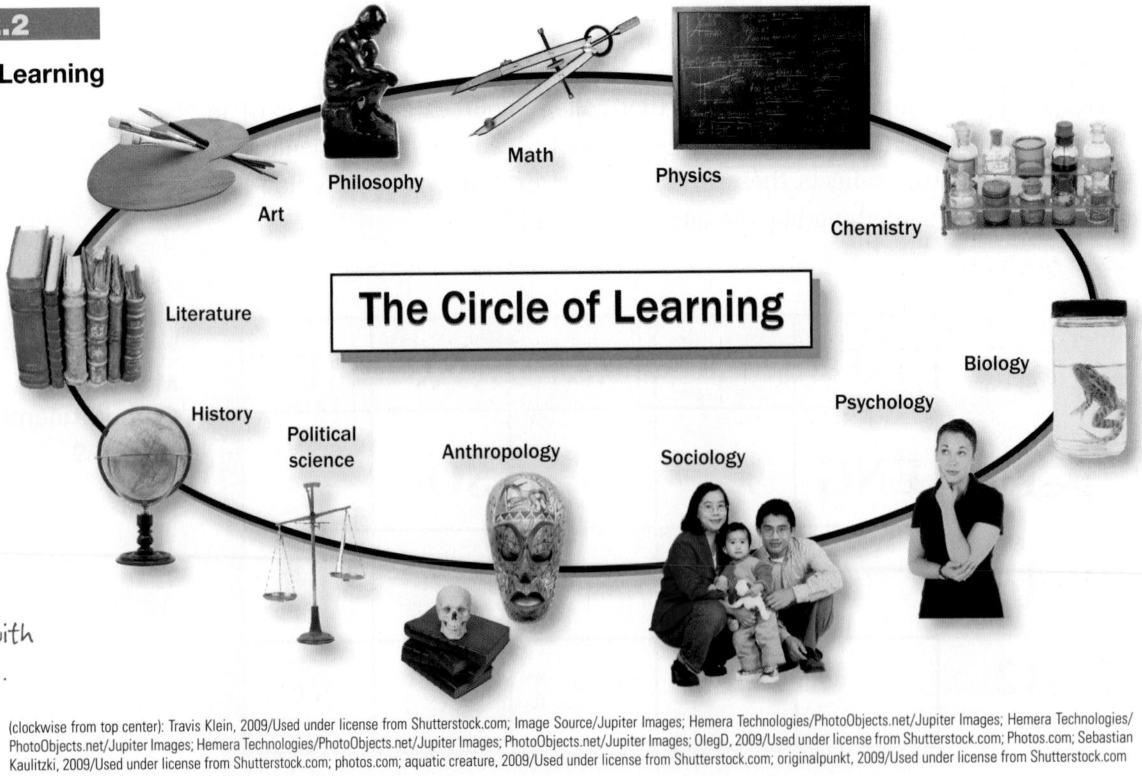

Really cool! Let me try with my courses . . .

(clockwise from top center): Travis Klein, 2009/Used under license from Shutterstock.com; Image Source/Jupiter Images; Hemera Technologies/PhotoObjects.net/Jupiter Images; Hemera Technologies/PhotoObjects.net/Jupiter Images; Hemera Technologies/PhotoObjects.net/Jupiter Images; PhotoObjects.net/Jupiter Images; OlegD, 2009/Used under license from Shutterstock.com; Photos.com; Sebastian Kaulitzki, 2009/Used under license from Shutterstock.com; photos.com; aquatic creature, 2009/Used under license from Shutterstock.com; originalpunkt, 2009/Used under license from Shutterstock.com

manipulate numbers and operations and functions, just as you manipulate sounds and words and sentences. Now, move clockwise around the circle.

Math is the fundamental language of *physics,* the study of atomic and subatomic particles. When atoms combine into elements, such as carbon and oxygen, the academic discipline is called *chemistry*. Chemicals combine to create living organisms studied in *biology* courses. Living organisms don't just exist, they think and behave, leading to the study of *psychology.* They also interact in groups, families, and organizations, which you study in *sociology.* You can also study units of living beings throughout time and across cultures in the discipline of *anthropology.* These units—people—who live and work together are typically governed or govern themselves, leading to *political science.* Let's keep going.

When an account of peoples and countries and their rulers is recorded, you study *history.* These written accounts, sometimes factual or sometimes fictional (for pleasure or intrigue) comprise the study of *literature.* Literature is one way to record impressions and provoke reactions—poetry is a good example—through the use of words. But images and symbols can do the same things—enter *art.* A particular question artists ask is "What is beauty?" otherwise known as *aesthetics,* which is also a particular topic of study in *philosophy.* Philosophy also includes another subspecialty called *number theory,* one of the earliest branches of pure mathematics. And now we're all the way around the Circle of Learning, arriving right back at *math.*

That's a quick rundown. Of course, many academic disciplines don't appear on this chart, but they could and should. A philosophy major might see her discipline at the center of the circle, or a geography major might say, "Hey, where's geography on this chart?" The circle, as it appears here, is representative. The point isn't which disciplines are represented. Instead, the Circle of Learning demonstrates that academic disciplines are interconnected because knowledge itself is interconnected. *Anthropology* (understanding people throughout time and across cultures) can provide an important foundation for *political science* (how people are governed or govern themselves), and *history* (a record of peoples and countries and rulers) can easily be the basis for *literature.* Capitalizing on what you're learning in one discipline can lead to deeper understanding in another.

In your career, you'll need to use knowledge without necessarily remembering in which course you learned it. You'll be thinking critically and creatively, solving problems, and calling upon all the skills you're cultivating in all the courses you're studying in college. The bottom line is that connections count. Recognize them, use them, and strengthen them to reinforce your learning.

> **No one can become really educated without having pursued some study in which he took no interest.**
>
> *T. S. Eliot, American-born poet (1888–1965)*

Building an Academic Map

Challenge: Considering all the different disciplines identified on the Circle of Learning, how would you answer these two general questions: *What* do students study in college? Secondly, *why* do they study these things? Identify two broad areas of study and two reasons why, as humans, we want to know.

Reaction:

____

____

____

Yeah! Why do we have to take all these courses!

Here's a model you can use to help you make sense out of your college education. Your education starts when you're born and continues until right about now when you begin choosing an academic major—and then, of course, you'll continue learning throughout your life. See if the process of building an Academic Map helps you better understand what looks like a long checklist of requirements involved in earning a college degree.

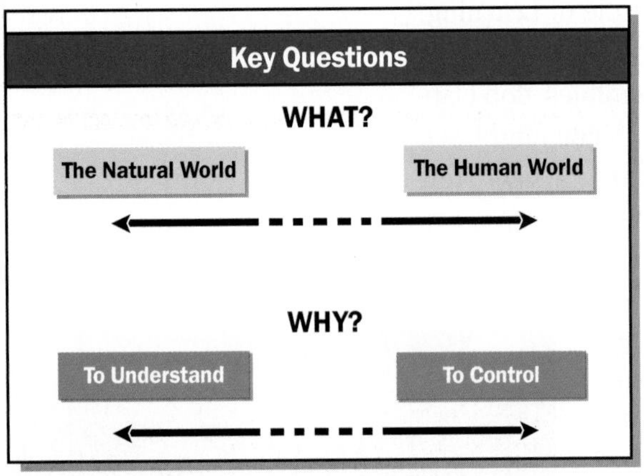

STEP 1: Start by Asking Two Key Questions—WHAT and WHY?

Earlier we noted that some students try to simplify their lives by only studying what's on the test. Another way in which college students are tempted to simplify is by streamlining their choice of classes. If a course isn't directly related to their major or doesn't fulfill a requirement, they ask, "What does *this* course have to do with anything? I'll never use this stuff!"

Two key questions about college may help explain why all this is so important.

- **WHAT?** *What* do college students study? English, math, physics, psychology—you can generate a long list. In fact, if you take your answer far enough, you'll eventually say—everything under the sun! Notice that the word university has the same origin as the word *universe.* But a convenient and meaningful way of putting it is to say that you look at things in two opposite directions. In college, you look outward, into the natural world; and you look inward, into the human world.

I always thought it was about the money, but this is a different, interesting approach.

- **WHY?** *Why* do college students study the natural world and the human world? At the most idealistic and theoretical end of the scale, human beings study to understand things. We're a naturally curious species, and we want to know how gravity operates, why the sky is blue, how Congress works (or maybe why it sometimes doesn't). But at the most practical end of the scale, we study not just to understand things but also to control them—to make things and people do what we want them to do. We want to "control" concrete and steel to build better bridges, to make information flow faster through computers, to erect indestructible buildings, to write more award-winning novels—maybe even to develop better, stronger, faster, healthier, smarter people. And by the way, in this discussion, the word *control* is the correct scientific term to use. It doesn't mean *manipulate* in a negative way, but rather *do something with, use,* or *change* as opposed to merely *understand* intellectually.

So in terms of the two questions posed, we've constructed two scales. René Descartes, the seventeenth-century French mathematician and philosopher, taught that if you really want to understand how two things (or in this case, scales) interact, put them on perpendicular axes.

STEP 2: From the WHAT and WHY Axes, Create Four Quadrants

Two Axes and Four Quadrants

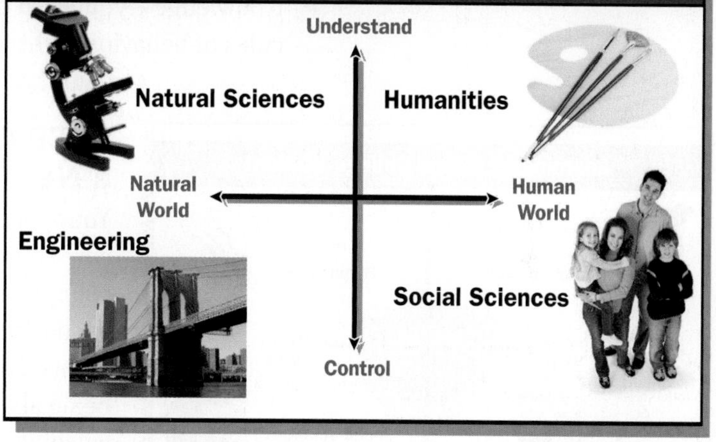

Clockwise from top left: Photos.com; Photos.com; iStockphoto.com/Sean Locke; iStockphoto.com/ziggymaj

What we've now so neatly set up are the four quadrants that identify how colleges and universities are organized. What do we call the academic departments that try to *understand*

- the natural world? The Natural Sciences (physics, chemistry, and biology, for example)
- the human world? The Humanities (history, literature, philosophy, et cetera)

And what do we call the disciplines that help us to control

- the natural world? The Engineering Sciences (mechanical, electrical, computer, et cetera)
- the human world? The Social Sciences (political science, psychology, communication, et cetera)

What we now see in this matrix is a representation of many, if not most, institutions of higher education. In fact, many schools are divided into Colleges or Divisions and have area requirements or core courses from these four quadrants.

STEP 3: Realize the Foundational Learning You Did As a Child

Learning as a Child

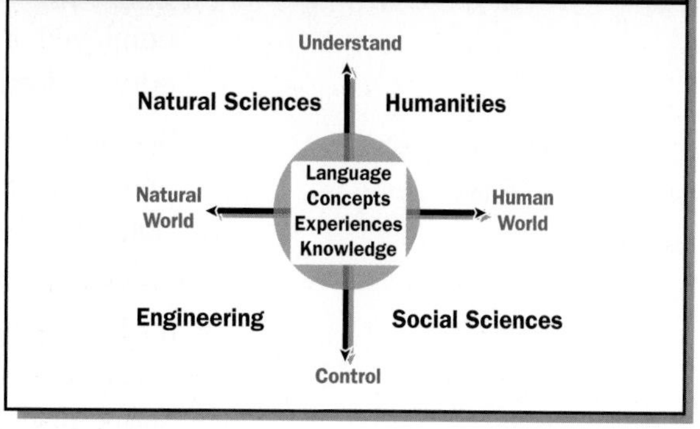

When does your education start? At birth, really—it starts right at the center of the matrix with language and basic knowledge and blows up like a balloon through grade school, middle school, and high school. Your education begins with things like this.

- Language—you learn how to transfer and work with information using *natural* languages (English, Spanish, and so on) and *artificial* languages (math, for example).
- Concepts—you learn that *big* and *little* are opposite sizes, that *before* precedes *after*, and that birds generally have feathers and fly, for example.
- Experiences—you learn what *hot* means when you touch the stove, sense being *wet* in the bathtub, and experience what *love* feels like from your family, for example.

CONTROL: *YOUR TOUGHEST CLASS*

Think about your most challenging class this semester. Is it a general education course or one required for your major? If it's a general education course, make a list of all the ways this course can help you either to further your career or to become a well-educated person. If this course is one in your major, ask yourself why the challenge is so great. Do you understand the course content? Do you keep up with readings and assignments? Can you follow your professor's teaching style? If appropriate, send your instructor in this class an e-mail indicating your specific efforts to do your best and detailing your progress.

- Knowledge—you learn common knowledge about our society and others', rules of behavior, right from wrong, and the history and culture of our country, for example.

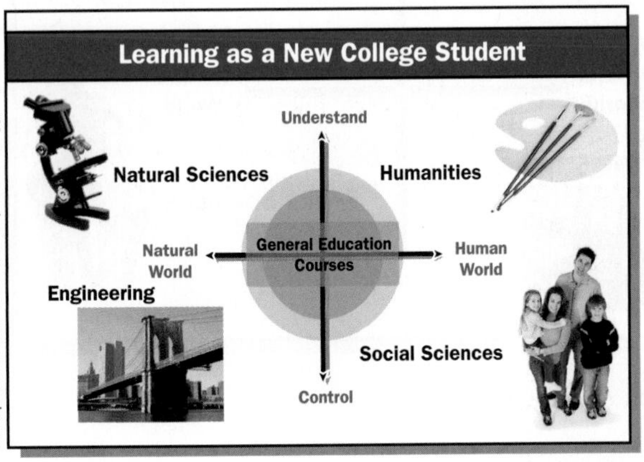

Clockwise from top left: Photos.com; Photos.com; iStockphoto.com/Sean Locke; iStockphoto.com/ziggymaj

STEP 4: Incorporate Core Learning As a New College Student

Your college or university may require general education or core courses from all four quadrants. At some institutions, the course for which you're using this textbook is the central or introductory course for all of the general education requirements. General education courses are about fluid knowledge, being able to shift between quadrants when you need to, critical thinking, and problem solving. In today's information-rich world, focused knowledge is critical, but it often takes crossover skills to understand highly complex problems.

Here are some other key reasons why knowing things from all four quadrants is important. Even after you graduate with a degree in the major you've chosen, your future isn't cast in concrete. Things change.[3]

- In today's high-tech world, old jobs die and are reborn as new ones. Yesterday's film developer has been replaced by today's online photo sharing websites. Even though the economy is challenging right now, at least 138 million people have jobs. And when the economy is sluggish, jobs sometimes just go away. But at least 138 million Americans are employed, and those who can transfer their skills because they're broadly educated will fare best if they do lose their jobs.
- Because salaries are lower, companies sometimes move jobs overseas—and as one expert says, "you never know whether it will be your job, or not."[4] The best way to ensure you're employed is to have broad-based skills you can use in more than one way.
- It's been estimated that approximately 45 percent of the working population in the United States would change jobs if they could. While that may sound discouraging, look at it this way: There are no perfect jobs, and your goals and values may change over time. Be educationally primed and ready for change when you want to make a move.
- When the economy is healthy, 2.4 million new jobs are born in the United States each year. Being well-educated means you're better able to snap up an opportunity as soon as it knocks.

I've seen my family go through stuff like this before ...

EXERCISE 12.1

Think Tank

Working in groups of three to five students, imagine you graduated from your college or university a few years ago, and you are now all rising young managers in a large corporation. Your boss calls one morning to tell you and your colleagues that she's naming all of you to a planning team to design a new product. You'll be part of a think tank, tasked with designing one of the following three items:

1. The next generation jumbo jet—the 797—which will be marketed worldwide in competition with European, Asian, Russian, and other American aircraft
2. A revolutionary new micro cell phone, which will have some features no other cell phone has ever had before
3. A hot new magazine for college students, which will sell on newsstands on college campuses everywhere and be available through e-subscriptions as well

Within the group, decide which of the three tasks to brainstorm. Your team is to come up with a basic concept for this new product that will win a competition as the best overall design of its class in the world.

Sketch a basic design for your product and draw the Academic Map (two axes/four quadrants) just discussed in this chapter. What various academic disciplines will your team need to draw upon as you develop your plans? If you choose task 1, for example, you'll surely need to draw from the field of aeronautical engineering—that's obvious. But what other kinds of knowledge must your think tank members bring to the table?

When all teams are ready, your instructor will ask each team to list its suggestions on an Academic Map a team member draws on the board. Try as best you can to write the disciplines in their appropriate quadrants. The point of this team exercise is to demonstrate visually the integrated nature of a truly productive education in the world of work.[5]

> When the economy is in a downturn, of course, these numbers change, and college enrollments surge with people going back to get degrees or to retool. They know the value of an education. You have the opportunity right now—make the best of it!

STEP 5: Identify Your Academic Major

On top of these basic courses to broaden your knowledge, you'll also take a concentration of courses in your academic major—say, in chemistry. Your personal Academic Map will continue to grow outward, but with a bulge in the direction of your major. It's skewed, but it still includes all four quadrants. Your Academic Map may not look exactly like someone else's, but it represents you and your college education, and the kinds of things you need to know in order to be a well-educated person.

Choosing an Academic Major

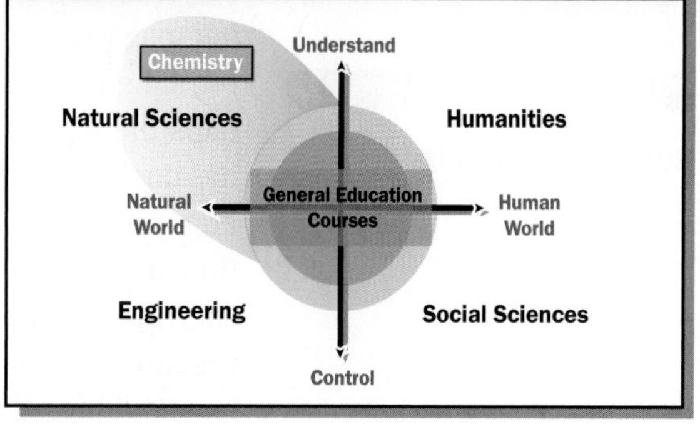

How to Choose a Major and a Career

Like many students, you probably put value in how well college prepares you for a profession.[6] Choosing a college major and directing yourself toward a prospective career can be stressful. Many students feel pressure to make the right decision—and make it right now! You might hear conflicting advice from family members that

> **That would never work in the real world. . . . The real world isn't a place, it's a justification for not trying.**
>
> *Jason Fried and David Heinemeier Hansson, Rework*

put a high priority on financial success above other important factors, and feel overwhelmed by the number of possibilities from which to choose.[7] You may know what you want to do with the rest of your life right now, but many of your classmates don't, and even if they *say* they do, they may well change their minds several times. Yes, these decisions are important. But where do you start? The decision-making process should involve these critical steps. If you're still deciding, or even if you think you already have, consider how they apply to you.

Pay attention here since I'm clueless!

1. Follow Your Bliss

In an ideal world, which major and career would you choose? Don't think about anything except the actual content you'd be studying. Don't consider career opportunities, requirements, difficulty, or anything else that might keep you from making these choices in an ideal world. What are you passionate about? Let's say you have a dream of becoming a famous athlete, for example a football player, like Peyton Manning or a skateboarder, like Tony Hawk, or a tennis player, like Venus Williams. Can you translate your dream into a goal and become a pro? Perhaps. Some pro athletes like these ones are extremely successful. Tony Hawk is said to earn as much as $10 million a year as a one-man sports franchise. Peyton Manning, who was called the most marketable player in the NFL, signed a record breaking multi-year contract for 99 million dollars in 2004 and earned 15.8 million dollars in 2010. He earned twice as much off the field (endorsements, etc.) than on the field.[8] If it's skateboarding, think about which majors might apply. Majoring in physics would help you understand skateboard ascent versus decent, trajectories, spin, and angles. Majoring in landscape architecture would allow you to design skateparks. You would spend time outdoors, build computer and 3-D models of parks, and perhaps even interview other skateboarders about desirable features. Majoring in journalism would put you in a good position to write for a skateboarding magazine.

Hey! Cool! This is what I would love to do!

> **Not all who wander are lost.**
>
> *J. R. R. Tolkien, English author (1892–1973)*

Like many students, you may be wondering what to do with your life. Perhaps the *idealist* in you has one potential career in mind and the *realist* in you has another. The $300,000 salary you'd earn as a surgeon may look very compelling until you consider the years of medical school required after college, the time invested in an internship and residency, and the still further years of necessary specialization. It takes long-term diligence, commitment, dedication, and resources—yours or borrowed ones—to make that dream come true. Do these factors lessen the appeal?

Perhaps there's conflict between your *idealism* and your family's *pragmatism*. Comedian Robin Williams once said, "When I told my father I was going to be an actor, he said, 'Fine, but study welding just in case.'"

I love this guy!

And perhaps you just don't know yet. If that's the case, don't panic. Despite the increased pressure these days to choose the right major because of rising tuition and a changeable economy, it's hard to have it all figured out from the start.[9] Some college students rush into something that doesn't suit them, which just increases their stress level later. Other students delay making a decision for many different reasons; they are instead waiters, wonderers, wanderers, or watchers. Many college graduates are still tweaking their plans! While you don't want to leap before you look, there's also a sense in which declaring a major can

I think I'm a wanderer.

EXERCISE 12.2

Wise Wanderings[10]

So just how to do you discover your passions? Do you examine your habits? (You watch football on television on Sunday afternoons and Monday nights, so you should be a football player, right?) Your easily identified "likes"? (You're crazy about ice cream; therefore you should open your own store so you can eat all you want?) Or do you simply list all the things you hate and then think of their opposites? Hmmm…

Try this method instead, created by Katharine Brooks, the author of *You Majored in What?* She calls it "a wandering map." It's a way to meander through people, places, and things, connect the dots in your life, and discover themes that are important to you (and your eventual career). Take a look at the wandering map created by a hypothetical student named Bill. He listed things that seemed significant—memories, past experiences, preferences, traits—and then he connected them. The process helped him discover themes that are probably very important about himself.

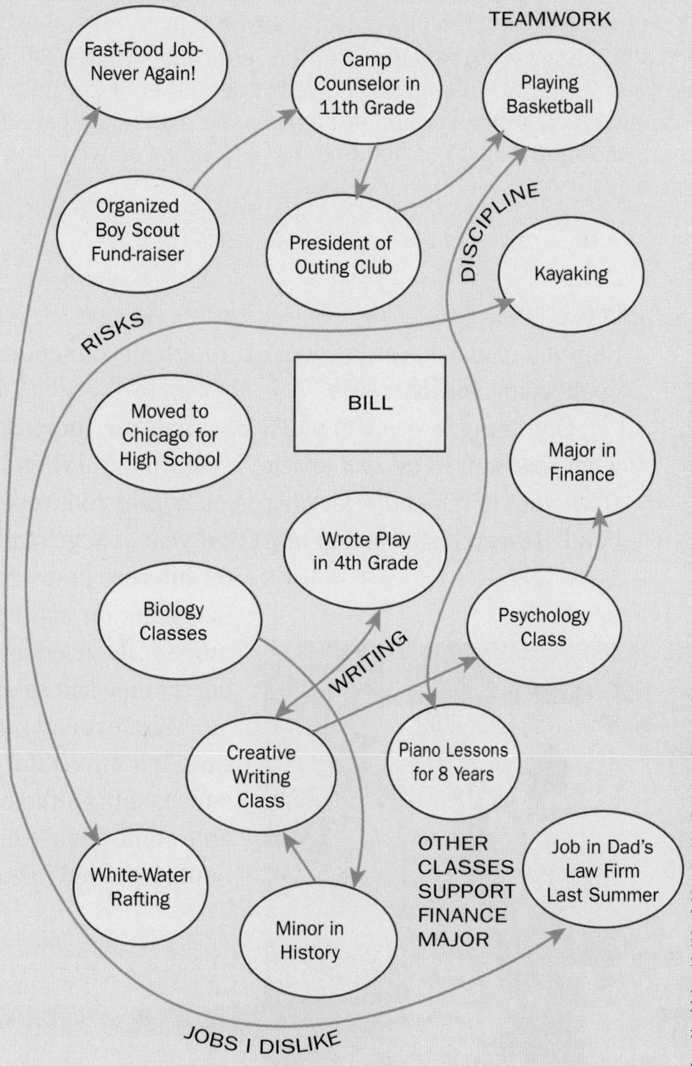

He identifies connections and labels them, and it's easy to see themes that stand out:

1. He seems to like creative pursuits, like writing and music.
2. He likes exciting things, rather than routine, boring ones.
3. He likes to work with people, organize, and lead.

(continued on next page)

Now get a large sheet of blank paper and try it for yourself. First, list all the things that seem significant in **your** life—memories, past experiences, dreams, preferences, skills, objects, traits—and place them on a large sheet of paper in any order. Then start linking these individual items as connections begin to make sense to you. Once you've completed the linking arrows (as Bill did above), then list the themes you discover here.

1.

2.

3.

Once you have identified your three personal themes, start pondering which sorts of career choices would match up best with your themes, and preferably with *all* your themes. Can you think of career options that would be ideal for Bill? If you can't think of a career that satisfies all your themes, zero in on one important one. If you remembered building model cars, for example, entering a soap-box derby, and reading automotive magazines, you might realize that one theme in your life has been a love of cars. From this realization, you might identify an engineering career in automotive design. Try it, and map career possibilities that capitalize on what you're already passionate about.

help you gain focus as you work through all your courses. That's the positive side of choosing wisely.

One thing is certain: you'll be a happier, more productive person if you do what *you* want to do *and* pursue it vigorously. When it comes to success, ability (*Can* you do it?) and effort (Are you *willing* to invest what it takes?) go hand in hand. Research shows that most first-year college students choose a major based on interest first. However, women base their decisions on aptitude second, while men are more influenced by career advancement opportunities and salary.[11]

Whatever your motivation, remember this. It's unusual for people to become truly successful halfheartedly. There are undeniable emotional and psychological components involved in success. Look at what some

Bryan Allen/Corbis

Follow your bliss and be what you want to be. Don't climb the ladder of success only to find it's leaning against the wrong wall.

Dr. Bernie Siegel, physician and writer

successful people have had to say, and note their use of emotional words such as *passion, love,* and *heart*:

- *God gave me a special talent to play the game... maybe he didn't give me a talent, he gave me a passion.* (Wayne Gretzky, called the greatest player in the history of hockey)
- *To waste time doing something you don't really love is, to me, the ultimate waste of time.* (Peter Jennings, ABC Nightly News, 1938–2005)
- *My father always told me, "Find a job you love and you'll never have to work a day in your life.* (Jim Fox, former player, LA Kings, NHL Hockey)

Cool quote! Remember this one to put in my room!

- *I am seeking, I am striving, I am in it with all my heart.* (Vincent van Gogh, Dutch painter, 1853–1890)
- *When love and skill work together, expect a masterpiece.* (John Ruskin, Oxford University scholar and writer, 1819–1900)
- *To love what you do and feel that it matters—how could anything be more fun?* (Katherine Graham, publisher, Washington Post, 1917–2001)
- *My heart is in the work.* (Andrew Carnegie, American industrialist, richest man in the world in 1901)

Having said that, what if your "bliss" just isn't feasible? You'd give anything to play for the NBA, but you're five foot two and female. You dream of being a rock star, but you can't carry a tune. Then it may be time to set aside the idealism and resurrect the realism in you. Maybe then it's time to translate—or shift—your dreams into goals.

Why do students tend to choose particular majors and careers? Research says these factors about you tend to be some of the most important:

1. **Your salary motivation.** While salary is certainly something you should be interested in, too much emphasis can force you to choose a major you're not really suited for, which can then lead you to decide college isn't for you.[12]
2. **Your brain.** Research indicates that students who are left-brained (whose left hemispheres are dominant) most often choose majors such as business, engineering, and science. Students who are right-brained choose majors such as education, nursing, communication, and law.[13]
3. **Your Mom.** While past research has focused on the effect fathers or both parents have on helping their children choose a major, recent studies show that mothers are influential, most readily through emotional channels, for example.[14]
4. **A faculty role model.** You may be attracted to a particular major because a teacher—a female, or a minority—someone like you, serves as a role model.[15]
5. **Your personality.** We'll explore this topic later in the "Your Type Is Showing" feature.

CURIOSITY: *FOCUS YOUR I'S*

The huge printing presses of a major Chicago newspaper began malfunctioning on the Saturday before Christmas, putting all the revenue for advertising that was to appear in the Sunday paper in jeopardy. None of the technicians could track down the problem. Finally, a frantic call was made to the retired printer who had worked with these presses for over forty years. "We'll pay anything; just come in and fix them," he was told.

When he arrived, he walked around for a few minutes, surveying the presses; then he approached one of the control panels and opened it. He removed a dime from his pocket, turned a screw ¼ of a turn, and said, "The presses will now work correctly." After being profusely thanked, he was told to submit a bill for his work.

The bill arrived a few days later, for $10,000.00! Not wanting to pay such a huge amount for so little work, the printer was told to please itemize his charges, with the hope that he would reduce the amount once he had to identify his services. The revised bill arrived: $1.00 for turning the screw; $9,999.00 for knowing which screw to turn. (Anonymous)

iStockphoto.com/Patryk Galka

So what does it take? After forty years on the job, the retired printer knew many things, including one elusive but critical piece of knowledge—which screw to turn. But perhaps you're just starting out, and experience is something you don't have yet. How will you achieve life and career success?

Some experts on growing up in our society say it's difficult to transition into adulthood. For many college students today, childhood was where they were given many opportunities: baseball, tennis, soccer, art, music, dance, travel. Their parents—with whom they have close ties—desperately want to help their children become successful. Many parents want to help solve their children's problems for them—with the best of intentions. They may be so eager to help that they try to motivate them with "ladder talk": "If you do well at the local campus, then you can get admitted to the big university, and if you graduate with a high grade point average there, you can get into a really good law school, and if you do well there, you'll be offered a job with a prestigious firm, and if you prove yourself to your superiors there, eventually you'll make partner." See how it goes—up the ladder of success? This type of communication, which is intended to encourage, can actually *discourage* some students. Such a long chain of challenging hurdles looks like an impossible dream.

Mel Levine, author of *Ready or Not, Here Life Comes,* says, "We are in the midst of an epidemic of work-life unreadiness because an alarming number of young adults are unable to find a good fit between their minds and their career directions.... Because they are not finding their way, they may feel as if they are going nowhere and have nowhere to go."[16]

How can anyone have nowhere to go with more than 12,000 different occupations or careers to choose from with 8,000 alternative job titles—for a total of over 20,000 options?[17] Some students start college and become overwhelmed. Sometime during the first year, or possibly later, they take a step back and announce in so many words, "There are too many choices. I refuse to choose at all."[18]

Here's another tough issue many college graduates face when entering the world of work. Many of them have already decided that work is boring because their part-time jobs in high school and college were boring. They don't want to climb the ladder of success. They'd like to skip the bottom and start somewhere closer to the top rung. But every job involves some element of grunt work, even those at the top. No job is round-the-clock fun, and in every new job, eventually the honeymoon is over, and the tough challenges begin. The simple truth is this: building a career takes time, persistence, dedication, and focus. Seemingly overnight successes like J. K. Rowling of Harry Potter fame are rare; steady progress toward a goal is the norm.[19]

So what does it take to launch your career successfully? You'll need to focus your I's on four things: Inner direction, Interpretation, Instrumentation, and Interaction—the four I's of career-life readiness. Here's what they mean.[20]

Inner direction. You've lived with yourself for some time now, but how well do you know yourself? How accurate is your view of yourself? Are you honest about your potential? You must first understand the inner you before you can direct it toward a career that fits.

Interpretation. Many students have memorized their way through countless classes, becoming very good at it, but often not fully understanding what they're learning. Somehow they get by, but they miss the larger principles beneath the specific facts they've memorized. On the job there's more required than repeating back what the boss has told you. You must interpret the information and apply it in your own way, which demonstrates whether you do (or don't) understand what you're doing.

Instrumentation. In your career, you'll need a toolkit filled with different kinds of abilities—engaging in high-level thinking, brainstorming, problem solving, making decisions, tapping your creativity, and cultivating both hard (technical) and soft (interpersonal) skills. And not only must you know how to use each of these tools, but you'll need to know when and why.

Interaction. Business (or any profession) isn't just about facts and figures. It's about people, values, and relationships. People will be what help you build your career. Without people to buy, sell, trade, consume, or produce, there is no business.

The more you focus your I's, the better prepared you'll be for the challenges ahead. Centuries ago, the German poet Johann Wolfgang von Goethe wrote these words—true then and true today: *Whatever you do or dream, you can begin it. Boldness has genius, power and magic in it. Begin it now.*

My I's are NOT focused yet, especially Inner Direction.

Becoming a famous athlete can certainly be a valid dream, one you're passionate about. Can you translate your dream into a goal and become a pro? Perhaps. But it's also important to be realistic. What about aging and injuries—not to mention real ability? And how many professional athletes are there—especially compared to other professionals such as teachers, architects, and physicians? When the statistics are against you, achieving success isn't impossible, but it might take more than expert skill. It might also take some luck. However, Barbara Bush once wisely said, "You just don't luck into things as much as you'd like to think you do. You build step by step, whether it's friendships or opportunities."

2. Conduct Preliminary Research

Has it ever occurred to you that you may not have all the facts—accurate ones—about your ideal major? Do you know what it *really* takes? Have you gotten your information from qualified sources—or are you basing your opinion on your roommate's reaction to one course he took in the major or on the campus grapevine?

Try an experiment. Choose three majors you're considering, one of which is your ideal major, and send yourself on a fact-finding mission. To find out if you're on target, get the answers to the following ten questions for each of the three possibilities. Go to the physical location (department) where each major is housed, and interview a professor. The experiment requires legwork; don't just let your fingers do the clicking.

1. What is the major?
2. Who is the interviewee?
3. What is the name of the academic department where this major is housed? Where are the department offices physically located on campus?

The privilege of a lifetime is being who you are.

Joseph Campbell, American professor and writer (1904–1987)

4. Which introductory courses in this major would inform you about your interests and abilities?

5. Which upper-level courses in this major interest you? (List three.)

6. What are the department's entry requirements to become a major?

7. How many students major in this discipline on your campus?

8. Which required course in the major do students usually find most challenging? Which is most engaging? Which is most valued? Why?

9. How would the interviewee describe the reputation of this department on campus? What is it known for?

10. From the interviewee's perspective, why should a student major in this discipline?

After you complete your interviews, review the facts. Did you change any of your opinions, based on what you learned?[21]

3. Take a Good Look at Yourself

EXERCISE 12.3

How Do You Look?

Take a good look at yourself and answer the following questions about how you prefer to work. Rank each item 1 or 2 based on your general preference. While many careers, if not most, require both, your task is to decide which of the two you prefer.

I prefer to work at a job:

		My answers:
1. Alone ______	With other people ______	alone
2. Indoors ______	Outdoors ______	outdoors!
3. With people ______	With equipment or materials ______	equipment
4. Directing/leading others ______	Being directed/led by others ______	??
5. Producing information ______	Managing information ______	??
6. In an organized, step-by-step way ______	In a big-idea, holistic way ______	big idea way
7. Starting things ______	Completing things ______	starting
8. Involving a product ______	Involving a service ______	product
9. Solving challenging problems ______	Generating creative ideas ______	creative ideas
10. Finding information ______	Applying information ______	applying
11. Teaching/training others in groups ______	Advising/coaching others one-on-one ______	one-on-one

Now look at your eleven first choices. Identify several career fields that come to mind that would allow you to achieve as many of them as possible.

“

Are you fit company for the person you wish to become?

”

Anonymous

© Larry Harwood Photography. Property of Cengage Learning

Here's a bottom-line question: Looking back at Dr. Bernie Siegel's quote several pages ago, what *is* the "right wall" to lean your ladder of success on? How do you know? Many first-year college students don't know. They don't have enough experience under their belts to plan for a lifetime. They're in college to *discover*. It all comes down to questions this book has been asking you all along: Who are you? And what do you want? If you're unsure of how to proceed in your decision making, follow these recommendations to see if they help you bring your future into focus.

Send in the SWOT Team!

A SWOT analysis is an excellent way to begin taking a good look at yourself in relation to your future. SWOT stands for Strengths, Weaknesses, Opportunities, and Threats. SWOT analyses are typically used in business, but creating one for yourself may be useful when it comes to deciding on a college major and a career.

Earlier this chapter asked you to build a personal Academic Map. Your SWOT analysis can borrow this format to help you create a potential career profile. Make a matrix with four quadrants, label each one, and fill them in as objectively as you can.

- **Strengths** are traits that give you a leg up. These are talents you can capitalize on and qualities you can develop.
- **Weaknesses** are traits that currently work against you. You can, however, work to reduce or eliminate them.
- **Opportunities** are conditions or circumstances that work in your favor, like a strong forecast for your prospective career's future.
- **Threats** are conditions that could have adverse effects. Some of these factors are beyond your control; however, sometimes you can successfully lessen their potential effects.

As you create the matrix, just as we did when building your Academic Map, begin with two basic questions:

What kinds of forces will impact your potential career?

Internal—forces inside you, such as motivation and skill

External—forces outside you that may affect your success: the job market or economy, for example

FIGURE 12.3

SWOT Analysis

Ah-ha! This helps!

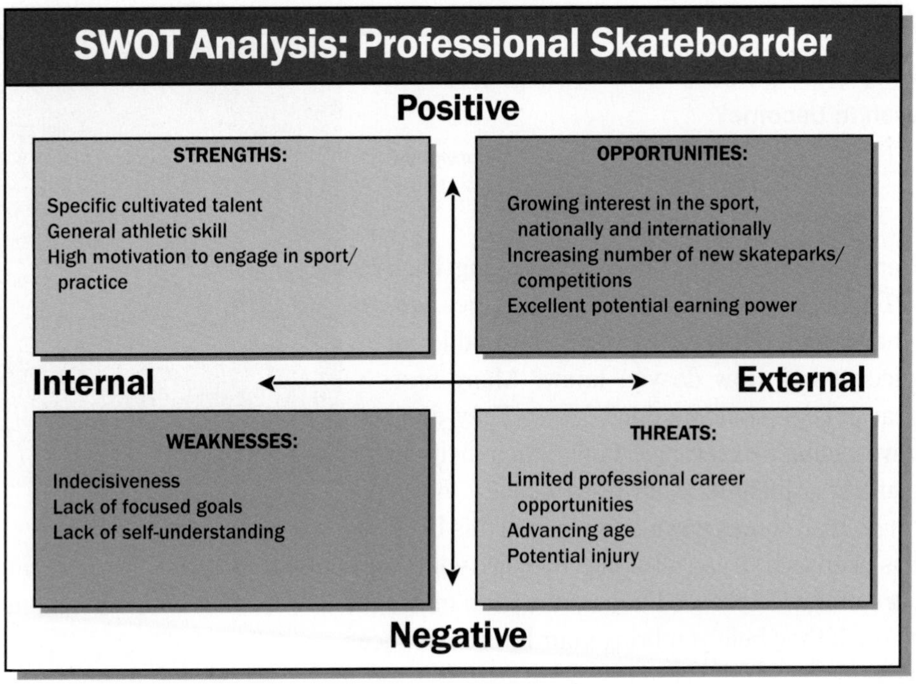

What kind of influence can these forces exert?

Positive—some forces will give you a boost toward your goals

Negative—other forces will work against you[22]

Let's complete a SWOT analysis for the earlier example of becoming a professional skateboarder. Of course, you might say that, technically, you don't need an academic degree for that particular career. But if you want to pursue related, more traditional careers—design a new skatepark or write for a skateboard magazine, for example—you would need an array of knowledge and enhanced skills from writing and design to finance and marketing. Besides, college isn't just about jobs, it's about living a fuller life as a well-educated person. Look at the SWOT analysis for a college student who dreams of becoming a professional skateboarder in Figure 12.3. What do you think? Is professional skateboarding a good career option for him? In your view, do the opportunities outweigh the threats? For example, does the potential earning power of a professional skateboarder outweigh the risks associated with possible incapacitating injuries? Do his well-cultivated athletic skills compensate for his lack of focus in other areas? If not, might he gravitate toward other potential careers, perhaps those that also involve skateboarding, like a degree in business to run a sports facility, for example, or a degree in journalism to write for a sports magazine?

> **The elevator to success is out of order, but the stairs are always open.**
>
> *Zig Ziglar*

EXERCISE 12.4

SWOT Analysis:

Looking at the model in Figure 12.3, try doing a SWOT Analysis of a career you're considering. If you have no idea where to begin, choose the career of someone you know—a friend or family member. Carefully analyze the career's Strengths, Weaknesses, Opportunities, and Threats as you see them. It may help to Google the career for specifics and check information-rich, accurate sites like OOH (Occupational Outlook Handbook), compiled by the U.S. Bureau of Labor Statistics. After you're done, write your conclusions below, and share your results in class, if asked. Is the career you've analyzed worth pursuing in your view?

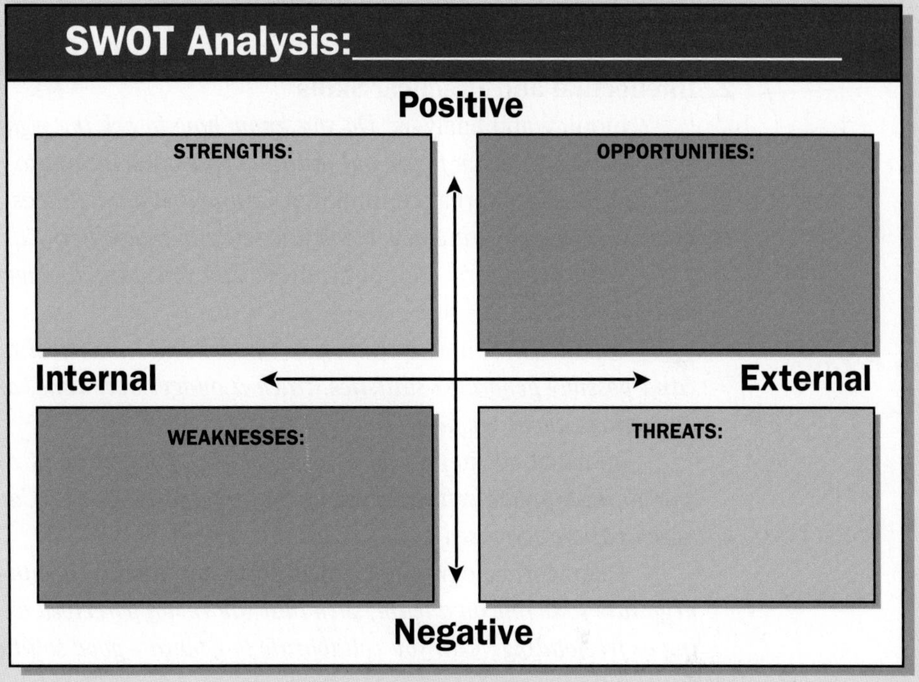

1. ______________________________

2. ______________________________

3. ______________________________

LEAP to Success[23]

What skills should all college graduates have? That's the question explored by a team of academic experts and leading employers, resulting in a ten-year national initiative (2005–2015)—LEAP. Leap stands for "**L**iberal **E**ducation and **A**merica's **P**romise." (And here liberal has nothing to do with politics. Instead, it's a time-honored approach to college learning that helps students learn to deal with complexity, diversity, and change—no matter which specific major they choose).

We live in a world where change—global, technological, cross-cultural, economic, ecological, you name it—is the only constant. How do you prepare for change? Can you prepare? What will get you ready? According to LEAP, four broad goals addressed in college will help you deal with twenty-first century challenges. As you look over the list below, assess your work-readiness in each area. In the blank that follows the examples, decide whether you'd rate yourself as 1 (making good progress) or 2 (need further development).

1. **Knowledge of Human Cultures and the Physical and Natural World**
   _____broad knowledge in science, math, social sciences, humanities, history, languages, and the arts: *Do you have a multidisciplinary background with fairly extensive cultural and cross-cultural knowledge? If someone mentions a painting like* **American Gothic**, *a word like* **octogenarian**, *a historical period like the* ***Peloponnesian Wars,*** *or* ***Pi*** *as the world's most famous number, can you follow? You don't have to know everything, of course, but you do need some knowledge about many different kinds of things.*

2. **Intellectual and Practical Skills**
   _____Inquiry and analysis: *Do you know how to ask the right questions of the right people? Can you figure out multiple possible solutions to real problems?*
   _____Critical and creative thinking: *Can you evaluate ideas other people propose? Can you generate new ideas yourself and judge their feasibility?*
   _____Written and oral communication: *Can you speak and write with precision and power?*
   _____Quantitative literacy: *Can you understand numerical data, comprehend (and possibly generate) statistics, track a budget over time, or make financial projections about the future?*
   _____Information literacy: *Can you use technology to find answers? Are you able to manipulate software, even for advanced purposes? Can you discern between valid and biased online information?*
   _____Teamwork and problem solving: *Do you "work well with others?" Can you negotiate your role on a team, such that you're not perceived as either domineering or freeloading? Can you collaborate to generate good solutions to problems?*

What are my strengths here???

3. **Personal and Social Responsibility**
   _____Civic knowledge and engagement, both locally and globally: *Are you engaged in your community and willing to stay informed or get involved? Do you have a basic knowledge of the role local, state, and federal governments play? Are you aware of global issues?*
   _____Intercultural knowledge and competence: *Are you interested in exploring the similarities, differences, and interrelationships between countries and cultures? Is your CQ strong? Can you interact well with others unlike you?*
   _____Ethical reasoning and action: *Do you think about the ethical ramifications of your decisions and take the right actions—ones that are not only best for you, but also others around you?*
   _____Foundations and skills for lifelong learning: *Do you want to continue learning beyond what's required of you in college? Are you setting learning goals now that will continue into your future?*

4. **Integrative and Applied Learning**
   _____Synthesis and application of what you know to new contexts and complex problems: *Can you connect knowledge from a variety of fields, rather than keeping it isolated in standard "compartments" (math, English, history, etc.)? Can you apply what you've learned, moving beyond memorization into real world usefulness?*

BOX 12.1 Five Ways to Open the Door (or Close It) during an Interview

By the time you graduate from college, you will have been interviewed many times to get a new job or to be admitted to graduate school. And after you graduate, you'll go through a series of interviews on your career path.

Often interviewers aren't particularly skilled at asking questions. They haven't been trained on how to interview prospective employees, so they just ask whatever questions come to them. And often, interviewees don't quite know what they're doing either.

Of course, you should always be honest, but there are various ways to communicate the same information. Telling an interviewer you "like to work alone" sounds antisocial. But if you say you "like to really focus on what you're doing without distractions," you've shown dedication to your work ethic. You also need to be aware of real pitfalls to avoid.

1. **"You've got to ac-centuate the positive; e-liminate the negative."** A trap question interviewers sometimes ask is, "What's your worst fault?" While you may be tempted to say the first thing that comes to mind, that could be a big mistake. "Umm . . . sleeping too much! I really like to sleep in." Not good. But some faults you could identify might actually be construed as strengths: "I have a little too much nervous energy. I'm always on the go. I like to stay busy."
2. **Stay focused.** "Tell me about yourself" is a common question interviewers ask. How much time do you have? Most of us like to talk about ourselves, but it's important to stay on track. Think possible questions through in advance, and construct some hypothetical answers. Keep your answers job-focused: what you liked about your last job, why you liked those aspects of it, what your long-term career goals are, and how this job can help you prepare. You don't need to go into your family background or your personal problems. And it's always a bad idea to bash a previous job or former boss. The interviewer may worry that you'll bring whatever didn't work there with you to this new job.
3. **Don't just give answers, get some.** A job interview is like a first date. Find out what you need to know. If the job is one you're interested in long-term, ask questions such as these three key ones:
   - **What does this company value?** Listen to the answer. Doing things by the book? The answer will tell you about the personality of the company.
   - **What's a typical day like for you?** An answer like "I get up at 5:00 a.m., get here at 6:30 a.m., and go home around 7:00 p.m.—and then I do paperwork all evening" tells you something. This may—or may not—be the job or the company for you.
   - **What happened to the last person in this job?** If you find out he was promoted, that's one thing. But if you learn he was fired or quit, see if you can find out why. Maybe he had job performance problems, or maybe this is an impossible job that no one could do well.

   Remember, too, that interviews are conversations with give and take, not just one person doing all the giving and the other doing all the taking. Listen to the interviewer. She may be looking for an opportunity to tell you things she thinks are important, too.
4. **Watch for questions out of left field.** Some companies like to get creative with their interviewing. Microsoft, for example, is known for asking problem-solving questions, such as "If you could remove any of the fifty states, which would it be? Be prepared to give specific reasons why you chose the state you did." There is no right or wrong answer, although some answers are better than others. ("We should just nuke state X. I had a bad experience there once" would probably furrow some brows, and naming Washington state, where Microsoft is located, might be a bad choice.) The interviewer just wants to hear how you think. Talk through your underlying reasoning.[24] Remember: Today's interviewers are looking for more than technical skills; they're looking for critical thinking skills, problem-solving skills, and creativity.[25]
5. **Don't start off with salary questions.** Make sure the first question out of your mouth isn't, "So tell me about the salary, again? Any way to notch that up a bit?" The last thing you want to do is give the interviewer the idea you're just in it for the money. Of course, you are, but not just for that. More importantly, in every job you have, you'll gain experience and knowledge that will always better prepare you for the next job to come.

I should practice for this!

LEAP is broad and comprehensive. As a first-year college student, you wouldn't be expected to have everything mastered now. But notice that even though *FOCUS* is about college success, many of the skills that are addressed throughout the book will help you get ready for your career—and hit the ground running. The skills you need for college and career success are more similar than you might imagine![26]

Test Your Strengths and Interests

If you're not sure which majors or careers might be good ones for you, consider using an assessment instrument to find out. Many such tools are available through your school's Counseling or Career Center, perhaps through your instructor for this course, or through particular career assessment workshops. These assessment tools don't focus on one specific job, but instead they give you general information about which types of work might fit you. And remember that's what you're looking for—general information, hints, suggestions, clues, something to go on. It's also a good idea to try more than one assessment tool. That way you can look for overlap—one test reinforcing the results of another. For the most part, standardized, published, paper-and-pencil assessments such as the Myers-Briggs Type Inventory and the Strong Interest Inventory are most reliable, but others, including popular online tests, can give you some helpful guidance as well. Here are several assessment tools that you may want to try that are available online. Some charge a fee to obtain your results; others are free.

I'll go online soon to look for these!

- Livecareer's Free Career Test
- The Princeton Review Career Quiz
- The Career Key
- The Career Interests Game
- John Holland's Self-Directed Search
- The Princeton Review Career Quiz
- Analyze My Career

4. Consider Your Major versus Your Career

? challenge

" reaction

Challenge: What is the relationship between choosing a major and choosing a career?

Reaction:

___

___

___

Which comes first, the chicken or the egg? The major or the career? Silly question? The obvious answer, of course, is that you must first major in something in college before you can build a career on it. But the question isn't as straightforward as it seems.

Should you choose a major based on an intended career? Perhaps you know you want to be a science teacher, first and foremost. You don't know whether to major in one of the sciences or in education. You like all sciences,

BOX 12.2 A Model Résumé

In today's competitive world, when literally hundreds of people may be applying for one choice position, how should a résumé be written? Can a résumé be appealing, but not flashy? Solid, but not stuffy? Professional, but still personal? Thorough, but brief? Take a look at Jared's and see what you think.

> This résumé uses a skills approach, rather than a chronological approach. A chronological approach works best if you have a career underway and can list various relevant positions that prepared you for this one.

JARED DANIELS

> Center your name, and use a standard résumé format. Many companies now scan résumés so that they can be read conveniently from one source. Skip the neon pink paper. Go for a highly professional look.

Current Address:
Evelyn Edwin Living-Learning Center
Rocky Mountain State University
Great Bluffs, CO 89898
(100) 555–6543 or jdaniels@rmsu.edu

Permanent Address:
1234 Aspen Way
Vail, CO 81657
(101) 555–9128

> Provide both your temporary address, if you're attending college away from home, and your actual home address. The employer may save your résumé and call you later, over the summer, for example, if the current opening is filled by someone else.

CAREER OBJECTIVE

> Build your career objective according to the position's advertised needs. "One size fits all" doesn't work when it comes to résumés.

To obtain a position as a communications specialist in a large company, designing web pages, creating internal e-newsletters, and planning corporate events.

EDUCATION

> Provide numbers whenever you can. Text can be glossed over, but numbers stand out and make your accomplishments more quantifiable.

Rocky Mountain State University, Great Bluffs, CO
Bachelor of Arts, Communication Major, 2011 (Minor: Spanish)
GPA 3.6/4.0
Personally financed 80% of college tuition through employment and athletic scholarship

Dog ear this page for when I need to write my resume!

HONORS

Vice President, RMSU Freshman Honor Society
Vail "Invest in the Future" League Soccer Scholarship (4 years, chosen from 150 applicants)

SUMMARY OF BEST ACADEMIC COURSEWORK

> Select coursework that applies directly to the advertised position.

Organizational Communication
Business and Professional Communication
Principles of Web Design
Advanced Composition
Emerging Technologies
Event Planning

SKILLS

> Technology is important in today's workplace. Don't underrate your competence. Many senior employees don't know as much as you do!

Technology
Part-time work, web page design
Proficient in Word, PowerPoint, Excel, Access, Macromedia Flash, Adobe Acrobat, and Photoshop
Event Planning
RMSU Freshman Honor Society, planned campus ceremonies for 1,000 guests (2 years)
Student Government, Campus Life Committee Chair (1 year)
Soccer Fundraising Events, Planning Committee Chair (3 years)
Writing
1st place winner, campus creative writing competition, 2011

EMPLOYMENT HISTORY

> If you're able, show that you have worked all throughout college to demonstrate your commitment to your goal.

Intern, Peak Industries, Human Resources Department, fall 2011
Student Assistant, Office of the Dean, Arts and Sciences, spring 2009
Residence Life, Floor Supervisor (2 years)
Hostess, Pancake Heaven, summers, 2007–2010

REFERENCES (available on request)

> Always obtain preapproval from your references, even if you don't list their names. You may be asked to provide them on a moment's notice.

BOX 12.3 Is College Worth It?

If it hasn't happened already, one day soon, you may be surfing the Web and run across articles with titles like "Who Really Needs a College Degree?" or "Newsflash: College Dropouts *Can* Get Rich." You become intrigued, jump from site to site, and find the ongoing debate over the value of a college education. As you read, thoughts like these may pop into your head:

- *Someday I'll have to pay all these loans back. I'm running up quite a tab here. How will I ever do that?*
- *How do I know I'll get a better job with a college degree? Maybe I should just pick a career that doesn't require one. Besides, are there even any good jobs out there?*
- *Should I really be going to college when my parents are struggling financially? They're sacrificing on my behalf, and I feel guilty.*
- *How can I keep my grades up and still earn enough money to work my way through college?*
- *Is all this stress really worth it?*

These are perfectly legitimate questions, and you're not alone in asking them. You should be reassured, however, by the results of recent, large-scale, national surveys:

1. College graduates (86 percent) say that "college has been a good investment for them personally."
2. College graduates believe that, on average, they make $20,000 per year more than their counterparts without college degrees. These beliefs are confirmed in actual salary data (although exact amounts vary by career).
3. Some people believe the primary role of college should be to help students prepare for a career. Others believe its primary role should be to foster intellectual and personal growth. College graduates emphasize the latter, and overall, they believe going to college helped them achieve these goals (74 percent).[31]
4. The current job market for college graduates is tight right now, but it's even worse for non-college graduates. According to *The New York Times*, the more education you have, the less vulnerable you are to unemployment woes. With a college degree, you'll be represented by the darkest (lowest) line below.

Unemployment Rates for Workers 25 Years and older, by Education

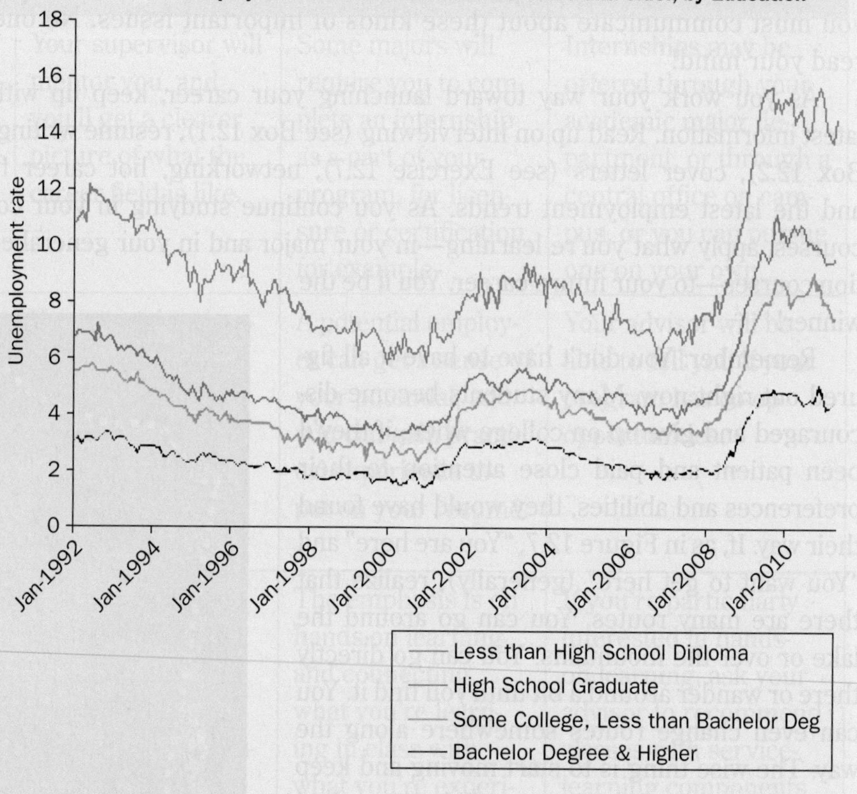

Source of data: U.S. Bureau of Labor Statistics.

An overwhelming majority of college graduates are glad they went to college. Only four percent say they wish they hadn't gone.[32] College is a better investment for most graduates and even more so today. A new study from Georgetown University[33] shows that a bachelor's degree can pay off for jobs that don't require one like secretaries, plumbers and cashiers. And, beyond money, education seems to make people happier and healthier.[34]

Ultimately, the decision is up to you. But if you're considering dropping out, do your homework first. Make the decision for the right reasons, not because you failed a test, dislike a class, or ran out of steam. A college education is an investment that's yours to keep for a lifetime. It has the power to create a better life for you, and in the opinion of many people who look back on theirs, it's possibly the best thing they've ever done.

Source: Based on Rampell, C. "Once Again: Is College Worth It?" *The New York Times*, June 6, 2011.

CAREER OUTLOOK: *ZOOM IN, ZOOM OUT*

"[It's] like driving at night in the fog. You can only see as far as your headlights, but you can make the whole trip that way."

E. L. Doctorow, in *Writers at Work*

Perhaps the most common question asked during hiring interviews is this one: "Where do you see yourself in five years?" Undoubtedly, it's a tough question. In today's uncertain economy, the most honest answer is "Are you kidding—who knows? I'm not even sure what I'll have for dinner tonight." Five years seems like forever. While your imaginary answer may be the most truthful one, it's not necessarily smart.[35]

One thing that trips up many first-year college students is thinking that they have to have it all figured out—now. They think there should be a linear path between their major and their career.[36] For example, a student should enter college having declared a business major, earn a business degree, and then land a good job in the business world. "On a clear day," as the old song goes, "you can see forever." It *should* be that easy.

iStockphoto.com/Dmitry Mordvintsev

Realistically, clarity typically unfolds as you go. Many students don't have a particular major or a career in mind. When things become increasingly foggy during their "trip" through college, they lose their way or maybe even give up. But as the quotation above indicates: you may only be able to see as far as your headlights shine in the fog, but if you had to, you could make the whole trip that way. Rather than being linear, the path is often non-linear. You may meet someone who knows someone, or one thing will need to another, and somehow you land somewhere else. (Jay Leno, for example, majored in speech therapy.) Success is "time-released," not a single-dose, magic pill. You work toward it by keeping two concurrent perspectives in mind: zooming out on your big-picture goals and zooming in on the "up close and personal" details of managing yourself on a daily basis. The ability to zoom in and out is a great tool to have on your cell phone, digital camera, or computer.[37] Likewise, while you're in college, you must be able to zoom in on your individual courses and zoom out to your overall degree plan. The same principle definitely holds in your career.

So when the time comes and the interviewer asks you the inevitable question, "Where do you see yourself in five years?" take this advice:

1. Reflect on what you will say beforehand.
2. Figure out what the interviewer is trying to learn about you. Does she expect a full-blown answer, or is she just trying to see how you think.
3. Shorten the time-frame so that you *can* answer: "I'm not really sure how many years it will take, but I do know that I want to join an organization just like this one and work on a highly creative team to learn all I can. Challenges are important to me."

On the other hand, don't:

1. Make up something so far-fetched that even *you* don't believe what you're saying.
2. Identify the exact job you want in the future. ("Honestly? I'd like your job. Are you planning to retire in the next five years?")
3. Feel obliged to answer the question literally, even if you don't really know for sure. Turn the question into one you can answer, communicating what you want the interviewer to know about you.[38]

Although you're being asked to zoom out, instead zoom in on who you are and what you want. It's important to keep both perspectives in mind in your journey toward success.

Think Ahead: Think about how you would answer the question identified in this section if you were applying for a job you could get today. When you graduate in four or five years, would you expect your answer to be different in some ways? Might it be the same in some ways?

CAST ON CAREERS

© Larry Harwood Photograph. Property of Cengage Learning

FOCUS: What was easiest for you as a college student—zooming in or zooming out?

DEREK: I was pretty foggy in general my first semester of college. It took all the energy I could muster just to focus on getting to all my classes and trying to do my best. To be honest, I didn't really think much about the big picture. But I'm starting to do that now, and I think everything I've learned thus far will help me build that future—but it will be a different future than the one I once would have imagined.

FOCUS: What are your career plans?

DEREK: My real passions are photography and graphic design, and I'd like to put them to good use in the field of advertising. Right now I'm looking into getting a paid internship, and then I'd like to work in South America, maybe Brazil. I know Spanish, and I'm learning Portuguese. Someday I'd like I'd like to start up my own creative/production agency.

EXERCISE 12.7

Cover Letter Critique

When you submit a résumé, either in person, through the mail, or online, you should send a well-written cover letter along with it that briefly outlines your qualifications for the job, expresses your interest, and gives the person who reviews your résumé some idea of who you are. Cover letters give you chance to make yourself stand out, especially when the average recruiter is said to spend 30 seconds on each resume. Take a look at the following cover letter from Jared Daniels and critique it. What has he done right, and what has he done wrong?

> 15 September
>
> To Whom It May Concern,
>
> I'd like to apply for your opening at BYB Industries. I have heard a lot about your company and it sounds great. A friend of mine works there, and he said his starting salary was unbelieveable. What exactly do you do at your company besides make electronics? He's told me a few things, but I'm eager to learn more!
>
> As you can see from my résumé, I don't have much experience. But I have just earned a degree in communication from Rocky Mountain State University, and I did pretty well. I want to start my career at a great company like yours.
>
> I hope to hear from you soon.
>
> Warmly,
>
> Jared Daniels

After finding the mistakes Jared made, rewrite this letter to bring to class or submit to your instructor.

▶▶ Your Type Is Showing

What does your psychological type have to do with your college major and career choices? Actually, a great deal. Your personality is the very core of who you are, so you need to know what possible effects it can have on your choices. Which type are you?

- **"I want to decide and move on."** ***EJ Types*** (ESTJ, ESFJ, ENFJ, ENTJ) like to make a decision quickly and get it over with. They may talk over the process of deciding and then jump in with both feet. They are organized students, keep track of credits, and work their way through a degree. If their intended major doesn't work out, they'll jump ship quickly and try another. The wiser decision might be to slow down and learn more about other options.
- **"I want to major in everything!"** ***EP Types*** (ESTP, ESFP, ENFP, ENTP) want to take their time deciding. Closing off options by making a choice provoke anxiety for them, so they'd rather experiment for a while. They may try one major, and then another, and then another until they find a fit—or run out of time or money. They want to plunge into co-curricular activities to experience it all! P students with J parents, however, can be at cross purposes. While the P student experiments, the J parent becomes frustrated. P students can stall out, too. When presented with too many options, they may opt out entirely.
- **"I want to be absolutely sure."** ***IJ Types*** (ISTJ, ISFJ, INFJ, INTJ) research, think, and reflect before coming to any conclusion. They read books, consult websites, and consider all the information carefully because they tend to stick with a decision once they've made it. Being introverts, they may spring their decisions on people (especially F's) who haven't been aware of what they're thinking.
- **"I wish I knew what I was going be when I grow up!"** ***IP Types*** (ISTP, ISFP, INFP, INTP) resist coming to a decision, so much so that they may miss important deadlines. Sometimes they need a nudge from someone, "Hey, did you know that you have to declare a major by your fifth semester?" IP's are wanderers. They'd rather believe that no decision is final so that they remain true to their inner values.[39]

Your Work Style

Each of the four dimensions of your type tells something about your likely work preferences. Here are some examples.

Extraverts (E)	**Introverts (I)**
Like activity and variety	Like to concentrate in quiet
Get impatient with long projects	Can focus on one project for a long time
Like to work with other people	Are content to work alone
Sensors (S)	**Intuitives (N)**
Like order and work steadily	Dislike routine and work in energy bursts
Like to use skills they already have	Like learning new skills
Are good at work that requires precision	Dislike taking time to be precise
Thinkers (T)	**Feelers (F)**
Like to work in an orderly setting	Like to work in a harmonious setting
Can reprimand someone when needed and are firm	Dislike telling people unpleasant things
Are analytically oriented	Are people-oriented and sympathetic with others
Judgers (J)	**Perceivers (P)**
Like to work according to plan	Can adapt to changes
Like to complete things	Like to leave things open to change
May not notice things that should get done	May put off things they don't like doing
Want only what they need to know to get started	Want to know everything about a new project[40]

Your Career Choice

Some studies show that the two middle letters (ST, SF, NT, or NF) of psychological type are relatively good predictors of what career fields people are attracted to. See if you find a career field you're considering in the four quadrants in Figure 12.8, and if what you're considering "fits" your type. But remember that research reports statistical regularities, not individual destinies.

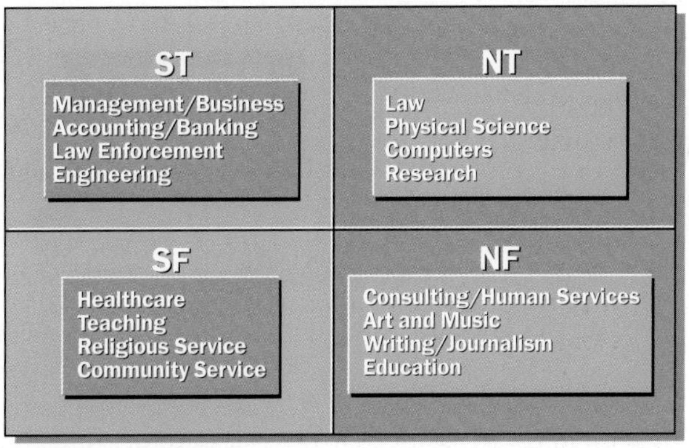

FIGURE 12.8

Career Choice and Psychological Type: What Do the Two Middle Letters Say?

Source: Based on J.K. DiTiberio & A.L. Hammer (1993). Introduction to Type in College. Palo Alto, CA: Consulting Psychologists Press.

My, How You've Grown! Goodbye and Good Luck!

Remember Aunt Ruth (or whatever her name was)? Every time she visited when you were a kid, she remarked about how much you'd grown. Or when you went to visit her, she'd measure you and mark a notch on the wall to compare your height now to the one from last year's visit. She loved watching you grow, and the fact that she noticed made you feel special. There's no doubt about it. In this first term of college, you have grown. You have gained new perspectives, new insights, and new ways of thinking about things. Like Aunt Ruth, others may notice. If those close to you are threatened by these changes, reassure them that your newfound knowledge hasn't made you

"**The self is not something that one finds. It's something one creates.**"

Thomas Szasz, Professor Emeritus in Psychiatry, State University of New York Health Science Center, Syracuse

think less of them. Remember: "You should have education enough so that you won't have to look up to people; and then more education so that you will be wise enough not to look down on people." If they are proud of you and your accomplishments, and have supported you along the way, thank them!

The important thing is to keep learning and never stop. Continuing to learn—whether in college or in life—is what will determine who you are and what you will become. This book, and the course for which you're reading it, have begun that process. Now the rest is up to you!

insight
action

Now What Do You Think?

1. At the beginning of this chapter, Ethan Cole, a frustrated and discouraged college student, faced a challenge. Now after reading this chapter, would you respond differently to any of the questions you answered about the "FOCUS Challenge Case"? Knowing what you know now, how would you advise him? Write a paragraph ending to the story, incorporating your best advice.
2. Plot the college courses you've taken this term on your own Academic Map. If you had to predict the quadrant you'll emphasize (major in), which one would it be? Why?
3. Assess your LEAP skills. Which areas are particular strengths of yours and which seem most challenging?
4. Have you taken a formal career strength or interest test? If not, locate one online, take it, and discuss the results.
5. Describe your academic anatomy. Is this something you've thought about before? What majors and careers might be "anatomically correct" for you?

Very funny video episode at www.cengage.com/success/staley/focus2e! :)

REALITY What did you LEARN?

On a scale of 1 to 10, answer the following questions now that you've completed the chapter.

low 1 2 3 4 5 6 7 8 9 10 high

In hindsight, how much did you already know about this overall subject before reading the chapter?

Can you answer these questions about choosing a major and a career more fully now that you've read the chapter? ________

1. What is an Academic Map?
2. What is a SWOT analysis and how might it help you choose a major and career?
3. How can you try on a career before actually entering it?

How useful might the information in this chapter be to you?

How much do you think this information might affect your success overall? ________

How much energy did you put into reading this chapter? ________

How long did it actually take you to complete this chapter (both the reading and writing tasks)? ________ Hour(s) ________ Minutes

Did you finish reading this chapter? ________

Did you intend to when you started? ________

If you meant to but didn't, what stopped you? ________

Challenge Yourself Online Quiz To find out just how much you've learned, access the College Success CourseMate via www.cengagebrain.com to take the Challenge Yourself Online Quiz.

Take a minute to compare these answers to your answers from the "Readiness Check" at the beginning of this chapter. What gaps exist between the similar questions? How might these gaps between what you thought before starting the chapter and what you now think after completing the chapter affect how you approach your next term of college?

REALITY FOCUS Exit Interview

INFORMATION ABOUT YOU

Although you have not quite completed your first term as a college student, we're interested in your reactions to college so far: how you have spent your time, what challenges you've experienced, and your general views about what college has been like. Please answer thoughtfully.

Name ______________________________

Student Number ______________ **Course/Section** ______________

Instructor ______________________________

Gender ______________ **Age** ______________

NOTE: Questions 1–10 were asked on the Entrance Interview and need not be repeated here. The numbering below begins with number 11 so that the Entrance and Exit Interview results can be compared, if you or your instructor would like to do that. It may be interesting to see how your original expectations of college compare to your actual experience. Note, too, that the Exit Interview contains several added questions at the end about your future education.

YOUR COLLEGE EXPERIENCE

Your Reactions to College

11. Which of the following reasons to finish your college degree seem important to you now? (Check all that apply.)

____ I want to build a better life for myself.
____ I want to be well off financially in the future.
____ My friends are going to college.
____ It is expected of me.
____ I want to continue learning.
____ I am unsure of what I might do instead.
____ I want to build a better life for my family.
____ I need a college education to achieve my dreams.
____ My family is encouraging me to continue.
____ I want to continue playing the sports for which I was recruited.
____ The career I am pursuing requires a degree.
____ other (please explain)

12. How did you find you learned best in college? (Check all that apply.)

____ by looking at charts, maps, graphs
____ by listening to instructors' lectures
____ by reading books
____ by going on field trips
____ by looking at color-coded information
____ by listening to other students during in-class discussions
____ by writing papers
____ by engaging in activities
____ by looking at symbols and graphics
____ by talking about course content with friends or roommates
____ by taking notes
____ by actually doing things

13. **The following sets of opposite descriptive phrases are separated by five blank lines. Put an X on the line between the two that best represents your response, like this:** For me, high school was easy ____:__X__:____:____:____ hard

My first term of college:

challenged me academically ____:____:____:____:____ was easy

was very different from high school ____:____:____:____:____ was a lot like high school

was exciting ____:____:____:____:____ was dull

was interesting ____:____:____:____:____ was uninteresting

motivated me to continue ____:____:____:____:____ discouraged me

was fun ____:____:____:____:____ was boring

helped me feel a part of this campus ____:____:____:____:____ made me feel like an outsider

14. **How many total hours per week did you study outside of class for your college courses?**

____ 0–5 ____ 6–10 ____ 11–15 ____ 16–20 ____ 21–25
____ 26–30 ____ 31–35 ____ 36–40 ____ 40+

15. **Now what do you expect your grade point average to be at the end of your first term of college?**

____ A+ ____ A ____ A− ____ B+ ____ B
____ B− ____ C+ ____ C ____ C− ____ D or lower

Your Strengths, Personality, and Interests

16. **Which of these *strengths* or personal characteristics contributed to your college success? (Check all that apply.)**

____ a. I am good at building relationships.
____ b. I can usually convince others to follow my plan.
____ c. I like to win.
____ d. I work toward future goals.
____ e. I like to be productive and get things done.
____ f. I have a positive outlook on life.
____ g. I'm usually the person who gets things going.
____ h. I enjoy the challenge of learning new things.
____ i. I am focused.
____ j. I can usually look at a problem and figure out a plan of action.
____ k. I work to keep everyone happy.
____ l. I'm a take-charge kind of person.
____ m. I help other people develop their talents and skills.
____ n. I'm a very responsible person.
____ o. I can analyze a situation and see various ways things might work out.
____ p. I usually give tasks my best effort.

17. **How confident are you now in yourself in each of the following areas? (1 = very confident, 5 = not at all confident)**

____ overall academic ability
____ mathematical skills
____ leadership ability
____ reading skills
____ public speaking skills
____ study skills
____ technology skills
____ physical well being
____ writing skills
____ social skills
____ emotional well being
____ teamwork skills

18. **For each of the following pairs of descriptors, which set sounds most like you based on what you've learned about yourself this term? (Please choose between the two options on each line and place a checkmark by your choice.)**

____ Extraverted and outgoing	or	____ Introverted and quiet
____ Detail-oriented and practical	or	____ Big-picture and future-oriented
____ Rational and truthful	or	____ People-oriented and tactful
____ Organized and self-disciplined	or	____ Spontaneous and flexible

19. ***FOCUS* is about 12 different aspects of college life. Which did you find to be most interesting as they applied to your academic success? (Check all that apply.)**

____ Building dreams, setting goals

____ Managing time, energy, and money

____ Developing information literacy, writing, and speaking skills

____ Developing your memory

____ Taking tests

____ Working toward wellness

____ Learning to learn

____ Thinking critically and creatively

____ Engaging, listening, and note-taking in class

____ Reading and studying

____ Building relationships, valuing diversity

____ Choosing a major and career

Your Challenges

20. **Of the 12 aspects of college life identified in the previous question, which were most challenging to apply to yourself in your academic work? (Check all that apply.)**

____ Building dreams, setting goals

____ Managing time, energy, and money

____ Developing information literacy, writing, and speaking skills

____ Developing your memory

____ Taking tests

____ Working toward wellness

____ Learning to learn

____ Thinking critically and creatively

____ Engaging, listening, and note-taking in class

____ Reading and studying

____ Building relationships, valuing diversity

____ Choosing a major and career

21. **Which one of your current classes was most challenging this term and why?**

Which class? (course title *or* department and course number) ____________________

Why? ____

Did you succeed in this course? ____ yes ____ no ____ Somewhat (please explain): ______________________________

22. **Please mark your *top three areas of concern* relating to your first term of college by placing 1, 2, and 3 next to the items you choose (with 1 representing your top concern).**

____ I did not fit in.

____ I was not academically successful.

____ I had difficulty handling the stress.

____ I overextended myself and tried to do too much.

____ I did not reach out for help when I needed it.

____ I did not put in enough time to be academically successful.

____ I am now tempted to drop out.

____ I was not organized enough.

____ I was distracted by other things, like spending too much time online.

____ Other (please explain) ____________________

____ I had difficulty making friends.

____ My grades disappointed my family.

____ I had financial problems.

____ I cut class frequently.

____ I procrastinated on assignments.

____ My professors were hard to communicate with.

____ I was homesick.

____ I was bored in my classes.

____ My job(s) outside of school interfered with my studies.

Your Future

23. **How certain are you now of the following (1 = totally sure, 5 = totally unsure)?**

____ Finishing your degree

____ Choosing your major

____ Deciding on a career

____ Completing your degree at this school

____ Continuing on to work toward an advanced degree after college

You may gain some personal insights if you compare the questions in this "Your College Experience" section of the Exit Interview with the matching questions from the "Your College Expectations" section in the Entrance Interview at the front of the book. Or your instructor may ask you to write about your Insights and intended Actions. Now continue on to these final questions about "Your Next Steps."

24. **What are you most looking forward to after this semester/quarter?**

25. **Did you achieve the outcomes you were hoping to achieve at the beginning of this first semester/quarter? Why or why not?**

YOUR NEXT STEPS

26. **Looking ahead, how satisfied do you expect to be with your decision to attend this school?**

____ very satisfied ____ satisfied

____ somewhat dissatisfied ____ very dissatisfied

____ not sure

27. **Which of the following statements best reflects your educational intentions?**

____ I plan to stay at this school until I complete my degree.

____ I plan to transfer to another institution (please identify which one ____________)

____ I plan to stop out of college for awhile (to work, for example) and then return to this school.

____ I plan to drop out of college.

28. **If you are thinking about transferring to another institution, why would you do so?**

This school does not offer my intended major (which is __________).

This school is too small.

This school is too large.

This school is too expensive.

I don't feel I fit in.

I want to go to a school closer to home.

I want to go to a school further from home.

I want to be closer to my boy/girlfriend.

I want to be closer to my friends.

I will change job locations.

I want to transfer from a two-year to a four-year institution.

I want to transfer from a four-year to a two-year institution.

other (please explain)

29. **What was the biggest difference between what you thought college would be like and what it was actually like for you?**

30. **How have you changed most over this first semester/quarter? In what ways are you different now that you've been in college? How will this introductory semester/quarter affect or change your future college experience?**

Notes

Chapter 1

1. Multi-tasking adversely affects brain's learning, UCLA psychologists report. (2006, July 26). *ScienceDaily.* Available at http://www.sciencedaily.com/releases/2006/07/060726083302.htm.
2. Bregman, P. (2010, May 20). How (and why) to stop multitasking. Available at http://blogs.hbr.org/bregman/2010/05/how-and-why-to-stop-multitaski.html#. *Harvard Business Review.* 'Infomania' worse than marijuana. Available at *BBC News.* http://news.bbc.co.uk/2/hi/uk_news/4471607.stm.
3. Seven, R. (2004, November 28). Life interrupted. *Pacific Northwest,* seattletimes.com. Available at http://seattletimes.nwsource.com/archive/?date=20041128&slug=pacificpinterrupt28; Richtel, M. (2010, June 6). Addicted to technology and paying a price. *The New York Times.* Available at http://www.nytimes.com/2010/06/07/technology/07brain.html?ref=yourbrainoncomputers; Richtel, M. (2010, August 24). Digital devices deprive brain of needed downtime. *The New York Times.* Available at http://www.nytimes.com/2010/08/25/technology/25brain.html?ref=yourbrainoncomputers.
4. Hamilton, J. (2008, October 9). Multitasking teens may be muddling their brains. *NPR: Your Health.* Available at http://www.npr.org/templates/story/story.php?storyId=95524385; Tierney, J. (2009, May 5). Ear plugs to lasers: The science of concentration. *The New York Times.* Available at http://www.nytimes.com/2009/05/05/science/05tier.html?scp=1&sq=%22ear%20plugs%20to%20lasers:%20the%20science%20of%20concentration%22&st=cse; Tugend, A. (2008, October 25). Multitasking can make you lose... um... focus. *The NewYork Times.* Available at http://www.nytimes.com/2008/10/25/business/yourmoney/25shortcuts.html?scp=1&sq=%22multitasking%20can%20make%20you%20lose%22&st=cse; Walls, C. (2006, March 19). genM: The multitasking generation. *Time.* Available at http://www.time.com/time/magazine/article/0,9171,1174696,00.html.
5. Spielberg finally to graduate. (2002, May 15). BBC News. Available at http://news.bbc.co.uk/2/hi/entertainment/1988770.stm.
6. Cranton, P. (1994). *Understanding and promoting transformative learning: A guide for educators of adults.* San Francisco: Jossey-Bass.
7. Davis, J. R. (1993). *Better teaching, more learning.* Phoenix, AZ: Oryx Press.
8. Sei, S. A. (2010, June). Intrinsic and extrinsic motivation: evaluating benefits and drawbacks from college instructors' perspectives. *Journal of Instructional Psychology, 37*(2), 153–160.
9. French, B. F., & Oakes, W. (2003). Measuring academic intrinsic motivation in the first year of college: Reliability and validity evidence for a new instrument. *Journal of the First-YearExperience, 15*(1), 83–102; French, B. F. Executive summary of instruments utilized with systemwide first-year seminars. Policy Center on the First Year of College.; French, B. F., Immerkus, J. C., & Oakes, W. C. (2005). An examination of indicators of engineering students' success and persistence. *Journalof Engineering Education, 94*(4), 419–425.
10. Based on Harrell, K. (2003). *Attitude is everything: 10 life changing steps to turning attitude into action.* New York: HarperBusiness.
11. Dweck, C. S. (2000). *Self-theories: Their role in motivation, personality, and development.* New York: Psychology Press, p. 1.
12. Brooks, D. (2009, May 1). Genius: The modern view. *The New York Times.* Available at http://www.nytimes.com/2009/05/01/opinion/01brooks.html.
13. Berglas, S. & Jones, E. E. (1978). Drug choice as a selfhandicapping strategy in response to noncontingent success. *Journal of Personality and Social Psychology, 36,* 405–417; Jones, E. E. & Berglas, S. (1978). Control of attributions about the self through self-handicapping strategies: The appeal of alcohol and the role of underachievement. *Personality and-Social Psychology Bulletin, 4,* 200–206; Dweck, C. S. (2006). *Mindset: The new psychology of success.* New York: Random House.
14. Dweck, *Mindset,* 7.
15. Ibid., 7.
16. Fischer, M. (2007, March-April). Settling into campus life; Differences by race-ethnicity in college involvement and outcomes. *The Journal of Higher Education,* 78(2), 125–161.
17. Dweck, C. S. (2000). *Self-theories: Their role in motivation, personality, and development.* New York: Psychology Press; Dweck, *Mindset.*
18. Anderson, S. (2009, May 17). In defense of distraction. *New York* (nymag.com). Available at http://nymag.com/news/features/56793/; Gallagher, W. (2009). *Rapt: Attention and the focused life.* New York: Penguin Press; Hamilton, J. (2008, October 2). Think you're multitasking? Think again. *NPR.* Available at http://www.npr.org/templates/story/story.php?storyId=95256794; Tierney, J. (2009, May 4). Ear plugs to lasers: The science of concentration. *The New York Times.* Available at http://www.nytimes.com/2009/05/05/science/05tier.html.
19. McCarron, G. P. & Inkelas, K. K. (2006). The gap between educational aspirations and attainment for first-generation college students and the role of parental involvement. *Journal of College Student Development, 47*(5), 534–549.
20. Martinez, J. A., Sher, K. J., Krull, J. L., Wood, P. K. (2009). Blue-collar scholars? Mediators and moderators of university attrition in first-generation college students. *Journal of College Student Development, 50*(1), 87–103; Collier, P. J., & Morgan, D. L., (2008). Is that paper really due today? *Higher Education, 55*(4), 425–446.
21. Cox, R. D. (2009). *The college fear factor: How students and professors misunderstand one another.* Cambridge, MA: Harvard University Press.
22. http://www.counselingcenter.illinois.edu/?page_id=142.
23. Association of American Colleges and Universities. (2002). *Greater Expectations: A New Vision of Learning as a Nation Goes to College.* Washington, DC:
24. Brooks, D. (2005, September 25). The education gap. *The New York Times,* pp. 4–11; Leonhardt, D. (2005, May 24). The collegedropout boom. *The New York Times.* Available at http://www.nytimes.com/2005/05/24/national/class/EDUCATION-FINAL.html.
25. Hoover, E. (2006, February 24). Study finds school-college "disconnect" in curricula. *The Chronicle of Higher Education, 52*(25), A1.
26. Omara-Otunnu, E. (2006, July 24). Conference examines transition from high school to college. University of Connecticut *Advance.* Available at http://advance.uconn.edu/2006/060724/06072407.htm.
27. Jacobs, L. F., & Hyman, J. S. (2010, 1 September). The five biggest mistakes college students make. *U.S. News & World Report.* Available at http://www.usnews.com/blogs/professors-guide/2010/09/01/the-5-biggest-mistakes-college-students-make.html.
28. Leonhardt, D. (2011, June 25). Even for cashiers, college pays off. The New York Times. Available at http://www.nytimes.com/2011/06/26/sunday-review/26leonhardt.html; http://cew.georgetown.edu/.

29. Data show value of college degree. (2005, April 8). *The Chronicle of Higher Education, 51*(31), A22.
30. Pascarella, E. T., & Terenzini, P. T. (2005). *How college affects students: A third decade of research.* San Francisco: Jossey-Bass, p. 403.

Chapter 2

1. Glenn, D. (2009, May 1). Close the book. Recall. Write it down. *The Chronicle of Higher Education.* Available at http://chronicle.com/article/Close-the-Book-Recall-Write/31819.
2. Chabris, C. F. (2009, April 27). How to wake up slumbering minds. *Wall Street Journal.* Available at http://online.wsj.com/article/SB124079001063757515.html.
3. Hallowell, E. M. (2011). *Shine. Using brain science to get the best from your people.* Boston: Harvard Business Review Press.
4. Brookfield, S. (1995). *Becoming a critically reflective teacher.* San Francisco: Jossey-Bass, p. 62.
5. Cousin, G. (2006), in Meyer, J. H. F., & Land. R. (eds.), *Overcoming barriers to student understanding: Threshold concepts and troublesome knowledge.* London and New York: Routledge. Cousin, G. (2006, December). Section I: Introduction to threshold concepts. *Planet,* 17. Available at http://www.gees.ac.uk/planet/p17/gc.pdf.
6. Leamnson, R. (1999). *Thinking about teaching and learning: Developing habits of learning with first year college and university students.* Sterling, VA: Stylus.
7. Doidge, N. (2007). *The brain that changes itself: Stories of personal triumph from the frontiers of brain science.* NewYork: Viking.
8. *Newsweek* writer with Ian Yarett. (2011, January 10 & 17). Can you build a better brain? *Newsweek,* pp. 40–45.
9. Jozefowicz, C. (2004, May–June). Sweating makes you smart. *Psychology Today.* Available at http://www.psychologytoday.com/articles/200405/sweating-makes-you-smart; Wu, A., Ying, Z., & Gomez-Pinilla, F. (2004). Dietary omega-3 fatty acids normalize BDNF levels, reduce oxidative damage, and counteract learning disability after traumatic brain injury in rats. *Journal of Neurotrauma, 21,* 1457–1467; PT Staff. (1998, March–April).Brain Boosters. *Psychology Today;* Alzheimer's Association. (2004). Think about your future. Maintain your brain today. Available at http://www.alz.org/we_can_help_brain_health_maintain_your_brain.asp.
10. Neergaard, L. (2005, June 20). Brain exercise is key to healthy mind. Available at http://www.msnbc.msn.com/id/8292945/ns/health-alzheimers_disease/t/fight-alzheimers-active-brain/.
11. Springer, M. V., McIntosh, A. R., Winocur, G., & Grady, C. L. (2005). The relation between brain activity during memory tasks and years of education in young and older adults. *Neuropsychology, 19*(2), 181–192.
12. Winne, P. H., & Nesbit, J. C. (2010). The psychology of academic achievement. *Annual Review of Psychology, 61,* 653–78.
13. Csikszentmihalyi, M. (2006). *Flow: The psychology of optimal experience.* New York: Academic Internet Publishers; Csikszentmihalyi, M. (1997). *Creativity: Flow and the psychology of discovery and invention.* New York: Harper Perennial; Gross, R. (1999). *Peak learning.* New York: Tarcher.
14. Caine & Caine, *Making connections;* Jensen, E. (2000). *Different brains, different learners.* San Diego: The Brain Store.
15. Willingham, D. T. (2009, Spring). Why don't students like school? *American Educator,* 4–13. Available at http://www.aft.org/pdfs/americaneducator/spring2009/WILLINGHAM(2).pdf.
16. Brandt, R. (1998). *Powerful learning.* Alexandria, VA: Association for Supervision and Curriculum Development, p. 29.
17. Campbell, B. (1992). Multiple intelligences in action. *Childhood Education, 68*(4), 197–201; Gardner, H., & Hatch, T. (1989). Multiple intelligences go to school: Educational implications of the theory of multiple intelligences. *Educational Researcher, 18*(8), 4–9; Gardner, H. (1983). *Frames of Mind: The Theory of Multiple Intelligences.* New York: Basic Books.Gardner, H. (2008). *5 minds for the future.* Boston: HarvardBusiness Press.
18. Christensen, C. M., Horn, M. B., & Johnson, C. W. (2008). *Disrupting class: How disruptive innovation will change the way the world learns.* New York: McGraw Hill.
19. Armstrong, T. (2000). *MI theory and cognitive skills.* Available at http://www.ascd.org/publications/books/109007/chapters/MI-Theory-and-Cognitive-Skills.aspx.
20. Law of Supply and Demand. Wikipedia Available at http://en.wikipedia.org/wiki/Supply_and_demand.
21. Armstrong, T. (1994). *Multiple intelligences in the classroom.* Alexandria, VA: Association for Supervision and Curriculum-Development; Gardner, *Frames of mind;* Gardner, H. (1993). *Multiple intelligences: The theory in practice.* New York: Basic Books.
22. Checkley, K. (1997). The first seven . . . and the eighth: A conversation with Howard Gardner, *Educational Leadership, 55*(1), 8–13.
23. Davis, B. (2009). *Tools for teaching, second edition.* San Francisco: Jossey-Bass, p. 273.
24. Fleming, N. D. (1995). I'm different; not dumb: Modes of presentation (VARK) in the tertiary classroom. In A. Zeimer (Ed.), *Research and Development in Higher Education, Proceedings of the 1995 Annual Conference of the Higher Education and Research Development Society of Australasia (HERDSA), HERDSA, 18,* 308–313; Fleming, N. D., & Mills, C. (1992). Not another inventory, rather a catalyst for reflection. *To Improve the Academy, 11,* 137–149. Available at http://www.ntlf.com/html/lib/suppmat/74fleming.htm.
25. Fleming, I'm different; not dumb.
26. Neil Fleming, personal communication, November 14, 2006.
27. Fleming, N., & Baume, D. (2006, November). Learning Styles Again: VARKing up the right tree!, *Educational Developments, 7.4,* 4–7.
28. Chabris, C. F. (2009, April 27). How to wake up slumbering minds. *Wall Street Journal.* Available at http://online.wsj.com/article/SB124079001063757515.html. (2008, May 10). Do the math dance: Mathematicians and choreographers use dance to teach mathematics. *Science Daily.* Available at http://www.sciencedaily.com/videos/2008/0503-do_the_math_dance.htm. Harold, H., Rohrer, D., & Bjork, R. (2008). Learning styles: Concepts and evidence. *Psychological Science in the Public Interest, 9*(3), 105–119. Available at http://www.psychologicalscience.org/journals/pspi/PSPI_9_3.pdf.
29. Schwartz, T., Gomes, J., & McCarthy, C. *The way we're working isn't working.* New York: Free Press, pp. 178–179.
30. Rock, D. (2009). *Your brain at work: Strategies for overcoming distraction, regaining focus, and working smarter all day long.* New York: HarperCollins Business.
31. Schwartz, T., Gomes, J., & McCarthy, C., pp. 104–105.
32. Fleming, N. D. (2005). *Teaching and learning styles: VARK strategies.* Christchurch, NZ: Microfilm Limited.
33. Based on DiTiberio, J. K., & Hammer, A. L. (1993). *Introduction to type in college.* Palo Alto, CA: Consulting Psychologists Press.
34. Komarraju, M., Karau, S. J., & Schmeck, R. R. (2009). Role of the big five personality traits in predicting college students' academic motivation and achievement. *Learning and Individual Differences, 19,* 47–52.
35. Check Consulting Psychology Press at http://www.cpp.com/ or the Center for Applications of Psychological Type at http://www.capt.org/for starters.
36. Pelley, J. W. (1997). *SuccessTypes for medical students: A program for improving academic performance.* Lubbock, TX: Texas Tech University, Extended Studies; Pelley, J. W. (2008). Success Types Learning Style Indicator. Available at http://www.ttuhsc.edu/SOM/success/page_LSTI/LSTI.htm.

37. Based on DiTiberio & Hammer, *Introduction to type in college.*

38. Ibid.

39. Winne, P. H., & Nesbit, J. C. (2010). The psychology of academic achievement. *Annual Review of Psychology, 61,* 653–78; Dembo, M. H., & Howard, K. (2007). Advice about the use of learning styles: A major myth in education. *Journal of College Reading and Learning, 37*(2). Available at http://www.swccd.edu/~asc/ED%20100-101%20docs/LS_Myth.pdf.

Chapter 3

1. Hallowell, E. M. (2006). *Crazy busy: Overstretched, overbooked, and about to snap! Strategies for coping in a world gone ADD.* New York: Ballantine Books.

2. Khawand, P. (2009). *The accomplishing more with less workbook.* On the Go Technologies, LLC.

3. Marklein, M, B. (2009, April 13). Facebook use linked to less textbook time. *USATODAY.com.* Available at http://www.usatoday.com/news/education/2009-04-13-facebook-grades_N.htm.

4. Khawand, P. (2009). *The accomplishing more with less workbook.* On the Go Technologies, LLC.

5. Eade, D. M. (1998). Energy and success: Time management. *Clinician News,* July/August. Available at http://finance.dir.groups.yahoo.com/group/HRinIndia/message/11186?l=1.

6. Loehr, J., & Schwartz, T. (2003). *The power of full engagement: Managing energy, not time, is the key to high performance and personal renewal.* New York: Free Press.

7. Bittel, L. R. (1991). *Right on time! The complete guide for time-pressured managers.* New York: McGraw-Hill, p. 16.

8. Bittel, Right on time! p. 16.

9. Loehr, *The power of full engagement;* Mokhtari, K., Reichard, C. A., and Gardner, A. (2009). The impact of Internet and television use on the reading habits and practices of college students. *Journal of Adolescent & Adult Literacy, 52*(7), 609–619.

10. Williams, R. L., Verble, J. S., Price, D. E., & Layne, B. H. (1995). Relationships between time management practices and personality indices and types. *Journal of Psychological Type, 34,* 36–42.

11. Demarest, L. (2001). *Out of time: How the sixteen types manage their time and work.* Gainesville, FL: Center for Applications of Psychological Type.

12. Nathan, R. (2005). *My freshman year: What a professor learned by becoming a student.* Ithaca, NY: Cornell University Press.

13. Fried, J., & Hanson, D. (2010). *Rework.* New York: Crown Business, p. 25–26.

14. Rock, D. (2009). *Your brain at work: Strategies for overcoming distraction, regaining focus, and working smarter all day long.* New York: HarperCollins Business.

15. Based on Covey, S. R., Merrill, A. R., & Merrill, R. R. (1996). *First things first: To live, to love, to learn, to leave a legacy.* New York: Free Press, 37.

16. Fortino, M. (2001). *E-mergency.* Groveland, CA: Omni Publishing.

17. Hobbs, C. R. (1987). *Time power.* New York: Harper & Row, pp. 9–10.

18. Can you really manage time? BusinessTown.com. Available at http://www.businesstown.com/time/time-can.asp.

19. Solomon, L. J., & Rothblum, E. D. (1984). Academic procrastination: Frequency and cognitive-behavioral correlates. *Journal of Counseling Psychology, 31,* 503–509.

20. Hoover, E. (2005, December 9). Tomorrow I love ya! *The Chronicle of Higher Education, 52*(16), A30–32. Available at http://chronicle.com/free/v52/i16/16a03001.htm. Zarick, L. M., & Stonebraker, R. (2009). I'll do it tomorrow: The logic of procrastination. *College Teaching, 57*(4), 211–215.

21. Ferrari, J. R., McCown, W. G., & Johnson, J. (2002). *Procrastination and task avoidance: Theory, research, and treatment.* New York: Springer Publishing.

22. Schouwenburg, H. C., Lay, C. H., Pychyl, T. A., & Ferrari, J. R. (Eds.). (2004). *Counseling the procrastinator in academic settings.* Washington DC: American Psychological Association.

23. Steel, P. (2007). The nature of procrastination. *Psychological-Bulletin, 133*(1), 65–94.

24. Hoover, Tomorrow I love ya!.

25. Felton, S., & Sims, M. (2009). *Organizing your day.* Grand Rapids, MI: Revell.

26. Sandholtz, K., Derr, B., Buckner, K., & Carlson, D. (2002). *Beyond juggling: Rebalancing your busy life.* San Francisco: Berrett-Koehler Publishers.

27. http://en.wikipedia.org/wiki/Juggling_world_records.

28. Adapted from K. Sandholtz, B. Derr, F. Buckner, D. Carlson (2002). *Beyond Juggling: Rebalancing your busy life.* San Francisco: Berrett-Koehler Publishing.

29. Farrell, E. F. (2005, February 4). More students plan to work to help pay for college. *The Chronicle of Higher Education, 50* (22), AI. Available at http://chronicle.com/weekly/v51/i22/22a00101.htm.

30. Norvilitis, J. M., & Santa Maria, P. (2002). Credit card debt on college campuses: Causes, consequences, and solutions. *College Student Journal, 36*(3), 356–364.

31. Credit cards. The Federal Reserve Board. Available at http://www.federalreserve.gov/creditcard/.

32. Muller, K. New credit card laws (2009) and students. *ezine@rticles.com.* Available at http://ezinearticles.com/?New-Credit-Card Laws-(2009)-And-Students&id=2410035; Miranda. (2009,May 21). Credit CARD Act of 2009: How it affects you. *Personaldividends*.com. Available at http://personaldividends.com/money/miranda/credit-card-act-of-2009-how-it-affects-you.

33. Kantrowitz, M. (2007) *FAQs about financial aid.* FinAid: The Smart Student Guide to Financial Aid. Available at http://www.finaid.org/questions/faq.html.

34. See http://www.dcccd.edu/about%20dcccd/News%20and%20Events/News/Pages/SAP05-09-11.aspx; http://www.independent.com/news/2011/feb/05/changes-financial-aid/.

35. Adapted from Sandholtz et al., *Beyond juggling.*

Chapter 4

1. Perry, W. (1970). *Forms of intellectual and ethical development in the college years.* New York: Holt, Rinehart & Winston; Perry, W. G. Jr. (1981). Cognitive and ethical growth: The making of meaning. In A. Chickering & Associates (Eds.), *The Modern American College: Responding to the New Realities of Diverse Students and a Changing Society.* San Francisco: Jossey-Bass; Erickson, B. L., Peters, C. B., & Strommer, D. W. (2006). Teaching first-year college students. San Francisco: Jossey-Bass; Belenky, M. F., Clinchy, B. M., Goldberger, N. R., & Tarule, J. M. (1986). *Women's ways of knowing.* New York: Basic Books; Pascarella, E. T., & Terenzini, P. T. (1991). *How college affects students.* San Francisco: Jossey-Bass; Magolda, M. B. (1988). *The impact of the freshman year on epistemological development: Gender differences.* Paper presented at the meeting of the American Educational Research Association, New Orleans; Magolda, M. B. B. (2006). Intellectual development in the college years. (2006, May/June). *Change, 38*(3), 50–54.

2. Halx, M. C., & Reybold, E. (2005). A pedagogy of force: Faculty perspective of critical thinking capacity in undergraduate students. *The Journal of General Education, 54*(4), 293–315.

3. Walkner, P. & Finney, N. (1999). Skill development and critical thinking in higher education. *Teaching in Higher Education, 4*(4), 531–548.

4. Diestler, S. (2001). *Becoming a critical thinker: A user friendly manual.* Upper Saddle River, NJ: Prentice Hall.

5. Halpern, D. F. (1996). *Thought and knowledge: An introduction to critical thinking.* Mahwah, NJ: Lawrence Erlbaum.

6. Barnett, R. (1997). *Higher education: A critical business.* Buckingham: SRHE and Open University Press.
7. Falcione, P. A. (1998). *Critical thinking: What it is and why it counts.* Millbrae, CA: California Academic Press.
8. Stupnisky, R. H., Renaud, R. D., Daniels, L. M., Haynes, T. L., & Perry, R. P. (2008). The interrelation of first-year college students' critical thinking disposition, perceived academic control, and academic achievement. *Research in Higher Education, 49,* 513–530.
9. Twale, D., & Sanders, C. S. (1999). Impact of non-classroom experiences on critical thinking ability. *NASPA Journal, 36*(2), 133–146.
10. Thomas, C., & Smoot, G. (1994, February/March). Critical thinking: A vital work skill. *Trust for Educational Leadership, 23,* 34–38.
11. Kaplan-Leiserson, E. (2004). Workforce of tomorrow: How can we prepare *all* youth for future work success? *Training & Development, 58*(4), 12–14.
12. Wade, C. (1995). Using writing to develop and assess critical thinking. *Teaching of Psychology, 22*(1), 24–28.
13. Schommer-Aikins, M., & Easter, M. (2009). Ways of knowing and willingness to argue. *The Journal of Psychology, 143*(2), 117–132.
14. Van den Brink-Budgen, R. (2000). *Critical thinking for students.* (3rd ed.). Oxford: How to Books; Ruggiero, V. R. (2001). *Becoming a critical thinker.* (4th ed.). Boston: Houghton Mifflin.
15. Career counselor: Bill Gates or Steve Jobs? *The New York Times. The Opinion Pages.* Available at http://www.nytimes.com/roomfordebate/2011/03/20/career-counselor-bill-gates-or-steve-jobs.
16. Wanted: Liberal arts grads. *Fortune* (1997, May 12), 135(9), 151.
17. Buddy, T. (2003, November 20). *About.com: alcoholism.* Crime and alcohol. Available at http://alcoholism.about.com/cs/costs/a/aa980415.htm.
18. Hamarta, E. (2009). A prediction of self-esteem and life satisfaction by social problem solving. *Social Behavior and Personality, 37*(1), 73–82.
19. Blakey, E., & Spence, S. (1990). Developing metacognition. ERIC Clearinghouse on Information Resources, Syracuse NY. Available at http://www.vtaide.com/png/ERIC/Metacognition.htm.
20. Schwartz, T., Gomes, J., & McCarthy, C. (2010). *The Way We're Working Isn't Working: The Four Forgotten Needs That Energize Great Performance.* New York: Free Press. pp. 128–129.
21. Schwartz, T., Gomes, J., & McCarthy, C. (2010). *The Way We're Working Isn't Working: The Four Forgotten Needs That Energize Great Performance.* New York: Free Press. p. 149.
22. Schwartz, T., Gomes, J., & McCarthy, C. (2010). *The Way We're Working Isn't Working: The Four Forgotten Needs That Energize Great Performance.* New York: Free Press. pp. 147–149.
23. Pink, D. H. (2006). *A whole new mind; Why right-brainers will rule the future.* New York: Riverhead Books.
24. Florida, R. (2002). *The rise of the creative class: And how it's transforming work, leisure, community and everyday life.* New York: Basic Books, xii.
25. Ibid.
26. Sternberg. R. J. (2004). Teaching college students that creativity is a decision. *Guidance & Counseling, 19*(4), 196–200.
27. Livingston, L. (2010). Teaching creativity in higher education. *Arts Education Policy Review, 111,* 59–62.
28. Vance, E. (2007, February 2). College graduates lack key skills, report says. *The Chronicle of Higher Education, 53*(22), A30.
29. Kurtz, J. R. (1998). It's all in your mind! Creative thinking essential in times of change. *Outlook, 66*(3), 5.
30. Rowe, A. J. (2004). *Creative intelligences: discovering the innovative potential in ourselves and others.* Upper Saddle, NJ: Pearson Education, pp. 3–6, 34.
31. Michalko, M. (2001). *Cracking creativity: The secrets of creative genius.* Berkeley, CA: Ten Speed Press.
32. Adapted from Adler, R., & Towne, N. (1987). *Looking out/Looking in.* (5th ed.) New York: Holt, Rinehart, and Winston, pp. 99–100.
33. Douglas, J. H. (1977). The genius of everyman (2): Learning creativity. *Science News, 111*(8), 284–288.
34. Harris, R. (1998). Introduction to creative thinking. *VirtualSalt.* Available at http://www.virtualsalt.com/crebook1.htm.
35. Eby, D. Creativity and flow psychology. *Talent Development Resources.* Available at http://talentdevelop.com/articles/Page8.html.

Chapter 5

1. Grant, D. M., Malloy, A. D., & Murphy, M. C. (2009). A comparison of student perceptions of their computer skills to their actual abilities. *Journal of Information Technology Education, 8.* Available at http://jite.org/documents/Vol8/JITEv8p141-160 Grant428.pdf.
2. Johnson, L., Smith, R., Willis, H., Levine, A., and Haywood, K., (2011). *The 2011 Horizon Report.* Austin, Texas: The New Media Consortium. Available at http://net.educause.edu/ir/library/pdf/HR2011.pdf.
3. Smith, S. D., & Caruso, J. B. (2010). ECAR study of undergraduate students and information technology, 2010. *Educause.* Available at http://www.educause.edu/Resources/ECARStudyofUndergraduateStuden/217333.
4. Ibid.
5. See http://en.wikipedia.org/wiki/Wikipedia.
6. Read, B. (2009, July 20). Students may not be as software savvy as they think, study says. *The Wired Campus: The Chronicle of Higher Education.* Available at http://chronicle.com/blogs/wiredcampus/students-may-not-be-as-software-savvy-as-they-think-study-says/7276. Grant, D. M., Malloy, A. D., & Murphy, M. C. (2009). A comparison of student perceptions of their computer skills to their actual abilities. *Journal of Information Technology Education, 8.* Available at http://jite.org/documents/Vol8/JITEv8p141-160Grant428.pdf.
7. *Internet World Stats.* Available at http://www.internetworldstats.com/stats.htm.
8. Bartlett, T. (2009, March 20). Cheating goes global as essay mills multiply. *Chronicle of Higher Education, 55*(28), p. A-1.
9. Billout, G. (2008, July/August). Is Google making us stupid? *The Atlantic.com.* Available at http://www.theatlantic.com/magazine/archive/2008/07/is-google-making-us-stupid/6868/.
10. Wood, G. (2004, 9 April). Academic original sin: Plagiarism, the Internet, and librarians. *The Journal of Academic Librarianship, 30*(3), 237–242. Carr, N. (2008, July/August). Is Google making us stupid? *The Atlantic.* Available at http://www.theatlantic.com/magazine/archive/2008/07/is-google-making-us-stupid/6868/. Nelson, F. (2009, April 29). Podcast: Is Twitter making us stupider? *Full Nelson: Information Week.* Available at http://www.informationweek.com/blog/229206696; Carr, N. (2010). *The Shallows: What the Internet is doing to our brains.* New York: W. W. Norton & Company.
11. (2010, June). Social insecurity. *Consumer Reports: Best and worst computers,* pp. 24–27.
12. Patchin, J. W., & Hinduja, S. (2011). A student's guide to personal publishing. Available at http://www.uwec.edu/patchinj/cyberbullying/Students_Guide_to_Personal_Publishing.pdf.
13. Holson, L. M. (2010, May 8). Tell-all generation learns to keep things offline. *The New York Times.* Available at http://www.nytimes.com/2010/05/09/fashion/09privacy.html.
14. (2010, June). Social insecurity. *Consumer Reports: Best and worst computers,* pp. 24–27.
15. (2011, March 26). What they're saying about sexting. *The New York Times.* Available at http://www.nytimes.com/2011/03/27/us/27sextingqanda.html?_r=1&ref=us. Hoffman, J. (2011, March 26). A girl's nude photo, and altered lives.

The New York Times. Available at http://www.nytimes.com/2011/03/27/us/27sexting.html?pagewanted=all.

16. See http://www.commonsensemedia.org/advice-for-parents/cyberbullying-tips; http://www.uwec.edu/patchinj/cyberbullying/Students_Guide_to_Personal_Publishing.pdf; http://www.cyberbullying.us/Bullying_and_Cyberbullying_Laws.pdf.
17. Fischman, J. (2008, December 30). Distance education becomes a major part of course catalogues. *The Chronicle of Higher Education.* Available at http://chronicle.com/article/Distance-Education-Becomes-a/42173/; Jaschik, S. (2008, April 7). Distance ed continues rapid growth at community colleges. *Inside Higher Ed.* Available at http://www.insidehighered.com/news/2008/04/07/distance.
18. Benner, J. (2005, 15 November). Facebook more than a way of life. *The BG News.*
19. Greene, L. (2006, March 8). You might be a Facebook stalker if. . . . *Winonan;* Hollister, L. (2005, October 5). Facebook addiction is needless, yet compelling. *The Volante Online.*
20. (2009, April 12). Study says Facebook can impact studies. *UPI.com.* Available at http://www.upi.com/Entertainment_News/2009/04/12/Study-says-Facebook-can-impact-studies/UPI-84181239555532/.
21. Turkle, S. (2011). *Alone together: Why we expect more from technology and less from each other.* New York: Basic Books; Turkel, S. (2011, March 30). Productivity, multitasking, and the death of the phone. *HBR Ideacast.* Available at http://blogs.hbr.org/ideacast/2011/03/productivity-multitasking-and.html.
22. Greenfield, D. N. (1999). *Virtual addiction.* Oakland, CA: New Harbinger Publications; Yair, E., & Hamburger, A. (2005). *The social net.* Oxford: Oxford University Press; Young, K. S. (1998). *Caught in the net.* New York: John Wiley.
23. Fischman, J. (2008, December 30). Distance education becomes a major part of course catalogues. *The Chronicle of Higher Education.* Available at http://chronicle.com/article/Distance-Education-Becomes-a/42173/.
24. Goode, J. (2010, September/October). Mind the gap: The digital dimension of college access. *Journal of Higher Education, 81*(5), 583–618.
25. Parry, M. (2009, June 19). The Online "Attrition Puzzle": New Study Revisits Dropout Debate. *Wired Campus: The Chronicle of Higher Education.* Available at http://chronicle.com/blogs/wiredcampus/the-online-attrition-puzzle-new-study-revisits-dropout-debate/7228.
26. Wighting, M. J., Liu, J., & Rovai, A. P. (2008). Distinguishing sense of community and motivation characteristics between online and traditional college students. *The Quarterly Review of Distance Education, 9*(3), 285–295.
27. Bollet, R. M., & Fallon, S. (2002). Personalizing e-learning. *Educational Media International, 39*(1), 39–45; Thompson, G. (2001–2002). Online student induction package.
28. What is research? In Leedy, P. (1997). *Practical Research: Planning and Design,* Sixth Edition, Upper Saddle River, NJ: Merrill Prentice Hall.
29. Christina Martinez, Reference Librarian, University of Colorado, Colorado Springs.
30. Fitzgerald, M. A. (2004). Making the leap from high school to college. *Knowledge Quest, 32*(4), 19–24; Ehrmann, S. (2004). Beyond computer literacy: Implications of technology for the content of a college education. *Liberal Education.* Available at http://www.aacu.org/liberaleducation/le-fa04/le-fa04feature1.cfm; Thacker, P. (2006, November 15). Are college students techno idiots? *Inside Higher Ed.* Available at http://www.insidehighered.com/news/2006/11/15/infolit.
31. Samson, S. (2010, May). Information literacy learning outcomes and student success. *Journal of Academic Librarianship, 36*(3), 202–10.
32. Ableson, H. Ledeen, K., & Lewis, H. (2008). *Blown to bits: your life, liberty, and happiness after the digital explosion.* Boston, MA: Pearson Education, Inc.
33. Thacker, P. (2006, November 15). Are college students techno idiots? *Inside Higher Ed.* Available at http://www.insidehighered.com/news/2006/11/15/infolit. Smith, S. D., & Caruso, J. B. (2010). ECAR study of undergraduate students and information technology, 2010. *Educause.* Available at http://www.educause.edu/Resources/ECARStudyofUndergraduateStuden/217333.
34. Young, J. (2006, June 12). Wikipedia founder discourages academic use of his creation. *The Chronicle of Higher Education, Wired Campus.* Available at http://chronicle.com/blogs/wiredcampus/wikipedia-founder-discourages-academic-use-of-his-creation/2305.
35. Jaschik, S. (2007, January 26). A stand against Wikipedia. *Inside Higher Education.* Available at http://www.insidehighered.com/news/2007/01/26/wiki.
36. Thacker, P. (2006, November 15). Are college students techno idiots? *Inside Higher Ed.* Available at http://www.insidehighered.com/news/2006/11/15/infolit. Smith, S. D., & Caruso, J. B. (2010). ECAR study of undergraduate students and information technology, 2010. *Educause.* Available at http://www.educause.edu/Resources/ECARStudyofUndergraduateStuden/217333.
37. http://compnetworking.about.com/od/dns_domainnamesystem/a/domain-name-tld.htm; http://lists.econsultant.com/top-10-domain-name-extensions.html; http://searchenginewatch.com/article/2048976/Major-Search-Engines-and-Directories.
38. Sullivan, D. (2008, March 27). Major search engines and directories. SearchEngineWatch.com. Available at http://searchenginewatch.com/article/2048976/Major-Search-Engines-and-Directories. (2008). Recommended search engines. *UC Berkeley Library. Regents of the University of California.* Available at http://www.lib.berkeley.edu/TeachingLib/Guides/Internet/SearchEngines.html; http://www.thesearchenginelist.com/.
39. McCarroll, C. (2001). To learn to think in college, write—a lot. *Christian Science Monitor, 93*(177), 20.
40. De Vos, I. (1988, October). Getting started: How expert writers do it. *Training & Development Journal,* 18–19.
41. Bean, J. C. (1996). *Engaging ideas: The professor's guide to integrating writing, critical thinking and active learning in the classroom.* San Francisco: Jossey-Bass.
42. Jensen, G., & DiTiberio, J. K. (1984). Personality and individual writing processes. *College Composition and Communication, 35*(3), 285–300; DiTiberio, J. K., & Hammer, A. L. (1993). *Introduction to type in college.* Palo Alto, CA: Consulting Psychologists Press; Sampson, E. (2003). *Creative business presentations.* London: Kogan Page.
43. Portions of this section are based on Staley, C., & Staley, R. (1992). *Communicating in business and the professions: The inside word.* Belmont, CA: Wadsworth.
44. Portions based on Staley & Staley, *Communicating in business and the professions.*
45. Smith, T. E., & Frymier, A. B. (2006). Get "real": Does practicing speeches before an audience improve performance? *Communication Quarterly, 54*(1), 111–125.
46. Engleberg, I. N. (1994). *The principles of public presentation.* New York: HarperCollins; Daley, K., & Daley-Caravella, L. (2004). *Talk your way to the top.* New York: McGraw-Hill.
47. Cassagrande, J. (2010). *It was the* best *of sentences, it was the* worst *of sentences.* Berkeley, CA: Ten Speed Press.
48. Selberg, A. (2011, March 19). Teaching to the text message. *The New York Times. Opinion Pages.* Available at http://www.nytimes.com/2011/03/20/opinion/20selsberg.html?_r=2&emc=tnt&tntemail1=y.
49. Gabriel, T. (2010, August 1). Plagiarism lines blur for students in the digital age. *The New York Times.* Available at http://www.nytimes.com/2010/08/02/education/02cheat.html?_r=2./.

Chapter 6

1. Based on http://www-sop.inria.fr/acacia/personnel/Fabien.Gandon/lecture/uk1999/history/.
2. Burchfield, C. M., & Sappington, J. (2000). Compliance with required reading assignments. *Teaching of Psychology, 27*(1), 58–60; Hobson, E. H. (2004). *Getting students to read: Fourteen tips.* IDEA Paper No. 40, Manhattan, KS: Kansas State University, Center for Faculty Evaluation and Development; Maleki, R. B., & Heerman, C. E. (1992). *Improving student reading.* IDEA Paper No. 26, Manhattan, KS: Kansas State University, Center for Faculty Evaluation and Development. Most Idea Center papers available at http://www.theideacenter.org/.
3. Gump, S. E. (2005). The cost of cutting class: Attendance as a predictor of student success. *College Teaching, 53*(1), 21–25.
4. Marburger, D. R. (2001). Absenteeism and undergraduate exam performance. *Journal of Economic Education, 32,* 99–109.
5. Perkins, K. K., & Wieman, C. E. (2005). The surprising impact of seat location on student performance. *The Physics Teacher, 43*(1), 30–33. Available at http://scitation.aip.org/journals/doc/PHTEAH-ft/vol_43/iss_1/30_1.html?bypassSSO=1.
6. Everding, G. (2009, May 28). Cell phone ringtones can pose major distraction, impair recall. *Washington University in St. Louis Record.* Available at http://news.wustl.edu/news/Pages/14225.aspx.
7. "Infomania" worse than marijuana. (2005, April 22). *BBC News.* Available at http://news.bbc.co.uk/2/hi/uk_news/4471607.stm; Bugeja, M. J. (2007, January 26). Distractions in the wireless classroom. *The Chronicle of Higher Education, 53*(21), C1. Available at http://chronicle.com/article/Distractions-inthe-Wireless/46664/; Young, J. R. (2006, June 2). The fight for classroom attention: Professor vs. laptop. *The Chronicle of Higher Education, 52*(39), A27. Available at http://chronicle.com/article/The-Fight-for-Classroom/19431; *2008 Campus Computing Project Executive Summary.* Available at http://www.campuscomputing.net/sites/www.campuscomputing.net/files/CC2008-Executive%20Summary_3.pdf; Cole, D. (2007, April 7). Laptops vs. learning. *Washington Post.* Available at http://www.washingtonpost.com/wp-dyn/content/article/2007/04/06/AR2007040601544.html.
8. Armbruster, B. B. (2000). Taking notes from lectures. In R. F. Flippo & D. C. Caverly (Eds.), *Handbook of college reading and study strategy research* (pp. 175–199). Mahwah, NJ: Erlbaum.
9. Staley, C. C., & Staley, R. S. (1992). *Communicating in business and the professions: The inside word.* Belmont, CA: Wadsworth, p. 223.
10. Adapted from Mackie, V., & Bair, B. Tips for improving listening skills; *International student and scholar services.* University of Illinois at Urbana-Champaign.
11. Hughes, C. A., & Suritsky, S. K. (1993). Notetaking skills and strategies for students with learning disabilities. *Preventing School Failure, 38*(1).
12. Allen, D. (2001). *Getting things done: The art of stress-free productivity.* New York: Penguin Books, p. 21.
13. Selby, J. (2004). *Quiet your mind.* Makawao, Maui, HI: Inner Ocean Publishing.
14. Staley & Staley, *Communicating in business and the professions,* pp. 229–236.
15. Kiewra, K. A., Mayer, R. E., Christensen, M., Kim, S., & Risch, N. (1991). Effects of repetition on recall and note-taking: Strategies for learning from lectures. *Journal of Educational Psychology, 83,* 120–123. Cheng, J. (2009, February 25). Study: Class podcasts can lead to better grades. *arstechnica.* Available at http://arstechnica.com/web/news/2009/02/study-listening-to-podcasts-better-than-going-to-lectures.ars.
16. Brock, R. (2005, October 28). Lectures on the go. *The Chronicle of Higher Education, 52*(10), A39–42; French, D. P. (2006). iPods: Informative or invasive? *Journal of College Science Teaching, 36*(1), 58–59; Hallett, V. (2005, October 17). Teaching with tech. *U.S. News & World Report, 139*(14), 54–58; *The Horizon Report.* (2006). Stanford, CA: The New Media Consortium.
17. DiTiberio, J. K., & Hammer, A. L. (1993). *Introduction to type in college.* Palo Alto, CA: Consulting Psychologists Press.
18. Van Blerkom, M. L., & Van Blerkom, D. L. (2004). Self-monitoring strategies used by developmental and non-developmental college students. *Journal of College Reading and Learning, 34*(2), 45–60.
19. Bloom, B. S. (Ed.). (1956). *A taxonomy of educational objectives (cognitive domain).* New York: Longman; http://www.odu.edu/educ/roverbau/Bloom/blooms_taxonomy.htm.
20. Peverly, S. T., Ramaswamy, V., Brown, C., Sumowski, J., Alidoost, M., & Garner, J. (2007). What predicts skill in lecture note taking? *Journal of Educational Psychology, 99*(1), 167–180.
21. Palmatier, R. A., & Bennett, J. M. (1974). Note-taking habits of college students. *Journal of Reading, 18,* 215–218; Dunkel, P., & Davy, S. (1989). The heuristic of lecture notetaking: Perceptions of American and international students regarding the value and practices of notetaking. *English for Specific Purposes, 8,* 33–50.
22. Armbruster, *Handbook of college reading and study strategy research.*
23. Van Meter, P., Yokoi, L., & Pressley, M. (1994). College students' theory of note-taking derived from their perceptions of note-taking. *Journal of Educational Psychology, 86,* 323–338.
24. Read, B. (2007, February 1). Lecture-hall laptops hurt students' grades, study says. *The Chronicle of Higher Education.* Available at http://chronicle.com/blogPost/Lecture-Hall-Laptops-Hurt/2812/; Fischman, J. (2009, March 16). Students stop surfing after being shown how in-class laptop use lowers test scores. *The Wired Campus: Chronicle of Higher Education.* Available at http://chronicle.com/blogPost/Students-Stop-Surfing-After/4576.
25. Davis, M., & Hult, R. (1997). Effects of writing summaries as a generative learning activity during note taking. *Teaching of Psychology 24*(1), 47–49; Boyle, J. R., & Weishaar, M. (2001). The effects of strategic notetaking on the recall and comprehension of lecture information for high school students with learning disabilities. *Learning Disabilities Research & Practice 16*(3); Kiewra, K. A. (2002). How classroom teachers can help students learn and teach them how to learn. *Theory into Practice 41*(2), 71–81; Aiken, E. G., Thomas, G. S., & Shennum, W. A. (1975). Memory for a lecture: Effects of notes, lecture rate and informational density. *Journal of Educational Psychology, 67,* 439–444; Hughes, C. A., & Suritsky, S. K. (1994). Notetaking skills of university students with and without learning disabilities. *Journal of Learning Disabilities, 27,* 20–24.
26. Bonner, J. M., & Holliday, W. G. (2006). How college science students engage in note-taking strategies. *Journal of Research in Science Teaching, 43*(8), 786–818.
27. Pauk, W. (2000). *How to study in college.* Boston: Houghton Mifflin.
28. Montis, K. K. (2007). Guided notes: An interactive method of success in secondary and college mathematics classrooms. *Focus on learning problems in mathematics, 29*(3), 55–68.
29. Pardini, E. A., Domizi, D. P., Forbes, D. A., & Pettis, G. V. (2005). Parallel note-taking: A strategy for effective use of Webnotes. *Journal of College Reading and Learning, 35*(2), 38–55.
30. Glenn, D. (2009, May 1). Close the book. Recall. Write it down. *The Chronicle of Higher Education.* Available at http://chronicle.com/article/Close-the-book-Recall-Write/31819.
31. De Simone, C. (2007). Applications of concept mapping. *College Teaching, 55*(1), 33–36.
32. Kiewra, How classroom teachers can help students learn and teach them how to learn.
33. Porte, L. K. (2001). Cut and paste 101. *Teaching Exceptional Children, 34*(2), 14–20.
34. Kiewra, K. A., DuBois, N. F., Christian, D., & McShane, A. (1988). Providing study notes: Comparison of three types of notes for review. *Journal of Educational Psychology, 80,* 595–597; Larkin, J. H., & Simon, J. A. (1987). Why a diagram is

(sometimes) worth ten thousand words. *Cognitive Science, 11,* 65–99; Robinson, D. H., Katayama, A. D., DuBois, N. F., & DeVaney, T. (1998). Interactive effects of graphic organizers and delayed review in concept acquisition. *The Journal of Experimental Education, 67,* 17–31; Winn, W. (1991). Learning from maps and diagrams. *Educational Psychology Review, 3,* 211–247.

35. Ancowitz, N. (2010, June 24). How to increase your self-promotion intelligence, or SPQ. *Psychology Today.* Available at http://www.psychologytoday.com/blog/self-promotion-introverts/201006/how-increase-your-self-promotion-intelligence-or-spq.
36. Tal-Or, N. (2010). Bragging in the right context: Impressions formed of self-promoters who create a context for their boasts. *Social Influence, 5*(1), 23–39.
37. Hanson, M. (2009, June 17). Is bragging good for your career? *LiveCareer.* Available at http://www.livecareer.com/news/Career/Is-Bragging-Good-for-Your-Career-_$$00858.aspx.
38. Kiewra, How classroom teachers can help students learn and teach them how to learn.
39. Craik, F. I. M., & Watkins, M. J. (1973). The role of rehearsal in short-term memory. *Journal of Verbal Learning and Verbal Behavior, 12,* 599–607.

Chapter 7

1. http://sci.gallaudet.edu/Physics12/Syllabus04.html.
2. Gordon, B. (1995). *Memory: Remembering and forgetting in everyday life.* New York: Mastermedia Limited.
3. Bolla, K. I., Lindgren, K. N., Bonaccorsy, C., & Bleecker, M. L. (1991). Memory complaints in older adults: Fact or fiction? *Archives of Neurology, 48,* 61–64.
4. Higbee, K. L. (2004). What aspects of their memories do college students most want to improve? *College Student Journal, 38*(4), 552–556.
5. Higbee, K. L. (1988). *Your memory: How it works and how to improve it* (2nd ed.). New York: Prentice Hall.
6. Ibid.
7. Nairine, J. S. (2006). *Psychology: The adaptive mind.* Belmont, CA: Wadsworth/Thomson Learning.
8. Associated Press. (2007, March 20). Studies focus on wandering thoughts. *CBCnews.* Available at http://www.cbc.ca/technology/story/2007/03/20/tech-thoughts.html.
9. Shenk, D. (1998). *Data smog.* New York: HarperOne.
10. Klingberg, T., Fernell, E., Olesen, P. J., Johnson, M., Gustafsson, P., Dahlström, K., Gillberg, C. G., Forssberg, H., Westerberg, H. (2005). Computerized training of working memory in children with ADHD—a randomized, controlled trial. *Journal of the American Academy of Child and Adolescent Psychiatry,* 44(2):177–86. Abstract available at http://www.ncbi.nlm.nih.gov/pubmed/15689731?dopt=Abstract.
11. Adams, S. (2011, April 9). How to get a real education. *The Wall Street Journal.* Available at http://online.wsj.com/article_email/SB10001424052748704101604576247143383496656-lMyQjAxMTAxMDEwMTExNDEyWj.html.
12. Coon, D. (2006). *Psychology: A modular approach to mind and behavior.* Belmont, CA: Wadsworth/Thomson Learning; Nairine, *Psychology.*
13. Nairine, *Psychology.*
14. Miller, G. A. (1956). The magical number seven plus or minus two: Some limits on our capacity for processing information. *Psychological Review, 63,* 81–97.
15. The neurological scratchpad: What is working memory? (2004, July 7). *Brain Connection.com.* Available at http://brainconnection.positscience.com/topics/?main=fa/working-memory2; Kotbagi, H. (1997). *Human memory.* Available at http://www.cc.gatech.edu/classes/cs6751_97_winter/Topics/human-cap/memory.html; Clark, D. *Memory: Learning and memory.* Available at http://www.nwlink.com/~donclark/hrd/learning/memory.html; Kerry, S. (1999–2002). Memory and retention time. *Education Reform.net.* Available at http://www.education-reform.net/memory.htm; Goodhead, J. (1999). The difference between short-term and long-term memory [On-line].
16. See http://www.usamemoriad.com/; http://en.wikipedia.org/wiki/World_Memory_Championships; http://www.worldmemorychampionship.com/.
17. Rozakis, L. (2003). *Test-taking strategies and study skills for the utterly confused.* New York: McGraw Hill; Meyers, J.N. (2000). *The secrets of taking any test.* New York: Learning Express; Ehren, B. J. *Mnemonic devices.* Available at http://itc.gsu.edu/academymodules/a304/support/xpages/a304b0_20600.html; Lloyd, G. (1998–2004). *Study skills: Memorize with mnemonics.* Available at http://www.back2college.com/memorize.htm.
18. Willingham, D. T. (2004). Practice makes perfect—but only if you practice beyond the point of perfection. *American Educator.* Available at http://www.aft.org/newspubs/periodicals/ae/spring2004/willingham.cfm.
19. Krueger, W. C. F. (1929). The effect of overlearning on retention. *Journal of Experimental Psychology, 12,* 71–78.
20. Tigner, R. B. (1999). Putting memory research to good use: Hints from cognitive psychology. *College Teaching, 47*(4), 149–152.
21. Murdock, B. B., Jr. (1960). The distinctiveness of stimuli. *Psychological Reports, 67,* 16–31; Neath, I. (1993). Distinctiveness and serial position effects in recognition. *Memory & Cognition, 21,* 689–698.
22. Cahill, L. (2003). Similar neural mechanisms for emotion induced memory impairment and enhancement. *Proceedings of the National Academy of Sciences, 100*(23), 13123–13124. Available at http://www.pnas.org/cgi/content/full/100/23/13123.
23. Dingfelder, S. F. (2005, September). Feelings' sway over memory. *Monitor on Psychology, 26*(8). Available at APA Online at http://www.apa.org/monitor/sep05/feelings.html.
24. Noice, H., & Noice, T. (2006). What studies of actors and acting can tell us about memory and cognitive functioning. *Current Directions in Psychological Science, 15*(1), 14–18.
25. Caine, M. (1990). *Acting in film: An actor's take on movie-making.* New York: Applause Theatre Books.
26. Noice, T., Noice, H., & Kennedy, C. (2000). The contribution of movement on the recall of complex material. *Memory, 8,* 353–363.
27. Glenberg, A. M., & Kaschak, M. P. (2002). Grounding language in action. *Psychonomic Bulletin & Review, 9,* 558–565.
28. Noice & Noice, What studies of actors and acting can tell us about memory and cognitive functioning.
29. Higbee, *Your memory.*
30. Ibid.
31. Weiss, P. (2011, March 10). How to remember anything: Lessons from a memory champion. *Shine.* Available at http://shine.yahoo.com/event/vitality/how-to-remember-anything-lessons-from-a-memory-champion-2463626; Horowitz, A. (2011, March 11). How to memorize everything. *The New York Times.* Available at http://www.nytimes.com/2011/03/13/books/review/book-review-moonwalking-with-einstein-by-joshua-foer.html?pagewanted=all.
32. Higbee, *Your memory.*
33. Bean, J. (1996). *Engaging ideas.* San Francisco: Jossey-Bass.
34. Tigner, Putting memory research to good use.
35. Higbee, *Your memory.*
36. Chan, J. C. K., McDermott, K. B., & Roediger, H. L. III. (2007). Retrieval-induced facilitation: Initially nontested material can benefit from prior testing of related material. *Journal of Experimental Psychology, 135*(4), 552–571; Karpicke, J. D., Butler, A. C., & Roediger, H. L. (2009). Metacognitive strategies in student learning: Do students practise retrieval when they study on their own? *Memory, 17*(4), 470–471. Abstract available at http://www.ncbi.nlm.nih.gov/pubmed/19358016.

37. Caine, R. N., & Caine, G. (1997). *Education on the edge of possibility.* Alexandria, VA: Association for Supervision and Curriculum Development.

38. Jenkins, E. (2003, June). Somewhere, the bard weeps. *Columbia Journalism Review.* Available at http://www.cjr.org/resources/lc/wherefore.php.

39. Berk, R. A. (2002). *Humor as an instructional defibrillator.* Sterling, VA: Stylus; Berk, R. A. (2003). *Professors are from Mars®, students are from Snickers®.* Sterling, VA: Stylus.

40. Offer, D., Kaiz, M., Howard, K. I., & Bennett, E. S. (2000). The altering of reporting experiences. *Journal of the American Academy of Child and Adolescent Psychiatry, 39,* 735–42.

41. Sleep strengthens your memory. (2007, April 25). *ScienceDaily.* Available at http://www.sciencedaily.com/releases/2007/04/070424180953.htm; Underwood, A. (2009, June 11). Can memory loss be prevented? *The New York Times.* Available at http://newoldage.blogs.nytimes.com/2009/06/11/can-dementia-be-prevented/; Low-carb diets can affect dieters' cognition skills. (2008, December 15). *ScienceDaily.* Available at http://www.sciencedaily.com/releases/2008/12/081211112014.htm.

42. Schacter, D. L. (2001). *The seven sins of memory: How the mind forgets and remembers.* Boston: Houghton Mifflin; Murray, B. (2003, October). The seven sins of memory. *Monitor on Psychology.* Available at APA Online at http://www.apa.org/monitor/oct03/sins.aspx.

43. Gibson, E. (2008, December 18). A boom in memory-enhancing drugs? *BusinessWeek.* Available at http://www.businessweek.com/magazine/content/08_52/b4114084625148.htm; DeNoon, D. J. (2008, December 11). Brain-boosting drugs FAQ: What you must know. *WedMD.* Available at http://www.webmd.com/brain/news/20081211/brain-boosting-faq-what-you-must-know; (2007, September 4). Memory-enhancement drugs show promise but face growing scrutiny. *ScienceDaily.* Available at http://www.sciencedaily.com/releases/2007/09/070903101826.htm.

44. Guterman, L. (2004, June 25). Gray matters. *The Chronicle of Higher Education, 50*(42), A22.

45. Ibid.

46. "Memory pill" for the forgetful. (2005, May 12). *BBC News.* Available at http://news.bbc.co.uk/2/hi/health/4539551.stm; Guterman, L. (2004, June 25). Gray matters. *The Chronicle of Higher Education, 50*(42), A22.

47. http://www.personalitypathways.com/type_inventory.html.

48. White, A. M., Signer, M. L., Kraus, C. L., & Swartzwelder, H. S. (2004). Experiential aspects of alcohol-induced blackouts among college students. *American Journal of Drug Alcohol Abuse, 30*(1), 205–224.

49. Crego, A., Holguín, S. R., Parada, M., Mota, N., Corral, M., & Cadaveira, F. (2009). Binge drinking affects attentional and visual working memory processing in young university students. *Alcoholism: Clinical and Experimental Research, 33*(11), 1870–1879.

50. Assefi, S. L., & Garry, M. (2003). Absolut® memory distortions: Alcohol placebos influence the misinformation effect. *Psychological Science, 14*(1), 77–80.

51. Gouzoulis-Mayfrank, E., Daumann, J., Tuchtenhagen, F., Pelz, S., Becker, S., Kunert, H-J., Fimm, B., & Sass, H. (2000). Impaired cognitive performance in drug free users of recreational ecstasy. *Journal of Neurology, Neurosurgery, and Psychiatry, 68,* 719–725. Available at http://jnnp.bmj.com/cgi/content/abstract/68/6/719?ijkey_3f8bc1cc460f69242c7f2f360d1ec74a41611d00&keytype2_tf_ipsecsha.

52. Study links ecstasy, long-term memory loss. (2004, January 15). *CNN.com.* Available at http://www.cnn.com/2004/HEALTH/01/15/ecstasy.memory.reut/index.html.

53. High-fat diets hammer memory, more than a waistline worry. (2004, October 25). *Society for Neuroscience.* Available at http://www.sfn.org/index.cfm?pagename=news_102504c.

54. Tagg, J. (2004, March–April). Why learn? What we may really be teaching students. *About Campus,* 2–10; Marton, F., & Säljö, R. On qualitative differences in learning: I-Outcome and process. (1976). *British Journal of Educational Psychology, 46,* 4–11.

Chapter 8

1. Rogers, M. (2007, March–April). Is reading obsolete? *The Futurist,* 26–27; Waters, L. (2007, February 9). Time for reading. *The Chronicle of Higher Education, 53*(23), 1B6.

2. Postman, N. (1985). *Amusing ourselves to death.* New York: Penguin Books; Stephens, M. (1991, September 22). The death of reading. *Los Angeles Times Magazine.* Available at http://www.nyu.edu/classes/stephens/Death%20of%20Reading%20page.htm.

3. Dillon, S. (2005, December 16). Literacy falls for graduates from college, testing finds. *The New York Times.* Available at http://www.nytimes.com/2005/12/16/education/16literacy.html; (2006). A first look at the literacy of America's adults in the 21st century. *National Center for Education Statistics.* Available at http://nces.ed.gov/NAAL/PDF/2006470.PDF; (2006, January 20). Reports on college literacy levels sobering. *MSNBC.* Available at http://www.msnbc.msn.com/id/10928755.

4. Mokhtari, K., Reichard, C. A. , & Gardner, A. (2009). The impact of Internet and television use on the reading habits and practices of college students. *Journal of Adolescent & Adult Literacy, 52*(7), 609–619; Clemmitt, M. (2008, Feburary 22). Reading crisis: Do today's youth read less than past generations? *CQ Researcher, 18*(8).

5. Stephens, The death of reading.

6. Caverly, D. C., Nicholson, S. A., & Radcliffe, R. (2004). The effectiveness of strategic reading instruction for college developmental readers. *Journal of College Reading and Learning, 35*(1), 25–49; Simpson, M. L., & Nist, S. L. (1997). Perspectives on learning history: A case study. *Journal of Literacy Research, 29*(3), 363–395.

7. Caverly, Nicholson, & Radcliffe, The effectiveness of strategic reading instruction for college developmental readers; Burrell, K. I., Tao, L., Simpson, M. L., & Mendez-Berrueta, H. (1997). How do we know what we are preparing students for? A reality check of one university's academic literacy demands. *Research & Teaching in Developmental Education, 13,* 15–70.

8. Bean, J. C. (1996). *Engaging ideas: The professor's guide to integrating writing, critical thinking, and active learning in the classroom.* San Francisco: Jossey-Bass; Wood, N.V. (1997). College reading instruction as reflected by current reading textbooks. *Journal of College Reading and Learning, 27*(3).79–95.

9. Saumell, L., Hughes, M. T., & Lopate, K. (1999). Underprepared college students' perceptions of reading: Are their perceptions different than other students? *Journal of College Reading and Learning, 29*(2), 123–125.

10. Buzan, T. (1983). *Use both sides of your brain.* New York: E. P. Dutton.

11. Ibid.

12. Sternberg, R. J. (1987). Teaching intelligence: The application of cognitive psychology to the improvement of intellectual skills. In J. B. Baron & R. J. Sternberg (Eds.), *Teaching thinking skills: Theory and Practice.* New York: Freeman. pp. 182–218.

13. Al-Jarf, R. S. (2002). Effect of online learning on struggling ESL college writers. San Antonio, TX: National Educational Computing Conference. Available at http://faculty.ksu.edu.sa/aljarf/My%20Press%20Room/al-jarf%20-%20NECC%20paper.pdf.

14. Based on Bean, *Engaging ideas.*

15. See http://www.americaslibrary.gov/jb/gilded/jb_gilded_whitman_2.html.

16. Hirsch, Jr., E. D., Kett, J. F., & Trefi l, J. (2002). *The new dictionary of cultural literacy: What every American needs to know.* New York: Houghton Mifflin.
17. http://dictionary.reference.com/browse/grit.
18. Halvorson, H. G., (2011, February, 25). Nine things successful people do differently. *Harvard Business Review Conversation.* Available at http://blogs.hbr.org/cs/2011/02/nine_things_successful_people.html#.
19. Wise, J. (2010, May 23). Extreme fear: How to thrive under stress. *Psychology Today.* Available at http://www.psychologytoday.com/blog/extreme-fear/201005/how-thrive-under-stress.
20. Based partly on Williams, S. (2005). Guiding students through the jungle of research-based literature. *College Teaching, 53*(4), 137–139.
21. (2010, May 20). Annual happiness index finds one-third of Americans are very happy. *Harris Interactive.* Available at http://www.harrisinteractive.com/NewsRoom/HarrisPolls/tabid/447/ctl/ReadCustom%20Default/mid/1508/ArticleId/394/Default.aspx.
22. Winne, P. H., & Nesbit, J. C. (2010). The psychology of academic achievement. *Annual Review of Psychology, 61*, 653–678. Available at http://psyc525final.wikispaces.com/file/view/The+Psychology+of+Academic+Achievement.pdf.
23. Soldner, L. B. (1997). Self-assessment and the reflective reader. *Journal of College Reading and Learning, 28*(1), 5–11. Jaschik, S. (2011, January 31). Can students learn to learn? *Inside Higher Ed.* Available at http://www.insidehighered.com/news/2011/01/31/colleges_try_to_use_metacognition_to_improve_student_learning.
24. Van Blerkom, M. L., & Van Blerkom, D. L. (2004). Self-monitoring strategies used by developmental and non-developmental college students. *Journal of College Reading and Learning, 34*(2), 45–60.
25. Melchenbaum, D., Burland, S., Gruson, L., & Cameron, R. (1985). Metacognitive assessment. In S. Yussen (Ed.), *The growth of reflection in children.* Orlando, FL: Academic Press. p. 5.
26. Hall, C. W. (2001). A measure of executive processing skills in college students. *College Student Journal, 35*(3), 442–450; Taylor, S. (1999). Better learning through better thinking: Developing students' metacognitive abilities. *Journal of College Reading and Learning, 30*(1), 34–45.
27. Learning to learn: Metacognition. Available at http://www.studygs.net/metacognition.htm.
28. Simpson, M. L. (1994/1995). Talk throughs: A strategy for encouraging active learning across the content areas. *Journal of Reading, 38*(4), 296–304.
29. Fast facts: Births and natality. *Centers for Disease Control and Prevention.* Available at http://www.cdc.gov/nchs/fastats/births.htm.
30. National Institutes of Health. Available at http://www.nhlbi.nih.gov/health/dci/Diseases/hs/hs_whatis.html.
31. Science on a Sphere. *NOAA.* Available at http://sos.noaa.gov/datasets/Atmosphere/air_traffic.html.
32. Elias, M. (2004, April 5). Frequent TV watching shortens kids'attention spans. *USA Today.* Available at http://www.usatoday.com/news/health/2004-04-05-tv-kids-attention-usat_x.htm.
33. Carey, B. (2010, September 8). Forget what you know about good study habits. *The New York Times.* Available at http://www.nytimes.com/2010/09/07/health/views/07mind.html.
34. Bol, L., Warkentin, R. W., Nunnery, J. A., & O'Connell, A. A. (1999). College students' study activities and their relationship to study context, reference course, and achievement. *College Student Journal, 33*(4).608–622.
35. When students study makes a difference too. (2005, November). *Recruitment & Retention.*
36. Friedrich, R., Peterson, M., & Koster, A. (2011). The rise of Generation C. *strategy+business magazine.* Booz & Company Inc. Reprint 11110. New York.
37. (2011). The future of the book. *Vimeo.* Available at http://vimeo.com/15142335.
38. Trainin, G., & Swanson, H. L. (2005). Cognition, metacognition, and achievement of college students with learning disabilities. *Learning Disability Quarterly, 28,* 261–272.
39. Jan, T. (2011, April 24). Tangled in an endless web of distractions. *Boston.com.* Available at http://articles.boston.com/2011-04-24/news/29469460_1_mit-social-networking-laptops.
40. Vergoth, K. (1995, July–August). Why you miss your deadlines. . . *Psychology Today.* Available at http://www.psychologytoday.com/articles/199507/why-you-miss-your-deadlines.
41. Meyers, D. (2001). *Psychology* (6th ed.). New York: Worth Publishers.
42. Huber, M. T., & Hutchings, P. (2004). *Integrative learning: Mapping the terrain.* Washington, DC: The Association of American Colleges and Universities. Available at http://www.carnegiefoundation.org/sites/default/files/publications/elibrary_pdf_636.pdf.
43. Moore, B. (2004). Interview by Betty Ann Boswer, *News Hour with Jim Lehrer*, PBS, September 9. In Huber, M. T., & Hutchings, P. (2004). *Integrative learning: Mapping the terrain.* Washington, DC: The Association of American Colleges and Universities. Available at http://www.carnegiefoundation.org/sites/default/files/publications/elibrary_pdf_636.pdf.
44. Youatt, J., & Wilcox, K. A. (2008). Intentional and integrated learning in a new cognitive age: A signature pedagogy for undergraduate education in the twenty-first century. *AAC&U Peer Review.* Available at http://www.aacu.org/peerreview/pr-fa08/pr-fa08_CognitiveAge.cfm.
45. Jensen, G. H. (1986). Learning styles. In J. A. Provost & S. Anchors (Eds.). *Application of the Myers-Briggs type indicator in higher education.* Palo Alto, CA: Consulting Psychologists Press; DiTiberio, J. K., & Hammer, A. L. (1993). *Introduction to type in college.* Palo Alto, CA: Consulting Psychologists Press.

Chapter 9

1. Petress, K. (2004). What do college examinations accomplish? *College Student Journal, 38*(4), 521–522.
2. Thalheimer, W. (2002). *E-learning's unique—and seemingly unknown—capability.* Somerville, MA: Work-Learning Research.
3. Coren, S. (1996). *Sleep thieves.* New York: Free Press; Cox, K. (2004, October 14). The lights are on, but nobody's home. *The Oxford Student.*
4. Grant, K. B. (2003, September 4). Popping pills and taking tests. *The Ithacan Online.* Available at http://www.ithaca.edu/rhp/ithacan/articles/0309/04/news/2popping_pill.htm.
5. Based on Green, K. (2003). *Survey of 300 A+ students.* Berkeley, CA: Crème de la Crème Press.
6. Frederickson, C. G. (1999). Multiple-choice answer changing: A type connection? *Journal of Psychological Type, 51,* 40–46.
7. Jensen, G. H. (1987). Learning styles. In J. A. Provost & S. Anchors (Eds.), *Applications of the Myers-Briggs type indicator in higher education.* p. 201. Palo Alto, CA: Consulting Psychologists Press.
8. Brinthaupt, T. M., & Shin, C. M. (2001). The relationship of academic cramming to flow experience. *College Student Journal, 35*(3), 457–472.
9. Tigner, R. B. (1999). Putting memory research to good use: Hints from cognitive psychology. *Journal of College Teaching, 47*(4), 149–152.
10. Small, G. (2002). *The memory bible.* New York: Hyperion.
11. Test anxiety. *University of Oregon Counseling & Testing Services.* Available at http://counseling.uoregon.edu/dnn/SelfhelpResources/StressandAnxiety/TestAnxiety/tabid/337/Default.aspx.

12. Tozoglu, D., Tozoglu, M. D., Gurses, A., & Dogar, C. (2004). The students' perceptions: Essay versus multiple-choice type exams. *Journal of Baltic Science Education, 2*(6), 52–59.

13. Schutz, P. A., & Davis, H. A. (2000). Emotions and self-regulation during test taking. *Educational Psychologist, 35*(4), 243–256.

14. Coren, *Sleep thieves.*

15. Perina, K. (2002). Sum of all fears. *Psychology Today.* Available at http://www.psychologytoday.com/articles/200211/sum-all-fears.

16. Perry, A. B. (2004). Decreasing math anxiety in college students. *College Student Journal, 38*(2), 321–324.

17. Perry, Decreasing math anxiety in college students.

18. Jonides, J., Lacey, S. C., & Nee, D. E. (2005). Processes of working memory in mind and brain. *Current Directions in Psychological Science, 14*(1), 2–5.

19. Ashcraft, M. H., & Kirk, E. P. (2001). The relationships among working memory, math anxiety, and performance. *Journal of Experimental Psychology: General. 130*(2), 224–237.

20. Beilock, S. L., Kulp, C. A., Holt, L. E., & Carr, T. H. (2004). More on the fragility of performance: Choking under pressure in mathematical problem solving. *Journal of Experimental Psychology: General, 133*(4), 584–600.

21. Mundell, E. (2005, March 9). Test pressure toughest on smartest. *HealthDay.com.* Available at http://domains.e-healthsource.com/?p=news1&id=524405.

22. Newman, E. (1996). *No more test anxiety.* Los Angeles, CA: Learning Skills Publications.

23. Arem, C. (2003). *Conquering math anxiety,* second edition. Belmont, CA: Brooks/Cole.

24. Kennedy, D. V., & Doepke, K. J. (1999). Multicomponent treatment of a test anxious college student. *Education & Treatment of Children, 22*(2), 203–217.

25. Firmin, M., Hwang, C., Copella, M., & Clark, S. (2004). Learned helplessness: The effect of failure on test-taking. *Education, 124*(4), 688–693.

26. Heidenberg, A. J., & Layne, B. H. (2000). Answer changing: A conditional argument. *College Student Journal, 34*(3), 440–451.

27. Sorokin, E. (2002, April 15). *Chewing gum expands the mind. BNET: The CBS Interactive Business Network.* Available at http://findarticles.com/p/articles/mi_m1571/is_13_18/ai_84804845/; Young, E. (2002, 13 March). *Chewing gum improves memory. NewScientist.com.* Available at http://www.newscientist.com/article/dn2039-chewing-gum-improves-memory.html; Carter, H. (2002, March 14). By gum, here's something for the memory to start chewing on. *The Guardian.* Available at http://www.guardian.co.uk/uk/2002/mar/14/research.medicalscience; Hayes, E. (2002, March 22). Here is something to chew on, by gum. *Orlando Sentinel.* Available at http://articles.orlandosentinel.com/2002-03-22/lifestyle/0203210377_1_chewing-gum-bubble-gum-teeth.

28. Placek, K. (2007, December 4). Study: Chewing gum can contribute to better test scores. *The Temple News Online.*

29. Ibid.

30. See http://news.bbc.co.uk/2/hi/uk_news/scotland/glasgow_and_west/4755297.stm.

31. Preparing for tests and exams. (2006). *York University.* Available at http://www.yorku.ca/cdc/lsp/skillbuilding/exams.html#Multiple.

32. Patterson, K., Grenny, J., McMillan, R. Switzler, Al, & Covey, S. R. (2002). *Crucial conversations: Tools for talking when stakes are high.* New York: McGraw-Hill; *Crucial conversations explained in two minutes.* Available at http://www.youtube.com/watch?v=qHRF8q3ltRw.

33. Patterson, K., Grenny, J., McMillan, R. & Switzler, A. (2009). University of California *ANR Leadership Development.* Available at http://groups.ucanr.org/ANR_Leadership/Book_Reviews/Crucial_Conversations-_Tools_for_Talking_When_the_Stakes_Are_Hig.htm.

34. Patterson, K., Grenny, J., McMillan, R. & Switzler, A. (1998–2009). Crucial conversations: Tools for talking when stakes are high. *LeadershopNow.* Available at http://www.leadershipnow.com/leadershop/0194-6excerpt.html.

35. Taking exams. *Brockport High School.* Available at http://www.frontiernet.net/~jlkeefer/takgexm.html. Adapted from Penn State University; On taking exams. *University of New Mexico.* Available at http://www.unm.edu/~quadl/college_learning/taking_exams.html; Lawrence, J. (2006). Tips for taking examinations. *Lawrence Lab Homepage.* Available at http://cobamide2.bio.pitt.edu/testtips.htm; The multiple choice exam. (2003). *Counselling Services, University of Victoria.* Available at http://coun.uvic.ca/learning/exams/multiple-choice.html; General strategies for taking essay tests. *GWired.* Available at http://gwired.gwu.edu/counsel/asc/index.gw/Site_ID/46/Page_ID/14565/; Test taking tips: Guidelines for answering multiple-choice questions. *Arizona State University.* Available at http://neuer101.asu.edu/additionaltestingtips.htm; Landsberger, J. (2007). True/false tests. *Study Guides and Strategies.* Available at http://www.studygs.net/tsttak2.htm; Landsberger, J. (2007). Multiple choice tests. *Study Guides and Strategies.* Available at http://www.studygs.net/tsttak3.htm; Landsberger, J. (2007). The essay exam. *Study Guides and Strategies.* Available at http://www.studygs.net/tsttak4.htm; Landsberger, J. (2007). Short answer tests. *Study Guides and Strategies.* Available at http://www.studygs.net/tsttak5.htm; Landsberger, J. (2007). Open book tests. *Study Guides and Strategies.* Available at http://www.studygs.net/tsttak7.htm; Rogers, T., & Kline, D. Test-taking advice: Especially for the multiple-choice challenged. *University of Calgary.* Available at http://members.shaw.ca/daprof/testtaking_advice.htm; Rozakis, L. (2003). *Test-taking strategies and study skills for the utterly confused.* New York: McGraw-Hill; Meyers, J. N. (2000). *The secrets of taking any test.* New York: Learning Express; Robinson, A. (1993). *What smart students know.* New York: Crown Trade Paperbacks.

36. Snyder, T. (2009, January 21). Cheating goes digital. *Edutopia.* Available at http://www.edutopia.org/technology-student-cheating-prevention.

37. *Plagiarism.org.* Available at http://www.plagiarism.org/facts.html; A cheating crisis in America's schools. (2007, 17 April). ABC News. Available at http://abcnews.go.com/Primetime/print?id=132376.

38. Gostick, A., & Telford, D. (2003). *The integrity advantage.* Salt Lake City, UT: Gibbs Smith Publishers.

39. Caught cheating. (2004, April 29). *Primetime Live,* ABC News Transcript. Interview of college students by Charles Gibson; Zernike, K. (2002, November 2). With student cheating on the rise, more colleges are turning to honor codes. *The New York Times,* p. Q10, column 1, National Desk; Warren, R. (2003, October 20). Cheating: An easy way to cheat yourself. Available at http://uwf.edu/voyager/archives/102903/page02.pdf; Thomson, S. C. (2004, February 13). Amid wave of cheating, universities push "academic integrity." *Knight Ridder/Tribune News Service.* Available at http://www.highbeam.com/doc/1G1-113209265.html; Heyboer, K. (2003, August 23). Nearly half of college students say Internet plagiarism isn't cheating. *The Star-Ledger Newark, New Jersey;* Kleiner, C., & Lord, M. (1999). The cheating game. *U.S. News & World Report.* Available at http://www.usnews.com/usnews/culture/articles/991122/archive_002427.htm.

40. Rogers & Kline, Test-taking advice; Rozakis, *Test-taking strategies and study skills for the utterly confused*; Meyers, *The secrets of taking any test.*

Chapter 10

1. Tinto, V. (1975). Dropout from higher education: A theoretical synthesis of recent research. *Review of Educational Research, 45,* 89–125; Tinto, V. (1993). *Leaving college: Rethinking the causes and cures of student attrition* (2nd ed.). Chicago: University of Chicago Press.

2. Paul, E. L., & Brier, S. (2001). Friendsickness in the transition to college: Precollege predictors and college adjustment correlates. *Journal of Counseling & Development, 79*(1), 77–89.
3. Pressman, S. D., Cohen, S., Miller, G. E., Barkin, A., Rabin, B. S., & Treanor, J. J. (2005). Loneliness, social network size, and immune response to influenza vaccination in college freshmen. *Health Psychology, 24*(3), 297–306; Hitti, M. (2005, May 2). Researchers say lonely college freshmen show weaker immune response. *WebMD Medical News.* Available at http://www.webmd.com/balance/news/20050502/loneliness-may-hurt-your-health.
4. Clifton, D. O., & Anderson, E. (2001–2002). *Strengths-quest: Discover and develop your strengths in academics, career, and beyond.* Washington, DC: The Gallup Organization.
5. Goleman, D. (1994). Emotional intelligence, quoted in *Funderstanding.* Available at http://www.funderstanding.com/v2/tag/emotional-intelligence-2/; Goleman, D. (1995). *Emotional intelligence.* New York: Bantam; Lawry, J. D. (2008, July–August). Are you emotionally intelligent? *About Campus,* 27–29.
6. Some situation topics suggested at Hay Group EI Quiz. Available at http://www.haygroup.com/leadershipandtalentondemand//Demos/EI_Quiz.aspx.
7. Gardner, H. (1993). *Multiple intelligences: The theory in practice.* New York: Basic Books; Checkley, K. (1997). The first seven . . . and the eighth: A conversation with Howard Gardner. Expanded Academic ASAP (online database). Original Publication: *Education,* 116.
8. Goleman, D. (2002, June 16). Could you be a leader? *Parade Magazine,* pp. 4–6.
9. Snarey, J. R., & Vaillant, G. E. (1985). How lower- and working-class youth become middle-class adults: The association between ego defense mechanisms and upward social mobility. *Child Development, 56*(4), 899–910.
10. Feist, G. J., & Barron, F. (1996, June). *Emotional intelligence and academic intelligence in career and life success.* Paper presented at the Annual Convention of the American Psychological Society, San Francisco, CA.
11. Emmerling, R. J., & Goleman, D. (2003). *Emotional intelligence issues and common misunderstandings.* The Consortium for Research on Emotional Intelligence in Organizations. Available at http://www.eiconsortium.org/pdf/EI_Issues_And_Common_Misunderstandings.pdf.
12. Grewal, D., & Salovey, P. (2005, July–August). Feeling smart: The science of emotional intelligence. *American Scientist, 93*(4), 330. Available at http://www.americanscientist.org/issues/feature/feeling-smart-the-science-of-emotional-intelligence.
13. Isen, A. M, Daubman, K. A., & Nowicki, G. P. (1987). Positive affect facilitates creative problem solving. *Journal of Personality and Social Psychology, 52*(6), 1122–1131; Ciarrochi, J., & Scott, G. (2006). The link between emotional competence and well-being: a longitudinal study. *British Journal of Guidance & Counselling, 34*(2), 231–243.
14. Parker, J. D. A., Duffy, J. M., Wood, L. M., Bond, B. J., & Hogan, M. J. (2005). Academic achievement and emotional intelligence: Predicting the successful transition from high school to university. *Journal of the First Year Experience & Students in Transition 17*(1), 67–78; Schutte, N. S., & Malouff, J. (2002). Incorporating emotional skills content in a college transition course enhances student retention. *Journal of the First Year Experience & Students in Transition 14*(1), 7–21; Di Fabio, A., & Palazzeschi, L. (2009). An in-depth look at scholastic success: Fluid intelligence, personality traits or emotional intelligence? *Personality and Individual Differences 46,* 581–585.
15. EQ-i: HEd, Multi-Health Systems, Inc. North Tonawanda, NY. Available at http://ei.mhs.com/. Used with permission.
16. Turning lemons into lemonade: Hardiness helps people turn stressful circumstances into opportunities. (2003, December 22). *Psychology Matters.* Available at APA Online at http://www.apa.org/research/action/lemon.aspx; Marano, H. E. (2003). The art of resilience. *Psychology Today.* Available at http://www.psychologytoday.com/articles/200305/the-art-resilience; Fischman, J. (1987). Getting tough: Can people learn to have disease-resistant personalities? *Psychology Today, 21,* 26–28; Friborg, O., Barlaug, D., Martinussen, M., Rosenvinge, J. H., & Hjemdal, O. (2005). Resilience in relation to personality and intelligence. *International Journal of Methods in Psychiatric Research, 14*(1), 29–42; Schulman, P. (1995). Explanatory style and achievement in school and work. In G. M. Buchanan & M. E. P. Seligman (Eds.), *Explanatory style* (pp. 159–171). Hillsdale, NJ: Lawrence Erlbaum; American Psychological Association. (1997). Learned optimism yields health benefits. *Discovery Health.* Available at http://health.discovery.com/centers/mental/articles/optimism/optimism.html.
17. Maher, K. (2004) Emotional intelligence is a factor in promotions. *CollegeJournal from the Wall Street Journal.*
18. Cherniss, C. (2000). *Emotional Intelligence: What it is and why it matters.* Paper presented at the Annual Meeting of the Society for Industrial and Organizational Psychology, New Orleans, LA. Available at http://www.eiconsortium.org/reports/what_is_emotional_intelligence.html.
19. Goleman, Could you be a leader? p. 4.
20. Boyatzis, R. E., Cowan, S. S., & Kolb, D. A. (1995). *Innovations in professional education: Steps on a journey from teaching to learning.* San Francisco: Jossey-Bass.
21. Davidson, R. J., Kabat-Zinn, J., Schumacher, J., Rosenkranz, M., Muller, D., Santorelli, S. F., Urbanowski, F., Harrington, A., Bonus, K., & Sheridan, J. F. (2003). Alterations in brain and immune function produced by mindfulness meditation. *Psychosomatic Medicine, 65,* 564–570. Available at http://dunntastic.com/sources/Davidson%202003%20-%20Alterations%20in%20brain%20and%20immune%20function%20produced%20by%20mindfulness%20meditation.pdf; Hughes, D. (2004). Interview with Daniel Goleman. Share Guide. Available at http://www.shareguide.com/Goleman.html.
22. Saxbe, D. (2004, November/December). The socially savvy. *Psychology Today.* Available at http://www.psychologytoday.com/articles/200501/the-socially-savvy.
23. Rath, T., & Clifton, D. O. (2004). *How full is your bucket?* New York: Gallup Press.
24. Bar-On, R. (2006). The Bar-On model of emotional-social intelligence (ESI). *Psicothema, 18* (Suppl.), 13–25. The Consortium for Research on Emotional Intelligence in Organizations. Available at http://www.eiconsortium.org/reprints/bar-on_model_of_emotional-social_intelligence.htm.
25. Knox, D. H. (1970). Conceptions of love at three developmental levels. *The Family Coordinator, 19*(2), 151–157; Fisher, *Why we love;* Cramer, D. (2004). Satisfaction with a romantic relationship, depression, support and conflict. *Psychology and Psychotherapy: Theory, Research and Practice, 77*(4), 449–461.
26. Fisher, H. (2004). *Why we love.* New York: Henry Holt.
27. Ibid.
28. Beach, S. R. H., & Tesser, A. (1988). Love in marriage; a cognitive account. In R. J. Sternberg & M. L. Barnes (Eds.), *The Psychology of Love.* 330–355 New Haven, CT: Yale University Press; Hatfield, E., & Walster, G. W. (1978). *A new look at love.* Lanham, MD: University Press of America.
29. Parker-Popel, T. (2009, April 20). What are friends for? A longer life. *The New York Times.* Available at http://www.nytimes.com/2009/04/21/health/21well.html; Ybarra, O., Burnstein, E., Winkielman, P., Keller, M. C., Manis, M. Chan, E., & Rodriguez, J. (2008). Mental exercising through simple socializing: Social interaction promotes general cognitive functioning. *Personality and Social Psychology Bulletin, 34,* 248–259.
30. Knox, D., Schacht, C., & Zusman, M. E. (1999, March). Love relationships among college students. *College Student Journal, 33*(1), 149–154. Available at http://www.findarticles.com/p/articles/mi_m0FCR/is_1_33/ai_62894068.
31. Schwartz, P. (2003, May–June). Love is not all you need. *Psychology Today.* Available at http://www.psychologytoday.com/articles/200302/love-is-not-all-you-need.

32. Bach, G. R., & Goldberg, H. (1974). *Creative aggression: The art of assertive living.* Garden City, NJ: Doubleday; Bach, G. R, & Wyden, P. (1972). *The intimate enemy: How to fight fair in love and marriage.* New York: Avon; Bach, G. R., Deutsch, R. M., (1985). *Stop! You're driving me crazy.* New York: Berkley Publishing Group; Tucker-Ladd, C. E. (1996–2006); *Driving each other crazy.* Psychological self-help. Available at http://psychologicalselfhelp.org/Chapter9/chap9_90.html.
33. Fisher, *Why we love.*
34. Fisher, R., & Brown, S. (1988). *Getting together: Building a relationship that gets to yes.* Boston: Houghton Mifflin, p. xi.
35. Hocker, J. L., & Wilmot, W. W. (2010). *Interpersonal conflict* (7th ed.). New York: McGraw-Hill.
36. Based in part on Marano, H. (2002). Relationship rules. *Psychology Today.* Available at http://www.psychologytoday.com/articles/200410/relationship-rules.
37. Dakss, B. (2006, March 3). Study: Bad relationships bad for heart. *CBS News.* Available at http://www.cbsnews.com/stories/2006/03/03/earlyshow/contributors/emilysenay/main1364889.shtml; (2005, December 5) Unhappy marriage: bad for your health. *WebMD.* Available at http://www.webmd.com/sex-relationships/news/20051205/unhappy-marriage-bad-for-your-health. Based on Keicolt-Glaser, J. (2005). *Archives of general psychiatry,* 62, 1377–1384.
38. Dusselier, L., Dunn, B., Wang, Y., Shelley, M. C., & Whalen, D. F. (2005). Personal, health, academic, and environmental predictors of stress for residence hall students. *Journal of American College Health, 54*(1), 15–24; Hardigg, V., & Nobile, C. (1995). Living with a stranger. *U.S. News & World Report, 119*(12), 90–91. Available at http://www.usnews.com/usnews/edu/articles/950925/archive_032964.htm; Nankin, J. (2005). Rules for roomies. *Careers & Colleges, 25*(4), 29.
39. Rytting, M., Ware, R., & Hopkins, P. (1992). Type and the ideal mate: Romantic attraction or type bias? *Journal of Psychological Type, 24,* 3–12; Sherman, R. G. (1981). Typology and problems in intimate relationships. *Journal of Psychological Type, 4,* 1–11.
40. Thomas, K. (1977). Conflict and conflict management. In M. D. Dunnette (Ed.), *Handbook of industrial and organizational psychology,* 889–935 Chicago: Rand McNally; Kilmann, R., & Thomas, K. W. (1975). Interpersonal conflict-handling behavior as reflections of Jungian personality dimensions. *Psychological Reports, 37,* 971–980; Rahim, M., & Magner, N. R. (1995). Confirmatory factor analysis of the styles of handling interpersonal conflict: First-order factor model and its invariance across groups. *Journal of Applied Psychology, 80,* 122–132; Wilmot, W. W., & Hocker, J. L. (2001). *Interpersonal* conflict (6th ed.). New York: McGraw-Hill. Kilmann, R. H., and K. W. Thomas. (1977). Developing a Forced-Choice Measure of Conflict-Handling Behavior: The MODE Instrument," *Educational and psychological measurement, 37*(2), 309–325.
41. Miller, G. R., & Steinberg, M. (1975). *Between people: A new analysis of interpersonal communication.* Chicago: Science Research Associates.
42. Bregman, P. (2010, July 21). How to avoid (and quickly recover from) misunderstandings. *Harvard Business Review Blog.* Available at http://blogs.hbr.org/bregman/2010/07/how-to-avoid-and-quickly-recov.html.
43. Ibid.
44. Bregman, P. (2011, January 3). The best way to use the last five minutes of the day. *Harvard Business Review Blog.* Available at http://blogs.hbr.org/bregman/2011/01/the-best-way-to-use-the-last-f.html.
45. Fulbeck, K. (2010). *Mixed: Portraits of multiracial kids.* San Francisco: Chronicle Books.
46. Bucher, R. D. (2004). *Diversity consciousness: Opening our minds to people, cultures, and opportunities* (2nd ed.). Upper Saddle River, NJ: Pearson Education.
47. *Race, the power of an illusion. PBS.* California Newsreel. Available at http://www.pbs.org/race/000_general/000_00-home.htm.
48. Based on "Sorting People" activity at http://www.pbs.org/race/002_SortingPeople/002_00-home.htm.
49. Wyer, K. (2007). Today's college freshmen have family income 60% above national average, UCLA survey reveals. *UCLA News.* Available at http://www.heri.ucla.edu/PDFs/PR_TRENDS_40YR.pdf.
50. Humphrey, D., & Davenport, A. (2004, Summer/Fall). What really matters in college: How students view and value liberal education. *Liberal Education.* Excerpt: Diversity and civic engagement outcomes ranked among least important. Available at http://www.diversityweb.org/Digest/vol9no1/humphreys.cfm.
51. Laird, T. F. (2005). College students' experiences with diversity and their effects on academic self-confidence, social agency, and disposition toward critical thinking. *Research in Higher Education, 46*(4), 365–387.
52. Lewin, T. (2009, July 7). Interracial roommates can reduce prejudice. *The New York Times.* Available at http://www.nytimes.com/2009/07/08/us/08roommate.html?adxnnl=1&adxnnlx=1312161887-Q1CKZUXsZ081TbxZkjR5w.
53. Moore, D. G. (2003, November 14). Toward a single definition of college. *The Chronicle of Higher Education, 50*(12), B7; Diversity defines new generation of college students. (2009, June 18). *The Chronicle of Higher Education.* Available at https://www.phoenix.edu/colleges_divisions/office-of-the-president/articles/diversity-defines-new-generation-college-students.html.
54. Pusser, B., Breneman, D. W., Gansneder, B. M., Kohl, K. J., Levin, J. S., Milam, J. H., & Turner, S. E. (2007). *Returning to learning: Adults' success in college is key to America's future.* Lumina Foundation. Available at http://www.luminafoundation.org/publications/ReturntolearningApril2007.pdf.
55. Gomstyn, A. (2003, October 17). Minority enrollment in colleges more than doubled in past 20 years, study finds. *The Chronicle of Higher Education, 50*(8), A25; Schmidt, P. (2003, 28 November). Academe's Hispanic future. *The Chronicle of Higher Education, 50*(14), A8.
56. Jaschik, S. (2007, November 28). Growth and consolidation of minority enrollments. *Inside Higher Ed.* Available at http://www.insidehighered.com/news/2007/11/28/minority.
57. Staley, C. (2003). *50 ways to leave your lectern.* Belmont, CA: Wadsworth, p. 67. Based on Defining "Diversity." (1995). In B. Pike & C. Busse, *101 games for trainers* (p. 11). Minneapolis: Lakewood Books.
58. Staley, C. (2003). *50 ways to leave your lectern,* Belmont, CA: Wadsworth, p. 32.
59. Carnes, M. C. (2005). Inciting speech. *Change, 37*(2), 6–11.
60. Lyons, P. (2005, April 15). The truth about teaching about racism. *The Chronicle of Higher Education, 51*(32), B5.
61. Epstein, G. (2005, June 5) More women advance, but sexism persists. *College Journal from the Wall Street Journal.* Women CEOs. *CNNMoney.com.* Available at http://money.cnn.com/magazines/fortune/fortune500/2008/womenceos/.
62. Farrell, E. F. (2005, August 5). Student volunteers are worth billions. *The Chronicle of Higher Education, 51*(48), A33.
63. Zlotkowski, E. (1999). Pedagogy and engagement. In R. G. Bringle, R. Games, & E. A. Malloy (Eds.). (1999). *Colleges and Universities as Citizens* (pp. 96–120). Needham Heights, MA: Allyn & Bacon.
64. Honnet, E. P., & Poulsen, S. J. (1989). *Principles of good practice for combining service and learning: A Wingspread special report.* Racine, WI: The Johnson Foundation.
65. Eyler, J., Giles, Jr., D. E., & Schmiede, A. (1996). *A practitioner's guide to refection in service-learning: Student voices and reflections.* Nashville, TN: Vanderbilt University Press.
66. Dewey, J. (1933). *How we think.* Boston: Heath.
67. Farrell, Student volunteers are worth billions.
68. Based on Nilsen, L. B. (1998). The circles of ________. *Teaching at Its Best.* Bolton, MA: Anker Publishing.

69. Wessel, D. (2003, September 9). Race still a factor in hiring decisions. *CollegeJournal from the Wall Street Journal.*
70. Beilke, J. R., & Yssel, N. (1999). The chilly climate for students with disabilities in higher education. *College Student Journal, 33*(3), 364–372.
71. Parker, P. N. (2006, March–April). Sustained dialogue: How students are changing their own racial climate. *About Campus, 11*(1), 17–23.
72. Gortmaker, V. J., & Brown, R. D. (2006). Out of the college closet: Differences in perceptions and experiences among out and closeted lesbian and gay students. *College Student Journal, 40*(3), 606–619.
73. Incidences and Statistics. (2009). Hate crime statistics 2009. *Department of Justice, Uniform Crime Reporting Program.* Available at http://www.fbi.gov/ucr/hc2005/incidentsoffenses.htm; *FBI Hate Crime Statistics.* Available at http://www2.fbi.gov/ucr/hc2009/incidents.html.
74. Parker, P. N. (2006, March–April). Sustained dialogue: How students are changing their own racial climate. *About Campus,* 17–34.
75. Based on Earley, P.C., Mosakowski, E. (2004, October). Cultural intelligence. *Harvard Business Review,* p. 143.
76. Earley, P. C., & Mosakowski, E. (2004, October). Cultural intelligence. *Harvard Business Review,* 139–146; Early, C. P., Ang, S., & Tan, J. (2006) CQ: *Developing Cultural Intelligence at Work.* Stanford, CA: Stanford University Press; Osborn, T. N., (2006). *"CQ": Another aspect of emotional intelligence.* Available at http://www.teaminternational.net/resources/docs/cultural%20intelligence.pdf.
77. Earley, P. C., & Mosakowski, E. (2004, October). Cultural intelligence. *Harvard Business Review,* 139–146.
78. Bucher, R. D. (2004). *Diversity consciousness: Opening our minds to people, cultures, and opportunities* (2nd ed.). Upper Saddle River, NJ: Pearson Education.
79. Dwyer, T., & Flannigan, K. (2001). Web globalization: Write once, Deploy worldwide. Available amazon.com; see http://www.internetworldstats.com/stats.htm.
80. General Education for global learning. American Association of American Colleges & Universities. Available at http://www.aacu.org/sharedfutures/gened_global_learning/.

Chapter 11

1. Davis, R., & DeBarros, A. (2006, January 25). In college, first year is by far the riskiest. *USA Today.* Available at http://www.usatoday.com/news/nation/2006-01-24-campus-deaths-cover_x.htm.
2. Monastersky, R. (2007, January 12). Who's minding the teenage brain? *The Chronicle of Higher Education, 53*(19), A14.
3. University of Minnesota (2008, October 22). Grades in college directly linked to health-related behaviors. *Science Daily.* Available at http://www.sciencedaily.com/releases/2008/10/081021120925.htm.
4. Common health problems in college students. (2000). Previously *Medem: Medical Library.* American Academy of Pediatrics. Health problems of college students. *Journal of American College Health, 45*(6), 243–250. (2009); The American College Health Association–National college health assessment spring 2008 reference group data report (abridged). *Journal of American College Health, 57*(5), 477–488.
5. Hales, D. (2006). *An invitation to health, brief.* Belmont, CA: Thomson Wadsworth, p. 32.
6. Kobau, R., Safran, M. A., Zack, M. M., Moriarty, D. G., & Chapman, D. (2004, July 30). Sad, blue, or depressed days, health behaviors and health-related quality of life, behavioral risk factor surveillance system, 1995–2000. *Health Quality of Life Outcomes, 2*(1).
7. Tanner, L. (2008, December 2). 1 in 5 young adults has personality disorder. *USA Today.* Available at http://www.usatoday.com/news/health/2008-12-02-mentalhealth_N.htm.
8. Hilts, P. J. (1993, May 22). U.S. defines mental illness as standard for treatment. *The New York Times.* Available at http://www.nytimes.com/1993/05/22/us/us-defines-mental-illness-as-standard-for-treatment.html.
9. Heredity and the Genetics of Schizophrenia. *Schizophrenia.com.* Available at http://www.schizophrenia.com/research/hereditygen.htm.
10. Scientists show how cannabis/marijuana may trigger schizophrenia. (2007, April 30). *Schizophrenia.com.* Available at http://www.schizophrenia.com/sznews/archives/004987.html.
11. MacInnes, N., Handley, S. L., & Harding, G. F. (2001). Former chronic methylenedioxy methamphetamine (MDMA or ecstasy) users report mild depressive symptoms. *Journal of Psychopharmacology, 15*(3), 181–186.
12. What is depression? (2000; updated 2006, September 13). *National Institute of Mental Health.* Available at http://www.nimh.nih.gov/publicat/depression.cfm.
13. Eisenberg, D., Golberstein, E., & Hunt, J. (2009, May). Mental health and academic success in college. B. E. *Journal of Economic Analysis & Policy.* Available http://www-personal.umich.edu/~daneis/papers/hmpapers/Eisenberg%20et%20al%20(2009).pdf.
14. National Institute of Mental Health. (1997; updated 2009, February 14). College depression: What do these students have in common? *Mental Health Matters.* Available at http://www.mental-health-matters.com/index.php?option=com_content&view=article&id=632.
15. Ibid.
16. Ibid.
17. Farrell, E. F. (2005, December 16). Need therapy? Check your in box. *The Chronicle of Higher Education, 52*(17), A35.
18. Celebrity meltdown. (1999, November/December). *Psychology Today.* Available at http://www.psychologytoday.com/articles/pto-19991101-000035.html.
19. Ibid.
20. Anxiety disorders: What you need to know. (2007). *Mental Health America.* Available at http://www.nmha.org/go/go/information/get-info/anxiety-disorders/anxiety-disorders.
21. Sieben, L. (2011, March 14). Nearly a third of college Students have had mental-health counseling, study finds. *The Chronicle of Higher Education.* Available at http://chronicle.com/article/Nearly-a-Third-of-College/126726/.
22. Marano, H. E. (2004). Up against the ivy wall in 2004. *Psychology Today.* Available at http://www.psychologytoday.com/articles/200405/against-the-ivy-wall-in-2004.
23. Benton, S. A., Robertson, J. M., Tseng, W., Newton, F. B., & Benton, S. L. (2003). Changes in counseling center client problems across 13 years. *Professional Psychology: Research and Practice, 34*(1), 66–72.
24. Astin, A. W., Astin, H. S., & Lindholm, J. A. (2010). *Cultivating the spirit: How college can enhance students' inner lives.* San Francisco: Jossey-Bass.
25. Astin, A. W., Astin, H. S., Lindholm, J. A., & Bryant, A. N. (2005). *The spiritual life of college students: A national study of college students' search for meaning and purpose.* Los Angeles: Higher Education Research Institute, UCLA.
26. Marsh, N. (2011, February). How to make work-life balance work. *TedTalks.* Available at http://www.ted.com/talks/nigel_marsh_how_to_make_work_life_balance_work.html.
27. Ibid.
28. Bregman, P. (2010, July 30). Don't regret working too hard. *Harvard Business Review Blog.* Available at http://blogs.hbr.org/bregman/2010/07/dont-regret-working-too-hard.html.
29. Astin et al., *The spiritual life of college students*; Bartlett, T. (2005, April 22). Most freshmen say religion guides them. *The Chronicle of Higher Education, 51*(33), A1. Available at http://chronicle.com/article/Most-Freshmen-Say-Religion/9956.

30. Saenz, V., & Wolf, D. (2006, February 16). Your First College Year Survey: Highlights from the 2005 YFCY. *National Resource Center Resources.* Available at http://www.sc.edu/fye/resources/assessment/essays/Saenz-2.16.06.html.

31. Nelms, L. W., Hutchins, E., Hutchins, D., & Pursley, R. J. (2007). Spirituality and the health of college students. *Journal of Religion and Health, 46*(2), 249–265.

32. Segerstrom, S. C., & Miller, G. E. (2004). Psychological stress and the human immune system: A meta-analytic study of 30 years of inquiry. *Psychological Bulletin, 130*(4), 601–630. (2004, July 4). Stress affects immunity in ways related to stress type and duration, as shown by nearly 300 studies. *APA Press Release.* Available at http://www.apa.org/news/press/releases/2004/07/stress-immune.aspx.

33. Adelson, R. (2005, January 1). Hard-hitting hormones: The stress-depression link. *Monitor on Psychology, 36*(1). Available at APA Online at http://www.apa.org/monitor/jan05/hormones.html.

34. Ross, S. E., Niebling, B. C., & Heckert, T. M. (1999). Sources of stress among college students. *College Student Journal, 33*(2), 312–317.

35. Largo-Wight, E., Peterson, P. M., & Chen, W. W. (2005). Perceived problem solving, stress, and health among college students. *American Journal of Health Behavior, 29*(4), 360–370.

36. Hudd, S. S., Dumlao, J., Erdmann-Sager, D., Murray, D., Phan, E., Soukas, N., & Yokozuka, N. (2000). Stress at college: Effects on health habits, health status and self-esteem. *College Student Journal, 34*(2), 217–227.

37. Miller, W. C., Staples, B. & Bravender, T. (2008). Risk factors associated with overweight and obesity in college students. *Journal of American College Health, 57*(1), 109–114; Gruber, K. J. (2008). Social support for exercise and dietary habits among college students. Adolescence, *43*(171), 557–575.

38. Strout, E. (2007, September 21). The obesity epidemic comes to campuses. *Chronicle of Higher Education, 54*(4), A1. Available at http://chronicle.com/article/The-Obesity-Epidemic-Comes-to/21074.

39. Racette, S. B., Deusinger, S. S., Strube, M. J., Highstein, G. R., & Duesinger, R. H. (2005). Weight changes, exercise, and dietary patterns during freshman and sophomore years of college. *Journal of American College Health, 53*(6), 245–251.

40. Obesity still a major problem. (2006, April 14). *National Center for Health Statistics, Centers for Disease Control and Prevention.* Available at http://www.cdc.gov/nchs/pressroom/06facts/obesity03_04.htm; Prevalence of Overweight, Obesity, and Extreme Obesity Among Adults: United States, Trends 1960–1962 through 2007–2008. *National Center for Health Statistics, Centers for Disease Control and Prevention.* Available at http://www.cdc.gov/nchs/data/hestat/obesity_adult_07_08/obesity_adult_07_08.htm.

41. Dietary guidelines for Americans (2005). Available at http://www.health.gov/dietaryguidelines/dga2005/document/pdf/DGA2005.pdf.

42. U.S. Department of Agriculture. (2010). Dietary guidelines for Americans. Available at http://www.cnpp.usda.gov/DGAs2010-PolicyDocument.htm.

43. U.S. Department of Agriculture. (2011). ChooseMyPlate.gov.

44. USDA Dietary Guidelines for Americans 2005. Available at http://www.health.gov/dietaryguidelines/dga2005/recommendations.htm.

45. USDA Food safety and inspection service. *Food facts sheet: How temperatures affect food.* Available at http://www.fsis.usda.gov/factsheets/how_temperatures_affect_food/index.asp.

46. 2000–2011. Eating disorders in college women, overview. *Healthyplace.com.* Available at http://www.healthyplace.com/eating-disorders/main/eating-disorders-in-college-women-overview/menu-id-58/.

47. Beavan, C. (2009). *No impact man.* New York: Farrar, Straus and Giroux.

48. Goldstein, K. (2009, September 11). "No impact man": The movie everyone is talking about. *Huffpost Green.* Available at http://www.huffingtonpost.com/2009/09/11/no-impact-man-the-movie-e_n_282472.html; No impact man: Official trailer. *YouTube.* Available at http://www.youtube.com/watch?v=Z9Ctt7FGFBo; Green, P. (2007, March 22). The year without toilet paper. *The New York Times.* Available at http://www.nytimes.com/2007/03/22/garden/22impact.html?pagewanted=all.

49. Prouty, A. M., Protinsky, H. O., & Canady, D. (2002). College women: Eating behaviors and help-seeking preferences. *Adolescence, 37*(146), 353–363.

50. Lowery, S. E., Kurpius, S. E. R., Befort, C., Blanks, E. H., Sollenberger, S., Nicpon, M. F., & Huser, L. (2005). Body image, self-esteem, and health-related behaviors among male and female first year college students. *Journal of College Student Development, 46*(6), 612–623.

51. Shuster, W. G. (2001). Less stress? Yes! *Jewelers' Circular Keystone, 172*(2), 98.

52. Bray, S. R., & Born, H. A. (2004). Transition to university and vigorous physical activity: Implications for health and psychological well-being. *Journal of American College Health, 52*(4), 181–188.

53. Seo, D., Torabi, M, R., Jiang, N., Fernandez-Rojas, X., & Park, B. (2009). Correlates of college students' physical activity: Cross-cultural differences. *Asia-Pacific Journal of Public Health.* Available at http://aph.sagepub.com/content/21/4/421.

54. Huggins, C. E. (2005, January 17). Best fitness routine may depend on personality. *American Medical Network.* Available at http://www.health.am/ab/more/best_fitness_routine_may_depend_on_personality/.

55. Jozefowicz, C. (2004, June). Sweating makes you smart. *Psychology Today,* 56–58.

56. Brown, F. C., & Buboltz, W. C., Jr. (2002). Applying sleep research to university students: Recommendations for developing a student sleep education program. *Journal of College Student Development, 43*(3), 411–416.

57. Jensen, D. R. (2003). Understanding sleep disorders in a college student population. *Journal of College Counseling, 6*(1), 25, 34.

58. (2008, June 15). The science of sleep. *60 Minutes* (CBS news transcript). Available at http://www.cbsnews.com/stories/2008/03/14/60minutes/main3939721.shtml.

59. Brown & Buboltz, Applying sleep research to university students.

60. Greer, M. (2004, July/August). Strengthen your brain by resting it. *Monitor on Psychology, 35*(7). Available at http://www.apa.org/monitor/julaug04/strengthen.html.

61. Pilcher, J. J., & Walters, A. S. (1997). How sleep deprivation affects psychological variables related to college students' cognitive performance. *Journal of American College Health, 46,* 121–126.

62. Kelly, W. E., Kelly, K. E. & Clanton, R. C. (2001). The relationship between sleep length and grade-point average among college students. *College Student Journal, 35*(1), 84–86.

63. Kelly, W. E. (2003). Worry content associated with decreased sleep-length among college students: Sleep deprivation leads to increased worrying. *College Student Journal, 37,* 93–95.

64. Kelly, W. E. (2004). Sleep-length and life satisfaction in a college student sample. *College Student Journal, 38*(3), 428–430; Teli, P. (2002, September 24, updated 2010, March 7). College students' sleep habits harmful to health, study finds. *The Daily Orange.* Available at http://www.dailyorange.com/2.8656/college-students-sleep-habits-harmful-to-health-study-finds-1.1251402; Facts and stats. DrowsyDriving.org. *National Sleep Foundation.* Available at http://drowsydriving.org/about/facts-and-stats/.

65. Killgore, W. D. S., Kahn-Greene, E. T., Lipizzi, E. L., Newman, R. A., Kamimori, G. H., Balkin, T. J. (2008). Sleep deprivation

reduces perceived emotional intelligence and constructive thinking skills. *Sleep Medicine,* 9, 517–526.

66. Facts and stats. Drowsy driving. *National Sleep Foundation.* Available at http://drowsydriving.org/about/facts-and-stats/.
67. Kelly, Sleep-length and life satisfaction in a college student sample.
68. Kerkstra, P. (2006, February 5). Online poker 101: A lesson in losing. *The Philadelphia Inquirer,* A01.
69. Farrell, E. (2005, September 2). Logging on, tuning out. *The Chronicle of Higher Education, 52*(2), A46.
70. Brown & Buboltz, Applying sleep research to university students.
71. Teli, College students' sleep habits harmful to health, study finds.
72. Coren, S. (1996). *Sleep thieves: An eye-opening exploration into the science and mysteries of sleep.* New York: Free Press.
73. Mohler-Kuo, M., Lee, J. E., & Wechsler, H. (2003). Trends in marijuana and other illicit drug use among college students: Results from 4 Harvard School of Public Health College Alcohol Study surveys: 1993–2001. *Journal of American College Health, 52*(1), 17–24; Hales, *An invitation to health,* p. 269.
74. Bon, S. R., Hittner, J. B., & Lawandales, J. P. (2001). Normative perceptions in relation to substance use and HIV-risky sexual behaviors of college students. *Journal of Psychology, 135*(2), 165.; Hales, *An invitation to health,* p. 269.
75. Hales, *An invitation to health,* p. 299.
76. College Alcohol Study. (2005). *Harvard School of Public Health.* Available at http://www.hsph.harvard.edu/cas/.
77. Killough, A. C. (2009, June 15). Study finds drinking by college students on the rise. *The Chronicle of Higher Education.* Available at http://chronicle.com/article/Study-Finds-Drinking-by/47745.
78. Malinauskas, B. M., Aeby, V. G., Overton, R. F., Carpenter-Aeby, T., & Barber-Heidal, K. (2007). A survey of energy drink consumption patterns among college students. *Nutrition Journal.* Available at http://www.nutritionj.com/content/6/1/35.
79. Bogle, K. A. (2008, March 21). "Hooking up": What educators need to know. *The Chronicle of Higher Education.* Available at http://chronicle.com/article/Hooking-Up-What-Educators/26465.
80. Nelson, T. F., Naimi, T. S., Brewer, R. D., & Wechsler H. (2005). The state sets the rate: The relationship of college binge drinking to state binge drinking rates and selected state alcohol control policies. *American Journal of Public Health, 95*(3), 441–446. Press release available at http://www.hsph.harvard.edu/cas/Documents/state/state_pr.html.
81. Ariniello, L. (2002, October). Young brains on alcohol. *Society for Neuroscience.* Available at http://www.sfn.org/skins/main/pdf/BrainBriefings/BrainBriefings_Oct2002.pdf.
82. Townshend, J. M., & Duka, T. (2005). Binge drinking, cognitive performance and mood in a population of young social drinkers. *Alcoholism: Clinical & Experimental Research,* 29(3), 317–325; (2005). Binge Drinking Impairs Mood, Cognitive Performance. *ACER News Release.* About.com: Alcoholism. Binge Drinking Impairs Mood, Cognitive Performance. Available at http://alcoholism.about.com/od/dementia/a/blacer050315.htm.
83. Heavy drinking among college students can be predicted. (2004, March 25). *Pacific Institute for Research and Evaluation.* Available at http://resources.prev.org/HeavyDrinkingAmongCollegeStudentsMediaRelease.pdf.
84. Hingson, R. W., Zha, W., & Weitzman, E. R. (2009). Magnitude of and trends in alcohol-related mortality and morbidity among U.S. college students ages 18–24, 1998–2005. *Journal of Studies on Alcohol and Drugs.*
85. Jennison, K. M. (2004). The short-term effects and unintended long-term consequences of binge drinking in college: A 10-year follow-up study. *The American Journal of Drug and Alcohol Abuse, 30*(3), 659–684.
86. Strano, D. A., Cuomo, M. J., & Venable, R. H. (2004). Predictors of undergraduate student binge drinking. *Journal of College Counseling, 7,* 50–63.
87. Sheffield, F. D., Darkes, J., Del Boca, F. K., & Goldman, M. S. (2005). Binge drinking and alcohol-related problems among community college students: Implications for prevention policy. *Journal of American College Health, 54*(3), 137–141.
88. Marczinski, C. A., Bryant, R., Fillmore, M. T. (2005). The relationship between cognitive preoccupation with alcohol and alcohol use in male and female college students. *Addiction Research and Theory, 13*(4), 383–394.
89. Nelson et al., The state sets the rate.
90. Gupta, S., & Abedin, S. (2007, May 7). Keg parties and cardiacs. *Time, 169*(19), 76; Sobering statistics. *California Polytechnic State University.* Available at http://www.hcs.calpoly.edu/content/pulse/sobering-stats.
91. Facts about alcohol poisoning. (2005). *College Drinking: Changing the Culture.* Available at http://www.collegedrinkingprevention.gov/OtherAlcoholInformation/factsAboutAlcoholPoisoning.aspx.
92. Get facts and statistics. Available at http://www.smartersex.org/resources/behind.asp.
93. Patterson, R. (2008, March 30). Students of virginity. *The New York Times.* Available at http://www.nytimes.com/2008/03/30/magazine/30Chastity-t.html; Yabroff, J. (2008). Campus sexperts. *Newsweek.* Available at http://www.thedailybeast.com/newsweek/2008/02/16/campus-sexperts.html.
94. Hales, *An invitation to health,* p. 216.
95. Ibid, p. 174.
96. Ibid, p. 163.
97. Laumann, E., Gagnon, J. H., Michael, R. T., and Michaels, S. (1994). *The social organization of sexuality: Sexual practices in the United States.* Chicago: University of Chicago Press.
98. Stammers, T. G. (2003, August). Abstinence under fire. *Postgraduate Medical Journal, 79,* 365–366.

Chapter 12

1. Gregory, M. (2003, September 12). A liberal education is not a luxury. *The Chronicle of Higher Education, 50*(3), B16.
2. Staley, R. S., II. (2003). In C. Staley, *50 ways to leave your lectern* (pp. 70–74). Belmont, CA: Wadsworth.
3. Bolles, R. N. (2007). *What color is your parachute?* Berkeley, CA: Ten Speed Press; Bolles, R. N. (2005). *What color is your parachute?* Berkeley, CA: Ten Speed Press; Bolles, R. N. (2009). *What color is your parachute?* Berkeley, CA: Ten Speed Press.
4. Bolles, R. N. (2005). p. xviii.
5. Staley, R. S., II, in Staley, *50 ways to leave your lectern.*
6. Farrell, E. F. (2006, December 12). Freshmen put high value on how well college prepares them for a profession, survey finds. *The Chronicle of Higher Education;* Farrell, E. F. (2007, January 5). Report says freshmen put career prep first. *The Chronicle of Higher Education, 53*(18), A32. Available at http://chronicle.com/article/Report-Says-Freshmen-Put-Ca/19260/.
7. Irvine, M. (2007, January 22). Polls say wealth important to youth. *NewsOK.* Available at http://newsok.com/polls-say-wealth-important-to-youth/article/3002446.DTL; Schwartz, B. (2004, January 23). The tyranny of choice. *The Chronicle of Higher Education, 50*(20), B6.
8. *Celebrity Net Worth.* Available at http://www.therichest.org/celebnetworth/athletes/nfl/peyton-manning-net-worth/; Skateboard hero Hawk looks beyond the board. *Ezilon Infobase.* Available at http://www.ezilon.com/information/article_5382.shtml.
9. Koeppel, D. (2004, December 5). Choosing a college major: For love or for the money? *The New York Times,* section 10, p. 1, column 4. Dunham, K. J. (2004, March 2). No ivory tower: College students focus on career. *Wall Street Journal* (Eastern Edition), pp. B1, B8.

10. Brooks, K. (2009). *You Majored in What?* New York: Viking, based on chapter 2.
11. Malgwi, C. A., Howe, M. A., & Burnaby, P. A. (2005). Influences on students' choice of college major. *Journal of Education for Business, 80*(5), 275–282.
12. Leppel, K. (2005). College persistence and student attitudes toward financial success. *College Student Journal, 39*(2), 223–241; http://wiki.answers.com/Q/What_are_the_highest_paying_jobs.
13. Saleh, A. (2001). Brain hemisphericity and academic majors: A correlation study. *College Student Journal, 35*(2), 193–200.
14. Simpson, J. C. (2003). Mom matters: Maternal influence on the choice of academic major. *Sex Roles, 48*(9/10), 447–460.
15. Rask, K. N., & Bailey, E. M. (2002). Are faculty role models? Evidence from major choice in an undergraduate institution. *The Journal of Economic Education, 33*(2), 99–124.
16. Levine, M. (2005). *Ready or not, here life comes.* New York: Simon & Schuster, p. 4; Levine, M. (2005, February 18). College graduates aren't ready for the real world. *The Chronicle of Higher Education, 51*(24), B11.
17. *Dictionary of occupational titles.* (1991). Washington, DC: Bureau of Labor Statistics. Or see *O*Net Online* (Occupational Information Network) at http://online.onetcenter.org/find/.
18. Based on Schwartz, The tyranny of choice.
19. See J. K. Rowling Biography at http://www.biography.com/people/jk-rowling-40998.
20. Levine, *Ready or not, here life comes.*
21. Based in part on Gordon, V. N., & Sears, S. J. (2004). *Selecting a college major: Exploration and decision making, 5th edition.* Upper Saddle River, NJ: Pearson Education.
22. Based on Hansen, R. S., & Hansen, K. *Using a SWOT analysis in your career planning. Quintessential Careers.* Available at http://www.quintcareers.com/SWOT_Analysis.html.
23. Association of American Colleges and Universities. (2011). *The LEAP vision for learning: Outcomes, practices, impact, and employers' views.* Washington, DC: Association of American Colleges and Universities.
24. *Job interviews get creative.* (2003, August 22). NPR. Available at http://www.npr.org/templates/story/story.php?storyId_1405340.
25. Vance, E. (2007, February 2). College graduates lack key skills, report says. *The Chronicle of Higher Education, 53*(22), A30.
26. Partenheimer, D. (2004, January 11). Abilities required for success in school don't differ greatly from those required in the real world. *APA Online.* Available at http://www.apa.org/news/press/releases/2004/01/success.aspx.
27. Rowh, M. (2003, February–March). Choosing a major. *Career World, 31*(5), 21–23.
28. Ezarik, M. M. (2007, April–May). A major decision. *Career World, 35*(6), 20–22.
29. Rask & Bailey, Are faculty role models?
30. Goldhaber, G. M. (1986). *Organizational communication* (4th ed.). Dubuque, IA: Wm. C. Brown, p. 236. In Staley, R. S., II, & Staley, C. C. (1992). *Communicating in business and the professions: The inside word.* Belmont, CA: Wadsworth.
31. Pew Social Trends Staff. (2011, May 15). *Pew Research Center.* Available at http://pewsocialtrends.org/2011/05/15/is-college-worth-it/.
32. Rampell, C. (2011, June 6). Once again: Is college worth it? *The New York Times.* Available at http://economix.blogs.nytimes.com/2011/05/20/once-again-is-college-worth-it/.
33. Georgetown University. *Center on Education and the Workforce.* Available at http://cew.georgetown.edu.
34. Leonhardt, D. (2011, June 25). Even for cashiers, college pays off. *The New York Times.* Available at http://www.nytimes.com/2011/06/26/sunday-review/26leonhardt.html.
35. Gallo, A. (2011, March 18). Where Will You Be in Five Years? *HBR Blog.* Available at http://blogs.hbr.org/hmu/2011/03/where-will-you-be-in-five-year.html.
36. Brooks, K. (2009). *You Majored in What?* New York: Viking.
37. Kanter, R. M. (2011, March). Managing yourself: Zoom in, zoom out. *HBR Blog.* Available at http://hbr.org/2011/03/managing-yourself-zoom-in-zoom-out/ar/1.
38. Gallo, A. (2011, March 18). Where Will You Be in Five Years? *HBR Blog.* Available at http://blogs.hbr.org/hmu/2011/03/where-will-you-be-in-five-year.html.
39. DiTiberio, J. K., & Hammer, A. L. (1993). *Introduction to type in college.* Palo Alto, CA: Consulting Psychologists Press; Hammer, A. L. (1993). *Introduction to type and careers.* Palo Alto, CA: Consulting Psychologists Press.
40. Myers, I. B., & McCaulley, M. H. (1985). *Manual: A guide to the development and use of the Myers-Briggs type indicator.* Palo Alto, CA: Consulting Psychologists Press. In Golden, V. J., & Provost, J. A. (1987). *"The MBTI and career development;" Application of the Myers-Briggs type indicator in higher education.* Palo Alto, CA: Consulting Psychologists Press.

Index

T